CONTENTS

How to use this book

The contents of this book are mapped exactly onto the AQA A AS specification. The book is divided into six chapters that match the topics in the specification, plus an introductory chapter.

Each chapter begins with an **introductory spread** where you will find:

A breakdown of the specification for the chapter contents.

A topic of interest related to the chapter.

A starter activity to help you prepare for what is to come.

The **content** of each chapter consists of around ten double-page spreads. All the features included in the book are highlighted on the two sample spreads on the right. The main text and all the other features together will help turn your psychological knowledge into effective exam performance. Each of the spreads is intended to be equivalent to around one double lesson, although you may find that you want to spend more time on some spreads.

Each chapter ends with some more useful features – an **end-of-chapter review** consisting of:

A diagrammatic summary of the chapter.

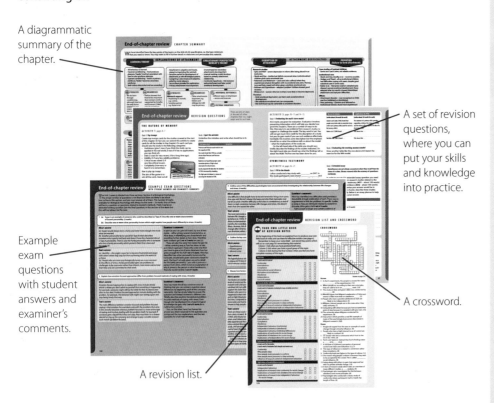

A set of revision questions, where you can put your skills and knowledge into practice.

Example exam questions with student answers and examiner's comments.

A crossword.

A revision list.

Suggested answers for questions throughout the book and to the crosswords can be found on our website: **www.folensblogs.com/psychcompanion**.

This book is called The Complete Companion because we wrote a book which we hoped would be like having a friendly examiner and teacher by your side, providing you with everything you need to do well at AQA A AS Psychology.

On each spread is an **introduction to the topic**, at the top left. This explains what the topic is about and what some of its main issues are.

The **main text** for the spread is in the middle of the page. We have provided more detail than you would require for an exam question on the topic,. However, the questions on the page (Can you …?) aim to help you select appropriate material to prepare for exam questions, and the diagrammatic summaries at the end of each chapter précis this down to the bare bones of each topic.

Internet research is a very occasional feature – when we could squeeze it in – but you can always do research on any area of the specification to update yourself or widen your horizons.

Sometimes we've added a **comment** to enhance understanding.

Validity or Reliability or Ethics. These boxes cover issues related to research methods. They are important evaluative matters that enhance or detract from the value of a particular piece of research.

Real-world applications. Most psychological research has additional impact because of its application in the real world. You can use such applications to demonstrate the value of that research as part of your AO2 commentary.

We invented a fictional family – **the Jackmans** – to help us pose some 'psychology in action' questions. These are a common feature of your exam – where you are asked to use your knowledge of psychology to explain or provide advice on an everyday kind of behaviour.

We have occasionally included a **cutting edge** feature that looks at some very recent research in a particular topic area. In general, throughout the book we have tried to seek out the most recent research in any area. But even better, you can look on our website to get bang up to date.

SECOND EDITION

Psychology AS

The Complete Companion

Folens

United Kingdom: Folens (Publishers) Ltd,
Waterslade House, Thame Road,
Haddenham, Buckinghamshire HP17 8NT
Email: folens@folens.com

Ireland: Folens Publishers,
Greenhills Road, Tallaght, Dublin 24
Email: info@folens.ie

Editor: Louise Wilson
Project development: Rick Jackman
Design and layout: Patricia Briggs
Cover design: Patricia Briggs with Chris Cardwell
Cover photographer: Chris Cardwell
Cover image of cat: courtesy of Clifton Photographic Company

First edition published 2003 by Nelson Thornes
Second edition first published 2008 by Folens Limited

British Library Cataloguing in Publication Data.
A catalogue record for this publication is available from the British Library.

ISBN 978-1-85008-288-0
Folens code: FD2880

Dedication

To Chris and Chloe (MC)

Acknowledgements

Our greatest thanks go to Rick Jackman and Patricia Briggs. Rick is simply the best; he has found us a new home and unstintingly dealt with all our queries and problems and worries, without ever complaining. Patricia is responsible for how our words look on the page and she has created a work of art, the product of enormous care and time. We appreciate her total willingness to go along with all of our crazy ideas. In addition we would also like to thank our editor, Louise Wilson, who did splendid work on editing the manuscript (and even said she enjoyed reading it!), and Sharon Wesselby for kindly allowing us to adopt her beloved Coco as our cover cat. Finally, our thanks go to Peter Burton and Folens for taking us on and being so appreciative of our efforts.

About our cover cat

Weighing in at little more than a couple of bags of sugar, Coco is a pedigree Birman. She lives in a tiny Somerset village with her sister Misty after they were rescued by their owner Sharon when they were just two years old. Fourteen years later they divide their time between proofreading their owner's business reports, sleeping for England and drinking tea. Like her sister, Coco is a constant reminder that you never own a cat, a cat always owns you.

Mike Cardwell

Cara Flanagan

Coco

Picture acknowledgements

The publishers would like to thank the following for permission to reproduce images in this book.

Mary Ainsworth, p. 40; Alamy, TNT Magazine, p. 18; Aquarius Collection, p. 183; ARC/www.deathcamps.org, p. 159; Solomon Asch, p. 149; Richard Atkinson, p. 9; Alan Baddeley, p. 14; Barking Dog Art, p. 83; www.beautycheck.de, p. 33; Phillip Burrows, p. 19; Cartoonstock.com, pp. 15, 117, 132; Corbis, pp. xi(r), 46, 50, 131, 146, 151, 152, 153, 154(b), 161, 167, 183, 184, 187; FLPA, pp. 2, 3(b). Fotolia.com: ©BOOJOO; ©jean-louis bouzou; ©Jose Alves; ©TAlex; ©vladislav susoy; ©Andres Rodriguez, p. ix; ©Cameron Collingwood, p. 182(b); ©caraman, p. 74; ©Diane Keys, p. 82; ©endostock, p. 150; ©enrico scarsi, p. 106; ©FotoWorx, p. viii; ©Fullvalue, p. 127; Goran Milic: pp. 181, 185, 187, 189, 191; ©iofoto, p. 147; ©LDiza, p. 106; ©Ludovic LAN, p. viii; ©Mat Hayward Photo, p. 88(l); ©MONIQUE POUZET, p. 36; ©Natalie Noelle, p. 67; ©Oleg Kozlov, p. 196; ©oscar johns, p. 196(b); ©Per Tillmann, p. 26; ©Brzozowski, p. 88(r); ©SFC, p. 71; ©Stasys Eidiejus, p. 106; ©Tan Kian Khoon, p. ix; ©valine, p. 122; ©Vladimir Mucibabic, p. 130; ©Yvonne_Bogdanski, p. 117. GettyImages, pp. 33, 179; Harvard Medical School/Center for the History of Medicine, p. 100; Holt-Studios, p. 32; Marie Jahoda, p. 180; Janice Kielcolt-Glaser, p. 120; Nick D. Kim, p. 179; Elizabeth Loftus, p. 16; Mary Evans Picture Library, pp. 194, 195; Donald Meichenbaum, p. 135; Alexandra Milgram, pp. 156, 157; Serge Moscovici, p. 152; New York Times, p. xi; Offthemarkcartoons, p. 21; PA Photos, pp. 3, 134, 147(t), 154/5, 160; Lloyd Peterson, p. 5; Margaret Peterson, p. 5; Rex Features, pp. 77, 123, 125, 166; James Roberton © Joyce Robertson, p. 48; Science Photo Library, pp. 117/8, 193; Still Pictures, p. 44; Dr. William Swann, p. 75; Tempest Photography, p. 165; Robert Thompson, p. 53; Topfoto, pp. xi(l), 79, 101; Philip Zimbardo/LuciferEffect, pp. xii, xiii.

Every effort has been made to contact copyright holders, but if any have been inadvertently overlooked, the publishers will be happy to make the necessary amendments at the first opportunity.

It is easy to forget that the names in this book (such as Milgram or Ainsworth) are real people. We have included brief biographies of some of the **researchers** covered in this book – and even sometimes included a message from them with an interesting or amusing anecdote.

We have provided **exam tips** all over the place but occasionally we have thought of a special one.

In all sections of the exam you will be asked **questions on research methods**. In Chapter 3 there are many questions on research methods but others are scattered through the book. At all times you should focus on the methods used by psychologists to conduct research and the strengths and weaknesses of these methods.

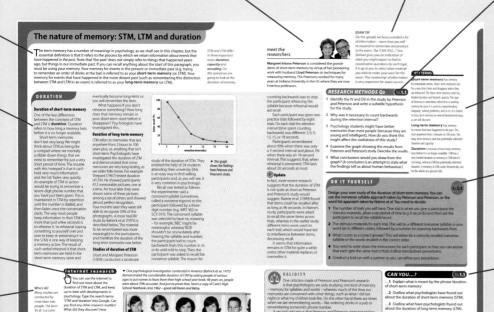

We have given on the page definitions of the **key terms** used in the specification plus some others that we think are very important.

DIY –we have provided a range of different ideas for practical activities that will enhance your understanding of research and your understanding of the topic.

On each spread we ask you some questions to help focus you on the level of knowledge and understanding that you will need for the exam. We have tried to find a balance between making material interesting and informative, but at the same time useful for your exam. You will not be required to reproduce the amount of detail on the spreads. These **Can you…?** boxes give you an indication of what you might expect to find in examination questions for each topic, and to ensure that you have at least that minimal level of understanding that will enable you to perform well in the exam.

This symbol means evaluation. Evaluation may be indicated by a ⊕ for **strengths** or a ⊖ for **weaknesses** or just an ⓔ for general **evaluation**:
Evaluation forms the AO2 commentary in extended essay-writing questions. For AO2 you can also include material on individual differences, real-life applications, validity, reliability or ethics.

The special **commentary corner** feature focuses on the special extended writing questions that require special strategies to do well – you need to plan what you are going to include and know how to present both description and evaluation. Skip over these at your peril!

LINK TO RESEARCH METHODS

In Chapters 0, 1 and 2 we have provided links to topics in the research methods chapter (Chapter 3) to help you interleave these topics – it might make it easier to study research methods bit by bit rather than doing the whole chapter at once.

There are blue boxes, with special symbols to show that they too are evaluation points. These may be **individual differences** (e.g. gender) or **cultural differences**, or **real-world applications**. Individual and cultural differences are important because they demonstrate that a finding is not universal (i.e. a weakness) whereas applications are important because they demonstrate usefulness (i.e. a strength).

You can find suggested answers to **can you…?** and **research methods** questions at: www.folensblogs.com/psychcompanion.

 We have also included the occasional **website** but as sites come and go, don't be disappointed if such links turn out to be nonexistent.

Scheme of work

This book is like a scheme of work.

- We have broken the specification down into lesson-sized chunks.
- There are links in Chapter 1 and Chapter 2 to the research methods chapter (Chapter 3) to help you, if you wish, interleave the research methods topics into the other chapters that comprise Unit 1.
- Each chapter has an end-of-chapter review for summative lessons.

You may decide to follow the book from front to back, or may prefer to start in the middle. If you intend take the Unit 2 exam in January, for example, then you will start with Chapter 4, 5 or 6. If you do wish to take the Unit 2 route, read the following notes.

The Unit 2 route

If you are studying the Unit 2 chapters (Chapters 4, 5 and/or 6) before the Unit 1 chapters (Chapters 1, 2 and 3) there are several things you need to do

1 Begin with the introductory chapter of this book, which covers validity and ethics and an introduction to conducting research in psychology. In the Unit 2 exam there will also be questions related to research methods, so you need to prepare for them.

2 In order to further prepare for research methods you may want to cover parts of Chapter 3 (Research methods) if you have time. In the Unit 2 exam you are likely to be asked questions about the validity and ethics of research in the areas covered, and also about the research methods used. For example, you might be asked about methods used to investigate stress topics (e.g. correlation); methods used to study social topics (e.g. Milgram's methods); and methods used to study abnormal topics (e.g. experiments). We have included some research methods questions in Chapters 4, 5 and 6, but on every spread you should be asking: 'How have psychologists investigated this?' and 'What are the strengths/weaknesses of this approach?'

3 Read the commentary corners in Chapters 1 and 2 because they give guidance on answering extended writing questions.

The AS examination

There are two AS exams: Unit 1 (PSYA1) and Unit 2 (PSYA2).

- In each exam all the questions will be compulsory.
- You will have one-and-a-half hours to answer around ten questions (some questions are parted).
- The total mark for each paper will be 72 marks.

Unit 1 Cognitive psychology, Developmental psychology and Research methods

The exam paper is divided into two sections, each worth 36 marks.

Section A Cognitive psychology and Research methods

In this section you will be asked questions on the topic of memory, given some brief descriptions of hypothetical studies of memory, and asked research methods questions in relation to these hypothetical studies or about actual studies.

Section B Developmental psychology and Research methods

In this section you will be asked questions on the topic of attachment and, again, will be asked research methods questions about hypothetical or actual studies of attachment.

Total marks: AO1 = 24, AO2 = 24 and AO3 = 24

Unit 2 Biological psychology, Social psychology and Individual differences

This exam paper is divided into three sections, each worth 24 marks.

Section A Biological psychology

Most of the questions in this section will be on the topic of stress. Four marks are allocated to a question or questions on research methods in relation to stress research, such as asking about the validity or ethics of such research, or asking how psychologists have investigated stress, or asking about the problems of correlational analysis (which is commonly used in stress research).

Section B Social psychology

This follows the same pattern as section A – mainly questions on the topic of social influence but there are also four marks worth of questions on research methods related to social psychology.

Section C Individual differences

This also follows the same pattern as section A – mainly questions on the topic of individual differences plus four marks worth of questions on research methods related to research on individual differences.

Total marks: AO1 = 30, AO2 = 30 and AO3 = 12

Assessment objectives

There are three assessment objectives (see right). In general you do not actually need to worry about these assessment objectives – you just simply answer the exam questions.

The only time you do need to think AO1 and AO2 is for the extended writing questions.

- These questions start with the word 'Discuss' or 'Describe and evaluate'.
- This means you need to provide description (AO1) and evaluation (AO2) in equal measure.
- These questions are worth more than other questions – perhaps 8 marks or 12 marks.
- Throughout this book we explain how to tackle such questions in our commentary corners.
- These questions are likely to be marked using the mark schemes shown on the right.

Detail and elaboration

The main difference between a good answer and a weak answer is the amount of *detail* (in AO1 answers) and *elaboration* (in AO2 answers).

AO1

If a question says 'identify' then you know a single word or phrase will usually be sufficient for your answer. But if the question says 'describe' or 'outline or 'explain' then you must provide some further information. Consider this question and answer:

Question: 'Describe **one** reason why people obey'.
Answer: 'Because it is justified'.

The answer, so far, is worth only one mark and needs more detail to attract further credit. You could add detail by:

- Providing an example – 'People obey because it is justified, for example during the Holocaust, Nazi propaganda portrayed the Jews as a danger to all Germans, thus justifying the horrific obedience that was to follow'.
- Adding a study – 'People obey because it is justified. This was shown in Milgram's study of obedience to authority where participants were given the initial justification of their role in delivering electric shocks that science wanted to help people improve their memory through the use of reward and punishment.'

Sample questions

AO1 (description)

- Outline key features of the multi-store model of memory. *(6 marks)*
- Describe the procedures in Milgram's study of obedience. *(3 marks)*

AO2 (evaluation and application of knowledge)

- Explain **one** strength of the multi-store model of memory. *(4 marks)*
- Sanjay is going to take his driving test but he always feels stressed when it comes to such tests. Suggest **two** strategies he might use, based on psychological research, to help cope with the stress he experiences in a test situation. *(4 marks)*
- Explain how conformity differs from obedience. *(2 marks)*

AO1 and AO2 (extended writing questions)

- Discuss how personality factors affect levels of stress. *(12 marks)*
- Outline and evaluate cultural variations in attachment. *(8 marks)*

AO3 (design, conduct and report research)

- Ainsworth conducted research on attachment. Describe **one** ethical issue raised by this research. *(2 marks)*
- Identify the sampling method used in the study described and give **one** strength of using this method in this study. *(3 marks)*

▶ Abbreviated mark scheme for 12-mark questions

Description (AO1)				
Marks	Detail	Knowledge and understanding	Selection of appropriate material	Presentation of information
6	Accurate and reasonably detailed	Sound	Appropriate	Clear and coherent
5–4	Generally accurate, less detailed	Relevant	Some evidence	Appropriate
3–2	Basic	Some relevant	Little evidence	Appropriate
1	Very brief/flawed	Very little	Largely or wholly inappropriate	

Evaluation (AO2)			
Marks	Use of material	Range of issues and/or evidence	Expression of ideas , specialist terms, spelling etc
6	Effective	Broad range in reasonable depth or narrower range in greater depth	Clear and good range, few errors
5–4	Not always effective	Range in limited depth or narrower range in greater depth	Reasonable, some errors
3–2	Basic	Superficial consideration of restricted range	Lacks clarity, some specialist terms, errors
1	Rudimentary	Just discernible	Poor, few specialist terms

AO2

Use the **three point rule** (explained on page 21)

(1) **Identify** your AO2 point (e.g. criticism, application, individual difference, etc.)
(2) **Justify** it (What evidence do you have for this?), and
(3) **Elaborate** it (How does this affect the topic being evaluated? Is this good or bad for it and why?).

For example, if your criticism of a study is 'lack of ecological validity', then you have identified it. You need to justify your claim in this context (e.g. studies of this phenomenon in other settings haven't produced the same results). Finally, you need to indicate why ecological validity is a problem in this study (e.g. this means that we can't generalise from the original study to other settings, which limits its explanatory usefulness).

Improving exam performance: A few key pieces of advice

What *does* the question require?

Throughout this book we try to prepare you for every conceivable question that might be thrown at you in an exam. However – and it is a big however – you have to play your part in this process. Questions make very specific requests, and examiners have marks available only for the specific requirements of the question. So, if a question asks you to describe the difference between two things, then that's what you must do in order to be awarded marks. You must not just describe the two things. Time spent reading questions carefully is time well spent, as it will stop you setting off on an answer that is not actually dealing with the question set. Being able to *read* questions accurately is a valuable skill, and one that can be usefully nurtured during your collaborative learning sessions (see 'Work with a friend', opposite).

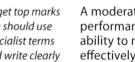

To get top marks you should use specialist terms and write clearly and coherently – these are very important marking criteria.

Don't panic

A moderate level of stress is good for performance, but too much can impair your ability to recall information and to use it effectively in the exam. A wise student learns to control their stress *before* the examination, and makes frequent use of stress management even during the revision stage. There are many excellent stress management techniques that are both free and portable (i.e. you can use them wherever you like). Use the Internet to find one that works for you, and practise it regularly.

One interesting fact is that physical activity (stretching your arms or feet) reduces stress because the activity tells the body that the stressor has been dealt with and therefore the sympathetic nervous system can 'stand down', putting you in a more relaxed state.

Time management is crucial

Many students waste *time* by writing too much for questions that don't require it, and waste *marks* by not writing enough for questions that do. The marks that are available for each question (as well as the space provided) inform you about how much you need to write. Do not waste important time *or* marks by providing answers that are inappropriately long or short for the number of marks available.

You might think of about 15–20 words per mark, so for a 12-mark extended writing question you should write an answer which is about 180–240 words. We are often asked by students what they should do if they run out of time in an exam. The answer is simple – don't!

Effective revision

Get yourself motivated People tend to do better when they are highly motivated. We have taught many mature students who all wished they had worked harder at school the first time around. You don't owe success to your teachers or your parents (although they would be delighted), you owe it to the person you will be ten years from now. Think what you would like to be doing in ten years, and what you need to get there, and let that thought prompt you into action now. It is always better to succeed at something you may not need later than to fail at something you will.

Work *with* your memory In an exam it is harder to access information learned by rote. When someone feels anxious it is easier for them to recall knowledge they *understand* well. Just reading or writing out notes may do little to help you create enduring memories or to understand the content. However, if you do something with your knowledge it will increase your understanding and make it more likely that material is accessible when you need it. Psychologists call this 'deep processing' as opposed to the 'shallow processing' that takes place when you read something without really thinking about it. Constructing spider-diagrams or mind-maps of the material, or even explaining it to someone else, involves deep processing and makes material more memorable.

Become multi-sensory Why stick to using just one of your senses when revising? Visual learners learn best by seeing what they are learning, so make the most of text, diagrams, graphs, etc. By contrast, auditory learners learn best by listening (and talking), taking in material using their sense of hearing. You may associate more with one of these styles than the other, but actually we can make use of *both* these types of learning styles. As well as *reading* your notes and *looking* at pictures and diagrams, try *listening* to your notes and *talking* about topics with other people, and even *performing* some of the material, e.g. by role-playing a study.

Short bursts are best One of the problems with revision is that you can do too much of it (in one go, that is…). As you probably know all too well, your attention is prone to wander after a relatively short period of time. Research findings vary as to the optimum time to spend revising, but 30–45 minutes at a time appears to be the norm. What should you do when your attention begins to wander? As a rule, the greater the physiological change (i.e. going for a walk rather than surfing the Internet), the more refreshed you will be when returning for your next 30–45 minute stint. There is another benefit to having frequent planned breaks – it increases the probability of subsequent recall.

Revisit regularly Have you ever noticed that if you don't use an icon on your computer for a long time, the cunning little blighter hides it. Your computer seems to take the decision that as you are not using it regularly, it can't be that important, so neatly files it away somewhere. Your brain works in a similar way, knowledge that is not used regularly becomes less immediately accessible. The trick, therefore, is to review what you have earned at regular intervals. Each time you review material, it will take less time, and it will surely pay dividends later on!

Work with a friend Although friends *can* be a distraction while you are trying to study, they can also be a very useful revision aid. Working together (what psychologists call 'collaborative learning') can aid understanding and make revision more interesting and more fun. Explaining something to someone else is a useful form of deep processing (see above), and by checking and discussing each other's answers to sample questions, you can practice your 'examiner skills' and therefore your understanding of what to put into an exam answer to earn the most marks.

Your own little book of revision notes

Students often buy a revision book just before the exam to help them in the final countdown. In fact some students buy more than one revision book. Such books have some value but it is much more valuable to produce your own little book of notes. It should be little for two reasons. First, you want it to be small so you can tuck it away in a pocket and whip it out in any spare moment to do some revision, and second, you want to reduce the amount of material to be memorised. What you want is brief cues that trigger you to recall a whole chunk of information.

Here is a chunk of information from our book:

> The most influential study of majority influence was carried out by Solomon Asch in 1956. Asch (1956) asked student volunteers to take part in a 'vision' test, although unbeknown to these volunteers, all but one of the participants were really confederates (i.e. colleagues) of the experimenter. The real purpose of the experiment was to see how the lone 'real' participant would react to the behaviour of the confederates.
>
> Participants were seated in a room and asked to look at three lines of different lengths. They were then asked to state, in turn, which of the three lines was the same length as a 'standard' line. Although there was always a fairly obvious solution to this task, amazingly (to the real participant), on some of the trials the rest of the group made the same wrong choice. Asch was interested in whether people would stick to what they believed to be right, or cave in to the pressure of the majority and go along with its decision.
>
> In total, 123 male American undergraduates were tested. Asch showed a series of lines to participants seated around a table. Participants always answered in the same order (with the real participant always answering second to last or last). The confederates were instructed to give the same incorrect answer on 12 of the 18 trials.

For your little book of notes you need to identify a few key points:

• Asch (1956) – 3 lines, standard line, 123 males, 12/18 critical

If you can learn and remember this essential information, you will be able to write a few sentences about Asch's research in the exam.

When you are studying topics in this book, select key points and write these in your little book of notes. Then, when you revise, these notes will be meaningful to you – because you wrote them. Rehearse them as you revise, as this will help make them memorable. In the end, just thinking 'Asch' could act as a trigger, prompting you to recall all the key points you need.

One other point about this approach to note-making – it is important that you select the material yourself, because the act of selecting makes you think about the content, and that is what makes the information memorable. When you read through Chapter 1 (on memory) you will find out how important elaborative processing is in memory.

What is psychology?

Psychology is the *science* of human behaviour and experience. You have probably already studied science and therefore know some things about the scientific method. You know, for example, that scientists:

- Conduct experiments and other kinds of studies.
- Try to find out about the causes of things.

Psychologists use the same methods as other scientists. They aim to find out about human behaviour by conducting research. However, psychological research is a little different from other scientific research because the objects of study are living, breathing, thinking human beings. This means that there are some differences, but also many similarities, with other sciences.

Let's look at an example of science in action, in one of the classic studies in psychology.

Science and pseudoscience

The two main features of science are (1) it aims to be objective and systematic, and (2) it is verifiable, e.g. you can check the results of a study by repeating it or cross-referencing it with another study – this means we can see whether the findings are true.

The aim of science is to discover natural laws (or theories) which then enable us to predict and control the world (e.g. build dams or treat schizophrenia). Without science, people are susceptible to superstition, and charlatans selling miracle cures or claiming knowledge of the future. Some people use science to sell their products or services, dishonestly claiming that this drug or that programme is 'scientifically proven'. One of the reasons for studying science is so that you too can learn to control your world and separate science from pseudoscience.

RIOTS IN AMERICAN PRISONS

In the 1970s in America there were many prison riots, but the most infamous occurred at Attica Prison in the state of New York in 1971. The riot started over poor prison conditions. The prisoners felt that they were illegally denied certain rights and were being held under inhumane conditions, as illustrated by the fact that the prison was designed to hold 1200 inmates but actually housed 2225. The riot was triggered when a rumour circulated that a prisoner was being held in his cell and was going to be tortured. A small group managed to gain control of part of the prison and eventually to take more than 40 officers and civilians hostage. They demanded that their needs be met before they would surrender. This led to a four-day-long standoff between prisoners and state police, during which time the prisoners gained support from various anti-government groups around the country. News crews were allowed inside to interview the leaders, all while preparations were being made on both sides for a major battle. On 13 September 1971, 1500 police and national guardsmen stormed the prison. The eventual death toll was 42, including 10 hostages.

The media speculated about the causes of the riot and many newspapers at the time blamed the prisoners. They were, they said, 'bad apples', basically people who were 'evil' by nature, and would always end up causing trouble no matter what was done with them.

▲ Philip Zimbardo, Emeritus Professor at Stanford University, California

Enter a young psychologist called Philip Zimbardo. He referred to the 'bad apple' account as a dispositional explanation – the belief that prison violence was due to the fact that both prisoners and guards have personalities, which makes conflict inevitable. Prisoners lack respect for law and order, and guards are domineering and aggressive. This dispositional explanation offers an account of behaviour in terms of the individual's disposition or personality.

Zimbardo argued that this dispositional explanation draws attention away from the complex matrix of social, economic and political forces that make prisons what they are, and thus prevents us making them better places. In Zimbardo's view, prisoners and guards behave as they do because of the situation they are placed in. They display a lack of respect because that is the kind of social role dictated by the prison situation. This is a situational explanation.

How can we tell which is the 'right' explanation – the dispositional or the situational hypothesis? The answer is 'by conducting a research study'.

Read on to find out what happened next …

Aim

Zimbardo designed a study to test the dispositional versus the situational explanation (Haney *et al.*, 1973). His **aim** was to see how 'ordinary' people would behave if you placed them in a prison environment and designated some of them as guards and others as prisoners. If the guards and prisoners in this mock prison behaved in a non-aggressive manner, this would support the dispositional hypothesis. On the other hand, if these ordinary people came to behave in the same way that we see in real prisons, then we must conclude that the environment plays a major part in the behaviour of guards and prisoners.

Hypothesis

Zimbardo's **hypothesis** was that 'assignment to the treatment of "guard" or "prisoner" would result in different reactions on behavioural measures of interaction, emotional measures of mood state and pathology and attitudes toward self, as well as other indices of coping and adaptation to this novel situation' (Haney *et al.*, p. 4). In other words he stated his belief that the role you are given to play will determine your behaviour (a situational explanation).

Procedures

An advertisement sought male volunteers for a psychological study of 'prison life', saying that they would be paid $15 a day. The 24 most stable (physically and mentally) men were selected and randomly assigned to being either a prisoner or a guard. There were two reserves and one dropped out, finally leaving 10 prisoners and 11 guards.

A mock prison was set up in the basement of the Psychology department at Stanford University in California, USA. The 'prisoners' were unexpectedly 'arrested' at home. On entry to 'prison' they were put through a delousing procedure, searched, given a prison uniform with ID number, nylon stocking caps (to make their hair look short), and an ankle chain. They were in prison 24 hours a day, whereas the guards worked shifts.

The guards referred to the prisoners only by number. The prisoners were allowed certain 'rights': three meals a day, three supervised toilet trips, two hours for reading or letter-writing, and two visiting periods and movies per week. They had to line up three times a day to be counted and tested on the prison rules.

The guards had uniforms, clubs, whistles, handcuffs and reflective sunglasses (to prevent eye contact). The aim was to reduce their sense of individuality so they would be more likely to act within their role rather than following their personal morals.

Findings

Over the first few days the guards grew increasingly tyrannical. They woke prisoners in the night and got them to clean the toilets with their bare hands. Some guards were so enthusiastic in their role that they even volunteered to do extra hours without pay.

The participants appeared at times to forget that they were only acting. Even when they were unaware of being watched, they still played their roles. When one prisoner had had enough, he asked for parole rather than saying he wanted to stop being part of the experiment. Had he come to think that he was actually a prisoner?

Five prisoners had to be released early because of their extreme reactions (crying, rage and acute anxiety) – symptoms that had started to appear within two days of the beginning of the study. In fact the whole experiment was ended after six days, despite the intention to continue for two weeks.

Conclusions

This study appears to demonstrate that both guards and prisoners conform to their social roles. In terms of the original aims of the experiment, we can conclude that situational factors seem to be more important rather than dispositional ones, because 'ordinary' students all too easily became brutal prison guards when placed in the right setting.

Not all psychologists believe that psychology is a science – but that's another story…

WWW You can read more about the SPE at www.prisonexp.org – a web site devoted to the Stanford Prison study – with a slide show, discussion questions, and links to other sites.

THE SCIENTIFIC METHOD*

Zimbardo's thoughts and research illustrate the **scientific method** – the method that underlies all scientific research.

1 Scientists observe things going on in the world about them.
2 They develop a tentative explanation for the things they observe and produce a hypothesis.
3 In order to establish whether the hypothesis is true, they design a study to test it.
4 If the hypothesis is shown to be true, then **conclusions** can be drawn.
5 If the hypothesis is false then … Think! Try again.

You will find that this method underlies much of what we cover in this book. Psychologists, like all scientists, seek to explain everyday phenomena and then to investigate their explanations in an objective and systematic way.

e Evaluation

There is one further aspect to research that we haven't mentioned – evaluation. This means looking at the *value* of the study. The findings of Zimbardo's study were plain for everyone to see. But if the techniques that were used in conducting the study were flawed then the results might be meaningless.

You know this from studying science. As part of your science course you were likely to have conducted various investigations or case studies. For example, you might have been given data about the benefits and hazards of using mobile phones, and been asked to weigh up this evidence. This would have included an *evaluation* of the methods used to collect the data. An important part of the process of science is being critical about the results. So we now need to evaluate Zimbardo's study. Psychologists are particularly concerned with three main issues when evaluating research: validity, ethics and usefulness.

What is research?

Anyone can have an opinion about human behaviour. You probably have lots of them, such as believing that if you eat less then you will lose weight or that girls have a better sense of humour than boys. But how do you know? Scientists aim to produce answers that are better than common sense. They do this by conducting well-controlled studies. Throughout this book we will look at how they do this.

Was Zimbardo's study valid?

If we want to draw conclusions about 'real life' then the behaviour we study must match up to 'real life' behaviour. One of the questions raised about Zimbardo's study was whether the participants were behaving like real prisoners and guards, or were simply playing the roles assigned to them? In real life people do act out roles but they also consider their individual sense of right and wrong. So if, for example, you were one of the guards you might order a 'prisoner' to clean the toilets with their bare hands because it was part of the 'game' whereas in real life you wouldn't do this because you felt it was wrong to treat a prisoner in such a dehumanising way.

In real life a prison guard (or a prisoner) would be likely to adapt the role to suit their personal beliefs and the requirements of the situation. Most of the guards later claimed that they had simply been acting a role. This means the study might tell us very little about people's behaviour in real life and would therefore mean that the findings are relatively meaningless – in scientific language, they would be seen as lacking **validity**.

However, there is an alternative view of the validity of this research. Zimbardo's analysis of the behaviour of his 'guards' showed that approximately 30% were 'cruel and tough'; about 50% were 'tough but fair'; and less than 20% were 'good guards' (i.e. generally helpful and kind to the 'prisoners'). In Chapter 5 of this book we touch briefly on the actions of Reserve Police Battalion 101, a German mobile killing unit of 500 men who shot dead over 38,000 Jews in just four months in 1942. These were not highly trained killers, but 'ordinary men', usually recruited because they were too old for the German Army. Historian Christopher Browning's analysis of the actions of this group (Browning, 1992) showed that, as with Zimbardo's guards, there was a nucleus of 'enthusiastic killers' who went out of their way to hunt Jews, a larger group who 'performed' only when assigned killing duties, and less than 20% who were classified as 'refusers and evaders', and found it difficult to carry out their terrible duty. Evidence such as this suggests that Zimbardo's findings perhaps do have some validity because they parallel events in the real world.

Was Zimbardo's study ethical?

We said at the beginning of this chapter that psychological research is a little different from other scientific research because the objects of study are living, breathing, thinking human beings. Therefore we have to think carefully about the effect of any study on the people who take part – the participants.

Participation in this study raised certain **ethical issues**, perhaps most importantly the issue of psychological harm. All participants experienced considerable emotional distress during the study. Five of the prisoners had to be released because of 'depression, crying, rage and acute anxiety' as well as one who had developed a 'psychosomatic rash'. The study was stopped after six days rather than being allowed to run the full two weeks. Zimbardo also tried to make amends by conducting **debriefing** sessions for several years afterwards and concluded that there were no lasting negative effects.

LINK TO RESEARCH METHODS

Ethical issues and how psychologists deal with them are discussed on pages 70–3. It might be useful to turn to this now in order to be able to assess all the research you are about to study.

Was Zimbardo's study useful?

As a result of this study, Zimbardo has been asked to testify before bodies concerned with prisons and prison reform. His testimony about the research influenced US Congress to change one law so that juveniles accused of federal crimes would no longer be housed with adult prisoners before trial (to prevent them from being abused). This was based on the abuse reported in the Stanford Prison Experiment. 'Quiet Rage', a video that Zimbardo and his Stanford undergraduate students produced from footage of the experiment, continues to be used in college classes and by civil, judicial, military and law enforcement groups to enlighten and arouse concern about prison life. The experiment has not, however, brought about the changes in prisons or even in guard training programmes that he would have liked. In fact, prisons have been radically transformed in the United States in the last 25 years to make them even less humane.

LINK TO RESEARCH METHODS

The chapter on research methods starts with a look at the important issue of validity (see pages 68–9). It might be useful to turn to this now.

▼ The guards' treatment of the prisoners was often quite sadistic. After the study was finished guards and prisoners were introduced to each other in 'encounter sessions'. This was just one part of the thorough debriefing procedures that took place months and years after the study ended.

DOING RESEARCH

Your study of psychology should be fun (!) and relevant to your life. So a good way to begin understanding the research process is to investigate something about human behaviour that interests you. However, before you get too excited, you can't study anything that would be unethical!

Observations of everyday life

You might think up your own idea but here is one possibility. Many students do their homework in front of the TV. Cara's daughter thinks she does it just as well in front of the TV as when working at a desk with no distractions. As you might imagine, Cara doesn't think this is true.

Research aim

To investigate whether people work just as well with the TV on, or whether their work will suffer as a result.

*This study is an experiment. The main characteristic of an **experiment** is that there is an **IV** which is changed (TV on or not) to see if this has any effect on the **DV** (quality of work). This permits us to draw causal conclusions – we can make a statement about whether having the TV on or off causes a change in the work that is done.*

LINK TO RESEARCH METHODS

Some of the key concepts for research are introduced on this page. You can learn more about them on page 000.

DO IT YOURSELF

1 Work with a small group of other students and discuss the following questions.
  • How could you find out whether people can work just as well with the TV on as in a quiet room?
  • What will you need to measure?
  • Will you have two different conditions? What will you change across the two conditions?
  • How many participants will you need? Will everyone take part in both conditions, or will you have two groups of participants?
  • What will you expect to find out?
  • What will the participants do?
  • What do you need to control?
2 When you have worked out what you will do, join with another group and explain your ideas to each other. The other group may ask useful questions which will help you refine your ideas.
3 Conduct your study. You may be able to do this in class or each member of your group could go away and collect some data.
4 Pool the data collected by your group and prepare a poster to present your results and conclusions.

ETHICAL ISSUES

Whenever you conduct research, you must always consider ethical issues carefully.

• Never use anyone under the age of 16 as a participant.
• Always obtain **informed consent** from all participants – tell your participants what they will be expected to do and allow them to refuse to take part.
• Debrief your participants after the study to tell them of any deception and to allow them to withdraw their data if they object, on reflection, to having taken part.

Before beginning any study, consult with others on the 'script' for the informed consent and the debrief.

Research design

You have just done what psychologists do – conducted a systematic study of human behaviour. You followed the scientific method: observe → explain → state expectations → design a study → see if your expectations were correct.

Psychologists use special words to describe aspects of the research process. We have used some of the terms already, and most of them are probably familiar to you from using them in science classes.

• *What will you expect to find out?* This should be your hypothesis, a statement of what you believe to be true. Your hypothesis might have been something like: *Students who do a memory task with the TV on produce work which is of lower quality than those who do the same task without the TV on.*
• *What will you measure?* This is called the **dependent variable (DV)**. When you decided exactly what you would measure, you **operationalised** the DV.

It isn't enough just to get people to do some work – you should have made sure that all participants were doing the same piece of work and would have specified what that piece of work was.
• *What are your two conditions?* This is called the **independent variable (IV)**. There are often two conditions of the IV – in this case having the TV on or having the TV off.
• *What will the participants do?* You worked out a set of **standardised procedures**. It is important to make sure that each participant did exactly the same thing in each condition, otherwise the results might vary because of changes in procedure rather then because of the IV.
• *What do you need to control?* You will have tried to control some **extraneous variables** such as time of day (people might do better on a test in the morning than in the afternoon, so all participants should do the test at about the same time of day).

Cognitive psychologists believe that human behaviour can be best explained if we first understand the mental processes that underlie behaviour. It is, therefore, the study of how people learn, structure, store and use knowledge – essentially how people think *about the world around them.*

Cognitive psychology: Memory

SPECIFICATION BREAKDOWN

Specification content	Comment
Models of memory	
• **The multi-store model, including the concepts of encoding, capacity and duration. Strengths and weaknesses of the model.**	In this first part of your study of memory you will look at two explanations of how your brain deals with incoming information and stores it. The first explanation or 'model' of memory is the multi-store model (MSM). This model is about 40 years old, but is important because it has influenced our understanding of memory for a long time. A key part of the MSM is the distinction between short- and long-term memory (STM and LTM). STM lasts a short time (duration) and can only hold a limited amount of information (capacity), whereas LTM lasts a long time and holds a potentially infinite amount of information. Information is stored in a different form (encoding) in STM and LTM, as we shall see.
• **The working memory model, including its strengths and weaknesses.**	The second model of memory is the 'working memory model' – a slightly more recent development. The working memory (WM) model focuses on one particular area of memory – immediate or working memory. This is the part of memory which is active when you are working on a problem or remembering someone's phone number. We will look at research evidence that supports or challenges each model, as well as its strengths and weaknesses.
Memory in everyday life	
• **Eyewitness testimony (EWT) and factors affecting the accuracy of EWT, including anxiety, age of witness.**	Memory research has many applications in everyday life. It can be used to explain our behaviour and the behaviour of people around us. One key application is in understanding our memory of events that occurred at the time a crime was committed – details of who committed the crime, what they did, and events surrounding the incident. If you are asked to provide such information this is called 'eyewitness testimony' (EWT).
• **Misleading information and the use of the cognitive interview.**	The big question about EWT is whether it is correct. It's not much use if it isn't, so psychologists have conducted many studies to try to understand the criteria that increase or decrease its accuracy. They have then tried to suggest techniques (such as the cognitive interview) which police can use to improve the accuracy of eyewitnesses' recall.
• **Strategies for memory improvement.**	Another application of memory, which is of particular interest to students, is how to improve the memory. The final part of this chapter looks at psychological research on strategies for memory improvement, such as the role of organisation – the extent to which organising information increases its memorability.

THE ORIGINS OF MEMORY

Have you ever been called 'bird-brained'? Well, that may not be as insulting as you might think. Scientists at the University of New Hampshire in the US are trying to learn more about the evolution of human memory by studying the Clark's nutcracker, a bird regularly faced with a particularly challenging task – remembering where it buried its supply of food for winter. Like many animals preparing for the winter, every autumn the Clark's nutcracker spends several weeks gathering food stores. What makes it unique among foraging animals is that it harvests more than 30,000 pine nuts, buries them in thousands of different food 'stores' over a 15-mile area, and then relies almost solely on its memory of where those stores are located to survive through winter. Evolution appears to have solved this problem for Clark's nutcrackers as they have developed a particularly good memory for spatial information. Nutcrackers have a better developed spatial memory than other corvidae (such as crows) that *are* not as dependent upon the recovery of food during the winter for their survival.

Memory and learning abilities in animals are in fact *adaptive specialisations* that have been shaped by natural selection to solve the specific problems posed by their environment. Darwin's theory of 'evolution by natural selection' is based on three main assumptions. First, only a small proportion of each generation survives to reproduce. Second, offspring are not identical to their parents, and so each generation exhibits a degree of variation, and at least some of this variation is heritable. Third, some characteristics give the animal that possesses them an advantage over others in the 'survive and reproduce' stakes. Heritable differences in memory will therefore evolve only if these differences lead to survival and reproductive success for those animals that possess them.

▲ Clark's nutcrackers – the memory skills of this bird are essential to survival during the long winter months.

But exactly how *does* memory benefit animals in the struggle for survival? An ability to remember and adjust later behaviour in line with previous learning is evident in many different aspects of animal behaviour. The impressive behaviour of Clark's nutcrackers would not be possible without a very efficient spatial memory which permits exploitation of available food resources. Animals must also compete over resources such as food, territory or mates, often with the same individuals, and on a regular basis. Retaining a memory for the outcome of previous contests, and being able to remember specific individuals would work to the advantage of both the winners and losers of previous contests. Reducing the incidence of fights would have the major advantage of reducing the likelihood of injury, thus making more time available for feeding and other activities. The same is true for social groups where animals rely on cooperation between individuals. Male olive baboons, for example, 'take turns' at keeping guard while the other mates, and so individuals must remember those with whom they have previously cooperated, so that the favour can be returned. By the same token, the ability to remember 'cheats' (who take but do not return the favour) is essential so that the same mistake is not made again.

These examples tell us that memory comes in many forms, and serves an important adaptive function for all animals. For Clark's nutcrackers, a good memory is essential if they are to survive a harsh winter where food is extremely scarce. For our own ancestors, also struggling to survive in a harsh environment, memory was an equally important adaptation for more or less the same reasons. What is clear, however, is that the type of task we face today is not the type that memory first evolved to solve. Remembering lengthy passages of factual information, or trying to recall several different usernames and passwords or the birthdays of all those nephews and nieces, was never a problem for our ancestors. As you embark on your study of memory, remember why it evolved in the first place.

Now if I could only remember where I left those pine nuts… .

▼ A male olive baboon. Remembering who you owe favours to and who owes you is essential in baboon society.

Now that *is* interesting…

Clark's nutcrackers are not the only animals capable of impressive feats of memory. We humans are pretty good at it as well. It appears, however, that we need to be *interested* in something in order to remember it well – the more interested we are, the better motivated we are to remember it. For example, Chase and Simon (1973) showed that expert chess players were much better at recalling chess positions than were novice players. Similarly, Morris *et al.* (1981) found that football enthusiasts could recall scores better than people with little or no interest in football. This particular relationship is fairly easy to test – simply get some people, test their knowledge (and therefore interest in…) football using the test below, then ask them to read through the football scores. These scores are randomly chosen from the 2002 season – you could choose a different day if you don't like the result for your team! Likewise you may have to change some of the questions if Tottenham sack their manager or Chelsea's owner sacks them. About 30 minutes or so later, give your participants the same list of matches, but this time with the scores removed. Their task is to fill the scores in. You might give 2 marks for a completely correct score and just 1 mark if the result is right (e.g. Aston Villa winning) although the score was wrong (e.g. 0–2).

FOOTBALL KNOWLEDGE TEST

1. What country does Chelsea's owner come from?
2. Who is manager of Tottenham Hotspur?
3. Which British club plays at 'The Stadium of Light'?
4. What was the name of the Liverpool goalkeeper whose heroics helped them to win the Champions League final in 2005?
5. How many substitutes can be used by one team during a Premier League match?
6. What colour shirts do Everton wear?
7. For which Spanish club did David Beckham play until his transfer in 2007?
8. Which team has the nickname 'The Canaries'?
9. England's 1966 World Cup winning captain Bobby Moore played for which club side?
10. Who is 'Motty'?

Premier League scores for May 11 2002		
Arsenal	4 – 3	Everton
Blackburn	3 – 0	Fulham
Chelsea	1 – 3	Aston Villa
Leeds United	1 – 0	Middlesbrough
Leicester	2 – 1	Tottenham
Liverpool	5 – 0	Ipswich
Manchester United	0 – 0	Charlton
Southampton	3 – 1	Newcastle
Sunderland	1 – 1	Derby County
West Ham	2 – 1	Bolton

When you have tested a few people and worked out their scores for the two tests, you can correlate them (see page 98 to read about correlation) to see if people who score higher on the football knowledge test also score higher on their recall of the scores. There should be a lesson in this for your own study of psychology – if you haven't worked out what that is, maybe you just aren't interested enough…!

The nature of memory: STM, LTM and duration

The term memory has a number of meanings in psychology, as we shall see in this chapter, but the essential definition is that it refers to the process by which we *retain information about events that have happened in the past*. Note that 'the past' does not simply refer to things that happened years ago, but things in our immediate past. If you can recall anything about the start of this paragraph, you must be using your memory. Your memory for events in the present or immediate past (e.g. trying to remember an order of drinks at the bar) is referred to as your **short-term memory** (or STM). Your memory for events that have happened in the more distant past (such as remembering this distinction between STM and LTM in an exam) is referred to as your **long-term memory** (or LTM).

STM and LTM differ in three important ways: duration, capacity and encoding. On this spread we are going to look at the duration of memory.

DURATION

Duration of short-term memory

One of the key differences between the concepts of STM and LTM is **duration**. 'Duration' refers to how long a memory lasts before it is no longer available.

Short-term memories don't last very long. We might think about STM as being like a notepad where we mentally scribble down things that we need to remember for just a very short period of time. The trouble with this 'notepad' is that it can't hold very much information and the 'ink' fades very quickly. An example of STM in action would be trying to remember a seven-digit phone number that you have just been given. This is maintained in STM by repetition until the number is dialled, and then fades once the conversation starts. The way most people keep information in their STM for more than just a few seconds is to *rehearse* it. So rehearsal (saying something to yourself over and over to keep re-presenting it to the STM) is one way of keeping a memory active. The result of such *verbal rehearsal* is that short-term memories are held in the short-term memory store and

eventually become long-term i.e. you will remember the item.

What happens if you don't rehearse something? How long does that memory remain in your short-term store before it disappears? Psychologists have investigated this.

Duration of long-term memory

LTM refers to memories that last anywhere from 2 hours to 100 years plus, i.e. anything that isn't short-term. Psychologists have investigated the duration of LTM and demonstrated that some memories are very long-lasting, as we older folks know. For example Shepard (1967) tested duration of LTM. He showed participants 612 memorable pictures, one at a time. An hour later they were shown some of these pictures among a set of others and showed almost perfect recognition. Four months later they were still able to recognise 50% of the photographs. A more 'real life' study by Bahrick *et al.* (1975) is described below. The material to be remembered was more meaningful to the participants, and therefore the duration of the long-term memories was better.

Studies of duration of STM

Lloyd and Margaret Peterson (1959) conducted a landmark

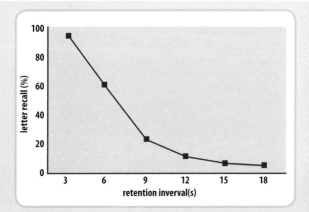

study of the duration of STM. They enlisted the help of 24 students attending their university (this is an easy way to find willing participants and, as you will see, it is very common in psychology).

Recall was tested as follows: the experimenter said a *consonant syllable* (sometimes called a *nonsense trigram*) to the participant followed by a three-digit number (e.g. WRT 303 or SCX 591). The consonant syllable was selected to have no meaning – for example, 'BBC' might be meaningful, whereas 'BCB' shouldn't be. Immediately after hearing the syllable and number, the participant had to count backwards from this number in 3s or 4s until told to stop. Then the participant was asked to recall the nonsense syllable. The reason for

▲ This graph shows the findings from Peterson and Peterson's study.

internet research

You can use the internet to find out more about the duration of STM and LTM, and keep up to date with developments in psychology. Type the search terms 'STM' and 'duration' into Google. Can you find any other research studies? What did they discover? How does that fit in with the research described on this spread?

Who's Al?
Many studies are conducted by more than two people. The term 'et al.' is a Latin phrase meaning 'and others'.

▼ *One psychological investigation conducted in America (Bahrick et al. 1975) demonstrated the considerable duration of LTM by asking people of various ages to put names to faces from their high school year book. 48 years on, people were about 70% accurate. And just to prove that, here's a copy of Cara's High School Yearbook circa 1962 – good old Karen and Betsy.*

CATHERINE FISHER "Cathy" Pet peeve: Brothers Hobby: T.V. Activities: Chorus, Swimming

KAREN FITZPATRICK "Fitzy" Pet peeve: Braces Hobby: Sports Activities: Chorus, Cheerleading, Hall Monitor, Hockey, Basketball

CARA FLANAGAN "Clara-Belle" Pet peeve: Riding bike to school on cold mornings Hobby: Sports Activities: Hockey, Basketball, Journalism, Junior Red Cross

ELIZABETH POGLESONG "Betsy" Pet peeve: School lunches Hobby: Talking on the telephone Activities: Hockey, Yearbook, Cafeteria monitor, Chorus, Swimming

KENNETH FRISBIE "Ken" Pet peeve: mooches Hobby: building slot racers Activities: Art Services

Margaret Intons-Peterson is considered the *grande dame* of short-term memory by virtue of her pioneering work with husband **Lloyd Peterson** on techniques for measuring memory. The Petersons worked for many years at Indiana University in the US where they are now Emeritus professors.

KEY TERMS

Short-term memory Your memory for immediate events. Short-term memories last for a very short time and disappear unless they are rehearsed. The short-term memory store has limited duration and limited capacity. This type of memory is sometimes referred to as *working memory* because it is used in comprehending language, solving problems, and so on. It is related to long-term memory in several fundamental ways, as we will discover.

Long-term memory Your memory for events that have happened in the past. This lasts anywhere from 2 minutes to 100 years. The long-term memory store has potentially unlimited duration and capacity.

Duration A measure of how long a memory lasts before it is no longer available. STM has a very limited duration (a memory in STM doesn't last long), whereas LTM has potentially unlimited duration. A memory in LTM could, theoretically, last for the whole of a person's life.

counting backwards was to stop the participant *rehearsing* the syllable because rehearsal would aid recall.

Each participant was given two practice trials followed by eight trials. On each trial the *retention interval* (time spent counting backwards) was different: 3, 6, 9, 12, 15, or 18 seconds.

Participants remembered about 90% when there was only a 3-second interval and about 2% when there was an 18-second interval. This suggests that, when rehearsal is prevented, STM lasts about 20 seconds at most.

℮ Update

In fact, more recent research suggests that the duration of STM is not quite as short as Peterson and Peterson's study would suggest. Nairne *et al.* (1999) found that items could be recalled after as long as 96 seconds. In Nairne's study, participants were asked to recall the *same* items across trials, whereas in the earlier study different items were used on each trial, which would have led to interference between items, decreasing recall.

It seems that information remains in STM for quite a while *unless* other material replaces or overwrites it.

RESEARCH METHODS Qs   No.**1.1**

1 Identify the IV and DV in the study by Peterson and Peterson and write a suitable hypothesis for the study.

2 Why was it necessary to count backwards during the retention interval?

3 Psychology students might have better memories than most people (because they are young and intelligent). How do you think this might affect the usefulness of this study?

4 Examine the graph showing the results from Peterson and Peterson's study. Describe the results.

5 What conclusions would you draw from the graph? (A conclusion is an attempt to state what the findings tell us about human behaviour.)

DO IT YOURSELF   No.**1.1**

Design your own study of the duration of short-term memory. You can use the nonsense syllable approach taken by Peterson and Peterson, or the word list approach taken by Nairne *et al.* You need to decide:

1 The number of trials you will have. One trial is when you give a participant the stimulus materials, allow a set period of time (e.g. 6 seconds) and then ask the participant to recall the syllable/word.

2 The stimulus materials for each trial. This will be a different nonsense syllable or your word set in different orders, followed by a number for counting backwards from.

3 What counts as a correct answer? This will either be a correctly recalled nonsense syllable or the words recalled in the correct order.

4 You need to write down the instructions for each participant so that you can ensure that each gets the same instructions (called standardised procedures).

5 Conduct a trial run with a partner so you can refine your procedures.

VALIDITY

One criticism made of Peterson and Peterson's research is that psychologists are only studying one kind of memory – memory for syllables and words – whereas much of the time our memories are concerned with other things, such as what I did last night or what my children look like. On the other hand there are times when we are remembering words – like ordering drinks in a pub or remembering someone's phone number.

A second criticism is that Peterson and Peterson were not testing duration. When the participants were counting backwards, the nonsense syllable could well have been *displaced* in STM by the numbers, thus wiping out the memory for the syllables.

CAN YOU...?   No.**1.1**

...**1** Explain what is meant by the phrase 'duration of short-term memory'.

...**2** Outline what psychologists have found out about the duration of short-term memory (STM).

...**3** Outline what have psychologists found out about the duration of long-term memory (LTM).

...**4** Suggest **two** reasons why research into duration of STM lacks validity.

The nature of memory: Capacity and encoding

There are three ways in which STM differs from LTM: duration, **capacity** and **encoding**. On the previous spread we looked at duration. On this spread we are going to consider what psychologists have discovered about capacity and encoding.

'Capacity' refers to how much can be held in a particular place. LTM has potentially unlimited capacity – it is a bit like having a library with virtually unlimited storage capacity. STM, on the other hand, has a very limited capacity. Beyond this capacity, new information can 'bump' out other items from STM. This is a form of forgetting. There are, however, ways in which the capacity of STM can be increased. We will see these later.

When we talk about 'encoding', we are referring to the way that information is changed so that it can be stored in memory. The basic unit of memory (the memory trace) is thought to be biochemical in nature. The precise mechanisms of memory are not fully understood, but most psychologists believe that a memory results from changes in the connections or connection strengths between neurons in the brain. For example, if two neurons are frequently active together, the connection between them will be strengthened. Over time, this means that activity in one neuron will tend to produce activity in the other neuron.

	STM	LTM
Duration	Measured in seconds and minutes	Measured in hours, days and years
Capacity	Less than 7 chunks	Potentially unlimited
Encoding	Acoustic or visual	Semantic (meaning)

▼ Cover up the picture below. How many dots were there? The capacity of STM is probably fewer than 9 items, which would predict that you wouldn't get the answer right because there were 12 dots. If there were 5 dots you would probably have coped.

INDIVIDUAL DIFFERENCES

Jacobs also found that recall (digit span) increased steadily with age; in one sample of school girls he found that 8-year-olds could remember an average of 6.6 digits whereas the mean for 19-year-olds was 8.6 digits.

Why does digit span increase with age? This might be due to a gradual increase in brain capacity, and/or it may be that people develop strategies to improve their digit span as they get older, such as chunking.

REAL-WORLD APPLICATIONS

One technique that maximises the efficiency of our memory is chunking. Alan Baddeley's PhD research was funded by the Post Office, and one of his discoveries was later to lay the foundations for the postcode system that we use in the UK today. Baddeley discovered that if the initial letters of a postcode made up something meaningful (e.g. BS for Bristol) it made the postcode easier to remember. Numbers were best remembered if they were placed between the city name and random letters. Compare the postcode for the University of Bristol (BS1 8TH) with that for the University of Toronto in Canada (M5S 1A1) and work out which was designed with the benefit of psychological research!

CAPACITY OF SHORT-TERM MEMORY

The capacity of STM can be assessed by using digit span, a technique used in the nineteenth century, in the early days of psychology.

Try this: Below is a string of digits each in a separate box. Cover all the boxes except the first and say the digit, then shut your eyes and recall it. Were you right? (Of course you were.) Now try it with two digits: look at the two digits, cover them up, recall them and check to see if you were correct. Keep going until you don't get them right.

2 4 3 7 5 9 4 6 2 1 5 3 2 8

How many digits could you recall correctly? This is the capacity of your immediate or short-term memory. The technique for assessing this is called the 'digit span technique'.

In one of the earliest studies in psychology, a London school teacher, Joseph Jacobs (1887), used this technique to assess the capacity of STM. He found that the average span for digits was 9.3 items, while it was 7.3 for letters. Why was it easier to recall digits? Jacobs suggests that it may be because there are only 9 digits whereas there are 26 letters.

Increasing the capacity of STM

The magic number 7 ± 2

George Miller (1956) wrote a memorable article called 'The magic number seven plus or minus two'. He reviewed psychological research and concluded that the span of immediate memory is 7; people can cope reasonably well with counting seven dots flashed onto a screen but not many more than this. The same is true if you are asked to recall musical notes, digits, letters and even words. Miller also found that people can recall 5 words as well as they can recall 5 letters – we **chunk** things together and can then remember more.

The size of the chunk matters

It seems that in fact the size of the chunk affects how many chunks you can remember. Simon (1974) found that people had a shorter memory span for larger chunks, such as 8-word phrases, than smaller chunks, such as one-syllable words.

ⓔ Update: The magic number 4 in STM

More recently, Cowan (2001) reviewed a variety of studies on the capacity of STM and concluded that STM is likely to be limited to about 4 chunks. This suggests that STM may not be as extensive as was first thought. Some researchers have also looked at the capacity of STM for visual information (rather than verbal stimuli) and also found that 4 items was about the limit (e.g. Vogel et al., 2001).

ENCODING

Acoustic and semantic encoding

We can compare the ways information is stored in STM and LTM in terms of the encoding of the memory trace. *Acoustic coding* involves coding information in terms of the way it sounds, and *semantic coding* involves coding information in terms of its meaning.

Baddeley (1966a and 1966b) tested the effects of acoustic and semantic similarity on short- and long-term recall. He gave participants lists of words which were acoustically similar or dissimilar and words that were semantically similar or dissimilar (see page 76). He found that participants had difficulty remembering acoustically similar words in STM but not in LTM, whereas semantically similar words posed little problem for short-term recall but led to muddled long-term memories.

(e) LTM and STM may sometimes use other codes

In general, STM appears to rely on an acoustic code for storing information. However, some experiments have shown that visual codes are also used in STM. For example, Brandimote *et al.* (1992) found that participants used visual encoding in STM if they were given a *visual* task (pictures) and prevented from doing any *verbal* rehearsal in the retention interval (they had to say 'la la la') before performing a *visual* recall task. Normally we 'translate' visual images into verbal codes in STM, but, as verbal rehearsal was prevented, they did use visual codes. Other research has shown that STM sometimes uses a semantic code (Wickens *et al.*, 1976).

Research has also shown that encoding in LTM is not exclusively semantic. Frost (1972) showed that long-term recall was related to visual as well as semantic categories, and Nelson and Rothbart (1972) found evidence of acoustic encoding.

LINK TO RESEARCH METHODS

The spread on experimental design (pages 76–77) looks at Baddeley's study in more detail and suggests how to replicate it.

KEY TERMS

Capacity This is a measure of how much can be held in memory. It is measured in terms of bits of information such as number of digits. STM has a very limited capacity (less than 7 'chunks' of information) whereas LTM has potentially unlimited capacity.

Encoding The way information is changed so that it can be stored in memory. Information enters the brain via the senses (e.g. eyes and ears). It is then stored in various forms, such as visual codes (like a picture), acoustic forms (sounds), or a semantic form (the meaning of the experience). Information in STM is mainly encoded *acoustically* (i.e. information is represented as *sounds*), whereas information in LTM tends to be encoded *semantically* (i.e. information is represented by its *meaning*).

Chunking Miller proposed that the capacity of STM can be enhanced by grouping sets of digits or letters into meaningful units or 'chunks'. For example it is easier to remember 100 1000 10 10000 than 10010001010000.

Acoustically similar: BIG rhymes with TWIG
Acoustically dissimilar: BIG does not rhyme with LARGE
Semantically similar: BIG means the same as LARGE
Semantically dissimilar: BIG does not mean the same as TWIG

CAN YOU...? No.1.2

...**1** Explain the terms duration, capacity and encoding in relation to memory.

...**2** Explain the difference between acoustic and semantic similarity.

...**3** Outline what psychologists have found out about (a) the capacity of short-term memory (STM) and (b) how information is encoded in STM and LTM. Provide evidence to support your answers.

COMMENTARY CORNER

Question: **Give a brief account of the differences between STM and LTM, and consider the extent to which research supports the distinction between them.** *(12 marks)*

There are some questions in the examination that are called 'extended writing' questions, where you are required to write a longer response of about 200 words. Such questions will always have two distinct parts – description (**AO1**) and evaluation (**AO2**). On many spreads in this book you will find commentary corners such as this where we are going to look at how you can deal with these challenging questions.

In the question posed above, the **AO1** content requires you to outline how STM and LTM differ in terms of *encoding*, *capacity* and/or *duration*. It is generally expected that exam candidates would be able to write about 100 words for this part of their answer, so this means we need to write about 35 words on each. The first one has been done for you.

> **STM and LTM differ in terms of duration.** *STM has a shorter duration, meaning that memories don't last very long (probably less than 20 seconds), whereas long-term memories can potentially last forever.* **(35 words)**
>
> **STM and LTM differ in terms of capacity.**
>
> **STM and LTM differ in terms of encoding.**

Okay, you have done the AO1 part of this essay, so now on to the AO2 part. Note that when we break up the 'essay' into these distinct 'chunks' they become shorter and more 'do-able'. For each difference we can provide evidence both for and against. The key here is to do something more than just *describe* supporting studies; you have to *use* the description as part of a critical sentence (which is what AO2 is all about).

> **Duration:** *Evidence to support the claim that STM and LTM are different with regard to duration.* **(about 20 words)**
>
> *e.g. Peterson and Peterson found that participants remembered almost no trigrams after 18, thus supporting the claim that short-term memories have a very limited duration.* **(24 words)**
>
> **However...** *(counter evidence, problems with supporting research etc.)* **(about 20 words)**
>
> **Capacity:** *Evidence to support the claim that STM and LTM are different with regard to capacity.* **(about 20 words)**
>
> **However...** *(counter evidence, problems with supporting research etc.)* **(about 20 words)**
>
> **Encoding:** *Evidence to support the claim that STM and LTM are different with regard to encoding.* **(about 20 words)**
>
> **However...** *(counter evidence, problems with supporting research etc.)* **(about 20 words)**

The multi-store model of memory

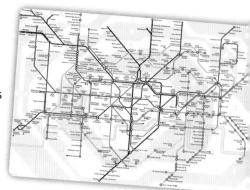

In psychology, a 'model' of something should never be taken as an exact copy of the thing being described, but as a representation of it. A map of the London Underground, for example, is a representation of the layout of the Underground that helps us appreciate how it works and where it goes. Of course direction, scale, etc. must be distorted somewhat to make it all fit neatly on the page. A model of memory is also a representation based on the evidence available. A model provides us with what is essentially an analogy of how memory works. Describing memory in terms of 'stores' or 'loops' makes our understanding more concrete, and simply conveys an approximate idea of how a particular psychologist has attempted to understand and explain the available evidence. These models change as the available evidence changes, so should not be seen as permanent fixtures.

On the following spreads we will be looking at two models – the multi-store model and the working memory model. They are not alternative models – the working memory model is an expansion of the original concept of a short-term store.

THE MULTI-STORE MODEL

The multi-store model of memory (MSM) is an explanation of how memory processes work. You hear and see and feel many things but only a very small number are remembered. Why are some things remembered and others aren't?

The multi-store model was first described by Richard Atkinson and Richard Shiffrin in 1968. It is illustrated in the diagram on the right. You should by now be quite familiar with the idea of a short-term store (STM) and a long-term store (LTM).

There is a third store in this model: the **sensory store** (or sensory memory). This is actually composed of several stores – the eyes, ears, nose, fingers, tongue etc., and the corresponding areas of the brain. The sensory stores are constantly receiving information, but most of this receives no attention and remains in the sensory stores for a very brief period. If a person's *attention* is focused on one of the sensory stores (for whatever reason), then the data is transferred to STM. Attention is the first step in remembering something.
Information held in STM is in a 'fragile' state. It will disappear (decay) relatively quickly if it isn't *rehearsed*. This may well be familiar to you. When you try to remember things for a test, what do you do? Possibly you repeat the things you want to remember over and over again – verbal rehearsal!

It will also disappear if new information enters STM pushing out (or *displacing*) the original information. This happens because STM has a limited capacity (probably about 4 chunks of information).

The second step is moving information from STM to LTM. Atkinson and Shiffrin said that this also happens through *rehearsal*. Initially rehearsal maintains information in STM but the more something is rehearsed, the more lasting the memory will be. This kind of rehearsal is referred to as *maintenance rehearsal* which is largely verbal.

Atkinson and Shiffrin proposed a direct relationship between rehearsal in STM and the strength of the long-term memory – the more the information is rehearsed, the better it is remembered.

So the multi-store model is what it says – a description of how memory works in terms of three 'stores': your senses (sensory memory), STM (limited capacity, short duration) and then LTM (potentially unlimited capacity and duration). Attention and rehearsal explain how data is transferred. Sounds good, or does it? We will consider the research evidence, here and on the next spread.

Have you ever had the experience of vaguely hearing someone say something and then hearing them say 'DID YOU HEAR ME???'? At which point you say 'What?' but simultaneously you 'hear' what was said. This is because the words are still in your sensory store.

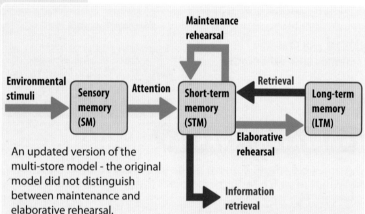

An updated version of the multi-store model - the original model did not distinguish between maintenance and elaborative rehearsal.

CAN YOU...? (No.1.3)

...**1** Identify **six** key pieces of information about the multi-store model. (This will enable you to construct your own précis* of the model.)

...**2** Explain what is meant by 'maintenance rehearsal'.

...**3** Outline **two** pieces of research evidence that support the distinction between STM and LTM.

...**4** Give a brief account of the sensory store.

...**5** Outline **one** case study related to the study of memory.

...**6** Suggest **two** reasons why this case study is a good way to study memory and **two** reasons why this case study is not a good way to study memory.

...**7** Describe the role of the hippocampus in memory.

...**8** Describe **two** ethical issues that are important when conducting memory experiments and explain how they can be dealt with.

Richard Atkinson (pictured) and Richard Shiffrin met at Indiana University in the US (where the Petersons also worked). Atkinson later moved to Stanford but continued to collaborate with Shiffrin as well as being a co-author on one of the best known psychology textbooks of all time – so famous that it is now called Atkinson and Hilgard's Introduction to Psychology. Atkinson has received a long list of honours but perhaps one of the more special ones was to have a mountain in Antarctica named after him.

KEY TERM

Sensory store / memory This is the information at the senses – information collected by your eyes, ears, nose, fingers and so on. Information is retained for a very brief period by the sensory registers. We are only able to hold accurate images of sensory information momentarily (less than half a second). The capacity of sensory memory is very large. The method of encoding depends on the sense organ involved, e.g. visual for the eyes or acoustic for the ears.

EVIDENCE FOR THREE SEPARATE MEMORY STORES

The key feature of the MSM is the proposal that memory can be separated into three distinct stores. On the previous two spreads of this chapter we have looked at evidence which supports a qualitative difference between STM and LTM in terms of duration, capacity and encoding. We will now look at some further evidence starting with research on the sensory store.

The sensory store

Evidence to indicate the duration of the sensory store was collected in a study by Sperling (1960). Participants saw a grid of digits and letters (as in the illustration below) for 50 milliseconds (a blink of an eye). They were either asked to write down all 12 items or they were told they would hear a tone immediately after the exposure and they should just write down that row. When asked to report the whole thing their recall was poorer (5 items recalled, about 42%) than when asked to give one row only (3 items recalled, 75%). This shows that information decays rapidly in the sensory store.

7	1	V	F	high tone
X	L	5	3	medium tone
B	4	W	7	low tone

Stimulus material used by Sperling

The serial position effect

Glanzer and Cunitz (1966) showed that, if you give participants a list of about 20 words, presented one at a time, and then ask them to recall any words they can remember, you can observe an interesting effect.

They tend to remember the words from the start of the list (a *primacy effect*) and from the end of the list (a *recency effect*) but are less good at recalling words in the middle. The primacy effect occurs because the first words are best rehearsed and transferred to LTM. The recency effect occurs because these words are in STM when you start recalling the list.

Areas of the brain associated with STM and LTM

One way to demonstrate the existence of separate stores in memory is to link STM and LTM to specific areas of the brain. Modern techniques of scanning the brain can be used (such as PET scans and fMRI which are used to detect brain tumours). These take images of the active brain and enable us to see what region is active when a person is doing particular tasks. Research has found that the *prefrontal cortex* is active when individuals are working on a task in short-term memory (Beardsley, 1997) whereas the *hippocampus* is active when long-term memory is engaged (Squire *et al.*, 1992).

Case studies

Psychologists have also learned about areas of the brain involved in different kinds of memory from their study of individuals with brain damage. One case involved a man referred to as HM (Scoville and Milner, 1957). His brain damage was caused by an operation to remove the hippocampus from both sides of his brain to reduce the severe epilepsy he suffered. HM's personality and intellect remained intact but he could not form new long-term memories, though he could remember things from before the surgery.

This suggests that the hippocampus may function as a memory 'gateway' through which new memories must pass before entering permanent storage in the brain for anything that happened since.

▼ The hippocampus looks like a seahorse and that's what the word means literally (Greek: hippos = horse, kampi = curve). In Alzheimer's disease, the hippocampus is one of the first regions of the brain to suffer damage. Memory problems and disorientation appear among the first symptoms.

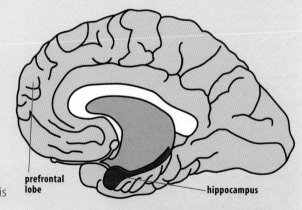

prefrontal lobe

hippocampus

* A précis is a summary. It isn't just shorter – it aims to include all the essential points.

REAL-WORLD APPLICATIONS

Some memories, such as the memory for new skills or habits, can sometimes be formed even without the hippocampus. A current research area is to determine exactly what kinds of learning and memory can survive hippocampal damage, and how these kinds of learning can be used to guide rehabilitation of people who have experienced such brain damage.

LINK TO RESEARCH METHODS

The case study method (strengths and weaknesses) is discussed on pages 100–1 including further details of the study of HM and of two other individuals with brain damage – Clive Wearing and KF.

Evaluating the multi-store model

On the previous spread we looked at various research studies that supported the MSM. It might appear, from reading these studies, that the MSM is an accurate representation of the way our memories work. On this spread we will take a more balanced view. It may seem, at first glance, that the weaknesses clearly outweigh the strengths – but don't forget all that research evidence on the previous pages.

STRENGTHS OF THE MULTI-STORE MODEL

First, as we have already noted, there is strong evidence (described on the first three spreads of this chapter) of three qualitatively different stores. This suggests that the basis of the MSM is sound.

Second, the model does provide an account of memory in terms of both structure and process. The structures are the three stores, and the processes are attention and verbal rehearsal. However, the model has been criticised for focusing too much on structure and too little on process.

Third, a great strength of this model is that MSM has clear predictions about memory which means psychologists can conduct studies to test it. This is a strength because psychologists need to be pushed into conducting research if they wish to find out about human behaviour. Without research we would not change the way we think about the causes of behaviour.

VALIDITY

An important criticism of the MSM is that the supporting evidence lacks validity for a number of reasons. First of all, memory research usually relates to semantic memory, so it is relevant to some everyday memory activities (such as remembering phone numbers), but not to all aspects of memory.

The studies have also largely involved college students studying psychology. It is quite likely that people aged 18–21 have rather different memories from people of other age groups, and students are also likely to be more than averagely intelligent. It is also likely that psychology students might try to guess at what the experiment is about and this may affect their behaviour (and the findings of the study). This is called *participant reactivity*.

The studies are also largely laboratory experiments. Such experiments are good because they can be highly controlled, but they tend to suffer from various threats to validity, such as *demand characteristics* and experimenter bias, even when the participants aren't students.

However, it isn't all bad. The studies related to the multi-store model are usually laboratory experiments, which means that *extraneous variables* are likely to be well controlled. We can therefore be more certain that any change in the dependent variable is due to the independent variable, and thus can reach conclusions about cause and effect. Therefore, in some way it can also be argued that this evidence has high validity.

WEAKNESSES OF THE MULTI-STORE MODEL

The bottom line is that most of the assumptions of the original multi-store model are either incorrect or, at best, only partially correct. Subsequent revisions of the model have tried to accommodate some of the criticisms. The main criticism of the MSM is that it oversimplifies memory *structures* and *processes*.

Structures: STM and LTM are not unitary stores

As far as structure is concerned, the MSM suggests that STM and LTM each operate in a single uniform fashion whereas the evidence suggests that this is not true.

Evidence for a non-unitary STM came from the case study of KF (Shallice and Warrington, 1970). KF suffered brain damage which resulted in difficulty dealing with verbal information in STM but a normal ability to process visual information. This suggests that STM is not a single store.

The MSM describes LTM as one single store whereas evidence from patients with amnesia indicates that there are different kinds of long-term memory. Schachter *et al.* (2000) have suggested that there are four long-term stores:

- *Semantic memory* – memory for knowledge about the world, including knowledge about words.
- *Episodic memory* – memory for what you did yesterday or a film you saw last week.
- *Procedural memory* – memory for riding a bicycle or learning how to read.

- *Perceptual-representation system (PRS)* memory related to perceptual priming – enhanced recognition of specific stimuli (such as words) which have been seen before (e.g. give a list of words and then a degraded version, e.g. TOBOGGAN and _O_ O_GA_. Ability to recognise the latter is an example of perceptual priming).

Spiers *et al.* (2001) studied memory in 147 patients with amnesia. In all cases their procedural memories and perceptual-representation systems were intact but the other two systems were not intact, showing that LTM is not unitary.

Processes: Rehearsal versus processing

In terms of process, research has also shown that maintenance rehearsal (repeating things) is not the only means by which enduring long-term memories are created. Craik and Lockhart (1972) proposed a different kind of model to explain lasting memories. They suggested that enduring memories are created by the *processing* that you do, rather than through maintenance rehearsal; things that are processed more deeply are more memorable just because of the way they are processed.

Consider the following study: Craik and Tulving (1975) gave participants a list of nouns (e.g. 'shark') and asked a question about each word. There were three kinds of question that each participant answered:

1 shallow processing – for example, 'Is the word printed in capital letters?'

LINK TO RESEARCH METHODS

See pages 78–9 for an explanation of participant reactivity, demand characteristics and experimenter bias.

...1 Explain why research related to the multi-store can be criticised for lacking validity but could also be said to have high validity.

...2 Identify and explain two strengths and two weaknesses of the multi-store memory model. For each, make sure you provide some elaboration to explain your criticism.

---

2 phonemic processing – for example, 'Does the word rhyme with "train"?'

3 semantic processing (deeper processing for meaning) – for example, 'Is the word a type of fruit?'

Participants remembered most words from condition 3 and least from condition 1. This suggests that deeper processing leads to enhanced memory.

There is no doubt that processing is important, and the work of Craik and Lockhart has led to a reformulation of the MSM, replacing 'maintenance rehearsal' with 'elaborative rehearsal'. Maintenance rehearsal involves repeating things, whereas *elaborative* rehearsal involves deeper or more semantic analysis. In fact Glenberg *et al.* (1977) showed that maintenance rehearsal does have some effect on creating enduring memories but not as much as elaborative rehearsal.

How separate are STM and LTM?

The multi-store model suggests that STM is involved before LTM. However Logie (1999) pointed out that STM actually *relies* on LTM and therefore cannot come 'first' as suggested in the MSM. Consider the following list of letters: AQABBCITVIBM. In order

to chunk this you need to recall the meaningful groups of letters and such meanings are stored in LTM.

Ruchkin *et al.* (2003) demonstrated this by asking participants to recall a set of words and pseudo-words (words designed to sound like real words but with no meaning). Brain activity was monitored and they found large differences in the two conditions. If words and pseudo-words involved just short-term memory then activity should have been the same for both conditions, but there was much more activity when real words were processed indicating the involvement of other areas of the brain. Ruchkin *et al.* (2003) concluded that STM is actually just the part of LTM which is activated at any given time.

This more recent view of a short-term store is embraced by the working memory model. The multi-store model's STM was a place to hold information as it is being moved into LTM, whereas the concept of working memory is that it is an end in itself – a place where information is held until it is put to use. Examples would include working on a maths problem or storing a phone number when telephoning someone.

DO IT YOURSELF

Demonstrating elaborative rehearsal   No.**1.2**

Here is a list of 10 words:

apple, dress, target, spoon, water, church, money, grate, house, onion

Each member of your class should find two participants. Participant 1 should be given 30 seconds to memorise the words. Participant 2 should be asked to rate each word for 'pleasantness' – giving a score of 5 if they think the word is very pleasant, 3 for neutral, and 1 for very unpleasant. Participant 2 should not be aware that they will be asked to recall the words.

The next day ask each of your participants to recall the words from the list. How did they do?

Hyde and Jenkins (1973) conducted this study and found as much as 50% higher recall for the group that had conducted elaborative rehearsal (rating words for pleasantness).

COMMENTARY CORNER

You may recall from the earlier commentary corner that questions in your AS psychology paper often end with a 'mini-essay' that tests your ability to engage critically with the material you have just learned. This is not something to be dreaded but rather a neat way to boost your marks by showing that you really do understand the implications of the preceding information. A typical question for the material we have just covered might be as follows:

Question: **To what extent does the multi-store model offer a reasonable account of human memory?** *(12 marks)*

There are several strategies for answering a question such as this although the end result should always mean that your answer is one-half description of knowledge and understanding (**AO1**) and one-half analysis and evaluation (**AO2**). For this first demonstration, we can choose the most straightforward technique – splitting the answer into two paragraphs, each one about 100 words long. The first of these paragraphs might then be a description of the multi-store model, and the second concentrating more on its general worth as an account of memory. For example:

Paragraph 1

Atkinson and Shiffrin (1968) proposed that memory could be explained in terms of three distinct stores. These were the sensory memory, which holds information for a very brief period; short-term memory (STM), characterised by limited capacity and relatively short duration; and long-term memory (LTM), which had potentially unlimited capacity and duration. If a person's attention is focused on material in the sensory memory, this would be transferred to STM. Atkinson and Shiffrin claimed that information was transferred from STM to LTM through the process of rehearsal. They proposed a direct relationship between rehearsal in STM and the strength of the long-term memory – the more the information is rehearsed, the better it is remembered.

Notice that this paragraph is entirely AO1 (descriptive) content, therefore everything that follows must be AO2 (analysis and evaluation) because half of the answer should be AO1 and half should be AO2.

Paragraph 2

Research studies have tended to support the distinction proposed by Atkinson and Shiffrin regarding differences between the stores with respect to capacity, encoding and duration. The existence of separate stores in memory is also supported by the use of modern brain scanning techniques (such as PET scans). These have shown, for example, that the prefrontal cortex is active when individuals are working on a task in immediate (i.e. short-term) memory whereas the hippocampus is active when LTM is engaged. Despite this research support, the multi-store model is probably an over-simplification of memory processes. For example, the multi-store model just proposes one long-term store, whereas research suggests several different forms of LTM (e.g. episodic, semantic and procedural memory).

Note that there is no one correct conclusion to be drawn here. You may choose to champion the multi-store model, or use your criticisms to totally destroy it. It really is your call.

The working memory model

On the previous two spreads we considered the multi-store model of memory. Now we will consider one alternative model – the working memory model (and its research evidence and strengths and weaknesses). The working memory model addresses one aspect of memory – short-term or immediate memory. On the previous spread we saw that the original formulation of short-term memory by Atkinson and Shiffrin was found lacking in several ways – it appears that immediate memory is not a unitary store as was first thought, and it appears that immediate memory has a different relationship with long-term memory from the one first suggested.

THE WORKING MEMORY MODEL

'Short-term memory is not a single unitary system; rather it is an amalgam (or alliance) of several temporary memory systems working together.' (Baddeley, 2004, p.33)

Baddeley and Hitch (1974) used the term 'working memory' to refer to that bit of memory that you are using when you are working on a complex task which requires you to store information as you go along. For example, if you are calculating a complex sum such as 21 + 12 + 52, you add 21 and 12 and hold that answer in working memory before adding the final number. Or, when reading a sentence, you store the individual words in working memory while determining the sentence's meaning.

Baddeley and Hitch felt that STM was not just one store but a number of different stores. Why did they think this?

- If you do two things at the same time and they are both visual tasks, you perform them less well than if you do them separately.
- If you do two things at the same time and one is visual whereas the other involves sound, then there is no interference. You do them as well simultaneously as you would do them separately.

This suggests that there is one store for visual processing and one store for processing sounds, as portrayed by the model.

The components of working memory

Central executive

This is the key component of working memory. The function of the **central executive** is to direct attention to particular tasks, determining at any time how *'resources'* are allocated to tasks. The 'resources' are the three slave systems listed below. Data arrives from the senses or from long-term memory. The central executive has a very limited capacity; in other words it can't attend to too many things at once.

Phonological loop

This too has a limited capacity. The **phonological loop** deals with auditory information and preserves the order of information. Baddeley (1986) further subdivided this loop into the phonological store and an articulatory process. The phonological store holds the words you hear, like an inner ear. The articulatory process is used for words that are heard or seen. These words are silently repeated (looped), like an inner voice, a form of *maintenance rehearsal*.

Visuo-spatial sketchpad

The **visuo-spatial sketchpad** is used when you have to plan a spatial task (like getting from one room to another, or counting the number of windows in your house). Visual and/or spatial information is temporarily stored here. Visual information is what things look like. Spatial information is the relationship between things.

Logie (1995) suggested that the visuo-spatial sketchpad can be divided into a visual cache (store) and inner scribe which deals with spatial relations.

Epidosic buffer

Baddeley (2000) added the **episodic buffer** because he realised the model needed a general store. The phonological loop and visuo-spatial sketchpad deal with processing and temporary storage of *specific* kinds of information. The central executive has no storage capacity; so there was nowhere to hold information that relates to both visual *and* acoustic information. The episodic buffer is an extra storage system that has, in common with all working memory units, limited capacity. The episodic buffer integrates information from the central executive, the phonological loop, the visuo-spatial sketch pad and also from long-term memory.

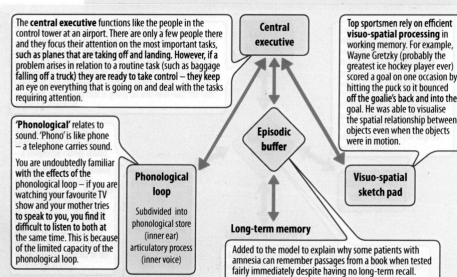

The **central executive** functions like the people in the control tower at an airport. There are only a few people there and they focus their attention on the most important tasks, such as planes that are taking off and landing. However, if a problem arises in relation to a routine task (such as baggage falling off a truck) they are ready to take control – they keep an eye on everything that is going on and deal with the tasks requiring attention.

'Phonological' relates to sound. 'Phono' is like phone – a telephone carries sound.

You are undoubtedly familiar with the effects of the phonological loop – if you are watching your favourite TV show and your mother tries to speak to you, you find it difficult to listen to both at the same time. This is because of the limited capacity of the phonological loop.

Top sportsmen rely on efficient **visuo-spatial processing** in working memory. For example, Wayne Gretzky (probably the greatest ice hockey player ever) scored a goal on one occasion by hitting the puck so it bounced off the goalie's back and into the goal. He was able to visualise the spatial relationship between objects even when the objects were in motion.

Central executive

Episodic buffer

Phonological loop

Subdivided into phonological store (inner ear) articulatory process (inner voice)

Visuo-spatial sketch pad

Long-term memory

Added to the model to explain why some patients with amnesia can remember passages from a book when tested fairly immediately despite having no long-term recall.

Try reading something while saying 'the the the ...' silently to yourself. Does this disrupt your reading? The working memory model suggests that the phonological loop is important in reading new material. If you read something you know well, is saying 'the the the ...' less disruptive? Try designing your own experiment to test this. You will need to make various design decisions:

- Will you use independent groups or repeated measures?
- What texts will you give to your participants? How can you ensure that they are equivalent?
- How will you measure the dependent variable – the extent to which reading is disrupted?

...**1** Identify **six** key pieces of information about the multi-store model? (This will enable you to construct your own précis of the model.)

...**2** Describe an everyday example of each of the four components of the WM model.

...**3** Outline **three** pieces of evidence that support the working memory model.

...**4** Give **one** criticism of each of the studies described in the previous question. (Hint: you might think about validity, or problems with case studies.)

EVIDENCE SUPPORTING THE WORKING MEMORY MODEL

Doing two tasks using the same or different components

Hitch and Baddeley (1976) gave participants two tasks to do simultaneously. Task 1 occupied the central executive (e.g. participants were given a statement 'B is followed by A' and shown two letters such as 'AB' and asked to say true or false). Task 2 either involved the articulatory loop (e.g. asked to say 'the the the' repeatedly), or both the central executive *and* the articulatory loop (saying random digits), or no additional task. Task 1 was slower when given a task involving both the central executive and the articulatory loop. Speed on task 1 was the same whether using the articulatory loop or no extra task. This shows that doing two tasks that involve the same component causes difficulty. It also suggests that, when different components are used, performance is not affected.

Evidence for the four components

Evidence for the central executive

Activity in the central executive should be increased when an individual has to perform two tasks simultaneously (dual-task) rather than one after the other (single-task). Bunge *et al.* (2000) used *fMRI* to see which parts of the brain were most active when participants were doing two tasks (reading a sentence and recalling the final word in each sentence). The same brain areas were active in either dual- or single-task conditions but there was significantly more activation in the dual-task condition indicating that increased attentional demands were reflected in brain activity.

Evidence for the phonological loop and articulatory process

The phonological loop explains why the **word-length effect** occurs – the fact that people cope better with short words than long words in working memory (STM). It seems that the phonological loop holds the amount of information that you can say in 2 seconds (Baddeley *et al.*, 1975a). This makes it hard to remember a list of long words such as 'association' and 'representative' compared to shorter words like 'harm' and 'twice'. The longer words can't be rehearsed on the phonological loop because they don't fit.

But the word-length effect disappears if a person is given an *articulatory suppression* task, for example if you are asked to say 'the the the ...' while reading the words. This repetitive task ties up the articulatory process and means you can't rehearse the shorter words more quickly than the longer ones, so the word-length effect disappears. This is evidence for the articulatory process.

Evidence for the visuo-spatial sketchpad

Baddeley *et al.* (1975b) demonstrated the existence of the visuo-spatial sketchpad. Participants were given a visual tracking task (they had to track a moving light with a pointer). At the same time they were given one of two other tasks: task 1 was to describe all the angles on the letter F, task 2 was to perform a verbal task. Task 1 was very difficult but not task 2, presumably because the second task involved two different components (or 'slave' systems). This is also evidence related to the effects of doing two tasks using the same or different components.

Evidence for the episodic buffer

Baddeley *et al.* (1987) found that, when participants were shown words and then asked for immediate recall, their performance was much better for sentences (related words) than for unrelated words. This supports the idea of an immediate memory store for items that are neither visual nor phonological and that draw on long-term memory (to link the related words).

Evidence from brain-damaged patients

Studies of individuals with brain damage also support the working memory model. As we have seen, the case study of KF (Shallice and Warrington, 1970) showed that STM works independently of LTM, as he had no problem with long-term learning but some aspects of his immediate memory were impaired. His short-term forgetting of auditory information was much greater than that of visual stimuli, and his auditory problems were limited in respect of verbal material such as letters and digits but not of meaningful sounds (such as a phone ringing). Thus his brain damage seemed to be restricted to the phonological loop.

Another patient, SC, had generally good learning abilities with the exception of being unable to learn word pairs that were presented out loud. This suggests damage to the phonological loop (Trojano and Grossi, 1995). Another patient, LH, who had been involved in a road accident, performed better on spatial tasks than those involving visual imagery (Farah *et al.*, 1988). This suggests separate visual and spatial systems.

KEY TERMS

Central executive Monitors and coordinates all other mental functions in working memory.

Phonological loop Encodes speech sounds in working memory, typically involving maintenance rehearsal (repeating the words over and over again). This is why this component of working memory is referred to as a 'loop'.

Visuo-spatial sketchpad Encodes visual information in terms of separate objects as well as the arrangement of these objects in one's visual field.

Episodic buffer Receives input from many sources, temporarily stores this information, and then integrates it in order to construct a mental episode of what is being experienced right now.

Word-length effect The observation that people remember lists of short words better than lists of long words.

Evaluating the working memory model

On the previous spread we saw that the working memory model has an impressive range of studies that provide support. Indeed the model is closely linked to research, having been developed on the basis of research findings. On this spread we will take a balanced look at the relative strengths and weaknesses of the model.

meet the researcher

Alan Baddeley has conducted a large amount of research on human memory. On page 7 we looked at his classic study on encoding in short- and long-term memory. His continued research on memory led him to formulate the working memory model, with colleague Graham Hitch. Baddeley continues to research and refine this model.

In addition to conducting research, Baddeley (2004) has also written many books, including a very readable one called, *Your memory: A user's guide.*

REAL-WORLD APPLICATIONS

The concept of working memory has been used in diagnosing mental illness. For example, Park *et al.* (1999) reviewed a number of studies and concluded that problems with working memory were a key distinction between normal individuals and patients with schizophrenia. In other words the concept of working memory is one means by which schizophrenia can be diagnosed.

EXAM TIP

It is important to be able to use all the specialist vocabulary linked to both models of memory – phrases such as 'semantic memory' and 'maintenance rehearsal' and 'phonological loop'. Being able to use these terms in the exam turns an answer that 'lacks detail' into one that 'is 'detailed'. Focus on getting familiar with these terms.

⊕ STRENGTHS OF THE WORKING MEMORY MODEL

First, the model explains observations made by psychologists, such as the word-length effect (see page 13) and the partial short-term memory difficulties experienced by individuals with brain damage such as KF and SC (see pages 13 and 101).

Second, there is a considerable amount of research evidence to support the model, especially more recent studies which show direct links between certain tasks and activation of parts of the brain demonstrating physical representations of the components of the WM model.

Third, the continuing development of this model reflects the shift from seeing 'memory' as one activity, to being able to distinguish an array of different kinds of memory. In the 1950s, psychologists (e.g. Karl Lashley) tried to find where memory was located in the brain. The MSM in the 1960s offered a first step in the right direction in identifying some sub-components of memory and linking these with areas of the brain such as the hippocampus. The working memory model has continued the refinement by identifying further components of memory.

Sternberg (2006) concludes: 'The working memory model is probably the most widely used and accepted today.'

Making comparisons with the multi-store model

There is abundant evidence of the existence of a brief memory store, and the WM model offers a better account than the STM component of the MSM. This is because it moves from describing immediate memory as a unitary store to one with a number of components. In comparison with the MSM, the working memory model includes verbal (maintenance) rehearsal as an optional process rather than the *only* means by which information is kept in immediate memory. The WM model also emphasises process more than the MSM, which emphasised structure. The WM model suggests that immediate memory holds the most recently activated portion of long-term memory, rather than portraying short-term memory as a way station on the way to and from long-term memory. WM moves the activated elements in and out of brief, temporary storage.

THE JACKMANS

Alice is rehearsing for a play at school and has to learn her lines.

1 Give her advice, based on the multi-store model, on how to learn her lines.
2 She still finds it difficult to learn the lines. What other suggestions can you offer her based on other psychological research.

Tom's mother gets very annoyed when she tries to speak to him when he is playing a game on the computer: he never seems to actually hear what she is saying.

3 Use both the multi-store model and the working memory model to explain why he doesn't seem to hear her.

On his way home from work, Rick witnessed an accident involving two cars, but when asked to make a statement to the police he can't remember many details.

4 Use the multi-store model to explain why his memory for the details is so poor.

WEAKNESSES OF THE WORKING MEMORY MODEL

The central executive

There is some concern about the central executive. What exactly is it? The answer appears to be that it allocates resources and is essentially the same as 'attention'. Some psychologists feel this is too vague and doesn't really *explain* anything.

Critics also feel that the notion of a single central executive is wrong and that there are probably several components. Eslinger and Damasio (1985) studied EVR who had had a cerebral tumour removed. He performed well on tests requiring reasoning which suggested that his central executive was intact, however he had poor decision-making skills (for example he would spend hours trying to decide where to eat) which suggests that in fact his central executive was not wholly intact.

In summary the account offered of the central executive is unsatisfactory because it fails to explain anything and because it is probably more complex than currently represented.

Evidence from brain-damaged patients

Some of the key evidence for the WM model comes from case studies of individuals who have suffered serious brain damage. There are a number of problems with using such evidence. First of all, you cannot make 'before and after' comparisons, so it is not clear whether changes in behaviour are *caused* by the damage. Second, the process of brain injury is traumatic, which may in itself change behaviour.

"This amnesia of yours ... can you remember how long you've had it?"

CAN YOU...? No.1.6

...1 Identify and explain two strengths and two weaknesses of the working memory model. For each, make sure you provide some elaboration to *explain* your criticism.

...2 Describe two differences between the multi-store model and the working memory model.

COMMENTARY CORNER

In the last 'Commentary Corner', we showed you *one* way to tackle the **AO1** + **AO2** extended writing question. Remember that this was only a suggestion, and you may well choose totally different material to express *your* view of the material being assessed.

A second technique is to decide in advance what your conclusion is going to be, and then construct an argument, based on research evidence or alternative viewpoints, that support that eventual conclusion. This is rather like a barrister who is trying to convince a jury of his client's innocence and must present an argument that will help the jury reach the same conclusion. Of course, this is only a partially appropriate analogy, as your 'conclusion' may simply be that there are clearly good *and* bad points about the theory or model being discussed. While this refreshing honesty is probably quite appropriate in an academic discussion, a barrister who presents an argument based on, 'Well…he might be innocent, but then again he might be guilty' would not get much work!

Taking the question at the top of the next column as your starting point, what material would you use to reach a conclusion that a) the working memory model is very worthwhile, b) the working memory model is not so good, and c) the working memory model has both strengths and weaknesses?

Question: **Give a brief account of and evaluate the working memory model of human memory.** *(12 marks)*

As with all these types of question, you are given 6 marks for the **AO1** content (in this case it is for a brief account of the working memory model) and 6 for the **AO2** content. Remember, you have to *use* material for it to count as **AO2**. An example of where this is *not* being done is:

'In a study of brain-damaged patients, LH, who had been involved in a road accident, performed better on spatial tasks than those involving visual imagery.'

Instead, an effective use of this same material might represent it thus:

'In a study of brain-damaged patients, LH, who had been involved in a road accident, performed better on spatial tasks than those involving visual imagery. This supports the working memory model because it suggests separate visual and spatial systems.'

The two paragraphs are different because the second one has an additional sentence, but can you explain *why* this turns the second paragraph into *effective* **AO2**?

Eyewitness testimony (EWT)

Eyewitnesses frequently play a critical role in criminal investigations, yet the psychological study of the accuracy of eyewitness memory suggests that it is actually far less reliable than we might imagine. The importance of this issue was highlighted in the Devlin Report of 1976, which found that in a large proportion of criminal cases in England and Wales, **eyewitness testimony** was the only evidence offered in court, and in approximately 75% of these cases the suspect was found guilty. In fact, research in the United States has shown that inaccurate eyewitness memory is the main factor leading to false convictions. One study estimated that there may be about 10,000 wrong convictions a year in the US through eyewitness testimony. In those cases, an innocent person is imprisoned, and the guilty person is still free.

Although there were no dramatic changes to the legal system as a result of psychological research, a precedent was set in Britain in the 1977 *Crown versus Turnbull* trial, where the Court of Appeal rejected eyewitness testimony that was presented without supportive evidence. Since then, prosecutions are unlikely to be brought on eyewitness evidence alone, and much greater use is now made of evidence like DNA and closed circuit TV recordings. However, eyewitness testimony is still a very important part of the evidence in many criminal trials, and presents a number of challenges to psychology.

meet the researcher

Elizabeth Loftus is Distinguished Professor at the University of California, Irvine. Her experiments have revealed how memories can be changed by things that we are told after the event. The legal field has been a significant application of her memory research.

Professor Loftus sent us the following anecdote about her life in psychology:

'In the mid '70s with my newly minted Ph.D. in hand, I spent a year at Harvard University. I sent a note to B.F. Skinner (a very famous Psychologist) explaining that I was ... at Harvard for the year, and, "nothing would give me greater pleasure than to have lunch with you." A couple of days later my office phone rang: "Hi it's Fred Skinner. I'd be happy to have lunch." We met at a restaurant near Harvard Yard, and as we walked toward the front door, he said "Women's lib aside, let me treat you this time." We talked about his multi-volume autobiography that he was currently working on. I could not believe that there I was, having lunch with the B.F. Skinner, and hearing about his autobiography before it was even finished. From my teen years, my personal motto has been "Nothing ventured nothing gained." Sometimes it pays off.'

WHAT *IS* EYEWITNESS TESTIMONY?

The term **eyewitness testimony** (EWT) is actually a legal term, referring to the use of eyewitnesses (or earwitnesses) to give evidence in court concerning the identity of someone who has committed a crime. Psychologists tend to use the term 'eyewitness memory' instead of 'testimony' when carrying out research to test the accuracy of eyewitness testimony.

Eyewitness memory goes through three stages:

- The witness *encodes* into LTM details of the event and the persons involved. Encoding may be only partial and distorted, particularly as most crimes happen very quickly, frequently at night, and sometimes accompanied by rapid, complex and often violent action.
- The witness *retains* the information for a period of time. Memories may be lost or modified during retention (most forgetting takes place within the first few minutes of a retention interval) and other activities between encoding and retrieval may *interfere* with the memory itself.
- The witness *retrieves* the memory from storage. What happens during the reconstruction of the memory (e.g. the presence or absence of appropriate retrieval cues or the nature of the questioning) may significantly affect its accuracy.

INDIVIDUAL DIFFERENCES

Who are the most accurate witnesses, males or females? Wells and Olsen's review of eyewitness testimony research (Wells and Olsen, 2003) concludes that although males and females may take an interest in different aspects of a scene, the overall abilities of males and females in eyewitness memory appears to be largely indistinguishable.

STUDIES OF THE *ACCURACY* OF EYEWITNESS TESTIMONY

Loftus and Palmer (1974) were interested in the accuracy of memory after witnessing a car accident, in particular to see if **leading questions** distorted the accuracy of an eyewitness's immediate recall. Forty-five students were shown seven films of different traffic accidents. After each film the participants were given a questionnaire which asked them to describe the accident and then answer a series of specific questions about it. There was one *critical question*. This question was 'About how fast were the cars going when they hit each other?' One group of participants were given this question. The other five groups were given the verbs *smashed*, *collided*, *bumped* or *contacted* in place of the word *hit*.

The mean speed estimate was calculated for each group, as shown in the table. The group given the word 'smashed' estimated a higher speed than the other groups (about 41 mph). The group given the word 'contacted' estimated the lowest speed (about 30 mph).

Verb	Mean speed estimate
smashed	40.8
collided	39.3
bumped	38.1
hit	34.0
contacted	31.8

Speed estimates for the different verbs

EWT in real life

Loftus' research suggested that EWT was generally inaccurate and therefore unreliable, but not all researchers agree with this conclusion. Yuille and Cutshall (1986) interviewed 13 people who had witnessed an armed robbery in Canada. The interviews took place more than 4 months after the crime and included two misleading questions. Despite these questions the witnesses provided accurate recall that matched their initial detailed reports. This suggests that post-event information may *not* affect memory in real-life EWT.

KEY TERMS

Eyewitness testimony The evidence provided in court by a person who witnessed a crime, with a view to identifying the perpetrator of the crime. The accuracy of eyewitness recall may be affected during initial encoding, subsequent storage and eventual retrieval.

Leading (misleading) question A question that, either by its form or by its content, suggests to the witness what answer is desired or leads him to the desired answer.

THE ROLE OF MISLEADING INFORMATION

The study by Loftus and Palmer indicates that the form of questioning can have a significant effect on a witness's answer to the question. It is possible that such *post-event information* may cause material to be altered *before* it is stored, with the result that memory of the event is permanently affected.

Loftus and Palmer conducted a second experiment to see if indeed memory was altered by misleading post-event information. A new set of participants was divided into three groups and shown a film of a car accident lasting one minute. Group 1 was given the verb *smashed*, group 2 was given the verb *hit*, and group 3 (the control group) did not have any question about the speed of the vehicles. The participants returned one week later and were asked a series of ten questions about the accident, including another *critical question*: 'Did you see any broken glass?' There was no broken glass in the film but, presumably, those who thought the car was travelling faster might *expect* that there would be broken glass. The findings are shown below. Participants gave higher speed estimates in the 'smashed' condition, as before. They also were more likely to think they saw broken glass. This suggests that misleading post-event information does change the way information is stored.

	Verb condition		
	smashed	hit	control
Yes	16	7	6
No	34	43	44

'Yes' and 'No' responses to the question about broken glass

In another experiment by Loftus *et al.* (1978) participants were shown slides of events leading up to a car accident. One group was shown a red Datsun stopping at a junction with a 'STOP' sign. The other group were shown a 'YIELD' sign. Later, all participants were given a set of questions. Half of each group had the question 'Did another car pass the red Datsun while it was at the YIELD sign?' and the other half had the same question but with STOP sign instead of YIELD sign. Finally they were shown pairs of slides and had to identify which slides were in the original sequence, including one pair showing the Datsun at either a STOP or a YIELD sign. The 75% of the participants who were given consistent questions picked the correct slide, whereas only 41% of those who were given a misleading question picked the correct slide. In other words, the misleading question was again shown to affect their recall.

Acquisition or retrieval

Does misleading information alter the way information is stored or the way it is retrieved?

Bekerian and Bowers (1983) replicated the stop sign/yield sign study by Loftus *et al.* (1978). In the recognition part of the experiment Loftus *et al.* had presented the slides out of sequence (in a random order). Bekerian and Bowers gave the slides in the original order and found that recall was now the same for the consistent and misleading groups. This shows that the participants' memories were intact in spite of misleading post-event information. Therefore misleading questions (post-event information) would appear to affect the retrieval of memories rather than their storage.

▲ Misleading information? This can affect the accuracy of recall.

DO IT YOURSELF

No.**1.4**

Try drawing a bar chart to represent the data in the two tables on this spread. (For information on graphs see page 81)

Why is a bar chart more useful than a table as a way to describe data?

INDIVIDUAL DIFFERENCES

Lindsay (1990) has explained the 'misinformation effect' in terms of 'source monitoring'. An eyewitness typically acquires information from two sources, from observing the event itself, and from subsequent suggestions. A number of studies (e.g. Schacter *et al.*, 1991) have found that compared to younger subjects, elderly people have difficulty remembering the source of their information, even though their memory for the information itself is unimpaired. As a result, they become more prone to the effect of misleading information when giving testimony.

REAL-WORLD APPLICATIONS

'The criminal justice system relies heavily on eyewitness identification for investigating and prosecuting crimes. Psychology has built the only scientific literature on eyewitness identification and has warned the justice system of problems with eyewitness identification evidence. Recent DNA exoneration cases have confirmed the warnings of eyewitness identification researchers by showing that mistaken eyewitness identification was the largest single factor contributing to the conviction of these innocent people.' (Wells and Olsen, 2003)

CAN YOU...?

No.**1.7**

...**1** Outline what psychologists have found out about the accuracy of eyewitness testimony.

...**2** Identify **two** factors which might affect accuracy.

...**3** Describe **two** individual differences in eyewitness testimony.

...**4** Explain whether misleading information alters the way information is stored or the way it is retrieved.

...**5** Suggest **two** reasons why the study by Loftus and Palmer lacks validity. (You might want to look at pages 68–9 to read about validity.)

VALIDITY

Laboratory experiments such as those carried out by Loftus may not represent real life because people don't take the experiment seriously and/or they are not emotionally aroused in the way that they would be in a real accident. Foster *et al.* (1994) found that if participants thought they were watching a real-life robbery, and also thought that their responses would influence the trial, their identification of a robber was more accurate.

Factors that influence the accuracy of EWT: *anxiety and age*

On the previous spread we looked at evidence related to the accuracy of EWT and considered one factor which may influence accuracy – the role of misleading questions. There are a number of other factors which influence the accuracy of EWT: anxiety and individual differences such as age are perhaps the most significant. On this spread we look at each of these in turn, and discover that the relationship between them, and the accuracy of EWT, is not always straightforward.

INDIVIDUAL DIFFERENCES

Deffenbacher *et al.* (2004) found that heightened stress had a debilitating effect on eyewitness recall for adults, but not for children.

ANXIETY

Many researchers have looked at the relationship between **anxiety** and accuracy in eyewitness testimony. From a review of 21 studies, Deffenbacher *et al.* (2004) carried out a meta-analysis of 18 studies published between 1974 and 1997, looking at the effects of heightened anxiety on accuracy of *eyewitness recall*. From these studies it was clear that there was considerable support for the hypothesis that high levels of stress negatively impacted on the accuracy of eyewitness memory. However, some studies have found that emotional arousal may actually *enhance* the accuracy of memory, as Christianson and Hubinette (1993) found when they questioned 58 real witnesses to bank robberies. Those witnesses who had been threatened in some way were more accurate in their recall, and remembered more details, than those who had been onlookers

and less emotionally aroused. This continued to be true even 15 months later.

Deffenbacher suggests that this apparent contradiction could best be explained with reference to the Yerkes-Dodson law (see right), which states that performance improves with increases in arousal up to some optimal point and then declines with further increases. Many researchers believe that anxiety effects in EWT are *curvilinear*. This means that *small to medium* increases in arousal may increase the accuracy of memory, but *high* levels interfere with accuracy. Those studies which had found improved memory accuracy were most likely dealing with increased arousal within the first part of the Yerkes-Dodson curve, whereas studies which showed that accuracy *decreases* with increased arousal were most likely operating in the second part of the curve.

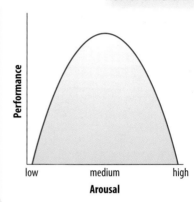

◀ There isn't a simple relationship between emotional arousal and accuracy – accuracy is poor when arousal is either low or high, but better under conditions of *moderate* arousal. This is a *curvilinear* relationship, also known as the Yerkes-Dodson law (1908).

The weapon-focus effect

There is evidence that in violent crimes, arousal may focus the witness on more central details of the attack (e.g. a weapon) than the more peripheral details (e.g. what else was going on). Loftus *et al.* (1987) identified the *weapon-focus effect*. In their initial experiment, Loftus *et al.* used two conditions, one involving a weapon and one not. In both conditions participants heard a discussion in an adjoining room. In condition 1 a man emerged holding a pen and with grease on his hands. In condition 2 the discussion was rather more heated and a man emerged holding a paperknife covered in blood. When asked to identify the man from 50 photos, participants in condition 1 were 49% accurate, compared with 33% accuracy in condition 2. This suggests that the weapon may have distracted attention from the person holding it and therefore might explain why eyewitnesses sometimes have poor recall for certain details of violent crimes.

A meta-analysis of studies concerned with the weapon-focus effect (Steblay, 1992) showed that the presence of a weapon does indeed reduce the chances of a witness correctly identifying the person holding it, but why would this be the case? Loftus *et al.* (1987) monitored eyewitnesses' eye movements and found that the presence of a weapon causes attention to be physically drawn towards the weapon itself and away from other things such as the person's face.

KEY TERM

Anxiety is an unpleasant emotional state where we fear that something bad is about to happen. People often become anxious when they are in stressful situations, and this anxiety tends to be accompanied by physiological arousal (e.g. a pounding heart and rapid, shallow breathing). Because of this, much of the research in this area is focused on the effects of arousal on EWT.

REAL-WORLD APPLICATIONS

A recent study by Riniolo *et al.* (2003) examined the accuracy of archival eyewitness testimony from survivors of the sinking of RMS Titanic in 1912, which resulted in the death of over 1500 people. Until the wreck of the Titanic was discovered in 1985, it was widely believed by historians that it had sunk intact, despite contrary evidence from eyewitnesses. Riniolo *et al.* discovered that 75% of the eyewitnesses who gave testimony at the time had reported that the Titanic was breaking apart as it sank, a memory that was eventually vindicated by Robert Ballard's discovery of the bow and stern sections lying some 2000 feet apart on the ocean floor. The Titanic survivors were still able to maintain an accurate recollection of an extremely traumatic event in less than ideal perceptual conditions (the Titanic sank at night). This study gives further support to the claim that central details of an event are often recalled accurately even when they are formed during traumatic conditions.

LINK TO RESEARCH METHODS

Christianson and Hubinette's study (1993) can be described as a natural experiment, while the study by Loftus *et al.* (1987) is a field experiment. You can read about these two different methods, and their relative advantages and disadvantages, on page 85.

...**1** Identify and explain **three** ways that eyewitness testimony may not be accurate.

...**2** For each of these, provide **one** piece of research evidence to support the influence on EWT.

...**3** Select **one** study on this spread and consider its validity.

...**4** Select a different study and consider any ethical issues that might have arisen in the study.

INDIVIDUAL DIFFERENCES

Research has shown that the accuracy of eyewitness memory may be compromised by anxiety, age or misleading information, but what about alcohol? Clifasefi *et al.* (2006) compared mildly intoxicated participants with those who were completely sober. Rather worryingly, 82% of the intoxicated participants (compared to 46% of sober participants) were not aware that someone dressed in a gorilla suit had slowly walked across the screen while they were watching a video of students throwing a basketball to each other. This can be explained by the psychological model of *alcohol myopia* (Steele and Josephs, 1990) – the more intoxicated a person becomes, the less attention they can allocate to peripheral tasks.

'I've never seen him before m'lud'.

AGE OF WITNESS

With a heightened concern over child abuse, children are becoming more evident in the courtroom, therefore there is a need to establish their credibility as witnesses. Similarly, research has tended to suggest a diminishing of cognitive skills among older adults, so can we expect a corresponding reduction in the accuracy of EWT among such individuals?

Age differences in accuracy

Parker and Carranza (1989) compared the ability of primary school children and college students to correctly identify a target individual following a slide sequence of a mock crime. In a photo identification task, child witnesses had a higher rate of choosing 'somebody' than adult witnesses, although they were also more likely to make errors of identification than the college students.

Yarmey (1993) stopped 651 adults in public places and asked them to recall the physical characteristics of a young woman to whom they had spoken for 15 seconds just 2 minutes earlier. Although young (18–29) and middle-aged (30–44) adults were more *confident* in their recall than the older (45–65) adults, there were no *significant differences* in the accuracy of recall that could be attributed to the age group of the witness.

Memon *et al.* (2003) studied the accuracy of young (16–33) and older (60–82) eyewitnesses. When the delay between an incident and its identification was short (35 min), there was no difference in the accuracy of the two age groups. However, when the identification task was delayed by one week, the older witnesses were significantly less accurate.

The own-age bias

Most studies have shown that older adults show poorer performance on tests of eyewitness memory, and face recognition in particular. However, part of this difference may result from the stimuli typically used in such studies. The majority of studies have tested college-aged students who are asked to correctly identify the faces of similar-aged targets. However, studies of older adults have also tended to present photographs of college-aged individuals. As a result, much of the work done on age differences in eyewitness memory has ignored the possibility that participants may simply have superior memory for faces in their own age group.

Anastasi and Rhodes (2006) used individuals from three age groups (18–25; 35–45; and 55–78) who were shown 24 photographs (representing the three different age groups), which they had to rate for attractiveness. After a short 'filler' activity, they were then presented with 48 photographs, 24 of which had been seen previously and 24 that acted as 'distractors'. Corrected recognition rates (hits minus 'false alarms') showed that the young and middle-aged participants were significantly more accurate than the older participants, but the most interesting finding was that all age groups were more accurate in identifying photographs from their own age group.

	Young photographs	Middle-aged photographs	Older photographs
Young participants	90	87	85
Middle-aged participants	85	93	87
Older participants	56	62	66

▲ Correct recognition rates (%) by age group of participant and age group of target photographs showing own-age bias (Anastasi and Rhodes, 2006)

Explaining the own-age bias

The findings from this research are consistent with the findings from research into the own-race bias, where typically people are better able to identify faces from their own ethnic group. The *differential experience hypothesis* (Brigham and Malpass, 1985) would suggest that the more contact we have with members of a particular age group or ethnic group, the better our memory would be for such individuals. Consequently, the less experience we have with a particular age group, the greater the own-age bias. Similarly, the *perceptual learning hypothesis* suggests that individuals differ in the amount of expertise they have acquired for processing same age and other age faces. Because individuals usually encounter members of their own age group more regularly, they become more expert at processing those faces, and would subsequently show better memory for them.

The Cognitive Interview

Although much of the research on eyewitness testimony has highlighted its fallibility, research has also looked at ways in which the accuracy of EWT can be improved. On this spread we take a look at the **cognitive interview** (CI), one of the most exciting developments in forensic psychology in recent years. This is a procedure designed for use in police interviews that involve witnesses. There were two main forces behind the development of the CI. The first was the need to improve the effectiveness of police interviewers when questioning witnesses. The second was to apply the results of psychological research to this area, particularly the work of Elizabeth Loftus, whose research had already dispelled the myth that eyewitness memory operates like a video camera.

WHAT IS THE COGNITIVE INTERVIEW?

Fisher and Geiselman (1992) reviewed the relevant psychological literature on memory, and related this to the way that interviews were carried out by the police in real life. They found, for example, that people remember events better when they are provided with retrieval cues. This could be accomplished in the police interview by mentally reinstating the context of the event being recalled. Fisher and Geiselman developed an interviewing technique, the cognitive interview, which was based on proven psychological principles concerning effective memory recall.

The original cognitive interview technique could be characterised by four distinct components:

1 *Report everything* – the interviewer encourages the reporting of every single detail of the event, even though it may seem irrelevant.
2 *Mental reinstatement of original context* – the interviewer encourages the interviewee to mentally recreate the environment and contacts from the original incident.
3 *Changing the order* – the interviewer may try alternative ways through the timeline of the incident, for example by reversing the order in which events occurred.
4 *Changing the perspective* – the interviewee is asked to recall the incident from multiple perspectives, for example by imagining how it would have appeared to other witnesses present at the time.

The first two components are based on the principle that if there is a consistency between the actual incident and the recreated situation, there is an increased likeliness that witnesses will recall more details, and be more accurate in their recall.

The latter two components are based on the assumption that information that has been observed can be retrieved through a number of different 'routes' into an individual's memory, therefore it is more productive to vary these routes during questioning.

Current research is focused on the relative contribution of each of the individual components of the cognitive interview in an attempt to make the technique more streamlined and time-efficient.

DO IT YOURSELF

No.**1.5**

You could have a go at cognitive interviewing yourself. Show a few friends a short extract of an 'incident' on video. Later you can interview half of them using a series of prepared direct 'interrogative' questions (e.g. 'Was the robber carrying anything in his hand?'). The other half could be asked the same questions, but following this instruction:

'I would like you to close your eyes and clear your head of all other thoughts. Focus only on the task at hand. I would like you to try and picture the events that you saw in the film as if they were happening right now, right before your eyes. Run through what happened; try to replay the event in your head as if it were a video that is replaying before you, which you are watching right now.'

You can then compare the accuracy of recall to see if a mental reinstatement of the original context made any difference.

KEY TERM

Cognitive interview A police technique for interviewing witnesses to a crime, which encourages them to recreate the original context in order to increase the accessibility of stored information. Because our memory is made up of a network of associations rather than of discrete events, memories are accessed using multiple retrieval strategies.

Research into the effectiveness of the cognitive interview

A meta-analysis of 53 studies found, on average, an increase of 34% in the amount of correct information generated in the CI compared with standard interviewing techniques (Köhnken *et al.*, 1999). However, most of these studies tested volunteer witnesses (usually college students) in the laboratory. The 'real world applications' on the right describes one of the few attempts to study the effectiveness of the CI technique outside the laboratory.

Milne and Bull (2002) examined the relative effectiveness of each of the four components of the CI. Undergraduate students and children were interviewed using just one individual component of the CI, and compared to a control condition (where they were instructed simply to 'try again'). Recall across each of the four individual components was broadly similar, and no different to that of the control group. However, when participants were interviewed using a combination of the 'report everything' and 'mental reinstatement' components of the CI, their recall was significantly higher than in all other conditions.

INDIVIDUAL DIFFERENCES

Ginet and Verkampt (2007) studied the effects of anxiety in the cognitive interview. They showed first-year undergraduates a video of a road accident. Electrodes were attached to their arms either a) to deliver electric shocks during the video (although no shocks were actually given), or b) simply to take physiological measurements. A week later they were interviewed using either a cognitive interview or a structured interview (SI – i.e. an interview that lacks the four CI components). Results showed that the CI participants recorded more and were more accurate in their recall of the accident than were the SI participants.

I HAVE A FEW ROUTINE QUESTIONS ABOUT YOUR HUSBAND'S DISAPPEARANCE MA'AM, BUT I THINK I'D RATHER STAND THAN HAVE A SEAT AT YOUR BUTCHER BLOCK TABLE...

CAN YOU...? No.1.9

...**1** Explain what is meant by the term 'cognitive interview'.

...**2** Explain how the cognitive interview works.

...**3** Outline research into the effectiveness of the cognitive interview (LTM).

...**4** Give **two** criticisms of the cognitive interview.

...**5** Comment on the *value* of the cognitive interview.

Ⓔ Evaluation of the cognitive interview

One of the problems with evaluating the effectiveness of the CI is that it is no longer just one 'procedure', but a collection of related techniques. For example, the cognitive interview in which the Merseyside and Thames Valley Police are trained is virtually the same as the technique first described by Fisher and Geiselman, although the Thames Valley Police do not use the 'changing perspectives' component. Other police forces that describe themselves as using the CI technique have tended to use only the 'reinstate context' and 'report everything' components of the CI (Kebbell and Wagstaff, 1996).

From their interviews with police, Kebbell and Wagstaff report an additional problem with the CI in practice. Police officers suggest that this technique requires more time than is often available and that instead they prefer to use deliberate strategies aimed to limit an eyewitness's report to the minimum amount of information that the officer feels is necessary.

An enhanced version of the CI (Fisher and Geiselman, 1992) includes additional cognitive techniques for probing a witness's mental image of an event. This creates additional problems because it places even greater demands on the interviewer. As a result, the quantity and quality of training of CI interviewers has become a critical issue. However, in a study by Memon *et al.* (1994) experienced detectives received only a relatively brief (4 hours) training session in the use of the CI, which did not produce any significant increases (compared to standard interviewing techniques) in the amount of information elicited from witnesses about an incident.

REAL-WORLD APPLICATIONS

Stein and Memon (2006) tested the effectiveness of the cognitive interview in Brazil, the first time this had been done in a developing country. In Brazil, the current model of police questioning is interrogative, and torture and other forms of ill treatment remain widespread throughout the criminal justice system. Women recruited from the cleaning staff of a large university were required to watch a video of an abduction. Compared to a standard police interviewing method, the CI increased the amount of correct information obtained from witnesses. In particular, the CI was far superior in producing forensically rich information, for example a detailed description of the man holding a gun, which would later have allowed police to determine which of the abductors was armed. These results suggest that techniques such as the CI may pave the way for a new approach to interviewing witnesses in Brazil and other developing countries, thus reducing the incidence of miscarriages of justice.

COMMENTARY CORNER

Question: **Discuss the use of the cognitive interview in obtaining evidence from eyewitnesses.** *(12 marks)*

In examinations, questions assess the degree to which you can apply prescribed knowledge. In this case, that is knowledge of the cognitive interview. However, over and above *describing* the cognitive interview (what it is, how it works, research that has used the cognitive interview, etc.), you should also be able to *evaluate* it. There are several ways to do this.

You could, for example, consider *effectiveness* to be a measure of the usefulness of the CI and so make use of the research studies on this spread.

You could also utilise *practical issues* in the implementation of the CI for this purpose. For example, Kebbell and Wagstaff report that many police officers tend not to use the CI technique in less serious crimes because they simply don't have the time.

Alternatively you could show the value of the CI in reducing miscarriages of justice in countries where these are likely to occur (see 'Real World Applications', above).

For all of these different types of 'evaluation', make sure you are addressing these three questions.

- **First**: what is the point I'm making? For example, that the CI is effective.
- **Second**: how do I know that? For example, because Köhnken *et al.* (1999) found a 34% increase in recall compared to standard interviewing techniques.
- **Third**: ask yourself 'So what?' For example, this shows that the CI is a more effective way to access memories for an incident than existing methods of interviewing are.

This is the **three point rule** – remember it whenever you are doing **AO2**.

21

Strategies for memory improvement

Throughout this chapter we have considered various ways in which psychological research has been *applied* to the real world. Application of knowledge is, after all, one of the key aims of conducting research, and there is no more important application of memory research than to increase our understanding of how to improve our own memories, especially for students with exams looming.

On this spread we will consider various techniques for memory improvement. What you will notice is that they all share one common characteristic – they all involve organisation.

◄ **The method of loci** – To remember something like the working memory model you imagine a journey through a familiar landscape or location, such as the house where you live. Imagine walking into your bathroom and finding an executive sitting in your bath (the central executive). In the next room there is a record player and your grandmother is listening to a record over and over again (phonological loop), and so on. In each room or special location in the room (a sofa, the fridge, etc.), place a piece of information – trying to create a memorable link – the weirder, larger, smellier, the more memorable it will be. Practise walking round the house and retrieving the items. When you want to remember the items, you imagine yourself walking around the house and you should recall the different pieces of information. Have fun during revision making up imaginary journeys.

*Can you remember the following letters:
TVCIAOMNILTMSTMNASA*

Would this be easier: TV CIA OMNI LTM STM NASA?

The task of memorising items becomes easier if you can produce smaller chunks of information which are memorable. The same is true for numbers, because 100100010000 is more memorable as 100 1000 10000 (hundred, thousand, ten thousand).

One mnemonist, SF, managed to remember more than 80 digits because he could give meaning to groups of digits. For example, if 3492 appeared in the sequence, he remembered this as '3 min 49.2 sec, a near world record for the mile. He had a detailed knowledge of running times and used this to remember an otherwise meaningless string of digits (Chase et al., 1981).

MNEMONIC TECHNIQUES

A mnemonic is any structured technique that is used to help people remember and (most importantly) recall information. We use these techniques when we have to recall large amounts of unfamiliar information, or to make associations between a number of things that are not otherwise associated.

Verbal mnemonics

A variety of memory improvement techniques focus on words.

1 An *acronym* is where a word or sentence is formed from the initial letters of other words. For example ROYGBIV (Roy G. Biv) is used to remember the colours of the rainbow: **R**ed, **O**range, **Y**ellow, **G**reen, **B**lue, **I**ndigo, **V**iolet.
2 An *acrostic* is a poem or sentence where the first letter in each line or word forms the item to be remembered. For example, **M**y **V**ery **E**asy **M**ethod **J**ust **S**peeds **U**p **N**aming **P**lanets is used to remember the order of the planets: Mercury, Venus, Earth, Mars, Jupiter, Saturn, Uranus, Neptune, Pluto.
3 *Rhymes* are groups of words with an identity and rhythm. Using the tune of 'Twinkle Twinkle Little Star' helps to remember the letters of the alphabet, or remembering the number of days in each month using the rhyme '30 days hath September, April, June, And November. All the rest have 31 save February'.
4 *Chunking* involves dividing a long string of information into memorable chunks (see Miller's research on page 6). The chunking of telephone numbers and post codes demonstrates this.

Visual imagery mnemonics

Some mnemonic techniques use visual images. Perhaps the best known is the *method of loci*, a technique first described by the Greeks who were extraordinarily gifted orators. They used these mental techniques to help them remember points they wanted to make in their long speeches. Loci literally means 'places' and the method requires the learner to associate parts of the material to be recalled with different places (usually, rooms in a familiar building, or sites along an often travelled road) in the order that they are to be recalled.

Another, considerably more recent method is the *keyword method* (Atkinson and Raugh, 1975) which is used when trying to associate two pieces of information. For example when learning a foreign language and wanting to remember a foreign word and its English equivalent, you think of an image to link the two words: the Spanish word for 'horse' is 'caballo', pronounced 'cob-eye-yo'; the keyword could be 'eye', so one might then visualise a horse with a large eye riding on its back. Conjuring up the visual image should trigger the recall of the word.

There are many other techniques that use visual imagery, such as *spider diagrams* and *mind maps*. These involve making notes of information in the form of a drawing, usually a branching pattern, with the main topic in the centre and component elements/ideas radiating outwards. Small sketches/doodles can be added, as well as colours (highlighters, felt-tips). Each page of notes therefore has a *unique, distinctive visual appearance* whereas pages of ordinary/linear notes all look very similar. This process, which adds a range of visual cues to the verbal material, has also been called 'mind mapping' (Buzan, 1993).

▲ A mind map about mind mapping.

As psychologists we ought to be able to explain why mnemonic techniques are successful. There are a variety of explanations.

The role of organisation

Probably the most important explanation is organisation. By organising data we establish links that help recall. Word associations and visual images create links or associations. Memory essentially involves making associations in the brain. Normally, the brain remembers new information through a self-organising process that builds associations among the most naturally fitting pieces of information. For example, you may find that whenever you smell bacon it makes you salivate. This is because, in the past you have eaten bacon and enjoyed the taste, thus your brain has learned a link between bacon and nice taste and both now make you salivate.

This is usually a time-consuming process. Mnemonic techniques accelerate the process by actively linking the new information with 'memory hooks' – artificial constructs created specifically for the stated purpose.

Organisation also refers to literally putting items in order, such as writing notes in a clear hierarchy. It's the same as trying to find things in your room – if your room is a mess it is harder to find them than if you had everything neatly ordered. Memory works in the same way, if it is organised you can find information much more quickly. The benefit of organisation was shown in a study by Bower *et al.* (1969). Participants were given 112 words to learn. If the words were organised into conceptual hierarchies, recall was two to three times better than if the words were presented in a random order. An example of one of the conceptual hierarchies is shown below right.

The role of elaborative rehearsal

A second explanation relates to the idea of elaborative rehearsal. Memory research has shown that enduring memories are created through the process of elaboration (see page 11). Mnemonic techniques make us elaborate the information to be remembered, for example when creating a mind map or developing the method of loci.

The *amount* of rehearsal is important (maintenance rehearsal) but the *nature* of rehearsal (elaboration) is more important.

Dual coding hypothesis

The value of visual techniques can be explained by both of the above accounts but there is an additional explanation for their value. Paivio (1971) proposed that words and images are processed separately, on the basis of his studies of patients who had damage to their temporal lobes and could not process images. According to Paivio, concrete words, which can be made into images, are double-encoded in memory. They are coded once in verbal symbols and once as image-based symbols. This double coding increases the likelihood that they will be remembered. Paivio called this the *dual coding hypothesis*. This can be linked to the phonological loop in the working memory model of Baddeley and Hitch (see page 12).

This explanation has been supported by many studies. For example, in one experiment, participants were given 100 different cards, one at a time; each card had two unrelated words, for example 'cat' and 'brick'. Participants in one group had to mentally produce an image linking the two. Participants in the other group were asked just to memorise the words. When given a cued recall test (i.e. given the first of each pair of words), the 'imagers' recalled 80% of words, while 'non-imagers' recalled just 45% (Bower, 1972).

```
                        Minerals
                 ┌──────────┴──────────┐
               Metals                 Stones
            ┌────┴────┐      ┌──────────┼──────────┐
           Rare    Common  Alloys    Precious   Masonry
            │         │       │          │          │
         Platinum  Aluminium Bronze   Sapphire  Limestone
            │         │       │          │          │
          Silver    Copper   Steel    Emerald    Granite
            │         │       │          │          │
           Gold      Lead    Brass    Diamond    Marble
```

...**1** Outline **three** memory improvement techniques.

...**2** Use psychological insights and research to explain *why* each of these techniques is successful.

...**3** Explain why organisation is important in learning and recall. Refer to psychological evidence in your answer.

VALIDITY

Remember that memory research often involves word lists and semantic memory rather than other kinds of memory. For this reason it has been regarded as lacking ecological validity. However, the topic on this spread – memory improvement – is related to semantic memory. Therefore memory research is perfectly valid as a basis for understanding this aspect of human behaviour.

DO IT YOURSELF

You could investigate the value of some of the methods on this page. One way to do this would be to select some material to be remembered, perhaps a new psychological study. Arrange for one group of students to use one technique to learn the study and a second group to use a different technique. After a period of time, test the recall of both groups. Which technique worked better?

REAL-WORLD APPLICATIONS

A rather ancient study (Woodrow, 1927) compared learning in three groups of participants. Group 1 spent 3 hours each week for 4 weeks memorising things such as poems and nonsense syllables, i.e. they were 'exercising their memories'. Group 2 spent the same amount of time being taught various memory techniques such as the ones on this spread. Group 3 was a control group that did nothing special. At the end of 4 weeks all participants were given some poetry to remember. Groups 1 and 3 performed about the same, while Group 2 was considerably better. This shows that memory techniques really can help your ability to remember and recall information.

LINK TO RESEARCH METHODS

You might try to collect both quantitative and qualitative data in your study. You can read about these on pages 80 and 103.

We have identified here the key points of the topics on the AQA (A) AS specification, i.e. the bare minimum that you need to know. You may want to fill in further details to elaborate and personalise this material.

MODELS OF MEMORY

DURATION
- LTM unlimited
- STM measured in seconds

- Shepard – 50% of photos recalled after 4 months.
- Bahrick *et al.* – yearbook photos, recall 70% accurate after 48 years.
- Peterson and Peterson – consonant syllables, max 18 secs.
- Nairne *et al.* – 96 seconds for same items across trials.

 VALIDITY
- Only one kind of memory (semantic memory) tested.
- Not actually testing duration – displacement instead.

CAPACITY
- LTM unlimited
- STM less than 7 chunks

- Miller – 7 ±2, chunking.
- Simon – size of chunk matters.
- Cowan – 4 rather than 7 chunks.

 INDIVIDUAL DIFFERENCES
- Jacobs (1887) age differences in digit span.

 APPLICATIONS
- postcodes based on chunking.

ENCODING
- LTM semantic
- STM acoustic or visual

- Baddeley– acoustic similarity decreases STM recall, semantic similarity decreases LTM recall.
- Brandimote *et al.* – visual encoding in STM if given visual task and verbal rehearsal prevented.
- Frost – visual coding in LTM.

THE WORKING MEMORY MODEL (WM)

Baddeley and Hitch (1974)
- Explains why you can do two different tasks at the same time but not two similar tasks (evidence from Hitch and Baddeley).
- Central executive – resource allocation, small capacity.
- Phonological loop – phonological store and articulatory process, maintenance rehearsal.
- Visuo-spatial sketchpad – visual cache and inner scribe.
- Episodic buffer – general store and integrates information from other stores and also from LTM.

THE MULTI-STORE MODEL (MSM)

Atkinson and Shriffrin (1968)

Structure
- Sensory memory – evidence from Sperling.
- STM – limited capacity and duration, mainly acoustic coding.
- LTM – unlimited capacity and duration, mainly semantic encoding.
- STM vs. LTM – serial position effect (Glanzer and Cunitz), role of hippocampus (Squire et al), case studies of brain damage (e.g. HM).

Processes
- Attention and maintenance rehearsal.

 STRENGTHS
- Applications – dealing with hippocampal damage.
- Strong evidence to support claims for duration, capacity and encoding.
- Includes details of structure and process.
- Has stimulated a lot of research which leads to increased understanding.

 WEAKNESSES
- Oversimplified.
- STM doesn't function as a unitary story e.g. KF (Shallice and Warrington).
- LTM is not a unitary store: semantic, episodic, procedural and perceptual-representation memories.
- Processing more important than maintenance rehearsal – Craik and Lockhart compared shallow, phonemic and semantic processing (MSM reformulated as elaborative rehearsal).
- STM is not independent of LTM – Ruchkin *et al.* compared words and pseudo-words involved different brain activity.

 VALIDITY
- Use of word lists.
- Participants often psychology students.
- Lab experiments (demand characteristics, experimenter bias but well controlled).

 STRENGTHS
- fMRI shows central executive more active when two tasks done (Bunge *et al.*).
- Explains word-length effect – remembering short rather than long words (Baddeley *et al.*).
- Visuo-spatial sketchpad shown in experiment with visual tracking task (Baddeley et al).
- Episodic buffer shown comparing recall of related and unrelated words (Baddeley *et al.*).
- Explains memory deficits of KF (STM OK for visual but not auditory) and SC (damage to phonological loop).
- Maintenance rehearsal is only an optional process.
- Emphasises process rather than MSM focus on structure.
- Model being continually updated by research.

 WEAKNESSES
- Central executive doesn't actually explain anything.
- Central executive is probably several components (Eslinger and Damasio).
- Problems with evidence from brain-damaged individuals e.g. no before and after comparisons.

 VALIDITY
- Same validity issues as for MSM.

MEMORY IN EVERYDAY LIFE

EYEWITNESS TESTIMONY
Involves encoding, retaining and retrieving memories

ACCURACY OF EWT

- Loftus and Palmer – leading question (hit vs contacted), inaccurate recall.
- Yuille and Cutshall – real-life robbery, accurate recall despite misleading questions.

 INDIVIDUAL DIFFERENCES

- Males and females same (Wells and Olsen).
- Older people have more difficulty remembering source of information but recall for event same as for younger people (Schachter *et al.*).

 APPLICATIONS

- Mistaken EWT largest single factor in wrongful convictions (Wells and Olsen).

MISLEADING INFORMATION
(post-event information)

- Loftus and Palmer – broken glass, misleading questions affect storage.
- Loftus *et al.* – STOP or YIELD sign.
- Bekerian and Bowers - repeated study with slides in sequence, misleading questions affect retrieval.

 VALIDITY

- Lab experiments may not be taken seriously.
- Ps not emotionally involved.
- Foster *et al.* – better identification with real-life set up.

FACTORS THAT INFLUENCE ACCURACY

Anxiety

- Deffenbacher *et al.* meta-analysis showed anxiety reduced accuracy of EWT.
- Christianson and Hubinette (1993) anxiety increased accuracy in real-life bank robberies.
- Contradiction explained by Yerkes-Dodson law.
- Loftus *et al.* – weapon-focus effect.

 APPLICATIONS

- Riniolo *et al.* EWT from Titanic was accurate.

Age of witness

- Yarney – describe young woman, younger Ps more confident but no age differences.
- Memon *et al.* – older less accurate when delay was one week.
- Anastasi and Rhodes – own-age bias.

 INDIVIDUAL DIFFERENCES

- Alcohol impairs attention (Clifasefi *et al.*).

COGNITIVE INTERVIEW (CI)

- What is it?
  1 Report everything
  2 Recreate original context
  3 Change order
  4 Change perspective (Fisher and Geiselman).
- Köhnken *et al.* – meta-analysis, 34% increase in correct recall.
- Milne and Bull – report everything and mental reinstatement gave best recall.
- Hard to evaluate because many versions of CI.
- Time-consuming.
- Training may not increase usefulness (Memon *et al.*).
- Individual differences – CI works better than SI (structured interview) (Ginet and Verkampt).

 APPLICATIONS

- CI used in Brazil (Stein and Memon).

STRATEGIES FOR MEMORY IMPROVEMENT

Mnemonic techniques
- Verbal – acronym, acrostic, rhymes, chunking.
- Visual imagery – method of loci, keyword method (Atkinson and Raugh), spider diagrams and mind maps.

Explaining how they work
- Organisation – creating memory hooks and organising material (Bower *et al.*).
- Elaborative rehearsal – amount and nature of rehearsal.
- Dual coding hypothesis – Paivio.

 APPLICATIONS

- Woodrow showed that memory techniques do improve memory.

 VALIDITY

- High because application relates to word lists (semantic memory).

End-of-chapter review   REVISION QUESTIONS

There are lots of ideas at the end of other chapters that you might adapt and try out here.

THE NATURE OF MEMORY

ACTIVITY 1 pages 4–7

Task 1 *Top trumps*

Create top trumps cards for the studies covered at the start of this chapter. (In fact you can extend this activity to create cards for all the studies in the chapter.) On each card you should rate the study in the following categories:

- Usefulness (give 5 stars if you think the study can be applied in the real world, 0 stars if it has no applications you can think of).
- Date (5 stars for very recent, 0 for a long time ago).
- Validity (5 if very few validity problems).
- Critical issues raised (5 if very few ethical issues).
- Complexity (how easy or hard it is to remember).

How to play top trumps

The aim of the game is to win all the cards. Deal out all the cards. Each player selects one card. The starting player selects a category from their own card which is likely to beat the others. If it does win, then that player takes all the cards and goes again.

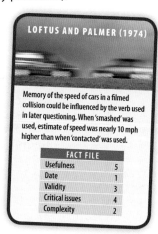

LOFTUS AND PALMER (1974)

Memory of the speed of cars in a filmed collision could be influenced by the verb used in later questioning. When 'smashed' was used, estimate of speed was nearly 10 mph higher than when 'contacted' was used.

FACT FILE	
Usefulness	5
Date	1
Validity	3
Critical issues	4
Complexity	2

Task 2 *Spot the mistake*

Underline the mistakes and write what should be in its place.

Text with error	Correction
Peterson and Peterson used words to test the capacity of LTM.	_____
One study found that STM was actually shorter than Peterson and Peterson estimated.	_____
Bahrick *et al.* found that people could remember photos of high school classmates for only 20 years.	_____
Jacobs proposed the idea that the duration of STM is increased by chunking.	_____
The digit span technique is a means of assessing the duration of STM.	_____
Nairne (1963) found that people remember about 8 chunks of information.	_____
Baddeley found that STM tends to use a semantic code.	_____
The words 'cat' and 'dog' are acoustically dissimilar.	_____
STM always uses an acoustic code.	_____

MSM AND WM

ACTIVITY 2 pages 8–9 and 12–13

Task 1 *Working visually*

In this chapter we have covered two influential *models* of memory – the multi-store model and the working memory model. Your responsibility in this process is to make yourself thoroughly familiar with both so that you can *describe*, *précis*, and *evaluate* each in turn. This exercise is designed to help you achieve this. You should start by addressing the MSM (some 'starter' points are included below) and then carry out the same exercise for the working memory model.

Without referring back to the spread for this topic, produce a diagram of the multi-store model of memory (Atkinson and Shiffrin, 1968). Check your answer.

Find a partner who hasn't seen the diagram of the MSM. Give them a pen and sheet of paper and try to describe the model to them so that they can draw it. How well did you do?

Now repeat this for the WM model.

Task 2 *From description to précis*

Being able to précis is the key to understanding. For any theory or study you need to be able to select the 'golden nuggets' – the key pieces of information – and then use these as 'coat pegs' on which you can hang your own description.

You have already done a précis of the MSM and WM (in the exercises on pages 8 and 13). Can you remember your six key points? Fill in the tables above right.

Identify 6 points related to the MSM

- _____
- _____
- _____
- _____
- _____
- _____

Identify 6 points related to the WM

- _____
- _____
- _____
- _____
- _____
- _____

Task 3 *From précis to description*

Now use your key points to write a 100-word description of each model.

Task 4 *Reducing it further*

Here's a final task for you. Try to produce an even shorter précis of each model. See how short you can make it while still covering the key points for each.

ACTIVITY 3 pages 10–11 and 14–15

Task 1 Evaluating the multi-store model

AO2 marks are given for evaluation. 'Evaluation' involves presenting information which will help you decide how good this model is. There are a number of ways to do this. One way is to use evidence from research studies to support or challenge the model. The key word is 'use'. You will not get much AO2 credit for the *description* of a study but you do gain marks if you use such evidence effectively. Inevitably this involves *some* description but the emphasis should be on what the evidence tells us about the model – what the implications of the study are.

On the left-hand side of the table you should very briefly describe the findings of the studies indicated. On the right-hand side you should say what the findings tell us about the MSM. The first one has been done for you.

Research evidence	Implications for MSM
(write about 20 words for each)	**(write about 20 words for each)**
Glanzer and Cunitz (1966) found that people were better able to remember items at the start (*primacy effect*) and the end of a list (*recency effect*).	The existence of a *primacy effect* provides supporting, evidence for a long-term store, and the *recency effect* supports the idea of a short-term store.
Nairne *et al.* (1999) found . . .	This shows that . . .
Ruchkin *et al.* (2003) found . . .	This shows that . . .

Task 2 Evaluating the working memory model

Draw another table like the one above and repeat the exercise for the WM model.

EYEWITNESS TESTIMONY

ACTIVITY 4 pages 16–21

Task 1 Fill in the blanks

Loftus conducted a key study with _____ on EWT. In this study participants were shown _____ and asked a series of questions including one critical question relating to the _____ of the cars. Participants were divided into _____ experimental groups. Each group was given a different _____, for example _____ or _____. They found that those participants who were given a question with the word _____ estimated the highest speed.

Task 2 Psychology in action

Rick is called to do jury service. A man has been accused of causing an offence at a football match, but he claims he wasn't even at the match. Eyewitnesses are going to be called, but when Rick's daughter hears this, she impresses her father with her knowledge about eyewitness testimony.

1 If you were Rick's daughter what **two** things would you tell your father about eyewitness testimony?
2 If you were being completely honest you would admit that psychologists don't know everything and sometimes their research is flawed. What would be the most important problem to mention to your father so he knows to take the advice with a pinch of salt?
3 How do *your* points compare to those of other class members?

Task 3 Extended writing

Eyewitnesses are not always accurate in what they recall from the scene of a crime. **Discuss research into the accuracy of eyewitness testimony.**

In order to answer this extended writing question you need to present evidence from research studies related to the accuracy of eyewitness testimony (**AO1** – about 100 words) and then evaluate the evidence (**AO2** – about 100 words). An effective way to organise your answer would be to break this down into six chunks: describe three studies and evaluate each study. Below is an essay planner to help guide you in producing your answer.

Essay planner
Study 1 (**AO1** about 35 words)
Evaluation of study 1 (**AO2** about 35 words)
Study 2 (**AO1** about 35 words)
Evaluation of study 2 (**AO2** about 35 words)
Study 3 (**AO1** about 35 words)
Evaluation of study 3 (**AO2** about 35 words)

MEMORY IMPROVEMENT

ACTIVITY 5 pages 22–23

Task 1 Mind maps

Produce a mind map of the information on memory improvement. Do you feel this has made it easier to remember the information? If so, you might try it for other spreads.

Task 2 Key words

Using all the key terms in this chapter create some cards. Write the key term on one card and write its definition on another.

One game you can play with these is called 'Concentration', which works best with 2 or 3 players. Place all the cards face down so that the key terms are on the left and the definitions are on the right. Turn two cards over – one from the left and one from the right. Do they match? If not, turn them face down again and let the next player have a go. If they do match then you keep the cards.

The Unit 1 exam is divided into two sections. Section A is Cognitive Psychology and Research Methods. The actual number of questions is not fixed but will always total 36 marks, 12 of which will be research methods questions (see end of Chapter 3). All questions are compulsory. There may be an extended writing question in this section of the exam (like question 4 below). Such questions are half AO1 and half AO2 and you must take care to provide enough of both. Some other questions are also AO2 questions, however there is a difference – in these questions you don't have to worry about AO2ing – just answer the question, and always give detail and elaborate your answers.

---

1 (a) The diagram below illustrates the multi-store model of memory. Write down appropriate labels for A and B. *(2 marks)*

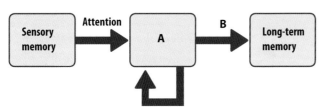

(b) Explain **one** strength of the multi-store model of memory. *(2 marks)*

Alice's answer

(a) A is short-term memory and B is rehearsal.
(b) One strength of the multi-store model is that it can explain memory in terms of three separate stores, each holding memories for an increasing amount of time. These are the sensory store, short-term store and the long-term store.

Tom's answer

(a) The box with A is STM and the arrow is rehearsal.
(b) The claims of the multi-store model of memory are well supported by research evidence. For example, Glanzer and Cunitz found evidence of a primacy effect (supporting the idea of a long-term store) and a recency effect (supporting the idea of a short-term store).

Examiner's comments

Alice gains all 2 marks for part (a) but no marks for part (b) because she has failed to give a strength of the model. She has *described* what the multi-store model can do but has not said why this is a strength. Why is it a good thing that there are three separate stores? **2 out of 4 marks**

Tom has answered this in his part (b) – it is a good thing because there is research evidence that suggests this is the case. Tom has given an accurate and detailed response, identifying the strength (it is supported by research) and providing evidence to support this. Tom also gains full marks for part (a); it is acceptable to use common abbreviations. **4 out of 4 marks.**

---

2 Explain why studies of memory have been criticised for lacking validity. *(5 marks)*

Alice's answer

Some studies of memory are criticised for lacking validity because they just use students as participants. Students are not really representative of the rest of the population. Studies also take place in laboratories, and so can lack ecological validity. Most studies involve remembering something pretty meaningless rather than something that might be useful in everyday life (like a telephone number or a round of drinks).

Tom's answer

In laboratory studies of memory the participants know they are taking part in a study, and so may change their behaviour accordingly. We find out little about how people react in real-life incidents. Also, because the majority of participants in such studies are students, they may regard memory tasks as intellectual challenges and therefore try harder to remember than usual. This means that any conclusions drawn from such studies may be restricted only to that type of situation and that type of participant.

Examiner's comments

Alice and Tom have used rather similar material in their answers. For example, they both mention the fact that participants tend to be students and also note that many memory studies are lab-based and unlike everyday life. The key difference lies in the way Tom has made his explanations effective. Alice says 'students are not representative of the population' whereas Tom goes on to say *why* they are not representative ('they may regard the tasks as intellectual challenges') and also to suggest why this is a problem ('therefore they may try harder than usual'). Such increased elaboration increases the *effectiveness* of the answer and thus the marks awarded.

Tom would receive **5 out of 5 marks** for an effective explanation demonstrating understanding of validity and knowledge of studies of memory, whereas Alice's answer is basic, with limited elaboration and thus receives **3 out of 5 marks**.

3 Mary witnesses a car accident on her way home from school. The next day the police come round to visit her and ask her to describe what she saw.

Identify and explain **two** techniques the police might use to help her recall the details of the accident accurately. *(4 marks)*

Alice's answer

The police could use two components from the cognitive interview. They could ask Mary to recall everything she remembers, regardless of how irrelevant it might appear (this could provide vital clues about the cause of the accident). They could also ask her to imagine how the scene looked from the perspective of other people who were there (e.g. the driver or a person on the other side of the road).

Tom's answer

Mary could be asked to try really hard to remember details of the accident, perhaps being helped by being shown pictures of different cars so she could identify the cars involved. The police should be careful not to ask any leading questions because these might mislead Mary and cause her to remember something that wasn't actually there.

Examiner's comments

Alice has used her knowledge of the cognitive interview to outline two techniques that might be used by the police. For each of these she has offered a brief explanation sufficient to gain **4 out of 4 marks**.

Tom has considered two techniques, as required by the question, but the first one is lacking psychology (she should 'try really hard to remember'). His second answer relates to leading questions and alone gains **2 out of 4 marks**.

Both students have wisely referred to Mary in their answers rather than simply describing techniques the police must use, thus acknowledging the particular form of this question which asks you to *use* your knowledge in a particular context rather than just describing it.

---

4 Outline and evaluate the working memory model. *(12 marks)*

Alice's answer

The working memory model has three separate components. The central executive system allocates attention to different inputs and monitoring the operation of the other two components. The phonological loop has two sub-components, the articulatory control system, where information is rehearsed subvocally, and the phonological store, where speech input is held for a very brief duration. The third component, the visuo-spatial sketchpad, deals with visual information coming either direct from the senses, or retrieved from long-term memory. The fourth component is the episodic buffer which acts as a store for visual and acoustic data.

The different components of the working memory model are well supported by research evidence. For example Bunge et al. (2000) found that the same parts of the brain were active during reading and recalling tasks, but were more active when participants had to perform two attentional tasks at the same time than when these were performed sequentially (evidence for the central executive). However, much of the key evidence for this model comes from the study of brain-damaged individuals, where it is impossible to make 'before and after' comparisons, thus limiting the validity of any conclusions drawn. Working memory has also been useful in understanding some of the cognitive changes associated with mental illnesses. For example, Park et al. (1999) found that working memory deficit may be an important indicator in schizophrenia.

Tom's answer

Working memory has three main parts. These are the central executive, which controls the other two parts, and decides where sensory input should go. The phonological loop is more to do with acoustic input (such as speech) and this goes round and round in a loop. The purpose of this is rehearsal, and this is sometimes called an 'inner ear'. The third part is the visuo-spatial sketch pad, and this holds visual information, for example an ice hockey player was able to hit a puck at a goalie's back because he could imagine it going in the goal.

There are many studies of working memory. Hitch and Baddeley gave participants either a task that just occupied the central executive, or one that occupied the central executive and another part of working memory. Participants performed slower when two parts of the working memory were used. Baddeley asked participants to track a moving light with a pointer. They also had to perform an extra task, either a visual task or a verbal task. They found it more difficult to track the moving light when they had a visual task than when they had a verbal task.

Examiner's comments

Questions that are worth 12 marks are called 'extended writing questions' and the marks are divided equally between description (AO1) and evaluation (AO2). Both Alice and Tom have organised their answers clearly so there is one paragraph of description (about 100 words) and one paragraph of evaluation (again about 100 words). This division of content is appropriate since the marks are equal and the *amount* that has been written is also about right.

Alice's description is more precise than Tom's (using more technical terms) and covers the fourth component of working memory. Nevertheless both could be described as 'accurate and reasonably detailed' and information has been presented in a 'clear and coherent' fashion. Tom may not have used quite as much jargon but he has identified three of the main components and given some information about each. His use of the ice hockey example provides evidence of understanding. Thus Alice would gain **6 out of 6 marks** for description and Tom would receive **5 out of 6 marks** for a slightly less detailed answer.

Alice continues her excellent response with a reasonable range of evaluative points each of which has been explained/elaborated. This elaboration is vital to gain AO2 marks. Top marks are awarded for evaluation which is *either* a 'broad range of evidence in reasonable depth' *or* a 'narrower range in greater depth'. Alice's AO2 material falls into the latter category and would get **6 out of 6 marks** for evaluation.

Tom has focused on just one piece of evidence – a study that supports the working memory model. At best this would be considered a 'restricted range of evidence', (the criteria for 2–3 marks), but Tom has simply *described* the evidence rather than using it *effectively* as part of a critical argument. Even just one sentence saying, 'This study supports the model' would raise this to a form of commentary, but as it stands it is only 'rudimentary' and evaluation is 'just discernible', therefore Tom gets only **1 out of 6 marks** for evaluation.

In total Alice would get **12 out of 12 marks** and Tom would get **6 out of 12 marks**.

YOUR OWN LITTLE BOOK OF REVISION NOTES

At the beginning of this book we explained how to produce your own little book of notes and use them for effective revision (see page x).

Remember to keep your notes brief – just record key points which will act as coat pegs for remembering the material.

Column 1: tick when you have produced brief notes.

Column 2: tick when you have a good grasp of this topic.

Column 3: tick during the final revision when you feel you have complete mastery of the topic.

Key terms

3 marks worth of material

Short-term memory ☐ ☐ ☐
Long-term memory ☐ ☐ ☐
Encoding ☐ ☐ ☐
Duration ☐ ☐ ☐
Capacity ☐ ☐ ☐
Eyewitness testimony ☐ ☐ ☐
Misleading question ☐ ☐ ☐

Research studies related to ...

6 marks worth of description
6 marks worth of evaluation (including the issues of validity and ethics)

Short-term memory ☐ ☐ ☐
Long-term memory ☐ ☐ ☐
Capacity ☐ ☐ ☐
Duration ☐ ☐ ☐
Encoding ☐ ☐ ☐
Multi-store model ☐ ☐ ☐
Working memory model ☐ ☐ ☐
Accuracy of eyewitness testimony ☐ ☐ ☐
Effect of age of witness on EWT ☐ ☐ ☐
Effect of anxiety on EWT ☐ ☐ ☐
Effect of misleading questions in EWT ☐ ☐ ☐
Cognitive interview ☐ ☐ ☐
Memory improvement ☐ ☐ ☐
Role of organisation ☐ ☐ ☐

Factors that affect ...

6 marks worth of material

Capacity of STM ☐ ☐ ☐
Duration of STM ☐ ☐ ☐
Encoding in STM and LTM ☐ ☐ ☐
Accuracy of eyewitness testimony ☐ ☐ ☐

Explanations/theories

6 marks worth of description
6 marks worth of evaluation (both strengths and weaknesses)

Multi-store model ☐ ☐ ☐
Working memory model ☐ ☐ ☐

Applications of memory research

6 marks worth of material

Memory improvement ☐ ☐ ☐

CROSSWORD

Answers on page 214.

Across

2 In 1976 this report made the recommendation that no court should convict on the basis of eyewitness testimony alone. (6)

5 A way of keeping information active in STM. (9)

6 A more contemporary view of short-term memory. (7,6)

10 The primary form of encoding in LTM. (8)

11 The evolutionary view on the origin of memory is that it is an _____ specialisation. (8)

12 The tendency to be less accurate when identifying people from different age groups than our own. (3,3,4)

15 A key researcher associated with the working memory model. (8)

17 This law predicts a curvilinear relationship between performance and arousal. (6, 6)

19 Research studies that are considered unrepresentative in some way might be criticised for lacking this. (8)

20 A way of extending the capacity of STM. (8)

Down

1 A limited capacity loop dealing with auditory information in 6 across. (12)

2 A measure of how long a memory lasts before it is no longer available. (8)

3 One of the two researchers who developed the cognitive interview in 1985. (9)

4 In the cognitive interview, witnesses are encouraged to report _____. (10)

7 This effect arises when people pay more attention to, for example, a gun, than to the person holding it. (6,5)

8 A type of study that combines the results of several similar studies to establish overall trends. (4,8)

9 In Loftus and Palmer's study of EWT, this verb produced the largest estimate of the car's speed. (7)

10 The first store in the multi-store model of memory. (7)

13 Atkinson and _____ developed the multi-store model of memory. (8)

14 A type of question likely to produce unreliable eyewitness testimony. (7)

16 Eyewitness accounts of the sinking of this ship in 1912 have recently proved to be more accurate than first thought. (7)

18 A number commonly believed to represent the capacity of STM. (5)

Developmental psychology is concerned with how children and adults change as they get older. Developmental psychology looks at various influences on development, such as parents, peers and others. These are all environmental influences (known as nurture). Changes also happen as a consequence of nature. 'Nature' refers to biological factors such as genes.

Developmental psychology: Early social development

Developmental psychology: Early social development

SPECIFICATION BREAKDOWN

Specification content	Comment
Attachment	
• **Explanations of attachment, including learning theory and evolutionary perspective, including Bowlby.**	The first part of this chapter is concerned with the process of attachment between infants and their caregivers, and the importance of this relationship in early social development. Explanations of attachments offer an account of how and why children become attached to a caregiver. The best-known and most developed explanation is Bowlby's theory, but there are others such as learning theory. The specification requires that you are familiar with at least two explanations, so we will look at learning theory and Bowlby's theory.
• **Types of attachment, including insecure and secure attachment and studies by Ainsworth.**	It is important to recognise that the quality of attachments varies between individuals (individual differences), for example some infants are *securely attached* whereas others are *insecurely attached*. The distinction between secure and insecure attachment stems from Ainsworth's research using the strange situation. You are required to study these different types of attachment as they are *included* in the specification.
• **Cultural variations in attachment.**	In addition to individual differences there are variations in childrearing methods in different cultures, which may be associated with differences in attachment. Research suggests that despite these differences secure attachment is the most common type of attachment in all cultures.
• **Disruption of attachment.**	Some children experience situations that lead to a disruption of attachment, for example when they have to spend time in hospital or when attending a day nursery. Such experiences cause separations between infant and attachment figure, disrupting attachment and may have a lasting effect if substitute emotional care is not provided.
• **Failure to form attachment (privation) and the effects of institutional-isation.**	The failure to form attachments during early development may have a profound effect on early social development. Such experiences of 'privation' may occur if a child is placed in an institution awaiting adoption (institutionalisation).
Attachment in everyday life	
• **The impact of different forms of day care on children's social development, including the effects on aggression and peer relations.**	Research on attachment has led some people to believe that when a child is placed in day care the consequent separation from his/her primary attachment figure will have detrimental effects on the child's early social development. Research has found that day-care experiences may have negative effects (such as increased aggression) or positive effects (such as improved abilities to cope with peer relationships).
• **Implications of research into attachment and day care for childcare practices.**	Psychological research can be used to shape childcare practices so that day-care facilities can offer the best possible care for children.

MOTHER GOOSE

Farmers often save the lives of motherless lambs by pairing them with a mother sheep whose own infant has died. The farmer takes the fleece from the dead lamb and wraps this round the other lamb. The mother thinks it is her own and will look after it without question. Within hours of birth the mother knows the smell of her own infant and will only care for this one. The mother forms an image of the infant: this is called imprinting. You can imagine that this is quite a useful characteristic, especially if you were a sheep surrounded by hundreds of lambs – it would be important to know your own infant, otherwise you would end up caring for any lamb and not ensuring the survival of your own genes.

Imprinting is reciprocal. It is even more important that infants imprint on a parent. A few summers ago the swans that live by Cara's house in Scotland had five cygnets. For the first few weeks the cygnets clung to their mother's rear end as she swam around the loch. Sometimes you couldn't even see the cygnets because they were tucked right underneath their mother. Being attached like this helped these young animals to survive. But how did they know to follow this particular individual rather than the ducks, or the dogs, or any of the other animals around the loch? Did they hatch out with an image of their mother in their heads and follow that image?

Konrad Lorenz (1952) famously demonstrated that animals aren't born with a ready-made image of their parents. Lorenz took a clutch of gosling eggs and divided them into two groups. One group was left with their natural mother while the other eggs were placed in an incubator. When the incubator eggs hatched, the first living (moving) thing they saw was Lorenz and they soon started following him around. To test this effect of imprinting Lorenz marked the two groups

▲ Farmers wrap the fleece of a dead lamb around an orphaned one so that the dead lamb's mother will care for the orphaned one.

to distinguish them and placed them together. The goslings quickly divided themselves up, one following their natural mother and Lorenz' brood following him. This suggests that a young animal *imprints* on the first object it sees. Another study (Guiton, 1966) showed that chicks would imprint on yellow rubber gloves!

Imprinting is important in the short-term for protection and being fed. It is also important in the long-term for mating. Studies have shown that mate choice is related to early imprinting experiences. The chicks which imprinted on the yellow rubber gloves tried to mate with them when older. Lorenz described how one of the geese who imprinted on him, called Martina, used to sleep on the end of his bed every night. When she reached maturity she became 'betrothed' to a gander (male goose) which Lorenz called Martin. On their first night the gander followed Martina upstairs to her usual bedtime spot, though he was not accustomed to being in a house. As the door banged shut he panicked at being enclosed and flew straight up into the chandelier in Lorenz's elegant bedroom, damaging himself considerably in the process.

Attachment in infants is similar to imprinting, as you will see. It is important in the short-term for survival, and is also related in the long-term to adult relationships – though in a different way to the

Here's looking at you

Which face would you select as the most attractive?

Psychologists have conducted studies using faces such as those above. They do this to investigate the *baby face hypothesis*. Have you ever noticed that most young mammals have the same distinctive facial features (big eyes, large forehead, squashed up nose)? We have been cooing over babies and 'aaahing' over young animals for thousands of years. If you haven't noticed this similarity, Walt Disney certainly did! These features act as a trigger for parenting behaviour, which is necessary for a young animal's survival. They elicit our desire to look after and care for babies.

However the effect doesn't end there. Since we have an innate tendency to find babyface features appealing, this spills over into the way we judge adult faces (Todd *et al.*, 1980). This is called the *baby face overgeneralisation*

hypothesis. People all over the world rate adult faces with an element of 'babyfaceness' as the most attractive (Langlois and Roggmann, 1990), and also describe people with baby-like faces as being socially, physically and intellectually weak (Zebrowitz, 1997).

The faces above were created by 'morphing' an adult woman's face with an average child face (formed by averaging four child photos). The first photo is 50% child/50% adult, the second photo is 30% child, the third photo is 20% child and the final one is 0% child/100% adult.

In a study using sets of faces similar to those above, only a few participants (9.5%) rated the totally adult face as being most attractive. Most of the participants preferred female faces that displayed between 10–50% childlike proportions (Gründl, 2007).

◀ Konrad Lorenz going for a swim, followed by his goslings.

birds' imprinting. A number of studies have shown that adults are *less likely* to mate with individuals with whom they were raised. For example, Shepher (1971) found that not one of the 3000 Israeli marriage records he studied was between individuals who had been raised together on the same communal farms (Kibbutz). This is called the *Westermarck effect* after Westermarck (1891) who

noted that, if children spend considerable time together before the age of six (a sensitive period), they avoid subsequently forming sexual relationships with these individuals – a kind of reverse imprinting. This would clearly be useful in avoiding incest, which is bioloically undesirable because it increases the chance of developing recessive genetic disorders.

Explanations of attachment

'An affectional tie that one person or animal forms between himself and another specific one – a tie that binds them together in space and endures over time. The behavioural hallmark of attachment is seeking to gain and to maintain a certain degree of proximity to the object of attachment. Attachment behaviours aim to maintain proximity or contact e.g. following, clinging and signalling behaviours such as smiling, crying and calling.'

What is meant by **attachment**? The definition on the left, written by the famous attachment researcher Mary Ainsworth (Ainsworth and Bell, 1970 p.50), captures the essence of what attachment is really all about. We can get a good feel for this idea by looking carefully at what she is saying. First, she describes attachment as an *'affectional'* tie that a person or animal forms between himself and another. What is an *'affectional'* tie? It is a tie based on emotions or *feeling* rather than any other need (such as bodily or cognitive needs). The way that a mother and young child cling to each other tells us that this is a bond that must be based on some pretty strong emotions. This tie 'binds them together in space and endures over time'. As we shall see, young children seek the company of their mother (or mother figure) and are disturbed when they are separated from her/him, even for short periods of time. This is not a one-way process, as any parent of a newborn baby will tell you. Even when we get much older and no longer need the security that our parents provided for us when we were young, that special emotional bond between us still exists.

How do we know if an attachment has developed? Ainsworth has that covered in her definition too. An infant tries to get close to and then maintain that proximity with the mother figure, and has a number of 'strategies' to bring the mother figure close and keep her there. Infants have one particularly powerful weapon in this process – the way they look, which you already know about from research on the baby face hypothesis on the previous page.

Explanations

In Chapter 1 we looked at models of memory. They could equally be called theories or *explanations* of memory. In this chapter we are going to talk about theories rather than models but they aim to achieve a similar sort of thing – to offer an account of behaviour that we see in everyday life. The scientific process (described on page xii) begins with observation of everyday life: 'scientists make observations about behaviour'. This is followed by making theories: 'scientists develop theories to explain what they have observed'.

So what have you observed about attachment? It is an experience familiar to all of us. It describes your relationships with your family members, friends and other people you know. You have varying degrees of attachment to these people but there is probably one person who you prefer to turn to at times of distress. John Bowlby produced the most comprehensive theory of attachment and we will look at his theory on the next spread. We start with an earlier explanation of attachment – learning theory. Psychologists in the 1950s did not call it attachment, they used the term 'love' to describe the emotional bond between a child and its mother figure or **primary attachment figure**.

Psychology is about all of us and our lives so it is not surprising that sometimes it touches on sensitive issues for some individuals. The issue of attachment may be a sensitive issue for some of you. One thing to bear in mind is that psychological theories are not facts; they are our best attempt to make sense of the world around us and hopefully use this information to improve people's lives.

LEARNING THEORY EXPLANATION OF ATTACHMENT

Learning theory was very popular in psychology in the first half of the twentieth century. In a nutshell, learning theory proposes that all behaviour is learned rather than inborn. When children are born they are like blank slates and everything they become can be explained in terms of the experiences they have.

Learning theory is put forward by *behaviourists* who prefer to focus their explanations solely on behaviour – what people do rather than what may or may not be going on in their minds. Behaviourists suggest that all behaviour (including attachment) is learned either through *classical* or *operant conditioning*.

Classical conditioning

Classical conditioning involves learning through association. Ivan Pavlov, a Russian physiologist, first described this type of learning. He was conducting research on the salivation reflex in dogs, recording how much they salivated each time they were fed. He noticed that they started salivating *before* they were fed. The dogs salivated as soon as they heard the door open, signalling the arrival of food. The dogs had come to *associate* the sound of the door with food. They had *learned* a new stimulus response (S-R). They learned to salivate (response) when the door opened (stimulus). This learning is summarised in the box below.

Before conditioning	During conditioning	After conditioning
Unconditioned stimulus (UCS) produces an unconditioned reflex (UCR)	Food and door opening occur together a number of times	Conditioned stimulus (CS) produces a conditioned response (CR)
Food (UCS) makes the dog salivate (UCR)		Door opening (CS) makes the dog salivate (now a CR)

The same principles can be used to explain attachment. Food (UCS) naturally produces a sense of pleasure (UCR). The person who feeds (CS) the infant becomes *associated* with the food. The 'feeder' eventually produces the pleasure associated with food; pleasure now becomes a *conditioned response* (CR). This association between an individual and a sense of pleasure is the attachment bond.

KEY TERMS

Attachment is an emotional bond between two people. It is a two-way process that endures over time. It leads to certain behaviours such as clinging and proximity-seeking, and serves the function of protecting an infant.

Primary attachment figure The person who has formed the closest bond with a child, demonstrated by the intensity of the relationship. This is usually a child's biological mother, but other people can fulfil the role – an adoptive mother, a father, grandmother and so on. Throughout this chapter when we say 'mother' we are referring to the person who fulfils the role of primary attachment figure.

Learning theory The name given to a group of explanations (classical and operant conditioning), which explain behaviour in terms of learning rather than any inborn tendencies or higher order thinking.

...1 Use classical conditioning to explain why cats come running when they hear the sound of a cupboard door opening (where their food is kept).

...2 Use operant conditioning to explain how you could get people to smile at you more often.

...3 Write a 100-word outline of the learning theory explanation of attachment.

...4 Write a 100-word *evaluation* of the learning theory explanation of attachment. (Remember that you should not *describe* research studies but must *use* them as part of an effective commentary.)

The learning theory explanation has been called the 'cupboard love theory' of attachment because it suggests that attachment is based on provision of food alone.

VALIDITY

Learning theory (based on classical and operant conditioning) is largely based on studies with non-human animals. Human behaviour may be similar in some ways but also is different because human behaviour is more influenced by higher order thinking and emotions. Behaviourist explanations may lack validity because they present an oversimplified version of human behaviour.

Behaviourists, on the other hand, believe that we are actually no different from other animals. Our behaviour patterns are constructed from the same basic building blocks of stimulus and response and therefore it is legitimate to generalise from animal experiments to human behaviour.

Operant conditioning

The second explanation used by the behaviourists is called operant conditioning. Learning also occurs when we are rewarded for doing something – rewards can be anything such as money or praise. Each time you do something and it results in a *pleasant consequence*, the behaviour is 'stamped in' or *reinforced*. It becomes more probable that you will repeat that behaviour in the future. If you do something and it results in an *unpleasant consequence*, it becomes less likely that you will repeat that behaviour. These two outcomes are called *reinforcement* and *punishment* respectively.

Dollard and Miller (1950) offered an explanation of attachment based on operant conditioning. They suggested that a hungry infant feels uncomfortable and this creates a drive to reduce the discomfort. When the infant is fed, the drive is reduced and this produces a feeling of pleasure (which is rewarding). Food becomes a *primary reinforcer* because it 'stamps in' (reinforces) the behaviour in order to avoid discomfort. The person who supplies the food is associated with avoiding discomfort and becomes a *secondary reinforcer*, and a source of reward in his/her own right. Attachment occurs because the child seeks the person who can supply the reward.

⊕ STRENGTHS OF LEARNING THEORY

The strength of learning theory is that it can provide an adequate explanation of how attachments form. We *do* learn through association and reinforcement. However, food may not be the main reinforcer; it may be that attention and responsiveness from a caregiver are important rewards that create the bond (such reinforcers were not part of the learning theory story).

⊖ WEAKNESSES OF LEARNING THEORY

The main weakness of this explanation is the role of food in attachment. People still seem to believe that feeding an infant plays a key role in developing a close relationship – fathers often feel relegated to a lesser position if their partner takes sole control of feeding. Yet there is strong psychological evidence to show that feeding has nothing to do with attachment. The most famous of such studies was conducted by Harry Harlow (1959) and entitled 'The Origins of Love'. Harlow had been conducting research on learning using rhesus monkeys when he noticed that the young monkeys, who were kept on their own in cages, became quite distressed when their cages were cleaned. The cages had 'sanitary pads' lining the bottom and it appeared that the monkeys became attached to these as a kind of 'security blanket'. This led Harlow to investigate the hypothesis that it was contact comfort (the security blanket) rather than food that was more important in the development of love (notice the scientific method at work here!).

Harlow created two wire mothers (see picture below). One (the lactating mother) had a feeding bottle attached and the other was wrapped in soft cloth but offered no food. According to learning theory the young monkeys should have become attached to the lactating mother who offered reduction of the hunger drive. In fact the monkeys spent most time with the cloth-covered mother and would cling to it, especially when they were frightened (a proximity-seeking behaviour which, as we saw, is characteristic of attachment).

Although this is a study with animals, and it may not apply to humans, it is supported by another study, this time with human infants. Schaffer and Emerson (1964) observed 60 babies from mainly working-class homes in Glasgow for a period of about a year. They found that in fact infants were not most attached to the person who fed them. They were most attached to the person who was most responsive and who interacted with them the most.

These studies suggest that 'cupboard love' is not likely to be the best explanation for attachment, although association and reinforcement may be part of the story.

◀ Orphaned monkeys spent most time with the 'cloth-covered mother', visiting the 'mother' with the feeding bottle for food. This suggests that attachment is related to contact comfort and not food.

Evolutionary perspective – Bowlby's attachment theory

Nowadays the main view of attachment is derived from the theory first proposed by John Bowlby in 1958 (the fuller version of the theory was published in 1969). John Bowlby worked as a psychiatrist in London, treating emotionally disturbed children. He observed that a number of children had experienced early separations from their families, and this led him to propose his first theory, the *maternal deprivation hypothesis* (1951), in which he suggested that a young child should 'experience a warm, intimate and continuous relationship with his mother (or permanent mother substitute) in which both find satisfaction and enjoyment'. He proposed that children deprived of such a relationship might suffer permanent long-term emotional maladjustment. Bowlby spent many years developing this first theory about the effects of deprivation into his more comprehensive theory of attachment, which focuses on why infants need to be attached to a caregiver and also how this attachment forms.

▶ It is no accident that all young animals have 'cute' faces: big eyes, small nose and chin, high forehead. These neonatal features elicit caregiving and this affects the way we view the attractiveness of adult features as well (see experiment on page 33).

*Notice the scientific method in action – Bowlby **observed** the behaviour of children ➜ this led him to develop a **theory** to account for his observations related to emotional development ➜ both he and other psychologists have developed **hypotheses** (such as the continuity hypothesis) from this theory, and have conducted studies to test the hypotheses.*

The theory of evolution

Evolution is a fact; evolution means change. Darwin's Theory of Evolution is an attempt to explain how such changes occur. We outlined this theory at the start of Chapter 1. Briefly, each new generation of animals shows some genetically caused variation from the previous one. If any such variations enhance the ability of that individual to survive, then the genes for these variations will appear in future generations.

Actually, it is not survival that matters. What matters is reproduction – unless an individual reproduces, their genes will not be perpetuated. Of course survival contributes to successful reproduction – you can't reproduce if you are dead!

We say that the variations, or traits, are *naturally selected*. This happens if a trait increases an individual's chances of survival and reproduction. For example, in Chapter 1, we argued that having a good memory is likely to enhance survival and thus reproduction, and thus will be naturally selected. Similarly an infant who sticks close to its mother is more likely to survive and therefore any trait related to such 'attachment' will be naturally selected.

One important thing to understand is that none of this is conscious. A baby does not think, 'If I look more attractive I will be more likely to survive because my mother will want to look after me', nor does a parent think, 'If I look after my child he is more likely to survive and reproduce my genes'. These behaviours are naturally selected only because they prove to be successful.

BOWLBY'S ATTACHMENT THEORY (1969)

Attachment is adaptive and innate

Bowlby's theory is an evolutionary theory (see left) because, in his view, attachment is a behavioural system that has evolved because of its survival value and, ultimately, its reproductive value. According to Bowlby, children have an **innate** drive to become attached to a caregiver because attachment has long-term benefits, similar to the benefits of **imprinting** (see page 32). Both attachment and imprinting ensure that a young animal stays close to a caregiver who will feed and protect the young animal. Thus attachment and imprinting are *adaptive* behaviours – behaviours that increase the likelihood of survival and, ultimately, reproduction. Infants who do not become attached are less likely to survive and reproduce. Attachment 'genes' are perpetuated, and infants are born with an innate drive to become attached (note that there is just one attachment gene, but lots of genes that are involved in this behaviour).

Sensitive period

Since attachment is innate, there is likely to be a limited window for its development i.e. a critical or **sensitive period**. Development of all biological systems takes place most rapidly and easily during a critical period but can still take place at other times (sensitive periods). For example, when a baby is growing in the womb there is a special time when the arms develop. Some forms of maternal illness during this period may prevent this happening at the critical time and the window for arm development passes forever. Bowlby applied the concept of a sensitive period to attachment. He suggested that the second quarter of the first year is when infants are most sensitive to the development of attachments. As the months pass it becomes increasingly difficult to form infant-caregiver attachments.

Caregiving is adaptive

It isn't just attachment that is innate; the drive to provide caregiving is also innate because it is adaptive (i.e. enhances survival of one's offspring). Infants are born with certain characteristics, called **social releasers**, which elicit caregiving. These social releasers include smiling and crying – who doesn't smile back at a baby's smile or feel uncomfortable when they hear a baby cry? Another example of a social releaser is a baby's face (see *baby face hypothesis*, page 33).

Attachment is the innate behavioural system in babies; caregiving is the innate response in adults. Both provide protection and thereby enhance survival. The formation of attachments depends on the *interaction* of these systems.

John Bowlby (1907–1990) was born into an upper-middle-class family and raised mainly by a nanny. His son, Sir Richard Bowlby explains how this led to his father's interest in attachment:

'The origin of my father's motivation for working on the conundrum of the parent-child attachment bond probably stems from a traumatic childhood. His father, my grandfather, was a successful surgeon who lived in a large London townhouse with his wife and six children. The children, as was normal for the time, were raised by nannies. The children only saw their mother for one hour each day, and even then the children went to see her all together, so there wasn't exactly individual quality time. My Father grew to love his nanny called Minnie, and I have little doubt that she was his surrogate primary attachment figure, but when he was four years old Minnie left the family. He lost his "mother figure", and his primary attachment bond was broken. He was then sent away to boarding school when he was eight years old, causing further trauma. I think one thing that saved him was that he did have those four years of secure attachment with Minnie.'

These early experiences of separation shaped him and also shaped his work. Like many psychologists he was drawn to investigate an area of behaviour that had been challenging for him in his own life.

A secure base

Attachment is important for protection, and thus acts as a secure base from which a child can explore the world and a safe haven to return to when threatened. Thus attachment fosters *independence* rather than dependence though some people mistakenly interpret attachment as dependence.

Monotropy and hierarchy

Bowlby believed that infants form a number of attachments but one of these has special importance. This bias towards one individual, the *primary* attachment, is called **monotropy**. Infants also have other secondary attachment figures that form a hierarchy of attachments. The one special attachment is most usually (but not necessarily) an infant's mother. Bowlby believed that sensitive responsiveness was the key – an infant becomes most strongly attached to the person who responds *most sensitively* to the infant's social releasers (the 'sensitivity hypothesis'). This person becomes the infant's *primary attachment figure*, providing the main foundation for emotional development, self-esteem and later relationships with peers, lovers and one's own children.

Secondary attachment figures are also important in emotional development; they act as a kind of safety net and also contribute to social development. Children brought up with no secondary attachment figures appear to lack social skills.

Internal working model

Attachment starts as the relationship between a caregiver and infant. This relationship may be one of trust or of uncertainty and inconsistency, and creates expectations about what all relationships will be like. Gradually the infant develops a model about emotional relationships: Bowlby called this an **internal working model**. This 'model' is a cluster of concepts about relationships and what to expect from others – about whether relationships involve consistent or inconsistent love, whether others make you feel good or anxious, and so on.

The continuity hypothesis

The internal working model means there is consistency between early emotional experiences and later relationships. This leads to the **continuity hypothesis** – the view that there is a link between the early attachment relationship and later emotional behaviour; individuals who are securely attached in infancy *continue* to be socially and emotionally competent, whereas insecurely attached children have more social and emotional difficulties later in childhood and adulthood.

INDIVIDUAL DIFFERENCES

There are different kinds of attachment – some babies form a secure attachment with their caregivers, whereas others form an insecure attachment. The main factor that determines the kind of attachment formed is the responsiveness of a caregiver. These individual differences in both infant and caregiver are discussed on pages 40–3 of this chapter.

CULTURAL VARIATIONS

In some cultures dependence rather than independence is promoted by secure attachment. In the West we value independence, whereas in Japan, for example, dependence is the desired outcome in social development. Cultural variations are examined on pages 44–7.

CAN YOU...?   (No.**2.2**)

...1 Outline **six** key points relating to Bowlby's theory of attachment.

...2 Use your key points to write a 100-word description of Bowlby's attachment theory.

KEY TERMS

Innate Refers to characteristics that are inborn, a product of genetic factors. Such traits may be apparent at birth or may appear later as a result of maturation (e.g. when a boy develops a beard).

Continuity hypothesis The idea that emotionally secure infants go on to be emotionally secure, trusting and socially confident adults.

Imprinting An innate readiness to develop a strong bond with a mother figure, which takes place during a critical or sensitive period.

Internal working model A mental model of the world that enables individuals to predict and control their environment. The internal working model based on attachment has several consequences: (1) In the short-term it gives the child insight into the caregiver's behaviour and enables the child to influence the caregiver's behaviour, so that a true partnership can be formed; (2) in the long-term it acts as a template for all future relationships because it generates expectations about how people behave.

Monotropy The idea that the one relationship that the infant has with his/her primary attachment figure is of special significance in emotional development.

Sensitive period A biologically determined period of time during which the child is particularly sensitive to a specific form of stimulation, resulting in the development of a specific response or characteristic. This is in contrast to the concept of a *critical period*, which suggests there is a more finite period during which change can take place.

Social releasers A social behaviour or characteristic that elicits a caregiving reaction. Bowlby suggested that these were *innate* and *adaptive*, and critical in the process of forming *attachments*. Examples include smiling, crying, making cooing noises, and the 'baby face' (large eyes, small nose, big forehead).

Evaluating Bowlby's theory of attachment

John Bowlby's theory of attachment has had an enormous influence on our understanding of emotional development. Today it is considered the dominant explanation for both *how* and *why* attachments develop. There is considerable research support for the theory, but also some criticisms and refinements.

The evolutionary approach in a nutshell

Attachment is adaptive and innate. Infants elicit caregiving and become attached to those individuals who respond most sensitively to their signals (social releasers). The relationship with a primary attachment figure acts as a template for all later relationships as a result of the internal working model.

➕ STRENGTHS OF BOWLBY'S THEORY OF ATTACHMENT

Imprinting in non-human animals

The research by Lorenz (see page 32) supports the view that imprinting is innate because the goslings imprinted on the first moving object they saw – whether it was a goose or Lorenz himself. A similar process is likely to have evolved in many species as a mechanism to protect young animals and enhance the likelihood of their survival.

Sensitive period

Later in this chapter we will look at research on what happens if attachments fail to develop. The conclusion from this research appears to be that once the sensitive period has passed it is difficult to form attachments. For example, Hodges and Tizard (see page 50) found that children who had formed no attachments had later difficulties with peers.

Universality

If attachment did evolve, as Bowlby suggests, to provide an important biological function, then we would expect attachment and caregiving behaviours to be universal i.e. found in all cultures. In one study of attachment, Tronick *et al.* (1992) studied an African tribe, the Efe, from Zaire, who live in extended family groups. The infants are looked after and even breastfed by different women but usually sleep with their own mother at night. Despite such differences in childrearing practices the infants, at six months, still showed one primary attachment. This supports the view that attachment and caregiving are universal and not influenced by different cultural practices. On pages 44–7 we will look further at studies of attachment in different cultures – not all of the research supports the universal view.

Monotropy and hierarchy

Bowlby suggested that infants form multiple attachments but these form a hierarchy, with one attachment having special importance in emotional development. There is much evidence to support this view such as the study by Tronick *et al.* (above). The study by Schaffer and Emerson (1964, see page 35) also found that most infants had many attachments – to mothers, fathers, grandparents, siblings, other relatives, friends and/or neighbours. However the infants maintained one *primary* object of attachment. This was most often the infant's mother, though it was frequently the infant's father. The primary attachment figure was not always the person who fed or bathed the infant; in fact Schaffer and Emerson reported that there was little relationship between time spent together and attachment. This suggests that it is the *quality* of caregiving (sensitivity) rather than the *quantity* that is important – the opposite of what learning theory would predict.

The importance of secondary attachments was shown in a study by Harlow where monkeys who were raised just with their mothers for the first six months were later socially abnormal – they didn't want to play or groom their peers (Blum, 2003). Of course monkeys are not the same as humans (in terms of, for example, emotional complexity), but human research supports this – for example research on the role of fathers described on the right.

Caregiver sensitivity

Schaffer and Emerson observed that strongly attached infants had mothers who responded quickly to their demands and who offered their child the most interaction. Infants who were weakly attached had mothers who failed to interact with them.

We might also consider Harlow's study (1959, see page 35). The infant monkeys formed only a one-way attachment with an unresponsive wire 'mother'. The result was that they all became quite maladjusted adults – they had difficulties in reproductive relationships and were poor parents. This underlines the importance of *interaction* in attachment. It is not enough to have something to cuddle, you need to be cuddled back. The findings are mirrored in studies of humans; Carlson (1998) found that insensitive caregiving was associated with *disorganised attachment* and having psychological problems in adulthood.

The continuity hypothesis

The Minnesota longitudinal study (Sroufe *et al.*, 2005) has followed participants from infancy to late adolescence and found continuity between early attachment and later emotional/social behaviour. Individuals who were classified as secure in infancy were rated the highest for social competence, were less isolated and more popular, and more empathetic. This demonstrates continuity. Further evidence for continuity is described on page 42 (see 'Effects of attachment type').

KEY TERM

Temperament hypothesis The belief that children form secure attachments simply because they have a more 'easy' temperament from birth, whereas innately difficult children are more likely to form insecure attachments and later relationships.

Bowlby's attachment theory has had a profound influence on many aspects of everyday life. Some of these are covered in the rest of this chapter – for example parenting programmes (see pages 43 and 56), dealing with the effects of separation (see page 48) and day-care programmes (see page 52).

⊖ WEAKNESSES OF BOWLBY'S THEORY OF ATTACHMENT

Multiple attachments

Many psychologists hold the view that all attachment figures are equally important (e.g. Rutter, 1995). In the multiple attachment model there are no primary and secondary attachments – all attachments are integrated into one single working model. However this may not be so very different from what Bowlby intended. Secondary attachments, in his theory, *do* contribute to social development, but healthy development requires one central person standing above all the others in a hierarchy. Research on infant-father attachment, for example, suggests a key role for fathers in social development (Grossmann and Grossmann, 1991). Relationships with siblings are important for learning how to negotiate with peers. Prior and Glaser (2006) conclude from a review of research that the evidence still points to the hierarchical model as suggested by Bowlby's concept of monotropy.

Alternative explanation

One of the key features of Bowlby's theory is the suggestion that there are continuities between early attachment and later social/emotional behaviours – the continuity hypothesis. However such continuity in development can be explained without using Bowlby's theory. An innately trusting and friendly personality could be the prime factor in secure attachments *and* the prime factor in forming close adult relationships. This is called the **temperament hypothesis** (Kagan, 1984) – certain personality or temperamental characteristics of the infant shape a mother's responsiveness.

There is evidence that children *are* born with innate temperamental differences. Thomas and Chess (1977) identified three basic infant personality types: easy, difficult and slow-to-warm-up. Further evidence comes from Bokhorst *et al.* (2003) who looked at twins and found greater similarity in terms of temperament for identical twins (twins who are genetically the same) than for non-identical twins.

There is also evidence that such temperamental differences contribute to attachment. Belsky and Rovine (1987) assessed babies aged one to three days old and found a link between certain physiological behaviours and later attachment types. They found that infants who were calmer and less anxious (aspects of temperament) were more likely to be securely attached. On the other hand Nachmias *et al.* (1996) found no association between early temperament and attachment strength.

CAN YOU...? No.2.1

...1 Bowlby's theory explains both how and why attachment develops. What is the 'how' explanation and what is the 'why' explanation?

...2 Describe **two** studies that support Bowlby's theory and explain why they provide support for it. (Describe the study briefly and then write a sentence 'So this shows that …')

...3 Describe **two** studies that do *not* support Bowlby's theory and explain in what ways they do not.

...4 Select **three** (or more) arguments in favour of Bowlby's theory, and for each of them present a counter-argument (i.e. an argument presenting the opposite view). (You may not find all the answers on this spread and, in fact, you may need to work out some of the counter-arguments for yourself.)

COMMENTARY CORNER

Question: **There are many explanations for attachment, such as learning theory and the evolutionary perspective (Bowlby).**

Discuss *one* explanation of attachment. *(8 marks)*

There are several things to note about this exam question:

1 It is a kind of 'extended writing' question. In chapter 1 we looked at these extended essay questions but we are now going to consider the different forms of such questions.

2 It starts with a statement. Some extended essay questions start with a brief statement for guidance. You must answer the question (not the statement) that follows and use the statement to provide some useful clues about what your answer might contain.

3 The question itself begins with the word 'discuss'. In Chapter 1 you were given various different versions of the extended writing question, using words like 'give a brief account' and 'consider'. One of the most common is the word 'discuss' – which means you must provide both description (**AO1**) and evaluation (**AO2**) in equal measure.

4 It is worth 8 marks and not 12 marks. In Chapter 1 all the extended writing questions were worth 12 marks whereas this one is 8 marks. This means you should not write as much. You might work on a rough rule that 1 mark is about 20–25 words, which means about 160-200 words for this answer (80–100 words of **AO1** and the same of **AO2**).

Consider the two theories of attachment we have covered so far: the learning theory approach and the evolutionary perspective (Bowlby). For an 8-, 10- or 12-mark question you will need to provide a lot less material than we have supplied for you. Your task is to represent the gist of your chosen theory in the appropriate number of words for the question. The requisite skill is the skill of *précis* (which we explained on page 26). You should practice writing descriptions and evaluations of different lengths to fit the possible questions.

AO1 *(description) 4 marks*

You could identify four important assumptions of the theory. Now write 25 words for each of these four points and you have your 100 words of AO1! Add another point and you're up to 125 words if needed.

AO2 *(evaluation) 4 marks*

How *plausible* an explanation (or theory) is largely depends on three factors:

1 Does it fit the facts?
2 Is it consistent with existing research findings?
3 Does subsequent research support its claims?

Each evaluative 'point' should be *elaborated* (remember the three point rule) and thus might be about 30 words, that would mean only three or four points are needed in total.

Types of attachment

Secure and insecure attachments are examples of a particular type or *style* of attachment bond that may be established between any two individuals (usually the mother and infant). These attachment styles are seen as patterns of thinking, feeling, and behaving in interpersonal situations. Mary Ainsworth is largely responsible for the original work on attachment types; her method of assessing attachment type (the strange situation), and her typology, have stood the test of time and are still used today.

AINSWORTH'S EARLY STUDIES

Infancy in Uganda (Ainsworth, 1967)

Mary Ainsworth came to London in the 1950s and worked with Bowlby as a research assistant. Initially she resisted Bowlby's ideas about attachment, preferring the more traditional learning theory. However that changed when she went to Uganda in 1954 to conduct a two-year naturalistic observation of mother-infant interactions. The participants were 26 mothers and their infants who lived in six villages surrounding Kampala. She observed that some mothers were more 'sensitive' to their infants' needs (e.g. they were able to provide more details about their infants) and these mothers tended to have 'securely attached' infants who cried little and seemed content to explore in the presence of their mother; secure attachment led to increasing competence and independence (the 'secure base'). Learning theory couldn't explain the importance of sensitivity in attachment, but Bowlby's evolutionary theory could.

The Baltimore study (Ainsworth *et al.*, 1971)

When Ainsworth returned to America she continued to study mother-infant interactions but this time in an urban setting. She observed 26 mothers and their infants from birth in the Baltimore area. She and her team didn't use behaviour checklists, preferring to use shorthand to record rich details about their observations.

The final interview with each mother and infant took place when the infant was one year old. The attachment relationship was assessed using the strange situation (described on the right). She found that the mothers of the infants subsequently classified as secure had behaved most sensitively with them at home during the first three months of life. Learning theorists found this difficult to understand: they were convinced that responsiveness to, for example, crying, should act as a reinforcer and *increase* the crying rather than Ainsworth's prediction that crying would decrease with caregiver responsiveness.

meet the researcher

Mary Salter Ainsworth (1913–1999), an American, had a considerable influence on Bowlby's thinking, and provided him with important empirical evidence for his theory. Bowlby focused on the universality of attachments, whereas Ainsworth was particularly interested in individual differences – the different types of attachment that infants formed with their caregivers.

Most importantly Ainsworth provided Bowlby with the concept of the attachment figure as a *secure base* from which an infant can explore the world, and pointed to the importance of *maternal sensitivity* in the development of mother-infant attachment patterns.

THE STRANGE SITUATION

Ainsworth and Wittig (1969) devised the strange situation to be able to test the nature of attachment systematically. The aim was to see how infants (aged between 9 and 18 months) behave under conditions of mild stress and also novelty. Stress is created in the strange situation by the presence of a stranger and by separation from a caregiver. This tests **stranger anxiety** and **separation anxiety** respectively. The strange situation also aims to encourage exploration by placing infants in a novel situation and thus tests the *secure base* concept.

Procedure

The research room is a *novel environment*, a 9 × 9 foot square marked off into 16 squares to help in recording the infant's movements.

The procedure consists of eight episodes, each designed to highlight certain behaviours as shown in the table below.

Episodes (about 3 minutes duration)	Behaviour assessed
1 Parent and infant play.	–
2 Parent sits while infant plays.	Use of parent as secure base
3 Stranger enters and talks to parent.	Stranger anxiety
4 Parent leaves, infant plays, stranger offers comfort if needed.	Separation anxiety
5 Parent returns, greets infant, offers comfort if needed; stranger leaves.	Reunion behaviour
6 Parent leaves, infant alone.	Separation anxiety
7 Stranger enters and offers comfort.	Stranger anxiety
8 Parent returns, greets infant, offers comfort.	Reunion behaviour

Why not draw a cartoon strip to illustrate what happens in the strange situation?

In the strange situation data is collected by a group of observers who record what the infant is doing every 15 seconds. The observer notes down which of the following behaviours is displayed and also scores the behaviour for intensity on a scale of 1 to 7: (1) proximity and contact-seeking behaviours, (2) contact-maintaining behaviours, (3) proximity and interaction-avoiding behaviours, (4) contact and interaction-resisting behaviours, (5) search behaviours.

LINK TO RESEARCH METHODS

All of the studies on this page involved the use of observational techniques – where the researcher observes and categorises the behaviour of target individuals. Observational techniques are described and evaluated on pages 86–9.

CAN YOU...? No.2.4

...1 When students are asked to describe the strange situation they often just list the eight episodes. Write a description of the eight episodes that doesn't involve a list.

...2 Summarise the way observations were recorded.

...3 Write a 25-word description of each of the four attachment types.

...4 In the strange situation there are actually independent variables (the caregiver goes, the stranger approaches the child and so on). Identify the DV in the strange situation.

...5 Describe **two** research methods used by Ainsworth.

▼ Behaviours displayed by infants in the strange situation (from Ainsworth *et al.*, 1978)

	Secure attachment (Type A)	Insecure-avoidant (Type B)	Insecure-resistant (Type C)
Willingness to explore	High	High	Low
Stranger anxiety	High	Low	High
Separation anxiety	Some easy to soothe	Indifferent	Distressed
Behaviour at reunion with caregiver	Enthusiastic	Avoids contact	Seeks and rejects
Percentage of infants in this category	66%	22%	12%

Findings from the strange situation

Ainsworth *et al.* (1978) combined the data from several studies, to make a total of 106 middle-class infants observed in the strange situation.

They found similarities and differences in the ways that infants behaved. In terms of similarity it was noted that exploratory behaviours declined in all infants from episode 2 onwards, whereas the amount of crying increased. Proximity-seeking and contact-maintaining behaviours intensified during separation and when the stranger appeared. Contact-resisting and proximity-avoiding behaviours occurred rarely towards the caregiver prior to separation.

In terms of differences, they found three main types of children, originally called A, B and C to avoid any descriptive labels. The characteristics of the main attachment types, with respect to the strange situation, are described below and summarised in the table below.

- The **secure attachment** style refers to those who have harmonious and cooperative interactions with their caregiver. They are not likely to cry if the caregiver leaves the room. When feeling anxious they seek close bodily contact with their caregiver and are easily soothed, though they may be reluctant to leave their caregiver's side prematurely. They seek and are comfortable with social interaction and intimacy. The securely attached infant uses the caregiver as a secure base from which to explore and thus is able to function independently.
- The **insecure-avoidant** (anxious) style of attachment is characterised by children who tend to avoid social interaction and intimacy with others. In the strange situation such children show little response to separation and do not seek the proximity of their caregiver on reunion. If the infant is picked up he/she shows little or no tendency to cling or resist being

put down. Such children are happy to explore with or without the presence of their caregiver. They are also characterised by high levels of anxiousness as well as avoidant behaviour, and may become quite angry because their attachment needs are not met.
- The **insecure-resistant** (ambivalent) style characterises those who both seek and reject intimacy and social interaction. Such children respond to separation from their caregiver with immediate and intense distress. On reunion, such children display conflicting desires for and against contact, they may angrily resist being picked up while also trying other means to maintain proximity.

All three of Ainsworth's attachment types show relatively *consistent* patterns of behaviour. However a re-analysis of over 200 strange situation videotapes led Main and Solomon (1986) to propose a fourth attachment type:

- The **insecure-disorganised** type which is characterised by a lack of consistent patterns of social behaviour. Such infants lack a coherent strategy for dealing with the stress of separation. For example, they show very strong attachment behaviour which is suddenly followed by avoidance or looking fearful towards their caregiver or displaying odd movements such as stumbling, but only when the caregiver is present (see also *disinhibited attachment* on page 51).

Secure Type B	Insecure-avoidant Type A	Insecure-resistant Type C	Insecure-disorganised Type D
62%	15%	9%	15%

▲ Van IJzendoorn *et al.* (1999) conducted a meta-analysis of nearly 80 studies in America covering over 6000 infants. This table shows the distribution of all four attachment types.

KEY TERMS

Secure attachment This is a strong and contented attachment of an infant to his or her caregiver, which develops as a result of sensitive responding by the caregiver to the infant's needs. Securely attached infants are comfortable with social interaction and intimacy. Secure attachment is related to healthy subsequent cognitive and emotional development.

Insecure attachment This is a form of attachment between infant and caregiver that develops as a result of the caregiver's lack of sensitive responding to the infant's needs. It may be associated with poor subsequent cognitive and emotional development.

Insecure-avoidant style of attachment characterises those children who tend to avoid social interaction and intimacy with others.

Insecure-resistant (ambivalent) attachment characterises those who both seek and reject intimacy and social interaction.

Insecure-disorganised The emphasis in the descriptions above is on 'consistency' of attachment-related behaviour. There are those who argue that there is also a type characterised by a lack of such consistent patterns of social behaviour.

Separation protest/anxiety The distress shown by an infant when separated from his/her primary attachment figure.

Stranger anxiety The distress shown by an infant when approached or picked up by someone who is unfamiliar.

Evaluating types of attachment

The importance of Ainsworth's strange situation technique is that it has provided a means by which attachment can be studied. Almost all studies of attachment use the strange situation technique to classify attachment type and then the type can be correlated to some other behaviour, for example maternal behaviours or a child's social behaviour in adolescence. This means that psychologists can discover, for example, what maternal behaviours are associated with secure and insecure attachment or how later behaviour relates to early attachment type. The strange situation is only appropriate for use with young children (up to 20 months) but related techniques have been developed for older children (e.g. preschool strange situation), and with adults (the AAI – adult attachment interview), and even with dogs (Topal *et al.*, 1998, see page 88).

VALIDITY

Validity concerns the extent to which we are measuring what we intended to measure. The strange situation aims to measure the attachment type of a child – secure, insecure-avoidant and so on. Does it measure this or does it measure the quality of a particular relationship?

For some the answer is that it only measures particular relationships. For example, Main and Weston (1981) found that children behaved differently depending on which parent they were with. This suggests that the classification of an attachment type may not be valid because what we are measuring is one relationship rather than something lodged in the individual.

Others take the view that this doesn't matter, as ultimately it is only one relationship (the one with the primary attachment figure) that determines attachment type. Bowlby suggested that attachment begins as the relationship between infant and primary attachment figure and later becomes internalised so that it is a characteristic of the child.

The fact that an infant responds differently with someone other than their primary attachment figure tells us something about that relationship but the attachment *type* is largely related to the one special relationship. Main (1999) tested a group of children and re-assessed them at age nine using the AAI (adult attachment interview), finding that attachment type seemed to be chiefly influenced by the mother, supporting Bowlby's concept of monotropy.

Validity of the strange situation can be demonstrated in other ways. For example, *construct validity* is demonstrated insofar as other studies have supported the four attachment types identified; they are confirmed as distinctly different categories. *Predictive validity* is demonstrated in the correlations found between early attachment types and later behaviours (see right).

RELIABILITY

A measurement is reliable if it is consistent. For example, if two or more people observe the same infant, the observations should be the same. Reliability of the strange situation has been assessed using inter-rater reliability – comparing the ratings made by a panel of experienced judges. Ainsworth *et al.* (1978) found almost perfect agreement when rating exploratory behaviour – they found .94 agreement between raters (1.00 would be perfect).

LINK TO RESEARCH METHODS

An important aspect of observational techniques is **reliability** – the extent to which several measurements of the same thing are consistent. This aspect of research methods is explained on page 90.

ETHICS

The intention of the strange situation is to cause mild distress. Is it acceptable to do this to infants? Ainsworth *et al.* (1978) claimed that the situation as a whole was intended not to be any more disturbing than ordinary life experiences. However, in episode six, 20% of the infants reportedly cried 'desperately'.

EFFECTS OF ATTACHMENT TYPE

Bowlby's theory predicted that there would be continuities between early attachment experiences and later social and emotional behaviour. On page 38 we looked at some evidence for this continuity hypothesis; now we will focus on the continuities of specific types of attachment.

Behaviour in later childhood

A number of longitudinal studies have demonstrated a link between early attachment experience and later social functioning. Prior and Glaser (2006) provide the following summary:

- *Secure attachment* is associated with positive outcomes such as less emotional dependence and higher achievement orientation and interpersonal harmony.
- *Avoidant attachment* is related to later aggressiveness, and generally negative affect.
- *Resistant attachment* is associated with greater anxiety and withdrawn behaviour.
- *Disorganised attachment* is linked to hostile and aggressive behaviour.

Adult romantic behaviour

According to Bowlby, later relationships are likely to be a continuation of these attachment styles because the mother's behaviour creates an *internal working model* of relationships that leads the infant to expect the same in later relationships. Hazan and Shaver (1987) investigated this hypothesis using a 'Love Quiz' in a newspaper. The quiz asked questions about early experiences (in order to classify attachment type), about current love experiences involvements and also about attitudes towards love (internal working model). Hazan and Shaver found that there were characteristic patterns of later romantic behaviour associated with each early attachment type (see table below). This supports Bowlby's theory, though we can't be certain that early attachment experiences *caused* later attachment types.

Attachment type	Secure adults	Insecure-avoidant adults	Insecure-resistant adults
Current love experiences	Relationships are positive	Fearful of closeness	Preoccupied by love
Attitudes towards love	Trust others and believe in enduring love	Love is not lasting nor necessary for happiness	Fall in love easily but have trouble finding *true* love

Tom and Alice are like chalk and cheese. Tom is outgoing and sociable whereas Alice seems to often be in a bad mood and is sometimes rather aggressive.

1 How can Ainsworth's research be used to explain these differences?

Clare is preparing a booklet for expectant mothers and wants to include some advice based on what psychologists know about the benefits of secure attachment and how caregivers might treat their babies to form the best attachments.

2 Based on your study of this topic, write a short piece of advice that Clare might include in her booklet.

Rick reads some research about how dogs are attached to their owners in the same way that children are attached.

3 Suggest how he might assess the attachment of the dogs to the different members of the family using a technique similar to the strange situation.

FACTORS INFLUENCING ATTACHMENT TYPE

Sensitivity

We looked at evidence related to the importance of sensitivity in attachment behaviours on page 38. Now we can consider the links between sensitivity and specific attachment types. Ainsworth developed the Maternal Sensitivity Scale to rate mothers' behaviours such as: sensivity-insensitivity to infants' signals, acceptance-rejection, cooperation-interference and accessibility-ignoring. Using this scale Ainsworth *et al.* (1978) found key group differences in maternal scores in the strange situation:

- Mothers of securely attached infants were more sensitive, accepting, cooperative and accessible.
- Mothers of insecurely attached infants were more unresponsive to crying and less affectionate.
- Mothers of avoidant infants were more rejecting, paid less attention to infants when entering the room.
- Mothers of resistant infants tended to be occupied with routine activities when holding the infant.

Maternal reflective functioning

Some studies have actually found rather low correlations between measures of maternal sensitivity and the strength of attachment (e.g. Raval *et al.*, 2001). Slade *et al.* (2005) found a greater role for *maternal reflective functioning* – the ability to understand what someone else is thinking and feeling. They suggest that maternal reflective thinking rather than sensitivity may be the central mechanism in establishing attachment type.

Temperament

On page 39 we examined evidence that temperament may be a component in attachment type, although the evidence is uncertain.

REAL-WORLD APPLICATIONS

In situations where disordered patterns of attachment develop between infant and caregiver, intervention strategies can be developed. For example 'the 'Circle of Security' project (Cooper *et al.*, 2005) teaches caregivers to understand their infants' signals of distress better and to increase their understanding of what it feels like to feel anxious. The project showed a decrease in the number of caregivers classified as disordered (from 60% to 15%) and an increase in infants classed as securely attached (from 32% to 40%).

CAN YOU...? No.2.5

...1 Explain why the strange situation has been accused of lacking validity.

...2 Explain why you think the strange situation is ethically acceptable or why it is not.

...3 Describe **two** behaviours which are affected by attachment type and **two** behaviours which affect attachment type.

COMMENTARY CORNER

Question: **Discuss research into different types of attachment. (12 marks)**

One of the secrets of effective AO2 commentary is making it obvious that that is what you are doing. It helps, therefore, to develop an AO2 'vocabulary' as below.

- This suggests that…
- So we can see that…
- This would imply…
- A consequence would be…
- An advantage of this is…
- An alternative explanation could be…

- This is supported by…
- This is challenged by…
- Not everyone reacts the same way, for example…
- There may be cultural variations…
- This has been applied to…

The advantages of this approach are that 1) it makes you *think* critically about your **AO1** material 2) it makes you think more broadly about the different possibilities for commentary and 3) it makes it more obvious to an examiner that this is **AO2** material (never a bad thing!). Of course just *describing* cultural variations in types of attachment, or the findings of a study that may (or may not) support the distinction between different types of attachment, is not sufficient. To really make your material *effective* you need to work with it as part of a critical argument i.e. you need to *elaborate* it.

For now, take a look at this and the previous spread and summarise two studies that have looked at different types of attachment (see page 9 for advice on précis). This is the **AO1** component of your answer, but for the **AO2** component you should pick four of the above 'lead-in sentences' and complete them (about 30 words total for each point made) using material from these spreads. For example, if we were to focus on *applications* of research in this area we might write something like…

'This has been applied to infant/caregiver interventions such as the "Circle of Security" project, which resulted in a decrease in the number of caregivers classed as disordered and an increase in infants classed as securely attached.'

Of course you could squeeze a lot more out of this point if you wanted to. You have *identified* the point of evaluation ('This has been applied to…'), followed by *justification* of that claim ('…such as the "Circle of Security" project which resulted in…'). What you could now do is state whether this would be a *desirable* application of research in this area and why – this is the 'So what?' part of the **three point rule** we introduced on page 21.

Cultural variations in attachment

Culture is an issue of central importance in Bowlby's theory because the theory suggests that attachment evolved to provide the biological function of protection for the infant, thus enhancing survival. If attachment is a biological and innate process, secure attachment should be the optimal form for all humans regardless of **cultural variations**. If, however, such attachments are found in particular cultures and not others, this suggests that attachment is not innately determined but is related to different childrearing methods used in different cultures. There may be a middle ground – the view that there is some variation between cultures, related to specific cultural childrearing practices but with some common ground e.g. the dominance of secure attachment.

One of the key dimensions on which cultures differ is the individualist-collectivist one. Western cultures such as ours and the American culture are classed as **individualist** cultures that value independence and the importance of the individual. By contrast, some other cultures are described as **collectivist**, emphasising the importance of the group or *collective*. Such cultures are characterised by the extent to which things are shared – groups live and work together sharing tasks, belongings and childrearing. They value *inter*dependence i.e. they aspire to be dependent on each other rather than function as self-determining individuals. Japan and Israel are examples of collectivist societies.

*The term **culture** refers to all the rules, customs, morals and ways of interacting that bind together members of a society or some other collection of people. We learn all these rules, customs etc. through the process of socialisation so that we too are able to interact appropriately with the other members of our culture. The term 'culture' doesn't necessarily equate to the term 'country' or even the term 'society', as many different groups, each with their own rules and customs, may co-exist within a country like the UK. The term 'subculture' is usually used to refer to a group within a country that, although it shares many of the dominant cultural characteristics of that country, may also have some special, different characteristics. Sociologists tell us that different social classes have different attitudes to, among other things, childrearing, and therefore might be regarded as different 'subcultures'.*

▲ Childrearing practices vary across different cultures. For example, in some cultures infants are cared for by many relatives, whereas in others an infant spends most time with his/her mother alone. In some cultures babies remain physically very close to their mothers, while in others separations are encouraged from the start (e.g. sleeping in a separate room).

CAN YOU...? — No.**2.6**

...1 Describe **three** findings from research into cultural variations in attachment.

...2 Select **two** studies on this spread that produce *contrasting* findings.

...3 Explain how research on cultural variations does or does not support Bowlby's theory of attachment.

STUDIES OF CULTURAL VARIATIONS

Some studies support Bowlby's view that attachment is universal – such studies show cultural similarities. In contrast there are also some studies that suggest there are important cultural differences.

Cross-cultural similarities

We have already described Ainsworth's Uganda study (1967) where she observed various universals in attachment behaviour. Infants in Uganda, like infants in the UK and America, used their mothers as a secure base for exploration, and mothers of securely attached infants showed greater sensitivity towards their infants than those who were insecurely attached.

Tronick *et al.* (1992) studied an African tribe, the Efe, from Zaire who live in extended family groups. The infants were looked after and even breastfed by different women but usually they slept with their own mother at night. Despite such differences in childrearing practices the infants, at six months, still showed one primary attachment.

Fox (1977) studied infants raised on Israeli kibbutzim who spent most of their time being cared for in a communal children's home by *metaplot* (nurses, one nurse is called a *metapelet*). Attachment was tested in the strange situation with either the metapelet or mother. The infants appeared equally attached to both caregivers except in terms of reunion behaviour, where they showed greater attachment to their mothers. This suggests that the mothers were still the primary attachment figure despite the shared care.

Cross-cultural differences

Grossmann and Grossmann (1991) found that German infants tended to be classified as insecurely rather than securely attached. This may be due to different childrearing practices. German culture involves keeping some interpersonal distance between parents and children, so infants do not engage in proximity-seeking behaviours in the strange situation and thus *appear* to be insecurely attached.

Takahashi (1990) used the strange situation technique to study 60 middle-class Japanese infants and their mothers and found similar rates of secure attachment to those found by Ainsworth *et al.* in the US sample. However, unlike the original sample, the Japanese infants showed no evidence of insecure-avoidant attachment and high rates of insecure-resistant attachment (32%). The Japanese infants were particularly distressed

LINK TO RESEARCH METHODS

Good questionnaires and interviews require careful design. Turn to pages 94–7 for advice on this.

RESEARCH METHODS Qs
No.**2.2**

1 The graph below shows the results from the study by van IJzendoorn and Kroonenberg. State **two** conclusions you can draw from this graph.

2 This study was based on data from other studies (a meta-analysis). Find out some limitations of this kind of research (see page 104).

3 The 32 studies examined all used the strange situation. Describe **two** criticisms of this technique.

KEY TERMS

Cultural variations
The ways that different groups of people vary in terms of their social practices, and the effects these practices have on development and behaviour.

Culture refers to all the rules, customs, morals and ways of interacting that bind together members of a society or some other collection of people.

Collectivist culture Any culture that places more value on the 'collective' rather than the individual, and on interdependence rather than independence. The opposite is true of **individualist culture**.

EXAM TIP
The topic of cultural variations is notoriously challenging for students. Life will be easier for you if you make sure you have a clear understanding of what is meant by 'culture' and 'subculture' – read the text on the facing page!

---

on being left alone; in fact their response was so extreme that for 90% of the infants the study was stopped at this point. This cultural variation can be explained in terms of different childcare practices. In Japan infants rarely experience separation from their mothers, which would explain why they were more distressed in the strange situation than their American counterparts. This would make them *appear* to be insecurely attached.

Conclusions

These studies suggest that, despite the fact that there are cultural variations in infant care arrangements, the strongest attachments are still formed with the infant's mother. The research also shows, however, that there are differences in the patterns of attachment that can be related to differences in cultural attitudes.

Meta-analysis

Van IJzendoorn and Kroonenberg (1988) conducted a meta-analysis of the findings from 32 studies of attachment behaviour. Altogether the studies examined over 2000 strange situation classifications in eight different countries, a larger sample of data than previously examined.. Van IJzendoorn and Kroonenberg were interested to see whether there would be evidence that *inter*-cultural differences did

exist i.e. differences between different countries/cultures. They were also interested to find out whether there were *intra*-cultural differences – differences in the findings from studies conducted *within* the same culture.

With reference to variation *between* cultures/countries, van IJzendoorn and Kroonenberg found that the differences were small (see graph below). Secure attachment was the most common classification in every country. Insecure-avoidant attachment was the next most common in every country except Israel and Japan.

With reference to variation *within* cultures, they found that this was *1.5 times* greater than the variation between cultures.

The conclusion to be drawn from this meta-analysis is that the global pattern across cultures appears to be similar to that found in the US. Secure attachment is the 'norm' – it is the most common form of attachment in all countries. This supports the idea that secure attachment is 'best' for healthy social and emotional development. These cross-cultural similarities support the view that attachment is an innate and biological process.

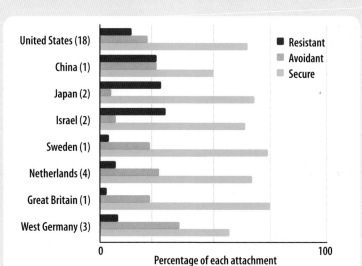

▲ Graph showing the findings from the study by van IJzendoorn and Kroonenberg (1988)

Evaluating cultural variations in attachment

The previous spread covered research on cultural variations in attachment. The conclusion suggested by many of these studies was that a bond develops with one primary attachment figure despite cultural differences in childcare (such as the number of caregivers who look after a child). It also appears that secure attachment is the norm all over the world. However these conclusions may not be justified if we find that the research itself is flawed. On this spread we will consider criticisms of the studies on cultural variations in attachment with a view to establishing overall conclusions.

▶ The Japanese encourage a dependent relationship (or 'sense of oneness') between mother and child. Doi (1973) called this *amae* (pronounced 'a-mah-yeh'). Doi claims that this is a natural tendency that is discouraged in Western cultures.

DO IT YOURSELF

No.**2.3**

It is often tempting to say to your teacher 'Just tell me what the answer is'. Often, however, there are no simple answers, or there may be several possible answers and it is up to each of us to decide which one best fits the facts *from our own point of view*. One way to decide on your own point of view is to have a debate in class.

For example, you may feel totally bewildered by the arguments on this page. Try to sort out what you think by conducting a debate in class. A debate is usually organised by having a proposition, such as, 'Research into cultural variations in attachment is flawed in many ways'. Divide your class into groups and let each group decide which position it wishes to take – either to support the proposition or to argue against it. Alternatively you can draw lots to see who takes which position.

Each group should then spend some time working out some specific arguments to present. It is also worth preparing your defence – that is, imagining the arguments that will be put forward by the other side and preparing counter-arguments to favour your position.

The debate should be conducted by allowing each individual or group a chance to put forward one argument and then allowing anyone to suggest counter-arguments. The debate will continue with a second argument and so on. At the end the class might vote for or against the proposition.

You can debate other topics in this chapter, or indeed in the rest of the book, for example, 'The strange situation is not ethically acceptable' or 'Learning theory is an outdated explanation of attachment'.

CRITICISMS OF RESEARCH ON CULTURAL VARIATIONS IN ATTACHMENT

Culture bias

Rothbaum *et al.* (2000) argued that attachment theory and research is not relevant to other cultures because it is so rooted in American culture. Rothbaum *et al.* looked in particular at the contrasts between American (Western) and Japanese culture.

1　The *sensitivity hypothesis*. Bowlby and Ainsworth promoted the view that secure attachment was related to caregiver responsiveness and sensitivity. Rothbaum *et al.* argue that this reflects Western ideas of autonomy, whereas in Japan, sensitivity is about promoting dependence rather than independence. Sensitivity has the opposite objectives in the two cultures.

2　The *continuity hypothesis*. Bowlby and Ainsworth proposed that infants who are more securely attached go on to develop into more socially and emotionally competent children and adults. However this competence is defined in terms of individuation – it means being able to explore, being independent and being able to regulate one's own emotions. In Japan the opposite is true; competence is represented by the inhibition of emotional expression (not showing your feelings) and being group-oriented rather than self-oriented.

3　The *secure base hypothesis*. In the West, secure attachments are seen as providing an infant with a secure base from which to explore, thus promoting independence. Attachment relationships in Japan are dependence-

oriented in keeping with the Japanese concept of *amae* ('to depend and presume upon another's love'). Behaviours associated with insecure ambivalent attachment are more typical of the characteristic *amae* relationship which may explain why such classifications are higher in Japan (see van IJzendoorn and Kroonenberg, page 45).

Rothbaum *et al.* suggest that psychologists should aim to produce a set of *indigenous* theories – explanations of attachment rooted in individual cultures. There may be a small set of universal principles, such as the need for protection, but in general, childcare practices will be related to cultural values.

It may be that Rothbaum *et al.* overstated the case. Posada and Jacobs (2001) note that there is actually a lot of evidence that supports the universality of attachment from many different countries: China, Columbia, Germany, Israel, Japan and Norway. Posada and Jacobs also point out that the issue is not whether sensitivity leads to independence, but simply that sensitivity is linked to secure attachment however secure attachment is manifested.

Prior and Glaser (2006) conclude that expressions of maternal sensitivity and manifestations of secure-base behaviour may vary across cultures but the core concepts are universal.

Nation versus culture

Rothbaum *et al.* talked about the behaviour of Japanese mothers and infants – yet this may be an unjustified generalisation as, within the country of Japan,

...1 Give **three** pieces of evidence that show how attachment theory and research is rooted in American culture.

...2 There are many problems with cross-cultural research. Select **two** problems and use these to criticise the conclusions of the studies on the previous spread.

there are different subcultures, each of which may have different childcare practices; one study of attachment in Tokyo (an urban setting) found similar distributions of attachment types to the Western studies, whereas a more rural sample found an over-representation of insecure-resistant individuals (van IJzendoorn and Sagi, 2001).

Indeed the van IJzendoorn and Kroonenberg study (1988, see previous spread) found more variation *within* cultures than between cultures. One explanation for the large within-culture variation is that some studies involved middle-class infants whereas others involved working-class infants. Rural societies in the US may be more similar to rural societies in Israel than they are to urban societies in the US. What this means is that data was collected on different *subcultures* within each country and that it is a mistake to think of behaviour within one country as representing a homogenous culture. Van IJzendoorn and Kroonenberg conclude that 'great caution should be exercised in assuming that an individual sample is representative of a particular (sub)culture'.

Cultural similarities

Van IJzendoorn and Kroonenberg suggest that the cross-cultural similarities they found might be explained by the effects of mass media (e.g. TV and books), which spread ideas about parenting so that children all over the world are exposed to similar influences. This means that cultural similarities may *not* be due to innate biological influences but are because of our increasingly global culture, certainly in urban areas.

Cross-cultural research

Many of the studies of cultural variations were conducted

by indigenous researchers i.e. psychologists who are native to the country in which the study is taking place. However this was not always true (e.g. Ainsworth's study of the Ganda). Even where researchers are indigenous they may belong to different cultures (e.g. city resident studying rural community). There are many problems with such cross-cultural research (research conducted across different cultures) not least problems with understanding the language used by people from different regions (if you come from Newcastle think about the difficulties of understanding the dialect of someone from Cornwall, and *vice versa*).

A particular issue for cross-cultural research is the 'tools' that are used. Psychologists measure behaviour using things like intelligence tests or observational methods such as the strange situation. Such tools or techniques are related to the cultural assumptions of the test/technique 'designer'. In the case of the strange situation it is assumed that willingness to explore is a sign of secure attachment. However, as we have seen, in some cultures this is not the case. In traditional Japanese culture, dependence rather than independence would be the sign of secure attachment. The term *imposed etic* is used to describe the use of a technique designed in one culture but imposed on another. The result of using this imposed etic to measure attachment is that Japanese children may *appear* to be insecurely attached according to Western criteria, whereas they are securely attached by Japanese standards.

LINK TO RESEARCH METHODS

The problems of cross-cultural research are examined on page 104.

COMMENTARY CORNER

Thinking critically

On this spread we have been evaluating research into cultural variations in attachment. There is a trick to doing this effectively and that lies in your ability to *think* critically. This is often as simple as elaborating material to indicate *why* a point you are making *is* an important critical point. Below you will find some of the points made on this spread, any of which could be used as a stand-alone critical point or as part of a critical argument for an extended answer. Try to think what you would write after each to make it a telling critical point (the first is done for you).

Examples for you to complete:

- Rothbaum *et al.* (2000) argued that attachment theory and research is not relevant to other cultures because it is so rooted in American culture... *However, this view is challenged by research (e.g. Posada and Jacobs, 2001), which shows that attachment theory applies to most cultures.*
- Cross-cultural research is important to our understanding of the attachment process because...
- Van IJzendoorn and Kroonenberg (1988) carried out a meta-analysis of 32 studies involving the strange situation in eight different countries. Although they found little variation in attachment styles *between* cultures, a surprising finding was that...
- The fact that secure attachment appeared to be the norm in most cultures led them to conclude...
- However, the validity of these conclusions can be questioned. The strange situation may not be a valid measure of attachment in all cultures because...
- An alternative explanation for van IJzendoorn and Kroonenberg's findings is that...
- A major problem for research in this area is the 'tools' (e.g. measurement techniques) that are used in such research. These limit the value of such research because...

If you can get used to elaborating all points in this way you will be developing your ability to think critically. You will also be developing your ability to elaborate important points and so earn much higher marks. This is not a skill limited to the extended 12-mark questions. Elaboration is essential wherever you are required to engage in a critical response. For example, a question may ask you to give one criticism of research on cultural variations, or to comment on why research in this area is important to our understanding of attachment. You always need to state your answer and then elaborate it – explain what you mean or provide an example. Elaboration does not mean 'say the same thing in a different way', which is what students often do. You need to come up with something further, and this is a skill we will develop throughout this book.

Disruption of attachment

Bowlby's theory suggests that attachment is essential for healthy social and emotional development. It therefore follows that a *disruption* of attachment might have a negative effect on social and emotional development. Such disruption may occur when an infant is separated from his or her attachment figure. Ainsworth's strange situation showed that *physical separation* from a primary attachment figure is distressing. However, in many cases, some degree of physical separation is unavoidable, as children must spend time in hospital, in day care or with a babysitter.

Psychologists are interested to discover the effects of such separations in order to provide important advice to parents, hospitals, day-care facilities and so on about how a child's social and emotional development should be safeguarded when attachment is disrupted.

◢ One of the children filmed by James Robertson was John, a 17-month-old boy who had to be cared for in a residential nursery while his mother was in hospital. Over the course of just nine days, John went from a happy, well-adjusted child to a child so distressed by the experience that upon reunion with his mother, his rejection of her was all too clear:

'A few minutes later his father entered the room and John struggled away from his mother into his father's arms. His crying stopped, and for the first time he looked directly at his mother. It was a long hard look, one she had never seen before.' (Robertson and Robertson, 1989)

VALIDITY

There are two points to make about the validity of the research described on this spread. First of all it can be argued that the research has high validity. The films were *naturalistic observations* – real-life events in a realistic setting. James Robertson was meticulous in the way he designed his observation record in order to avoid any bias (i.e. lack of *observer bias*) and the record is available for others to inspect and check his observations.

Second, we could also argue the opposite case. The conclusions of this study are based on *case studies* made of only a few children. These children may share certain characteristics that differentiate them from other children (such as being British children from urban communities), and therefore it is not appropriate to think that all children would respond in the same way. For example some children may be familiar with separations and therefore may not show the same signs of distress. Further criticisms of *case studies* are considered on page 100.

THE EFFECTS OF PHYSICAL SEPARATION

In the 1930s and '40s psychologists studied children who had experienced prolonged separations from their families. They observed that such children were often profoundly disturbed and lagged behind in intellectual development. For example, Spitz and Wolf (1946) observed that 100 'normal' children who were placed in an institution became severely depressed within a few months. Skeels and Dye (1939) found that similar children scored poorly on intelligence tests.

These effects were quite a surprise because, before these studies, no one really thought about the effects of separation on infants and children. It was assumed that a good standard of physical care was all that would be required when infants and children were separated from attachment figures. The work of James Robertson, and his wife Joyce, increased our understanding of the effects of separation and, in particular, how the negative effects might be avoided. The Robertsons (1967–73) made a landmark series of films of young children in situations where they were separated from their primary attachment figure.

A two-year-old goes to hospital

In the first film James Robertson used a cine camera to meticulously record his observations of daily life in a hospital ward, focusing on one little girl, Laura, who was admitted to hospital for an eight-day stay. The film shows Laura alternating between periods of calm and distress. She is visited occasionally by her parents and begs to go home, but as time goes on tries to cope with the disappointment of having to stay. Laura's obvious struggle to control her feelings over the course of the film is hard to watch.

Jane, Lucy, Thomas, Kate and John

Jane, Lucy, Thomas and Kate were all under three years of age and placed in foster care for a few weeks with the Robertsons while their mothers were in hospital. The Robertsons endeavoured to sustain a high level of substitute emotional care and keep routines similar to those at home. Fathers' visits were arranged regularly to maintain emotional links with home. Kate was taken to visit her mother in hospital and was much more settled after this. All the children seemed to adjust well. They showed some signs of distress, for example Thomas rejected attempts to cuddle him but in general they slept well and did not reject their mothers when reunited. Some were reluctant to part with the foster mother, demonstrating the formation of good emotional bonds.

John's experiences were quite different. John was placed in a residential nursery for nine days while his mother was having a baby. His father visited regularly. During the first two days in the nursery the film shows John behaving fairly normally. Gradually this changes as he makes determined efforts to get attention from the nurses, but cannot compete with the other, more assertive children. The nurses are always friendly but also always busy. When John fails to find anyone who will respond to him, he seeks comfort from an over-sized teddy bear, but this isn't enough. Over the next few days he gradually breaks down and refuses food and drink, stops playing, cries a great deal, and gives up trying to get the nurses' attention. The nurses change shift regularly so there is no constant care.

In the first week he greets his father enthusiastically but by the second week he just sits quietly when his father is there and doesn't say anything. For long periods of the day he lies with thumb in mouth, cuddling his large teddy bear. On the ninth day, when his mother comes to take him home, John screams and struggles to get away from her.

For many months afterwards he continued to have outbursts of anger towards his mother.

PHYSICAL VERSUS EMOTIONAL DISRUPTION

The observational record made by the Robertsons appears to demonstrate a clear difference between physical and emotional disruption. Other studies support this. For example in the study described earlier by Skeels and Dye (1939) some of the children who showed IQ deficits were transferred to a home for mentally retarded adults. When the children's IQs were tested again, they had increased. Why? Could it be that the retarded adults enjoyed having children to look after and provided the missing emotional care. To test this idea Skodak and Skeels (1949) arranged for some more infants to be placed in a home for the mentally retarded while a control group remained in the orphanage. When the children's IQs were tested after one-and-a-half years they found that the IQs of the control group had, on average, fallen from 87 to 61 points while the transferred group's IQ had risen from 64 to 92 points.

There are other studies that support the conclusion that emotional ill effects can be reversed by providing good emotional care – i.e. attachments. For example, Bohman and Sigvardsson (1979) also found evidence that emotional ill effects can be reversed. They studied over 600 adopted children in Sweden. At the age of 11, 26% of them were classified as 'problem children'. In a follow-up study ten years later, none of the children were any worse off than the rest of the population. This would suggest that early, negative effects were reversed.

The research therefore indicates that disruption of attachment can have negative effects but these can be avoided or reversed when alternative emotional care is provided. For some children, sadly, this does not happen and therefore disruption of attachment leads to permanent difficulties, as we will see on the next spread.

It is also the case that negative effects of deprivation may only surface if there are 'triggers' later in life. For example, Bifulco et al. (1992) studied 249 women who had lost mothers through separation or death before they were 17. This group was twice as likely to suffer from depressive or anxiety disorders when the children became adults. This suggests that early disruptions in attachment may make an individual psychologically more vulnerable and, if triggered by stressful events later in life, mental disorders may develop.

INDIVIDUAL DIFFERENCES

Research has shown that not all children are affected by emotional disruption in the same way. Barrett (1997) reviewed various studies on separation and concluded that securely attached children may sometimes cope reasonably well, whereas insecurely attached children become especially distressed.

A similar conclusion was drawn from another study by Bowlby (Bowlby et al., 1956) of 60 children under the age of four who had TB. Treatment of this condition involves a prolonged stay in hospital. The nurses in the TB hospital could not provide substitute maternal care and the children were visited only once a week, therefore probably experiencing prolonged early *deprivation*. When these children were assessed in adolescence, some members of the TB group were more maladjusted (63%) than the 'normal' children, but there were no significant differences between them and their 'normal' peers in terms of intellectual development. Bowlby et al. suggest that those children who coped better may have been more securely attached and thus more resilient.

CAN YOU...? No.2.8

...1 Identify **three** effects that disruption of attachment has on a child's social and emotional development.

...2 For each effect provide some research support.

...3 Describe **two** factors that are important when considering the effect disruption of attachment may have on a child's development.

...4 Describe **two** strengths and **two** limitations of the research by Robertson and Robertson.

REAL-WORLD APPLICATIONS

The research by Robertson and Bowlby may not seem that significant to you – but that's because care of children is different now, thanks in part to their work. Some of you may have had to spend time in hospital during your childhood and would probably have been visited daily by family and friends; your parents may even have stayed overnight in a parents' suite. In the 1950s the situation was completely different; a survey by the *Nursing Times* in 1952 found that only 25% of children's hospitals allowed daily visiting and 12% prohibited visiting altogether. When Robertson showed his films to medical professionals they were outraged. They believed that children in hospital were quite happy and discouraged visiting by parents because children appeared to get only more distressed by such visits; the children *appeared* to be happier when left alone.

COMMENTARY CORNER

One of the characteristic features of your AS psychology specification is that it emphasises the *application* of knowledge as well as its description. On this spread we have covered two aspects of attachment disruption that could, you might imagine, so easily be avoided. This is where you come in, as exam questions may well ask you to put your psychology into action by offering advice to others. For example, consider the following question:

Q: Debbie is due to go into hospital to have her second child, but has no family in the area to look after her first child (James, aged 18 months) while she is there. She is considering leaving James in a residential nursery while she is in hospital. Using your psychological knowledge, suggest two things she should consider before doing this.

A: *Debbie should look for a nursery where the staff are able to pay especial attention to the emotional needs of her son. She might watch how the staff treat the other children. She might also look for signs that parents are encouraged to keep in touch and where links with home, such as bringing in some of James' own toys, are also encouraged.*

Suggest a second piece of advice that would help Debbie make her decision.

Q: Imagine you have been appointed as a government advisor with a special responsibility for the emotional well-being of children. You have been asked to come up with two initiatives to ensure that any effects arising from disruption of attachment in early childhood are minimised.

A: *Hint – when answering a question such as this remember to be psychological, i.e. base your suggestions on psychological theory or evidence rather than personal speculation.*

Failure to form attachment

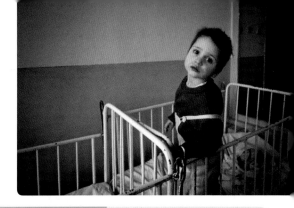

There are many common situations that can lead to a disruption of attachment, such as hospital care or day care. Much less common are situations where children fail to form any attachments, called '**privation**'. This may occur in situations where attachment has been disrupted, such as prolonged stays in hospital, or it may be due to abusive or neglectful parenting as seen, for example, in rare cases of isolated children. Perhaps the most common cause of privation has been institutional care.

ISOLATED CHILDREN

Throughout the course of history there have been cases recorded where individual children have been raised in conditions of extreme isolation – and privation, i.e. apparently *lacking* emotional care. Two of the best-known cases are that of Genie and of the Czech twins (Andrei and Vanya).

Genie was locked in a room by her father until she was 13½ (because he thought she was retarded). When she was 'found' she could not stand erect, and could not speak. She never fully recovered socially. She apparently showed a *disinterest* in other people. Her lack of recovery may be due to her extreme early emotional privation. Or it may be due to the late age at which she was 'discovered' (well past Bowlby's sensitive age for effective attachment), which would mean that recovery was not possible (Curtiss, 1977; Rymer, 1993).

The Czech twins (Koluchová, 1976) spent the first seven years of their lives locked up by a stepmother – their own mother died when they were infants. When they were first 'discovered' they couldn't talk. After discovery they were cared for by two loving sisters and by age 14 had near normal intellectual and social functioning. By the age of 20, they were of above average intelligence and had excellent relationships with the members of their foster family (Koluchová, 1991). It is possible they were 'discovered' at a young enough age and therefore could recover.

ⓔ Evaluation

People find these case studies very moving and memorable – but how good are they as psychological evidence? Each individual has unique characteristics – we don't know whether Genie was retarded from birth, nor do we know if she did actually form an attachment with her mother. The Czech twins may have formed important attachments to each other. Therefore it is difficult to reach any firm conclusions from these cases.

⚖ ETHICS
Genie's mother sued the psychologists for their excessive and outrageous testing – which was disputed by the psychologists. However it is clear that Genie's own interests were not best served by the interests of science.

WWW Read more about Genie and other case histories at kccesl.tripod.com/genie.html and www.feralchildren.com/en/children.php?tp=2

INSTITUTIONAL CARE

Children in institutional care are likely to experience privation. We have already examined a number of such studies of the effects of **institutionalisation** on the previous spread. These studies provide a consensus that young children admitted to institutional care usually respond with acute distress.

Longitudinal study

Perhaps the most well-controlled study of privation was conducted by Jill Hodges and Barbara Tizard (Hodges and Tizard, 1989). They followed a group of 65 British children from early life to adolescence. The children had been placed in one institution when they were less than four months old. At this age children have not yet formed attachments. There was an explicit policy in the institution against the 'caretakers' forming attachments with the children. An early study of the children found that 70% were described as not able 'to care deeply about anyone'. Thus we can conclude that most, if not all, of these children had experienced early emotional privation (a *lack* of attachment rather than simply a disruption of attachments).

The children were assessed at regular intervals up to the age of 16. Some of the children remained in the institution, but most had left it (were 'ex-institutional'), and had either been adopted or restored to their original families. The 'restored' children were less likely to have formed attachments with their mothers, but the adopted children were as closely attached to their parents as a control group of 'normal' children. However both groups of ex-institutional children had problems with peers. They were less likely to have a special friend and less likely to be liked by other children. They were also more quarrelsome and more likely to be bullies, and also sought more attention from adults (a sign of **disinhibited attachment**).

These findings suggest that early privation had a negative effect on the ability to form relationships even when given good subsequent emotional care. This supports Bowlby's view that the failure to form attachments during the sensitive period of development (see page 36) has an irreversible effect on emotional development. The children coped well at home, when the other person in the relationship was working hard on their behalf, but the same was not true for peer relationships.

Romanian orphanages

In the last 15 years there have been further opportunities to study the effects of institutionalisation because wars in Eastern Europe have left many children homeless. Rutter *et al.* (2007) studied a group of about 100 Romanian orphans and assessed them at four, six and eleven years old. Those children who were adopted by British families before the age of six months have shown 'normal' emotional development when compared with UK children adopted at the same age. However, many of those Romanian orphans adopted after six months showed disinhibited attachments and had problems with peers. This suggests that long-term consequences may be less severe than was once thought *if* children have the opportunity to form attachments. However, when children do not form attachments (i.e. continuing failure of attachment) then the consequences are likely to be severe.

◀ One thing to note about the research on this spread is that much of it is very old. This is mainly because institutional care changed dramatically after the 1950s, as a result of the early psychological research, and this meant it was no longer possible to conduct such studies (there was no one to study).

Possible effects	Source
Disinhibited attachment	Rutter *et al.* (Romanian orphans); Hodges and Tizard (ex-institutional children)
Intellectual underfunctioning	Genie; Skeels and Dye (orphans)
Poor parenting	Harlow (monkeys); Quinton *et al.* (ex-institutional mothers)
Mental disorder	Depression (Spitz and Wolf, Bifulco *et al.*); Attachment disorder
Physical underdevelopment	Genie; Gardner (deprivation dwarfism)
Little long-term effect	Czech twins; Bowlby *et al.*, Rutter *et al.* (individual differences)

THE EFFECTS OF PRIVATION AND INSTITUTIONALISATION

Attachment disorder

Attachment disorder has recently been recognised as a distinct psychiatric condition and included in the DSM (see page 178). It is essentially what psychologists like Sptiz and Bowlby and Rutter have been writing about for 50 years: when some children experience disruptions of early attachments this affects their social and emotional development. Children with attachment disorder have:

- no preferred attachment figure.
- an inability to interact and relate to others that is evident before the age of five.
- experience of severe neglect or frequent change of caregivers.

There are two kinds of attachment disorder:

- *reactive* or *inhibited*: shy and withdrawn, unable to cope with most social situations.
- *disinhibited* attachment: over-friendly and attention seeking.

Poor parenting

Earlier in this chapter we looked at the study by Harlow (1960) which showed that monkeys raised with a surrogate mother went on to become poor parents. This is supported in a study by Quinton *et al.* (1984) who compared a group of 50 women who had been reared in institutions (children's homes) with a control group of 50 women reared at home. When the women were in their 20s it was found that the ex-institutional women were experiencing extreme difficulties acting as parents. For example, more of the ex-institutional women had children who had spent time in care.

Deprivation dwarfism

Children in institutional care are usually physically small; one suggestion is that lack of emotional care rather than poor nourishment is the cause of such 'dwarfism'. Gardner (1972) provided evidence from case studies such as one case where a girl was born with a malformation that meant she had to be fed through a tube, and her mother, in fear of dislodging the tube, never cuddled or picked up the girl. At 8 months this child was severely withdrawn and physically stunted and admitted to hospital for treatment. She thrived on the attention she was given there and soon returned to normal, despite no change in her diet. Gardner suggests that emotional disturbance may affect the production of hormones such as growth hormones, and this would explain the link between emotional deprivation and physical underdevelopment (dwarfism).

Evaluation

Some research suggests that individuals who do not form a primary attachment within that early sensitive period are unable to recover and they display signs of disinhibited attachment. However this is not true of *all* children who experience privation. In the study of Romanian orphans, one-third recovered well. Therefore it seems that privation alone cannot explain negative outcomes. It is more likely that damage only occurs when there are multiple risk factors such as privation followed by poor subsequent care, or insecure attachment with early separations and parental disharmony (Turner and Lloyd, 1995).

There are a few important issues to bear in mind. First, we cannot be certain that the children studied had failed to form attachments. For example, in the Tizard and Hodges study we assume that in early life none of the children had formed attachments. It could be that they had formed attachments and that later problems were due to other factors such as feelings of rejection.

Second, we do not know to what extent the effects of privation extend into adult life. We do know that the Czech twins appeared to recover well but this is not a well-controlled study. In the Romanian study the last assessment at age 11 showed a lower number of children with disinhibited attachment. In the Hodges and Tizard study it was not possible to recontact a large enough group of the children later in life (Tizard, 2005). It may be that ex-institutional children need more time than normal to mature sufficiently and learn how to cope with relationships. We may find that children who have failed to form attachments early in life *can* eventually recover given the right kind of care.

CAN YOU...? No.2.9

...1 Outline the findings *and* conclusions from **three** studies of privation/ institutionalisation

...2 Describe **two** effects of privation/ institutionalisation and provide research support for these effects.

...3 Explain **two** criticisms of the research you have described in your answer to question 2.

KEY TERMS

Disinhibited attachment A type of *disorganised* attachment where children do not discriminate between people they choose as attachment figures. Such children will treat near-strangers with inappropriate familiarity (overfriendliness) and may be attention-seeking.

Institutionalisation describes the result of institutional care. An 'institution' is a place dedicated to a particular task, such as looking after children awaiting adoption, or caring for the mentally ill, or looking after patients in hospital. An institution is a place where

people live for a period of time as opposed to day care or outpatient care where people go home every day. In the past such institutions had fairly strict regimes and offered little emotional care. Many institutions today strive to avoid this, especially where children are involved. However, in some countries limited resources mean that it is still not possible to offer very much emotional care in institutions.

Privation The lack of having any attachments due to the failure to develop such attachments during early life.

The impact of day care

EXAM ADVICE

Note that the specification says you need to know about the 'impact of different forms of day care on children's social development, including the effects on aggression and peer relations'. This means that you may be asked any of the following questions:

- *'Describe the impact of day care on children's social development.'*
- *'Describe the impact of day care on children's aggression.'*
- *'Describe the impact of day care on children's peer relations.'*

If you are asked the first question you can use research on aggression and/or peer relations.

If you are asked specifically about aggression or peer relations you must focus on that specific research.

We have just examined a range of studies on the effects of disruption to attachment. Of all the everyday situations, **day care** is probably the most common one where infants and children experience physical separation from their primary attachment figure. Day care is a very important issue because, in the UK, about 70% of women with children under the age of one year go out to work (Gregg *et al.*, 2005). The resulting *physical* separation may or may not also involve a loss of *emotional* care. If it does, then the evidence we have reviewed so far would suggest that the day-care experience is likely to have negative effects on children's **social development**, especially for those who are insecurely attached.

People are sharply divided on the issue of day care:

'While they are babies or young toddlers, even the very best day care seldom gives them anything they positively need, and being there all day and every day often deprives them of what they need from mothers. The vital continuous one-to-one attention can rarely be achieved in group care, however excellent the facility may be.' (Penelope Leach, 1994, p.70)

Kristin Droege, a research associate at Milken Family Foundation, argues that children in high-quality childcare arrangements tend to be less timid and fearful than children who spend a preponderance of their time at home. Her conclusion: quality day care breeds well-adjusted children who tend to be more outgoing and cooperative with unfamiliar peers.

What is meant by 'day care'?

The term 'day care' is not a precise concept. In general it refers to a form of temporary care (i.e. not all day and night long) that is not provided by parents, and usually takes place outside the home. Recent research has tended to use the phrase 'non-maternal' or 'non-parental' care which includes childminding and day nurseries. Many of you reading this will have first-hand experience of one or both of these.

Childminders take care of small groups of children in their own home and are registered with the local authority. Some people regard this as a preferable form of day care, because the care the child receives is more likely to be similar to the care they would receive in their own home. Carers have to be registered.

Another commonly used form of day care is the *day nursery*. Day nurseries can be found in a variety of locations including schools, churches and women's shelters. There are many other different types of day care including home day care, where a childcare professional cares for the child in their own home (remember Mary Poppins?). One of the most rapidly growing forms of day care is the nursery within the workplace. This is gaining popularity because employers recognise that providing on-site day care is not only a good benefit for employees but it also makes good business sense.

The difference between day care and institutional care

As well as knowing what day care *is*, it is important to understand what it is *not*. Other forms of care that are part of a more formal institutional programme of childrearing (such as fostering and community homes) or that are health-related (such as hospitalisation) is not what is meant by day care in this context.

RESEARCH ON THE IMPACT OF DAY CARE

Negative effects on social development

One of the conclusions drawn from Bowlby's research in the 1950s was that prolonged separation of an infant from his/her mother figure could cause long-term maladjustment. This was applied by others to the day-care situation and, over the years, many studies have supported the conclusion. For example, Violata and Russell (1994) conducted a meta-analysis of the findings from 88 studies, concluding that regular day care for more than 20 hours per week had an unmistakably negative effect on socio-emotional development, behaviour and attachment of young children.

Increased aggressiveness

The National Institute of Child Health and Human Development (NICHD) in America started a longitudinal study in 1991 to study many aspects of child development. Over 1000 children from diverse families and from 10 different locations continue to be involved. The children and their parents have been assessed at regular intervals in order to establish the effects of various experiences such as day care on children's development. When the cohort of children was studied at age five, the data showed that the more time a child spent in day care of any kind or quality, the more adults rated them as assertive, disobedient and aggressive (NICHD, 2003). Children in full-time day care were close to three times more likely to show behaviour problems than those cared for by their mothers at home. The behaviour problems included frequent arguing, temper tantrums, lying, hitting and unpredictable conduct.

The latest reports (e.g. Belsky *et al.*, 2007) looked at the same children at the end of their primary education and still found a link between day-care experience and increased aggressiveness.

A UK study (Melhuish, 2004) also found evidence that high levels of day care, particularly nursery care in the first two years, may elevate the risk of developing anti-social behaviour.

Peer relations

We saw earlier in this chapter that secure attachment is linked to better peer relations – the Minnesota longitudinal study found that securely attached infants go on to be more popular (Sroufe *et al.*, 2005, see page 38). There is evidence that children in day care are less likely to be securely attached. For example Belsky and Rovine (1988) assessed attachment (using the strange situation) in infants who had been receiving 20 hours or more of day care per week before they were one year old. These children

What is meant by 'social development'?

When we consider the *social* development of children, we are interested in two related aspects of the growing-up process.

First, we are interested in the development of *sociability* in children, i.e. the tendency to seek and enjoy the company of others and to make personal relationships with them. Sociability is an important characteristic because having good relationships with others (such as friends, colleagues and love partners) is so helpful in our lives.

Second, we are interested in the *socialisation* process, i.e. the process by which an individual acquires the knowledge, values, social skills and sensitivity to others that enables them to become a part of society. With both of these aspects of social development there is an assumption that children acquire *appropriate* behaviours that are adaptive for their particular society.

DO IT YOURSELF   No.**2.4**

The studies on this page all make use of existing data – they observe and/or interview children and parents to find out about their early care experiences. An alternative approach would be to conduct an experiment to see if day care *causes* aggressive behaviour. How might you design such a study and what would be the pros and cons?

▶ Some women become depressed being at home looking after young children with little adult company; depressed mothers are likely to form insecure attachments with their children which would have a negative effect on development.

HI DAD, WHAT A DAY I'VE HAD, SHE'S DONE NOTHING BUT CRY

Robert Thompson

were more likely to be insecurely attached compared with children at home.

This would lead us to expect that children in day care are more likely to be insecurely attached and therefore less successful in peer relationships.

Positive effects on social development

There are good reasons to believe that day care might actually have a positive influence on children's social development. Harlow's study on lone mother-infant monkey pairs indicated how social interaction in infancy is as important to social development as primary attachments (see page 35). Good day care can provide plenty of social stimulation, whereas children at home, especially if they have little contact with other children, may lack such social interaction. In addition, mothers at home on their own may feel isolated and bored, finding interaction difficult. In a classic study of depression, Brown and Harris (1978) found that many depressed women claimed their low mood was due to the isolation of being at home with children. This may be a particular problem of isolated, nuclear families in urban communities where children may lack important social interactions in infancy.

As we might therefore expect, there are many studies that have found positive effects associated with day care. For example Alison Clarke-Stewart and associates (1994) studied 150 children and found that those in day care were consistently more advanced in their social development than children who stayed at home with their mothers. These advances were in social development, independence, dinnertime obedience, compliance requests, and social interactions with peers. The EPPE (Effective Provision of Pre-School Education Project) followed the development of 3000 children in various pre-school educational settings in the UK. This study found increased independence and sociability in children who attended day care (Sylva *et al.*, 2003).

Peer relations

Day care exposes children to their peers and thus permits them time to develop social strategies, such as the ability to negotiate and to make friends. Research supports this link between day care and social strategies. Field (1991) found that the amount of time spent in full-time day care was positively correlated to the number of friends children had once they went to school. Clarke-Stewart *et al.* (1994) found that those children who attended day care could negotiate better with peers. Creps and Vernon-Feagans (1999) found that children who started day care before the age of six months were actually *more* sociable than those who started later.

CUTTING EDGE

We have referred to a number of longitudinal studies of the effects of day care but there are many others. A new project is underway in the UK following 1201 UK children from birth to school age, conducted in London and Oxfordshire – the Families, Children and Child Care (FCCC) project. Have a look at its website for recent findings: www.familieschildrenchildcare.org/fccc_frames_home.html

CAN YOU...?   No.**2.10**

...1 Describe the effect of day care on aggression. (You should write about 100 words.)

...2 Describe the effect of day care on peer relations. (You should write about 100 words.)

...3 Explain why there may be differences in the effects of different forms of day care.

...4 Suggest **two** strengths of the NICHD study. (Hint: You need to work these out for yourself based on the information provided.)

KEY TERMS

Day care This refers to a form of temporary care (i.e. not all day and night long), not given by family members or someone well known to the child, and usually outside the home. It is sometimes referred to as 'non-parental care'.

Social development That aspect of a child's growth concerned with the development of sociability, where the child learns how to relate to others, and with the process of socialisation, in which the child acquires the knowledge and skills appropriate to that society.

Evaluating research on day care

The evidence presented on the previous spread painted a mixed picture for the impact of day care. There appear to be strong arguments and evidence on both sides of the debate. But what of the criticisms? On this spread we will look at criticisms of the two main claims – that day care leads to higher levels of aggression and that it leads to better peer relations. We will also look at some mediating factors – the fact that quality of care, number of hours spent in day care and age can all affect the later outcomes. This means it isn't quite as simple as saying that day care is good or bad; we must consider the circumstances under which it might have positive or negative outcomes.

 ## WEAKNESSES OF RESEARCH ON DAY CARE

Aggression and day care

The research reported on the previous spread indicates that children who spend more time in day care are more aggressive. Not all studies support this finding. For example Prodromidis *et al.* (1995) studied Swedish first-borns, and concluded that childcare arrangements were *not* associated with aggression or non-compliance.

Perhaps more importantly there are two other findings from the NICHD study that haven't received quite as much media attention as the aggression/day-care link. First, one of the NICHD workers, Sarah Friedman, has pointed out that the results related to aggression can be stated differently – the study found that 83% of children who spend 10 to 30 hours in day care did *not* show higher levels of aggression. Friedman claims that the study results so far actually tell us very little (reported in Lang, 2006).

The second finding to consider is that the NICHD data actually showed that a mother's sensitivity to her child was a better indicator of reported problem behaviours than was time in childcare, with more sensitive mothering being linked to fewer problem behaviours. Higher maternal education and family income also predicted lower levels of children's problem behaviours. These findings put the aggression findings in perspective (NICHD, 2003). The 2006 data again suggest that children's development is more strongly affected by factors at home than those in day care (Belsky *et al.*, 2007).

A final important consideration is that the findings are not causal – the data cannot show that day care *caused* aggression. Instead, the data show that day care and aggressiveness are linked in some way. The American Psychological Association (Dingfelder, 2004) suggests that the results are meaningless unless one knows the processes by which aggression is increased; for example it could be that aggression only increases when children are inadequately supervised.

Peer relations and day care

The issue about correlation versus cause (see above) applies to the peer-relations and day-care link. We cannot assume that experiences in day care *cause* later sociability – we have merely uncovered a link. It might be, for example, that shy and unsociable children have mothers who are also shy and unsociable (because temperament is inherited) and such mothers may prefer to stay at home to care for their children. Therefore it is more outgoing children who attend day care, which explains why day-care children are more sociable!

Day care has no effects

The point is made over and over again in the conclusions presented by different day-care researchers that day care is not the only influence on a child's development. In fact there are so many influences that it is difficult to disentangle the direct effects of day care as opposed to, for example, the effects of type of attachment between mother and child. Clarke-Stewart (1985) concluded that, while day-care programmes had some direct effects on development, they clearly were not operating alone.

Gregg *et al.* (2005) analysed data from the Avon Longitudinal Study of Parents and Children (ALSPAC, also known as 'Children of the 90s' study) which has followed 14,000 children born during 1991–92 in the UK, and concluded that for the majority of children, maternal employment in the first three years of life appears to have no adverse effect on later behaviour. Any negative effects found in this study were very small and restricted to certain special circumstances that we will look at when considering the moderating factors.

DO IT YOURSELF

No. **2.5**

Is there a link between day care and sociability (the tendency to be friendly towards and get on with others)? If day care has a positive effect on sociability then we would expect people who have spent more time in day care to be more sociable (this is a positive correlation). In order to see if this is true we could conduct a study to score each person on two variables:

1 *Time spent in day care* – measure this by asking each participant to estimate the number of months they spent in day care before starting school.

2 *Sociability* – you need to develop a measure of sociability. This might consist of a number of questions such as, 'How many close friends do you have?' or, 'Do you prefer to spend time on your own, with one close friend or in a group of people?' Use the answers to produce a score for each participant.

You then correlate the two scores (see DIY on page 98).

This research raises an important ethical issue of psychological harm – measuring a person's sociability and relating this to past experiences may create anxiety. Therefore you should only conduct this research within your class and certainly never with children under the age of 16. Alternatively, you might just want to make up some data to see how correlation works.

LINK TO RESEARCH METHODS

The link between day care and aggression is a correlation. The study suggested above requires a correlational analysis. You can find out more about correlations on pages 98–9.

Exciting news! Rick and Clare are expecting a new baby. One thing worries Clare – she has recently gone back to work and really enjoys having her own life outside the home. She would like to continue working after the new baby is born. Rick would prefer Clare to stay at home as she did with the other children. They have both read our book.

1 Suggest **three** arguments that Rick could present to Clare to convince her that she ought to stay at home.
2 Suggest what responses Clare might make to Rick.

EXAM TIP
It is difficult to see clear patterns in the research on day care because there are so many factors involved. It may help you, when answering exam questions, to select particular pieces of research to build up an argument. In psychology there are no 'right' answers – just a well-argued and well-evidenced answer.

ⓔ MEDIATING FACTORS

A 'mediating factor' is something that forms a connecting link between two other things; in this case it is intervening between the effects of day care and social development.

Quality of care

The reason why people believe that day care may be harmful to children is because physical separation from a primary attachment figure appears to leave a child with no emotional care. However if suitable substitute emotional care is provided, then there may be no ill effects, as James and Joyce Robertson demonstrated (see page 48). In day-care situations where the staff-to-child ratio is poor and/or there is a high turnover of staff, children will be looked after by a series of familiar strangers who cannot act as secondary attachment figures. We would expect this to be associated with negative effects. Research does show a difference. For example the NICHD study (1997) reported that low-quality day care was associated with poor social development.

Even when high-quality day care is provided, it is unlikely that day-care staff provide the commitment and interest that parents provide. Parents have a much greater investment in the well-being and development of their child, and may provide a different kind of attention for the child as well as more intense empathy (consideration of the child's feelings). Day-care providers and childminders may look for peace and quiet, rather then stimulation and empathy, especially when they are caring for a number of young children at the same time.

This view has been supported in various research studies. For example, Bryant *et al.* (1980) found that some children in a childminding setting were actually disturbed, and suggested that this may be because childminders don't feel that they have to form emotional bonds with the children. Howes and Hamilton (1992) found that secure attachments occurred with only 50% of day-care staff, but with 70% of mothers. The lower rate of attachment probably reflects the lower quality and closeness of the caregiver relationship, which is probably due to the fact that day-care assistants are less committed to the child, less attached and engage in less intense interactions. Gregg *et al.* (2005) reported that the only group of children affected by day care were children whose care consisted solely of unpaid care by a friend, relative or neighbour. This implied that in such situations carers feel less responsibility for emotional care because they are unpaid.

Individual differences

Some children find day care harder to cope with than others. For example, children who have a shy nature may find it quite frightening (Pennebaker *et al.*,1981).

We have already discussed (page 52) the fact that insecurely attached children may find separation more difficult. The NICHD study (1997) found that children whose mothers lacked responsiveness (and thus might be insecurely attached) did less well in day care. On the other hand, Egeland and Hiester (1995) found that insecurely attached children did best in day care, whereas securely attached children were the ones that became more aggressive – this might be due to the fact that insecurely attached children *needed* compensatory care, and therefore benefited from day care, whereas the securely attached children did not need this extra attention.

Child's age and number of hours

Two important variables, when considering whether day care has good or bad effects, are the age of the child when he/she starts day care and how long a child spends each day or week in day care. It may be that there is a limit to how much day care a small child can take. Gregg *et al.* (2005) found that negative effects were more likely to be found in children who are placed in day care before they were 18 months old. The magnitude of these effects was small, and only a quarter of working mothers are in full-time work this early.

On the other hand Clarke-Stewart *et al.* (1994) found no difference in attachment between children spending a lot of time in day care (30 hours or more a week from age three months) with children who spent less time (less than 10 hours a week). Other studies have reported similar findings – no ill effects were found when children were placed in day care under the age of one and even for more than 20 hours per week (e.g. Scarr and Thompson, 1994; Andersson, 1992).

Applications

The fact that there are no clear effects of day care on children's social development suggests that such research serves no purpose. However it may be worth focusing on the factors associated with good outcomes – such as quality of day care and age of child when starting day care. We will turn to this on the next spread.

CAN YOU...? No.2.11

...1 Describe **three** criticisms of day-care research.

...2 Explain why both a child's age when starting day care, and the number of hours spent per week in day care would be significant factors in the effect of day care on social development.

Implications of research into attachment and day care

The final spread of this chapter concerns a very important aspect of psychological research – how can research into day care be applied in everyday life, particularly in terms of what constitutes high-quality day care? On this spread we examine how research translates into the practical issues of childcare provision in the UK. In Sweden, for example, public day care is heavily subsidised and flexible work schedules are common. Similarly, in France, childcare facilities are subsidised by the government, with younger children being entitled to full-day childcare. Initiatives in the UK such as the Sure Start programme show that our government is also taking the development of young children seriously.

ATTACHMENT RESEARCH

Attachment research has been applied to situations where children experience physical separation from primary attachment figures. Research by, for example, the Robertsons (see page 48) showed that the negative effects of emotional disruption could be avoided if substitute emotional care was provided as well as links with existing attachment figures. This research led to major changes in the visiting arrangements for parents with children in hospital. It also affected institutional care of children, for example in foster homes.

Another application of attachment research has been to child adoptions. In the past, mothers who were going to give a baby up for adoption were encouraged to nurse the baby for a significant period of time. By the time the baby was adopted, the sensitive period for attachment formation may have passed, making it difficult to form secure attachments. Bowlby's research led to changes in adoption protocols. Today most babies are adopted within the first week of birth, and research shows that adoptive mothers and children are just as securely attached as non-adoptive families (Singer et al., 1985).

Another application of attachment research is to improve the quality of parenting, especially in situations where a mother-infant relationship is not thriving. It is important to remember that emotional deprivation or privation may occur even when no separation has occurred, as in the case of a depressed or abusive parent. Earlier in this chapter we looked at one programme (the 'Circle of Security', see page 43) which helped caregivers learn to respond more sensitively to their young children and thus promote secure attachment.

And finally, understanding of attachment processes can be applied to improving the quality of day care, as is the aim of one innovative project in London, the Soho Family Centre. The centre's day-care programme is based on attachment theory. The centre believes that childcarers must function as secondary attachment figures who support and complement the primary attachment figure. In order to ensure this, each carer is assigned a maximum of only three children and is paired with another carer who can step in if need be. Thus each child is ensured close emotional relationships. In addition, continuity of care is valued, and one way this is achieved is to allow the carers to include their own children in their 'care group'. This allows mature women to return to this kind of work, and the children benefit from the women's experience.

DAY-CARE RESEARCH

On the previous spread we looked at various factors that mediate the effects of day care on children's social development. Perhaps the most important factor is the quality of day care. Research shows that high-quality day care is associated with positive outcomes, whereas negative effects may be due to low-quality care. But what do psychologists mean by high quality?

Characteristics of high-quality day care

Psychologists have identified the following key characteristics of high-quality day care:

- *Low child-to-staff ratios.* The NICHD study (1999) found that its day-care staff could provide sensitive care only if the ratios were as low as 3:1. Even then, day-care staff might be overwhelmed and unable to offer consistent care.
- *Minimal staff turnover.* Schaffer (1998) identifies consistency of care as one of the most important factors in good outcomes. When staff come and go, children may either fail to form attachments to the staff or, if they have formed an attachment, may suffer the anxiety associated with deprivation when the staff go.
- *Sensitive emotional care.* The NICHD study found that about 23% of infant-care providers give 'highly' sensitive infant care, 50% of them only 'moderately' sensitive care, and 20% are 'emotionally detached' from the infants under their care.
- *Qualified staff.* Sylva et al. (2003) reported from EPPE study that quality was associated with the qualification levels of the day-care staff. The higher the qualifications of staff, particularly the manager of the centre, the better the outcomes for the children in terms of social development.

Availability of high-quality day care

In the UK the availability of high-quality day care is monitored in a number of ways. First, it is controlled legally. For example, there are legal standards that must be met, which include issues such as minimum staffing ratios in relation to age of children and minimum levels of qualification for day-care staff. Second, day-care nurseries are inspected by Ofsted (who inspect schools as well) to ensure high-quality care. Finally, the UK government has initiated the Sure Start programme that aims to deliver the best start in life for every child, including top-quality day care, by ensuring the quality of childcare services. The success of this initiative is the focus of the NESS project (*National Evaluation of Sure Start*, Melhuish et al., 2005), which is studying the outcomes of the Sure Start programme. Early findings from the NESS study suggest that intervention in the form of high-quality day care produces greater benefits for children from moderately disadvantaged families than for children from more severely disadvantaged families. You can read about the Sure Start programme and the NESS project at www.surestart.gov.uk and www.ness.bbk.ac.uk.

CAN YOU...? No.2.12

...1 Describe **two** implications of attachment research for childcare practices.

...2 Describe **two** implications of day-care research for childcare practices.

...3 Give **two** limitations that should be considered when considering the implications of the above research.

No.**2.6**

What is day care today really like? You could conduct some qualitative research into the quality of day care using the internet. 'Qualitative research' is research that doesn't only take into account how many people like something or what ratings are given to a certain thing. Instead it takes a more open-ended approach and information is collected to provide a broad picture. Such information can later be reduced to numbers.

1 In order to do this you might start by looking at advertisements for day-care provision that are on the web and drawing up a list of the factors that they use to advertise themselves.
2 You could also look at your notes on day care and decide on criteria that are likely to be important (e.g. the number and quality of staff, the activities offered, the physical surroundings).
3 You might also look at the childcare checklist offered on www.extension.iastate.edu/Publications/PM1805.pdf
4 Now you can devise your own system of assessing day-care providers.
5 Finally, use your rating system to produce a report on one or more centres. Such reports can be quantitative (perform a content analysis using the criteria selected) or qualitative (write a commentary related to the criteria selected, but including particular details).

LINK TO RESEARCH METHODS

Read more about qualitative research and analysis, and content analysis on pages 102–3.

COMMENTARY CORNER

Question: **Outline and evaluate research into the effects of day care on social development (e.g. aggression, peer relations).** *(12 marks)*

When people have a discussion they do not usually follow the 'two paragraph rule' – one side states their entire case then the opposition states theirs. Inevitably there are lots of 'yeah buts, no buts…' going on. The following approach is a slightly more sophisticated version of the slanging match that we know and love! In this approach, outlining a research conclusion would represent the **AO1** component with the 'yes, but…' second sentence representing the **AO2** component. For example,

'Clarke-Stewart et al. (1994) studied 150 children and found that those who were in day care were consistently more advanced in their development than were children who stayed home with mothers.' 'Yes, but… day care is not the only influence on a child's development. There are so many influences, that it is difficult to disentangle the direct effects of day care from other influences on a child's behaviour. Clarke-Stewart (1985) concluded that, while day-care programmes had some direct effects on development, they clearly were not operating alone.'

Similarly

'Gregg et al. (2005) analysed data from the 'Children of the 90s' study and concluded that for the majority of children, maternal employment in the first three years of life appears to have no adverse effect on later behavioural outcomes.' 'Yes, but… some children find day care harder to cope with than others. For example, Pennebaker et al. (1981) found that children who have a shy nature may find it quite frightening.'

You can try this 'debate' approach yourself on the following research conclusions by offering an alternative *critical* perspective on that conclusion. Don't feel constrained to comment on the *specific* conclusion of a study, but consider how such a conclusion may be challenged in more general terms.

1 'Violata and Russell (1994) conducted a meta-analysis of the findings from 88 studies, concluding that regular day care for more than 20 hours per week had a negative effect on socio-emotional development, behaviour and attachment of young children.' *'Yes, but….'*
2 'The NICHD study found that children in full-time day care were close to three times more likely to show behaviour problems than those cared for by their mothers at home.' *'Yes, but….'*
3 'The EPPE (Effective Provision of Pre-School Education Project) study found increased independence and sociability in children who attended day care.' *"Yes, but….'*
4 'Field (1991) found that the amount of time spent in full-time day care was positively correlated to the number of friends children had once they went to school.' *"Yes, but….'*
5 'Gregg et al. (2005) found that negative effects occurred in children who are placed in day care before they are 18 months old.' *'Yes, but….'*

ROUND UP

In the first two chapters of this book we have provided a range of tips to help you tackle the more challenging extended writing questions. Here is a round up of our tips.

What is an extended writing question?

- It is a question that requires you to include equal amounts of description *and* evaluation (AO1 and AO2). Such questions are likely to start with words such as 'describe and evaluate' or 'discuss'.

How do I provide AO2?

- Identify critical points that you can make (e.g. research support, individual differences etc.).
- Elaborate your critical points using the *three point rule* (see page 21).
- Use the AO2 *vocabulary* to make your evaluation effective (see page 43).

How do I structure my answer?

- Write one AO1 paragraph and then one AO2 paragraph.
- Use the 'yes but no but' approach (described on the left).

How much should I write?

- About 20–25 words per mark is a useful guideline, which means about 240–300 words for a 12-mark question (120–150 words of AO1 and the same for AO2).

What do I do when a question begins with a statement?

- Make sure you answer the question that follows and not the initial statement. The statement is there to give you some hints about how to answer the question.

End-of-chapter review ⟩ CHAPTER SUMMARY

W e have identified here the key points of the topics on the AQA (A) AS specification, i.e. the bare minimum that you need to know. You may want to fill in further details to elaborate and personalise this material.

EXPLANATIONS OF ATTACHMENT

LEARNING THEORY

- All behaviour is learned.
- Classical conditioning – food produces pleasure. 'Feeder' (mother) associated with food so also produces pleasure.
- Operant conditioning – food is a primary reinforcer, 'feeder' becomes secondary reinforcer.
- Both reduce discomfort and are rewarding.

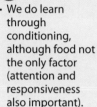 **STRENGTHS** ⊖ **WEAKNESSES**

- We do learn through conditioning, although food not the only factor (attention and responsiveness also important).
- Harlow showed that food is less important than contact comfort, supported by Schaffer and Emerson (1964) who found infants most attached to adult who fed them.

⚖ **VALIDITY**

- Largely animal studies.

EVOLUTIONARY PERSPECTIVE BOWLBY'S THEORY

- Attachment is adaptive and innate, related to imprinting (for survival).
- Sensitive period for development of attachment, as with all biological systems.
- Caregiving is also innate and adaptive, aided by social releasers.
- Secure base provided for exploration.
- Primary attachment most important (monotropy) but secondary attachments also important.
- Internal working model develops based on primary attachment relationship.
- Continuity hypothesis – link between early attachment and later social/emotional development.

 STRENGTHS ⊖ **WEAKNESSES**

Research support
- Imprinting in animals, e.g. Lorenz.
- Sensitive period, e.g. Rutter et al.
- Universality of attachment, e.g. Tronick et al.
- Monotropy (primary attachments), e.g. Shaffer and Emerson.
- Caregiver sensitivity, e.g. Harlow.
- Continuity hypothesis, e.g. Sroufe et al.

- Other attachments important, e.g. fathers and siblings, but still may be primary and secondary attachments.
- Temperament hypothesis offers an alternative explanation, supported by Belsky and Rovine.

 INDIVIDUAL DIFFERENCES

- Different types of attachment – secure and insecure.

CULTURAL VARIATIONS

- Attachment may lead to dependence rather than independence in some cultures.

 APPLICATIONS

- Parenting programmes, dealing with separation and day care.

DIFFERENCES IN ATTACHMENT

TYPES OF ATTACHMENT

Research
- Ainsworth's early studies in Uganda and Baltimore – showed importance of secure attachment and sensitive responsiveness.
- Strange Situation – assessed response to mild stress, separation and stranger anxiety.

Findings
- Secure attachment (62%).
- Insecure-avoidant (15%).
- Insecure-resistant (9%).
- Insecure-disorganised (15%) (Main and Solomon).
- Also 'disinhibited' as a type.

⚖ **VALIDITY**

- Measures a particular relationship not an individual – e.g. Main and Weston evidence with fathers.
- But *primary* attachment creates attachment type – Bowlby.
- Construct validity demonstrated by research support for 4 types.
- Predictive validity demonstrated, e.g. Hazan and Shaver ('love quiz').

⚖ **RELIABILITY**

- High inter-rater reliability (.94) in strange situation.

EFFECTS

- Longitudinal studies show continuities, e.g. secure attachment → positive outcomes.
- Love quiz (Hazan and Shaver) looked at adult romantic styles.

CONTRIBUTORY FACTORS

- Sensitivity.
- Maternal reflective functioning.
- Temperament.

 APPLICATIONS

- 'Circle of Security', increases maternal sensitivity.

CULTURAL VARIATIONS

- Similarities – Ainsworth (Uganda), Tronick et al. (The Efe), Fox (Israeli kibbutzim).
- Differences – insecure attachments, Grossmann and Grossmann (German interpersonal distance), Takahasi (Japanese dependence).
- On balance research supports monotropy, although distinct cultural differences.
- Van IJzendoorn and Kroonenberg – meta-analysis, global patterns of attachment similar suggesting attachment is innate, biological process.

CULTURE BIAS (Rothbaum et al.)

- Attachment theory rooted in US culture: sensitivity hypothesis, continuity hypothesis and secure base are all related to Western ideals.
- Should instead create a set of indigenous theories.
- However, core attachment concepts may be universal, e.g. evidence from other countries (Posada and Jacobs).

OTHER CRITICISMS

- Nation versus culture – large variations within countries, e.g. Van Ijzendoorn and Kroonenberg.
- Subcultural differences within countries, e.g. rural vs urban.
- Cultural similarities due to shared media rather than biology.
- Cross-cultural research flawed because of e.g. research bias and use of imposed etics (the strange situation has a different meaning in different cultures).

ATTACHMENT DIFFICULTIES

DISRUPTION OF ATTACHMENT

Research studies
- Spitz and Wolf – severe depression in infants after being placed in an institution.
- Skeels and Dye – intellectual deficits recovered when institutionalised children given extra emotional care.
- Robertson and Robertson – Laura and John suffered when they experienced physical disruption with no emotional care; Jane, Thomas, Lucy and Kate coped well when given substitute emotional care.
- Bohman and Sigvardsson – adopted 'problem' children showed good recovery.
- Bifulco et al. – women who lost mothers more likely to become depressed.

Therefore:
- Early emotional deprivation can harm early social/emotional development.
- But substitute emotional care can compensate.
- But individual may be vulnerable to emotional disorders.

 VALIDITY
- High validity because naturalistic studies.
- Low validity because case studies with unique characteristics.

 INDIVIDUAL DIFFERENCES
- Securely attached children cope better (Bowlby et al. TB sanatorium).

🌍 **APPLICATIONS**
- Hospitals today encourage parents to visit children.

PRIVATION (failure to form attachment)

Case studies of isolated children
- Genie and Czech twins, not reliable evidence.

Institutional care
- Skeels and Dye, Bowlby et al. – recovery possible.
- Hodges and Tizard – all ex-institutional children had difficulties coping with peers, despite good substitute care in some cases.
- Rutter et al. – Romanian orphans adopted early showed normal emotional development; those adopted after six months showed disinhibited attachment and had peer difficulties.

Effects
- Attachment disorder – now recognised on DSM; reactive (inhibited) or disinhibited.
- Poor parenting – Quinton et al. followed ex-institutional women, found most experienced difficulties as parents.
- Deprivation dwarfism – Gardner.

 EVALUATION
- Privation alone can't explain poor outcome – cumulative effect of risk factors, e.g. insecure attachment, lack of sensitivity.
- Research questionable because can't be sure what attachments had formed, nor have sufficient long-term studies been conducted.

ATTACHMENT IN EVERYDAY LIFE

DAY CARE

Negative effects on social development
- Long-term maladjustment – Bowlby's claim, supported by Violata and Russell.
- Increased aggressiveness shown in NICHD study, also disobedience and assertiveness; Melhuish also found increased risk in UK sample.
- Peer relations – day-care children less likely to be securely attached (Belsky and Rovine) and this is linked to poorer peer relations (Sroufe et al.).

Positive effects on social development
- Good day care provides social stimulation; children at home may feel more isolated, mothers may be depressed (Brown and Harris).
- More advanced social development – Clarke-Stewart et al. and Sylva et al., also found more independence and compliance.
- Peer relations – day-care children had more friends at school (Field), negotiated better with peers (Clarke-Stewart et al.) and were more sociable (Creps and Vernon-Feagans).

➖ **WEAKNESSES**
- Some studies have found no link with aggression (e.g. Prodromidis et al.).
- Day-care children may be more aggressive than non-day care but 83% were not aggressive at all (Friedman).
- Mother's sensitivity and home factors are a better predictor of aggressiveness (Belsky).
- Data is correlational, not causal.
- Many studies have found no effects, e.g. Gregg et al. (ALSPAC study).

ⓔ **MEDIATING FACTORS**
- Low quality of care associated with poorer outcome (NICHD).
- Generally day care may provide lower-quality care, and less-secure attachment, than a mother can (Howes and Hamilton).
- Individual differences – secure children cope better.
- Child's age and number of hours also important.

IMPLICATIONS

Implications of attachment research
- Visiting arrangements for children in hospital.
- Adoptions – avoiding late adoptions.
- Parenting, e.g. 'Circle of Security' to improve maternal sensitivity.
- Improving day-care quality, e.g. Soho Family Centre focuses on role of secondary attachment figures.

Implications of day-care research
- Improve quality through:
  - Low child-to-staff ratios – 3:1 (NICHD).
  - Minimal staff turnover – consistency of care (Shaffer).
  - Sensitive emotional care – only 20% provide highly sensitive care (NICHD).
  - Qualified staff (Sylva et al.).
- Quality monitored by Sure Start and NESS.

End-of-chapter review REVISION QUESTIONS

There are lots of ideas at the end of other chapters that you might adapt and try out here.

EXPLANATIONS OF ATTACHMENT

ACTIVITY 1 pages 34–9

Task 1 Research evidence

Draw a table like the one below. Select six studies from pages 34–9 and write down the researcher's name(s) in the left-hand column. In the right-hand column state which explanation the study supports and explain why it supports that explanation. One example has been completed for you.

Study	Explanation
Harlow (1960)	Supports Bowlby's theory because it showed that contact comfort was more important than feeding, and also that lack of responsiveness was linked to maladjustment.

Task 2 Key concepts

Here is a list of the key concepts involved in Bowlby's theory. Copy the table out and write a brief explanation for each.

Concept	Explanation
Adaptiveness	
Sensitive period	
Social releaser	
Monotropy	
Secure base	
Internal working model	

Task 3 Writing exam advice

One possible exam question would be

Describe and evaluate one explanation of attachment. *(12 marks)*

Imagine you are writing a book for AS level students. Write down **four** (or more) top tips for students about how to answer this question and get maximum marks.

When you have finished writing the advice you might prepare two example answers to the essay question:

1 An answer that *does not* follow your advice.
2 A model answer that does follow the advice, with notes showing where the advice has been followed.

After you have written both versions, give them to someone else to read and ask them to identify which is the better one. Then explain to them why the essays are different.

TYPES OF ATTACHMENT

ACTIVITY 2 pages 40–3

Task 1 Fill in the blanks

Ainsworth developed a technique to assess _____ called the _____ _____ . Various aspects of infant behaviour are tested. For example, when the caregiver leaves, this tests _____ _____, and when the infant is left with a stranger this tests _____ _____ . Ainsworth found that most infants were _____ _____ ___ and found two different kinds of insecure attachment – _____ and _____ .

Task 2 The strange situation

The table below presents the episodes of the strange situation in the wrong order. Work out the correct order.

	Parent returns, greets infant, offers comfort.
	Parent returns, greets infant, offers comfort if needed; stranger leaves.
1	Parent and infant play.
	Stranger enters and talks to parent.
	Stranger enters and offers comfort.
	Parent sits while infant plays.
	Parent leaves, infant alone.

Task 3 Evaluating the strange situation technique

Draw up a table like the one below and list arguments for and against the strange situation technique.

When thinking about arguments *for* the strange situation, you might ask yourself, 'Why is it useful?' and 'Why has it been valuable?'

When thinking about arguments *against* the strange situation you might ask yourself, 'Why isn't it useful?' and 'What are the ethical issues that are raised?'

Arguments *for* the strange situation	Arguments *against* the strange situation

Task 4 Ainsworth's studies

Three studies by Ainsworth are described in this chapter. List all three studies and for each one record brief details of the procedures, the findings and the conclusion.

CULTURAL VARIATIONS IN ATTACHMENT

ACTIVITY 3 pages 44–7

Task 1 van IJzendoorn and Kroonenberg

- Without rereading the study, write down anything you can remember about it (even if it is only one sentence).
- Now turn to page 45 and reread the description of the study and write a list of key words – about 10.
- Close your book and now try to describe the study again.

Task 2 Extended writing

Childrearing methods vary in different cultures but attachments are the same. **Discuss research into cultural variations in attachment.**

In order to answer this extended writing question you need to present evidence from research studies (**AO1** – about 100 words) and then evaluate the evidence (**AO2** – about 100 words). An effective way to organise your answer would be to break this down into six chunks. Here is an essay planner to help guide you in producing your answer.

Essay planner
Study 1 (**AO1** about 35 words)
Evaluation of study 1 (**AO2** about 35 words)
Study 2 (**AO1** about 35 words)
Evaluation of study 2 (**AO2** about 35 words)
Study 3 (**AO1** about 35 words)
Evaluation of study 3 (**AO2** about 35 words)

Task 3 Writing a conclusion

The essay plan above ignores the quote at the beginning:

'Childrearing methods vary in different cultures but attachments are the same.'

You could now write a final paragraph (of about 30 words) deciding what conclusions you would draw from the research evidence mentioned.

DISRUPTION/FAILURE TO FORM ATTACHMENT

ACTIVITY 4 pages 48–51

Task 1 Psychology in action

When Alice was only one year old she burned her arm badly and had to stay in hospital for two weeks. When she came home her family thought she would be pleased to leave the hospital but instead she seemed sad and very detached from everyone.

1 Using your knowledge of psychology, explain why she might be so sad and detached.
2 Suggest how this might have been prevented.
3 How do *your* points compare to those of other class members?

Tom has got a job as a babysitter. On his first visit to the family he looks after the children for two hours and the youngest child, Emily, becomes very upset. The next day he asks a friend who is studying psychology for advice.

1 Based on your psychological knowledge, what advice would you give Tom so that he can help Emily be more settled the next time he babysits?

Task 2 Teacher for a day

Your teacher has been asked to talk to a group of childcare students about the effects that institutional care may have on young children, and she (or he) is so impressed by your grasp of the topic that she/he decides you should deliver the lesson. Prepare a presentation for the students – a poster or Powerpoint display or a handout on the effects of institutionalisation.

Task 3 Useful applications

Research on disruption of attachment and failure to form attachment has led to important changes in the care of children. Draw up a list of as many applications as you can think of. You could do this in a group and see which group does best.

DAY CARE

ACTIVITY 5 pages 52–67

Task 1 Happy day care

Imagine that you have been employed by the HAPPY FAMILY DAY-CARE CENTRE to produce a leaflet or a poster for parents. Include information based on psychological research to convince prospective parents that this nursery would be an excellent place for their child.

Task 2 True or false?

	T or F
The NICHD study started in 2001 and involved over 1000 American children.	☐ ☐
The more day care a child experiences the more likely they are to be aggressive.	☐ ☐
The NICHD study found that maternal sensitivity was the best indicator of reported problem behaviours.	☐ ☐
Day-care research shows that day care causes aggressive behaviour.	☐ ☐
Children who start day care early (before the age of one) are more likely to experience negative outcomes from it than children who are placed in day care at a later age.	☐ ☐
Belsky found that day-care children were more sociable than children raised at home.	☐ ☐
High-quality day care is associated with good child-to-staff ratios of about 5:1.	☐ ☐

Task 3 Dominoes

Draw up a list of 30 concepts from the whole chapter (e.g. maternal responsiveness, deprivation, aggression) and also make a list of 30 studies.

Produce 30 rectangular cards (about 3 cm × 6 cm). Draw a line down the middle to look like a domino. On the left-hand side write one concept, on the right-hand side write the name of a study.

You play the game by dealing out all the cards/dominoes and placing the last one in the centre of the table. The first player has to lay a 'brick' that matches either end of the domino. For example if one end says 'aggression' you could match this with the NICHD day study that found aggressiveness was linked to day care.

The game finishes when no player can make another move and the winner is the one with fewest dominoes left.

Task 4 Multiple choice questions

Working on your own or in groups, write multiple choice questions and answers related to the material in this chapter (and Chapter 1 if you wish). Then pool your questions with the rest of the class. You can answer the questions individually or as a group.

End-of-chapter review

EXAMPLE EXAM QUESTIONS
WITH STUDENT ANSWERS AND EXAMINER'S COMMENTS

The Unit 1 exam is divided into two sections. Section B is Developmental Psychology and Research Methods. The actual number of questions is not fixed but will always total 36 marks, 12 of which will be research methods questions (see end of Chapter 3). All questions are compulsory. There may be an extended writing question in this section of the exam (like question 5 below). Such questions are half AO1 and half AO2, and you must take care to provide enough of both. Some other questions are also AO2 questions, however there is a difference – in these questions you don't have to worry about AO2ing – just answer the question, and always give detail and elaborate your answers.

---

1 *The baby did not cry much when his mother left the room and greeted her return with enthusiasm. He was happy to explore the room when his mother was there though he checked occasionally to see where she was. He clung to his mother when a stranger entered the room.*

  (a) Identify the type of attachment displayed by the infant. *(1 mark)*

  (b) Describe **one** other type of attachment. *(2 marks)*

Alice's answer

(a) The attachment type is secure. This is when an infant demonstrates a willingness to explore their environment and is easily soothed when confronted with strangers.
(b) Another type of attachment is insecure attachment. This can either be insecure-ambivalent or insecure-resistant.

Tom's answer

(a) The type of attachment displayed is secure attachment.
(b) Another type of attachment is insecure-ambivalent attachment, where the infant appears to reach out for the mother but then pulls away from her as if undecided how he feels about her.

Examiner's comments

Alice has given appropriate answers but hasn't focused on the exact demands of the question. Part (a) is worth only one mark so a simple identification was all that was required, as Tom has done. Both students get **1 mark**.

In part (b) Alice has not given enough detail this time. She has *identified* another type of attachment but has not *described* it, which is what the question requires. What she has done is to elaborate the type (insecure attachment) by identifying two sub-types, but this doesn't count as description. Tom has identified one type and described some characteristics. Thus Alice gets **1 out of 2 marks** and Tom gets **2 out of 2 marks**.

---

2 Learning theory has been used to explain attachment. How does this explanation differ from the evolutionary explanation of attachment? *(4 marks)*

Alice's answer

Learning theory proposes that attachment occurs because an infant associates the person who feeds it with a sense of pleasure and this is attachment. Learning theory also proposes that attachment may develop through reinforcement because the person who feeds the infant reduces hunger and this is rewarding so the person becomes a secondary reinforcer.

Bowlby's evolutionary explanation suggests that attachment occurs because infants are born with a drive to become attached and become attached to someone who provides sensitive responsiveness.

Tom's answer

Learning theory explains attachment in terms of learning, whereas evolutionary theory suggests that attachment occurs because it is an innate drive that promotes survival.

Examiner's comments

You might, at first glance, assume that Alice will gain more marks than Tom. She certainly seems to know more about the two explanations. However Alice hasn't answered the question. She gains **1 out of 3 marks** because, although there is an implicit contrast between learned and innate characteristics, she has not made this *explicit*. She has answered a slightly different question – outlining the two explanations – rather than identifying and explaining the difference. Tom receives **2 out of 3 marks** for making the contrast explicit but does not give sufficient detail for full marks. He could have achieved full marks by giving further elaboration of the difference or by providing a second difference.

---

3 **(a)** Describe what psychologists have found about cross-cultural variations in attachment. *(4 marks)*

  (b) Describe **one** criticism that has been made of research into cross-cultural variations in attachment. *(2 marks)*

Alice's answer

(a) One meta-analysis was conducted that looked at cross-cultural variations in attachment in 32 studies across 8 different countries. They found that secure attachment was the most common classification in all of the countries however there was quite a bit of difference in the relative rates for different kinds of insecure attachment. For example in Japan and Israel there was quite a high rate of resistant-insecure attachment compare to insecure-avoidant whereas the opposite was true in most other countries.
(b) A criticism that is made of this research is that the strange situation technique was used in all of the studies even though it might not have been a valid measure to use.

Tom's answer

(a) Ainsworth conducted an observational study of Ugandan women and their children, observing their interactions. This led her to conduct similar research in America. This research was good because it was naturalistic and related to real life. Another study, by Fox, involved Israeli children brought up on a kibbutz, where they were cared for by a metapelet and only spent a short amount of time with their real parents. The recordings were often made by Western observers of people in a different culture and their observations may have been biased because they imposed their own understanding on what they observed.

Examiner's comments

Alice has provided detailed findings from one study. The amount of detail given means that she can be given the full **4 out 4 marks** for this part of the question. A student can access all four marks either by providing findings from a number of studies or a number of findings from one study. Alice has not given the name of the researchers (van IJzendoorn and Kroonenberg) but the details provided make it clear exactly what study she is describing. Her criticism is appropriate but not sufficiently elaborated for full marks – thus **1 out of 2 marks**.

Tom has chosen different but nevertheless creditworthy research studies but fails to score more than **1 out of 4 marks** because he has not provided any information about what the studies *found*; an easy mistake to make but a shame as it seems that he has detailed knowledge of research in this area but has failed to turn this knowledge into good exam performance. For part (b) Tom has identified and explained an appropriate criticism and thus receives **2 out of 2 marks**.

---

4 Margaret has just had a baby and wishes to go back to work. Suggest **two** factors that she might consider when selecting day care. *(3 marks)*

Alice's answer

The frequency of staff turnover is an important factor. One study found that a high turnover of staff left children being cared for by familiar strangers.

If a child is left with a neighbour or friend, they feel personally responsible and invest more in their emotional welfare.

The NICHD study found that a low quality of day care is also associated with poor social development, so she needs to ensure it is of a high quality.

Tom's answer

It is important to consider the emotional impact on the child, and also if day care is close to where the family lives. A long car journey for a child every day may negatively affect them.

If Margaret decided to move to Sweden, where Andersson found positive effects on day-care children, then day care would be worth consideration as there is a good staff-child ratio.

Examiner's comments

Alice has again misread the question and described three instead of two factors. In such cases an examiner will read all three and award credit to the best two (this is called *positive marking*). In this case her second answer is not as good as the other two because it is not clearly based on psychological research. There is one mark for each factor and one mark for the justification, which she has done in both, therefore Alice gets **4 out of 4 marks**.

Tom's first paragraph actually contains two answers. Insufficient detail has been given for 'emotional impact' and the 'car journey' is not based on psychological research. The second paragraph provides a positive effect rather than a negative one but it isn't realistic, therefore **1 out of 4 marks** because at lease there is the implication that quality matters.

---

5 Discuss research into the effects of failure to form attachment (privation). *(8 marks)*

Alice's answer

Hodges and Tizard used a longitudinal approach to study the effects of early experiences and later development. They found that children who were raised in an institution during the sensitive period were unlikely to form an attachment, even when restored to their biological parents.

The Czech Twins (Koluchová, 1976) were detained in a basement by their stepmother until the age of seven. Although they were severely affected, they had a normal social and intellectual capability by the age of 14, and at the age of 20 they were above average intelligence.

A weakness to Hodges and Tizard's research is that the parents may not have invested emotionally the same in their children. The biological parents in Hodges and Tizard's sample may not have been as interested in their children, which is why they were less attached.

Although the Czech twins suffered from privation, this did demonstrate that a person without a bond with a primary caregiver could then go out and function adequately in society.

Rutter's study shows that recovery from extreme privation can be achieved given adequate care, although adoption (at age two) was still within Bowlby's 'sensitive period'.

Tom's answer

It has been found by psychologists that absence of a primary caregiver can have many effects, for example the Robertsons looked at how children were affected when their mothers had to spend time in hospital. They filmed a number of children under the age of 3 in foster care or in a hospital nursery. The children were OK if they were cared for emotionally. These were case studies. Other work includes Genie who was a victim of severe neglect. She suffered from privation and couldn't speak properly. Her state of mind may not have been because she was a victim of no attachment but because she was retarded. This was another case study. There are also the Czech twins who were locked in a cellar but rescued when they were 7 and then raised by two kind sisters. Later in life they appeared to be fine, which shows that privation doesn't always have negative effects.

Examiner's comments

Alice has taken a no-nonsense approach to this essay and written four paragraphs which are clear in their intent. The first two paragraphs are clearly AO1, accurate and detailed. Thus Alice gets **4 out of 4 marks for AO1**.

The final two paragraphs are all AO2, each one matching a descriptive paragraph. The evaluation of Hodges and Tizard's research is not well developed – why is this a weakness of the research? It is an explanation of the findings but not an evaluation. The second evaluative point is a more of a conclusion than a criticism and contains unsubstantiated claims – what evidence is there to support the claim that they functioned adequately? Remember the three point rule – always present evidence to support your claim. Alice gets **3 out of 4 marks**.

Tom's answer is less effective than Alice's in many ways. Most importantly Tom has failed to focus on the question and included evidence about disruption of attachment rather than focusing solely on privation, as required. Tom would receive only **2 out of 4 marks**.

There is rather little AO2 material – the statement about being a case study and the conclusion drawn from the Czech twin study are both potential AO2 points but have not been made effectively. For example just stating that 'this was another case study' lacks that all important AO2 vocabulary to make it clear that this is a critical point (e.g. add 'however'). So **0 out 4 marks** for evaluation.

Alice's total for this question is **7 out of 8 marks** and Tom's is **2 out of 8 marks**.

YOUR OWN LITTLE BOOK OF REVISION NOTES

At the beginning of this book we explained how to produce your own little book of notes and use them for effective revision (see page x).

Remember to keep your notes brief – just record key points which will act as coat pegs for remembering the material.

Column 1: tick when you have produced brief notes.

Column 2: tick when you have a good grasp of this topic.

Column 3: tick during the final revision when you feel you have complete mastery of the topic.

Key terms

3 marks worth of material

Attachment	☐	☐	☐
Secure attachment	☐	☐	☐
Insecure attachment	☐	☐	☐
Disruption of attachment	☐	☐	☐
Privation	☐	☐	☐
Institutionalisation	☐	☐	☐
Day care	☐	☐	☐

Research studies related to ...

6 marks worth of description
6 marks worth of evaluation (including the issues of validity and ethics)

Bowlby's theory of attachment	☐	☐	☐
Types of attachment	☐	☐	☐
Ainsworth's studies	☐	☐	☐
Cultural variations in attachment	☐	☐	☐
Disruption of attachment	☐	☐	☐
Failure to form attachment (privation)	☐	☐	☐
Institutionalisation	☐	☐	☐
Impact of day care on social development	☐	☐	☐
Impact of day care on aggression	☐	☐	☐
Impact of day care on peer relations	☐	☐	☐

Factors that affect ...

6 marks worth of material

Types of attachment	☐	☐	☐
Effects of disruption of attachment	☐	☐	☐
Effects of privation	☐	☐	☐
Effects of institutionalisation	☐	☐	☐
Impact of day care on social development	☐	☐	☐

Explanations/theories

6 marks worth of description
6 marks worth of evaluation (both strengths and weaknesses)

Learning theory	☐	☐	☐
Bowlby's theory (evolutionary perspective)	☐	☐	☐

Implications of attachment and day-care research

6 marks worth of material

Implications of attachment research	☐	☐	☐
Implications of day-care research	☐	☐	☐

CROSSWORD

Answers on page 214.

Across

1. Type of attachment associated with a failure to form attachments. (12)
3. Term used to describe an infant's main caregiver: _____ attachment figure. (7)
7. Term used by psychologists to describe the failure to form attachments. (9)
10. Type of insecure attachment where infant both seeks and rejects contact with caregiver. (10)
13. Type of attachment resulting from sensitive responsiveness from primary attachment figure. (6)
16. They conducted a longitudinal study of children who were adopted or returned home from an institution (Hodges and T-----) (6)
17. A UK government programme set up to investigate the effects of temporary separations on infants. (4,5)
18. Psychologist who demonstrated imprinting in geese. (6)
19. Important longitudinal study of over 1000 American children. (5)
20. Name of female psychologist who conducted research with Ugandan mothers and children. (9)
21. The method developed for assessing type of attachment s_____ s_____. (7,9)

Down

2. The psychologist who showed that contact comfort was more important than feeding in rhesus monkeys. (6)
4. The type of society where members are more concerned with independence than interdependence. (13)
5. Type of culture where members more concerned with group needs and interdependence. (12)
6. Number of attachment types listed in this chapter. (4)
8. Husband and wife team who investigated the effects of temporary separations on infants. (10)
9. A kind of conditioning where learning occurs through association. (9)
11. The hypothesis that innate personality type affects the kind of attachments that are formed with one's caregiver. (11)
12. Term used by Bowlby to describe the importance of one emotional relationship to an infant. (9)
14. The name of girl studied by Curtiss. (5)
15. Close emotional bond between two people. (10)

Research methods are systematic approaches to discovering things about the world. Psychologists use a wide range of different methods to obtain and analyse data about people's behaviours and experience. If we are to fully understand and evaluate psychological theories and concepts, we must understand the research procedures which have provided the evidence for these theories.

Research methods

The content of this chapter is different from the content of the other chapters of this book for a variety of reasons:

1 *You will be asked questions on research methods in all parts of the AS exam.* There are five topic areas (cognitive, developmental, biological, social and individual differences) and in each of these you will be asked questions about research methods in addition to the questions specific to the topic area. For example, in Unit 1, the section in the exam on memory will contain some questions on memory, whereas others will be about validity, ethics and/or how to design and conduct research into memory.

2 *Research methods concepts are an integral part of the study of all areas of psychology.* For example, one of the ways to evaluate any study is in terms of its validity, or in terms of ethical issues raised, or criticisms of the research methods used. Therefore you will be applying your knowledge from this chapter to all other chapters when you evaluate research studies.

SPECIFICATION BREAKDOWN

Specification content	Comment
Methods and techniques	
Candidates will be expected to demonstrate knowledge and understanding of the following research methods, their advantages and weaknesses:	
• **Experimental method including laboratory, field and natural experiments** • **Studies using a correlational analysis** • **Observational techniques** • **Self-report techniques including questionnaire and interview** • **Case studies**	Psychologists (and all scientists) use many different research methods and techniques when conducting research. The specification focuses on the most common methods and techniques as listed on the left. You will be asked questions on these, and about their advantages and weaknesses.
Investigation design	
Candidates should be familiar with the following features of investigation design:	
• **Aims** • **Hypotheses including directional and non-directional** • **Experimental design (independent groups, repeated measures, and matched pairs)** • **Design of naturalistic observations including the development and use of behavioural categories** • **Design of questionnaires and interviews** • **Operationalisation of variables including independent and dependant variables** • **Pilot studies** • **Control of extraneous variables** • **Reliability and validity** • **Awareness of the BPS Code of Ethics** • **Ethical issues and ways in which psychologists deal with them** • **Selection of participants and sampling techniques including random, opportunity and volunteer sampling** • **Demand characteristics and Investigator effects**	In the introductory chapter of this book we outlined the scientific method. In order to test any explanation of behaviour, a scientist needs to state research aims and (usually) a hypothesis. The next step is to design the study – the design of the study will differ depending on the method/technique that is selected. The specification requires that you are able to design experiments, naturalistic observations, and self-report techniques (questionnaires and interviews). There are some issues common to most kinds of methods/techniques: operationalisation, use of pilot studies, control of extraneous variables, reliability and validity, consideration of ethical issues and how to deal with them, selection of participants, and understanding of the factors that influence participants (most notably demand characteristics and investigator effects). Exam questions will be set which assess your ability to deal with all of these issues, for example asking you to explain what a pilot study is or to explain how you would conduct a pilot study or why you would conduct one.
Data analysis and presentation	
Candidates should be familiar with the following features of data analysis, presentation and interpretation:	
• **Presentation and interpretation of quantitative data including graphs, scattergrams and tables** • **Analysis and interpretation of qualitative data** • **Measures of central tendency including median, mean, mode** • **Measures of dispersion including ranges and standard deviation** • **Analysis and interpretation of correlational data – positive and negative correlations and the interpretation of correlation coefficients** • **Presentation of qualitative data** • **The processes involved in content analysis**	A key part of any research is the analysis of data – presenting the results and working out what they mean. The data may be presented graphically and/or in terms of measures of central tendency (e.g. mean) and dispersion (e.g. range). If your results are numerical, then they are described as 'quantitative'. Sometimes psychologists collect data which is 'qualitative', for example collecting data about what people do or say. Content analysis is a means of dealing with qualitative data by putting complex behaviours into categories.

WHAT DO PSYCHOLOGISTS DO?

Psychologists try to explain human behaviour. They develop explanations of behaviour and then have to work out ways to test these explanations to see whether or not they are true. This is where research methods come in – they are the means by which psychologists test their explanations. There are many different kinds of research methods/techniques: some of these are listed in the specification on the left and we will focus on these.

Let's look at one area of behaviour. You may have heard the advice 'eat five items of fruit/vegetables a day in order to be healthy'. Are people who eat fruit and vegetables actually healthier than people who don't? In order to see whether this is true we could use a variety of methods – experimental methods or non-experimental ones:

Experimental

- You could control what people eat for a specific period of time (e.g. six months). One group would eat five pieces of fruit/vegetables per day. The other group would eat no fruit or vegetables. Over the six-month period each group would keep a record of any illnesses. After six months you could compare the two groups in terms of number of days of illness (the dependent variable).

Non-experimental

- **Observational techniques**. You could conduct a study in your local supermarket, observing how much fruit/vegetables each person buys.
- **Self-report**. In the supermarket you could ask people about their health and produce a healthiness score for each person.
- **Correlational analysis**. You could correlate the number of fruit/vegetables for each person with their healthiness score.
- **Case studies**. You could focus on a few individuals and ask them to record what they eat every day. You could also record various aspects of their health such as heart rate and body temperature, and test the functioning of their immune system. You could extend such a study to cover a wide selection of people and would then be able to make generalisations from this data.

In this book you will see that psychologists use these different methods and techniques when investigating behaviour.

STARTER ACTIVITY

Flanwell University is currently conducting research on 16–18 year olds and has asked your class to help them with their research programme. At present they are undertaking research in the following areas:

- Gender differences in the use of mobile phones.
- The differences between arts and science students.
- The kind of dreams that students have.
- Exercise and well being.

Select one research topic and decide on a specific research aim and hypothesis. You should then suggest an appropriate research method and technique(s) and briefly describe how you think you might investigate it.

Note: if you want to conduct your study you should only use participants from your class and/or close friends/family members.

A very shy guy goes into a pub and sees a beautiful woman sitting at the bar. After an hour of gathering up his courage, he finally goes over to her and asks, tentatively, 'Um, would you mind if I chatted with you for a while?'

She responds by yelling, at the top of her voice, 'NO! I won't sleep with you tonight!' Everyone in the bar is now staring at them. Naturally, the guy is hopelessly embarrassed and slinks back to his table.

After a few minutes, the woman walks over to him and apologises. She smiles and says, 'I'm sorry if I embarrassed you. You see, I'm a psychology student, and I'm studying how people respond to embarrassing situations.'

To which he responds, at the top of his voice, 'What do you mean £200?!'

Validity

How science works

1 Observe human behaviour.
2 Develop explanation/hypothesis.
3 Test hypothesis.
4 Collect results.
? ? ? ? ? ? ? ?
5 Draw conclusions.

The key theme throughout your psychology course is the theme of *'how science works'*. In the introduction to this book we looked at an example of the scientific method at work in Zimbardo's Stanford Prison Experiment – Zimbardo *observed* behaviour in the world around him and then developed an *explanation* for this behaviour. In order to test this explanation he designed a study (the SPE) and concluded that this study supported the situational explanation. This process is outlined in the diagram on the right. You will notice that there is a row of red question marks – this is where we have to consider validity. A study produces results; these are facts which cannot be argued with. The next step is to draw conclusions from the results; conclusions are interpretations of the facts. But if the study lacks validity then such conclusions are unjustified.

CONTROL

Consider the following experiment:

A class of psychology students conducted the study on page xiv with the aim of finding out whether students could do their homework effectively while in front of the TV. The study involved two conditions – doing a memory test in silence and doing it with the TV on. It might be that all the participants in the silent condition did the memory test in the morning and all the participants in the 'TV on' condition did the memory test in the afternoon.

The independent variable (IV) was whether the TV was on or not. The dependent variable (DV) was the participants' score on the memory test. If TV is a distraction, the silence group should do better on the test.

But were there other things that might have affected their score on the memory test?

- It might be that people are more alert in the morning and that is why they do better on the morning test.
- It might be that the students in one group had naturally better memories than those

in the other group and that would explain why one group did better.

These are called *extraneous variables*.

If an experimenter fails to control such extraneous variables then the results of the study will be *meaningless*. The experimenter may claim that the IV caused a change in the DV but in fact this may not the case – changes in the DV may actually be caused by something else – the extraneous variable(s). *Consequently the experimenter may not have actually tested what he (or she) intended to test.* Instead the influence of a different variable has been tested.

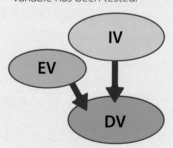

Therefore **control** is vital in experiments. An experimenter seeks to control as many *relevant* extraneous variables as possible i.e. those extra to the IV.

REALISM

The aim of any psychological study is to provide information about how people behave in 'real life'. If the set-up of a study is too artificial or contrived then the participants will not act as they would normally.

For example, the study by Loftus and Palmer investigated eyewitness testimony by showing participants a film of a car accident and asking questions about the speed of a car (see page 16).

But how realistic is this? Is watching the film the same as seeing a real accident?

Many things affect the *realism* of a psychological study. The term **mundane realism** refers to how an experiment mirrors the real world. 'Mundane' means 'of the world' – commonplace, ordinary. Watching a car accident on film in a laboratory lacks mundane realism and this means that the results of the study may not be very useful in terms of understanding behaviour in the real world.

In defense of artificial lab experiments

Which drops faster – a kilo of feathers or a kilo of lead?

Theoretically they both drop at the same rate. However, if you try to test this you will find the kilo of feathers drops more slowly because of air resistance. The air resistance is an extraneous variable. To test the proposition properly the study would need to be done in an artificial and contrived set-up of a vacuum with no air to impede the feathers' fall.

Coolican (2004a) argues in defence of contrived laboratory experiments that appear to lack realism. He points out that such settings are deliberately artificial in order to eliminate those extraneous variables that are normally present in the real world. The lab is intended as a place to test theory. If a study is successful here then further studies might test the results in a more real-life, everyday context.

Sometimes the contrived nature of the lab doesn't matter. For example, if you want to test the accuracy of eyewitness testimony then doing this in a lab may be just like real life – you could arrange for participants to be doing a memory experiment in a lab, while they are doing this a 'thief' comes in the room, steals a handbag and runs out. If you asked participants to try to identify the thief, how is this different from a real-life robbery? And remember that studies conducted in a natural environment may also lack validity because of lack of control. **Think outside the box** – all studies have some validity, the question is how much and why.

Invariably, studies in psychology involve a trade-off between control and realism. The greatest control can be achieved in the laboratory. However, it is debatable to what extent findings from the laboratory can be generalised to other environments, especially the less controllable environments in which everyday life is lived.

Some psychologists argue that we can only discover things about behaviour if we uncover cause-and-effect relationships in highly controlled laboratory experiments. Others argue that studies in the natural environment are the only real option for psychologists who are interested in how life is actually lived.

control

realism

Learning about research methods is a bit like learning a foreign language. When you learn a foreign language you have to learn a new set of words and, more especially, what they mean. One of the best ways to do this is to speak the language – the same is true for research methods. Don't hold back, don't be scared – use the words.

To help you learn the language you could create your own Research Methods Vocabulary Book to record all the terms used, their meanings and their advantages and weaknesses. You can include a copy of the specification for research methods in your book, and tick off each term when you have recorded the details and again when you feel you understand it (see list at the end of this chapter).

What is validity? The term 'validity' refers to how true or legitimate something is as an explanation of behaviour. It involves the issues of control, realism and generalisability.

Students often believe that validity is about 'being correct'. This is both right and wrong. It is right because a researcher seeks to find out whether the hypothesis is true i.e. correct, but it is wrong if you think that being correct means finding out that the predicted expectations have been confirmed. Validity is not about confirming your expectations.

GENERALISABILITY

The point of realism in psychological research is to be able to *generalise* the results beyond the particular unique research setting – in particular to be able to understand behaviour in everyday life (the 'real world').

A study may be very 'natural' or real (i.e. high realism) but can still lack generalisability.

- If all the participants in a study are American university students, it may not be reasonable to generalise the findings to the behaviour of all people because Americans (and students) have unique characteristics.
- If a study about obedience is conducted in a hospital with real nurses (see Hofling *et al.*, page 159) this may not tell us much about obedience in everyday life because part of a nurse's job is to obey doctors, which differs from other obedience relationships.

It is very important to remember this – just because a study is conducted in a natural environment (such as a hospital) doesn't mean the findings can be generalised to the real world.

INTERNAL AND EXTERNAL VALIDITY

Validity can be separated into **internal validity** and **external validity**.

Internal validity

Internal validity concerns what goes on *inside* a study. It is concerned with things such as:

- Whether the IV produced the change in the DV (or did something else affect the DV?).
- Whether the researcher tested what he intended to test. For example if you want to find out whether watching TV affects the quality of homework, you cannot be certain you are doing this by just having the TV on (the person may not be listening to it).
- Whether the study possessed (or lacked) mundane realism.

To gain high internal validity you must design the research carefully, controlling extraneous variables, and ensuring that you are testing what you intended to test.

External validity

External validity is affected by internal validity – you cannot generalise the results of a study that was low in internal validity because the results have no real meaning for the behaviour in question.

External validity concerns the ability to generalise the results of a study to:

- Different places or settings (called *ecological validity*)
- Different people or populations (called *population validity*)
- Different times (e.g. the 1950s or 2000s) (*historical validity*)

RESEARCH METHODS Qs

No.**3.1**

1 Select one or more studies that you are familiar with and explain why you think the study might be:

- High in internal validity.
- High in external validity.
- Low in internal validity.
- Low in external validity.

2 An area of study that has interested psychologists is massed versus distributed practice i.e. whether learning is better if you practice something repeatedly (massed) or space your periods of practice (distributed). This topic has been studied in different settings.

Study 1: Participants were required to recall nonsense syllables on 12 occasions spread over either 3 days or 12 days (Jost, 1897). Recall was higher when spread over 12 days. This finding has been supported by subsequent research.

Study 2: Post office workers had to learn to type postcodes either using massed or distributed practice (Baddeley and Longman, 1978). Distributed practice was again found to be superior.

Present arguments for why each of these studies could be viewed as having high and low external validity.

Internal validity is about control and realism. External validity is about generalising.

KEY TERMS

Internal validity Whether the study has tested what it set out to test; the degree to which the observed effect was due to the experimental manipulation rather than other factors such as extraneous variables.

External validity The degree to which a research finding can be generalised: to other settings (ecological validity); to other groups of people (population validity); over time (historical validity).

Control Refers to the extent to which any variable is held constant or regulated by a researcher.

Mundane realism Refers to how a study mirrors the real world. The simulated task environment is realistic to the degree to which experiences encountered in the environment will occur in the real world.

Ethical issues

What is an *issue*? It is a conflict between two points of view. In psychology, an ethical issue is a conflict between (1) what the researcher needs in order to conduct useful and meaningful research, and (2) the rights of participants. Ethical issues are conflicts about what is acceptable. On this spread we consider various ethical issues which arise in psychological research.

ETHICAL ISSUES

1 informed consent

From the researcher's point of view, **informed consent** means revealing the true aims of the study – or at least telling participants what is actually going to happen. This might cause participants to guess the aims of the experiment. For example, a psychologist might want to investigate whether people obey a male teacher more than a female teacher. If the participants are told the aim of this experiment before the study takes place, it might change the way they behave – they might try to be equally obedient to both. Researchers therefore may not always want to reveal the true aims.

From the participants' point of view they should be told what they will be required to do in the study so that they can make an informed decision about whether they wish to participate. This is a basic human right, established during the Nuremburg war trials: in the Second World War Nazi doctors conducted various experiments on prisoners without their consent and the war trials afterwards decided that consent should be a basic human right for participants involved in any study.

Even if researchers have sought and obtained informed consent, that does not guarantee that participants really do understand what they have let themselves in for. Epstein and Lasagna (1969) found that only a third of participants volunteering for an experiment really understood what they had agreed to take part in.

Another problem is the requirement for the researcher to point out any likely benefits or risks of participation. Researchers are not always able to accurately predict the risks of taking part in a study.

2 Deception

As we have just seen, it can be necessary to deceive participants about the true aims of a study otherwise participants might alter their behaviour and the study could be meaningless. A distinction, however, should be made between withholding some of the details of the research aims (reasonably acceptable) and deliberately providing false information (less acceptable).

From the participant's point of view, **deception** is unethical – you should not deceive anyone without good cause. Perhaps more importantly, deception prevents participants being able to give informed consent. They may agree to participate without really knowing what they have let themselves in for and they might be quite distressed by the experience.

Deception can also lead people to see psychologists as untrustworthy. It might also mean that a participant may not want to take part in psychological research in the future.

Baumrind (1985) argued that deception is morally wrong on the basis of three generally accepted ethical rules in Western society: the right of informed consent, the obligation of researchers to protect the welfare of the subject, and the responsibility of researchers to be trustworthy. However, others point out that sometimes deception is relatively harmless, for example a participant may have little reason to refuse to take part in a memory study (no distress, quick experiment) and therefore the deception seems less objectionable.

3 The right to withdraw

From the participant's point of view, the **right to withdraw** from a study is important. If a participant begins to feel uncomfortable or distressed they should be able to withdraw. This is especially important if a participant has been deceived about the aims and/or procedures. However, even if a participant has been fully informed, the actual experience of taking part may turn out to be rather different, so they should be able to withdraw.

From the researcher's point of view, if participants do leave during the study this will bias the results because the participants who have stayed are likely to be more obedient, or they might be more hardy.

Sometimes the right to withdraw is compromised by payment of participants. In such cases participants may not feel able to withdraw.

4 Protection from physical and psychological harm

From the researcher's point of view, studying some of the more important questions in psychology may involve a degree of distress to participants. It is also difficult to predict the outcome of certain procedures (such as in the Stanford Prison Experiment, see Introduction) therefore it is difficult to guarantee **protection from harm**.

From the participant's point of view, nothing should happen to them during a study that causes harm. It is considered acceptable if the risk of harm is no greater than in ordinary life. There are many ways harm can be caused to participants, some physical (e.g. getting them to smoke, or drink coffee excessively), some psychological (e.g. making them feel inadequate, or embarrassing them). Participants should be in the same state after an experiment as they were before, unless they have given their informed consent to be treated otherwise.

5 Confidentiality

From the researcher's point of view it may be difficult to protect **confidentiality** because the researcher wishes to publish the findings. A researcher may guarantee *anonymity* (withholding the participants' names) but even then it may be obvious who has been involved in a study. For example, knowing that a study was conducted on the Isle of Wight could permit some people to be able to identify participants.

From the participants' point of view, the Data Protection Act makes confidentiality a legal right. It is only acceptable for personal data to be recorded if the data are not made available in a form which identifies the participants.

6 Privacy

From the researcher's point of view it may be difficult to avoid invasion of **privacy** when studying participants without their awareness.

From the participants' point of view, people do not expect to be observed by others in certain situations e.g. when in the privacy of their own homes, while they might expect this when sitting on a park bench in public.

Everyone conducting psychological research, including psychology students, is expected to be aware of their responsibility to ensure participants are treated in an ethically appropriate manner. Whenever you conduct any research you must ensure that you deal properly with all ethical issues.

KEY TERMS

Confidentiality A participant's right to have personal information protected.

Deception Where a participant is not told the true aims of a study (e.g. what participation will involve) and thus cannot give truly informed consent.

Informed consent Participants have the right to be given comprehensive information concerning the nature and purpose of the research and their role in it, in order that they can make an informed decision about whether to participate.

Privacy A person's right to control the flow of information about themselves. Contrast with confidentiality.

Protection from harm During a research study, participants should not experience negative physical or psychological effects, such as physical injury, lowered self-esteem or embarrassment.

Right to withdraw Participants should have the right to withdraw from participating in a study if they are uncomfortable in any way, and should also have the right to refuse permission for the researcher to use any data they produced.

Subjects or participants?

In early psychological research the people in the studies were called 'subjects'. In the 1990s there was a move to use the term 'participant' instead of 'subject'.

One reason for the change of terminology is that the term 'participant' reflects the fact that such individuals are not passive members of a study but are actively involved. They search for cues about what to do and this may mean that they behave as researchers expect rather than as they would in everyday life. The use of the term 'participants' acknowledges this active involvement.

A further reason for the change is that the term 'subject' implies that those involved must be obedient and are powerless. The BPS guidelines (see page 72) say, 'psychologists owe a debt to those who agree to take part in their studies and [believe] that people who are willing to give up their time, even for remuneration, should be able to expect to be treated with the highest standards of consideration and respect. This is reflected in the change from the term "subjects" to "participants".' On the next spread we look further at these BPS guidelines.

Confidentiality and privacy – what's the difference?

The words 'confidentiality' and 'privacy' are sometimes used interchangeably, but there is a distinction between them. **Confidentiality** *concerns the communication of personal information from one person to another, and the trust that this information will then be protected.* **Privacy** *refers to a zone of inaccessibility of mind or body, and the trust that this will not be 'invaded'.*

In other words, we have a right of privacy. If this is invaded, confidentiality should be respected.

Ethical issues are *issues* because there are no easy answers. Below are descriptions of various studies for your consideration. When considering them it might be useful to discuss your thoughts in small groups and then present your views to the class. In each study:

a Identify any ethical issues raised in the study.
b Consider to what extent they are acceptable from the researcher's point of view.
c Consider to what extent they are acceptable from the participants' point of view.
d Decide whether you think the study was ethically acceptable, or not, giving your reasons.
e Suggest what you think the researcher might have done to make the study more ethically acceptable.

Study A – In the Stanford Prison Experiment (see Introduction) Zimbardo *et al.* took great care to inform the prospective participants about what would be involved in the study. However the participants who were selected to be the prisoners were not informed that they would be arrested in their own homes, and did not know the amount of psychological distress that would be caused by participating.

Study B – Craik and Lockhart (see page 10) conducted a study on memory where participants had to read thirty questions and for each of the questions either respond 'yes' or 'no'. Afterwards they were asked to recall as many of the words as they could. They were not informed of the true aims of the study (to compare deep with shallow processing) and were not told they would have to recall the words.

Study C – Middlemist *et al.* (1976) investigated invasion of personal space by conducting a field experiment in a men's urinal. There were three conditions: a confederate (ally of the researcher) stands either immediately next to a participant, one urinal away, or is absent. An observer recorded onset of micturation times (how long they took before they started to urinate) as an indication of how comfortable the participant felt. Some psychologists regard this as an important study of personal space.

Study D – Piliavin *et al.* (1969) investigated the behaviour of bystanders in an emergency situation to see how quickly they would offer help to someone (a confederate) who collapsed on a New York subway train. The confederate either acted as if he was drunk (carried a bottle in a brown bag) or as if he was disabled (carried a black cane). Observers recorded how long it took for anyone to offer help. There was no opportunity to debrief participants.

Study E – Orne (1962) observed that people behave in quite unusual ways if they think they are taking part in a psychology experiment. For example, in one experiment he asked participants to add up columns of numbers on a sheet of paper and then tear the paper up and repeat this again. If people believed this was part of a psychology experiment some were willing to continue the task for over six hours!

✋ internet research

You might want to investigate some of these studies more fully in order to decide about the associated ethical issues. A search on the internet should give further information.

How psychologists deal with ethical issues

The most obvious way of dealing with ethical issues is through the use of guidelines produced by a professional organisation. All professionals (police officers, doctors, teachers, etc.) have a professional body whose job it is, among other things, to ensure that certain standards are maintained. In the UK psychologists have the British Psychological Society (BPS), in the US there is the American Psychological Association (APA), in Canada the Canadian Psychological Association (CPA), and so on.

Psychologists, like other scientists, have other ways of dealing with ethical issues such as the use of ethics committees, the consideration of costs and benefits and punishment.

DEALING WITH ETHICAL ISSUES

Ethical guidelines

The BPS regularly updates its **ethical guidelines**. The current version is the 'Code of Ethics and Conduct' (BPS, 2006), see right. The intention of such guidelines is to tell psychologists what behaviours are not acceptable and give guidance on how to deal with ethical dilemmas.

This 'rules and sanctions' approach is inevitably rather general because of the virtual impossibility of covering every conceivable situation that a researcher may encounter. The Canadians take a slightly different approach – they present a series of hypothetical dilemmas and invite psychologists to discuss these. The strength of this approach is that it encourages discussion, whereas the BPS and APA approach tends to close off discussions about what is right and wrong because the answers are provided. Guidelines also absolve the individual researcher of any responsibility because the researcher can simply say, 'I followed the guidelines so my research is acceptable'.

Ethics committees

All institutions where research takes place have an **ethics committee**, and the committee must approve any study before it begins. It looks at all possible ethical issues raised in any research proposal and at how the researcher suggests that the issues will be dealt with, weighing up the *benefits* of the research against the possible costs to the participants. In some cases the cost-benefit balance is seen to be reasonable, in other cases it is decided that the costs are simply too great, or the research simply not of sufficient value.

Cost-benefit analysis

The problem with cost-benefit decisions is that it is difficult, if not impossible, to predict both costs and benefits *prior* to conducting a study. In fact it is difficult to assess them even *after* conducting a study. How are costs and benefits quantified? How much does personal distress cost?

If we judge the costs and benefits from a participant's point of view, we might list distress and loss of time versus payment for participation and a feeling of having contributed to scientific research. If we judge costs and benefits in terms of society at large, we can consider the value in improving people's lives versus the possibility that individuals may be less trusting in future. You could also judge costs/benefits in terms of the *group* to which an individual belongs – when research is done to investigate cultural differences, the research may not harm the individual but the findings may lead to biased treatment of the individual's cultural group (for good or bad).

Diana Baumrind (1959) argued that the cost-benefit approach solves nothing because you simply exchange one set of dilemmas (the ethical issues) for another. Baumrind also argued that the cost-benefit approach could be said to legitimise unethical practices. For example it suggests that deception and harm *are* acceptable in many situations *provided* the benefits are high enough.

Punishment

If a psychologist does behave in an unethical manner, such as conducting unacceptable research, then the BPS reviews the research and may decide to bar the person from practising as a psychologist. It is not a legal matter (the psychologist won't be sent to prison) but it could affect the psychologist's livelihood.

Issues versus guidelines

Issues are not the same as guidelines even though informed consent is both an issue and a guideline. An issue is a conflict; a guideline is a means of resolving this conflict.

Note that debriefing is not an issue, it is a way of dealing with ethical issues such as deception, psychological harm and lack of informed consent.

Some examples of the BPS code of ethics

On deception

Psychologists should supply information as fully as possible. The central principle is the reaction of participants when deception is revealed; if this leads to discomfort, anger or objections from participants then the deception is inappropriate.

On informed consent

Whenever possible, an investigator should inform all participants of the objectives of an investigation, and of all aspects of the research or intervention that might reasonably be expected to influence their willingness to participate. Failure to make full disclosure prior to obtaining informed consent requires additional safeguards to protect the welfare and dignity of the participants.

Children

Research with children (under age 16), or with participants who have impairments that limit understanding and/or communication, to the extent that they are unable to give their consent requires special safe-guarding procedures.

On protection from harm

Investigators have a primary responsibility to protect participants from physical and mental harm during an investigation. Normally the risk of harm must be no greater than in ordinary life i.e. participants should not be exposed to risks greater than, or additional to, those encountered in their normal lives.

If harm, unusual discomfort, or other negative consequences for the individual's future life might occur, the investigator must obtain the disinterested approval of independent advisors, inform the participants, and obtain real, informed consent from each of them.

WWW Read the BPS guidelines in full at www.bps.org.uk/the-society/ethics-rules-charter-code-of-conduct/code-of-conduct/ethical-principles-for-conducting-research-with-human-participants.cfm

Dealing with ethical issues

Ethical issue	How to deal with it	Limitations
Informed consent	Participants are asked to formally indicate their agreement to participate and this should be based on comprehensive information concerning the nature and purpose of the research and their role in it. An alternative is to gain *presumptive consent* (see right). Researchers can also offer the right to withdraw.	If a participant is given information concerning the nature and purpose of a study this may invalidate the purpose of the study. Even if researchers have sought and obtained informed consent, that does not guarantee that participants really do understand what they have let themselves in for. The problem with presumptive consent is that what people expect that they will or will not mind can be different from actually experiencing it. (Consider Milgram's study, Chapter 5).
Deception	The need for deception should be approved by an *ethics committee*, weighing up benefits (of the study) against costs (to participants). Participants should be fully *debriefed* after the study and offered the opportunity to withhold their data.	Cost-benefit decisions are flawed because they involve subjective judgements, and the costs are not always apparent until after the study. Debriefing can't turn the clock back – a participant may still feel embarrassed or have lowered self-esteem.
The right to withdraw	Participants should be informed at the beginning of a study that they have the right to withdraw.	Participants may feel they shouldn't withdraw because it will spoil the study. In many studies participants are paid or rewarded in some way (e.g. university students may be given course credits), so they may not feel able to withdraw.
Protection from harm	Avoid any risks greater than everyday life. Stop the study.	Researchers are not always able to accurately predict the risks of taking part in a study.
Confidentiality	Researchers should not record the names of any participants; they should use numbers or false names.	It is sometimes possible to work out who the participants were on the basis of the information that has been provided, for example the geographical location of a school. In practice, therefore, confidentiality may not be possible.
Privacy	Do not observe anyone without their informed consent unless it is in a public place. Participants may be asked to give their retrospective consent or withhold their data.	There is no universal agreement about what constitutes a public place. Not everyone may feel this is acceptable, for example lovers on a park bench.

Debriefing

One way to deal with deception is to debrief participants after the research has taken place, and inform them of the true nature of the study. Participants should be offered the opportunity to discuss any concerns they may have and to withdraw their data from the study – so it is as if they never took part.

A researcher may also use this opportunity to ask participants for further information, for example asking why a participant behaved as they did, or asking if they guessed what the study was about.

Presumptive consent

An alternative to gaining informed consent from participants is to gain informed consent from others (**presumptive consent**). This can be done, for example, by asking a group of people whether they feel a planned study is acceptable. We then *presume* that the participants themselves would have felt the same, if they had been given the opportunity to say so.

DO IT YOURSELF

Set up an ethics committee

No.**3.2**

Divide your class into groups. Each group should devise a study that raises one of the ethical issues described on this spread. Don't think up wild ideas, just something that would make an ethics committee have to think about whether or not such a study would be acceptable. You might look through this book for ideas.

The group should write a research proposal for the study (as all researchers have to do). This proposal should contain an outline of the research aims and the procedure to be followed. It must also identify any ethical issues and how they will be dealt with.

Then present your proposal to an ethics committee. This committee should be composed of people who represent the different interests such as the university authorities, psychology department and participants, all role-played by members of your class.

RESEARCH METHODS Qs　No.**3.3**

Re-examine the studies on page 71, and consider again how you would *deal* with the ethical issues raised.

KEY TERMS

Ethics committee (also called institutional review board, IRB) A group of people within a research institution that must approve a study before it begins.

Ethical guidelines Concrete, quasi-legal documents that help to guide conduct within psychology by establishing principles for standard practice and competence.

Presumptive consent A method of dealing with lack of informed consent or deception, by asking a group of people who are similar to the participants whether they would agree to take part in a study. If this group of people consents to the procedures in the proposed study, it is presumed that the real participants would also have agreed.

It is often claimed that some early studies in psychology (such as Milgram's study discussed in Chapter 5) were able to be carried out because there were no ethical guidelines. In fact the APA produced its first set of ethical guidelines in 1953, including quite detailed advice on informed consent.

Experiments and hypotheses

In the Introduction we gave you an opportunity to conduct your own experiment. An experiment is a way of conducting research in which:

- One variable is made to change (by the experimenter). This is called the *independent variable* or *IV*.
- The effects of the IV on another variable are observed or measured. This is called the *dependent variable* or *DV*.

The first step in conducting any study (an experiment or an observational study or a questionnaire) is to decide on research aims. For example: 'Is revision more effective when it is done in short bursts?'

The next step is to develop a hypothesis to focus on one specific expectation.

HYPOTHESES

A **hypothesis** states what you believe to be true. It is a precise and testable statement of the relationship between two variables. Note that it is a statement and not a question.

A possible hypothesis for the research on memory could be:

'People remember more when they study in short bursts.'

There are several problems with this hypothesis, as we will see.

Levels of the IV

The independent variable (IV) is 'study in short bursts'. In order to conduct an experiment we need to compare this condition with another condition – studying in short bursts versus studying for longer sessions. These two conditions are different levels of the IV. A good study and good hypothesis should always include two (or more) levels of the IV or a condition where the IV is absent. If we don't have these different conditions or levels, we have no basis for comparison. So the hypothesis should be:

'People remember more when they study in short bursts than when studying for longer sessions.'

Operationalisation

A further problem is that a good hypothesis must be written in a testable form i.e. a way that makes clear the specific way the experiment tests the hypothesis. In particular we need to *operationalise* the *IV* and *DV*. Consider our hypothesis: 'People *remember more* when they study in *short bursts* than when studying for *longer sessions*'. What do we mean by 'remember more' and 'short bursts' and 'longer sessions'? In order to test this hypothesis we need to specify a set of behaviours or *operations* that can be measured or manipulated for the IV and DV.

Operationalising two levels of the IV

'Short bursts' of study can be operationalised as 10-minute study sessions repeated three times over a period of three hours. 'Longer sessions' can be operationalised as one 30-minute session.

Operationalising the DV

'Remember more' can be operationalised by deciding how to assess recall – we could do this by giving students a chapter of a book to revise and giving them a set of questions to see how many questions they get right.

So the final fully operationalised hypothesis should be:

'People get more questions right on a test of recall when they study in short bursts (ten minutes at a time repeated three times) than when studying for longer sessions (one 30-minute session).'

You actually know all about experiments – you conduct them without thinking. For example, when you start a new class with a new teacher you see how he or she responds to your behaviour – you might make a joke or hand your homework in on time (both IVs) to see if the teacher responds well (the DV). You are experimenting with cause and effect.

However – don't make the mistake of calling every research study an experiment – it has to have an IV and DV to be an experiment – there are many non-experimental methods such as observations and questionnaires.

RESEARCH METHODS Qs — No.3.4

Study A *In order to study the effects of sleep deprivation, students are asked to limit their sleep to five hours a night for three nights and then sleep normally for the next three nights. Each day the students' cognitive abilities are assessed using a memory test.*

Study B *Participants volunteer to take part in a study. They are told the study is about public speaking but the real aim is to see how people respond to encouragement by others. Some participants speak in front of a group of people who smile at them, while others talk to a group who appear disinterested.*

Study C *Marathon runners are assessed on how much sleep they have the night before and the night after a race to see what the effects of exercise are on sleep.*

Study D *A teacher is doing a psychology course and decides to try a little experiment with her class of eight-year-olds. She gives half the class a test in the morning, and half of them do the same test in the afternoon to see if time of day affects performance.*

For each study, answer the following questions:

1. Identify the IV and DV (including both levels of the IV).
2. How could you operationalise the IV and DV?
3. Identify **one** possible extraneous variable.
4. In what way is this study high or low in validity?
5. Identify at least **two** possible ethical issues.
6. Describe how you would deal with each ethical issue.
7. Describe **one** limitation for each of your methods of dealing with the ethical issues.

Ivy Deevy

Many students find it difficult to remember which is the IV and which is the DV – think of the silly woman.

The thing that comes first (Ivy) is the IV which leads to a change in the DV.

Directional and non-directional hypotheses

The hypothesis on the far left is a **directional hypothesis** – it states the expected *direction* of your results, i.e. you are expecting that people will remember *more* when studying in short bursts. If you changed the hypothesis to *'people remember less when they study in short bursts than longer sessions'* this is still a directional hypothesis – you are then stating that the results are expected to go in the opposite direction.

A **non-directional hypothesis** predicts that there will be a difference between two conditions or two groups of participants: *'Recall is different when studying in short bursts than in longer bursts'*. This time we have not stated whether the difference will be more or less, just different.

Directional	People who do homework without the TV on, produce *better* results than those who do homework with the TV on.
Non-directional	People who do homework with the TV on, produce *different* results than those who do homework with no TV on.

(Note that, for clarity, the IV and DV haven't been operationalised in the above examples.)

Which should you use?

Why do psychologists sometimes use a directional hypothesis instead of a non-directional one (or *vice versa*)? Psychologists use a directional hypothesis when past research (a theory or a study) suggests that the findings will go in a particular direction. Psychologists use a non-directional hypothesis when there is no past research or past research is contradictory.

A FEW OTHER THINGS

Pilot studies

If you have tried any of the experiments in this book you were probably aware that there were flaws in your design. Did you realise that there would be flaws beforehand? Or did some of the flaws become apparent after conducting the experiment?

Scientists deal with this problem by conducting a **pilot study** first. A pilot study is a small-scale trial run of a research design before doing the real thing. It is done in order to find out if certain things don't work. For example, participants may not understand the instructions or they may guess what an experiment is about. They may also get bored because there are too many tasks or too many questions. If you try out the design using a few typical participants you can see what needs to be adjusted without having invested a large amount of time and money.

Confederates

Sometimes a researcher has to use another person to play a role in an experiment or other investigation. For example, you might want to find out if people respond differently to orders from someone wearing a suit compared with someone dressed in casual clothes. In this experiment the IV would be the clothing worn by someone briefed to behave in a certain way by the experimenter. The experimenter would arrange for this person to give orders either dressed in a suit or dressed casually. This person is called a **confederate**.

1. For each of the following, decide whether it is a directional or non-directional hypothesis.
   a. Boys score differently on aggressiveness tests than girls.
   b. Students who have a computer at home do better in exams than those who don't.
   c. People remember the words that are early in a list better than the words that appear later.
   d. People given a list of emotionally-charged words recall fewer words than participants given a list of emotionally-neutral words.
   e. Hamsters are better pets than budgies.
   f. Words presented in a written form are recalled differently from those presented in a pictorial form.

2. Now write your own. Below are listed research aims for possible experiments. For each one identify and operationalise the IV and DV and then write two hypotheses: a directional one and a non-directional one.
   a. Do girls watch more television than boys?
   b. Do teachers give more attractive students higher marks on essays than students who are less attractive?
   c. Does lack of sleep affect schoolwork?
   d. A researcher believes older people sleep more than younger people.
   e. Do people rate food as looking more attractive when they are hungry?
   f. A teacher wishes to find out whether one maths test is harder than another maths test.

3. Select one of the experiments from question 2. Explain *why* you would conduct a pilot study for this experiment and describe *how* you would do it. (You are not required to explain *what* a pilot study is – make sure you answer the specific questions of 'why' and 'how'.)

Try designing your own study to investigate the research aim on the far left (studying in short bursts or longer sessions).

- Decide on your *IV* (and the different conditions), and the *DV* and how it will be measured (operationalised).

- Identify any *extraneous variables* that should be controlled.

- How many participants will you need? Will everyone take part in both conditions, or will you have two groups of participants?

- Conduct a pilot study to check your design. Are there any changes you would make to the final design?

▼ The woman on the left (a confederate) talks 'blirtatiously' (loudly and effusively) to see what effect this has on the person who is studying.

KEY TERMS

Directional hypothesis states the direction of the predicted difference between two conditions or two groups of participants.

Non-directional hypothesis predicts simply that there will be a difference between two conditions or two groups of participants, without stating the direction of the difference.

Pilot study A small-scale trial run of a study to test any aspects of the design, with a view to making improvements.

Confederate An individual in a study who is not a real participant and has been instructed how to behave by the investigator/experimenter. May act as the independent variable.

Experimental design

On this spread we are going to find out a little more about experiments. We are going to look at **experimental design**.

Baddeley's experiment (outlined on page 7 and described in more detail below) used an **independent groups** design.

- Each participant was tested in only one condition.
- There were four separate (independent) groups of participants (groups A, B, C, D).

We could redesign this as a **repeated groups design**.

- Each participant would then be tested on all four conditions: lists A, B, C and D.

BADDELEY'S STUDY OF STM CAPACITY

Baddeley's (1966a) study is an *experiment*. As you know, an experiment is a particular kind of study where there is an *independent variable (IV)* and a *dependent variable (DV)*. In Baddeley's experiment the IV was the kind of list (acoustic or semantic, similar or dissimilar) and the DV was recall – how many sequences a participant recalled correctly.

The experiment involved procedures similar to the following:

1 There were four groups of participants: A, B, C, D. Each group was given one of the lists below.
2 Group A heard 12 sets of five words drawn from List A. For example one set might be: cab, can, mad, man, max, another set might be: mat, map, cap, cad, cab. The words were read out at a rate of one per second.
3 After each set of five words the participants were asked to recall the five words in the correct order. The participants had a card with all the ten words from the list; it was the order of recall that mattered.
4 Group B did the same with list B and so on.

List A acoustically similar	cat, cab, can, cad, cap, mad, max, mat, man, map
List B acoustically dissimilar	pit, few, cow, pen, sup, bar, day, hot, rig, bun
List C semantically similar	great, large, big, huge, broad, long, tall, fat, wide, high
List D semantically dissimilar	good, huge, hot, safe, thin, deep, strong, foul, old, late

Analysing the results

A score was calculated for each participant on the condition that they took part in. Their score was the number of sets they had remembered in the correct order, so the maximum score would be 12 for each participant.

Extraneous variable

Poor hearing could be an extraneous variable that might affect the dependent variable (recall) and potentially confound the findings. Baddeley did give participants a hearing test.

DO IT YOURSELF
No.**3.4**

Conduct your own study of encoding in STM following Baddeley's design, but this time using **repeated measures**. You can do this in class as long as you promise not to spoil it by letting what you know affect your behaviour!

- Produce 12 sets of five words for each of the four word lists A, B, C, D.
- You will need a master copy of each list to aid participants when recalling word sets, which is given to participants.
- List A: One person should read each of the 12 sets to the class, one at a time. After each set, give the participants time to write down the five words in the correct order on an answer sheet.
- Repeat the same for lists B, C and D.
- After going through all four lists (48 sets), each participant should work out their total score for each list. They get one point for each set where the five words were recalled in the correct order. Each participant should have four scores – one each for lists A, B, C and D.
- Combine the results from the whole class. Using your knowledge of graphs, work out a way to present the results.

1 What did you find?

2 What problems did you encounter?

3 How could you use counterbalancing (see facing page) to improve the design of this study?

4 What do you *conclude* from this study?

EXAM TIP *A conclusion is an interpretation of the results – an attempt to generalise from the particular research study to wider issues. In this case, making a statement about short-term memory generally, rather than a statement about the participants in the study.*

RESEARCH METHODS Qs
No.**3.6**

1 Consider your study on noise and memory. Did this use repeated measures or independent groups?
2 Consider Baddeley's experiment. What are the advantages of doing this as an independent groups design? What are the advantages of doing it as a repeated measures design?
3 If you were doing the noise and memory experiment as a repeated measures design, explain how you would use counterbalancing to overcome order effects.

For each of the following experiments, state whether it is repeated measures, independent groups or **matched pairs** design. When trying to decide, it might help you if you ask yourself 'Would the findings be analysed by comparing the scores from the same person or by comparing the scores of two (or more) groups of people'? If it is two or more groups of people, then are the people in the different groups related (i.e. matched) or not?

4 Boys and girls are compared on their IQ test scores.
5 Hamsters are tested to see if one genetic strain is better at finding food in a maze than another.
6 Reaction time is tested before and after a reaction time training activity to see if test scores improve after training.
7 Students are put in pairs based on their GCSE grades, and then one member of the pair is given a memory test in the morning and one in the afternoon.
8 Three groups of participants are given different word lists to remember, in order to find out whether nouns, verbs or adjectives are easier to recall.
9 Participants are asked to give ratings for attractive and unattractive photographs.

Comparing experimental designs

Weaknesses	Ways of dealing with the weaknesses
Repeated measures design	
In an experiment one condition may be more difficult than another. For example, if you wanted to see whether people remembered more in the morning or afternoon, you could give participants a memory test in the morning and a different test in the afternoon. However, it might be that participants did better in the morning because the test was easier than the test in the afternoon. In this case changes in the DV would be due to an extraneous variable (easier test) rather than the IV.	You can make sure the tests are equivalent. Create a list of 40 words and randomly allocate these to two lists so that both lists are equivalent.
When participants do the second memory test they may guess the purpose of the experiment, which may affect their behaviour. For example, some participants may purposely do worse on the second test because they want it to appear as if they work less well in the afternoon.	You can use a cover story about the purpose of the test to try to prevent them guessing what it is about (single blind).
The order of the conditions may affect performance (an order effect). Participants may do better on the second test because of a *practice effect* or because they are less anxious OR they may do worse on the second test because of being bored with doing the same test again (*boredom* or *fatigue* effect).	You can use counterbalancing (explained on the right).
Independent groups design	
No control of participant variables (i.e. the different abilities or characteristics of each participant). For example participants in Group 1 might happen to have better memories than those in group 2.	Randomly allocate participants to conditions which (theoretically) distributes participant variables evenly.
You need twice as many participants.	Be prepared to spend more time and money!
Matched pairs design	
Very time-consuming to match participants on key variables. You probably have to start with a large group of participants to ensure you can obtain matched pairs on key variables.	Restrict matching variables to make it easier.
May not control all participant variables because you can only match on variables known to be relevant, but it could be that others are important. For example, in a memory experiment you might match on memory abilities but later find that some of the participants had been involved in a teaching programme to boost memory skills and you should have matched on this.	Conduct a pilot study to consider key variables.

Matched pairs design

This is a third kind of experimental design. It involves the use of two different groups of participants; each participant in Group A is paired with one in Group B. This is done by pairing participants on key variables (e.g. IQ, memory ability, gender) and then placing one member of each pair in each group. It is important to realise that the characteristics for matching *must* be relevant to the study. In other words you wouldn't match participants on gender if you were testing memory – unless there was some evidence that women had better memories than men.

Counterbalancing

Counterbalancing ensures that each condition is tested first or second in equal amounts. If participants do the same memory test first in the morning and then in the afternoon, we might expect them to do better on the second test because they have had some practice – or they might do worse because they are bored with the task. These are called **order effects** which can be dealt with using counterbalancing.

There are two ways to counterbalance order effects. In each case, we have two conditions:

Condition A – test done in the morning
Condition B – test done in the afternoon

Way 1. AB or BA

Divide participants into two groups:

Group 1: each participant does A then B
Group 2: each participant does B then A

Note that this is still a repeated measures design even though there are two groups of participants, because comparison will be made for each participant on their performance on the two conditions (morning and afternoon).

Way 2. ABBA

This time, all participants take part in each condition twice.

Trial 1: Condition A (morning)
Trial 2: Condition B (afternoon)
Trial 3: Condition B (afternoon)
Trial 4: Condition A (morning)

Then we compare scores on trials 1+4 with trials 2+3. As before, this is still a repeated measures design because we are comparing the scores of the same person.

KEY TERMS

Counterbalancing An experimental technique used to overcome order effects. Counterbalancing ensures that each condition is tested first or second in equal amounts.

Experimental design A set of procedures used to control the influence of factors such as participant variables in an experiment.

Independent groups Participants are allocated to two (or more) groups representing different experimental conditions. Allocation is usually done using random techniques.

Matched pairs Pairs of participants are matched in terms of key variables such as age and IQ. One member of each pair is placed in the *experimental group* and the other member in the *control group*.

Order effect In a repeated measures design, an extraneous variable arising from the order in which conditions are presented, e.g. a practice effect or fatigue effect.

Random allocation Allocating participants to experimental groups or conditions using random techniques (see page 93).

Repeated measures Each participant takes part in every condition under test.

Single blind A type of research design in which the participant is not aware of the research aims or of which condition of the experiment they are receiving.

Extraneous variables

On page 68 we looked at the concept of validity, including the problem of extraneous variables (EVs). If EVs are not controlled they confound the results of a study because the change in the dependent variable (DV) may be due to the EV rather than the independent variable (IV). On this spread we are going to look at a number of different EVs. Any researcher worth his salt (including you) must understand and control EVs in order for a study to be valid.

Sometimes the term 'confounding variable' is used instead of extraneous variable – the terms have different meanings but at AS level it is considered acceptable for you to assume they are the same.

Participants may want to offer a helping hand. If they know they are in an experiment they usually want to please the experimenter and be helpful, otherwise why are they there? This sometimes results in them being over-cooperative – and behaving artificially. There is also the 'screw you' effect where a participant deliberately behaves in a way that spoils an experiment.

PARTICIPANT VARIABLES

A participant variable is any characteristic of individual participants. Participant variables act as extraneous variables only if an independent groups design is used. When a repeated measures design is used, participant variables are controlled.

Age, intelligence, motivation, experience

Participants in one condition may perform better because they have certain characteristics in common rather than because of the IV they receive. In the noise and memory experiment it might be that the members of one group of participants were younger (and thus had better memories), or that they were more intelligent, more highly motivated or more experienced at doing memory tests. These factors would act as EVs, making the results meaningless.

Gender

Males and females are psychologically different in many ways partly because of the way they are socialised. For example, research suggests that women are more compliant than men because they are more oriented to interpersonal goals (Eagly, 1978). This means that if there are more women than men in one condition of an experiment this might mask the effects of the IV. However, it is important to realise that gender only acts as an EV in some circumstances. For example, we would not control gender in a memory experiment unless we had a reason to expect that it would matter.

Irrelevant participant variables

When considering participant variables as EVs we need only focus on those that are relevant to the task. Therefore, in the noise and memory task, liking of spicy food would not be an EV (at least, it would be hard to see why it would be).

SITUATIONAL VARIABLES

Situational variables are those features of a research *situation* that may influence participants' behaviour and thus act as EVs.

Order effects

One example of a situational variable is order effects, which were described on page 77. Improved participant performance may be due to practice (an EV) rather than the IV.

Time of day, temperature, noise

When we considered 'control' earlier in this chapter (page 68) we used the example of doing a test in the morning or afternoon. Any environmental variable, such as time of day, temperature or even noise levels at the time of testing, may act as an EV but only if

- *It does affect performance on the behaviour tested* – e.g. if the task is cognitive, time of day may be significant because people are more alert in the morning, but if the task is concerned with obedience, time of day may not matter.
- *It varies systematically with the IV* e.g. participants in group 1 are all tested in the morning and those in group 2 are all tested in the afternoon. If some members of each group

PARTICIPANT EFFECTS (PARTICIPANT REACTIVITY)

Participant effects are different from participant variables. Participant effects may occur because participants actively seek cues about how to behave. An obvious difference between psychological research and other scientific research is that the object of study is animate rather than inanimate objects. The problem with such animate beings is that they may try to guess what they are supposed to be doing, (though sometimes participants are not aware they are being studied, in which case there isn't a problem). Participants can seek cues about how they should behave because they want to help, or because they are unsure about what is expected.

Another kind of participant effect is called the **Hawthorne effect**, named after a study conducted at the Hawthorne Electric factory in Chicago (see a description of the research study on page 83, study E). This describes the fact that participants' performance may change not because of the IV but merely because they are responding to the extra attention they are receiving as research participants.

Social desirability bias is another example of a participant effect. Participants sometimes wish to present themselves in the best possible way and therefore may not behave according to personal preference but in the way they consider most socially acceptable in this situation.

Dealing with participant effects

Researchers can use a *single blind design* where the participant doesn't know the true aims of the study. This prevents the participant from seeking cues about the aims and reacting to them. Another strategy is to make the experimental task sufficiently engaging so that the participant pays attention to the task and not the fact that they are being observed. This is called **experimental realism**.

▶ **Clever Hans** (Hans Von Osten) was a stallion owned by Wilhelm Von Osten. Hans demonstrated an astonishing ability with arithmetic. Someone would ask a simple arithmetic question, for example 'What's 7 times 4?', and they would then start counting aloud. When they reached 28 the horse would start stamping its hooves. However, rigorous testing showed that he was not adding, he was responding to subtle unconscious cues from his owner – Wilhelm was communicating expectations which acted as *demand characteristics*. The reason the horse did as expected was because of the cues, not his ability. Fulfilling expectations is the outcome of demand characteristics.

Investigator/ experimenter bias
This is the term used to describe the effects of an experimenter's expectations on a participant's behaviour. A classic demonstration of this was in the experiment by Rosenthal and Fode described on page 112, which showed that even rats are affected by an experimenter's expectations.

are tested in the morning, whereas the rest are tested in the afternoon, then time of day would not be an EV because it will not have a systematic effect on the DV.

Investigator effects

Investigator effects are any cues (other than the IV) from an investigator that encourage certain behaviours in the participant, leading to a fulfillment of the investigator's expectations. Such cues act as an EV.

The way in which an investigator asks a question may *lead* a participant to give the answer the investigator 'wants' (similar to leading questions, see page 16). Alternatively, the way the investigator responds to a participant may encourage some participants more than others. For example, research has found that males are more pleasant, friendly and encouraging with female participants than with other male participants (Rosenthal, 1966).

There are also indirect investigator effects, such as the *investigator experimental design effect*. The investigator may operationalise the measurement of variables in such a way that the desired result is more likely, or may limit the duration of the study for the same reason.

Demand characteristics

A **demand characteristic** is an aspect of the research situation which triggers a predictable response in participants, causing most, if not all of them, to respond in a similar way. Particular cues in an experimental situation may communicate to participants what is expected of them (or 'demanded' of them) and what the investigator hopes to find. Participants respond to demand characteristics because, as we have seen, they are actively searching for cues about how to behave. Demand characteristics may act as an alternative IV (confounding variable) because they explain the change in the DV. The outcome is that the results are biased in favour of the research hypothesis, confirming the researcher's initial beliefs.

Orne (1962), who coined the term 'demand characteristics', described them as 'the totality of cues which convey an experimental hypothesis to [a participant]'. Orne's study on tearing up paper was an example (see page 71) – he claimed that participants only do this because they are responding to the demand characteristics of the study. They would not do this in everyday life.

Dealing with situational variables

Some situational differences are controlled by good research design. One particular way to control situational variables such as experimenter bias is to use *standardised procedures* to ensure that all participants are tested under the same conditions. Standardised procedures include *standardised instructions* which are important in control investigator/experimenter effects. Another way to control experimenter effects is to use a **double blind** design where the experimenter cannot communicate cues about the research aims because he/she doesn't know them.

RESEARCH METHODS Qs No.**3.7**

1 How might investigator bias affect the results of a case study?

2 In each of the studies listed below give an example of a possible (i) participant variable, (ii) situational variable, (iii) example of participant reactivity, (iv) investigator effect and (v) demand characteristic. For each one, if you can, suggest how the problem might be dealt with.

a *In a study, participants' memory was tested in the morning and in the afternoon, to see if there was any difference in their ability to recall numbers.*

b *Participants were given a list of adjectives describing Mr Smith. One group had positive adjectives first, followed by negative adjectives. The other group had the adjectives in reverse order. They were all then asked to describe Mr Smith.*

KEY TERMS

Demand characteristics A cue that makes participants aware of what the researcher expects to find, or how participants are expected to behave. Demand characteristics can change the outcome of a study because participants will often change their behaviour to conform to the expectations.

Double blind Neither the participant nor the experimenter are aware of the research aims and other important details and thus have no expectations. In a single blind study only the participant is unaware.

Experimental realism The extent to which participants become involved in an experiment and become less influenced by cues about how to behave.

Hawthorne effect The tendency for participants to alter their behaviour merely as a result of knowing that they are being observed.

Investigator/experimenter bias The effect that an investigator/experimenter's expectations have on the participants and thus on the results of a research study.

Investigator effect Anything that the investigator/experimenter does which has an effect on a participant's performance in a study, other than what was intended. This includes direct effects (as a consequence of the investigator/experimenter interacting with the participant) and indirect effects (as a consequence of the investigator designing the study).

Social desirability bias A tendency for respondents to answer questions in a way that will present them in a better light.

Investigator versus experimenter
In many experiments the person who designs the experiment is not the same as the person who actually deals with the participants. To distinguish these roles we talk of investigators and experimenters.

The person who conducts the study has a direct effect on participants, whereas the person who designs the study has an indirect effect.

Quantitative data analysis

The information collected in any study is called 'data' or, more precisely a 'data set' (a set of items). Data are not necessarily numbers; they could be words used to describe how someone feels. Numerical data are described as **quantitative**, whereas data which are non-numerical are called **qualitative**. Once a researcher has collected data, it needs to be analysed in order to identify trends or to see the bigger picture. On this spread we will look at methods of **quantitative data analysis**. Qualitative data analysis is discussed on page 103.

These methods are sometimes referred to as 'descriptive statistics' because they are methods of describing quantitative data.

MEASURES OF CENTRAL TENDENCY

Measures of central tendency inform us about central (or middle) values for a set of data. They are 'averages' – ways of calculating a typical value for a set of data. An average can be calculated in different ways:

The **mean** is calculated by adding up all the numbers and dividing by the number of numbers.

- It makes use of the values of all the data.
- It can be misrepresentative of the data as a whole if there are extreme values.
- It cannot be used with nominal data (see below).

The **median** is the *middle* value in an *ordered* list.

- Not affected by extreme scores.
- Not as 'sensitive' as the mean because not all values are reflected in the median.

The **mode** is the value that is *most* common.

- Useful when the data are in categories i.e. nominal data.
- Not a useful way of describing data when there are several modes.

EXAM TIP *Many candidates find it hard to remember the link between 'measures of central tendency' and 'mean, median, mode'. One way to help you remember connections is to produce memorable pictures – the more outrageous the better!*

Nominal – *The data are in separate categories, such as grouping people according to their favourite football team (e.g. Liverpool, Inverness, Caledonian Thistle, etc.).*

Ordinal – *Data are ordered in some way, for example asking people to put a list of football teams in order of liking. Liverpool might be first, followed by Inverness and so on. The 'difference' between each item is not the same, i.e. the individual may like the first item a lot more than the second, but there might only be a small difference between the items ranked second and third.*

Interval – *Data are measured using units of equal intervals, such as when counting correct answers or using any 'public' unit of measurement. Many psychological studies use* plastic interval scales *where the intervals are arbitrarily determined, and we can't therefore know for certain that there are equal intervals between the numbers. However, for the purposes of analysis, such data may be accepted as interval.*

Ratio – *There is a true zero point as in most measures of physical quantities.*

NOIR – *an acronym to help remember the four levels of measurement of data:* nominal, ordinal, interval *and* ratio.

MEASURES OF DISPERSION

A set of data can also be described in terms of how dispersed or spread out the numbers are.

The easiest **measure of dispersion** to use is the **range**. Consider the data sets below:

3, 5, 8, 8, 9, 10, 12, 12, 13, 15   mean = 9.5   range = 12 (3 to 15)

1, 5, 8, 8, 9, 10, 12, 12, 13, 17   mean = 9.5   range = 16 (1 to 17)

The two sets of numbers have the same mean but a different range, so the range is helpful as a further method of describing the data. If we just used the mean, the data would appear to be the same. The range is the difference between the highest and lowest number.

There is a more precise method of expressing dispersion, called the **standard deviation**. This is a measure of the spread of the data around the mean. The standard deviations for the two sets of numbers above are 3.69 and 4.45 respectively. These can be calculated using a mathematical calculator.

	Advantages	Weaknesses
Range	**Provides you with direct information.** **Easy to calculate.**	**Affected by extreme values.** **Doesn't take into account the number of observations in the data set.**
Standard deviation	**More precise measure of dispersion because all values taken into account.**	**May hide some of the characteristics of the data set (e.g. extreme values).**

RESEARCH METHODS Qs   No.**3.8**

1 For each of the following sets of data (data sets)
   a calculate the mean,
   b calculate the median,
   c calculate the mode,
   d state which of the three measures of central tendency would be most suitable to use and why.

   Data set 1: **2, 3, 5, 6, 6, 8, 9, 12, 15, 21, 22**
   Data set 2: **2, 3, 8, 10, 11, 13, 13, 14, 14, 29**
   Data set 3: **2, 2, 4, 5, 5, 5, 7, 7, 8, 8, 8, 10**
   Data set 4: **cat, cat, dog, budgie, snake, gerbil**

2 Why is it better to know about the mean and range of a data set rather than just the mean?

3 Explain why it might be better to know the standard deviation of a data set rather than the range.

4 Look at the following data sets. Which one do you think would have the *smaller* standard deviation?

   Data set A: **2 2 3 4 5 9 11 14 18 20 21 22 25**
   Data set B: **2 5 8 9 9 10 11 12 14 15 16 20 25**

5 There are three graphs on the right.
   a What can you conclude from Graph C?
   b Write a title that would be suitable for all three graphs.
   c Describe the *y* axis of all three graphs.

A picture is worth 1000 words! Graphs provide a means of 'eyeballing' your data and seeing the findings at a glance.

- **Tables** The numbers you collect are referred to as 'raw data' – numbers that haven't been treated in any way. These data can be set out in a table or summarised using measures of central tendency and range.
- **Bar chart** The height of the bar represents frequency. Shows data in categories but also suitable for numbers.
- **Line graph** As with a bar chart, the *y* axis represents frequency but, in this case, the values along the *x* axis must be continuous i.e. data that have some implicit order such as numerical data but not categories of things such as favourite football teams.
- **Scattergram** A kind of graph used when doing a correlational analysis (see page 98).

Each of the graphs below presents the data collected in an experiment on memory and organisation (see 'DIY' on right). Only one of these graphs is useful, two of them are a waste of time – which is the useful one?

Graph A

Participant number 1 in the random word group is placed next to participant number 1 in the organised word group. Students like to draw 'participant charts', *but they are totally meaningless*.

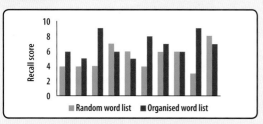

Graph B

The findings from each participant are shown in this graph. They are grouped together so that you can see all the scores from participants in the random word group and all the scores from the participants in the organised word group.

This is *slightly better* than Graph A because we can just about tell that the random word list led to better recall – but a glance at the means (as in Graph C) shows this effortlessly.

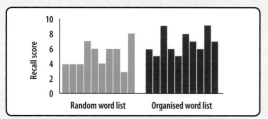

Graph C

This graph shows the mean scores for each group. The findings are immediately obvious, which is the point of using a graph.

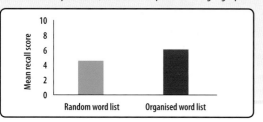

Memory and organisation

No.**3.6**

In the days when psychology students had to do coursework, this was a top choice. On page 23 we described a study by Bowers *et al.* (1969); this is an adaptation of that study. You can use the word lists below. The column of words on the left is organised in categories, whereas the column on the right shows the same words in random order.

Your task is to design a study using these words.

Dogs	Pear
Labrador	Beagle
Beagle	Clarinet
Boxer	Hail
Spaniel	Rain
Fruit	Drinks
Apple	Rose
Pear	Squash
Plum	Hand
Orange	Boxer
Weather	Iron
Snow	Coke
Rain	Gold
Sleet	Harp
Hail	Piano
Flowers	Metal
Daffodil	Apple
Rose	Body
Pansy	Fruit
Tulip	Instruments
Instruments	Daffodil
Harp	Plum
Piano	Nose
Flute	Weather
Clarinet	Copper
Drinks	Labrador
Water	Water
Milk	Flowers
Squash	Brass
Coke	Foot
Body	Tulip
Nose	Pansy
Foot	Dogs
Toe	Sleet
Hand	Milk
Metal	Orange
Brass	Toe
Gold	Snow
Copper	Flute
Iron	Spaniel

1 Write your own list of design decisions that need to be made, based on your experience of designing other studies. Ensure that you consider ethical issues carefully.

2 Write a fully operationalised hypothesis.

3 Conduct a pilot study to check your design and make any alterations to the design that are necessary.

4 Now collect your data (or, if this is not possible, invent a set of data).

5 Present the data you have collected in a
- Table – show raw data, and *appropriate* measures of central tendency and dispersion.
- Graph – draw an *appropriate* bar chart.

6 What conclusions would you draw from your study?

A graph should be simple. It should clearly show the findings from a study.

There should be a short but informative title.

The x axis must be labelled (x axis goes across the page, it's usually the IV).

The y axis is usually the DV or 'frequency' (y axis goes up vertically).

Always use squared paper if you are hand-drawing graphs.

KEY TERMS

Mean The arithmetic average of a group of scores. Takes the values of all the data into account.

Measure of central tendency A descriptive statistic that provides information about a 'typical' response for a data set.

Measure of dispersion A descriptive statistic that provides information about how spread-out a set of scores is.

Median The middle value in a set of scores when the scores are placed in rank order.

Mode The most frequently occurring score in a data set.

Qualitative Data that expresses the 'quality' of things – descriptions, words, meanings, pictures, texts and so on. Qualitative data cannot be counted or quantified but they can be turned into quantitative data by placing them in categories.

Quantitative Data that represent how much or how long, or how many, etc. there are of something; i.e. a behaviour is measured in numbers or quantities.

Quantitative data analysis Any means of representing trends from numerical data, such as measures of central tendency.

Range The difference between the highest and lowest score in a data set.

Standard deviation shows the amount of variation in a data set. It assesses the spread of data around the mean.

Laboratory and field experiments

On page 74 we considered experiments. There are different kinds of experiments. We will start by looking at two kinds: laboratory (lab) experiments and field experiments. All experiments have one thing in common, they all have an independent variable and a dependent variable.

Laboratory experiment – An experiment conducted in a *special environment* where variables can be *carefully controlled*. Participants are *aware* that they are taking part in an experiment, though they may not know the true aims of the study.

Field experiment – An experiment conducted in a more *natural environment*, i.e. in 'the field' (as distinct from 'a field' – 'the field' is anywhere outside a laboratory). As with the laboratory experiment, the IV is still *deliberately manipulated* by the researcher. Participants are *often not aware* that they are participating in an experiment.

*An experiment permits us to study **cause and effect**. It differs from non-experimental methods in that it involves the manipulation of one variable (the independent variable – IV), while trying to keep all other variables constant. If the IV is the only thing that is changed then it must be responsible for any change in the dependent variable (DV).*

Note that it is possible to do research in a laboratory which is not an experiment. For example, controlled observations are conducted in a laboratory (we will look at these on page 86).

*Note also that there are field studies as well as field experiments. Any study which is conducted in a natural environment is called a **field study** – it is only a field experiment if there is an IV that has been manipulated by an experimenter.*

EVALUATING LAB AND FIELD EXPERIMENTS

Lab experiments are 'contrived'

- Participants know they are being studied and this is likely to affect their behaviour.
- The setting is not like everyday life. This is described as being low in mundane realism. People behave more like they 'normally' do when a study is high in mundane realism.
- The IV or DV may be operationalised in such a way that it doesn't represent everyday experiences e.g. using consonant syllables to test how memory works. This may, of course, happen in field experiments as well.

For all these reasons participants in a lab experiment are less likely to behave as they would in everyday life.

Many of the problems outlined above for lab experiments may also arise in field experiments, for example the IV in a field experiment may lack realism. Therefore field experiments are not *necessarily* more like everyday life than lab experiments.

Field experiments have less control

Field experiments may be more natural but it is more difficult to control extraneous variables.

There is also a major ethical issue – if participants don't know they are being studied and it is difficult to debrief them, is it right to manipulate and record their behaviour?

Balancing act

Lab experiments tend to make control easier but also tend to be less natural especially because participants are aware they are being studied.

Field experiments tend to be more natural and more representative of everyday life but this means less control and greater ethical problems.

Paying homage to formal terms*

As we have already said, learning about research methods is a bit like learning a foreign language. You have to learn to use a whole new vocabulary and you have to learn the meaning of this vocabulary. The problem with the vocabulary is that people often focus too much on the words and fail to really grasp the underlying meaning. This is the case with the terms 'field' and 'lab' experiment. It isn't always easy to decide whether a study is one or the other. What matters more are the underlying issues of validity and ethics. So don't get too hung up on the terms – focus on the meaning.

An excellent phrase 'invented' by Hugh Coolican (2004) to explain this problem.

KEY TERMS

Field experiment A controlled experiment conducted outside a laboratory. The IV is still manipulated by the experimenter, and therefore causal relationships can be demonstrated. Field experiments tend to have lower internal validity (more difficult to control EVs) and higher external validity (greater mundane realism). Participants are usually unaware that they are participating in an experiment, thus reducing participant effects.

Laboratory experiment An experiment carried out in a controlled setting. Lab experiments tend to have high internal validity and low external validity, though this isn't always the case.

Field or lab experiment?

Sometimes it isn't very easy to work out whether a study is a lab or field experiment.

On page 18 we described the weapons effect study by Loftus *et al.* (1987). The study might seem, on the surface, to be a lab experiment: it was conducted under controlled conditions in a room unfamiliar to the participants. But the actual behaviour that was being measured (the participants' ability to identify the man running through the room) reflected natural behaviour. The participants were not aware that it was this behaviour that was being studied and therefore were not primed to respond to participant effects or relevant demand characteristics.

Is this a lab or a field experiment? What do you think? How would you rate its internal and external validity?

LAB VERSUS FIELD EXPERIMENTS

It may help you to understand the difference between lab and field experiments to look at the examples below and answer the questions on the right.

Study A

Bickman (1974) tested the effects of perceived authority on obedience. Confederates dressed in a sports jacket and tie, a milkman's uniform, or as a guard, and made requests to passers-by, for example, asking them to pick up some litter or to give some one money for a parking meter. Participants obeyed most when the confederate was dressed as a guard. This study shows what most of us know – we are more likely to obey someone who looks like they have authority than someone who does not.

Study B

Participants were asked to wait in a room before an experiment began. There was a radio playing either good or bad news and a stranger was present. When they were asked to rate the stranger, the degree of liking was related to the kind of news they had been listening to, showing that people like others who are associated with positive experiences (Veitch and Griffitt, 1976).

Study C

The participants were children aged from three to five years. Each child was taken on its own to an experimental room where there were lots of toys including, in one corner, a 5-foot inflatable Bobo doll and a mallet. The experimenter invited the 'model' (another adult) to join them and then left the room for about 10 minutes. Half of the children watched the model playing aggressively with the Bobo doll while the others watched the model play non-aggressively with the doll. Later they were given an opportunity to play with toys including the Bobo doll and were observed through a one-way mirror. The children who saw the aggressive behaviour were more likely to behave aggressively (Bandura et al., 1961).

Study D

One group of school pupils were given information about how their peers had performed on a maths task. They were either told that their peers had done well or done poorly on the test. The children were later given a maths test in class. Those who expected to do well did better than those led to expect to do poorly (Schunk, 1983).

Study E

Researchers were asked to study what factors led to increased worker productivity at the Hawthorne Electrical factory. The study found that increased lighting led to increased productivity – but then also found that *decreased* lighting led to increased activity (Roethlisberger and Dickson, 1939). The researchers finally realised that the persistent increase in productivity was not related to lighting conditions at all (the IV) but because the workers were responding positively to the attention they were receiving and this was enhancing their performance.

Study F

Participants were tested in their teaching room and given nonsense trigrams (e.g. SXT) and then asked to count backwards until told to stop. Then participants were asked to recall the trigram. The counting interval was used to prevent - trigram being rehearsed. When the counting interval was three seconds, participants could recall most trigrams; when it was 18 seconds they couldn't recall many trigrams (Peterson and Peterson, 1959).

RESEARCH METHODS Qs — No.3.9

Answer the questions below for the experiments A–F described on the left.

1. Identify the IV and DV.
2. Was the task required of participants contrived?
3. Was the study conducted in a natural setting?
4. Was the setting high or low in mundane realism?
5. Did the participants know they were being studied?
6. Were the participants brought into a special situation, or did the experimenter go to them?
7. What relevant variables might not have been controlled?
8. Do you think this was a lab or field experiment?

Discuss: What is the point of distinguishing between laboratory and field experiments?

DO IT YOURSELF — No.3.7

You can try to replicate the weapon-focus study by Loftus *et al.* (1987, see page 18). Field experiments raise important ethical issues, so it will only be possible to conduct this study using other students in your school or college, and they must be aged over 16.

You will need to conduct the study with independent groups – one group will see a *confederate* (someone who is not known to the group) come into the room either (a) holding nothing or (b) holding something very unusual (but not a weapon!).

Both groups of participants will need to be engaged in a task which is interrupted by the entry of the confederate. You could arrange for the groups to be doing the memory and organisation study on page 81.

1. Consider the design questions in question 8 below (in Research Methods Qs 3.10).
2. Approach a member of staff and ask if you can conduct a psychology experiment in two of their classes. Give them the full details of what you intend to do.

RESEARCH METHODS Qs — No.3.10

You can answer these questions whether or not you actually conduct the study above.

1. Identify the conditions of the IV.
2. How would you operationalise the DV?
3. Are there any extraneous variables that should be controlled?
4. Write a suitable directional hypothesis.
5. Why should the same person act as the stranger in both conditions?
6. What was the experimental design?
7. Can you think of **two** ethical issues raised in this study (i.e. something that may harm participants) and say how you can deal with them.
8. Invent a set of data that might be collected from this experiment and display this in a table and a graph. (This is useful to do before conducting the study , with some dummy data, because it helps you understand the design and may lead you to make some changes).

Natural experiments

There is a third kind of experiment, called a **natural experiment**. In a natural experiment, the environment is natural as in a field experiment, but the change in the IV is also 'natural'. The experimenter makes use of a naturally varying IV instead of deliberately manipulating it, which is what happens in a field experiment. The reason for this is that there are some IVs that cannot be manipulated directly for practical or ethical reasons. For example, when studying the effects of privation (discussed in Chapter 2), you couldn't deliberately take some people away from their families. In a natural experiment the effects of the IV on the DV are observed by the experimenter, just as in field and lab experiments, but it is possible that some extraneous variables are not controlled. For example, in a study comparing children who have experienced privation with those who haven't, it might be that many of the children who experienced privation also came from families who were less wealthy.

Strictly speaking an experiment involves the deliberate manipulation of an IV by an experimenter, therefore natural experiments are not 'true experiments' because no one has *deliberately* changed the IV to observe the effect this has on the DV. Such experiments are sometimes called **quasi-experiments** instead.

RESEARCH METHODS Qs   No.**3.11**

1 Answer the following questions for the four studies described on the right.
   a Identify the IV and DV.
   b How was the IV manipulated?
   c Identify at least **two** threats to internal validity.
   d What were the aims of this study?
   e Write a suitable hypothesis for this experiment.
   f What was the experimental design?
   g Explain why this is a natural experiment.

2 The study by Schellenberg (below) is not a natural experiment. What kind of experiment is it? Explain the reasons for your answer.

EXAMPLES OF NATURAL EXPERIMENTS

On page 18 a study by Christianson and Hubinette (1993) is described, which investigated the effects of anxiety on eyewitness recall. This is a natural experiment. In Chapter 2 there is another natural experiment by Hodges and Tizard (1989), see page 50.

The influence of TV on aggressive behaviour

A recent study was conducted in St. Helena, to see whether the introduction of television would produce an increase in anti-social behaviour (Charlton et al., 2000). The residents of this tiny island (47 square miles) received television for the first time in 1995. The vast majority of the measures used to assess pro- and anti-social behaviour showed no differences in either after the introduction of television. This finding is in contrast with an earlier natural experiment by Williams (1986) in a Canadian town where TV was introduced for the first time. In this study anti-social behaviour was found to increase.

DO IT YOURSELF   No.**3.8**

You may of course think of your own natural experiment, but here is one you could try.

Music lessons can boost IQ

A recent study looked at the effects of music lessons on IQ (Schellenberg, 2004). The participants (aged six years) had their IQs tested before the study began. They were allocated to one of four groups: two groups had 36 weeks of extra-curricular music tuition (one had singing-based tuition, the other studied keyboard). A third group had extra drama lessons on top of normal school, and the last, baseline group, simply attended school as usual. The children completed IQ and other tests at the end of each school year. Schellenberg found that the IQ performance of the two music groups increased significantly more than that of the drama and baseline groups.

You can conduct similar research making use of existing data – the fact that some people have had music lessons and others haven't. Thus you will be conducting a natural experiment.

IV Divide your class into those who have received extra music lessons and those who have not. You must operationalise this IV – i.e. decide what constitutes 'having music lessons'. Would one week of lessons count, or one year?

DV For each member of your class calculate a GCSE score as a rough measure of IQ. One way to do this is to assign a value to each grade, add all scores together and divide by the number of GCSE subjects. This gives you a final score for each student. You can use the table below to record your raw data.

Ethics Individuals may record their data anonymously.

Analysis Calculate a mean GCSE score for the group of pupils who have had music lessons and compare this to the mean GCSE score for the group who haven't had music lessons. Draw a graph to illustrate this data. What can you conclude?

| Participant | GCSE SCORES Grade A*=9, A=8, B=7, C=6, D=5, E=4, F=3, G=2, U=1, X=0 |||||||||||||||||||| Total score (add white column numbers) | Final score (total score/ number of scores) | Music lessons (Y/N) |
	Grade	Score	Grade	Score	Grade	Score	Grade	Score	Grade	Score	Grade	Score	Grade	Score	Grade	Score	Grade	Score	Grade	Score			
1																							
2																							
etc.																							

GENERALISABILITY OF NATURAL EXPERIMENTS

Drawing valid conclusions from natural experiments is problematic because:

- Participants are not randomly allocated to conditions and this means that there may be biases in the different groups of participants. For example, in the study on music and IQ (below left) there may have been other factors that differentiated between the music lesson and non-music lesson group (e.g. the music lesson group came from families with more money or who were better motivated generally). These factors would act as an extraneous variable.
- The sample studied may have unique characteristics. For example, in the St. Helena study the people were part of a pro-social community which means that the findings can't be generalised to other cultures.

DIFFERENCE STUDIES

Some people consider that studies of gender differences are natural experiments. An example of a study of gender differences would be comparing whether boys or girls have higher IQs. It might be claimed that gender is the IV and IQ score is the DV.

However the variable 'gender' has not been manipulated (or changed). It is a naturally *occurring* variable not a naturally *manipulated* one. In any experiment the IV has to have been, in some way, 'applied to someone' (Coolican, 2004a). Therefore gender is not an IV. The same is true of studies looking at personality (extraverts and introverts) or at age (younger versus older) – these conditions are not applied to the individual, they are an existing part of that person.

Such studies are difference studies. They are not experiments; they could be called quasi-experiments. We cannot draw causal conclusions. We cannot, for example, say that gender caused an individual to have a higher IQ. We can only conclude that gender is related to IQ. An IV must be manipulated in some way in order to count as a true experiment; it cannot be an existing state of affairs.

Comparing lab, field and natural experiments

	Advantages	Weaknesses
Laboratory experiment *To investigate causal relationships under controlled conditions.*	**Well controlled; extraneous variables are minimised, thus higher internal validity.** **Can be easily replicated (repeated) to check if the same results occur which supports the external validity of the results.**	**Artificial, contrived situation where participants may not behave as they do in everyday life because of a lack of mundane realism, participant effects, investigator effects and demand characteristics. This reduces internal validity.**
Field experiment *To investigate causal relationships in more natural surroundings.*	**Less artificial, usually higher mundane realism and thus higher internal validity.** **Avoids participant effects (because participants not aware of study), which may increase internal validity.**	**Extraneous variables less easy to control because the experiment is taking place in the real world, thus reducing internal validity.** **There may still be demand characteristics, for example the way an IV is operationalised may convey the experimental hypothesis to participants.**
Natural experiment *To investigate causal relationships in situations where IV cannot be manipulated by an experimenter.*	**Allows research where IV can't be manipulated for ethical or practical reasons, e.g. studies of privation.** **Enables psychologists to study 'real' problems such as the effects of disaster on health (increased mundane realism and validity).**	**Cannot demonstrate causal relationships because IV not directly manipulated.** **Inevitably many extraneous variables (e.g. lack of random allocation), which are a threat to validity.** **Can only be used where conditions vary naturally.** **Participants may be aware of being studied causing participant effects, investigator effects and demand characteristics.**

RESEARCH METHODS Qs No.3.12

1 Five studies are described below. Identify each study as a lab, field or natural experiment, and explain your decision:

   A *Two primary schools use different reading schemes. A psychological study compares the reading scores at the end of the year to see which scheme was more effective.*

   B *Children take part in a trial to compare the success of a new maths programme. The children are placed in one of two groups – the new maths programme or the traditional one – and taught in these groups for a term.*

   C *The value of using computers rather than books is investigated by requiring children to learn word lists, either using a computer or with a book.*

   D *The effect of advertisements on gender stereotypes is studied by showing children ads with women doing feminine tasks or neutral tasks and then asking them about gender stereotypes.*

   E *A study investigates the anti-social effects of TV by monitoring whether people who watch a lot of TV (more than five hours a day) are more aggressive than those who don't.*

2 For each of the studies above (A–E) explain why you think it would have high or low validity.

the see-saw illustrated on page 68.

KEY TERMS

Difference studies Studies in which two groups of participants are compared in terms of a *DV* (such as males versus females, or extraverts versus introverts). This is not a true *experiment* because the apparent *IV* (gender or personality) has not been manipulated.

Natural experiment A *research method* in which the experimenter cannot manipulate the *independent variable* directly, but where it varies naturally and the effect can be observed on a *dependent variable*. Strictly speaking, an experiment involves the deliberate manipulation of an IV by the experimenter, so causal conclusions cannot be drawn from a natural experiment. In addition, participants are not *randomly allocated* to conditions in a natural experiment, which may reduce *validity*.

Quasi-experiments Studies that are 'almost' experiments but lack one or more features of a true experiment, such as full experimenter control over the IV and random allocation of participants to conditions. This means that they cannot claim to demonstrate causal relationships.

EXAM TIP
The key thing to remember about lab, field and natural experiments is they all have an IV and a DV. They differ in terms of factors such as control and realism – the see-saw illustrated on page 68.

Observational methods and techniques

In an observational study participants are observed engaging in whatever behaviour is being studied and the observations recorded.

- In a **naturalistic observation** behaviour is studied in a natural situation where *everything has been left as it is normally*.
- In a **controlled observation** some variables are controlled by the researcher, reducing the 'naturalness' of behaviour being studied. Participants are likely to know they are being studied and the study may be conducted in a laboratory.
- Observation may also be used in an experiment – in which case observation is a research *technique* instead of a research *method*.

*In **controlled observations** it is the participants' environment that is controlled, not the techniques used to obtain observational data.*

***Systematic techniques** are used in **naturalistic and controlled observations**.*

EXAMPLES OF DIFFERENT KINDS OF OBSERVATION

In Chapter 2 we looked at research by Mary Ainsworth and associates. Her research involved the use of:

- **Naturalistic observation** – in her study of Ugandan women and children she spent time observing their interactions. Her observations were structured, i.e. she didn't simply sit there all day and write down everything she saw. She spent short periods of time noting specific behaviours. Naturalistic observation means that the behaviour being studied is not interfered with, but the researcher may be quite structured in terms of how observations are recorded. On the facing page we will look at how and why observations are structured, but first you might try the 'Do it yourself' below to experience at first hand some of the problems involved.
- **Controlled observation** – the strange situation technique involved structuring the behaviour of the participants as well as those of the observers. The participants had to follow eight episodes and the observers had a checklist of five behaviours they had to rate every 15 seconds (see page 40).
- **Observational techniques in an experiment** – one could take the view that Ainsworth's study was an experiment rather than a controlled observation. The IV is the behaviour of the parent and stranger, and the DV is the infant's behaviour. In this case the observations are a technique used to assess the infant's behaviour.

An example of a naturalistic observation

Do little boys 'reward' each other for sex-appropriate play? Is the same true for little girls? One study observed boys and girls aged three to five years during their free play periods at nursery school. The researchers classified activities as male, female or neutral and recorded how playmates responded. The researchers found that children generally reinforced peers for sex-appropriate play and were quick to criticise sex-inappropriate play (Lamb and Roopnarine, 1979).

An example of a controlled observation

The same research described above could have been conducted by controlling some of the variables. For example, the researchers might have set up a special playroom in their laboratory with certain types of toys available (male, female and neutral). They could have observed the children through a one-way mirror so the children would be unaware of being observed.

An example of an experiment with controlled observational techniques

In the 'Bobo doll study' described on page 83 (Bandura *et al.*, 1961) the children's aggressiveness was observed at the end of the experiment to see if those exposed to the aggressive model behaved more aggressively. Each child was taken to a room which contained some aggressive toys (e.g. a mallet and a dart gun), some non-aggressive toys (e.g. dolls and farm animals) and a Bobo doll.

The experimenter stayed with the child while he/she played for 20 minutes, during which time the child was observed through a one-way mirror. The observers recorded what the child was doing every five seconds, using the following measures:

- Imitation of physical aggression.
- Imitative verbal aggression.
- Imitative non-aggressive verbal responses.
- Non-imitative physical and verbal aggression.

DO IT YOURSELF
No.**3.9**

Making observations

Work with a partner and take it in turns to observe each other. One of you will be Person A and the other will be Person B.

Person A should have a difficult task to do (e.g. answering one set of questions in this book).

Person B should have a boring task to do (e.g. copying from a book).

Each person should spend five minutes on their task, while the other person observes them, noting down any aspect of their partner's behaviour.

RESEARCH METHODS Qs
No.**3.13**

Answer the following questions about the observational study on the left.

1 Suggest a suitable hypothesis for the study.
2 If you carried out the activity, summarise your observations.
3 What uncontrolled factors might affect your findings?
4 What can you conclude from your research?
5 In this study is observation the method or the technique?
6 Are the observations controlled or naturalistic?
7 Describe **one or more** difficulties that you encountered.

You might think that making observations is easy, but if you tried the DIY on the left, you should now realise it is difficult for two main reasons:

- It is difficult to work out what to record and what not to record.
- It is difficult to record everything that is happening even if you do select what to record and what not to record.

Observational research, like all research, aims to be objective and rigorous. For this reason it is preferable to use **observational techniques**.

Structured observations
The researcher uses various 'systems' to organise observations.

- **Behavioural categories**
  How to record the behaviour you are interested in.
- **Sampling procedures**
  Who you are observing and when.

Unstructured observations
The researcher records all relevant behaviour but has no *system*. The behaviour to be studied is largely unpredictable.

The most obvious problem with this is that there may be too much to record. Another problem is that the behaviours recorded will often be those which are most visible or eye-catching to the observer but these may not necessarily be the most important or relevant behaviours.

Behavioural categories

One of the hardest aspects of the observational method is deciding how different behaviours should be categorised. This is because our perception of behaviour is often seamless; when we watch somebody perform a particular action we see a continuous stream of action rather than a series of separate behavioural components.

In order to conduct systematic observations, one needs to break up this stream of behaviour into different behavioural categories. What is needed is *operationalisation* – breaking the behaviour being studied into a set of components. For example, when observing infant behaviour, you can have a list including things like smiling, crying and sleeping, etc., or, when observing facial expressions, including expressions such as those shown on page 88.

The behavioural categories should:

- Be *objective*: the observer should not have to make inferences about the behaviour, but should just record explicit actions.
- Cover *all possible component behaviours* and avoid a 'waste basket' category.
- Be *mutually exclusive*, meaning that you should not have to mark two categories at one time.

Sampling procedures

When conducting a *continuous* observation the observer should record every instance of the behaviour in as much detail as possible. This is useful if the behaviours of interest do not occur very often.

However, in many situations, continuous observation is not be possible because there would be too much data to record, therefore there must be a systematic method of sampling observations:

- **Event sampling** Counting the number of times a certain behaviour (event) occurs in a target individual or individuals.
- **Time sampling**. Recording behaviours in a given time frame. For example, noting what a target individual is doing every 30 seconds. At that time the observer may tick one or more categories from a checklist.

1 In each of the following observations state which sampling procedure would be most appropriate and explain how you would do it:
   a Recording instances of aggressive behaviour in children playing in a school playground.
   b Vocalisations (words, sounds) made by young children.
   c Compliance to controlled pedestrian crossings by pedestrians.
   d Litter-dropping in a public park.
   e Behaviour of dog owners when walking their dogs.

2 *A group of students decided to study student behaviour in the school library.*
   a Suggest **one or more** hypotheses that you might investigate.
   b List **five** behaviours you might include in a behaviour checklist.
   c Identify a suitable sampling procedure and explain how you would do it.
   d How could you observe the students so that they were not aware that they were being observed?
   e What ethical issues might be raised in this observational study?
   f For each issue identified in your answer to (e), explain how you could deal with this issue and whether this would be acceptable.
   g Explain in what way this would be a naturalistic observation.
   h In this study is observation a method or a technique?

KEY TERMS

Behavioural categories Dividing a target behaviour (such as attachment or sociability) into a subset of behaviours. This can be done using a behaviour checklist or a coding system (explained on the next spread).

Controlled observation A form of investigation in which behaviour is observed but under controlled conditions, in contrast with a naturalistic observation.

Event sampling An observational technique in which a count is kept of the number of times a certain behaviour (event) occurs.

Naturalistic observation A research method carried out in a naturalistic setting, in which the investigator does not interfere in any way but merely observes the behaviour(s) in question, though this is likely to involve the use of structured observations.

Observation techniques The application of systematic methods of observation in an observational study, experiment, or other study.

Sampling The process of taking a sample which is intended to be a representative selection of a target population (see page 92 for more on sampling).

Structured (systematic) observations An observer uses various 'systems' to organise observations, such as behavioural categories and sampling procedures.

Time sampling An observational technique in which the observer records behaviours in a given time frame, e.g. noting what a target individual is doing every 30 seconds. You may select one or more categories from a checklist.

Unstructured observations An observer records all relevant behaviour but has no system. This technique may be chosen because the behaviour to be studied is largely unpredictable.

Designing observational research

In order to make systematic and objective observations, researchers need to develop behavioural categories – they may do this themselves or use something developed by another researcher. The method is called a coding system or behaviour checklist.

Using a **coding system** means that a code is invented to represent each category of behaviour. A **behaviour checklist** is essentially the same thing though a *code* for each behaviour may not be given (see DIY on facing page). A further method is to provide a list of behaviours or characteristics and ask observers to rate each one using a *rating scale*.

A BEHAVIOUR CHECKLIST

Secure attachment in pets (Topal *et al.*, 1998)

Psychologists in Hungary used the strange situation technique (see page 40) to explore the attachments between dogs and their owners. For 10,000 years dogs have been bred for certain traits, among them their willingness to become attached to their owners. This makes it quite likely that dogs and owners will behave like infants and caregivers. The presence of a caregiver (the owner) should reduce anxiety and increase willingness to explore in the dog.

In this study owners and their dogs went through the eight episodes of the strange situation and their behaviours were recorded using the checklist on the right. A tick could be entered at regular intervals (e.g. every 15 seconds). Owners were not informed of the purpose of the study.

The findings of the study were that dogs, like people, were either securely or insecurely attached.

Behaviour checklist for the strange situation	
EXPO	exploration when with owner
EXPS	exploration when with stranger
PLYO	playing when with owner
PLYS	playing when with stranger
PASO	passive behaviours when with owner
PASS	passive behaviours when with stranger
CONTO	physical contact with the owner
CONTS	physical contact with the stranger
SBYO	standing by the door when with owner
SBYS	standing by the door when with stranger

A CODING SYSTEM

The Facial Action Coding System (FACS) for observing facial expressions (Ekman and Friesen, 1978).

Paul Ekman and others have developed the coding system below to code non-verbal behaviours. This can be used to investigate, for example, what expressions are shown on a person's face when they are lying.

Code	Description	Code	Description
1	Inner Brow Raiser	26	Jaw Drop
2	Outer Brow Raiser	27	Mouth Stretch
4	Brow Lowerer	28	Lip Suck
5	Upper Lid Raiser	41	Lid droop
6	Cheek Raiser	42	Slit
7	Lid Tightener	43	Eyes Closed
9	Nose Wrinkler	44	Squint
10	Upper Lip Raiser	45	Blink
11	Nasolabial Deepener	46	Wink
12	Lip Corner Puller	51	Head turn left
13	Cheek Puffer	52	Head turn right
14	Dimpler	53	Head up
15	Lip Corner Depressor	54	Head down
16	Lower Lip Depressor	55	Head tilt left
17	Chin Raiser	56	Head tilt right
18	Lip Puckerer	57	Head forward
20	Lip Stretcher	58	Head back
22	Lip Funneler	61	Eyes turn left
23	Lip Tightener	62	Eyes turn right
24	Lip Pressor	63	Eyes up
25	Lips part	64	Eyes down

A RATING SYSTEM

Early Child Environment Rating Scale (ECERS) (Harms *et al.*, 1998)

This scale has been used in numerous studies of child development to record observations of a child's early environment and then relate this to other developmental outcomes such as school success. In general, research has found positive correlations.

The observer rates each of the 43 items on seven-point scale: 1 (inadequate), 3 (minimal), 5 (good), and 7 (excellent). The 43 items were:

▲ Outer brow raiser

▲ Lip corner depressor

You can see illustrations of all the other codes at www-2.cs.cmu.edu/afs/cs/project/face/www/facs.htm

Space and furnishings	Personal care routines	Language reasoning	Activities	Interaction	Programme structure	Parents and staff
1 Indoor space	9 Greeting/ departing	15 Books and pictures	19 Fine motor	29 Supervision of gross motor activities	34 Schedule	38 Provisions for parents
2 Furniture for routine care, play and learning	10 Meals/snacks	16 Encouraging children to communicate	20 Art	30 General supervision of children (other than gross motor)	35 Free play	39 Provisions for personal needs of staff
3 Furnishings for relaxation and comfort	11 Nap/rest	17 Using language to develop reasoning skills	21 Music/movement	31 Discipline	36 Group time	40 Provisions for professional needs of staff
4 Room arrangement for play	12 Toileting/nappy-changing	18 Informal use of language	22 Blocks	32 Staff-child interactions	37 Provisions for children with disabilities	41 Staff interaction and cooperation
5 Space for privacy	13 Health practices		23 Sand/water	33 Interactions among children		42 Supervision and evaluation of staff
6 Child-related display	14 Safety practices		24 Dramatic play			43 Opportunities for professional growth
7 Space for gross motor play			25 Nature/science			
8 Gross motor equipment			26 Maths/number			
			27 Use of TV, video, and/or computers			
			28 Promoting acceptance of diversity			

Method and technique

Remember that all research involves making observations. In some research the overall method is observational where the emphasis is on observing a relatively unconstrained segment of a person's freely chosen behaviour. However observational techniques are used in almost all studies, even experiments.

Controlled and naturalistic

Both kinds of observation use systematic methods to record observations i.e. there is control over how the observations are made. Control over the environment is only true in a controlled observation, for example the setting may be moved from the person's normal environment or some of the items in the environment may be deliberately chosen.

Participant and non-participant

In many cases the observer is merely watching the behaviour of others and acts as a non-participant. In some studies observers also participate, which may affect their objectivity. A classic example of a participant observation is described on the right.

Overt and covert

One-way mirrors are used to prevent participants being aware that they are being observed. This is called **covert** or undisclosed observation. Knowing that your behaviour is being observed is likely to alter your behaviour, and therefore observers often try to be as unobtrusive as possible, though this has ethical implications.

Naturalistic observation and natural experiment

Both involve naturally occurring variables that have not been manipulated by the researcher. However, in a natural experiment, there is an IV and its effect on a DV is observed so that we can draw tentative causal conclusions. In a naturalistic observation there is no IV.

Making systematic observations

No.**3.10**

The coding system below is adapted from one used by Fick (1993) in a study which looked at the effects of having a dog on the nature and frequency of social interactions in nursing home residents.

You can use this shortened version below to make observations of other students in a common room or cafeteria.

- *Non-attentive behaviour*: Participant is not engaged in group activity.
- *Attentive listening*: Participant maintains eye contact with other group members.
- *Verbal interaction with another person*: Participant initiates or responds verbally to another person.
- *Non-verbal interaction with another person*: Participant touches, gestures, smiles, nods etc. to another person.

1 Decide on your research aims, for example you could compare social interactions in the morning and afternoon, or differences between boys and girls, or between different environments (such as in class and in the cafeteria).

2 State your hypothesis.

3 Draw up a grid to record your observations.

4 Decide on a sampling procedure.

5 Present your findings using descriptive statistics.

A PARTICIPANT, COVERT OBSERVATION

In the 1950s the social psychologist Leon Festinger read a newspaper report about a religious cult that claimed to be receiving messages from outer space. These predicted that the end of the world would take place on a certain date in the form of a great flood. The cult members were going to be rescued by a flying saucer so they all gathered with their leader, Mrs Keech. Festinger was intrigued to know how the cult members would respond when they found their beliefs were unfounded, especially as many of them had made their beliefs very public. In order to observe this at first hand Festinger and some co-workers posed as converts to the cause and were present on the eve of destruction. When it was apparent that there would be no flood, the group leader Mrs Keech said that their prayers had saved the city. Some cult members didn't believe this and left the cult, whereas others took this as proof of the cult's power (Festinger *et al.*, 1956).

1 With reference to the study by Lamb and Roopnarine on the previous spread (which was an example of a naturalistic observation), give examples of **one** advantage and **one** weakness of studying children in this way.

2 With reference to the example of a controlled observation on the previous spread, give **one** advantage and **one** weakness of studying children in this way.

3 Explain **two** strengths of the study conducted by Festinger *et al.* (described above).

4 What distinguishes a successful teacher from an unsuccessful one? A group of students decide to observe various teachers while they are teaching.
   a Identify **two** behavioural categories that could be used to record 'successful teaching behaviour'.
   b Describe **one** way in which you could minimise the intrusive nature of your observations.
   c How would you record the data in this observational study?
   d Suggest **one** advantage and **one** weakness of conducting an observational study in this context.
   e Describe **two** ways of ensuring that this study would be carried out in an ethically acceptable manner.
   f In this study is observation a method or a technique?

Behaviour checklist A list of the behaviours to be recorded during an observational study.

Coding system A systematic method for recording observations in which individual behaviours are given a code for ease of recording.

Covert observations Observing people without their knowledge, e.g. using one-way mirrors. Knowing that behaviour is being observed is likely to alter a participant's behaviour.

Evaluating observational research

Like all research methods there are advantages and weaknesses with observational techniques and methods. The main concerns are related to validity and ethical issues and a new concept, reliability.

VALIDITY

External validity

Observational studies are likely to have high ecological validity because they involve more natural behaviours (but remember that naturalness doesn't always mean greater ecological validity).

Population validity may be a problem if, for example, children are only observed in middle-class homes, because we cannot generalise such findings to children from all classes.

Internal validity

Observations will not be valid (or reliable) if the coding system/behaviour checklist is flawed. For example some observations may belong in more than one category, or some behaviours may not be codeable.

The validity of observations is also affected by **observer bias** – what someone observes is influenced by their expectations. This reduces the objectivity of observations.

Improving validity

A researcher can improve validity by conducting observations in varied settings with varied participants, which makes the findings more generalisable to other settings and other people.

The researcher can also use more than one observer to reduce observer bias and averaging data across observers (which balances out any biases).

ETHICAL ISSUES

In studies where participants are observed without their knowledge there are issues relating to informed consent. Some observations may be an invasion of privacy, in which case participant confidentiality should be respected. The use of one-way mirrors often involves deception.

In observations where participants *are* aware of being studied there are still issues similar to those in all studies, such as informed consent, right to withdraw etc.

Dealing with ethical issues

The same general principles apply to dealing with ethical issues that apply to all other research. For example ethics committees can be used to approve observational designs, and researchers should consult ethical guidelines. One particular BPS guideline concerns observational research – this type of research is acceptable where those observed would expect to be observed by strangers. In addition researchers should be aware that it is not acceptable to intrude upon the privacy of individuals who, even while in a normally public space, may believe they are unobserved.

RELIABILITY

Reliability refers to whether something is consistent.

If you use a ruler to measure the height of a chair today and check the measurement tomorrow, you expect the ruler to be reliable (consistent) and provide the same measurement. You would assume that any fluctuation was because the chair had changed size. If the fluctuation was due to some change in the ruler it would be pretty useless as a measuring instrument – not dependable, consistent or reliable.

Any tool used to measure something must be reliable, such as a psychological test assessing personality, or an interview about drinking habits, or observations made by two observers of a target individual.

If the 'tool' is measuring the same thing it should produce the same result on every occasion. If the result is different then we need to be sure that it is the thing (chair or personality) that has changed or is different, and not our measuring tool.

Reliability of observations

Observations should be consistent, which means that ideally two observers should produce the same record. The extent to which two (or more) observers agree is called inter-rater or **inter-observer reliability**. A general rule is that if there is more than 80% agreement on the observations, the data have inter-observer reliability.

$$\frac{\text{Total agreements}}{\text{Total observations}} > 80\%$$

Improving reliability

Observers should be trained in the use of a coding system/behaviour checklist. They should practise using it and discuss their observations. The investigator can then check the reliability of their observations.

1. Training observers

The Behavioural Observation unit (BEO) at the University of Bern trains people in the use of observational techniques using its coding system (below) (BEO, 2004). The unit has a nursery school where the children can be observed by trainees through a one-way mirror.

Coding system KaSo 12:		
No social participation	1	Occupied alone
	2	Hanging around alone
	3	Alone – onlooker
	4	Alone – unclear
Social participation	5	Parallel behaviour 1
	6	Parallel behaviour 2
	7	Loosely associated but interactive
	8	Role play – identifiable
	9	Social participation unclear
Not identifiable	10	Child not in view, generally unclear

2. Assessing reliability

The graphs below show observations made by three observers (blue, red and green lines) of two children in the nursery class using KaSo 12 (see left).

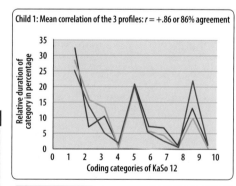

Child 1: Mean correlation of the 3 profiles: $r = +.86$ or 86% agreement

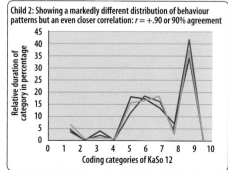

Child 2: Showing a markedly different distribution of behaviour patterns but an even closer correlation: $r = +.90$ or 90% agreement

VALIDITY AND RELIABILITY

Different archers produce the patterns of arrows shown below.

Being reliable is being consistent, being valid is being on target (related to what you are aiming to do).

A study that lacks reliability will therefore lack validity, but you can have a study that is reliable but not valid.

For example, if an observer is inconsistent in the observations he makes (e.g. recording some observations when he wasn't sure what the target individual was doing) then the results are meaningless.

If an observer uses a behaviour checklist which is not very thorough, and sometimes the target individual does things which can't be recorded, the observations may be perfectly reliable but lack validity because the behaviour checklist was poor.

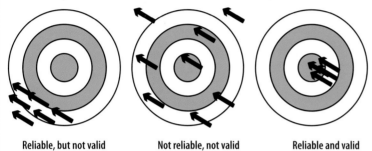

Reliable, but not valid   Not reliable, not valid   Reliable and valid

Evaluation of observational research

Advantages	Weaknesses
• What people say they do is often different from what they actually do, so observations may be more valid than questionnaires/interviews.	• There can be little or no control of extraneous variables which may mean that something unknown to the observer may account for the behaviour observed.
• Gives a more realistic picture of spontaneous behaviour. It is likely to have high *ecological validity*.	• The observer may 'see' what he/she expects to see. This is called **observer bias**. This bias may mean that different observers 'see' different things, which leads to low **inter-observer reliability**.
• Provides a means of conducting preliminary investigations in a new area of research, to produce hypotheses for future investigations.	• If participants don't know they are being observed there are ethical problems such as deception and invasion of privacy. If participants do know they are being observed they may alter their behaviour.

RESEARCH METHODS Qs   No.3.16

1 On the facing page are two graphs showing the observations of two children made by three observers. Do you think that the graphs indicate an acceptable level of inter-observer reliability?

2 Identify **one** advantage of a natural experiment when contrasted with a naturalistic observation.

3 Identify **one** advantage of a naturalistic observation when contrasted with a natural experiment.

4 *A psychologist decided to observe the non-verbal behaviours between two people having a conversation. (Non-verbal behaviours are those which don't involve language, such as smiling, touching, etc.)*
   a Explain why it would be desirable to conduct a pilot study in this investigation.
   b If this is to be a naturalistic observation, where might the student researchers make their observations?
   c Each conversation is observed by two students. Identify **one** way in which you could ensure reliability among the different observers, and explain how you might put this into practice.
   d Describe **two** features of the study that might threaten its validity.
   e Explain how you could deal with the two features that might threaten validity.
   f Draw a suitable table for recording observations, showing some of the possible behavioural categories that could be used.

g Describe **one** way of ensuring that this study would be carried out in an ethically acceptable manner.
h Evaluate your method of dealing with the ethical issues in this study.

5 *Imagine that you wished to investigate interpersonal deception to see if it was possible to use facial expressions to tell whether someone is lying or not.*
   a Describe how you would design a study using observational techniques to investigate this. Record at least **six** design decisions, and describe each one carefully.
   b Identify **one** problem that might occur concerning validity, **one** problem concerning reliability and **one** problem concerning ethics.
   c For each of the three problems identified above, suggest how you might deal with the problem.
   d Would you describe your study as a naturalistic observation, a controlled observation or a natural, field or lab experiment? Explain why.
   e How could the same study be carried out using a different method?
   f What would be the relative advantages of carrying out this study as a naturalistic observation and as a lab experiment?

6 Main and Solomon (1990) reported inter-observer reliability rates for observations in the strange situation of between .77 and .80. Is this very good, good, reasonable or poor? Give reasons for your answer.

KEY TERMS

Inter-observer reliability The extent to which there is agreement between two or more observers involved in observations of a behaviour. A general rule is that if the total number of agreements divided by the total number of observations is more than 80%, then the data have high inter-observer reliability.

Observer bias In observational studies, there is the danger that observers might 'see' what they expect to see. This reduces the validity of the observations.

Reliability A measure of consistency both within a set of scores or items (*internal reliability*) and also over time, such that it is possible to obtain the same results on subsequent occasions when the measure is used (*external reliability*). The reliability of an experiment can be determined through replication.

Selection of participants

When making observations, a researcher usually uses some method of sampling to reduce the number of observations – as we saw on page 87. However, sampling isn't used only in observational studies – researchers have to do this in all studies. For example, it would be impossible to conduct an experiment with all the schoolchildren in Britain, so if we wanted to find out about British schoolchildren we would select a sample from this target population.

The most obvious way to do this is to use the people who happen to be around at the time (called an **opportunity sample**). This is probably the method you have been using up to now when doing your own experiments. Most psychologists use this method or a **volunteer sample**. The 'ideal' method is a **random sample** because it is the least biased.

SAMPLING TECHNIQUES

Opportunity sample

How? Ask people walking by you in the street, i.e. select those who are available.

➕ The easiest method because you just use the first participants you can find, which means it takes less time to locate your sample than if using one of the other techniques.

➖ Inevitably biased because the sample is drawn from a small part of the target population, for example if you selected your sample from people walking around the centre of a town on a Monday morning then it would be unlikely to include professional people (because they are at work) or people from rural areas.

Volunteer sample

How? Advertise in a newspaper or on a noticeboard.

➕ Access to a variety of participants (e.g. all the people who read a newspaper) which would make the sample more representative and less biased.

➖ Sample is biased because participants are likely to be more highly motivated and/or with extra time on their hands (= **volunteer bias**).

Random sample

How? See 'randomness' on right.

➕ Unbiased, all members of the target population have an equal chance of selection.

➖ The researcher may end up with a biased sample (e.g. more boys than girls) because the sample is too small (see facing page).

▼ In any study there is a **target population**, which is the group of individuals a researcher is interested in. The researcher aims to take a representative *sample* from this target population using a sampling method. The sample should be representative so that generalisations about the target population can be made on the basis of the sample.

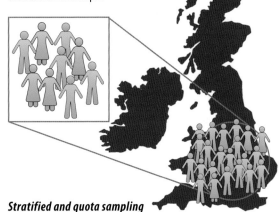

Stratified and quota sampling

You are not required to know about stratified and quota sampling, however this is the method most often used in questionnaires and also the method students quite often want to use to get a representative sample.

How? Sub-groups (or strata) within a population are identified (e.g. boys and girls, or age groups: 10–12 years, 13–15 etc.). Participants are obtained from each of the strata in proportion to their occurrence in the target population. Selection is done randomly (**stratified sample**) or by another method such as opportunity sampling (**quota sampling**).

➕ More representative than an opportunity sample because there is equal representation of sub-groups.

➖ Although the sample represents sub-groups, each quota taken may be biased in other ways, for example if you use opportunity sampling you only have access to certain sections of the target population.

HYPOTHESES AND CONCLUSIONS

A research hypothesis and the research conclusion(s) should be about the *target population* and not the specific *participants* in the research study. The intention of any research is to be able to *generalise* from a particular group of people (the participants) to people in general. The hypothesis is the researcher's initial statement of what he or she believes to be true. The conclusions are an interpretation of the results in terms of what they tell us about the population from which the sample was drawn.

For this reason both the hypothesis and conclusions should:

- Always be about the target population rather than the actual participants.
- Always be in the present tense i.e. 'People learn list A faster', not the future e.g. 'People will learn list A faster' or in the past 'People learned list A faster'.

EXAM TIP

A sampling method is about how participants are identified, NOT about who eventually takes part. Whatever the sampling method, it may be that some participants refuse to take part, which then leaves the researcher with a biased sample – a sample of only those who are willing participants.

However, this doesn't apply in most field experiments – when participants aren't aware they are being studied, they can't refuse.

All sampling methods aim to produce a representative sample but are inevitably biased – bias means 'distorted' in some way. There are lots of biases, such as: experimenter bias, interviewer bias, observer bias, social desirability bias, sample bias, volunteer bias.

EXAM TIP

*Many students mistake a **systematic sample** for a random sample – selecting every tenth person is not random, it is a systematic method of selection. However if you select a number using a random method and start with this person, and then you select every tenth person, this would be a random sample.*

RANDOMNESS

'Random' means each member of the population having an equal chance of being selected. The easiest way to obtain a random selection is to draw numbers or names *'out of a hat'*. This is sometimes called the 'lottery method'.

An alternative *random technique* is to give each participant a number and then select participants using a random number table or random function on a calculator or computer.

Random selection is used to obtain a random sample of participants or for *random allocation* of participants to conditions when using an independent measures design.

Each of the balls has an equal chance of being drawn – i.e. the draw is random.

RESEARCH METHODS Qs No.3.17

1 Identify the sampling method in each of the studies below.

   a *A researcher wished to study memory in children aged between 5 and 11. He contacted the headmaster of his local primary school and arranged to test the children in the school.*

   b *A university department undertook a study of mobile phone use in adolescents, using a questionnaire. The questionnaire was given to a group of students in a local comprehensive school, selected by placing all the students' names in a container and drawing out 50 names.*

   c *A class of psychology students conduct a study on memory. They put a notice on the noticeboard in the sixth form common room asking for participants who have an hour to spare.*

2 In each of the studies above state the advantage of using that sampling method *in that particular study*.

3 A research study is conducted comparing the ability of boys and girls aged 5–12 to remember words. Their memories are tested giving them 30 words to remember. The results are:

	Boys	Girls
Mean score	10.3 words	15.7 words
Standard deviation	9.8	7.6

   a Write a suitable non-directional hypothesis for the study above.

   b How would you describe the target population?

   c Suggest a suitable method of selecting participants.

   d Describe **one** weakness with this method of selection.

   e What experimental design would you use?

   f Give **two** examples of words that might be suitable to use to test their memory, and explain why these words would be suitable.

   g After giving the children the lists to learn, how long should the researcher wait before testing their recall? Explain your answer.

   h How might demand characteristics be a problem in this study?

   i What does the standard deviation tell us about the boys' scores.

   j Describe **one** conclusion you could draw from the data in the table.

DO IT YOURSELF

How random is random? No.3.11

Take 40 pieces of paper and write 20 boys' names and 20 girls' names on each slip. Put them in a hat and draw out 10 slips of paper. If the selection is representative you ideally should get five boys and five girls.

Put the slips of paper back and draw 10 out again. Repeat this four times and then try drawing a larger sample e.g. of 20 slips of paper. Each time, record how many boys' and girls' names were drawn. You can record your results in the table below.

	Sample size 10					Sample size 20		
	1	2	3	4	5	6	7	8
Boys								
Girls								

The point is that, in principle, random selection results in an unbiased and representative sample, *but only if the sample is large enough*. Is this what you found? What happens if you try the same task with a random number table or using the random function on your calculator?

KEY TERMS

Opportunity sample A sample of participants produced by selecting people who are most easily available at the time of the study.

Random sample A sample of participants produced by using a random technique such that every member of the target population being tested has an equal chance of being selected.

Stratified sample Groups of participants are selected according to their frequency in the population in order to obtain a representative sample. Groups or strata are selected from the target population that need to be represented, and then individuals are sampled from the strata. If this final sample is carried out using a random technique it is a stratified sample, otherwise it is a **quota sample**.

Systematic sample A method of obtaining a representative sample by selecting every fifth or tenth person. This can be a random sample if the first person is selected using a random method; you then select every fifth or tenth person after that.

Target population The group of people that the researcher is interested in. The group of people from whom a sample is drawn. The group of people about whom generalisations can be made.

Volunteer bias A form of sampling bias (distortion) because volunteer participants are usually more highly motivated than randomly selected participants.

Volunteer sample A sample of participants produced by a sampling technique that relies solely on volunteers to make up the sample. Also called a self-selected sample.

Self-report techniques

Psychologists aim to find out about behaviour. One way to do this is to conduct experiments; we have also looked at one non-experimental method – observations. Another non-experimental method or technique is to ask people questions about their experiences and/or beliefs. These are called self-report methods (because the person is reporting their own thoughts/feelings), and include questionnaires and interviews. A **questionnaire** can be given in a written form or it can be delivered in real-time (face-to-face or on the telephone) in which case it is called an **interview**.

1 QUESTIONNAIRES

A questionnaire is a set of questions. It is designed to collect information about a topic or topics.

The two great strengths of questionnaires are:

1 You can collect the same information from a large number of people relatively easily (once you have designed the questionnaire, which is not so easy).
2 You can access what people think – observations and experiments rely on 'guessing' what people think and feel on the basis of how they behave. With a questionnaire you can ask people directly; whether they can, and do, give you truthful answers is another matter.

*A questionnaire or interview can be a **research method** or a **research technique**.*

The aims of a study may be to find out about smoking habits in young people. The researcher would design a questionnaire to collect data about what people do and why. In this case the questionnaire is the research method.

The aims of a study might be to see if children who are exposed to an anti-smoking educational programme have different attitudes towards smoking than children not exposed to such a programme. The researcher would use a questionnaire to collect data about attitudes, but the analysis would involve a comparison between the two groups of children – an experimental study using a questionnaire as a research technique to assess the DV.

Designing questionnaires

Writing good questions

When writing questions there are three guiding principles:

- *Clarity*. Questions need to be written so that the reader (respondent) understands what is being asked. One way to do this is to operationalise certain terms. There should be no ambiguity.
- *Bias*. Any bias in a question might lead the respondent to be more likely to give a particular answer (as in a leading question). The greatest problem is probably social desirability bias. Respondents prefer to select answers that portray them in a positive light rather than reflect the truth.
- *Analysis*. Questions need to be written so that the answers are easy to analyse. If you ask, 'What do you like most about your job?' or, 'What makes you feel stressed at work?' you may get 50 different answers from 50 people. These are called **open questions**. Alternatively one can ask **closed questions** where a limited range of answers is provided, such as listing 10 things people usually like about their work, or 10 sources of stress. Such closed questions are easier to analyse but respondents may be forced to select answers which don't represent their real thoughts or behaviour.

Writing good questionnaires

A good questionnaire should contain good questions. Some other things to consider when designing a good questionnaire are:

- *Filler questions*. It may help to include some irrelevant questions to distract the respondent from the main purpose of the survey. This may reduce demand characteristics.
- *Sequence for the questions*. It is best to start with easy ones, saving questions that might make someone feel anxious or defensive until the respondent has relaxed.
- *Sampling technique*, i.e. how to select respondents. Questionnaire studies often use stratified or quota sampling (see page 92).
- *Pilot study*. The questions can be tested on a small group of people. This means the questions can later be refined in response to any difficulties encountered.

KEY TERMS

Closed questions Questions that have a range of answers from which respondents select one; produces quantitative data. Answers are easier to analyse than those for open questions.

Interview A research method or technique that involves a face-to-face, 'real-time' interaction with another individual and results in the collection of data.

Open questions Questions that invite the respondents to provide their own answers rather than select one of those provided. Tend to produce qualitative data.

Questionnaire Data are collected through the use of written questions.

Structured interview Any interview in which the questions are decided in advance.

Unstructured interview The interview starts out with some general aims and possibly some questions, and lets the interviewee's answers guide subsequent questions.

Examples of open questions

1 What factors contribute to making work stressful?
2 How do you feel when stressed?

Examples of closed questions

1 Which of the following makes you feel stressed? (You may tick as many answers as you like.)

☐ Noise at work   ☐ Lack of control
☐ Too much to do   ☐ Workmates
☐ No job satisfaction

2 How many hours a week do you work?

☐ 0 hours ☐ Between 11 and 20 hours
☐ Between 1 and 10 hours
☐ More than 20 hours

3 *Likert scale*

Work is stressful:
☐ Strongly agree ☐ Agree ☐ Not sure
☐ Disagree ☐ Strongly disagree

4 How much stress do you feel? (Circle the number that best describes how you feel.)

At work:
A lot of stress   5 4 3 2 1   No stress at all
At home:
A lot of stress   5 4 3 2 1   No stress at all
Travelling to work:
A lot of stress   5 4 3 2 1   No stress at all

5 Forced choice question

A   The worst social sin is to be rude
B   The worst social sin is to be a bore

An interview can be very structured or can be unstructured.

A **structured interview** has pre-determined questions i.e. a questionnaire that is delivered face-to-face with deviation from the original questions.

An **unstructured interview** has less structure! New questions are developed as you go along. The semi-structured approach combines both structured and unstructured interviews, similar to the way your GP might talk to you when you are feeling ill. He or she starts with some pre-determined questions but further questions are developed as a response to your answers. For this reason this semi-structured approach is also called the *clinical interview*.

Examples of interviews

Lawrence Kohlberg (1978) interviewed boys about their moral views. Interviewers gave the boys an imaginary situation and then asked a set of questions.

In Europe, a woman was near death from a rare type of cancer. There was one drug that the doctors thought might save her. It was a form of radium that a druggist in the same town had recently discovered. The drug was expensive to make but the druggist was charging 10 times what the drug cost him to make. He paid $400 for the radium and charged $4000 for a small dose of it. The sick woman's husband, Heinz, went to everyone he knew to borrow the money, but he could only get together about $2000 which is half of what it cost. He told the druggist that his wife was dying and asked him to sell it cheaper or let him pay later. But the druggist said, 'No. I discovered the drug and I'm going to make money from it'. Heinz got desperate and broke into the man's store to steal the drug for his wife.

- Should Heinz steal the drug?
- Why or why not?
- (If interviewee originally favours stealing, ask:) If Heinz doesn't love his wife, should he steal the drug for her?
- (If interviewee originally favours not stealing, ask:) Does it make a difference whether or not he loves his wife?
- Why or why not?
- Suppose the person dying is not his wife but a stranger. Should Heinz steal the drug for the stranger?
- Why or why not?

Carol Gilligan also investigated moral principles (Gilligan and Attanucci, 1988). Participants were asked a set of questions about their own experiences of moral conflict and choice:

- Have you ever been in a situation of moral conflict where you had to make a decision but weren't sure what was the right thing to do?
- Could you describe the situation?
- What were the conflicts for you in that situation?
- What did you do?
- Do you think it was the right thing to do?
- How do you know?

The interviewer asked other questions to encourage the participants to elaborate and clarify their responses, such as saying, 'Anything else?' A special focus was put on asking participants to explain the meaning of words they used.

RESEARCH METHODS Qs   No.3.18

1 Would you describe Kohlberg's and Gilligan's interviews as structured, unstructured, or semi-structured (i.e. a mix of the structured and unstructured approach)? Explain your answer.

2 In the interviews above, find an example of a closed question and an example of an open question.

3 On page 80 we defined the terms *quantitative and qualitative*. In the interviews above, find an example (not the same examples as for question 2) of a question that would produce quantitative data and a question that would produce qualitative data.

4 A psychology student designed a questionnaire about attitudes to eating. Below are some questions from this questionnaire:
(1) Do you diet? always sometimes never (circle your answer)
(2) Do you think dieting is a bad idea?
(3) Explain your answer to question 2.

For each question:
a State whether it is an open or closed question.
b State whether the question would produce quantitative or qualitative data.
c Give **one** criticism of the question.
d Suggest how you could improve the question in order to deal with your criticism.
e Suggest **one** strength of the question.
f Write **one** further question that would produce quantitative data and **one** that would produce qualitative data.

DO IT YOURSELF

Design and use your own questionnaire   No.3.12

Select a suitable topic, for example, 'Methods of exam revision'; 'Places people go for a good night out'; 'Why people choose to study psychology'; or 'How emotional are you?'. You could alternatively choose a topic related to your studies such as a questionnaire on day-care experiences or on stress.

Steps in questionnaire design

- Write the questions. Keep the questionnaire short, somewhere between 5 and 10 questions. Include a mixture of open and closed questions.
- Consider ethical issues and how to deal with them.
- Construct the questionnaire including standardised instructions.
- Pilot the questionnaire.
- Decide on a sampling technique.

Conduct the questionnaire

- Analyse the data. (Just select a few questions for analysis. For quantitative data you can use a bar chart. For qualitative data you can identify some trends in the answers and summarise these.)
- Write the report.

Try your own interview

Try out the moral interviews with a partner in class. Take turns being the interviewer and interviewee for both kinds of interview.

Discuss

- What you found out.
- The differences in the information obtained.
- Which questions worked best and why.
- How truthful you were and why.

Evaluating self-report techniques

Self-report techniques can be evaluated as always, with reference to the key issues of validity, ethics and reliability.

VALIDITY

External validity

The external validity of questionnaires and interviews concerns the extent to which the findings can be generalised to other situations and other people. A major factor will be the representativeness of the sample used to collect data. For example, if a questionnaire collected data only from shoppers on a weekday morning in London it is not reasonable to generalise this to all people in the UK.

Internal validity

The internal validity of self-report techniques is related to the issue of whether the questionnaire or interview (or psychological test) really measures what it intended to measure.

There are several ways to assess this, the most common being:

- *Face validity*: Does the test *look* as if it is measuring what the researcher intended to measure. For example, are the questions obviously related to the topic?
- *Concurrent validity*: This can be established by comparing the current questionnaire or test with a previously established test on the same topic. Participants take both tests and then the two test scores are compared.

Improving validity

Validity is improved firstly by assessing the validity of a questionnaire or interview. If such measures of validity are low then:
External validity: Use a more appropriate sampling method to improve population validity because then the findings could be generalised to a wider population.
Internal validity: If one or more measures of internal validity are low, then the items on the questionnaire/interview/test need to be revised in order to produce a better match between scores on the new test and an established one.

ETHICAL ISSUES

- *Deception* about true research aims may sometimes be necessary in order to collect truthful data.
- *Psychological harm* Respondents may feel distressed by certain questions or having to think about certain sensitive topics.
- *Privacy* questions may be related to sensitive and personal issues, invading an individual's privacy.
- *Confidentiality* must be respected; names and personal details should not be revealed without permission. No personal data may be stored.

RELIABILITY

Internal reliability is a measure of the extent to which something is consistent within itself. For example, all the questions on an IQ test (which is a kind of questionnaire) should be measuring the same thing. This may not be relevant to all questionnaires, because sometimes internal consistency is not important, e.g. a questionnaire about day-care experiences might look at many different aspects of day care and its effects.

External reliability is a measure of consistency over several different occasions. For example, if an interviewer conducted an interview, and then conducted the same interview with the same interviewee a week later, the outcome should be the same – otherwise the interview is not reliable.

Reliability also concerns whether two interviewers produce the same outcome. This is called **inter-interviewer reliability**.

Assessing reliability

Internal reliability	Split-half method: A single group of participants all take a test once. Their answers to the test questions are divided in half. This is done by, for example, comparing all answers to odd number answers with all answers to even number answers. The individual's scores on both halves of the test should be very similar. The two scores can be compared by calculating a correlation coefficient (see page 98).
External reliability	Test-retest method: A group of participants is given a test or questionnaire or interview once and then again sometime later (when they have had the chance to forget it). The answers can be compared and should be the same. If the tests produce scores, these can be compared by calculating a correlation coefficient.

Improving reliability

It is possible to improve internal reliability by removing those items which are most inconsistent. The only way to do this is by trial and error – remove one test item and see if the split-half correlation coefficient improves. If it does, then the removed item should be permanently left out.

RESEARCH METHODS Qs

No.**3.19**

1 *A group of students wishes to study mobile phone use in people aged 14–18. Why might it be preferable to*
   a Conduct an interview rather than a questionnaire?
   b Conduct a questionnaire rather than an interview?
   c Collect quantitative data?
   d Collect qualitative data?

2 *Imagine instead that the students wished to find out about drug taking.* Answer the same questions a–d as in question 1.

3 For each of the studies described in 1 and 2, suggest **two** ethical issues that should concern the students and suggest how they might deal with these.

4 *In a study on self-esteem (a person's feeling about their own worth), the researcher constructs a scale to measure it. The scale consists of 30 questions.*
   a How could the researcher assess the reliability of the self-esteem scale?
   b *Why* would it matter if the reliability of the scale was poor?
   c How could the researcher improve the reliability of the scale?
   d How could the researcher assess the validity of the self-esteem scale?
   e Why would it matter if the validity of the scale was poor?

Comparing questionnaires and interviews

	Advantages	Weaknesses
Questionnaires *Respondents record their own answers.*	• Can be easily repeated so that data can be collected from large numbers of people relatively cheaply and quickly. • Respondents may feel more willing to reveal personal/confidential information than in an interview.	• Answers may not be truthful, for example because of leading questions and social desirability bias. • The sample may be biased because only certain kinds of people fill in questionnaires – literate individuals who are also willing to spend time filling in a questionnaire and returning it.
Structured interview *Questions predetermined.*	• Can be easily repeated because the questions are standardised. • Requires less interviewing skill than an unstructured interview. • More easy to analyse than an unstructured interview because answers are more predictable.	• The interviewer's expectations may influence the answers the interviewee gives (a form of investigator bias called **interviewer bias**). • Reliability may be affected by the same interviewer behaving differently on different occasions or different interviewers asking different questions (low inter-interviewer reliability).
Unstructured interviews *Interviewer develops questions in response to respondent's answers*	• More detailed information can generally be obtained from each respondent than in a structured interview. • Can access information that may not be revealed by predetermined questions.	• More affected by interviewer bias than structured interviews because in an unstructured interview the interviewer is developing new questions on the spot which might be less objective. • Requires well-trained interviewers, which makes it more expensive to produce reliable interviews compared with structured interviews which don't require specialist interviewers.

EXAM TIP

Often students write something like, 'The advantage of a questionnaire is that you can collect lots of data'. The problem with this is that it is not clear what 'lots of data' means. Compared to what? In fact you can also collect lots of data in an experiment or an interview.

• *You need to provide clear detail. (What is 'lots of data'? Why is there 'lots of data'?)*

• *You need to offer a comparison. (Compared to what? E.g. compared to an interview.)*

A good answer would say 'The advantage of a questionnaire is that you can collect data from more people than you would if using the interview method.'

DO IT YOURSELF No.3.13

How daring are you?

Answer YES or NO to the questions below.

1 Do you get scared on fast roller coasters?
2 Are you scared of flying?
3 Would you rather read a good book than play a computer game?
4 Do you prefer staying in rather than going out?
5 Have you ever lied to your parents?
6 Do you use the internet every day?
7 Do you arrange your CDs in alphabetical order?
8 Have you ever played truth or dare?
9 Are you too shy to tell people what you really think?
10 Do you dislike answering questions in class?

If you answered yes to more than five questions above you're a bit of a pussycat.

• Have you got any criticisms of the questionnaire?

• Try assessing the internal and external reliability of the questionnaire, as well as its face validity.

• To assess concurrent validity you can compare the outcome with an established psychological test. For example, psychologists measure sensation-seeking using Zuckerman's (1994) Sensation Seeking Scale (you can take the test and get your score at: www.bbc.co.uk/science/humanbody/mind/surveys/sensation/).

• Rewrite the quiz to deal with your criticisms and try to improve reliability and validity.

RESEARCH METHODS Qs No.3.20

1 Explain the difference between a structured and an unstructured interview.

2 Explain the difference between a questionnaire and an interview.

3 How can 'leading questions' be a problem in interviews or questionnaires?

4 Explain the difference between qualitative and quantitative data.

5 You have been asked to construct a questionnaire about peoples' attitudes towards smoking
   a Write **one** closed question that would collect quantitative data.
   b Write **one** open question that would collect qualitative data.
   c Write an example of a leading question for this questionnaire.
   d Explain how social desirability bias might affect the validity of the responses to your questionnaire.
   e Describe **one** advantage of using questionnaires to collect data in this study.
   f Describe **one** weakness of using questionnaires to collect data in this study.

KEY TERMS

Inter-interviewer reliability The extent to which two interviewers produce the same outcome from an interview.

Interviewer bias The effect of an interviewer's expectations, communicated unconsciously, on a respondent's behaviour.

WWW Look at some other online questionnaires and psychological tests at www.queendom.com/ (claims to be the world's largest testing centre, tests and questionnaires on everything) and www.atkinson.yorku.ca/~psyctest/ (site providing access to psychological tests that can be downloaded and used by student researchers including dieting beliefs scale and self-esteem scales).

Studies using a correlational analysis

The concept of a correlation should be familiar to you from GCSE maths. A **correlation** is a relationship between two variables.

Age and beauty co-vary. As people get older they become more beautiful. This is a **positive correlation** because the two variables *increase* together.

You may disagree, and think that as people get older they become less attractive. You think age and beauty are correlated but it is a **negative correlation**. As one variable increases the other one decreases.

Or you may simply feel that there is no relationship between age and beauty. This is called a **zero correlation**.

When conducting a study using a correlational analysis you need to produce a correlational **hypothesis**, which states the expected relationship between **co-variables**. In our case age and beauty are the co-variables; the study expects to find a relationship between these co-variables, so possible hypotheses might be:

• Age and beauty are positively correlated (directional).
• As people get older they are rated as more beautiful (directional).
• Age and beauty are correlated (non-directional).

SCATTERGRAMS

A correlation can be illustrated using a **scattergram**. For each individual we obtain two scores which are used to plot one dot for that individual – the co-variables determine the *x* and *y* position of the dot. The scatter of the dots indicates the degree of correlation between the co-variables.

A statistical test is used to calculate the **correlation coefficient**, a measure of the extent of correlation that exists between the co-variables.

• A correlation coefficient is a number.
• A correlation coefficient has a maximum value of 1 (+1 is a perfect positive correlation and –1 is a perfect negative correlation).
• Some correlation coefficients are written as –.52, whereas others are +.52. The plus or minus sign shows whether it is a positive or negative correlation.
• The coefficient (number) tells us how closely the co-variables are related. –.52 is just as closely correlated as +.52, it's just that –.52 means that as one variable increases the other decreases (negative correlation), and +.52 means that both variables increase together (positive correlation).

The top scattergram illustrates a positive correlation. The middle scattergram shows a negative correlation. The bottom scattergram is a zero correlation.

The correlation coefficients for all three graphs are: (1) +.76 (2) –.76 (3) –.006. The plus or minus sign shows whether it is a positive or negative correlation. The coefficient (number) tells us how closely the co-variables are related. –.76 is just as closely correlated as +.76.

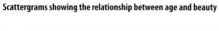

Scattergrams showing the relationship between age and beauty

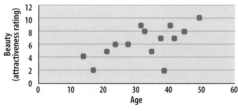

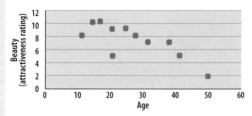

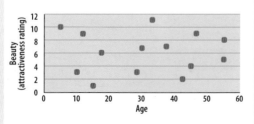

Linear and curvilinear

The correlations we have considered are all **linear** – in a perfect positive correlation (+1) all the values would lie in a straight *line* from the bottom left to the top right.

However there is a different kind of correlation – a **curvilinear** correlation. The relationship is not linear, but curved. However, there is still a predictable relationship. For example, stress and performance do not have a linear relationship. Performance on many tasks is depressed when stress is too high or too low; it is best when stress is moderate. (See the illustration on page 18.)

DO IT YOURSELF

No.**3.14**

Playing with correlation coefficients: The Excel method

Using Excel (the Microsoft Office application) you can enter and alter pairs of numbers to see how this affects a scattergram and correlation coefficient. Both are produced by Excel:

1 Open a new document in Excel (select <file> <new> <blank workbook>).
2 Select <insert> <chart> <XY (scatter)> and press <next>.
3 Place cursor at very top left of the page, click and drag across two rows and then down 16 rows. Press <next> <next> <finish>.
4 Now enter your pairs of scores (these can be invented or you could try entering a real set of numbers – such as height and shoe size of your class) to see if they are correlated. Do not enter data in the top row.
5 To calculate correlation coefficient: Place the cursor in an empty box. Select <insert> <function>. In top box type 'correl' and press 'go' and then <OK>.
6 Screen now says 'array1' and 'array2'. Click in 'array1' and then move cursor to top of first column of your numbers, click and drag to bottom of column. Do the same for array2.
7 Try changing some of the numbers and see how this alters your scattergram and the correlation coefficient.

You an also play with correlations on various websites such as www.stattucino.com/berrie/dsl/regression/regression.html

Evaluation of studies using correlational analysis

Advantages	Weaknesses
• Can be used when it would be unethical or impractical to manipulate variables and can make use of existing data.	• People often misinterpret correlations and assume that a cause and effect have been found, whereas this is not possible.
• If correlation is significant then further investigation is justified.	• There may be other, unknown variables (**intervening variables**) that can explain why the co-variables being studied are linked.
• If correlation is not significant then you can probably rule out a causal relationship.	
• As with experiments, the procedures can be repeated again which means that the findings can be confirmed.	• As with experiments, may lack internal/external validity, for example method used to measure IQ may lack validity or sample used may lack generalisability.

A correlation is not a research method. Therefore we don't talk about a correlational study but a study using a correlational analysis.

KEY TERMS

Correlation / correlational analysis Determining the extent of a relationship between two variables; co-variables may not be linked at all (**zero correlation**), they may both increase together (**positive correlation**), or as one co-variable increases, the other decreases (**negative correlation**). Usually a **linear** correlation is predicted, but the relationship can be **curvilinear**.

Correlation coefficient A number between −1 and +1 that tells us how closely the co-variables in a correlational analysis are related.

Intervening variable A variable that comes between two other variables which is used to explain the relationship between those two variables. For example, if a positive correlation is found between ice cream sales and violence this may be explained by an intervening variable – heat – which causes the increase in ice cream sales and the increase in violence.

Scattergram A graphical representation of the relationship (i.e. the correlation) between two sets of scores.

Significance A statistical term indicating that the research findings are sufficiently strong for us to accept the research hypothesis under test.

Significance is the extent to which something is particularly unusual.

When we look at a correlation coefficient we need to know whether it is strong or weak. In order to do this we use tables of significance which tell us how big the coefficient needs to be in order for the correlation to count as significant (unusual).

The table on the right gives an approximate idea of the values needed. The more pairs of scores you have, the smaller the coefficient can be.

A coefficient of either −.45 or +.45 would be significant if there were 16 pairs of data, but not if there were 14 pairs.

The magnitude of the number informs us about significance, while the sign tells us which direction the correlation is in (positive or negative).

Significance table	
N=	
4	1.000
6	0.829
8	0.643
10	0.564
12	0.503
14	0.464
16	0.429
18	0.401
20	0.380
22	0.361
24	0.344
26	0.331
28	0.317

These values are for Spearman's test of correlation.

RESEARCH METHODS Qs

No.**3.21**

1 Identify two variables that are likely to be positively correlated (such as height and weight).

2 Identify two variables that are likely to be negatively correlated.

3 What does a correlation coefficient tell you about a set of data?

4 Give an example of a positive correlation coefficient and a negative correlation coefficient.

5 Explain what the following correlation coefficients mean:
   +1.00   −1.00   .00   −.60   +.40   +.10

6 Consider the number +.36.
   a Identify the magnitude and sign of this number.
   b If this value was obtained after testing 20 people, would it be significant?
   c Sketch a scattergram to approximately illustrate this correlation.
   d If you conducted a study with 30 participants, would a correlation of +.30 be significant?

7 *A study investigates whether there is a negative correlation between age and liking for spicy foods. Participants are asked to rate their liking for spicy foods on a scale of 1 to 10 where 10 means they liked it a lot and 1 not at all.*
   a What is meant by the term 'negative correlation' in this context?
   b Why might you expect to find a negative correlation between these variables?

c Suggest **three** suitable descriptive statistics that could be used in this study.
d Describe **one** advantage and **one** weakness of conducting a correlational analysis.

8 *Guiseppe Gelato always liked statistics at school and now that he has his own ice cream business he keeps various records. To his surprise he found an interesting correlation between his ice cream sales and aggressive crimes. He has started to worry that he may be irresponsible in selling ice cream because it appears to cause people to behave more aggressively. The table below shows his data.*

All data rounded to 1000s	Jan	Feb	Mar	Apr	May	Jun	Jul	Aug	Sep	Oct	Nov	Dec
Ice cream sales	10	8	7	21	32	56	130	141	84	32	11	6
Aggressive crimes	21	32	29	35	44	55	111	129	99	36	22	25

a Sketch a scattergram of Guiseppe's data.
b What can you conclude from the data and the scattergram? (Remember that conclusions are an *interpretation* of the findings.)
c What intervening variable might better explain the relationship between ice cream and aggression?
d Describe how you would design a study to show Guiseppe that ice cream does (or does not) cause aggressive behaviour. (You need to operationalise your variables, decide on a suitable research design and sampling method, etc.).

Case studies

A **case study** involves the detailed study of a single individual, institution or event. It uses information from a range of sources, such as from the person concerned and also from their family and friends. Many techniques may be used – the people may be interviewed or they might be observed while engaged in daily life. Psychologists might use IQ tests or personality tests or some other kind of questionnaire to produce psychological data about the target person or group of people. They may use the experimental method to test what the target person/group can or can't do. The findings are organised to represent the individual's thoughts, emotions, experiences and abilities. Case studies are generally *longitudinal*, in other words they follow the individual or group over an extended period of time.

On this spread we are going to look at some case studies which provide insights into human memory and the workings of the brain.

KEY TERM

Case study A research method that involves a detailed study of a single individual, institution or event. Case studies provide a rich record of human experience but are hard to generalise from.

THE CASE OF PHINEAS GAGE

In 1848 Phineas Gage was working on the construction of a railway track in Vermont USA, blasting rock with gunpowder. He would fill a hole with dynamite, then cover the dynamite with sand and insert a tamping iron which was 3 feet 7 inches long. This was then hammered into the hole to pack down the gunpowder, only on one occasion he forgot to put in the sand, and as soon as he hammered the tamping iron it exploded, driving the tamping iron right through his skull. It went in under his left cheek bone and completely out through the top of his head. Not only did he survive, but he was able to speak, despite massive bleeding and substantial loss of brain tissue. After a short spell in hospital he went back to work, and he lived for a further 12 years. Some years after he died, his body was exhumed (along with the tamping iron which he had he kept) and his skull placed on display at Harvard University.

▲ Phineas' skull on display and an artist's impression of how the tamping iron would have passed through his head.

Phineas Gage was able to function fairly normally, showing that people can live despite the loss of large amounts of brain matter. However, the accident did have a significant effect on Phineas' personality. Before the accident he was hard-working, responsible, and popular, whereas afterwards he became restless and indecisive and swore a lot.

This case was important in the development of brain surgery because it showed that parts of the brain could be removed without having a fatal effect. Thus surgeons started to remove brain tumours, no longer fearful that this would cause a patient's death. Phineas' injury also suggested that damage to the frontal lobe leads to personality changes. This may have influenced the development of frontal lobotomies – a form of psychosurgery to disconnect the frontal lobes from the rest of the brain.

THE CASE OF HM

In the 1940s psychosurgery was at its peak. Dr William Scoville was one of the surgeons at the forefront of this work, performing over 200 lobotomies. Scoville used the operation to help a patient known simply as Henry M or HM. On his sixteenth birthday HM experienced his first severe epileptic fit. For the next few years these fits became progressively more debilitating and uncontrollable by medication. Scoville believed that HM's epilepsy might be cured by removing the parts of his brain thought to be causing the fits.

The effect on HM's epilepsy is not clear, but it seems to have got slightly better – however this was overshadowed by a much greater problem. HM was no longer able to form any new memories. His personality and intellect remained intact but he had lost some of his memories from the ten years prior to the operation (anterograde amnesia). More importantly, he lost the ability to form any new long-term memories (retrograde amnesia). For many years he reported that his age was 27 and the year was 1953. After a while he realised this was absurd and tried guessing the answer. He happily reread magazines with no loss of interest. He couldn't memorise lists of words or recall faces of people he met. He didn't remember that his mother had died and every time they told him, he mourned all over again.

HM only vaguely understood: 'Right now, I'm wondering, have I done or said anything amiss? You see, at this moment everything looks clear to me, but what happened just before? That's what worries me. It's like waking from a dream.' (Hilts, 1995)

HM's loss was psychology's gain. For the next 50 years he was tested by different psychologists at MIT in Boston. On one occasion, when he arrived at the lab, a researcher asked him if he remembered the way to the testing rooms. He said he didn't, but as he said it, his body turned in the right direction (Hilts, 1995). This suggests that his memory for skills (*procedural memory*) was intact but his memory for the events of life (*episodic memory*) was not, supporting the distinction between different types of long-term memory (see page 9).

HM also provided some interesting evidence in relation to STM. If HM was asked to estimate time he seemed to be able to do so for a maximum of 20 seconds, which fits with the estimates given by Peterson and Peterson concerning the duration of short-term memory (see page 4).

Ethical issues

If HM had no memory for things that happened to him, how could he have given his consent for psychologists to study him? He did not understand what was being done to him (which included electric shocks) or who was doing it. Psychologists need to ask themselves whether the means justify the ends.

HM himself (who is still alive) adopts a philosophical stance on his problems: 'It does get me upset, but I always say to myself, what is to be is to be. …what I keep thinking is that possibly I had an operation. And somehow the memory is gone… it isn't worrisome… to me, because I know that if they ever performed an operation on me, they'd learn from it. It would help others.'

THE CASE OF CLIVE WEARING

One of the difficulties with a case study is that it concerns a unique case and therefore generalisations should be made with caution. The conclusions drawn from the study of HM have, however, been confirmed by another case study. Baddeley (1990) described the same symptoms in a British man, Clive Wearing, who contracted a viral infection which attacked his brain, damaging the hippocampus and associated areas. Like HM, Wearing lost all his ability to transfer memories from STM (or working memory) to LTM. He remembers some aspects of his life before the infection, but not others. For example, he knows that he has children from an earlier marriage, but cannot remember their names. He recognises his second wife, Deborah, and greets her joyously every time they meet, believing he has not seen her in years, even though she may have just left the room to fetch a glass of water. Like HM his *procedural memory* is intact – he had been a conductor and pianist, working for the BBC and can still conduct a choir and play the piano but he has no recollection of his musical education (*episodic memory*). Also like HM, his STM is functional and he is perpetually convinced that he has only just recovered consciousness. In his diary, page after page is filled with entries like this:

8:31 AM: Now I am really, completely awake.
9:06 AM: Now I am perfectly, overwhelmingly awake.
9:34 AM: Now I am superlatively, actually awake.

▲ Clive Wearing and his wife, Deborah, who divorced him after he developed amnesia but decided she couldn't live without him and they have remarried.

WWW Two videos of Clive Wearing at www.learner.org/resources/series150.html#

THE CASE OF KF

In contrast to HM and Clive Wearing, KF's brain damage (from a motorcycle accident) left him with normal long-term recall but variable problems with short-term memory. He has a digit span of one (i.e. when given a string of 20 numbers to recall in sequence he usually can only remember one of them). This suggests he has almost no short-term recall. These deficits support the *multi-store model* because they show that STM and LTM are separate.

However, other of KF's deficit support the *working memory model*. If KF is given a paired associates task (he is given time to learn pairs of unrelated words such as 'nail' and 'map', and later prompted with the first word and asked to recall the second), KF's performance is only slightly poorer than normal control participants. This shows that only some areas of his STM are damaged. In addition KF does better on short-term recall tasks if material is presented visually than when it is presented auditorily, which again fits the working memory model.

Evaluation of case studies

Advantages	Weaknesses
• The method offers rich, in-depth data so information that may be overlooked using other methods is likely to be identified. • Can be used to investigate instances of human behaviour and experience that are rare, for example investigating cases of children locked in a room through childhood to see what effects such deprivation has on emotional development. It would not be ethical to generate such conditions experimentally. • The complex interaction of many factors can be studied, in contrast with experiments where many variables are held constant.	• It is difficult to generalise from individual cases as each one has unique characteristics. • It is often necessary to use recollection of past events as part of the case history and such evidence may be unreliable. • Researchers may lack objectivity as they get to know the case, or because theoretical bias may lead them to overlook aspects of the findings. • There are important ethical issues such as confidentiality – many cases are easily identifiable because of their unique characteristics, even when real names are not given.

VALIDITY

It is difficult to make generalisations to the wider population from a case study of one or a few individuals. In the case of the brain-damaged individuals this is especially true for a variety of reasons. First, we don't know how 'normal' their abilities were before the damage occurred. HM's disabilities may have been due to his epilepsy. Without causing deliberate damage to a normal brain (which would be unethical) we cannot claim to demonstrate a causal relationship between specific cognitive functions and brain areas.

Second, just because an area of the brain (such as the hippocampus) is *associated* with an inability to create new long-term memories doesn't mean that part of the brain is responsible. It may be that the hippocampus acts as a relay station and thus damage to the hippocampus has an effect. So we cannot demonstrate with certainty that one area of the brain is the causal component.

However, on the plus side, such case studies do provide additional evidence to support existing experimental studies.

RESEARCH METHODS Qs   No.3.22

1 Consider your understanding of the topic of memory after reading this spread. In what way has the information here enhanced your understanding?
2 Why do you think there are so many case studies related to memory?
3 Describe what research methods were likely to be used in the case studies described on this spread.
4 Suggest **two** advantages of using case studies rather than experiments to collect data about memory.
5 Suggest **two** weaknesses.
6 A hospital is interested to find out why some patients with head injuries recover faster than others. *Why* would you recommend using a case study and *how* would you do it?

Content analysis

A content analysis is what it says – the analysis of the content of something. For example a researcher might study the gender content of magazine advertisements and attempt to describe this content in some systematic way so that conclusions could be drawn (see DIY on the right). Content analysis is a form of indirect observation, indirect because you are not observing people directly but observing them through the artefacts they produce. These artefacts can be TV programmes, books, songs, paintings etc. The process involved is similar to any observational study, the researcher has to make design decisions about:

1 *Sampling method* – what material to sample and how frequently (e.g. which TV channels to include, how many programmes, what length of time).
2 *Behavioural categories* to be used:
   - Quantitative analysis: Examples in each category are counted. For example, when performing a content analysis of adolescent behaviour from letters in teen magazines, the researcher would decide on a set of topics (categories), and then count how many letters included the topics.
   - Qualitative analysis: Examples in each category are described rather than counted. For example, when performing a content analysis of adolescent behaviour from letters in teen magazines the researcher would provide quotes from different letters to illustrate the category.

EXAMPLE OF QUANTITATIVE CONTENT ANALYSIS

Manstead and McCulloch (1981) analysed ads on British TV to look at gender stereotypes. They observed 170 ads over a one-week period, ignoring those that contained only children and animals. In each ad they focused on the central adult figure and recorded frequencies in a table like the one on the right. For each ad there might be no ticks, one tick or a number of ticks.

In this study, women were found to be more likely than men to be portrayed as product users, to be cast in a dependent role, to produce no arguments in favour of the product and to be shown at home.

	Male	Female
Credibility basis of central character		
Product user	☐	☐
Product authority	☐	☐
Role of central character		
Dependent role	☐	☐
Independent role	☐	☐
Argument spoken by central character		
Factual	☐	☐
Opinion	☐	☐
Product type used by central character		
Food/drink	☐	☐
Alcohol	☐	☐
Body	☐	☐
Household	☐	☐

Evaluation of content analysis

Advantages	Weaknesses
• Has high ecological validity because they are based on direct observations of what people actually do; real communications which are current and relevant, such as recent newspapers or children's books in print.	• Observer bias reduces the objectivity and validity of findings because different observers may interpret the meaning of the behavioural categories differently.
• When sources can be retained or accessed by others (e.g. back copies of magazines or videos of people giving speeches) findings can be replicated and so tested for reliability.	• Likely to be culture-biased because interpretation of verbal or written content will be affected by the language and culture of the observer and behavioural categories used.

EXAMPLE OF QUALITATIVE CONTENT ANALYSIS

A Finnish study considered the role of the family in adolescents' peer and school experiences. Joronen and Åstedt-Kurki (2005) conducted semi-structured interviews with 19 adolescents aged 12–16, using questions such as, 'What does your family know about your peers?' and, 'How is your family involved in your school activities?' These interviews produced 234 pages of notes which were were analysed using a qualitative content analysis.

1 All answers to the same question were placed together.
2 Each statement was compressed into a briefer statement and given an identifier code.
3 These statements were compared with each other and categorised so that statements with similar content were placed together and a category (or theme) identified.
4 The categories were grouped into larger units producing eight main categories, for example
   - *Enablement* e.g. 'Yeah, ever since my childhood we've always had lots of kids over visiting.' (girl, 15 years)
   - *Support* e.g. 'They (family members) help if I have a test by asking questions.' (boy, 13 years)
   - *Negligence* e.g. 'My sister is not at all interested in my friends.' (girl, 16 years)

One of the conclusions drawn from this study is that schools should pay more attention to the multiple relationships that determine an adolescent's behaviour.

RESEARCH METHODS Qs — No.3.23

1 Explain in what way a content analysis is a form of observation.

2 Describe **two** advantages of conducting this kind of research.

3 How might observer bias affect the findings of a content analysis?

4 A university department was given funding to investigate the stereotypes presented in children's books (age stereotypes, gender stereotypes, etc.). They were to compare books that children read today with those from 20 years ago to see how and if stereotypes had changed.

   a Suggest **three** items that could be used as behavioural categories in this study.
   b Write operationalised definitions for these items.
   c How might you ensure that two researchers were using the behavioural categories in the same way?

5 On this page there is an example of a qualitative content analysis. In what way is it a content analysis? In what way is it qualitative?

Qualitative data

On page 80 we identified the difference between *quantitative* and *qualitative* data. It is sometimes said that qualitative data concerns 'thoughts and feelings' – but you can also have *quantitative* data about thoughts and feelings, for example a researcher could ask participants to rate their feelings about a film on a scale of 1 to 5. The result would be a number – a quantity. The difference between quantitative and qualitative research runs much deeper than 'thoughts and feelings'.

Qualitative research aims to produce an in-depth understanding of behaviour, and, because of the open-ended nature of the research, produce new explanations. The goal is to understand behaviour in a natural setting and also to understand a phenomenon from the perspective of the research participant and understand the *meanings* people give to their experience. The researcher is concerned with asking broad questions that allow the respondent to answer in their own words, or to observe behaviour.

PRESENTING QUALITATIVE DATA

Qualitative research uses smaller samples than quantitative research but usually involves the collection of a large amount of data – pages of written material and/or audio/video recordings. The challenge when presenting qualitative data is to find ways to summarise it so that conclusions can be drawn.

The first step is to *categorise* the data in some way.

- *Pre-existing categories* – i.e the researcher decides on some appropriate categories before beginning the research.
- *Emergent categories* – i.e. the categories or themes emerge when examining the data (as in the qualitative analysis on the left).

Later the behavioural categories can then be used to summarise the data.

- The categories or themes may be listed.
- Examples of behaviour within the category may be represented using quotes from participants or descriptions of typical behaviours in that category.
- Frequency of occurrences in each category may be counted, thus qualitative data are turned into quantitative data.

Finally a researcher may draw conclusions.

Comparing quantitative and qualitative data

	Advantages	Weaknesses
Quantitative data	• **Easier to analyse because the data are given in numbers that can be summarised using measures of central tendency and dispersion as well as simple graphs.** • **Can produce neat conclusions because numerical data reduces the variety of possibilities.**	• **Oversimplifies reality and human experience (statistically significant but humanly insignificant).**
Qualitative data	• **Represents the true complexities of human behaviour.** • **Gains access to thoughts and feelings that may not be assessed using quantitative methods with closed questions.** • **Provides rich details of how people behave because participants are given a free range to express themselves.**	• **More difficult to detect patterns and draw conclusions because of the large amount of data usually collected.** • **Subjective analysis can be affected by personal expectations and beliefs (though quantitative methods may only appear to be objective but are equally affected by bias).**

What research techniques produce qualitative data?

Quantitative and qualitative data may be produced in all kinds of studies:

- Unstructured observations generally produce *qualitative* data because the data that is collected is not placed in categories but, instead, everything that is observed is recorded.
- Structured observations produce numerical data in categories (*quantitative*). For example, Ainsworth *et al.*'s study using the strange situation counted *how often* infants engaged in certain behaviours (see page 40).
- Questionnaires or interviews using open questions produce *qualitative* data, whereas closed questions produce *quantitative* data.
- An unstructured interview is more likely to produce *qualitative* data because of the questions that develop (e.g. 'Why do you feel that?').
- A content analysis of television programmes could produce *qualitative* data and then the frequency of key themes could be counted producing *quantitative* data.
- Case studies can produce *quantitative* data but tend to include unique details of an individual's life and quotes to highlight unique experiences, thus they are more *qualitative* than quantitative. For example, the case study of HM (on page 100) includes records of experiences and what he said.
- Experiments produce numerical data (*quantitative*), for example Peterson and Peterson's study (page 4) found out *how many* words were correctly recalled.
- In some experiments participants are interviewed afterwards to find out if they have any important insights. For example, Asch interviewed participants after his conformity study (see page 148) and he analysed their *qualitative* responses to produce three broad categories which were the reasons why people conformed.

DO IT YOURSELF

No.**3.15**

Sexism in the media.

You could try to replicate the study by Manstead and McCulloch on the far left.

1 You might try a pilot study to see if the categories work and adapt them if necessary.

2 Decide on sampling methods. You can share the work with other class members.

3 Count the frequency of occurrences in each category.

4 Display your findings using one or more graphs.

KEY TERM

Content analysis A kind of observational study in which behaviour is observed indirectly in written or verbal material such as interviews, conversations, books, diaries or TV programmes. Behaviour is categorised (qualitative analysis) and may be counted (quantitative analysis).

Other research methods and techniques

This chapter (and the AS specification) covers only some of the research methods and techniques that are used by psychologists. On this page we will very briefly mention some other methods and techniques that you are likely to encounter when you read about research in psychology. It is useful to know something about them and their advantages and weaknesses.

OTHER RESEARCH METHODS AND TECHNIQUES

Investigations

In this chapter we have looked at a range of different research methods – experiments, observations, case studies etc. There are some occasions when a study doesn't fit into any of these categories. The study on the next spread, on the Barnum effect, is just that – it's not an experiment (no IV and DV); it's not a case study nor an observation; and it doesn't use a correlational analysis. It does use a questionnaire as a technique to collect data. In such cases a study is just an investigation.

The multi-method approach

In reality very few studies simply use one method. Many studies reported in this book use the *multi-method approach* – a combination of all sorts of different techniques and methods to investigate the target behaviour. For example, Schaffer and Emerson's study of infant attachment in 1964 (see page 38) was basically a non-experimental study, using naturalistic observation, interviews and rating scales, but it also included an experimental element, when mothers were asked to record infants' responses (a DV) to seven everyday situations (an IV).

Meta-analysis

A **meta-analysis** is a technique used in a number of research studies we have looked at in this book. A researcher or team of researchers combines the result of several studies that have addressed similar aims/hypotheses. The researcher(s) use **effect size** as the DV in order to assess overall trends. We use effect sizes in our everyday lives, for example a weight loss programme may boast that it leads to an average weight loss of 30 pounds. This is the size of the effect.

In Chapter 1 we looked at a meta-analysis of 53 studies related to the cognitive interview (Köhnken *et al.*,1999) which demonstrated the effectiveness of the CI compared with standard interviewing techniques. The effect size was 34% which means that of all the studies, the CI technique improved recall by 34%.

➕ Analysing the results from a group of studies rather than from just one study can allow more reliable conclusions to be drawn. Often studies produce rather contradictory results (e.g. some studies may find no effect, some studies a small effect, and others a larger effect). A meta-analysis allows us to reach an overall conclusion.

➖ The research designs in the different studies sampled may vary considerably, which means that the studies are not truly comparable, and thus the conclusions are not always valid.

Cross-cultural studies

In **cross-cultural studies** psychologists compare behaviours in different cultures. This is a way of seeing whether cultural practices affect behaviour. It is a kind of natural experiment where the IV is, for example, childrearing techniques in different cultures and the DV is some behaviour, such as attachment.

➖ There are many limitations with such studies. For example, researchers may use tests or procedures that have been developed in the US and are not equally valid in their country. This may make the individuals in the researcher's culture appear 'abnormal' or inferior. The term used to describe this is an **imposed etic** – when a technique or psychological test is used (i.e. imposed upon) in one culture even though it was designed for use in another culture. We discussed the problems of imposed etics in Chapter 2 – using the strange situation technique, which was developed in the US, to measure attachment in other cultures.

➖ A second limitation is that the group of participants may not be representative of the culture, and yet researchers might make generalisations about the whole culture – or even the whole country.

➕ This technique does enable psychologists to see whether some behaviours are universal i.e. not affected by cultural differences. For example the meta-analysis by van IJzendoorn and Kroonenberg showed that secure attachment was a universal behaviour.

Longitudinal and cross-sectional studies

When a study is conducted over a long period of time it is said to be a **longitudinal study** (it's long!). The reason for such studies is to be able to observe long-term effects and to make comparisons between the same individual at different ages.

An alternative way to do this is to conduct a **cross-sectional study.** In this instance one group of participants of a young age is compared to another, older group of participants at the same point in time e.g. in 2008.

➖ **Attrition** is a problem in a longitudinal study. The people who drop out are more likely to have particular characteristics (e.g. be the ones who are less motivated or more unhappy), which leaves a biased sample.

➖ A problem with cross-sectional studies is that the two groups of participants may be quite different. The *participant variables* in a cross-sectional design are not controlled, because the participants in each group are different.

➖ In a longitudinal study participants are likely to become aware of the research aims and their behaviour may be affected.

➖ **Cohort effects** cause difficulties for both longitudinal and cross-sectional studies. A group (or cohort) of people who are all the same age share certain experiences, such as children born just before the war who experienced poor diets in infancy due to rationing. In a longitudinal study we may not be able to generalise the findings from a study that looks at only one cohort because of the unique characteristics of that cohort. In a cross-sectional study cohort effects may produce spurious results, for example one cross-sectional study might compare the IQs of people aged twenty-something with eighty-somethings and find that the IQs of the latter group were much lower, concluding that ageing led to a decrease in IQ. The real reason, however, might well be because the eighty-somethings had lower IQs when they were twenty-something (due to e.g. poorer diet).

Attrition The loss of participants from a study over time which is likely to leave a biased sample or a sample which is too small.

Cohort effects One group of participants (cohort) may have unique characteristics because of time-specific experiences during the development of its members, such as being a child during the Second World War. This can affect both cross-sectional studies (because one group is not comparable with another) or longitudinal studies (because the group studied is not typical).

Control condition In a repeated measures experiment, the condition that provides a baseline measure of behaviour without the experimental treatment (IV), so that the effect of the experimental treatment may be assessed.

Control group In an independent groups experiment, a group of participants who receive no treatment. Their behaviour acts as a baseline against which the effect of the IV may be measured.

Cross-cultural study A kind of natural experiment in which the IV is different cultural practices and the DV is a behaviour such as attachment. This enables researchers to investigate the effects of nature and nurture.

Cross-sectional study One group of participants of a young age are compared with another, older group of participants, with a view to finding out the influence of age on the behaviour in question.

Effect size A measure of the strength of the relationship between two variables.

Experimental condition In a repeated measures design, the condition containing the experimental treatment (IV).

Experimental group In an independent groups design, a group of participants which receives the experimental treatment (the IV).

Imposed etic A technique or theory is developed in one culture and then used to study the behaviour of people in a different culture which has different norms, values, experiences etc.

Longitudinal study Observation of the same items over a long period of time. Such studies usually aim to compare the same individuals at different ages, in which case the IV is age. A longitudinal study might also observe a school or other institution over a long period of time.

Meta-analysis A researcher looks at the findings from a number of different studies in order to reach a general conclusion about a particular hypothesis.

Role play A controlled observation in which participants are asked to imagine how they would behave in certain situations, and act out the part. This method has the advantage of allowing the study of certain behaviours that might be unethical or difficult to find in the real world.

Role play

In some investigations participants are required to take on a certain role and then their behaviour can be observed as if it were real life. For example they might be asked to imagine that they are lying, or to pretend that they are a prison guard as in Zimbardo's study (see Introduction). **Role play** is a form of *controlled observation*.

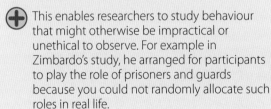

This enables researchers to study behaviour that might otherwise be impractical or unethical to observe. For example in Zimbardo's study, he arranged for participants to play the role of prisoners and guards because you could not randomly allocate such roles in real life.

The question is whether people really do act as they would in real life. In Zimbardo's study the participants acting as guards may have been following what they *thought* was guard-like behaviour, as seen in films. If they were real-life guards they may have acted more in accordance with personal principles rather than according to social norms.

1 In each of the following, identify the research method and, where relevant, the research technique(s) or design.
   a Scores from a questionnaire, 'How good is your memory', are related to GCSE results.
   b A male or female confederate stands by the roadside with a broken-down car to see if people are more likely to help a male or a female.
   c Psychology A-level results from two classes are compared to see if teacher A's teaching style was better than that of teacher B.
   d Children are shown two films, one that shows a child being helpful and another that shows a child not being helpful. They then are given free play time to see if they are more helpful.
   e Students are asked to explain what methods they find most successful for revision.
   f A group of children is assessed every year on various measures such as IQ, self-esteem and personality.
   g Interactions between first-time mothers and their newborn babies are compared with interactions of second-time mothers and their newborn babies.
   h A study on gambling is based around the experiences of one individual.
   i The effect of age on IQ is studied by comparing a group of young people with a group of older people.

2 In each of the following, identify the experimental and control group/condition.
   a A study looking at the effects of organisation on recall; one group is given an organised list of words to remember and the other has an unorganised list to remember.
   b A study looking at the effects of day care on IQ at age 10; some children have had two years in day care and the others have not had any.
   c A study looking at the effects of alcohol; each participant is asked to learn and recall a list of words and then given four units of alcohol and asked to repeat the same task.

A DIFFERENT KIND OF CONTROL

We have discussed the importance of controls in experimental research – to control extraneous variables. However researchers also use the word 'control' in a different context – as a means of establishing a baseline in an experiment. You may recall seeing the words *experimental group* and *control group*.

For example, a researcher might want to investigate the effects that rewards have on performance. To do this children could be asked to collect rubbish from a playground and offered a chocolate bar as a reward. They collect ten bags of rubbish.

We cannot conclude anything about the effects of the reward because we don't know if ten bags of rubbish is more or less than 'normal'. We don't know if they would have collected as many bags even if offered no reward. We need to have a control group so that we can make a comparison.

We need two groups of children (independent groups design): an **experimental group** (offered a reward) and a **control group** (offered no reward). This allows us to compare the effects of the reward (IV) on collecting rubbish (DV).

Or we can do a repeated measures study and then need to have two conditions: an **experimental condition** (children offered a reward on one occasion) and a **control condition** (offered no reward on another occasion). In this case 'control' refers to establishing a baseline for comparison rather than control of EVs.

In an independent groups design we would have experimental and control *groups* (each participant is assigned to one group). In a repeated measures design we would have experimental and control *conditions* (each participant experiences both conditions).

Science and pseudoscience

Let us end this chapter where we began the book. In the introductory chapter to this book we considered the value of science and the scientific approach. Research methods provide the systems for studying our world in an objective and systematic manner. They alert researchers to the potential biases and variables that may challenge the validity of any study. Despite such checks and balances, scientific conclusions are not always correct. It is important to replicate previous research to double-check findings and slowly move our knowledge and understanding forward.

It is critical to understand that science is not perfect, but without it we are easily fooled.

Read the statements below. For each statement rate how much it applies to you – zero is 'very poor', and a rating of five is 'excellent'. How many of them accurately describe you? Add up your total and divide by 13.

1   You have a great need for other people to like and admire you.
2   You have a tendency to be critical of yourself.
3   You have a great deal of unused capacity which you have not turned to your advantage.
4   While you have some personality weaknesses, you are generally able to compensate for them.
5   Your sexual adjustment has presented problems for you.
6   Disciplined and self-controlled outside, you tend to be worrisome and insecure inside.
7   At times you have serious doubts as to whether you have made the right decision or done the right thing.
8   You prefer a certain amount of change and variety and become dissatisfied when hemmed in by restrictions and limitations.
9   You pride yourself as an independent thinker and do not accept others' statements without satisfactory proof.
10 You have found it unwise to be too frank in revealing yourself to others.
11 At times you are extroverted, affable, sociable, while at others you are introverted, wary, reserved.
12 Some of your aspirations tend to be pretty unrealistic.
13 Security is one of your major goals in life.

Now read about the Barnum Effect.

THE BARNUM EFFECT

Bertram R. Forer (1949) gave a personality test to his students and told them that he would produce a unique personality analysis for each of them, based on the test. He asked each of the students to rate the analysis on a scale of 0 (very poor) to 5 (excellent) in terms of how much it related to themselves. Most of the students endorsed the statements as being true about them – the average was 4.26 (i.e. very close to 'excellent').

He then revealed that each student had in fact been given the same analysis – those statements on the left. He had copied these from a newspaper astrology column!

This is an excellent example of scientific enquiry and it also gives us some insight into the appeal of the pseudosciences. Many people love to read their horoscope and put great store in their uncanny accuracy. But the truth of the matter is that such predictions work only because we love to hear information about ourselves. This has been called the Forer or *Barnum Effect*, named after P.T. Barnum, the famous North American showman.

► Some people believe that the popularity of horoscopes is due to the Barnum effect. Will a course in psychology change your mind?

MORE INVESTIGATION OF PSEUDOSCIENCE: SHEEP AND GOATS

A recent study looked at the effect a course on the scientific method had on students' belief in the paranormal (Keeports and Morier, 1994). The course, called 'Science and pseudoscience', explored legitimate methods of scientific inquiry and compared them to the faulty, and often fraudulent, methods of the pseudosciences. Students doing an alternative course on 'psychology and law' were used as a control. At the beginning of term all the students completed the *Belief in the Paranormal Scale* (on the right) and they completed this again at the end of term. The students in the 'Science and Pseudoscience' class demonstrated a substantially reduced belief in the paranormal relative to the control class.

▲ People who believe in paranormal phenomena are the 'sheep'; those who don't are 'goats'.

You can use the scale to try another interesting study (see DIY opposite). One explanation that has been proposed for belief in the paranormal is that some people are less comfortable with the notion that occasionally things happen by chance rather than because they have been caused by something. Such people are more likely to be 'sheep' because they look to paranormal explanations to explain such events (Brugger *et al.*, 1990). 'Sheep' should also be less good at *probabilistic reasoning* – i.e. making judgements related to probability. For example, which of the following is more likely?

- I throw 10 dice at the same time and get 10 sixes.
- I throw one dice 10 times in succession and get 10 successive sixes.

In fact they are both equally likely – if you didn't think so, it suggests you are not good at probabilistic reasoning.

Belief in the Paranormal Scale

This questionnaire represents an attempt to discover which of the various paranormal events and phenomena you believe to be most likely and which you believe to be least likely. There are no right or wrong answers. Moreover, this is not an attempt to belittle or make fun of your own beliefs. Therefore please indicate your true feelings as well as you can. If you are unsure or ambivalent indicate this by marking 'undecided' and proceed to the next item. Indicate your answers in the following format:

1 = strongly disagree with this statement
2 = disagree with statement
3 = undecided or don't know
4 = agree with statement
5 = strongly agree with statement

Investigating belief in the paranormal

1 A measure of the degree to which someone believes in paranormal phenomena.

You can use the *Belief in the Paranormal Scale* (below) or produce your own questionnaire. A high score on the scale indicates that you believe in paranormal phenomena.

2 A measure of probabilistic reasoning.

You can do this by asking participants to 'mimic' the rolling of a dice: they should write down (or say) 100 digits between 1 and 6.

This can be scored by placing a tick whenever a number is repeated consecutively. The participant's score is the total number of ticks. A low score indicates that they are not good at probabilistic reasoning.

You will need to debrief participants after collecting data because you cannot provide full information about this study beforehand. When debriefing you can conduct a short interview (or present a questionnaire) asking them about their thoughts relating to paranormal events.

- Describe the aims of the sheep-goat study.
- Would the hypothesis predict a positive or a negative correlation?
- State a fully operationalised directional hypothesis.
- Design decisions: Decide on a suitable method of sampling (each member of the class might collect data from two or three people), and decide on standardised procedures and write standardised instructions.
- Consider ethical issues and how you will deal with them. Write a post-research debrief.

Analysing your data

1 Draw a scattergram to show the relationship between the co-variables (belief in the paranormal and probabilistic reasoning).

2 Calculate the correlation coefficient (using the Excel method on page 98).

- What do the graph and correlation coefficient tell you about your findings? Is the correlation strong, moderate or weak?

3 Calculate the mean, median and mode for both sets of data (belief in the paranormal and probabilistic reasoning).

- Which measure of central tendency is the most useful? Why?
- Which measure of central tendency is the least useful? Why?
- Use a measure of dispersion to describe your data.

4 Sort your participants into three groups: sheep, goats and neutral. You need to decide how to define each group, for example you might decide that the sheep are all those who scored more than 45.

Draw a bar chart to show the mean probabilistic reasoning score for each group.

- Compare the scattergram and the bar chart. Which do you think is more informative?

5 Summarise the responses given by participants in the post-research interview.

- What conclusions can you draw from your qualitative analysis?

Record your agreement in the boxes using the numbers 1 2 3 4 5

1 I believe psychic phenomena are real, and should become part of psychology and be studied scientifically.

2 All UFO sightings are either other forms of physical phenomena (such as weather balloons) or simply hallucinations.

3 I am convinced the Abominable Snowman of Tibet really exists.

4 I firmly believe that ghosts and spirits do exist.

5 Black magic really exists and should be dealt with in a serious manner.

6 Witches and warlocks do exist.

7 Only the uneducated or demented believe in the supernatural.

8 Through psychic individuals it is possible to communicate with the dead.

9 I believe the Loch Ness Monster of Scotland exists.

10 I believe that once a person dies his spirit may come back from time to time in the form of ghosts.

11 Some individuals are able to levitate (lift objects) through mysterious mental forces.

12 I believe that many special persons throughout the world have the ability to predict the future.

13 The idea of being able to tell the future through the means of palm reading represents the beliefs of foolish and unreliable persons.

14 I am firmly convinced that reincarnation has occurred throughout history.

15 I firmly believe that, at least on some occasions, I can read another person's mind via ESP (extrasensory perception).

16 ESP is an unusual gift that many persons have and should not be confused with elaborate tricks used by entertainers.

17 Ghosts and witches do not exist outside the realm of the imagination.

18 Supernatural phenomena should become part of scientific study, equal in importance to physical phenomena.

19 All of the reports of 'scientific proof' of psychic phenomena are strictly sensationalism with no factual basis.

20 Through the use of mysterious formulas and incantations it is possible to cast spells on individuals.

21 With proper training anyone could learn to read other people's minds.

22 It is advisable to consult your horoscope daily.

23 Plants can sense the feelings of people through a form of ESP.

24 ESP has been scientifically proven to exist.

25 There is a great deal we have yet to understand about the mind of Man, so it is likely that many phenomena (such as ESP) will one day be proven to exist.

Scoring for the Belief in the Paranormal Scale (Jones *et al.*, 1977)

Reverse the responses for questions 2, 7, 13, 17, 19 i.e. for question 2 if a person responded with 5, then change this to 1, 4 then change this to 2, 3 stays the same, 2 changes to 4 and 1 changes to 5.

Now add all responses, giving a maximum score of 125.

In the trial of this scale (with 475 undergraduates) 10% scored less than 50 (low believers) and 10% scored more than 85 (high believers).

(The reason for the reverse of some questions is to prevent participants getting into a habit of always giving a high or low rating – this way, if you tend towards paranormal belief you sometimes give high and sometimes give a low rating. A *response set bias* is the tendency for respondents to answer questions in the same way, regardless of context.)

We have identified here the key points of the topics on the AQA (A) AS specification, i.e. the bare minimum that you need to know. You may want to fill in further details to elaborate and personalise this material.

METHODS AND TECHNIQUES

EXPERIMENTS AND HYPOTHESES

Experiment – IV → DV

Hypothesis
- **Directional** (predicting one condition better than other).
- **Non-directional** (no direction predicted.
- Hypotheses must be **operationalised**.

OBSERVATION

- **Naturalistic** – behaviour not manipulated.
- **Controlled** – some variables can be controlled.
- **Content analysis** – indirect observation of behaviour.

Observational design:

- **Structured** and **unstructured**.
- **Behavioural categories** (operationalisation) – e.g. behaviour checklist, coding system, rating system.
- **Sampling** – **event** and **time**.
- **Participant** and **non-participant**.
- **Overt** and **covert**.

- **External validity** – high for naturalistic observation but population validity may be a problem.
- **Internal validity** – depends whether behavioural categories are appropriate.
- **Reliability** – established with inter-observer reliability, improves with training of observers.
- **Ethical issues** – informed consent, privacy and confidentiality.

CASE STUDIES

Study of a single person, institution or event.

- Rich data; possible unusual insights into rare cases.
- Generalisation is a problem; research bias; ethical issues such as privacy and confidentiality.

EXPERIMENTAL DESIGN

- **Repeated measures** – order effects (e.g. practice effect); Participants may guess purpose of experiment.
- **Independent groups** – no control of **participant variables**; twice as many participants required.
- **Matched pairs** – time-consuming and only partially effective at controlling participant variables.
- **Counterbalancing** (e.g. ABBA) to control for order effects.

SELF-REPORT

Good questions

- Clear (operationalised).
- Unbiased – no leading questions, avoid **social desirability bias**.
- Constructed to aid analysis – **closed** (quantitative) or **open** (qualitative) questions.

Good questionnaires

- Filler questions.
- Sequence of questions.
- Sampling technique.
- Pilot study.

- **Questionnaires** – easily repeated and more impersonal but answers may not be truthful.
- **Unstructured interviews** – more detail may be obtained by adapting questions but more affected by interviewer bias.

- **External validity** – affected by representativeness of sample.
- **Internal validity** – can be assessed using face or concurrent validity.
- **Internal reliability** – check with split-half method.
- **External reliability** – check with test-retest.
- **Ethical issues** – deception, psychological harm, privacy and confidentiality.

LAB, FIELD AND NATURAL EXPERIMENTS

- **Lab** – controlled environment often lacks mundane realism.
- **Field** – natural environment but IV controlled by experimenter, control more difficult, ethical issues.
- **Natural (quasi)** – IV varies naturally, doesn't show cause-and-effect because participants not randomly allocated to conditions.
- **Extraneous variables** can be controlled in all three.

STUDIES USING CORRELATIONAL ANALYSIS

- **Scattergram** to show correlation graphically.
- **Correlation coefficient** – numerical measure of relationship between co-variables.
- **Positive** – co-variables increase together.
- **Negative** – one co-variable increases as other decreases.
- Most relationships are linear, **curvilinear** is a more complicated relationship.

- Can be used when variables can't be manipulated (practically or ethically); Lack of correlation may rule out causal relationship.
- Results often misinterpreted as showing a causal link; real cause may be an unknown **intervening variable**.

Other methods/techniques used in psychological research include:

- Meta-analysis (a study of studies).
- Cross-cultural studies (comparison of same behaviour in different cultures).
- Longitudinal and cross-sectional studies (study of how a particular behaviour changes across different age groups).
- Role play (participants act out specific roles to recreate a situation of interest to the researcher).

INVESTIGATION DESIGN

VALIDITY

How true or legitimate something is; whether a study or test measures what it intended to measure.

- Determined by control of extraneous variables.
- **Mundane realism** (mirroring the real world) – tends to be low when control is high.
- **Generalisability** is related to both control and realism.
- **Internal validity** concerns what goes on inside a study e.g. control, realism.
- **External validity** concerns what goes on outside a study, e.g. ecological validity.

SELECTION OF PARTICIPANTS

- **Opportunity** – easy but biased.
- **Volunteer** – varied sample but volunteer bias.
- **Random** – unbiased in theory but not necessarily in practice.
- **Stratified** and **quota sampling** may be used in questionnaires.

EXTRANEOUS VARIABLES

Participant variables affect independent groups design only.

- Age
- Gender
- Personality
- Intelligence, motivation, etc.

Situational variables

- Order effects (e.g. practice).
- Time of day, temperature, noise.
- Investigator effects (e.g. leading questions).
- **Demand characteristics.**

Can be dealt with using **standardised procedures/instructions** and/or **double blind**.

Participant effects

- **Hawthorne effect**
- **Social desirability bias**

Can be dealt with by **single blind** design and/or increased **experimental realism**.

ETHICAL ISSUES

- **Informed consent** - information that may affect participants' willingness to take part.
- **Deception** – lying or withholding key information may bring psychology into disrepute.
- **Right to withdraw.**
- **Protection from harm**.
- **Confidentiality**.
- **Privacy**.

DEALING WITH ETHICAL ISSUES

- **Ethical guidelines** (BPS code of ethics) e.g. debriefing.
- **Ethics committees**.
- **Cost-benefit analysis** – may raise as many problems as it solves.
- **Punishment** – being barred from professional association.
- **Presumptive consent** – presume consent of actual participants.

Some other design matters:

- **Pilot studies** (small-scale trial run of the main study).
- **Confederates** (instructed by the experimenter to play a particular role in the study).

DATA ANALYSIS

QUANTITATIVE DATA

- **Measures of central tendency** (mean, median, mode).
- **Measures of dispersion** (range, standard deviation).
- **Visual display** (tables, bar chart, line graph, scattergram).
- **Measurement scales** (NOIR – nominal, ordinal, interval and ratio data).

Quantitative data:

- Easier to analyse; produces neat conclusions.
- Oversimplifies reality and human experience.

QUALITATIVE DATA

- Produce categories
  – pre-existing
  – emergent.
- List themes/examples.
- Convert to quantitative data.

- Represents complexity of human behaviour; rich details; gains access to thoughts and feelings.
- More difficult to detect patterns and draw conclusions; subjective analysis may lead to bias.

Task 1 Graphs

For each of the graphs below

a Identify the type of graph.
b Describe **one or more** conclusions that could be drawn from the graph.

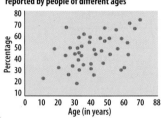

Driving under the influence of an illicit drug, reported by people of different ages

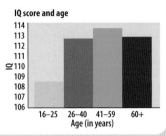

IQ score and age

Task 2 Research methods and techniques

The specification requires that you know about the research methods and techniques listed below. For each one, identify **two** advantages and **two** weaknesses and **two** ethical issues which may be difficult to deal with.

• Laboratory experiment
• Field experiment
• Natural experiment
• Studies using a correlational analysis
• Observational techniques
• Questionnaire
• Interview
• Case studies

Task 3 Knowing the words

You may recall that right at the beginning of this chapter there was a note about how learning about research methods was a bit like learning a foreign language – you have to learn a new set of words and what they mean. The best way to do this is to *use* your new language. The exercises throughout this book were intended to help you do this.

Write down now all the new words you have learned (that you can remember) and then check through your Research Methods Booklet (suggested on page 69) to see what words you had forgotten. You might work with a partner and when you have finished get another pair to check your list. See who in the class can correctly identify the most terms.

Task 4 Knowing the meaning

Create a card game by writing down all the key terms in this chapter on cards and then writing all the definitions onto other cards. Place all cards face down. Each player turns two cards over; if they match, you keep the cards and have another go. If they don't match, the next player takes their turn. At the end, the winner is the one with the most cards.

There are lots of ideas at the end of other chapters that you might adapt and try out here.

Task 5 Research methods questions

1 *A psychologist conducted a study to look at whether watching certain films made children more helpful (one film was about being helpful, the other was neutral). He advertised for participants in the local newspaper. A large number of children volunteered, and a sample of 30 was selected for the actual experiment.*
  a What is the IV in this experiment?
  b What is the DV?
  c How could you operationalise the DV?
  d State a suitable research prediction for this study.
  e Is your prediction directional or non-directional?
  f Explain your choice of direction.
  g What kind of experimental design would you use in this study?
  h Describe **one** weakness of this experimental design.
  i How could you deal with this problem?
  j Describe the target population.
  k What kind of sample was obtained?
  l Suggest how the experimenter might select the sub-sample from all those who applied.

2 *A psychology experiment aims to investigate how preschool children differ from those already at school in terms of their ability to remember symbols that look like letters.*
  a If the experimenter wanted to obtain a random sample of each of the two age groups how might this have been done?
  b Explain the purpose of using a random sample.
  c What is the IV in the experiment?

  d What is the DV?
  e The children were shown 20 different symbols. Why was it better to use 20 symbols rather than just two symbols?
  f Why might it be better to use two rather than 20 symbols?

3 *Mary Smith organises a project to enable her psychology class to have a go at using matched pairs design. The class is divided into two groups, one will receive word list A (nouns) and the other word list B (verbs). They will be tested on recall.*
  a Suggest **two** participant variables that could be used to match classmates.
  b Explain why each of the variables you chose would be important to control in this study.
  c What are the two conditions in the experiment?
  d If she decided to use an independent measures design, suggest **two** ways that participants could have been allocated to conditions.
  e The teacher used words that were all of two syllables and of similar length. Give **one** reason why.
  f The teacher decided to repeat the study using all the pupils in the school. She selected every fifth pupil in the register. Why is this not a random sample?

4 *A psychologist wishes to investigate whether people are more likely to give a donation when they walk past a person collecting money for charity if they see someone else in front of them giving money. How would you design an experiment to test these aims?*

Task 6 Multiple choice questions

1 One reason for using a directional hypothesis would be because
a Past research suggests that participants will do better on one condition than another.
b Past research is uncertain about how participants will perform.
c There is no past research.
d The researcher wants to make a strong statement.

2 A student plans to investigate the effects of practice on IQ test performance. Some participants are given a practice test prior to the IQ test, whereas others do no test beforehand. The dependent variable in this study is
a The participants.
b The effects of practice.
c IQ test performance before the study.
d IQ test performance at the end of the study.

3 The study described in question 2 above is a
a Repeated measures design.
b Independent groups design.
c Matched pairs design.
d Careful design.

4 One advantage of doing a matched pairs design is
a You need fewer participants than for repeated measures.
b You can control some participant variables.
c Order effects are not a problem.
d b and c

5 The letters 'ABBA' refer to a research design
a Created by a Swedish rock band.
b To control participant variables.
c To counterbalance for order effects.
d b and c.

6 Which of the following could *not* be an extraneous variable in a study
a An investigator effect.
b A confederate.
c An order effect.
d Lack of standardised procedures.

7 An individual who is instructed in how to behave by the researcher, often acting as the IV, is called
a An extraneous variable.
b A dependent variable.
c The investigator.
d A confederate.

8 Which of the following is a random sample?
a Names drawn from a hat.
b Asking people if they would like to take part.
c Every tenth name in a register.
d Taking whoever happens to be there.

9 Which of the following is a measure of central tendency?
a Range.   b Bar chart.
c Mode.   d Interval.

10 Mundane realism refers to
a Using video film to capture participants' behaviour.
b An experiment being boring and therefore not holding participant's interest.
c The extent to which an experiment mirrors the real world.
d A Spanish football team.

11 A case study may concern
a A single individual.
b An institution.
c An event.
d All of the above.

12 Which method is good for collecting lots of data?
a Experiment.
b Questionnaire.
c Naturalistic observation.
d All of the above.

13 The key feature of a naturalistic observation is that
a No set categories are used to record behaviour.
b Behaviour is observed.
c There is an independent variable.
d Everything has been left as it normally is.

14 A coding system is a method used in observational research for
a Sampling behaviours.
b Making systematic observations.
c Analysing the findings.
d All of the above.

15 A correlation coefficient of +.65 indicates
a No correlation.
b A weak positive correlation.
c A moderate positive correlation.
d A strong positive correlation.

16 Respondents often answer questions in a way that makes them look good rather than being truthful. This is called
a A response set.
b A leading question.
c Social desirability bias.
d The Hawthorne Effect.

17 Closed questions tend to produce
a Qualitative data.
b Quantitative data.
c Questionable data.
d a and c.

18 Debriefing is an
a Ethical issue.
b Ethical guideline.
c An ethical issue and an ethical guideline.
d A folder for research notes.

19 Which of the following ethical issues is not likely to be a problem in a naturalistic observation?
a Informed consent.
b Privacy.
c Confidentiality.
d Protection from psychological harm.

20 When observations are made from data in a newspaper, this is called
a Direct observation.
b Indirect observation.
c Content analysis.
d b and c.

21 Low reliability in an observational study can be dealt with by
a Using more than one observer.
b Conducting observations in varied settings with varied participants.
c Training observers to use the coding system.
d a and c.

22 Variables in an experiment are operationalised, which means they are
a Understandable by participants.
b Used in a medical experiment.
c Described in a way that can be easily measured or manipulated.
d Turned into numbers.

23 Internal validity is concerned with
a The generalisability of research findings.
b The population that was studied.
c Whether a researcher tested what he intended to test.
d Whether the findings are what the experimenter expected.

24 External validity refers to
a The generalisability of research findings.
b Whether the findings are what the experimenter expected.
c Whether an observed effect can be attributed to the IV.
d All of the above.

Answers are on page 214.

The Unit 1 exam is divided into two sections – Section A: Cognitive psychology and Research methods and Section B: Developmental psychology and Research methods. In total on the Unit 1 exam there are 24 marks on research methods questions, split between cognitive and developmental psychology. There are also research methods questions on Unit 2, with 12 marks in total (4 marks in each section).

---

1   A classic experiment in psychology looked at the effect of experimenter expectations. Rosenthal and Fode (1963) asked students to train rats to learn the route through a maze. The students were told that there were two groups of rats: one group consisted of 'fast learners' having been bred for this characteristic, while the other comprised 'slow learners'. In fact there were no differences between the rats. Despite this, the findings of the study showed that the supposedly brighter rats actually did better. When the students were asked about their rats afterwards those with 'fast learning' rats described them as smarter, more attractive, and more likeable. The only explanation can be that the students' expectations affected the rats' performance.

   (a)   Identify the independent variable in this experiment. (*2 marks*)

Alice's answer

The IV is expectations, either expecting the rat was bright or dull.

Tom's answer

IV is the students' expectations about the rats.

Examiner's comments

Alice gets the full **2 out of 2 marks** because she has fully operationalised the IV, identifying both levels. Tom gets only **1 out of 2 marks** because his is not operationalised.

   (b)   (i)   Identify **one** ethical issue that might arise in this study. (*1 mark*).

         (ii)   Explain how the investigators might have dealt with this issue. (*2 marks*)

Alice's answer

(i) Deception.
(ii) Debrief the participants after the study and tell them the true aims of the study and see if they are feeling distressed in any way.

Tom's answer

(i) Debriefing.
(ii) Tell the participants at the end what the true aims are.

Examiner's comments

Alice again gets **full marks** as she has given a correct answer for (i) and provided sufficient detail of what she would do in (ii). Unfortunately Tom gets **zero marks** as his answer for (i) is wrong – debriefing is judged to be an ethical guideline but not an issue. Because (i) is wrong, part (ii) automatically receives no marks.

   (c)   (i)   Is this study a repeated measures design or independent groups design? (*1 mark*)

         (ii)   Explain why a matched participants design is preferable to an independent groups design. (*2 marks*)

Alice's answer

(i) Repeated measures.
(ii) Matched pairs is better because it means you can control participant variables (which you can't with independent groups) and also avoid order effects (which are a problem for repeated measures).

Tom's answer

(i) Independent groups.
(ii) When you use matched pairs it means that you are essentially using two groups like in an independent groups design but you match the participants on certain key variables.

Examiner's comments

In part (ii) both Alice and Tom have provided lengthy answers but Tom's fails to answer the question. He explains what a matched pairs design is but not why it is better. Alice, on the other hand, provides two reasons why matched pairs is a better design, though really only one of her reasons is relevant – the participant variables part, and for full marks she should have explained this a bit more; she might have given an example of a participant variable that could be controlled, such as intelligence.

So both students get **1 out of 3 marks**.

   (d)   This study is a laboratory experiment. Give **one** strength of laboratory experiments. (*2 marks*)

Alice's answer

One strength is the extraneous variables can be controlled.

Tom's answer

Lab experiments are conducted in a contrived environment where the experimenter can control variables better than in a field experiment, which is a strength of the lab experiment.

Examiner's comments

Alice's answer is correct but again not sufficient detail for full marks and again an example would have helped, **1 out of 2 marks**.

   Tom could have specified which variables can be converted – both independent and extraneous variables can be better controlled so he wins the day and gets the full **2 out of 2 marks**.

(e) Explain what demand characteristics are, using a possible example from this study. (*3 marks*)

Alice's answer

A demand characteristic is a cue in the research environment which invites participants to behave in predictable ways. For example in the experiment on rats in mazes the students are likely to have tried to figure out what the experiment was about and therefore they were affected more than usual by the labels given to the rats.

Tom's answer

Demand characteristics spoil an experiment because they help people to guess what the experiment is about. For example the horse Clever Hans seemed able to add things up but in fact he was responding to his owner's cues.

Examiner's comments

Alice has given a detailed explanation and an appropriate example from the study so she gets **3 out of 3 marks**. Tom's explanation is reasonable though it lacks detail. His example is not appropriate – the question required an example from the study so he would get only **1 out of 3 marks**.

---

2   A school decides to conduct a study on the pre-school experiences of the students in the school using a questionnaire. They want to collect data about whether students were looked after at home, or spent some time in a day nursery, and to see if this was related to the students' social development.
      A part of this questionnaire is shown on the right.

   (a)   Outline **one** advantage of using a questionnaire. (*2 marks*)

> 8   Before you went to school, who looked after you? (tick as many boxes as apply)
>   ☐ Mother or father
>   ☐ Childminder
>   ☐ Nursery school
>
> 9   If you did have care outside your home, how long was this for (give your answer in months)?
>
> 10 Describe what kind of person you are (in terms of shyness, friendliness etc.)

Alice's answer

They are quick and easy to use and collect lots of data.

Tom's answer

One advantage is that you can collect lots of data because you can give the questionnaire to lots of people quickly and relatively easily.

Examiner's comments

Alice is not up to her usual high standard here and has given three answers to a question requiring just one. Only her first answer ('they are quick') will be considered and it isn't clear why a questionnaire is quick – they can take a long time – so she gets **0 out of 2 marks**, while Tom gets the full **2 out of 2 marks**.

   (b)   Explain **one** reason why a pilot study might have been carried out in the context of this study. (*2 marks*)

Alice's answer

You would do it so that any problems might be detected, such as some questions that were not clear, and these can then be put right.

Tom's answer

A pilot study is a small-scale trial run of a full-scale study conducted with a small sample of participants.

Examiner's comments

Alice is back on form and has written a fuller answer, but she has failed to spot the all-important phrase 'in this study'. Her answer does not relate to the particular study and therefore she gets **1 out of 2 marks**. Tom gets nothing as he has failed to answer the question – which asked 'why' not 'what' (**0 out of 2 marks**).

   (c)   (i) Identify **one** question in the extract above that would provide qualitative data. (*1 mark*)

         (ii) With reference to the question you have identified in part (i), explain why this question would produce qualitative data. (*3 marks*)

Alice's answer

(i) Question 10. (ii) The question would provide a range of answers which would not be easily quantifiable.

Tom's answer

(i) Question 10. (ii) This question is about what people think and feel and therefore it is qualitative.

Examiner's comments

Both students have correctly identified question 10 but Tom's reason is not sufficient – in fact questions about thoughts and feelings can be quantitative or qualitative, but qualitative questions do tend to be more about thinking/feeling so he can receive some credit. Tom gets **2 out of 3 marks** and Alice gets **3 out of 3 marks**.

   (d)   Explain what the term 'reliability' means and how you would check the reliability of this questionnaire. (*3 marks*)

Alice's answer

Reliability means consistency. You could check reliability by doing a test-retest which would involve giving the questionnaire to a group of people and then giving it to the same people again a while later, and then comparing their answers on the two occasions.

Tom's answer

Reliability refers to how trustworthy something is. You can check reliability by asking someone else to confirm that a person's answers are honest.

Examiner's comments

Alice has given a full and correct answer for **3 out of 3 marks**. Tom starts on a bad foot because validity is about trustworthiness, not reliability. Tom goes on to give a method of checking validity and not reliability, so **0 out of 3 marks** for him.

YOUR OWN LITTLE BOOK OF REVISION NOTES

At the beginning of this book we explained how to produce your own little book of notes and use them for effective revision (see page x).

Remember to keep your notes brief – just record key points which will act as coat pegs for remembering the material.

For this chapter we have provided only the list of terms and concepts that need to be mastered – you will need to create your own tick list (see end of other chapters):

Experimental method
- Laboratory, field, natural
- Experimental design (independent groups, repeated measures, and matched pairs)
- Evaluation

Studies using a correlational analysis
- Analysis and interpretation of correlational data
- Positive and negative correlations
- Interpretation of correlation coefficients
- Evaluation

Observational techniques
- Design of naturalistic observations
- Development and use of behavioural categories
- Evaluation

Self-report techniques
- Design of questionnaires and interviews
- Evaluation

Case studies
- Evaluation

Validity
- Control of extraneous variables
- Demand characteristics and Investigator effects

Reliability

Ethical issues
- Ways in which psychologists deal with them
- Awareness of the BPS Code of Ethics

Selection of participants and sampling techniques
- Random, opportunity and volunteer sampling

Aims, Hypotheses
- Directional and non directional

Operationalisation of variables
- Independent and dependant variables

Pilot studies

Quantitative data, presentation and interpretation
- Graphs, scattergrams and tables
- Measures of central tendency including median, mean, mode
- Measures of dispersion including ranges and standard deviation

Qualitative data, analysis and presentation
- Processes involved in content analysis

CROSSWORD

Answers on page 214.

Across

7 A measure of dispersion that measures the difference between the highest and lowest score in a set of data. (5)

8 A research design where neither the participant nor the experimenter is aware of the condition that an individual participant is receiving. (6,5)

11 In an interview or questionnaire, questions that invite the respondent to provide their own answer rather than select one of those provided. (4)

12 A graphical representation of the relationship (i.e. the correlation) between two sets of scores. (11)

14 The middle value in a set of scores when they are placed in rank order. (6)

15 The arithmetic average of a group of scores, calculated by dividing the sum of the scores by the number of scores. (4)

16 In an experiment, the variable that is measured by the experimenter (initials). (2)

18 The kind of data that best expresses what people think or feel, and cannot be counted. (11)

19 A research method that involves a face-to-face interaction with another individual and results in the collection of data. (9)

20 In a repeated measures design, a confounding variable arising from the sequence in which conditions are presented, e.g. a practice or boredom effect. (5,6)

Down

1 A graph used to represent the frequency of data. (3,5)

2 The most frequently occurring score in a set of data. (4)

3 Data which represent how much or how long, or how many etc. there are of something. (12)

4 Predicts the kind of difference (e.g. more or less) between two groups of participants or between different conditions: _____ hypothesis. (11)

5 A small-scale trial run of a study to test any aspects of the design, _____ study. (5)

6 A measure of consistency within a set of scores or items, and over time such that it is possible to obtain the same results on subsequent occasions when the measure is used. (11)

9 Kind of sampling where people are selected who are most easily available. (11)

10 A technique for selecting participants such that every member of the population being tested has an equal chance of being selected. (6)

12 A type of research design where the participant is not aware of the research aims. (6,5)

13 A sampling technique which relies solely on people who offer to participate, usually in response to an advertisement. (9)

17 In an experiment, the variable that is manipulated by the experimenter (initials). (2)

Biological psychology explains behaviour in terms of the systems that operate in our bodies – such as blood, hormones, nerves and the brain – and also in terms of genes. The way you think and feel has important influences on these biological systems, as illustrated by the study of stress.

CHAPTER

4

Biological psychology: Stress

SPECIFICATION BREAKDOWN

Specification content	Comment
Stress as a bodily response	
• **The body's response to stress, including the pituitary-adrenal system and the sympathomedullary pathway in outline**	This section of the specification starts with some technical terms that may be new to you – 'pituitary-adrenal' (HPA) and 'sympathomedullary'. You'll soon be familiar with these terms, which relate to what's going on in the body when it is aroused!
• **Stress-related illness and the immune system**	Research has shown that stress is associated with various illnesses, including heart attacks and even the common cold. One reason for this is that stress generally reduces the ability of the immune system to fight off invaders such as bacteria and viruses. In this section you will look at psychological research on the link between stress and the immune system and other stress-related illness (cardiovascular and psychiatric disorders).
Stress in everyday life	
• **Life changes and daily hassles** • **Workplace stress**	There are many sources of stress in our everyday lives. One source is life changes – events such as marriage, moving house and even Christmas – which have a psychological 'cost'. It isn't just the big events that are stressful – according to psychologists everyday hassles also wear you down and act as stressors. A further common source of stress comes from the workplace – job demands and responsibilities are linked to illness.
• **Personality factors, including Type A behaviour**	Some people are more affected than others by stress. One such personality type is called 'Type A' – people who are competitive and assertive, and also in a rush to do things. The concept of hardiness has also been used to explain why some people cope better than others with stress.
• **Distinction between emotion-focused and problem-focused approaches to coping with stress**	People who do experience high levels of stress may seek ways to reduce their stress levels. The methods may be emotion-focused and deal with the emotional side of feeling stressed, or they may be problem-focused and tackle the problem that is creating stress.
• **Psychological and physiological methods of stress management, including Cognitive Behavioural Therapy and drugs**	Methods of *coping* may not be that helpful in the long-term *management* of stress. Methods of stress management aim to provide more comprehensive techniques for dealing with stress. These may be psychological and deal with the subjective experience of stress, or physiological and deal with what is happening in your body when you experience stress. We will look at different examples of each of these, as well as the strengths and weaknesses of each method.

THE EVOLUTIONARY ORIGINS OF THE STRESS RESPONSE

As we saw in Chapter 1, evolution is the process by which traits are shaped by natural selection. As with many other human traits (such as caring for our young and priorities in mate selection), the stress response has been shaped by this process. Because stress is so often associated with its negative effects (e.g. 'feeling stressed', 'suffering from stress'), its usefulness has often been overlooked. By changing certain aspects of the body in times of danger, the stress response increases our ability to cope with the physical challenges that might arise. Nesse and Young (2000) suggest that the first step in understanding the adaptive nature of stress, therefore, is to understand the exact situations in which the stress response is useful.

In order to do this, we need to go back millions of years. Today, people like you face very different challenges from those of your earliest ancestors. You are faced with challenges such as AS examinations, the uncertainty of new relationships, and a never-ending lack of money, and you may be forgiven for thinking that your life is far more stressful than the tranquil existence of early humans. However, life was hard for early humans, and their stressors were usually physical, unlike those of many modern-day humans who face mostly social and mental stressors.

Early humans evolved a coordinated pattern of bodily changes that would snap into action when faced with imminent danger. This was first identified by physiologist Walter Cannon, who labelled it the 'fight or flight response'. This response is hard-wired into our brains and represents an adaptation fine-tuned by natural selection, designed to protect us from bodily harm. Cannon observed that during the fight or flight response, a variety of changes prepare the body for *physical* action, including increased heart rate and depth of breathing, increased glucose synthesis for energy, increased muscle tension for greater strength and increased blood clotting in preparation for possible tissue damage.

The stress response was clearly a beneficial adaptation for our ancestors, but it was not without its costs. It was expensive in terms of calories expended, and therefore early humans could not afford to stay in this state of readiness for any great length of time. It also interfered with other activities (such as finding food, forming alliances and mating). Finally, as we will see later, chronic stress has an adverse effect on the body's ability to defend itself against infection. Despite these costs, the benefits of this adaptation (staying alive being the main one) meant that the benefits clearly outweighed the costs.

However, the fight or flight response, so admirably suitable for the physical dangers faced by early humans, is less suitable for twenty-first century humans living in a technological world. Whereas for our ancestors the costs of the stress response were outweighed by its benefits, to most modern humans, the physiological and chemical changes associated with stress usually bring only costs.

Clearly this is the case, given the preoccupation of modern humans for 'coping with stress' and 'stress management'. The legacy we are left with from our early human ancestors is, therefore, an adaptation shaped for the ancient dangers of life millions of years ago, yet clearly inappropriate for dealing with most modern stressors.

So, what makes us stressed in our world? The commonly accepted definition of stress is 'a mismatch between the demands made upon an

▲ Early humans such as Homo ergaster, depicted here, lived nearly two million years ago in the eastern Rift Valley of Africa. The stressors they faced on a daily basis led to the evolution of our stress response.

individual and their ability to meet these demands'. We tend to think about these 'demands' as being mainly external (e.g. a difficult examination, a boring or particularly demanding job, a stressful argument with a parent), yet many stressors arise more from our desire for personal goals that are too numerous and often not attainable.

When our efforts to achieve these goals (do well in exams, be liked by everyone, be happy etc.) are frustrated, or when we can't pursue all our goals at once (run a home and family, study for A level) the stress response is activated. As Randolph Nesse puts it, much of what we experience as stress arises '…not from a mismatch between our abilities and the environment's demands, but from a mismatch between what we desire and what we can have'. Perhaps that is worth remembering as you embark on this chapter. Will you understand and remember it all? Possibly not. Will you understand and remember enough to do well in your AS examination? Hopefully, yes. We may still have the burden of a stress response that is on a hair trigger, and can be activated by receiving a phone bill or by a malfunctioning computer. However, unlike our ancestors, we are unlikely to be clubbed over the head, or ripped limb from limb as a consequence.

STARTER ACTIVITY

What does happen when people are stressed? You have probably had the experience yourself many times – a racing heart, sweaty palms, a dry mouth. These are all characteristic changes of the stress response. Did you know, for example, that one of the selective advantages of sweating when faced with danger is that it makes the body slippery and more difficult to catch hold of!

▶ Modern humans face very different stressors to those faced by early humans, yet are equipped with the same stress response.

Test out your own stress responses, or at least the stress responses of those around you. Arrange for volunteers to engage in mildly stressful tasks, such as giving a presentation to the class or doing the particularly frustrating Stroop task (see faculty.washington.edu/chudler/words.html).

Take physiological measurements before, during and after (repeated measures), e.g. pulse rate, size of pupils (when aroused they are dilated), dryness of mouth, sweat (check underarms!) and perhaps even blood pressure if you have a blood pressure monitor.

You could also use biodots as a way of measuring (relatively crudely) how stressed someone is. These are small self-adhesive temperature-sensitive discs which indicate changes in temperature by changing colour. When a person is tense, the skin blood vessels constrict, reducing the blood flow, and the biodot appears yellow, amber or black. When people are calm and relaxed, the skin blood vessels dilate, increasing blood flow, and the biodot appears turquoise, blue or violet.

You could also ask participants to produce a subjective report of their sensations.

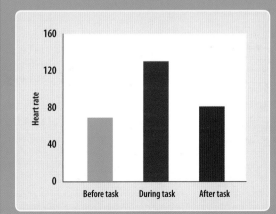

- How did the physiological measurements change over the three phases? (For example, calculate mean heart rate for your volunteers and represent it on a graph.)
- Did you find individual differences in your volunteers? (For example, were males more or less stressed than females?)
- Did people's subjective report match their physiological data?
- What did you learn about the stress response from this activity?

The body's response to stress

Stress is experienced when a person's perceived environmental, social, and physical demands exceed their perceived ability to cope, particularly when these demands are seen as endangering the person's well-being in some way. For example, a person who has built up an examination to be something that is incredibly demanding, and yet knows they have done very little revision, will experience stress, *but only if* failing the exam will result in pretty unpleasant consequences for them. It is clear from this definition that the experience of stress is as strongly influenced by our *perception* of a situation as it is by the actual situation itself. People are constantly evaluating events in their life (exams, jobs, relationships etc.), deciding whether they threaten well-being, and determining whether they have the resources available for meeting the demands posed by them. The stress response was especially important for our ancestors because the bodily changes associated with stress were essential in conditions of **fight or flight**, helping them deal with stressors that were current at the time. Nowadays however, although the stress *response* has stayed the same, the nature of the stressors we typically face has clearly changed, with the result that the response we are about to describe may not be universally adaptive. The body's response to stress involves two major systems, one for *acute* (i.e. sudden) stressors such as a personal attack, and the second for *chronic* (i.e. ongoing) stressors such as a stressful job.

There is a link between stress and attachment research. In Chapter 2 we looked at secure and insecure types of attachment. Research suggests that an additional advantage of secure attachment is that securely attached offspring are less likely to show elevated cortisol levels in response to stressful situations (Gunnar et al., 1996).

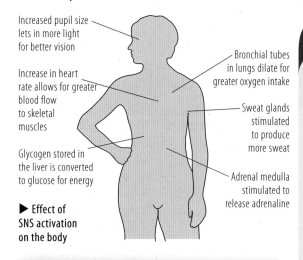

- Increased pupil size lets in more light for better vision
- Increase in heart rate allows for greater blood flow to skeletal muscles
- Glycogen stored in the liver is converted to glucose for energy
- Bronchial tubes in lungs dilate for greater oxygen intake
- Sweat glands stimulated to produce more sweat
- Adrenal medulla stimulated to release adrenaline

▶ Effect of SNS activation on the body

INDIVIDUAL DIFFERENCES

One of the most basic behavioural differences between men and women is how they respond to stress. Taylor *et al.* (2000) found that men usually react to stress with a 'fight or flight' response, but women may show a 'tend and befriend' response. This gender difference is seen in many species, with females responding to stressful conditions by protecting and nurturing their young (the 'tend' response), and by seeking social contact and support from other females (the 'befriend' response).

What makes this gender difference? *Oxytocin*, a **hormone** secreted in both men and women as a response to stress, has been shown to make people less anxious and more sociable. Taylor *et al.* (2000) found that higher levels of oxytocin were associated with reduced *cortisol* responses to stress and with faster recovery following acute stress. Male hormones appear to reduce the effect of oxytocin, but the female hormone *oestrogen* amplifies it. As a result, men are more vulnerable to the adverse health effects of stress and more likely than women to develop stress-related disorders such as hypertension and coronary heart disease. Because the tend-and-befriend regulatory system may protect women against stress, this may explain why women live an average of seven-and-a-half years longer than men.

ACUTE STRESS: THE SYMPATHOMEDULLARY PATHWAY

Immediate (acute) stressors arouse the *autonomic nervous system* (*ANS*). The ANS is one part of the nervous system. It is called 'autonomic' because it governs itself (i.e. it is automatic). This system is necessary because some bodily functions, such as your heartbeat, might not work as well as they need to if you had to think about them. The ANS is divided into the *sympathetic branch* (sympathetic nervous system or SNS) and the *parasympathetic* branch. The SNS arouses an animal to be ready for fight or flight, the parasympathetic branch returns the animal to a state of relaxation.

When an animal is exposed to an acute stressor, the SNS is activated, preparing the body for fight or flight. A key part of this response is the sympathetic adrenal medullary system (SAM); together the SNS and SAM system make up the **sympathomedullary pathway**.

The SNS

Neurones from the SNS travel to virtually every organ and gland within the body, preparing the body for the rapid action necessary when an animal is under threat. Responses include an increase in heart rate, blood pressure and cardiac output, increased pupil size and metabolic changes such as the mobilisation of fat and glycogen (a kind of sugar) in the bloodstream. *Noradrenaline* (also known as *norepinephrine*) is the **neurotransmitter** released by the SNS to activate these internal body organs.

The SAM system

At the same time that the SNS is activated, the SAM system alerts the animal through the release of *adrenaline* (also known as *epinephrine*) into the bloodstream, where it is transported rapidly throughout the body to prepare the animal for fight or flight. The SAM system is regulated by the SNS and also the adrenal medulla.

The adrenal medulla

Each *adrenal gland* has two distinct zones, the *adrenal medulla*, in the centre of the gland, and the *adrenal cortex* around the outside. Neurons of the SNS travel to the medulla, so that when it is activated it releases adrenaline into the bloodstream. Once in the blood, adrenaline has widespread effects on the body's physiological systems, e.g. boosting the supply of oxygen and glucose to the brain and muscles, and suppressing non-emergency bodily processes such as digestion.

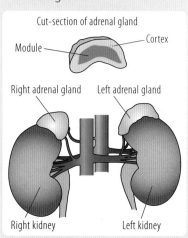

Cut-section of adrenal gland

- Module
- Cortex
- Right adrenal gland
- Left adrenal gland
- Right kidney
- Left kidney

...1 Summarise the sympathomedullary pathway and pituitary adrenal system responses in just 100 words each.

...2 Outline each of these in just 50 words.

...3 Draw a rough diagram for each, illustrating the main components and what they do during the stress response.

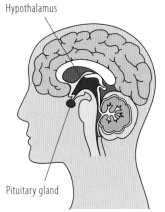

Hypothalamus

Pituitary gland

CHRONIC STRESS: THE PITUITARY-ADRENAL SYSTEM

The **pituitary-adrenal system** (also known as the hypothalamic-pituitary-adrenal axis or HPA) has traditionally been seen as the body's 'stress system', controlling levels of *cortisol* (CORT) and other important stress-related hormones. Although both physical and emotional stressors activate the HPA, compared to the sympathomedullary (SAM) system, activation of the HPA is much less easy to achieve, occurring in response to chronic (ongoing) stress situations. A diagrammatic representation of this system can be seen below.

The role of the hypothalamus

When stressors are perceived by the higher centres of the brain, a message passes to a small cone-shaped part of the brain, the *hypothalamus*. The hypothalamus is the control system for most of the body's hormonal systems, including those involved in the stress response. Activation of a particular region of the hypothalamus, the *paraventricular nucleus* (PVN) leads to the production of a chemical messenger, *corticotrophin-releasing factor* (CRF), which is released into the bloodstream in response to the stressor.

```
Perception of stressor
by higher brain centres
        ↓
   Hypothalamus
CRF     ↓
 Pituitary Gland
ACTH    ↓          Negative
 Adrenal Cortex    feedback
CORT    ↓
Cortisol causes stress
effects in the body
```

▲ The pituitary-adrenal system

The pituitary gland

On arrival at the anterior lobe of the *pituitary gland*, CRF causes the pituitary to produce and release *adrenocorticotrophic hormone* (ACTH). From the pituitary, ACTH is transported in the bloodstream to its target site in the adrenal glands, located on top of the kidneys.

The adrenal cortex

Cortisol, released by the adrenal cortex, is responsible for several stress-related effects in the body. Some of these are positive (e.g. a quick burst of energy and a lower sensitivity to pain), whereas others are negative (e.g. impaired cognitive performance, higher blood pressure and lowered immune response). Prolonged release of ACTH causes the adrenal cortex to increase in size in order to cope with increased cortisol production. Long-term ACTH deficiency causes it to shrink.

Feedback

It takes about 20 minutes for this process to be complete, with cortisol levels typically rising sharply 20 minutes after the initial perception of an acute stressor. This system is also very efficient at regulating itself. Both the hypothalamus and pituitary gland have special receptors that monitor circulating cortisol levels. If these rise above normal levels, they initiate a reduction in CRF and ACTH levels, thus bringing cortisol levels back to normal.

CONSEQUENCES OF THE STRESS RESPONSE

The physiological responses outlined on these two pages are adaptive for stress responses that require an energetic behavioural response, but the stressors of modern life rarely require such levels of physical activity. The problem for modern humans arises when the stress response system is repeatedly activated, with the consequence that the cardiovascular system (heart and blood vessels) begins to suffer from abnormal wear and tear. The increased blood pressure that is characteristic of SNS activation can lead to physical damage in the delicate lining of blood vessels, and eventually to heart disease. Similarly, although cortisol may assist the body in fighting a viral infection or healing damaged tissue, too much cortisol suppresses the immune response, shutting down the very process that fights infection. Some researchers believe that the feedback system that is such an important part of the pituitary-adrenal system may break down when individuals are exposed to chronic (ongoing) stress.

KEY TERMS

Fight or flight A term which literally means that an animal is energised to either fight or run away, but has come to mean a general state of energised readiness.

Hormones Any substance produced by a gland or organ of the body and circulated in the blood, only affecting specific target cells in the body.

Neurotransmitter A substance released from the end of a neuron into the synapse (gap between neurons), causing the adjacent neuron to be excited or inhibited.

Pituitary-adrenal system A stress response system involving the hypothalamus, pituitary gland and adrenal cortex, which helps the body deal with chronic stressors.

Stress The subjective experience of a lack of fit between a person and their environment (i.e. where the perceived demands of a situation are greater than a person's perceived ability to cope).

Sympathomedullary pathway The influence of the SNS and adrenal medulla prepares the body for flight or flight when faced with an acute stressor.

DO IT YOURSELF

No.4.1

On this spread we have introduced a rather challenging new vocabulary – all the big words are listed below, some of them with definitions. You don't need to know all of them, but the more important ones need to be committed to memory. One way to do this is to use more familiar ideas to represent the different words. For example you might try to remember those Spanish cousins 'Adrena Cortez' (the adrenaline junkie) and 'Adrena Medulla' (with her cortisol habit).

List of words for you to remember

Adrenal cortex	Corticotrophin-	Paraventricular
Adrenal glands	releasing factor (CRF)	nucleus (PVN)
(produce adrenaline)	Cortisol	Pituitary gland
Adrenal medulla	Hormone	Pituitary-adrenal
Adrenaline	Hypothalamus	system (HPA)
Adrenocortico-	Neurotransmitter	Sympathetic
trophic hormone	Noradrenaline	nervous system
(ACTH)	Oestrogen	(SNS)
Autonomic nervous	Oxytocin	Sympathomedullary
system (ANS)	Parasympathetic	(SAM) system
	branch	

Stress-related illness: The immune system

On the previous spread we hinted at the fact that stress can have some undesirable effects on our health and well-being. The belief that stress leads to illness is fundamental for most people. In one UK survey (Pollock, 1988) there was found to be a general belief that stress could be a direct cause of illness. Statements concerning the link between stress and heart disease, and stress and psychiatric illness (the so-called 'nervous breakdown') appear regularly in the press as well as in the psychological literature. Both the stress response systems discussed earlier (SAM and HPA) have also been shown to have a direct effect on the **immune system**, for example the autonomic nervous system sends nerves directly into the tissues that form and store cells of the immune system. These cells of the immune system are also sensitive to levels of circulating cortisol, so the scene is set for an interaction between stress and immune system functioning. The main function of the immune system is to protect the body from infectious agents such as viruses and other toxins. The immune system can fail us in two ways – either by becoming *under-vigilant*, letting infections enter the body, or *over-vigilant*, so that it is the immune system itself, rather than an infectious agent, that causes illness. Research suggests that stress might be associated with both types of immune dysfunction (Evans *et al.*, 2000).

KEY TERM

Immune system
This is a system of cells within the body that is concerned with fighting against intruders such as viruses and bacteria. White blood cells (leucocytes) identify and eliminate foreign bodies (antigens).

▼ Components of the immune system.

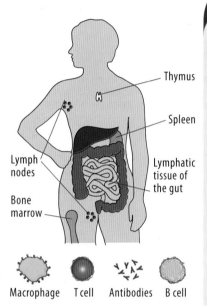

Thymus

Spleen

Lymph nodes

Lymphatic tissue of the gut

Bone marrow

Macrophage   T cell   Antibodies   B cell

RESEARCH INTO STRESS AND IMMUNE SYSTEM FUNCTIONING

Most studies of the relationship between stress and immune system functioning have focused on acute (i.e. short-lived) stressors and have found a *decrease* in immune cell function (e.g. Kiecolt-Glaser *et al.*, 1984). However, other studies have shown an *increase*. For example, Fischer *et al.* (1972) found higher *lymphocyte* (a kind of leucocyte – i.e. immune cell) counts in Apollo astronauts during splashdown. Other research has focused on the effects of chronic stressors: for example, Arnetz *et al.* (1987) studied the effect of unemployment in Sweden, and found a decrease in lymphocyte response to *antigens*.

Acute stressors: Examination stress

Kiecolt-Glaser *et al.* (1984) carried out a natural experiment investigating whether the stress of short-term, stressors (important examinations) had an effect on immune system functioning in medical students. Blood samples were taken one month before (low stress) and during the exam period itself (high stress). Immune system functioning was assessed by measuring *NK cell activity* (see below) in the blood samples. NK cell activity was significantly reduced in the second blood sample compared to the sample taken one month before. This suggests that short-term, predictable stressors reduce immune system functioning, increasing vulnerability to illness.

Exam-related immune changes have also been shown to have a dramatic effect on the rate at which wounds heal. Marucha *et al.* (1998) inflicted a 'punch biopsy' in the mouth of students either during the summer holidays or three days before an exam. The wounds given before the exam took 40% longer to heal than the wounds during the holidays.

What is the immune system?
The immune system is designed to defend the body against millions of antigens (i.e. bacteria, viruses, toxins and parasites) that would otherwise invade it. None of these things are able to get in when your immune system is working efficiently, but the moment your immune system stops functioning properly, the door is wide open.

How does the immune system operate?
The immune system protects you in three different ways:

1. *It creates a barrier that prevents antigens from entering your body.*
2. *If an antigen (such as a virus) does get into the body, the immune system tries to detect and eliminate it before it can make itself at home and reproduce.*
3. *If the virus is able to reproduce and start causing problems, the immune system is responsible for eliminating it.*

Cells of the immune system
Probably the most important part of the immune system is the white blood cells, known as leucocytes. Leucocytes are produced in the bone marrow. Some remain there but others migrate to the thymus gland, spleen or lymph nodes for storage. Those that remain in the bone marrow are known as B (for bone*) cells, whereas the ones that migrate elsewhere are known as T (for* thymus*) cells. Macrophages are another kind of cell in the immune system. They are often referred to either as scavengers, because they pick up and ingest foreign materials, or as antigen-presenting cells, because they present antigens to other cells of the immune system such as B cells and T cells.*

Th1 and Th2 immunity
*A specific B cell is tuned to a specific antigen, and when that antigen is present in the body the B cell produces millions of specialised immune proteins (*antibodies*) to eliminate it. This type of immune response is known as Th2 immunity.*

The T cells are responsible for a more aggressive form of immunity, detecting cells in the body that are harbouring antigens. When they detect such a cell, they bump up against it and destroy both the antigen and the cell. This is known as Th1 immunity. Natural killer (NK) cells are an important part of the Th1 response, and protect against cancer cells as well as viruses.

Cytokines
These two types of immune response (Th1 and Th2) are counter-regulatory. When one branch is active it produces chemicals called cytokines *that inhibit the action of the alternate branch. In this way the body is able to maintain a balance between the two types of immune response with Th2 active during the day and Th1 during the night. Stress can influence the balance between the two branches so that one is inhibited more than the other. For example, chronic stress, characterised by repeated HPA activation, is associated with a shift away from Th1 immunity towards Th2 immunity to ward off cancer.*

meet the researcher

Janice Kiecolt-Glaser's research has led her to a position of international prominence in the study of the impact of stress on the immune system. She and her colleagues at Ohio State University have helped bring this area of research from infancy to its current status as a thriving area of study.

CAN YOU...? No.4.2

...1 Provide **two** physiological explanations of how stress may affect a person's health.

...2 Describe **two** pieces of evidence of the effect stress has on the functioning of the immune system.

...3 For each piece of evidence, give **one** criticism of the research it is based on.

DO IT YOURSELF No.4.2

You could try a natural experiment similar to the one by Kiecolt-Glaser *et al.* – compare illness before and during any stressful time such as exams. You need to work out a method of assessing illness (e.g. you could ask each participant to keep a record of any illness using a rating scale for each day to record how well or ill they were, for example 'on a scale of 1 to 5 state how well you are, where 5 is very well and 1 is feeling ill'). Then compare their average score before the stressful period and during the stressful period.

Chronic stressors: Relationship stress

Examinations represent a relatively short-term stressor, so we might expect to find an even greater effect on immune system functioning under conditions of chronic (ongoing) stress. Marital relationships can be stressful, as can separation from a marital partner. Kiecolt-Glaser *et al.* (2005) tested the impact of interpersonal conflict on wound healing. She found that blister wounds on the arms of married couples healed more slowly after they had discussions which were conflicting rather than supportive. Kiecolt-Glaser *et al.* (1987) compared women separated from their partners with matched married controls. They found poorer immune system functioning in women who had separated during the last year.

What about couples at the beginning of their relationship? Malarkey *et al.* (1994) studied 90 newly-wed couples over a 24-hour period. They were asked to discuss and resolve marital issues likely to produce conflict (e.g. finances). Marital conflict produced significant changes in adrenaline and noradrenaline, which could lead to poorer immune functioning.

The effects of stress can sometimes *enhance* the immune system

Evans *et al.* (1994) looked at the activity of one particular antibody – sIgA – which coats the mucous surfaces of the mouth, lungs and stomach, and helps protect against infection. Evans *et al.* (1994) arranged for students to give talks to other students (mild but acute stress). These students showed an increase in sIgA, whereas levels of sIgA decreased during examination periods which stretched over several weeks. Evans *et al.* (1997) propose that stress may have two effects on the immune system: up-regulation (i.e. increased efficiency) for short-term acute stress and down-regulation for chronic stress.

A meta-analysis (Segerstrom and Miller, 2004)

A meta-analysis of 293 studies conducted over the past 30 years found:

- Short-term, acute stressors can boost the immune system, prompting it to ready itself for infections or other challenges to the integrity of the body.
- Long-term, chronic stressors led to suppression of the immune system – the most chronic stressors were associated with the most global suppression of immunity.
- The longer the stress, the more the immune system shifted from potentially adaptive changes to potentially detrimental changes.

EVALUATION

Lazarus (1992) suggests there are various reasons why a relationship between stress and illness is difficult to establish.

1. Health is affected by many different factors (including genetic influences, lifestyle etc.). As a result, there may be little variance left that can be accounted for by stress.
2. Health is generally fairly stable and slow to change. As a result, it makes it difficult to demonstrate that exposure to particular stressors have caused a change in health.
3. To demonstrate how stress affects long-term health would involve continuous measurement over time. This would be expensive and impractical, therefore most research has concentrated on relatively short periods of time.

INDIVIDUAL DIFFERENCES

Research has shown consistent gender and age differences in the stress/immune system relationship. Women show more adverse hormonal and immunological changes in the way they react to marital conflict (Kiecolt-Glaser, *et al.*, 2005). As people age, stress has a greater effect on immune system functioning, making it harder for the body to regulate itself (Segerstrom and Miller, 2004).

REAL-WORLD APPLICATIONS

Knowledge of how stress affects immune system functioning has led to many new programmes for a 'healthy lifestyle'. Stress-coping behaviours can be taught to groups of all ages and backgrounds. Techniques include deep breathing and expressive writing (for example, 15 minutes writing about a stressor then discarding the writing without reading it). People who use stress-coping behaviours generally report improvement in their physical and psychological well-being. Towards the end of this chapter we will look at methods of coping with and managing stress.

121

Stress-related illness: Cardiovascular and psychiatric disorders

In the previous spread, we described the relationship between stress and immune system functioning. More and more evidence suggests a relationship between prolonged exposure to stressors and the risk of **cardiovascular disorders**, i.e. any disorder of the heart (e.g. coronary heart disease) and circulatory system (e.g. hypertension – high blood pressure). It is also a commonly held belief (de Ridder, 1996) that psychological factors such as stress are related to psychiatric disorders such as anxiety and **depression**. In de Ridder's survey, stress was the second most popular explanation of the causes of mental disorders.

▶ Why should we be cautious about accepting the view that stress causes cardiovascular disorders?

- Exposure to stress and cardiovascular outcomes are often based on self-report (e.g. questionnaires). A general tendency toward negative perceptions (i.e. remembering more unpleasant events than pleasant ones) may lead to an unjustified association between higher perceived stress and cardiovascular symptoms.
- Stress may directly cause illness, however it may also indirectly lead to illness because stressed individuals are more likely to engage in unhealthy behaviours to distract them from the stressful situation. Thus, it may be these behaviours (e.g. smoking, drinking and drug-taking) that cause illness, rather than the stressor itself.

The AS psychology specification only requires you to study the effects of stress on the immune system, but questions may allow a more general definition of 'illness', in which case you would be able to use the material on this spread. Another (perhaps more relevant) reason for covering this material is that it is both interesting and appropriate to all of us who lead stressful lives.

INDIVIDUAL DIFFERENCES

Recent research suggests that the sympathetic branch of the ANS in some individuals is more reactive than in others (Rozanski *et al.*, 1999). This would mean that some people (described as '*hyperresponsive*') respond to stress with greater increases in blood pressure and heart rate than others, and this would lead to more damage to the cardiovascular system in hyperresponsive individuals.

Later in this chapter (pages 130–1) we will look further at research into the relationship between individual differences and stress – at evidence that some *types* of people get more stressed and are also more likely to have heart attacks and other cardiovascular disorders than others.

STRESS AND CARDIOVASCULAR DISORDERS

Acute and chronic stress may affect many different aspects of the cardiovascular system (i.e. the heart and circulatory system), for example:

- Hypertension (high blood pressure).
- Coronary heart disease (CHD) caused by *atherosclerosis* (the narrowing of the coronary arteries).
- Stroke (damage caused by disruption of blood supply to the brain).

Although such cardiovascular disorders (also known as cardiovascular *disease*) are affected by lifestyle, diet, smoking etc., stress has become increasingly implicated in the development of all the disorders listed above. A number of suggestions have been put forward to explain how stress might cause cardiovascular problems. For example,

- Stress activates the sympathetic branch (SNS) of the autonomic nervous system, leading to a constriction of the blood vessels and a rise in blood pressure and heart rate.
- An increase in heart rate may wear away the lining of the blood vessels.
- Stress leads to increased glucose levels, leading to clumps blocking the blood vessels (*atheroschlerosis*).

Cardiovascular disorders and anger (an acute stressor)

Williams (2000) conducted a study to see whether anger was linked to heart disease: 13,000 people completed a 10-question anger scale, including questions on whether they were hot-headed, if they felt like hitting someone when they got angry, or whether they got annoyed when not given recognition for doing good work. None of the participants suffered from heart disease at the outset of the study. Six years later, the health of participants was checked; 256 had experienced heart attacks. Those who had scored highest on the anger scale were over two-and-a-half times more likely to have a heart attack than those with the lowest anger ratings. People who scored 'moderate' in the anger ratings were 35% more likely to experience a coronary event. This suggests that anger may lead to cardiovascular disorders. Williams concluded that 'individuals who find themselves prone to anger might benefit from anger management training'.

Cardiovascular disorders and work-related stress (a chronic stressor)

Russek (1962) looked at heart disease in medical professionals. One group of doctors was designated as high-stress (GPs and anaesthetists) while others were classed as low-stress (pathologists and dermatologists). Russek found heart disease was greatest among GPs (11.9% of the sample) and lowest in dermatologists (3.2% of the sample). Supporting the view that stress is linked to heart disease.

The effects of stress on existing conditions

Sheps *et al.* (2002) conducted a landmark study, the first study large enough to show that stress can be fatal for people with existing coronary artery disease. Sheps *et al.* focused their research on volunteers with *ischemia* (reduced blood flow to the heart). They gave 173 men and women a variety of psychological tests, including a public speaking test. Their blood pressure typically soared dramatically, and in half of them, sections of the muscle of the left ventricle began to beat erratically. Of all the participants, 44% of those who had shown the erratic heartbeats died within three to four years, compared to just 18% who had not. This shows that psychological stress can dramatically increase the risk of death in people with poor coronary artery circulation.

A study by Orth-Gomér *et al.* (2000) showed that among married or co-habiting women, marital conflict was associated with a 2.9 fold increase in recurrent events (e.g. heart attack) for women with existing coronary heart disease. Interestingly, work conflict did not have the same effect.

CAN YOU...? No.4.3

...1 Describe **two** studies of stress-related illness.

...2 Explain the link between stress, the immune system and stress-related illness.

...3 Describe **two** gender differences in the way people respond to stress.

KEY TERMS

Cardiovascular disorder Refers to any disorder of the heart (e.g. coronary heart disease, CHD) and circulatory system (e.g. hypertension – high blood pressure).

Depression A common mental disorder characterised by feelings of sadness, lack of interest in everyday activities, and a sense of worthlessness. Depression can be triggered by a stressful life event or by biological changes.

► American singer Mariah Carey's well-publicised bout of depression in 2001 was blamed on the chronic stress of a punishing work schedule.

STRESS AND PSYCHIATRIC DISORDERS

The relationship between chronic stress and psychiatric disorders such as anxiety and depression is so commonly reported in the media that it seems reasonable to assume that exposure to extreme stressors would lead to more serious psychiatric illness. We start, however, by looking at a relatively common mental disorder – depression.

Stress and depression

Brown and Harris (1978) found that women who suffered chronic stress conditions (such as having more than three children under the age of 14 at home, and being unemployed) were more likely to develop depression. They also reported that working-class women were more prone to depression than middle-class women because of the stress of having to leave home to work, and having to leave their children in the care of others.

Melchior et al. (2007) carried out a survey over a period of one year among 1000 people aged 32 in a wide range of occupations in New Zealand. They found that 15% of those in high-stress jobs suffered a first episode of clinical depression or anxiety during that year, compared with 8% in low-stress jobs. Women were generally worse affected than men.

Stress and other disorders

After the Vietnam War ended in 1975, the mass incidence of psychiatric symptoms among war veterans led to the 'discovery' of *post traumatic stress disorder* (PTSD). PTSD has been observed in war veterans and rape victims, as well as the victims of chronic stressors such as poverty and abuse. Perpetration Induced Traumatic Stress (PITS) (MacNair, 2002) is a form of PTSD caused by being an active participant in *causing* trauma (e.g. soldiers, executioners, or police officers, where it is socially acceptable or expected for them to kill). For example, Rohlf and Bennett (2005) found that 1 in 10 workers, whose occupations required euthanising animals, experienced moderate levels of PITS symptoms.

The evidence for stress being linked to other psychiatric conditions is less strong. For example, a study by Stueve et al. (1998) compared the role of stressful life events in causing depression, schizophrenia and other disorders. They found that stressful events were only associated with depression, and not with the other disorders.

The diathesis-stress model

In order for a person to develop a psychiatric disorder, they must possess a biological vulnerability to that disorder (the diathesis). An individual's vulnerability is determined by genetic or early biological factors (such as exposure to viral infection when in the womb). Stress can have an impact on that vulnerability, either triggering the onset of the disorder or worsening its course. If the person is not capable of adapting to the stressful situation, psychiatric symptoms will develop or worsen. In the Brown and Harris study described above, for example, stressful experiences alone did not predict the onset of depression. Rather it was the absence of a close confiding relationship in the women's lives that made them more vulnerable to life stressors, and therefore more vulnerable to depression. We will look again at the *diathesis-stress model* in Chapter 6.

e EVALUATION

Problems with determining a causal link between stress and depression include:

1 It is frequently not possible to assess whether stressful events in the period before diagnosis of a psychiatric disorder have caused the disorder or have been a consequence of the person's deteriorating state.

2 Most studies have made use of retrospective methodology, in which recall of events tends to be somewhat unreliable. Prospective studies, where people who have experienced a stressful event are followed over time, are rare.

3 Although the relationship between stress and depression has been demonstrated by some researchers, others (e.g. Rabkin, 1993) claim that the effects are small, accounting for less than 10% of the variance observed.

COMMENTARY CORNER

Question: **To what extent does research support a link between stress and illness?** *(12 marks)*

After reading the last two spreads, you may have a sneaking feeling that stress *does* lead to illness. In constructing a response to this question, therefore, you could work up a series of arguments to support this. If you glance back at the content on the previous spread you will see a number of different possibilities for justifying that relationship. Some of these are *research* based (e.g. Kiecolt-Glaser, Segerstrom and Miller) and some are *explanations* about why such a relationship might exist. Although the question specifies 'research', the explanations of *why* there might be a link between stress and immune system dysfunction would be useful as AO2 'commentary'. Be careful, however, with descriptions of *how* the immune system works. Most of the material on the workings of the immune system has been presented to aid your understanding and is not likely to be creditworthy in an examination answer.

What if the question made reference to '*stress and the immune system*' rather than illness? In that case you would need to restrict yourself to discussing material from the previous spread only.

In either case it is obvious that you can only include a very small proportion of the material presented here, so be selective, and construct your answer carefully so that you have equal amounts of AO1 description and AO2 critical commentary.

Life changes

What sort of things actually cause the chronic stress reaction we described earlier? On the next two spreads we look at two related, yet very different, types of stressors, **life changes** and daily hassles. Life changes are those events (such as getting married or dealing with bereavement), that necessitate a major transition in some aspects of our life. Because they have such an impact on us, they are sometimes referred to as *critical* life changes. There is considerable variation in the impact of these 'critical' life changes. What might be profoundly stressful for one person (such as the death of a spouse) may be a blessed relief for another. Likewise, something as minor as the death of a much-loved pet may be devastatingly stressful to some people. Although the term 'life change' suggests that something must happen in order to cause a person such stress, the same reaction can be found when something *doesn't* happen. For example, *not* being promoted, or *not* getting to university are extremely stressful life 'not-changes' for many people.

CAN YOU...? No.4.4

...1 Explain why life changes are thought to cause stress.

...2 Explain why it can be argued that life changes do not cause stress.

...3 Describe **two** studies of life changes and give **two** criticisms for each of them. Try to make all four of your criticisms different.

RESEARCH ON LIFE CHANGES

Two medical doctors, Holmes and Rahe (1967) played a key role in developing the idea that life changes are linked to stress and illness. In the course of treating patients, they observed that it was often the case that a range of major life events seemed to precede physical illness. These changes were both positive and negative events that had one thing in common – they involved change. Change requires psychic energy to be expended i.e. it is stressful. Holmes and Rahe suggested that this affected health.

Using life changes to measure stress

In order to test the idea that life changes are related to physical illness, it was necessary to have some means of measuring life changes. Holmes and Rahe (1967) developed the Social Readjustment Rating Scale (SRRS) based on 43 life events taken from their analysis of over 5000 patient records.

In order to establish the stressfulness of each event they enlisted the help of about 400 participants. The participants were asked to score each event in terms of how much readjustment would be required by the average person. The participants were asked to provide a numerical figure for this readjustment, taking marriage as an arbitrary baseline value of 50. If an event would take longer to readjust to than marriage, then they were told to give the event a larger score. Scores for all participants were totalled and averaged to produce life change units (LCUs) for each life event (shown in the table on the right).

Classic study of life changes

Rahe *et al.* (1970) used the SRRS to test Holmes and Rahe's hypothesis that the number of life events a person experienced would be positively correlated with illness. Rahe *et al.* aimed in particular to study a 'normal' population as distinct from the populations previously studied of individuals who were already ill in hospital.

A military version of the SRRS was given to all the men aboard three US Navy Cruisers – a total of over 2700 men. The men filled the questionnaire in just before a tour of duty, noting all the life events experienced over the previous six months.

An illness score was calculated on the basis of the number, type and severity of all illnesses recorded during the tour of duty (about seven months).

Rahe *et al.* found a positive correlation between LCU score and illness score of +.118. You may think that .118 is not a particularly strong correlation, but given the number of participants it is significant.

The findings support the hypothesis that there is a positive correlation between life changes and physical illness. Why would this be the case? We know that life changes cause stress and we know that stress causes illness. As both positive and negative events are included in the SRRS (even Christmas is stressful), it appears that it is change rather than the negativity of change that is important. It is the overall amount of 'psychic energy' required to deal with a life event that creates the stress.

Recent research on life changes

Michael and Ben-Zur (2007) studied 130 men and women, half of whom had been recently divorced and half recently widowed. They looked at levels of life satisfaction. In the widowed group this was found to be higher *before* their bereavement than after the loss. This isn't particularly surprising, yet divorced individuals showed the opposite pattern *after* separation from their partners. They had higher levels of life satisfaction (and lower levels of stress) after separation than before. One explanation suggested was that they might now have been dating or living with a new partner, and another that they may have been using problem-focused coping during separation or loss, turning the life change into a positive, instead of a negative experience.

The Social Readjustment Rating Scale (SRRS)

Example items

Rank	Life event (LCU)
1	**Death of a spouse (100)**
2	**Divorce (73)**
4	**Jail term (63)**
6	**Personal injury or illness (53)**
7	**Marriage (50)**
8	**Fired at work (47)**
10	**Retirement (45)**
12	**Pregnancy (40)**
17	**Death of a close friend (37)**
22	**Change in responsibilities at work (29)**
23	**Son or daughter leaving home (29)**
25	**Outstanding personal achievement (28)**
27	**Begin or end school (26)**
28	**Change living conditions (25)**
30	**Trouble with boss (23)**
33	**Change in schools (20)**
36	**Change in social activities (18)**
41	**Holiday (13)**
42	**Christmas (12)**
43	**Minor violations of the law (11)**

KEY TERM

Life changes
Events in a person's life (such as divorce or bereavement) that require a significant adjustment in various aspects of a person's life. As such, they are significant sources of stress.

1 What term is used to describe the graph on the right?

2 How would you describe the correlation in this graph (positive or negative, weak or strong)?

3 Explain difficulties in drawing conclusions from this data.

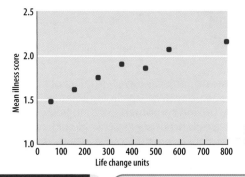

◄ **Hypothetical correlation between total life change units and mean illness score.**

e EVALUATION OF THE LIFE CHANGES APPROACH

The life changes approach has generated a huge amount of research, with many adaptations of the SRRS turning up in self-help publications and magazines. Despite the apparent success of the approach, however, it is not without its problems (Jones and Bright, 2001).

Positive and negative events

Research using the SRRS appears to suggest that any life-changing event has the potential to damage health because of the significant readjustment it entails. However, some critics now suggest that it is the *quality* of the event that is crucial, with 'undesired, unscheduled and uncontrolled' changes being the most harmful.

Life changes and daily hassles

Lazarus (1990) suggests that as major life changes are relatively rare in the lives of most people, it is the minor daily stressors (i.e. hassles) of life that are the more significant source of stress for most people. For example, DeLongis *et al.* (1988) studied stress in 75 married couples. They gave the participants a life events questionnaire and a Hassles and Uplifts scale (see next spread). They found no relationship between life events and health, but did find a significant positive correlation of +.59 between hassles and next-day health problems such as flu, sore throats, headaches and backaches.

Individual differences

The SRRS ignores the fact that life changes will inevitably have different significance for different people. For example, the untimely death of a much-loved spouse will undoubtedly have a devastating effect on the surviving partner, but the death of an elderly spouse after a long and painful illness may not be quite so stressful for the survivor. Similarly, what are relatively minor stressors for some people, such as a son or daughter leaving home or even a particularly busy Christmas, would be major stressors for some people.

Spurious relationship

Most studies of the relationship between life changes and illness have produced correlational data, i.e. they do not tell us about any possible *causal* relationship between the two. It is possible that an observed relationship may result from a third variable – anxiety. Brown (1974) suggests that people with high levels of anxiety would be more likely to report negative life events and would also be more prone to illness.

⚖ VALIDITY AND RELIABILITY

The life changes approach relies on people's memory for events in their life being (a) accurate and (b) consistent. There have been concerns that retrospective reports may not be particularly accurate (i.e. they lack validity). For example, Brown (1974) suggests that people who are unwell may feel the need to provide an explanation for their illness, and therefore are more likely to report stressful events than those who are not ill. He cites the fact that in the days before it was properly understood that Down's syndrome was a chromosomal abnormality, mothers of Downs' children reported far more traumatic events in their pregnancy than did mothers of non-Downs' children. This was despite the fact that there were no real differences in the experiences of Downs and non-Downs mothers during pregnancy.

The reliability of retrospective reports has also been questioned. For example, Rahe (1974) found that test-retest reliability (see page 96) varies depending on the time interval between testing. However, most researchers have reported acceptable levels of reliability for retrospective reports of life events. Hardt *et al.* (2006) interviewed 100 patients with a history of childhood abuse with a time lag of 2.2 years between interviews. Reliability of reports of family situation (e.g. separation of parents) were assessed as well as physical and sexual abuse. The results show moderate to good reliability for most childhood experiences.

🌍 REAL-WORLD APPLICATIONS

Research into the relationship between life changes and stress has provided an important insight into suicide. Heikkinen and Lönnqvist (1995) examined life events during the last three months preceding suicide among 219 suicide victims in Finland. Differences in life events were found across age groups: family discord, loss (through separation or death), financial troubles and unemployment were more common among younger victims, whereas physical illness appeared to be the most important stressor in elderly suicides, particularly for men. Contrary to popular belief, living alone and diminished opportunities for social interaction were not common factors in late-life suicides.

▲ Comedian Kenneth Williams committed suicide in 1988, at the age of 62. In his later years he suffered from stomach ulcers and severe back pain. His last diary entry read: 'By 6.30 pain in the back was pulsating as it's never done before ... so this, plus the stomach trouble combines to torture me – oh – what's the bloody point?'

Daily hassles

EXAM TIP
Try not to confuse 'life changes', which are major events requiring significant individual readjustment, with 'daily hassles' which are relatively minor stressors that we experience on a day-to-day basis.

Although major life changes undoubtedly have a significant impact on our well-being, they are relatively rare in our day-to-day lives. Psychologists have turned their attention instead to the daily stressors, such as a broken computer, a missed bus, or arguments with our families. These **daily hassles** may have a significant part to play in our psychological well-being.

Daily hassles are relatively minor events that arise in the course of a normal day. They may involve the everyday concerns of work, such as a disagreement with a colleague or issues arising from family life. Although such issues and their associated emotional effects are usually short-lived, they may linger if left unresolved, and the 'after-effects' of unresolved issues may then intensify over time as they accumulate with subsequent hassles (see 'Real-World Applications' on this spread). The negative effects of daily hassles can in turn be offset to some degree by the more positive experiences that we have every day. Such **daily uplifts**, such as a smile from someone in the street or an e-mail from a long lost friend, are thought to counteract the damaging effects of stress.

Items from the Hassles and Uplifts Scale (Delongis et al., 1982)

This scale contains 53 items worded so that the respondent can indicate whether a given event is a hassle (on the left), uplift (on the right), or both. For example:

0 = None or not applicable   2 = Quite a bit
1 = Somewhat   3 = A great deal

0 1 2 3	Time spent with family	0 1 2 3
0 1 2 3	Your physical appearance	0 1 2 3
0 1 2 3	The weather	0 1 2 3
0 1 2 3	Pets	0 1 2 3
0 1 2 3	Social commitments	0 1 2 3

 You can download the whole scale from home.cc.umanitoba.ca/~mdlee/Teaching/hassles.doc or try a different scale at www.bhicares.org/pdf/manual/indepthassessment/dhauscale.pdf

REAL-WORLD APPLICATIONS
Daily hassles and road rage

Individuals experience a wide range of daily hassles during the course of a day. These frequently accumulate, with the consequence that new stressors appear before existing issues have been resolved. The influence of hassles that have not been dealt with effectively can persist (even when no longer in conscious awareness), and add to the pressure of subsequent stressors. Gulian *et al.* (1990) found that participants who reported a difficult day at work subsequently reported higher levels of stress on their commute home. When unresolved 'non-driving' hassles are carried forward into the driving situation, events (such as mechanical failure and the actions of other road users) are more likely to be interpreted as stressful by the driver.

RESEARCH ON DAILY HASSLES

Measuring hassles and uplifts

The Hassles and Uplifts Scales, or HSUP (Delongis *et al.*, 1982), measures respondents' attitudes toward daily situations. Instead of focusing on the more highly stressful life events, the HSUP provides a way of evaluating both the positive and negative events that occur in each person's daily life.

Daily hassles

Bouteyre *et al.* (2007) investigated the relationship between daily hassles and the mental health of students during the initial transition period from school to university. First-year psychology students at a French university completed the hassles part of the HSUP and the Beck Depression Inventory as a measure of any symptoms of depression that might be attributable to the hassles of the transition. Results showed that 41% of the students studied suffered from depressive symptoms, and there was a positive correlation between scores on the hassles scale and the incidence of depressive symptoms. This study shows that the transition to university is frequently fraught with daily hassles, and that these can be considered a significant risk factor for depression.

Daily uplifts

Gervais (2005) asked nurses to keep diaries for a month, recording all their daily hassles and uplifts while at work. They were also asked to rate their own performance over the same period. Typical entries were:

'Lack of beds meant cancellation of elective admissions; this was left to me; I had to deal with people's anger despite not being responsible.' (Nurse, General Ward)

'A bit of a hassle at work today due to being on duty with staff who don't pull their weight. Felt not appreciated today at work.' (Nurse, Medical Ward)

At the end of the month, it was clear that daily hassles were found to increase job strain and decrease job performance. Nurses felt that some of the uplifts they experienced (such as a compliment from a patient or praise from a superior) counteracted the negative effects of their daily hassles. As well as overcoming the stress associated with their daily hassles, these daily uplifts also improved their performance on the job.

Daily hassles versus life changes

Daily hassles are now broadly accepted as comparable to, if not greater than, life changes as a significant source of stress. For example, in an Australian study (Ruffin, 1993) daily hassles were linked to greater psychological and physical dysfunction than major negative life events. Flett *et al.* (1995) found that major life-changing events may differ from daily hassles in the extent to which a person would receive and/or seek social support. A total of 320 students (160 men, 160 women) read a scenario describing a male or female individual who had experienced either a major life event or daily hassles. They then rated the amount of support (both emotional and practical) that the person would receive and would seek from others. Individuals who had suffered major life events were rated higher in both seeking and receiving support from significant others. The findings suggest that, compared to major life events, the greater negative influence of daily hassles on psychological adjustment may be due, in part, to the reduced social and emotional support received from others.

CAN YOU...? No.**4.5**

...**1** Outline **two** explanations of why daily hassles might cause stress.

...**2** Outline the role of daily uplifts with regard to stress.

...**3** Describe **two** studies of daily hassles and for each of them give **two** criticisms of each. Try to make all four of your criticisms different.

RESEARCH METHODS Qs No.**4.2**

1 Briefly describe how the relationship between daily hassles and stress has been investigated using correlational analysis.

2 Describe **two** strengths and **two** weaknesses of using this method of research.

3 Identify **one** alternative method that has been used to investigate the relationship between stress and daily hassles.

(You can answer the same questions for life events.)

INDIVIDUAL DIFFERENCES

Miller *et al.* (1992) studied 250 people over 50 years of age and their relationships with their pets. They found that pets appear to serve different roles for female and male pet owners. For females, pets were commonly associated with *uplifts* (e.g. leisure and lack of psychological pressure), but for males, pets were more likely to be associated with *hassles* (e.g. time and money necessary to care for them).

▲ Cat... complete companion or daily hassle?

℮ EVALUATION OF RESEARCH INTO DAILY HASSLES

Explaining daily hassles

The accumulation effect

As already noted, a number of studies (e.g. Ruffin, 1993) have shown that daily hassles provide a more significant source of stress for most people than major life events. One explanation for this is that an accumulation of minor daily stressors creates persistent irritations, frustrations and overloads which then result in more serious stress reactions such as anxiety and depression (Lazarus, 1999).

The amplification effect

An alternative explanation is that chronic stress due to major life changes may make people more vulnerable to daily hassles. For example, a husband trying to come to terms with a recent divorce may find the relatively minor squabbling of his children to be a major irritation. As a result, he may experience higher than expected levels of distress given the relatively trivial nature of the irritation. As the person is already in a state of distress, the presence of associated minor stressors may amplify the experience of stress. The presence of a major life change may also deplete a person's resources so that they are less able to cope with minor stressors than they would be under normal circumstances.

Methodological problems

The problems of retrospective recall

Strangely, for a measure which assesses daily hassles, participants are usually asked to rate the hassles experienced over the previous month. The same problems with retrospective reporting that were discussed on the previous spread therefore apply. Some researchers have overcome this problem by using a diary method, where participants rate minor stressors and feelings of well-being on a daily basis.

What does research tell us?

Most of the data from research on daily hassles is correlational. This means we cannot draw *causal* conclusions about the relationship between daily hassles and well-being. However, as with all correlations, they indicate that daily hassles in our lives can *potentially* have adverse effects on our health and well-being. As a result, we would be unwise to ignore the message in such research.

DO IT YOURSELF No.**4.3**

You could construct your own daily hassles scale, drawing on the ideas represented here. Schafer (1992) suggested items that might be suitable for a scale used by students: library too noisy; too little money; boring teacher; not enough close friends; conflicts with family; writing essays; fixing hair in the morning, etc. In order to conduct a study using this scale, you would also again need some way to assess illness (or health). The issue of questionnaire design is considered on page 94.

THE JACKMANS

Both Tom and his mum Clare are taking driving lessons. This is a stressful experience for anyone, but Clare is finding it especially stressful.

1 Give **two or more** reasons, based on psychological research, why driving lessons might be more stressful for Clare than for Tom.

Clare's mother has recently moved into a nursing home, and, after passing her driving test, Clare tries to call in on her on her way home from work each day. She finds her mother's demands quite stressful and recently snapped at her.

2 From your knowledge of research in this area, explain to Clare why she was so short-tempered with her mother.

3 What would you advise Clare to do to prevent this from happening again?

COMMENTARY CORNER

Throughout this book we have dedicated this commentary corner feature to helping you tackle extended writing questions. These questions differ from other exam questions because they carry more marks (marks you don't want to lose) and also because you have to understand the difference between describing and evaluating (AO1 and AO2). In the commentary corners throughout this book we have provided all sorts of useful tips for answering this type of question – and also don't forget the round up of key points on page 57.

Workplace stress

Stress at work is a priority issue for all of us who work, and for all who employ us. The European Foundation's 1996 report on working conditions in the European Union reported that over half of the workers questioned believed that their work adversely affected their health. Defining what is stressful about the workplace is not always that straightforward. You may remember from our initial discussion of stress and stressors that whether a particular stressor causes a stress reaction in an individual depends on how the individual perceives its demands and their ability to cope with those demands. So, to label 'responsibility' or 'workload' as automatic stressors without considering their impact on particular individuals, ignores the important fact that each of us interacts with our working environment differently, and so perceives it differently.

However, there are still a number of characteristics of the working environment that are commonly reported as being 'stressful'. These might be divided into *physical stressors* (such as noise and length of working day) and *psychosocial stressors* (such as relationships with co-workers and role responsibility). Each of these two broad types of workplace stressor has the *potential* to cause a stress reaction, and thus affect physical and psychological health. Whether they do have this effect or not, depends on many other factors including an individual's ability to cope and available social support.

RESEARCH ON WORKPLACE STRESSORS

Workload and control

Marmot *et al.* (1997) investigated the *job-strain model* of workplace stress. This model proposes that the workplace creates stress and illness in two ways: (1) high workload (creating greater job demands) and (2) low job control (e.g. over deadlines, procedures etc.). Marmot *et al.* suggested that in the civil service, higher-grade employees would experience high workload whereas low-grade civil servants would experience low job control. Therefore, both grades are likely to experience high levels of stress, but for different reasons. A total of 7372 civil servants working in London agreed to answer a questionnaire on workload, job control and amount of social support, and to be checked for signs of cardiovascular disease (e.g. ischemia or chest pains). Five years later participants were re-assessed.

Workload

Marmot *et al.*'s study found no link between high workload and stress-related illness, and therefore concluded that job demand was not a significant factor in stress. However other studies have examined different aspects of 'demand' or 'workload'. For example, Johansson *et al.* (1978) looked at the effects of performing repetitive jobs that require continuous attention and some responsibility (i.e. high job demand). The sawyers in a Swedish sawmill (high-risk group) have a stressful job – repetitive tasks, with an unrelenting pace and a sense of responsibility for the whole company because if they fall behind on their

work, the production of the whole company is slowed down. The high-risk group were found to have higher illness rates and also higher levels of *adrenaline* in their urine than a low-risk group (e.g. maintenance workers who had less monotonous jobs and more flexibility). The high-risk group also had higher levels of stress hormones on work days than on rest days.

Control

At the end of Marmot *et al.*'s study it was found that participants in the higher grades of the civil service had developed the fewest cardiovascular problems, and those in the lowest grades the most. Why might this be the case? Civil servants in the higher grades expressed a high sense of job control and good levels of social support, whereas those in the lower grades expressed a lower sense of job control and also had the poorest social support.

Role conflict

Role conflict occurs when experiences at work interfere with family life, and *vice versa*. An employee who continually has to take work home, or who is often absent from work because of childcare issues, may well experience role conflict. Conflict between work and family is associated with higher levels of absenteeism, lower levels of performance, and poorer physical and mental health. A study of 226 hospital doctors (Pomaki *et al.*, 2007) showed that role conflict was directly associated with emotional exhaustion, depressive symptoms, and somatic complaints.

KEY TERM

Workplace stressors Aspects of our working environment (such as work overload or impending deadlines) that we experience as stressful, and which cause a stress reaction in our body.

internet research

You can look at the European Agency for Safety and Health at Work's report on workplace stressors: osha.europa.eu/publications/reports/203/stress_en.pdf.

If you are less ambitious but still interested enough to read something extra on this topic, a summary of the report is available at: osha.europa.eu/publications/factsheets/8.

Alternatively, a factsheet on the risk factors and symptoms of workplace stress is available at: osha.europa.eu/publications/factsheets/22.

INDIVIDUAL DIFFERENCES

The role of control

The study by Marmot *et al.* suggested that lack of control was a source of stress in the workplace. However, there may be individual differences. Schaubroeck *et al.* (2001) found that some workers respond differently to lack of control – they are *less* stressed by having no control or responsibility. In this study Schaubroeck *et al.* measured saliva and could assess immune system functioning directly from the saliva. They found that some people had higher immune responses in low-control situations. Some people view negative work outcomes as being their fault. For these employees control can actually exacerbate the unhealthy effects of stress.

EVALUATION OF RESEARCH INTO WORKPLACE STRESS

Consequences of workplace stress

Stress and coronary heart disease

Kivimäki *et al.* (2006) carried out a meta-analysis of 14 studies (including the Marmot *et al.* study opposite) looking at the relative risk of *coronary heart disease* (CHD) in association with work stress. The analysis, which involved over 83,000 employees across Europe, the US and Japan, found that employees with high levels of job strain were 50% more likely to develop CHD.

Russek (1962) (see page 122) studied the incidence of CHD in medical professionals. Heart disease was greatest among GPs (classified as a high-stress medical occupation) and lowest in dermatologists (classified as low-stress).

Workplace stress and mental health

Work is generally good for our mental health, but there are times when it can be harmful. Although workplace stress may not cause depressive illness directly, high levels of stress at work combined with other problems (such as difficulties at home or daily hassles), can make depression more likely to occur. Warr (1987) used the analogy of 'vitamins' to explain how certain features of the workplace might contribute to the mental health of the worker. Low levels of vitamins lead to poor physical health, so low levels of these work-related features may lead to poor *mental* health. Some examples are:

- *Opportunity for control* – do situations offer the opportunity for personal control over activities and events?
- *Opportunity for skill use* – does the job allow for the use of existing skills or the development of new skills?
- *Opportunity for interpersonal contact* – important for meeting needs of friendship and social support.

Problems with the study of workplace stress

The impact of workplace stressors

Lazarus (1995) claims that the study of stressful factors in the workplace misses the point that there are wide individual differences in the way people react to and cope with individual stressors. Lazarus' *transactional approach* emphasises that the degree to which a workplace stressor is perceived as stressful depends largely on the person's perceived ability to cope. Therefore high job demands and role ambiguity may be perceived as stressful to one person, but not to another, particularly those high in 'hardiness' (see page 131).

The evolution of work and work stressors

The changing nature of the work environment, with the advent of new technology, virtual offices and the blurring of home/work environments means that our current knowledge of workplace stressors rapidly becomes out of date. As the ultimate purpose of research in this area is to help people manage the stresses of their working day, psychological research may inevitably lag behind actual work practices.

REAL-WORLD APPLICATIONS

Research on workplace stress has led to many different suggestions about how to deal with its negative consequences. Ritvanen *et al.* (2007) investigated whether aerobic fitness could reduce the physiological stress responses teachers experienced during working hours. Twenty-six male and female teachers participated in the study, which involved exercise tests, measurement of physiological responses (i.e. levels of adrenaline and noradrenaline, cortisol, blood pressure, heart rate and muscle tension) as well as measurement of perceived stress.

Results showed that teachers with the highest levels of aerobic fitness had lower levels of heart rate, muscle tension and perceived stress. This study suggests that improving aerobic fitness may therefore reduce the negative effects of work stress in teachers.

COMMENTARY CORNER

Question: **Outline and evaluate the contribution of two or more factors to stress in the workplace. *(12 marks)***

Understanding the impact of workplace stressors is important because all of us (except the very lucky or the very unfortunate) will need to work at least for part of our lives. The fact that we are also asking you to represent your understanding of this area through an examination question should not distract you from that fact. So, what better way to kill two birds with one stone than to do a little research yourself! If you are really ambitious, you could read (or just dip into) the European Agency for Safety and Health at Work's report on workplace stressors, available online (see 'internet research' on the opposite page).

Reading 'real-life' material like this is an excellent way of both furthering your understanding of a topic (in this case the impact of workplace stressors) and increasing your motivation and enthusiasm for a subject. Armed with so much useful and informed information, addressing questions like the one above should be far more straightforward. However, doing your own research does create an extra problem – what do you put in and what do you leave out? That's the beauty of psychology – there is no one prescribed way to answer an exam question. YOU choose what to include in an answer, and the examiner simply marks the relevance, accuracy and detail of the material you give them.

Personality factors and stress

There *are* important differences in the way that people react to stress as there are differences in the way they react to many other influences in their lives. Some people appear to be able to face horrendously stressful living conditions and still remain relatively healthy, whereas others buckle at the slightest bit of pressure. The term 'personality' is an elusive term that defies precise definition. In its broadest terms, personality can be thought of as a set of characteristic behaviours, attitudes and general temperament that remain relatively stable and distinguish one individual from another. Perhaps an easier way to define it is in more everyday terms – it is that fundamental 'thing' that makes us who we are, and makes us different from everybody else. Of course, we are different because of the peculiar mix of temperament, attitudes etc. that defines *us*, but there are inevitably some personality *traits* that we share with those around us. It is this fact that interests psychologists who study the mediating influence of personality on the impact of stressors. Research has established that *some* personality characteristics make us more vulnerable to the negative effects of stress, while others make us more resistant.

WWW Interested in whether you have a Type A personality? Take the test online at: www.queendom.com

The terms 'Type A personality' and 'Type A behaviour' are used interchangeably in the literature. They essentially mean the same thing.

▶ The Type A personality is ambitious and competitive with a strong sense of time urgency.

INDIVIDUAL DIFFERENCES

Riska (2002) claims that psychology's preoccupation with the Type A personality was a reflection of the importance of traditional masculinity in the 1950s and 60s. The behaviours and attributes of Type A man were those ideally required of ambitious and successful men in a competitive, capitalist society. The Type B male, in stark contrast, was doomed to flounder in the wake of the ambitious and competitive Type As. For women to be successful in the same climate meant that they too must embrace the 'masculine' behaviours of the Type A male. As coronary-prone Type A men were alerted to the unhealthy life they were living, a *hardy* personality became more important for the successful executive. Unlike the Type A personality, reflecting mainly male behaviour, hardiness, with its emphasis on the acquisition of positive health behaviours in men *and* women, portrays the personality characteristics of all those able to cope with stressful circumstances.

THE TYPE A PERSONALITY

Type A personality describes a person who is involved in an incessant struggle to achieve more and more in less and less time. Friedman and Rosenman (1959) believed the Type A individual possessed three major characteristics:

- Competitiveness and achievement striving
- Impatience and time urgency
- Hostility and aggressiveness

These characteristics would, they believed, lead to raised blood pressure and raised levels of stress hormones, both of which are linked to ill health, particularly the development of coronary heart disease (CHD). In contrast *Type B* (or *non-Type A*) was proposed as a personality relatively lacking these characteristics, being patient, relaxed, and easy-going, and therefore less vulnerable to stress-related illness.

Research on the Type A personality

In order to assess the hypothesis that CHD was associated with Type A personality, Friedman and Rosenman set up the Western Collaborative Group Study in 1960. Approximately 3000 men aged 39 to 59, living in California, were examined for signs of CHD (in order to exclude any individuals who were already ill) and their personalities were assessed using a structured interview. The interview included questions about how they responded to everyday pressures. For example, respondents were asked how they would cope with having to wait in a long queue. The interview was conducted in a provocative manner to try to elicit Type A behaviour. For example, the interviewer might speak slowly and hesitantly, so that a Type A person would want to interrupt.

WESTERN COLLABORATIVE GROUP STUDY		
	TYPE A	TYPE B
Heart attacks	12.8%	6.0%
Recurring heart attacks	2.6%	0.8%
Fatal heart attacks	2.7%	1.1%

The findings were alarming. After 8½ years, twice as many Type A participants had died of cardiovascular problems. As can be seen from the table, over 12% of the Type A personality participants had experienced a heart attack, compared to just 6% of the Type Bs. Type As also had higher blood pressure and higher cholesterol. They were also more likely to smoke and have a family history of CHD, both of which would increase their risk.

Evaluation of the Type A personality

- Ragland and Brand (1988) carried out a follow-up study of the Western Collaborative Group participants in 1982–3, 22 years after the start of the study. They found that 214 (approximately 15%) of the men had died of CHD. This study confirmed the importance of the CHD risk factors (age, smoking and high blood pressure), but found little evidence of a relationship between Type A behaviours and mortality, thus challenging the earlier conclusion that Type A personality was a significant risk factor for CHD mortality.
- Myrtek (2001) carried out a meta-analysis of 35 studies on this topic, and found an association between CHD and a component of Type A personality – *hostility*. Other than this, there was no evidence of an association between Type A personality and CHD.

The concept of hardiness has been used to explain why some soldiers remain healthy under war-related stress. In the 1990s Gulf War, the higher the hardiness level, the greater the ability of soldiers to experience combat-related stress without negative health consequences such as post-traumatic stress disorder or depression (Bartone, 1999). Applicants for elite military units, such as the US Navy Seals (above), are now screened for hardiness, with hardiness training becoming more widespread throughout the military.

Type A personality The Type A behaviour pattern is characterised by constant time pressure, competitiveness in work and social situations, and anger, i.e. being easily frustrated by other people.

The hardy personality provides defences against the negative effects of stress. These are control over one's life, commitment (i.e. a sense of involvement in the world), and challenge (i.e. life changes are opportunities rather than threats).

THE HARDY PERSONALITY

Although Type A behaviour is claimed to be a risk for CHD, many Type A individuals appear resistant to heart disease. Kobasa and Maddi (1977) suggested that some people are more psychologically 'hardy' than others. **The hardy personality** includes a range of characteristics which, if present, provide defences against the negative effects of stress.

- *Control* – Hardy people see themselves as being in control of their lives, rather than being controlled by external factors beyond their control.
- *Commitment* – Hardy people are involved with the world around them, and have a strong sense of purpose.
- *Challenge* – Hardy people see life challenges as problems to be overcome rather than as threats or stressors. They enjoy change as an opportunity for development.

Research on the hardy personality

Kobasa (1979) studied about 800 American business executives, assessing stress using Holmes and Rahe's SRRS. Approximately 150 of the participants were classified as high stress according to their SRRS scores. Of these, some had a low illness record whereas others had a high illness record. This suggests that something else was modifying the effects of stress because individuals experiencing the same stress levels had *different* illness records. Kobasa proposed that a hardy personality type encourages resilience. The individuals in the high-stress/low-illness group scored high on all three characteristics of the hardy personality, whereas the high-stress/high-illness group scored lower on these variables.

Maddi *et al.* (1987) studied employees of a US company (Illinois Bell Telephone) that was, over a year, dramatically reducing the size of its workforce. Two-thirds of employees suffered stress-related health problems over this period, but the remaining third thrived. This 'thriving' group showed more evidence of hardiness attributes, i.e. commitment, control and challenge.

Lifton *et al.* (2006) measured hardiness in students at five US universities to see if hardiness was related to the likelihood of their completing their degree. The results showed that students scoring low in hardiness were disproportionately represented among the drop-outs, and students with a high score were most likely to complete their degree.

ⓔ Evaluation of the hardy personality

Hardiness and negative affectivity (NA)

Some critics argue that the characteristics of the hardy personality (i.e. commitment, control and challenge) can be more simply explained by the concept of negative affectivity (NA) (Watson and Clark, 1984). High-NA individuals are more likely to report distress and dissatisfaction, dwell more on their failures, and focus on negative aspects of themselves and their world. NA and hardiness correlate reasonably well, suggesting that 'hardy individuals' are simply those who are low on NA.

Problems of measurement

Most of the research support for a link between hardiness and health has relied upon data obtained through self-report questionnaires. More recent efforts have led to the development of the Personal Views Survey. This new questionnaire addresses many of the criticisms raised with respect to the original measure, such as long and awkward wording and negatively worded items. However, not all of the problems have been resolved. For example, some studies show low internal reliability for the challenge component of hardiness.

CAN YOU...? No.4.7

...1 Explain how Type A behaviour modifies the effects of stress, using research evidence in your answer.

...2 Describe **four** research findings relating to the relationship between personality and stress, and give **one** criticism of each of these findings.

DO IT YOURSELF No.4.4

Even if you don't intend applying for the SAS or the US Navy Seals, hardiness helps people resist many of the harmful effects of stress in daily life. As we can see in the Lifton *et al.* study on the left, hardy students are more likely to complete academic courses. The test below provides a measure of hardiness. It is then up to you to decide what you might correlate respondents' scores with. As with any test of personality, there are important ethical issues to be considered before you begin testing other people (see page 70).

Write down how much you agree or disagree with the following statements.

| 0 = strongly disagree | 1 = mildly disagree |
| 2 = mildly agree | 3 = strongly agree |

A Trying my best at work makes a difference.

B Trusting to fate is sometimes all I can do in a relationship.

C I often wake up eager to start on the day's projects.

D Thinking of myself as a free person leads to great frustration and difficulty.

E I would be willing to sacrifice financial security in my work if something really challenging came along.

F It bothers me when I have to deviate from the routine or schedule I've set for myself.

G An average citizen can have an impact on politics.

H Without the right breaks, it is hard to be successful in my field.

I I know why I am doing what I'm doing at work (school or office).

J Getting close to people means I'm then obligated to them.

K Encountering new situations is an important priority in my life.

L I really don't mind when I have nothing to do.

(See page 214 for how to score the statements.)

Approaches to coping with stress

So far we have concentrated on the effects of stress, but now we turn our attention to how people *cope* with stress. Folkman and Lazarus (1980) define coping responses as 'cognitions and behaviours that a person uses to reduce stress and to moderate its emotional impact'. They measured a person's *style* of coping using the Ways of Coping Questionnaire (WCQ), which indicated that people use two major types of coping strategy to deal with stressful events. These are **problem-focused coping**, which involves the use of strategies designed directly to alleviate the stressful situation itself, and **emotion-focused coping** which involves the use of strategies which deal only with the emotional distress associated with stressful events. Emotion-focused coping is viewed as being more passive because it is an internal process that involves changing thoughts or feelings associated with a stressful event as opposed to taking direct behavioural action against it.

EXAM TIP

The key distinction between problem-focused and emotion-focused coping is that one deals with the stressor itself and the other deals only with the emotions generated by the stressor.

When is each strategy used?

Whether problem or emotion-focused coping is used in response to a stressor depends partly on personal style (some people make more use of emotional strategies, and others problem-solving strategies), and partly on the *type* of stressful event. Research has shown that people typically use problem-focused coping with events that are potentially controllable (e.g. dealing with debt) and emotion-focused coping with stressors perceived as less controllable (e.g. bereavement). Problem-focused coping is the more effective coping strategy *provided* that the individual has a realistic chance of changing those aspects of the situation that are causing them stress. Emotion-focused coping can reduce arousal levels prior to a more constructive problem-solving approach, or may help people to deal with stressful situations where there are few options to change the stressful situation itself.

KEY TERMS

Problem-focused coping The use of strategies designed directly to alleviate the stressful situation itself.

Emotion-focused coping The use of strategies that deal only with the emotional distress associated with stressful events.

PROBLEM-FOCUSED AND EMOTION-FOCUSED COPING

Problem-focused coping

Although the actual coping response would vary with the nature of a particular stressor, some common problem-focused strategies are:

- *Taking control* of the stressful situation (e.g. finding out as much as possible about a disease or taking active steps to deal with debt).
- *Evaluating the pros and cons* of different options for dealing with the stressor (e.g. choosing whether or not to have surgery or planning a new life after bereavement).
- *Suppressing competing activities* (e.g. avoiding the temptation to put off surgery because of work commitments).

Some strategies, such as seeking social support, can be both problem-focused *and* emotion-focused. For example, people with supportive social relationships may feel more in control of a situation because they are able to rely on these relationships. They may, as a result, feel able to engage in more problem-solving coping behaviours. The existence of social support (e.g. having a shoulder to cry on) may also decrease the amount of psychological distress associated with a stressor (i.e. emotion-focused coping).

Emotion-focused coping

Likewise, emotion-focused coping will vary with the nature of the stressor, as different stressors create different types of emotion. Examples include:

- *Denial* (e.g. going on as if nothing had happened) and *distancing* (e.g. just not thinking about it).
- *Focusing* on and venting emotions (e.g. crying or getting angry with others).
- *Wishful thinking* (e.g. dwelling on what might have been if this hadn't happened).

Some forms of emotion-focused coping are *positive* (e.g. reinterpreting the event in a positive light), whereas some are negative (e.g. repeatedly thinking about the problem without trying to change it). While positive emotion-focused coping can be helpful, negative emotion-focused coping tends to be associated with maladaptive health outcomes (the use of denial when experiencing the symptoms of CHD may lead to a delay in seeking treatment).

Research

Health outcomes

A study of nursing students (Penley *et al.*, 2002) found that problem-focused coping was positively correlated with overall health outcomes, whereas *negative* emotion-focused coping (e.g. avoidance and wishful thinking) was associated with poor overall health outcomes. Gilbar (2005) examined the associations among coping strategies and psychological distress in patients with breast cancer, a major life-change stressor. The results showed that use of emotion-focused coping (e.g. avoidance, distraction) was associated with high psychological distress, whereas use of problem-focused strategies (e.g. the use of social support resources) was beneficial in allaying this distress.

Examination stress

Folkman and Lazarus (1985) investigated the different coping responses used by students in the run-up to exams, and during the wait for results. They found that both problem-focused and emotion-focused strategies were used at both stages, but different forms dominated during each stage. Problem-focused coping was more evident before the exam, and emotion-focused (mostly distancing) was more evident during the wait for results.

Threat and coping

Rukholm and Viverais (1993) examined the relationship between stress, threat and coping. They concluded that if a person feels a significant degree of threat when confronted by a stressor, they may need to deal with the resultant anxiety through emotion-focused coping first. Only when this is under control can they make use of problem-focused coping.

e EVALUATION

Problems of measurement

Stone *et al.* (1991) have argued that many of the items in the Ways of Coping measure are more appropriate to some types of stressor than others. They found most of the scale was relevant to relationship stressors (e.g. problems involving boyfriends or girlfriends) but approximately three-quarters of the items were inappropriate for health problems. Similarly some statements on the scale (e.g. 'finding a new faith') may seem of little relevance if the stressor is a broken-down car or crippling debt.

Is emotion-focused coping always maladaptive?

Although most studies appear to indicate that emotion-focused coping is ineffective as a way of dealing with stress, there are reasons to doubt that this is always the case. For example, Lazarus suggests that emotion-focused coping (such as denial or distraction) may be unhelpful when experiencing serious symptoms of ill health, as it delays the individual from seeking appropriate treatment. However during the recovery period (e.g. after an operation) this may be a very useful way of coping. Despite this, if this type of coping continues for too long it may distract the person from making the necessary lifestyle changes (e.g. not smoking and taking regular exercise) to prevent the same thing happening in the future.

INDIVIDUAL DIFFERENCES

Can everybody use problem-focused coping?

Mullis and Chapman (2000) studied the relationship between adolescents' self-esteem (a subjective assessment of a person's self-worth) and the coping strategy used. Adolescents between the ages of 11–17 from four US schools were asked to complete questionnaires on self-esteem and coping strategies. Adolescents with higher scores for self-esteem used more problem-focused coping and less emotion-focused coping strategies than adolescents who scored lower for self-esteem. This finding emphasises the importance of positive self-worth among adolescents who must cope effectively with stress in their lives.

THE JACKMANS

Rick is having a very trying time with a subordinate at work who is clearly struggling to deal with his workload, and yet will always claim that 'everything is okay'. When Rick tries to address the problem with him, he either changes the subject or gets angry.

From your study of problem-focused and emotion-focused coping:

1 What do you think is happening here?
2 Suggest **two** things that Rick might do to help his colleague deal constructively with the problem.

INDIVIDUAL DIFFERENCES

Research has often found evidence of gender differences in coping, with males more likely to use problem-solving coping and females more likely to use emotion-focused coping (Brody and Hall, 1993). Rosario *et al.* (1988) describe two theories that might explain these apparent gender differences.

- *Socialisation theory* – women are taught to express their emotions more openly, and so use more emotion-focused coping, whereas men are taught to approach stressful situations in a more active, problem-focused manner.
- *Role constraint* theory – gender differences in coping are a product of the *roles* that males and females tend to occupy.

Rosario *et al.* (1988) found that males and females in the *same* social roles did not differ in their reported use of problem-focused or emotion-focused coping strategies, which supports role constraint theory.

COMMENTARY CORNER

The specification requires you to be able to 'distinguish' between problem-focused and emotion-focused coping. This is fairly straightforward, i.e. one deals directly with the stressor itself and the other deals only with the emotions generated by the stressor. However, it should be fairly obvious that in the exam more will be required that just a simple distinction. Therefore, as well as *distinguishing* between these two strategies you should be able to describe each type of coping response, outline research related to each, *and* offer some appropriate critical commentary. As we have emphasised throughout this book, the key to effective examination answers lies in reading the questions carefully and tailoring the material at your disposal to the exact demands of the question. Before putting pen to paper, ask yourself the following:

- What is the exact requirement of the question? For example, does it ask for an outline of these two approaches, or *also* an explanation of the distinction between them? Maybe the words 'research' or 'studies' appear in the question to prompt you to include supporting research studies.
- How many marks are available? This would determine how long you spend on the question and approximately how many words you write.

Remember that exam answers only ever require a small proportion of the material you have available, so don't panic when you find that you are leaving out much of the information on this spread!

Psychological methods of stress management

You may remember that the *problem-solving approach* to coping with stress involves the use of techniques that help the person to cope with the situation itself rather than just dealing with the symptoms. A person can focus on the specific problem or situation that has arisen, trying to find some way of changing it or avoiding it in the future, or may learn techniques that minimise the negative effects of stressful situations. Although some of the most often-used psychological approaches to stress management are relaxation and meditation, some experts believe that the really effective techniques involve specific psychological interventions that either train individuals to appraise stressful situations differently or to increase the resistance to the negative effects of stress. We will examine two psychological approaches – **stress inoculation training** (which is an example of **Cognitive Behavioural Therapy**) and **hardiness training**.

'There is nothing either good or bad, but thinking makes it so.' (Hamlet, William Shakespeare)

Cognitive Behavioural Therapy (CBT)

'Therapy' is a term usually used by psychologists when dealing with mental disorders. In Chapter 6 we will look at some of the therapies commonly used to treat mental disorders. One such approach is the cognitive behavioural approach. The cognitive behavioural approach is actually a combination of two approaches – the *cognitive approach* and the *behavioural approach* (both discussed in detail in Chapter 6). The cognitive approach is based on the belief that the key influence on behaviour is how an individual *thinks* about a situation. Therefore cognitive therapy aims to change unwanted or maladaptive thoughts and beliefs. Behaviourists believe that undesirable behaviours have been learned, therefore behavioural therapy aims to reverse the learning process and produce a new set of more desirable behaviours. *Cognitive Behavioural Therapy* links the two, and involves cognitive techniques, such as challenging negative thoughts (e.g. 'What makes you think you won't be able to beat this?'), and behavioural techniques, such as rewarding desirable behaviours.

COGNITIVE BEHAVIOURAL THERAPY

Stress inoculation training

Meichenbaum (1985) believed that although we cannot (usually) change the *causes* of stress in our life (e.g. a stressful job is still a stressful job), we can change the way that we *think* about these stressors. As negative thinking (e.g. 'I failed to hit a deadline, people must think I'm hopeless') may lead to negative outcomes such as anxiety and depression, positive thinking (e.g. 'My boss will still be delighted by what I've achieved') leads to more positive attitudes and feelings. These reduce the stress response and help us to cope better in the future.

Meichenbaum's therapy, called stress inoculation training (SIT), is a form of Cognitive Behavioural Therapy developed specifically to deal with stress. It is different from other stress treatments because Meichenbaum suggested that an individual should develop a form of coping before the problem arises. He suggested that a person could *inoculate* themselves against the 'disease' of stress in the same way that they would receive inoculations against infectious diseases such as measles.

Meichenbaum proposed three main phases to this process:

1 Conceptualisation phase

The therapist (trainer) and client establish a relationship, and the client is educated about the nature and impact of stress. For example, the client is taught to view perceived threats as problems to be solved, and to break down global stressors into specific components that can be coped with. This enables the client to think differently about (i.e. reconceptualise) their problem.

2 Skills acquisition phase (and rehearsal)

Coping skills are taught and practised primarily in the clinic and then gradually rehearsed in real life. A variety of skills are taught and tailored to the individual's own specific problems. These include positive thinking, relaxation, social skills, methods of attention diversion, using social support systems and time management. Clients may be taught to use coping self-statements, e.g. 'relax, you're in control'. The skills taught are both cognitive and behavioural: cognitive because they encourage the client to think in a different way, and behavioural because they involve learning new more adaptive behaviours.

3 Application phase (and follow-through)

Clients are given opportunities to apply the newly learned coping skills in different situations, which become increasingly stressful. Various techniques may be used such as imagery (imagining how to deal with stressful situations), modelling (watching someone else cope with stressors and then imitating this behaviour), and role playing (acting out scenes involving stressors). Clients may even be asked to help train others. Booster sessions (follow-through) are offered later on.

REAL-WORLD APPLICATIONS

Many sportsmen and women unwittingly respond to stress with maladaptive thoughts that greatly hinder their performance. Once they understand how this way of thinking is keeping them from reaching their full potential, they begin to develop new coping strategies which can have a profoundly positive impact on their performance. Studies of the effects of stress inoculation training on sports performance have generally been very positive: SIT has been linked with improved performance during cross-country running, squash and basketball, and has been particularly effective at boosting the performances of gymnasts (Kerr and Leith, 1993). If Ryan Babel's performances for Liverpool are anything to go by, it has worked pretty well in football as well!

▼ Liverpool footballer Ryan Babel admitted that he had always been susceptible to pressure from the crowd, and struggled to handle fans turning against him. That is now a thing of the past thanks to manager Rafa Benitez .'He (Benitez) told me that the abuse ought to make me stronger, saying the more the opposing fans swore at me, the more afraid of me they were.'

meet the researcher

As well as being named the most cited psychology researcher within Canadian universities, **Donald Meichenbaum** was voted 'one of the ten most influential psychotherapists of the century' by American clinicians. He worked with victims of Hurricane Katrina in 2005, and the 1993 Oklahoma bombing, as well as with Canadian soldiers serving in Afghanistan and the native Inuit population in northern Canada.

STRENGTHS OF SIT

Effectiveness

Meichenbaum (1977) compared SIT with another form of treatment called *systematic desensitisation* (described on page 196). Patients used SIT or desensitisation to deal with their snake phobias. Meichenbaum found that although both forms of therapy reduced the phobia, SIT was better because it helped clients deal with a second, non-treated phobia. This shows that SIT can inoculate against future stressful situations as well as offering help in coping with current problems.

Sheehy and Horan (2004) examined the effects of SIT on the anxiety, stress and academic performance of first-year law students. Participants received four weekly sessions of SIT, each lasting 90 minutes. Results showed that all participants who received SIT displayed lower levels of anxiety and stress over time. The academic ranks of participants predicted to finish in the bottom 20% of their class also reflected conspicuous and significant improvement after SIT. More than half of these significantly improved their predicted class rank.

Preparation for future stressors

A major advantage of this method of stress management is that it doesn't just deal with current stressors, but also gives the client the skills and confidence to cope with future problems. The focus on skills acquisition provides long-lasting effectiveness so that the individual is less adversely affected by stressors in the future.

WEAKNESSES OF SIT

Time-consuming and requires high motivation

SIT requires a lot of time, effort, motivation and money. Its strengths are also its weaknesses – it is effective because it involves learning and practising many new skills, but this complexity makes it a lengthy therapy which would suit only a limited range of determined individuals.

Unnecessarily complex

It may be that the effectiveness of SIT is due to certain elements of the training rather than all of it. This means that the range of activities (and time) could be reduced without losing much of the effectiveness. For example, it might be equally effective to just learn to talk more positively and relax more.

HARDINESS TRAINING

On pages 130–1, we considered the role of personality in modifying the effects of stress. Suzanne Kobasa identified a personality type that was especially resistant to stress – the hardy personality. Kobasa argued that this concept could be usefully turned into a stress management technique. If some people were naturally resistant to stress (because they were hardy) then perhaps it would be possible to teach others how to become more 'hardy', and thus manage stress better.

How can you teach hardiness?

Salvatore Maddi, who worked with Kobasa, founded the Hardiness Institute in California. The aim of the hardiness training programme is to increase self-confidence and sense of control so that individuals can more successfully navigate change. Both Maddi and Kobasa suggested the following ways to train hardiness

- *Focusing*. The client is taught how to recognise the physiological signs of stress, such as muscle tension and increased heart rate, and also to identify the sources of this stress.
- *Reliving stress encounters*. The client relives stress encounters and is helped to analyse these situations and their response to them. This gives them an insight into their current coping strategies and how

they might be more effective than they thought.
- *Self-improvement*. The insights gained can now be used to move forward and learn new techniques of dealing with stress. In particular the client is taught to focus on seeing stressors as challenges that they can take control of, rather than problems that they must give in to.

 Does it work?

The Student Support Services at Utah Valley State College has offered hardiness training to their at-risk students. Hardiness training helps these students to stay in, and to graduate from, school by mastering the many stresses they encounter while they work to develop themselves professionally and personally (from Hardiness Institute website).

Hardiness training has been used effectively by Olympic swimmers to ensure that they are committed to the challenge of increased performance levels, and are able to control the stressful aspects of their daily lives that might otherwise interfere with their training (Fletcher, 2005).

However, hardiness training has the problem that it must first address basic aspects of personality and learned habits of coping that are notoriously difficult to modify. It cannot, therefore, be seen as a rapid solution to stress management.

 Learn more about hardiness training at www.hardinessinstitute.com

KEY TERMS

Cognitive Behavioural Therapy (CBT) A combination of *cognitive* therapy (a way of changing maladaptive thoughts and beliefs), and *behavioural* therapy (a way of changing behaviour in response to these thoughts and beliefs).

Stress inoculation therapy A type of CBT which trains people to cope with anxiety and stressful situations more effectively by learning skills to 'inoculate' themselves against the damaging effects of future stressors.

Hardiness training The aim of hardiness training is to increase self-confidence and sense of control so that individuals can more successfully navigate change in their lives.

CAN YOU...? No.4.9

...**1** Describe **one** cognitive behavioural method of stress management in about 150 words.

...**2** Reduce this description to 75 words.

...**3** Describe **two** strengths and **two** weaknesses of this method.

...**4** Describe **one** other psychological method of stress management in about 75 words, and give **two** criticisms of it.

Physiological methods of stress management

On page 132 we saw that in *emotion-focused* coping, a person can just focus on alleviating the emotions associated with the stressful situation, even if the situation itself cannot be changed. They may achieve this in a number of ways including the use of drugs to reduce the anxiety associated with stress (drug therapies). These approaches are referred to as the *physiological* approach to stress management. You will learn more about drug therapies in Chapter 6, but for now we will focus on two of the most common anti-anxiety drugs, and how they are used to combat stress.

'Physiological' refers to processes in the body, whereas 'psychological' refers to processes in the mind.

WWW Watch Dr Heather Ashton explain some of the problems of BZs on a YouTube video: www.youtube.com/watch?v=osg7ZP5h3Pw

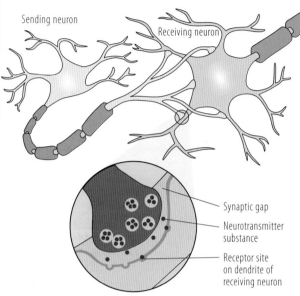

Sending neuron

Receiving neuron

Synaptic gap

Neurotransmitter substance

Receptor site on dendrite of receiving neuron

▲ GABA is released from one neuron across the synaptic gap where it reacts with special receptors on the second (receiving) neuron. BZs are carried to special booster sites on these receptors, where they enhance the action of GABA.

DRUG THERAPIES

Benzodiazepines (BZs)

The group of drugs most commonly used to treat anxiety and stress are *benzodiazepines* (e.g. Librium or Valium), which slow down the activity of the central nervous system.

- *GABA* is a neurotransmitter that is the body's natural form of anxiety relief. About 40% of the neurons in the brain respond to GABA which, when released, has a general quietening effect on many of the neurons in the brain. It does this by reacting with GABA receptors on the outside of receiving neurons. When GABA locks into these receptors it opens a channel which increases the flow of chloride ions into the neuron. Chloride ions make it harder for the neuron to be stimulated by other neurotransmitters, thus slowing down its activity and making the person feel more relaxed.
- *BZs enhance the action of GABA* by binding to special sites on the GABA receptor and boosting the actions of GABA. This allows *more* chloride ions to enter the neuron, making it even *more* resistant to excitation. As a result, the brain's output of excitatory neurotransmitters is reduced, and the person feels calmer.
- *BZs and serotonin* – Serotonin is a neurotransmitter that has an arousing effect in the brain. BZs reduce any increased serotonin activity, which then reduces anxiety.

Beta-blockers (BBs)

- *Sympathetic arousal* – as we saw earlier (page 118), stress leads to arousal of the sympathetic nervous system and this creates raised blood pressure, increased heart rate, elevated levels of cortisol, and so on. These symptoms can lead to cardiovascular disorders and also reduce the effectiveness of the immune system.
- *How do they work?* – Beta-blockers reduce the activity of adrenaline and noradrenaline which are part of the sympathomedullary response to stress. Beta-blockers bind to receptors on the cells of the heart and other parts of the body that are usually stimulated during arousal.
- *What do they achieve?* – By *blocking* these receptors, it is harder to stimulate cells in, for example, the heart, so it beats slower and with less force, and blood vessels do not contract so easily. This results in a fall in blood pressure, and therefore less stress on the heart. The person feels calmer and less anxious. Beta-blockers are often used by sportsmen (e.g. snooker players) and musicians to reduce arousal because sympathetic arousal may have a negative effect on performance.

DO IT YOURSELF

No.**4.6**

1 There is a lot of detail and a lot of complicated terminology here, but relax – you only need to be able to outline it. We have the luxury of about 1500 words on this topic (physiological methods of stress management) so can afford to stretch it a bit to help you understand what it's all about. However, the most you would have to reproduce in an exam would be 200–250 words. Rather than bogging yourself down with all this biological detail, précis it into the type of outline you might be expected to reproduce in the exam.

2 Try summarising the action of BZs into just 100 words. Choose your words carefully, concentrating on clearly written and informative content. Now do the same exercise with just 50 words, and another 50 words for beta-blockers. In fact, just to really get you used to the skill of précis, try doing these in *exactly* 100 and 50 words. Keep tweaking them until you're happy with what you've produced.

3 Now practise dividing these different outlines into bullet points. Perhaps you've made six points for your 100-word version and three for your 50-word version. This exercise will not only provide you with useful outlines for your revision, you will also be actively processing the material, making it more likely that you'll remember it in the exam.

REAL-WORLD APPLICATIONS

Beta-blockers have been shown to significantly reduce the symptoms of anxiety that can hinder some musicians' playing. Lockwood (1989) studied over 2000 musicians in major US symphony orchestras and found that 27% reported taking beta-blockers. The musicians in this study said they felt better about their performance after taking beta-blockers, and music critics consistently judged their performances to be better.

...1 Explain the difference between BZs and BBs.

...2 Describe **two** physiological methods of stress management (see 'Do it yourself').

...3 For each give **one** strength and **one** weakness.

...4 Give **two** reasons why using drugs is better than using Cognitive Behavioural Therapy to deal with stress, and **two** reasons why drugs are less effective.

STRENGTHS OF DRUG TREATMENTS

Effectiveness

Drugs can be very effective in combating the effects of stress. One way to assess effectiveness is to compare outcomes – one group of anxious patients is given a drug and another group is given a placebo – a substance that has no *pharmacological* effects (i.e. it has no effect on the body). Patients are given medication but do not know whether it is the real thing or the placebo. This enables us to determine whether the effectiveness of the drug is due to its pharmacological properties or to something psychological (e.g. simply believing that taking the drug will make you better).

- Kahn *et al.* (1986) followed nearly 250 patients over eight weeks and found that BZs were significantly superior to a placebo. A meta-analysis of studies focusing on the treatment of social anxiety (Hildalgo *et al.*, 2001) found that BZs were more effective at reducing this anxiety than other drugs such as antidepressants.
- Beta-blockers are effective in reducing anxiety in a variety of stressful situations e.g. among musicians (see 'Real-world applications'), and in sports where accuracy is more important than physical stamina (e.g. snooker and golf).

Ease of use

One of the great benefits of using drugs for stress is that the therapy requires little effort from the user. You just have to remember to take the pills. This is much easier than the time and effort needed to use psychological methods. For example, stress inoculation therapy requires a lot of time, effort and motivation on the part of the client if it is to be effective.

What's the difference between physiological and psychological methods of stress management?

- The main difference between a *physiological* and a *psychological* approach to stress management is that in the former a person focuses on alleviating the emotions associated with the stressful situation rather than dealing with the situation itself. This is a form of *emotion-focused coping*.
- The psychological approach to stress management involves the use of techniques that help the person to cope with the situation itself rather than just dealing with the symptoms of their stress. Because psychological approaches frequently involve learning constructive ways to deal with stressful situations (thus minimising their stressful impact), this is a form of *problem-focused coping*.

WEAKNESSES OF DRUG TREATMENTS

Addiction

BZs were first introduced over 40 years ago and replaced barbiturates which tended to be addictive, i.e. patients exhibited withdrawal symptoms when they stopped taking the drug, indicating a physiological dependence. It is only recently that the problems of addiction and BZs have been recognised, especially the problems of low-dose dependence on BZs. Patients taking even low doses of BZs show marked withdrawal symptoms when they stop taking them. Because of such addiction problems there is a recommendation that use of BZs should be limited to a maximum of four weeks (Ashton, 1997).

Side effects

Side effects of BZs include 'paradoxical' symptoms (so-called because they are the opposite of what might be expected) such as increased aggressiveness and cognitive side effects. These cognitive side effects include impairment of memory, especially the ability to store acquired knowledge in long-term memory.

Most people who take beta-blockers do not experience any side effects, although some studies have linked them with an increased risk of developmental diabetes.

Treating the symptoms rather than the problem

Drugs may be very effective at treating symptoms but the effect only lasts while a person takes the drugs. As soon as they stop taking the drugs the effectiveness ceases. It may be that the problem has passed, but in cases of chronic stress, it may not be appropriate to simply put a temporary bandage on the problem especially if the treatment produces further problems of its own (such as addiction). This means that it may be preferable to seek a treatment that addresses the problem itself (i.e. a *psychological* method) rather than one that deals only with the symptoms.

COMMENTARY CORNER

Question: **Consider the effectiveness of physiological approaches to stress management.** *(8 marks)*

An effective way of handling the requirements of this question is to decide at the outset what your conclusion will be and to work towards that.

You may, for example, decide that physiological approaches are not particularly effective forms of stress management and proceed to justify that in your choice of material. For example, drugs may be very effective at treating the symptoms of stress, but this only lasts as long as one takes the drugs. As soon as you stop, the effectiveness ceases.

On the other hand, you may decide that physiological approaches *are* effective in the management of stress, and so you choose to emphasise slightly different aspects of the same material. For example drugs do appear to work, particularly in the way they reduce the general anxiety associated with stressful situations. This claim is supported by the research of Kahn *et al.* (1986), who followed nearly 250 patients over eight weeks and found that BZs were significantly superior to placebo in the treatment of stress-related anxiety.

It is a useful exercise for you to construct *two* answers to this question, one the case for the prosecution (i.e. that physiological approaches are *not* effective), and one the case for the defence (i.e. that they *are* effective). Having thought about the arguments from both sides, you are then in a much better position to construct a more well-rounded answer to this question. It is unlikely that physiological approaches are *completely* ineffective, but then again it is equally unlikely that they are *completely* effective.

You should also be prepared for a question that is worth 12 marks instead of 8 marks – the mark allocation is important in adjusting how much you write. If you write too much you may waste valuable time that could have been spent elsewhere.

End-of-chapter review CHAPTER SUMMARY

We have identified here the key points of the topics on the AQA (A) AS specification, i.e. the bare minimum that you need to know. You may want to fill in further details to elaborate and personalise this material.

STRESS

BODY'S RESPONSE TO STRESSORS

Acute stress Sympathomedullary pathway (SAM)
- SNS → noradrenaline → fight or flight changes in the body.
- SNS → adrenal medulla → adrenaline → fight or flight changes.

 INDIVIDUAL DIFFERENCES
- Men → fight or flight, women → tend and befriend (Taylor *et al.*).
- Higher levels of oxytocin reduce cortisol which reduces stress.
- Oxytocin reduced by male hormones; amplified by female hormones.

Chronic stress Pituitary-adrenal system (HPA)
- Hypothalamus → CRF → pituitary → ACTH → adrenal cortex → cortisol.
- System is self-regulatory – high levels of cortisol lead to reduction in CRF and ACTH.

 CONSEQUENCES
- SNS activation → high blood pressure → heart disease.
- Too much cortisol suppresses immune system.

STRESS-RELATED ILLNESS

The immune system
- Research by Kiecolt-Glaser *et al.* – shows poorer immune system functioning during:
  (i) Acute (e.g. examinations) and
  (ii) Chronic (e.g. marital conflict) stressors.
- Short-term (acute) stress may enhance efficiency of immune system whereas ongoing (chronic) stress reduces it.
- Meta-analysis (Segerstorm and Miller) 293 studies confirm above trend.

 INDIVIDUAL DIFFERENCES
- Female immune systems are more reactive to stress of marital conflict.
- Stress has greater effect on immune system functioning in older people.

 APPLICATIONS
- Creating healthy life-style programmes.
- Stress-coping behaviours associated with improvement in psychological well-being.

 EVALUATION
- Lazarus – difficult to establish relationship between stress and illness as health changes slowly and determined by many different factors.

Cardiovascular disorders
- Williams – people with high anger ratings (acute stressor) had more heart attacks.
- Russek – high-stress medics had more heart disease than low-stress medics.
- Sheps *et al.* – effects of stress worse in people with existing coronary conditions.

Psychiatric disorders
- People in high-stress jobs more prone to depression (Melchior *et al.* 2007).
- PTSD and PITS caused by traumatic stress e.g. conflict or euthanising animals (Rohlf and Bennett).
- Diathesis-stress model sometimes explains role of stress in mental disorder, e.g. depression.

 INDIVIDUAL DIFFERENCES
- Hyperresponsive people have greater physiological response to stress.

 EVALUATION
- Use of self-report measures may be unreliable.
- May be indirect rather than direct links, e.g. stress leads to smoking and drinking which leads to illness.
- Link between stress and depression may be other way around (e.g. depression causes stress).

STRESS IN EVERYDAY LIFE

APPROACHES TO COPING WITH STRESS

Problem-focused coping
- Deals with problem itself, e.g. taking control, suppressing competing activities.
- Active rather than passive.

Emotion-focused coping
- Deals with emotions caused by stress.
- e.g. denial, wishful thinking.
- Can be positive or negative.

- Gilbar – breast cancer patients did best with problem focus.
- Folkman and Lazarus – students used problem focus before exams, emotion focus while waiting for results.
- Rukholm and Viverais – emotion focus first for problems that create threat, then problem focus when threat reduced.

 INDIVIDUAL DIFFERENCES
- Males more likely to use problem focus.
- Adolescents with higher self-esteem use problem focus (Mullis and Chapman).

 EVALUATION
- 'Ways of Coping' measure not appropriate for all stressors.
- Emotion focus unhelpful for serious illness but good for recovery.

PSYCHOLOGICAL METHODS OF STRESS MANAGEMENT

Stress inoculation training (Meichenbaum)
- Prepares person for stress now and in the future.
- Steps in therapy: Conceptualisation, skills acquisition and rehearsal, application phases.

 STRENGTHS
- Meichenbaum found SIT more effectiveness than systematic desensitisation for snake phobia, and generalised to another phobia.
- Sheehy and Horan – students given SIT improved their academic rank.
- Long-lasting and useful for other problems.

WEAKNESSES
- Time-consuming and need for high motivation.
- Overcomplicated – effectiveness may be due to some rather than all elements.

 APPLICATIONS
- Kerr and Leith – SIT successfully used with gymnasts, runners, etc.

Hardiness training
- Kobasa – hardy people more resistant to stress.
- Maddi – Hardiness Institute, increase self-confidence and sense of control.
- Steps in therapy: Focusing, reliving stress encounters, self-improvement.

 EVALUATION
- Successfully used by at-risk students and by Olympic swimmers (Fletcher, 2005).
- Not a rapid method because involves change to personality and learned habits.

LIFE CHANGES

- Holmes and Rahe created the SRRS.
- Rahe *et al.* tested naval men over 6 months. Positive correlation between ill health and LCUs.
- Michael and Ben-Zur – life changes (divorced vs bereaved) had different effects.

APPLICATIONS
- Life events may predict suicide among young (Heikken and Lönnqvist).

EVALUATION
- Quality of event important.
- Daily hassles may matter more e.g. DeLongis *et al.* found less of a link between life events and health.
- Individual differences for meaning of life events.
- Correlation but not cause.

VALIDITY AND RELIABILITY
- Memory for life events may be poor → low validity and reliability.
- Hardt *et al.* found good test-retest for interviews over 22 years.

DAILY HASSLES

- Delongis *et al.* created HSUP.
- Bouteyre *et al.* – positive correlation between HSUP and depression in undergraduates.
- Gervais (2005) qualitative analysis of nurses, uplifts counteracted hassles.
- Daily hassles may have more impact than life events because less social support (Folett *et al.*).

APPLICATIONS
- Road rage linked to daily hassles (Gulian *et al.*).

INDIVIDUAL DIFFERENCES
- Pets can be an uplift for females.

EVALUATION
- Effect may be due to accumulation of hassles over the day.
- Major life event may make a person more vulnerable to hassles.
- Problems with retrospective recall – can use diary method.
- Correlation not cause.

WORKPLACE STRESSORS

- Marmot *et al.* – low job control and lack of social support linked to stress in civil service study.
- Pomaki *et al.* – role conflict had less effect if health promoting behaviours used.

INDIVIDUAL DIFFERENCES
- Some workers more stressed by high control (Schaubroeck *et al.*).

APPLICATIONS
- Aerobic fitness reduced effects of work stress (Ritvanen *et al.*).

EVALUATION
- Consequences – may lead to CHD or depression.
- Lazarus' transactional approach – workplace stress depends on perceived ability to cope.
- The workplace is constantly changing so research goes out of date.

PERSONALITY FACTORS

Type A personality
- Respond to stress with impatience, hostile and competitive.
- Freidman and Rosenman – conducted structured interviews to establish type. 8½ years later twice as many Type As had died of heart attacks.

INDIVIDUAL DIFFERENCES
- Type A man reflects 1960s, hardiness more relevant today.

EVALUATION
- Ragland and Brand didn't find link between Type A and mortality after 22 years.
- Myrtek – hostility component of Type A more important.

Hardy personality
- Kobasa and Maddi – 'hardy' people cope because of control, commitment and challenge.
- Kobasa – US executives had different illness records if they were hardy.
- Maddi *et al.* – hardiness attributes in 'thriving' employees.
- Lifton – 'hardy' students more likely to graduate.

EVALUATION
- More simply just negative affectivity – NA (Watson and Clark).
- Questionnaire used has low reliability, even improved version (Personal Views Survey) has problems.

PHYSIOLOGICAL METHODS OF STRESS MANAGEMENT

Benzodiazepines (BZs)
- GABA is a natural calming neurotransmitter.
- BZs bind to sites on GABA receptors and enhance the action of GABA by allowing more chloride ions into the neuron, making it more resistant to excitation and thus making the person more relaxed.
- Serotonin has an arousing effect – BZs reduce increased serotonin activity associated with anxiety.

Beta-blockers (BBs)
- BZs reduce sympathetic activity by binding to receptors on heart and other parts of body usually aroused by adrenaline.

STRENGTHS OF DRUG TREATMENTS
- Kahn *et al.* – BZs superior to placebos.
- Lockwood – BBs helped musicians overcome stage fright.
- Ease of use.

WEAKNESSES OF DRUG TREATMENTS
- Addiction – even low-dose BZs seem to lead to withdrawal symptoms. Limit use to 2 weeks.
- Side effects of BZs – paradoxical symptoms, e.g. aggressiveness and poor memory.
- Side effects of BBs – rare but possibly diabetes.
- Treats symptoms and not the problem – problem reappears once drugs stopped, though problem may have passed.

Psychological methods deal with the emotion associated with a situation (emotion-focused), whereas physiological methods deal with the situation itself (problem-focused).

End-of-chapter review | REVISION QUESTIONS

There are lots of ideas at the end of other chapters that you might adapt and try out here.

THE BODY'S RESPONSE TO STRESS

ACTIVITY 1 pages 118–19

Task 1 Questions

Here are a few questions, reviewing some of the points raised in this part of the chapter.

1 What is the ANS and in what way is it 'automatic'?
2 What is the difference between acute and chronic stress?
3 What is the name of the physiological system linked to acute stress?
4 What is the SNS?
5 The SNS activates the body for fight or flight. Which branch of the ANS is related to the relaxed state?
6 Which hormone is linked to fight or flight?
7 Where in the adrenal gland is this hormone produced?
8 Briefly outline the sympathomedullary pathway.
9 Identify **two** effects of sympathetic arousal.
10 What role does the pituitary gland play in the stress response?
11 Which hormone is linked to chronic stress?
12 What part of the brain first deals with stress perception?
13 What chemical messenger is released from the paraventricular nucleus (PVN)?
14 What stress hormone is released from the pituitary?
15 What part of the adrenal gland is linked to chronic stress?
16 Outline the pituitary-adrenal system.

Task 2 Evaluating the stress response

On pages 118–19 we have provided some points of evaluation. Use these to write a short paragraph (about 150 words) of evaluation, for example:

- In what way the response is not universal (i.e. doesn't apply to everyone)?
- In what way it is actually not that adaptive (i.e. may not always be that helpful)?

STRESS-RELATED ILLNESS AND THE IMMUNE SYSTEM

ACTIVITY 2 pages 120–3

Task 1 Research studies

We looked at a number of studies on stress and the immune system, some of which are listed below. For each of them see if you can briefly remember the key points (method, findings and conclusions):

- Kiecolt-Glaser et al. (1984)
- Marucha et al. (1998)
- Kiecolt-Glaser et al. (2005)
- Evans et al. (1994)
- Segerstrom and Miller (2004)

Task 2 Psychology in action

Rick has been working on a major book project for the last two months. This has meant him frequently working for 12 hours a day and also constantly having his boss on the phone asking when he would be able to meet various deadlines.

1 Use your psychological knowledge to advise him of some of the physiological effects that working like this will have.
2 There have been some criticisms of research in this area. Suggest **one** reason to feel uncertain about the validity of the advice you have given.
3 How do *your* points compare to those of other class members?

LIFE CHANGES AND DAILY HASSLES

ACTIVITY 3 pages 124–7

Task 1 Fill in the blanks

Some studies use a correlational analysis, such as the study by Rahe *et al.* In this study the co-variables were _____ and _____. The study expected to find a _____ correlation which is when one variable increases while the other variable _____.

Rahe *et al.* found that the correlation _____ was .118. For _____ participants this was significant, which means that _____.

If you wanted to represent these findings on a graph you would use a _____. The x-axis would be labelled _____ and the y-axis would be labelled _____. A suitable title for the graph would be _____ _____. Each dot on this graph represents _____.

One problem with correlational research is that _____.

Task 2 Life events versus daily hassles

List as many differences as you can think of. For example, life events are major changes in one's life, whereas daily hassles are minor but ongoing; the evidence suggests that life events have less effect on stress levels than daily hassles.

Task 3 Jigsaw technique

Divide your class into groups with four members in each group. It is best if the groups are not 'friendship groups'. Give each person in your group a letter – A, B, C and D. Each person has to perform their letter-specific task which is listed below. They must (i) prepare a set of brief and memorable notes on their topic, (ii) brief the group on their topic, (iii) write three questions for a test on their topic.

Person A: Research on life changes
Person B: Evaluation of research on life changes
Person C: Research on daily hassles
Person D: Evaluation of research on daily hassles

Your teacher should collect all the questions that have been written and use them to produce a class test. Each person will take the test individually – your performance will depend on how well you were briefed in your group!

WORKPLACE STRESS

ACTIVITY 4 pages 128–9

Task 1 Psychology in action

We have pointed out the importance of understanding workplace stress – both for employees and employers. The UK Work Task Force has asked you to produce a fact sheet for employees or employers (choose one). Present psychological advice about how stress can be decreased in the lives of workers, referring to the evidence on which the advice is based.

Task 2 Design your own research

Flanwell University has approached your class to ask for help in conducting research on workplace stress. You should work in a small group to design an appropriate study. The university wants to find out what factors cause stress in the workplace and whether these differ depending on age and/or gender (or any other individual differences).

- Decide what research method to use – you might collect data using a questionnaire and then conduct a correlational analysis, or you might design an experiment.
- Decide on particular features of design – see Chapter 3 for advice for your particular research method, and also look at sampling (page 92).
- Ethical issues should be considered and decisions made about how to deal with them.
- Collect some real data or invent some answers, and present your findings in graphical form.

PERSONALITY FACTORS

ACTIVITY 5 pages 130–1

Task 1 Timed essay

It is very important to practice the extended writing questions to time. If you had to answer a 12-mark question you probably should spend about 15 minutes, and write a total of 240–300 words.

Students often have a false idea of what they can do because, before the exam, they have plenty of time to write quite reasonable essays and they also use their notes. Write an answer to the following question without any notes and allow yourself only 15 minutes:

Discuss what psychological research has shown about the way personality affects a person's experience of stress. *(12 marks)*

***Before you begin, write a very short plan of the key points to be covered – you might use one of our essay planners (e.g. see page 61).

Task 2 Mark your essay

When you have finished you should swap your essay with someone else and each of you mark the other's essay. You can find example mark schemes on page vii.

Each of you should consider each sentence in the essay and decide whether it is relevant and if it is, whether it is AO1 or AO2. At the end decide on a mark for AO1 and a mark for AO2.

Task 3 Improve your essay

With your marking partner you should discuss the marks each of you gave to the other's essay and then spend time improving both essays. You can use your textbook or class notes to improve the essays. You will probably find that you will take out as much material out as you put in – students often include irrelevant material just to pad out an essay.

COPING WITH STRESS AND STRESS MANAGEMENT

ACTIVITY 6 pages 132–7

Task 1 Psychology in action

Below are descriptions of different people's experiences of stress. For each:

(a) Suggest an *appropriate* coping strategy or method of stress management.
(b) Explain in what way this strategy/method is appropriate.
(c) Identify **two** weaknesses of this strategy/method.

1   Yasmin has two lovely little boys who are usually very well behaved. However there are occasional days when the boys are quite demanding and when she has had a long day at work she ends up feeling very stressed.
2   William is a university student. He has always worked very hard at his studies but now is finding the pressure of academic work harder and harder to cope with.
3   Tina's mother is stressing her out! She is always on about how she should tidy her room or work harder at school or go out less. Nag nag nag!
4   Ahmed has had a difficult year. First his marriage broke up, then he had to change jobs and move house, finally he also had to deal with the death of his father over a particularly stressful Christmas season.

Task 2 Match the terms

For each term or name in the list, state whether it is linked to SIT, hardiness, or one of the two drug therapies: BZs or BBs.

Kobassa	Meichenbaum	Focusing
Sympathetic arousal	GABA	Coping self-statements
Reliving stress	Noradrenaline	Side effects
CBT	Conceptualisation phase	Serotonin

Task 3 Mock exam

You have now completed Chapter 4. On the next spread we show you an example of what the section on Biological Psychology will look like in the exam. We also outline the rules by which the questions are set. Read those rules and try to set an exam paper yourself. You can also look on the AQA website to see examples of sample questions and, after January 2009, there will also be past papers to look at.

Set a mock exam and get another group to consider whether your questions would be legitimate.

Task 4 Ethical issues

In each section of the Unit 2 exam you will be asked a 4-mark question on research methods, such as, 'Identify an ethical issue in this area and say how you would deal with it'.

For each ethical issue listed on page 70 find an example in this chapter to illustrate it and say how you would deal with it.

The Unit 2 exam is divided into three sections. Section A is Biological Psychology. The actual number of questions is not fixed but there are likely to be about four or five in this section, and you must answer all of them. The number of marks available for Biological Psychology will always be the same – 24 marks; four of these will be in a question or questions related to research methods. There may be an extended writing question (see the final question) in this section of the exam but this will not always be the case.

---

1 (a) Susan is an example of someone who could be described as 'Type A'. Describe **one or more** characteristics of Susan's personality. (*2 marks*)

   (b) Describe **one or more** other personality factors which might explain how people react differently to stress. (*4 marks*)

Alice's answer

(a) Susan would always be in a hurry and never have enough time to do what she wanted.

(b) Another personality factor would be Type B which describes someone who is pretty laid back and doesn't have the characteristics of a Type A personality. There is also the hardy personality who is someone who has a hardy personality which protects them from stress and becoming ill.

Tom's answer

(a) Hostility – this might cause her to become frustrated and angry with others when they stop her from achieving what she wants to achieve.

(b) People who are more psychologically hardy are more resistant to the effects of stress. Hardy personality types see problems as challenges to be overcome rather than threats, have more control over their lives and are committed to their work.

Examiner's comments

In part (a) you can gain full marks by one of two routes – either giving several characteristics, as Alice does, or identifying one characteristic and providing further detail, as Tom does. Therefore both students get **2 out of 2 marks** for part (a).

There are also the same two routes for part (b) – either covering one, as Tom has done, or lots, as in Alice's approach. If you only cover one then you have to give a lot of extra detail and Tom has given enough for the full **4 out of 4 marks**. Alice has identified two other personality factors and for full marks should have given some extra detail for each. She hasn't actually given any extra detail for the hardy personality – just said it protects a person from stress, which is not an explanation of why it protects the person or what hardiness is, thus she would receive **3 out of 4 marks**.

---

2 Explain how emotion-focused approaches differ from problem-focused methods of coping with stress. (*4 marks*)

Alice's answer

Emotion-focused approaches to coping with stress include denial, which is where you don't admit to yourself that something is happening. For example, someone might still lay the table for their husband, even after he has died. Problem-focused approaches include dealing with the problem, for example, the bereaved wife might start dating again and stop being lonely that way.

Tom's answer

The main difference between emotion-focused and problem-focused coping is that emotion-focused deals only with the emotions that arise in the stressful situation whereas problem-focused is a more active type of coping and involves dealing with the problem itself. For example if someone gets a big bill that they can't pay, they may hide it in a drawer (denial) or ring up the company and arrange to pay a smaller amount each month (problem-focused).

Examiner's comments

Alice has made the all-too-common error of thinking that you can answer a question about differences by explaining each of the concepts separately. She has simply failed to answer the question and instead answered a different one 'Briefly describe emotion-focused and problem-focused methods of coping with stress'. Even though she has displayed lots of psychological knowledge she gets only **1 out of 4 marks** for a rudimentary answer.

Tom, on the other hand, has framed his answer as a direct response to this question and juxtaposed the two explanations and the two examples for a full **4 out of 4 marks**.

3 Outline some of the difficulties psychologists have encountered when investigating the relationship between life changes and stress. (*4 marks*)

Alice's answer

One difficulty is that people have to try and remember things from some time ago, and this isn't always that easy and also their memories may not be accurate. Another difficulty is that data is correlational, so even if there is a high correlation between life changes and stress, this doesn't mean that one caused the other.

Tom's answer

The most commonly used method of researching the relationship between life changes and stress is the SRRS. This has been used in research by Rahe et al. (1970). They found that the more life changes (such as divorce or bereavement) sailors had experienced in the previous six months, the more likely they were to have suffered from a stress-related illness. However, this doesn't distinguish between relatively positive life changes (like Christmas) and negative life changes (like divorce). Also, it uses American sailors, therefore this is a restricted sample.

Examiner's comments

Alice has identified two difficulties and provided a reasonable enough explanation of each. There was no requirement to link the problems to specific studies as long as they are obviously related to research in this area. Alice gets a full **4 out of 4 marks**.

Tom's answer is longer and contains evidence of good psychological knowledge, but this time it is Tom who is not focused on the question. He has provided a lot of background information of one appropriate piece of research but only concentrated near the end on the *difficulties* encountered with using the SRRS, therefore only **2 out of 4 marks**.

---

4 Outline the key components of the pituitary-adrenal system. (*2 marks*)

Alice's answer

1 *Hypothalamus*
2 *Pituitary gland*
3 *Adrenal cortex*

Tom's answer

The hypothalamus releases CRF which stimulates the pituitary gland to release ACTH into the bloodstream. This activates the adrenal cortex which releases cortisol. This travels to various sites throughout the body.

Examiner's comments

The key things to note in this question are that it says 'outline' and also is only worth 2 marks. Therefore Alice's answer is perfectly adequate. Tom has gone above and beyond the call of duty, which is fine, but he still only gets the same as Alice – **2 out of 2 marks** – and may have wasted important examination time. Lesson to be learned – look for the clues in the question as an indication of how much to write.

---

5 Discuss how factors in the workplace may affect stress. (*8 marks*)

Alice's answer

Two factors are workload and control. High amounts of workload and low levels of control are thought to increase levels of stress. However, Marmot's research with civil servants found that those workers who were high on workload did not suffer unduly from stress. His research did, however, support the claim that low levels of control produce high levels of stress. Workers who were in jobs where they had very little control over what happened to them were more likely to experience cardiovascular disorders such as high blood pressure. However, this may have more to do with the fact that, compared to workers in the higher grades, these workers were lower paid, and had lower levels of social support, something which is known to help people resist the harmful effects of stress.

Tom's answer

There are three main factors which may affect whether people suffer from stress at work. Workload has been studied by Marmot et al. (1997), who found no relationship between level of workload and stress, and Johansson et al. (1978), who did, with workers in a sawmill who experienced the highest workloads also suffering from the most stress-related illnesses. The second factor is control. In Marmot et al.'s study, civil servants in higher grade positions, who experienced more control over their jobs than civil servants in lower grade positions, experienced lower levels of stress at work. The third factor is role conflict, where work and home demands interfere with each other, which has been found to contribute to stress.

Lazarus criticises studies in this area, saying there are individual differences in how people are affected, and that this research doesn't take modern types of workplace (each working from home) into account.

Examiner's comments

Alice has provided both description (AO1) and evaluation (AO2) but are they balanced? She has identified and briefly described two possible factors (AO1), then given evidence to challenge one factor and support the other (AO2). The middle sentence 'Workers who were in jobs …' is really an amplification of the AO2 point. The final sentence can be counted as AO1 as it introduces two further factors which may affect stress in the workplace. In general this is a rather short answer – it is about 130 words whereas 160 is probably a minimum (20–25 words per mark) but it is balanced. In a slightly longer answer Alice would have had space to describe the factors in more detail and provide more evaluation, therefore **3 out of 4 marks for AO1** and the same for **AO2**.

Tom has presented a very clearly organised answer to the question and given three factors – enough in a question worth 8 marks. He would gain all **4 out of 4 AO1 marks**. On the downside, his evaluation is fairly basic though two points have been made, therefore a somewhat generous **2 out of 4 AO2 marks**.

Both Alice and Tom would get a total of **6 out of 8 marks**.

YOUR OWN LITTLE BOOK OF REVISION NOTES

At the beginning of this book we explained how to produce your own little book of notes and use them for effective revision (see page x).

Remember to keep your notes brief – just record key points which will act as coat pegs for remembering the material.

Column 1: tick when you have produced brief notes.

Column 2: tick when you have a good grasp of this topic.

Column 3: tick during the final revision when you feel you have complete mastery of the topic.

Candidates will be expected to demonstrate knowledge and understanding of the following research methods, their advantages and weaknesses:

Key terms

3 marks worth of material

- Pituitary-adrenal system
- Sympathomedullary pathway
- Immune system
- Stress-related illnesses
- Life changes
- Daily hassles
- Workplace stressors
- Type A behaviour
- Emotion-focused approaches to coping with stress
- Problem-focused approaches to coping with stress
- Cognitive Behavioural Therapy

Research studies related to ...

6 marks worth of description

6 marks worth of evaluation (including the issues of validity and ethics)

- The body's response to stress
- The immune system
- Stress-related illness
- Life changes
- Daily hassles
- Workplace stress
- Personality factors
- Emotion-focused approaches to coping with stress
- Problem-focused approaches to coping with stress
- Psychological methods of stress management
- Physiological methods of stress management

Explanations/theories

6 marks worth of description

6 marks worth of evaluation (both strengths and weaknesses)

- The body's response to stress
- Pituitary-adrenal system
- Sympathomedullary pathway
- Applications of stress research

6 marks worth of material

6 marks worth of evaluation (both strengths and weaknesses)

- Emotion-focused and problem-focused approaches to coping with stress
- **Two** psychological methods of stress management
- **Two** physiological methods of stress management

CROSSWORD

Answers on page 214.

Across

1. A drug that lowers stress by reducing heart rate and blood pressure. (4,7)
4. First stage of stress inoculation training. (17)
10. Part of the brain which first perceives stressors. (12)
11. Gland in the brain that controls release of many different hormones. (9)
12. Research suggests that lack of this is a significant workplace stressor. (7)
13. Branch of the nervous system associated with 'fight or flight'. (11)
15. Abbreviated name for neurotransmitter that is the body's natural form of anxiety relief. (4)
16. Walter _____, the physiologist who first described the 'fight or flight' response to stress. (6)
18. Abbreviation used for the acute stress response. (3)
19. SIT is a form of Cognitive _____ Therapy. (11)
20. Hormone produced by the adrenal cortex in times of stress. (8)

Down

2. Abbreviation for hormone produced by the pituitary gland as part of the pituitary-adrenal response. (4)
3. The opposite of daily hassles are daily _____. (7)
5. Chemical substance produced by the paraventricular nucleus (PVN) which causes the pituitary gland to produce adrenocorticotrophic hormone. (3)
6. Personality type that Friedman and Rosenman found was linked with a greater likelihood of heart attack. (4,1)
7. A word for white blood cells – an important part of the immune system. (10)
8. Relatively minor stressors, but research suggests they are a significant source of stress. (5,7)
9. Personality type that Kobasa proposed could cope better with stress. (5)
11. A type of coping response which involves directly addressing the source of the stress: _____-focused. (7)
14. Substance that has no pharmacological effects. (7)
17. A scale developed by Holmes and Rahe, and used to measure life changes. (4)

Social psychology is the study of the nature and causes of human social behaviour. In particular, social psychologists are interested in the influence that other people have on our behaviour as we interact with them in our social world.

Social psychology: Social influence

Social psychology: Social influence

SPECIFICATION BREAKDOWN

Specification content	Comment
Social influence	
• **Types of conformity, including internalisation and compliance**	Your study of social influence starts with the topic of conformity – human behaviour is in part influenced by what *most* people do (i.e. majority influence). Behaviour is also sometimes influenced by the views and actions of small numbers of individuals (the minority). In the case of conformity, individuals are usually merely *complying* i.e. following the behaviour of others but not changing what they believe. In the case of minority influence, personal views may be changed because the behaviour of others has become *internalised*.
• **Explanations of why people conform, including informational social influence and normative social influence**	We will also look at explanations for why people conform. The two most common explanations are informational social influence (we conform in order to do the right thing) and normative social influence (we conform to gain acceptance and not be rejected by the 'crowd').
• **Obedience, including Milgram's work** • **Explanations of why people obey**	Your behaviour is not only indirectly influenced by others but may be changed by *direct* orders from others i.e. you obey them. The classic study of obedience was conducted by Stanley Milgram because he wanted to investigate why German officers in the Second World War were so obedient (see right). Milgram conducted a range of obedience studies in different settings that demonstrated that obedience can be explained in terms of situational factors (i.e. obedience occurs because of factors in the situation that trigger it). There are other explanations for obedience that offer alternative views to those of Milgram.
Social influence in everyday life	
• **Explanations of independent behaviour, including how people resist pressures to conform and pressures to obey authority**	It may be more valuable to look at the 'reverse' side of why people conform and why they obey – looking at how people resist social influences and behaviour independently. In some situations it is *desirable* to conform/obey, but in other situations independent behaviour is more appropriate.
• **The influence of individual differences on independent behaviour**	Psychologists are interested to know about the factors that lead to independent behaviour, and particularly to understand why some people are more independent than others. One possible explanation is locus of control – whether an individual feels they are responsible for their own behaviour (an internal locus of control) or that they are controlled by external forces (an external locus of control).
• **Implications for social change of research into social influence**	We end this chapter looking at how social influence research can be used to understand the process of social change – how the views and behaviour of all social groups change over time. Many of these implications can be gleaned by studying how different forms of social influence have been demonstrated in real-life social change.

THE FINAL SOLUTION

'The Nazi extermination of European Jews is the most extreme instance of abhorrent immoral acts carried out by thousands of people in the name of obedience.' (Milgram, 1974)

The study of social influence has produced some of the most startling insights into human behaviour. Stanley Milgram's studies of obedience in the 1960s provided a chilling insight into the darker side of human nature that was tragically demonstrated in the European Holocaust during World War II.

The Nazi extermination policy toward the Jews (known as 'the Final Solution') started in 1941 when special killing units operating along the Eastern Front began shooting Jews in mass graves. In 1942, battalions of German Order Police were added to the extermination force and carried out more mass shootings and deportations.

To increase the efficiency with which the annihilation could be achieved, Jews were ferried without food or water to labour-death camps such as Treblinka and Auschwitz-Birkenau. Some camps were specifically equipped for mass killing by means of gas chambers and crematoria for the disposal of the remains. Those who were not gassed immediately were forced to live on a starvation diet and to endure harsh physical labour and unending brutality.

Auschwitz was the most efficient camp established by the Nazi regime for carrying out the 'Final Solution'. The total number of Jewish dead in Auschwitz-Birkenau will never be known for certain because most were not registered. Estimates vary between one million and two-and-a-half million, with a conservative estimate of the total number murdered during the Holocaust being closer to six million.

But was such brutality a product of evil and sadistic minds, or was this *extraordinary* behaviour performed by *ordinary* people? In 1960, just as Milgram was beginning his studies at

▲ 'Unable to defy the authority of the experimenter, [participants] attribute all responsibility to him. It is the old story of "just doing one's duty", that was heard time and again in the defence statement of the accused at Nuremberg… a fundamental mode of thinking for a great many people once they are locked into a subordinate position in a structure of authority.' (Milgram, 1967)

Yale University, Adolf Eichmann, who had been in charge of implementing 'the Final Solution', was captured in Argentina by the Israeli secret service. His demeanour during the ensuing trial was hardly that of the vicious war criminal many had expected, as documented by Hannah Arendt in her book, 'Eichmann in Jerusalem: A Report on the Banality of Evil'.

'It would have been comforting indeed to believe that Eichmann was a monster… The trouble with Eichmann was precisely that so many were like him, and that the many were neither perverted nor sadistic, that they were, and still are, terribly and terrifyingly normal.' (Arendt, 1965)

The disturbing implication was that, 'in certain circumstances the most ordinary decent person can become a criminal' (Arendt, 1965), and it is exactly this proposition that Milgram's studies attempt to address. Eichmann's own excuse for his crimes was the familiar claim that he was acting on orders. Milgram's studies provided, at least in part, a test of the viability of such an explanation.

ABU GHRAIB

Milgram's experiment showed that ordinary people were prepared to deliver potentially lethal electric shocks to others because they were encouraged to do so by authority figures. A study by Milgram's former classmate, Philip Zimbardo (the Stanford Prison Experiment (SPE), which we described in the introductory chapter) also showed how ordinary well-balanced people could be turned into tyrannical guards or cowering prisoners simply because of the situation in which they found themselves. The major lesson from both Milgram and Zimbardo's research was that people underestimate the power of the situation to influence and shape their behaviour.

When the Abu Ghraib prison abuses in Iraq came to light in 2004 there were striking similarities with the SPE. Isolated within the confines of the prison, a group of guards appeared to expand their assigned roles to include horrific acts of abuse against Iraqi prisoners. One of the main reasons why psychologists carry out research in social influence is to help understand the complex social and psychological forces behind incidents like the Abu Ghraib abuse. By understanding the situational forces that cause people to act in this way, such evil actions can be better prevented in the future.

Research not only shows us why people act in this way, but also shows us how to *reduce* these social influence effects. As we shall discover in the obedience experiments of Stanley Milgram, the presence of just one other person who also refused to obey was sufficient to produce defiance in the research participant. If just one person is brave enough to defy the commands of a malevolent authority, it can dramatically reduce that authority's influence on others. This was evident in Abu Ghraib, where the actions of one person who stood up to authority, Private Joe Darby, brought the abuses to light and caused their termination.

How does all of this affect us in our everyday life? Rather like the technological advances that start their life in NASA spacecraft and then find their way into our everyday items (e.g. smoke detectors, golf ball design, sports bras…), social influence research affects us all. Throughout this chapter we look at how *we* are influenced by the situation in which we find ourselves, and how, when needed, we can resist that influence.

▲ An Iraqi prisoner is forced to stand motionless, believing that any movement with bring instant electrocution.

STARTER ACTIVITY

THE POWER OF TOUCH

In this chapter we look at some of the more traditional areas of research such as majority influence and obedience, but social psychology's interest in social influence does not end there.

One of the more unusual avenues of research interest is the effect that *touching* someone has on their compliance to a request. Although lightly  touching the arm or shoulder of a person when making a request may seem a pretty trivial thing to do, research has shown that such brief non-verbal contact can have some pretty powerful effects. Touch has been shown to have a positive effect on compliance in a wide range of behaviours, including helping behaviour, returning library books, participation in market surveys and even tipping in a restaurant.

In a US study, waiters and waitresses experienced a 25% increase in the size of their tips when they lightly touched the shoulder of the customer when delivering the bill. In a recent French study (Guéguen, 2007), men were more successful in persuading a woman to dance with them and also more successful at getting phone numbers when their request was accompanied by a light touch on the woman's forearm.

What does this tell us about the practical implications of social influence? Well, this is for you to find out, if you are game enough to try. For those of you who work in an occupation where persuading clients (to tip, to leave quietly, to tidy up after themselves) is a part of the job, try this out for yourselves. For those of you interested in the social influence involved in moving in on a member of the opposite sex on a crowded dance floor, see if this increases your success rate. Remember though, that touching doesn't equal grabbing or groping, and that some people find any sort of physical contact intrusive, so exercise some caution!

Given the sensitive nature of touching, you may feel on safer ground designing and carrying out a laboratory experiment to test the power of touch. Construct a hypothesis, select your **IV** and **DV**, think about what **extraneous variables** you would need to control, and decide which **experimental design** to use. Most importantly of all, consider the **ethical issues** and how you will deal with them. When you are happy with your design see what happens…

Some researchers suggest that touching is associated with the perception of dominance, and may also be seen to enhance the perceived sexual attractiveness of the toucher. Other researchers have explained the positive effects of touching on compliance by arguing that touch produces a more positive evaluation of the toucher generally. This advantage may not extend across all cultures, as tactile contact is more common in some cultures than others. In non-contact cultures, touch may be viewed negatively and be associated with *less* rather than more compliance.

Conformity to majority influence

An individual is said to *conform* if they choose a course of action that is favoured by the majority of other group members, or is considered socially acceptable. In contrast, an individual would be described as *deviating* if they chose to behave in a way that was not socially acceptable or that the majority of group members did not appear to favour. Because the individual is clearly influenced by how the *majority* think or behave, this form of social influence is sometimes referred to as *majority influence*. The fact that an individual goes along with the majority in *public* does not indicate that they have changed their *private* attitudes or beliefs (attitude conversion). Although attitude conversion can follow exposure to a majority position (e.g. 'If everybody believes that then it must be the case'), it is more usually **compliance** rather than true attitude change. Therefore most **conformity** is characterised by *public compliance* rather than *private acceptance* (**internalisation**).

EXAM TIP
The terms 'compliance' and 'internalisation' are identified on the specification, so it is important to know the difference between them.

TYPES OF CONFORMITY

Kelman (1958) proposed three types of conformity:

- *Compliance* – going along with others to gain their approval or avoid their disapproval.
- *Internalisation* – going along with others because you have accepted their point of view because it is consistent with your own.
- *Identification* – going along with others because you have accepted their point of view but only because of a desire to be like them.

What is compliance?

When exposed to the views or actions of the majority, individuals may engage in a process of *social comparison*, concentrating on what others say or do so that they can adjust their own actions to fit in with them. Because identification with the majority is desirable, if there is a difference between the individual's point of view and that expressed by the majority, they may simply go along with the majority without analysing why such a difference exists. This results in public *compliance*, with little or no private attitude change.

What is internalisation?

When exposed to the views of other members of a group, individuals are encouraged to engage in a *validation* process, examining their own beliefs to see if they or the others are right. Close examination of the group's position may convince the individual that they are wrong and the group is right. This can lead to acceptance of the group's point of view both publicly *and* privately.

What is identification?

In some instances, an individual might accept influence because they want to establish a relationship with another person or group. By adopting their attitudes and behaviours, they feel more a part of the group. This has elements of both compliance *and* internalisation, as the individual accepts what they are adopting as right and true (internalisation), but the *purpose* of adopting them is to be accepted as a member of the group (compliance).

Although Kelman (1958) originally intended his distinction between compliance and internalisation to apply to the influence of a majority, for the AQA examination it is appropriate to equate compliance with majority influence and internalisation with minority influence.

RESEARCH INTO MAJORITY INFLUENCE – ASCH (1956)

Asch (1956) asked student volunteers to take part in a 'vision' test, although unbeknown to these volunteers, all but one of the participants were really confederates (i.e. colleagues) of the experimenter. The real purpose of the experiment was to see how the lone 'real' participant would react to the behaviour of the confederates.

Participants were seated in a room and asked to look at three lines of different lengths. They were then asked to state, in turn, which of the three lines was the same length as a 'standard' line (see right). Although there was always a fairly obvious solution to this task, amazingly (to the real participant), on some of the trials the rest of the group made the same *wrong* choice. Asch was interested in whether people would stick to what they believed to be right, or cave in to the pressure of the majority and go along with its decision.

Standard line

Comparison lines

Procedures

In total, 123 male American undergraduates were tested. Asch showed a series of lines to participants seated around a table. Participants always answered in the same order (with the real participant always answering second to last or last). The confederates were instructed to give the same incorrect answer on 12 of the 18 trials.

Findings

On the 12 critical trials, 36.8% of the responses made by true participants were incorrect i.e. they conformed to the incorrect response given by the unanimous decision of the other group members. One quarter of the participants never conformed on any of the trials.

To confirm that the stimulus lines were indeed unambiguous, Asch conducted a control trial with no confederates giving the wrong answers. In this condition he found that people do make mistakes about 1% of the time, but this could not explain the relatively high levels of conformity in the main study.

Why did people conform?

Asch (1956) interviewed some of his participants and found that they tended to give one of three reasons for why they did conform: (1) *distortion of perception* – a small number of participants came to see the lines in the same way as the majority, (2) *distortion of judgement* – they felt doubt about the accuracy of their judgement and therefore yielded to the majority view, (3) *distortion of action* – the majority of participants who conformed continued privately to trust their own perceptions and judgements, but changed their public behaviour, giving incorrect answers to avoid disapproval from other group members (i.e. they *complied*).

CUTTING EDGE

Asch's post-experimental interviews (see opposite) indicated that people conformed for different reasons, but only recently has research suggested *why* this might be the case. Berns *et al.* (2005) took a brain scan of the working brain. They found that conformity showed up as activity in regions of the brain that were entirely devoted to perception, whereas independence of judgement – i.e. going against a deviant majority – showed up as activity in brain areas involved in emotion. This study suggests that information from other people changes our perception deep within the brain, leading to the possibility that exposure to the attitudes or beliefs of a leader or powerful majority may actually change the way individuals think and feel.

VARIATIONS IN THE ASCH STUDY

Asch carried out many variations of his original study to find out which variables had significant effects on the amount of conformity:

The difficulty of the task

In one variation, Asch made the differences between line lengths much smaller (so that the 'correct' answer was less obvious and the task more difficult). Under these circumstances, the level of conformity increased. More recent research has taken this relationship a little further. Lucas *et al.* (2006) found that the influence of task difficulty on conformity is moderated by the *self-efficacy* of the individual. These researchers found that when exposed to maths problems in an Asch-type task, high-self-efficacy participants (i.e. participants who were confident in their own abilities) remained more independent than low-self-efficacy participants, even under conditions of high task difficulty. This shows that situational differences (task difficulty) and individual differences (self-efficacy) are both important in determining conformity.

Size of the majority

Asch found that there was very little conformity when the majority consisted of just one or two individuals. However, under the pressure of a majority of three, the proportion of conforming responses jumped to about 30%. Further increases in the size of the majority did not increase the level of conformity substantially, indicating that the size of the majority is important but only up to a point.

The unanimity of the majority

In Asch's original study, the confederates unanimously gave the same wrong answer. What would happen if this unanimity was disturbed? When the real participant was given the support of either another real participant or a confederate who had been instructed to give the right answer throughout, conformity levels dropped significantly, reducing errors from 32% to just 5.5%.

What would happen if the lone 'dissenter' gave an answer that was both different from the majority *and* different from the true answer (i.e. more extreme)? In this condition, conformity rates dropped from 32% to 9%, nearly as great a fall as when the dissenter provided support for the real participant by giving the same answer. This led Asch to conclude that it was breaking the group's consensus that was the major factor in conformity reduction.

INDIVIDUAL DIFFERENCES

Eagly and Carli (1981) carried out a meta-analysis of 145 studies and found that women were generally more compliant than men. This may be explained by differences in sex roles whereby women are more interpersonally-oriented than men and thus predisposed to conform to others – Eagly and Carli also found that male researchers were more likely than female researchers to find gender differences, possibly because they used experimental materials that were more familiar to males than to females. Females complied more because they were less confident, not because they were more conformist.

meet the researcher

Solomon Asch (1907–1996) was a pioneer of social psychology. He was born in Warsaw and emigrated to the US as a teenager, studying psychology at Columbia University in New York and influencing a generation of social psychologists including Stanley Milgram whose PhD he supervised.

Asch is probably best known for his studies of conformity in the 1950s and his name is synonymous with the topic to the extent that the finding that individuals will frequently acquiesce to the majority is known as the *Asch effect*.

WWW You can listen to Asch's landmark experiment in a BBC radio programme www.bbc.co.uk/radio4/science/mindchangers1.shtml

CAN YOU...? No.5.1

...1 Summarise Asch's original study into just 120 words.

...2 Outline the findings *and* conclusions from **two** other studies of conformity.

DO IT YOURSELF No.5.1

Try carrying out a version of the Asch experiment yourself, using male and female participants.

What would you need to consider when designing this experiment?

- What are your independent, dependent and extraneous variables?
- What would your hypothesis be?
- What ethical issues might arise in this experiment, and how might you deal with them?

What did you find out? Are females more conformist than males?

Are there any *other* explanations for your results?

KEY TERMS

Conformity is a form of social influence that results from exposure to the majority position and leads to *compliance* with that position. It is the tendency for people to adopt the behaviour, attitudes and values of other members of a reference group.

Compliance occurs when an individual accepts influence because they hope to achieve a favourable reaction from those around them. An attitude or behaviour is adopted not because of its content, but because of the rewards or approval associated with its adoption.

Internalisation occurs when an individual accepts influence because the content of the attitude or behaviour proposed is consistent with their own value system.

Evaluating research into conformity

What is the value of Asch's research? We can establish this by looking at subsequent research to see to what extent the findings agree or disagree with those of Asch. On this page we look at various studies that deal with possible criticisms of the original research. On the facing page we examine the question of whether conformity is culture-specific, investigated by Smith and Bond.

VALIDITY

Asking people to judge the length of lines is a rather insignificant task and one where they would probably be willing to conform to save face. On a more important task we would expect conformity levels to drop. The fact that the participants had to answer out loud and in a group of strangers means that there were special pressures on them to conform, such as not wanting to sound stupid and wanting to be accepted by the group. The findings may, therefore, only tell us about conformity in special circumstances. For example, Williams and Sogon (1984) tested people who belonged to the same sports club and found that conformity may be even higher with people you know.

REAL-WORLD APPLICATIONS

The most obvious application of research into conformity is the jury. Insights from Asch's research suggest that many jurors would not want to appear deviant from what they believe to be the attitudes of their fellow jurors. Pressure to conform to the majority view is particularly strong in juries, as demonstrated by the finding that the first vote of the jury determines the outcome of the deliberations in over 95% of cases (Tanford and Penrod, 1986). This suggests that conformity pressure is a major issue in jury decision-making.

ETHICS
Deception and lack of informed consent

The participants in Asch's study did not know they were being tricked – they did not know the real purpose of the experiment, nor did they know that the other 'participants' were actually confederates of the experimenter. They could not have been told the true purpose of the experiment or it would have been pointless. To some extent our objections can be overcome if the researchers did properly inform the participants *after* the experiment (during debriefing) and offer them the right to withhold their data from the study. This right to withhold data is a means of compensating for the deception – the participants did not have the right to informed consent at the start of the study but, in a sense, were offered this afterwards.

THE JACKMANS

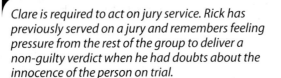

Clare is required to act on jury service. Rick has previously served on a jury and remembers feeling pressure from the rest of the group to deliver a non-guilty verdict when he had doubts about the innocence of the person on trial.

With your knowledge of research into majority influence, what advice would you give to Clare that would help her deal with jury deliberations?

WWW You can read more about McCarthyism online at en.wikipedia.org/wiki/McCarthyism

CRITICISMS OF ASCH'S RESEARCH

Is the study a 'child of its time'?

It is possible that these findings are unique to one culture – particularly as the participants were all men and all American, and the research was conducted in the 1950s, the era of *McCarthyism* (a period of strong anti-Communist feeling in America when people were scared to be different)? This was the claim made by Perrin and Spencer (1980) who tried to repeat Asch's study in England in the late 1970s using science and engineering students. In their initial study they obtained only *one* conforming response out of 396 trials. In a subsequent study, Perrin and Spencer used youths on probation as participants, and probation officers as the confederates: this time they found similar levels of conformity to those found by Asch. This suggests that conformity is more likely when the perceived costs of *non*conformity are high.

Nicholson *et al.* (1985) also replicated Asch's experiment and found some evidence for conformity among British students. They explained the difference between their results and Perrin and Spencer's in terms of the greater feeling of national cohesion in Britain arising from the Falklands War.

The Asch Effect: Stable or unpredictable?

Lalancette and Standing (1990) modified Asch's methodology to make the test stimuli more ambiguous and so increase the likelihood of obtaining conformity in an experiment with undergraduates. As with Perrin and Spencer's study, no conformity was observed. They concluded that the so-called Asch effect appeared to be an unpredictable phenomenon rather than a stable tendency of human behaviour.

Conformity or independence?

We should remember that only about one-third of the trials where the majority unanimously gave the wrong answer, produced a conforming response. In other words, in *two-thirds* of these trials the participants resolutely stuck to their original opinion *despite* being faced by an overwhelming majority expressing a totally different view. Asch believed that rather than showing human beings to be overly conformist, his study demonstrated a commendable tendency to stick to what we believe, i.e. to show *independent* behaviour.

CAN YOU...? No.5.2

...1 Explain why research on conformity may be criticised as lacking validity.

...2 Describe **three** other criticisms of Asch's research. (Hint: you can use both positive and negative points as criticisms.)

◄ Senator Joseph McCarthy, who waged a relentless anti-Communist crusade in 1950s America.

e CULTURE AND CONFORMITY: A META-ANALYSIS (SMITH AND BOND, 1998)

It has long been held that conformity is, to a degree, a product of cultural conditions with some cultural groups being stereotyped as conforming and submissive and others as more independent and assertive. Some researchers (e.g. Perrin and Spencer, 1981) have contended that the relatively high levels of conformity found in Asch's research in the 1950s are more indicative of the particular social climate operating in the US at the time (e.g. McCarthyism) than of a universal human behaviour. Both of these possibilities were investigated in an influential meta-analysis of conformity studies by Smith and Bond.

Procedures

Smith and Bond analysed conformity studies carried out between 1952 and 1994 that had used the same (or similar) procedures as Asch's original study. This resulted in a total of 133 studies carried out in 17 countries. Some countries (such as the US and UK) were classified as individualist, and others (such as Japan and Fiji) as collectivist. For the second part of the analysis, which was to investigate changes in conformity over time, only studies carried out in the US (97 of the 133) were used.

Results

Collectivist countries tended to show higher levels of conformity than individualist countries. The impact of the cultural variables on conformity levels was greater than any other variable (such as gender).

Levels of conformity in the US had declined steadily since Asch's studies in the 1950s, with the date of study negatively correlated with the level of conformity found in the study.

Consistent with the findings of Asch, however, conformity was significantly higher with (a) larger majority sizes, (b) a greater proportion of female participants, and (c) more ambiguous stimuli.

Limitations of this analysis

1. Cultures are not homogenous and differences between individualist and collectivist values *within* different cultures have been established in other research (e.g. Schwartz, 1992). Drawing conclusions based on differences *between* cultures may, therefore, be an oversimplification.
2. In cross-cultural comparisons, there is the problem of cultural differences in the relevance or meaningfulness of the materials used. It is possible that the task was more meaningful for one culture than the other, and that it was *these* differences, rather than differences in conformity, that were being measured.

INDIVIDUAL DIFFERENCES

In individualist cultures, most people's behaviour is determined primarily by personal goals that may or may not overlap with the goals of their 'collective' (i.e. family, work group etc.). In collectivist cultures, social behaviour is determined largely by goals shared with the collective rather than separate from it. In individualist cultures, if there is a conflict between personal and collective goals, personal goals take preference. This priority is reversed in collectivist cultures. As a result, people from collectivist cultures should be more likely to yield to the majority than people from individualist cultures. This proposition is tested in the Smith and Bond meta-analysis above.

COMMENTARY CORNER

Question: **Has research supported the view that the majority exerts a significant degree of influence over the individual?** *(12 marks)*

An effective way to tackle a more 'thoughtful' question such as this is by imagining two sides of a debate, with one side being the AO1 position, and the other the contradictory AO2 position. In this example, Tom and Alice get argumentative.

Tom: Asch's research on majority influence seems to provide convincing evidence for the importance of majority influence.

Alice: Maybe, but you seem to have forgotten that Asch also found that *despite* the pressure exerted by the majority, a large proportion of his participants remained independent in their judgements. Let's face it, asking people to judge the length of lines is a pretty insignificant task. They would probably be willing to conform to save face.

Tom: True, but Asch's research still shows that group pressure can be so strong that people are willing to deny the evidence of their own eyes for the sake of conformity with the rest of the group.

Alice: Hmm… I remember reading Perrin and Spencer's claim that the Asch studies reflected a particular period of American history – the era of McCarthyism – when conformity was highly valued. In fact, when they tried to repeat Asch's study twenty years later they found that out of 396 trials, only once did they get a conforming response.

Tom: Yes, but remember that they used science and engineering students who may have felt more confident about their ability to estimate line length. In fact in another study by Perrin and Spencer where they used youths on probation as the participants, and probation officers as the confederates, they got very similar levels of conformity to those found by Asch in the 1950s.

Alice: I bet you're popular at school…

Tom: I'll ignore that. Also, in a review of studies of conformity all over the world, Smith and Bond found that conformity to a majority is more likely in collectivist cultures than in individualist cultures. They claim that conformity may be seen as a positive feature in cultures where interdependence is more highly valued than independence.

Alice: So how come the US was shown to be such a conformist society? You surely can't get a more individualist culture than that!

Tom: Okay, enough, call it a draw?

Alice: In your dreams.

Conformity to minority influence

So far, our discussion of social influence has focused on compliance and the power of the *majority*. Serge Moscovici, one of the foremost critics of this perspective, claims that the idea of an all-powerful majority simply does not fit with historical reality. History has shown us just how powerful a persuasive *minority* can be. For example, the suffragette movement of the 1920s gradually changed public and political opinion so that eventually women were given the vote. Minorities such as the suffragettes tend not to have much power or status, and may even be dismissed as troublemakers, extremists or simply 'weirdos'. How then, do they ever have any influence over the majority?

Minorities that are active and organised, and that advocate and defend their position *consistently*, can create social conflict, doubt and uncertainty among members of the majority. This may ultimately lead to *internalisation* of the minority's beliefs and opinions, as it converts others to its point of view.

In order for **minority influence** to take place, there must be a conversion within individuals who were formerly part of the majority. This involves a careful thinking through of the arguments of the minority and the gradual internalisation of its point of view. As a result, the process of internalisation tends to be relatively slow, whereas conformity to a majority is a far more rapid and passive process, as individuals *comply* with the majority position without a great deal of thought.

meet the researcher

Serge Moscovici (1928–) was born in Romania into a Jewish family. From an early age, Moscovici suffered the effects of anti-Semitic discrimination, and in 1938 was expelled from school on the basis of newly issued anti-Semitic legislation. In 1939, he joined the Communist Party (which was then illegal), although he later became disillusioned with Communist politics. During the Cold War between Eastern and Western Europe, he helped Jewish dissidents cross the border illegally. For this, he was tried in 1947 and eventually left Romania for good, arriving in France a year later. In Paris, helped by a refugee fund, he studied psychology at the Sorbonne. As one of the founding influences in European social psychology, his name is synonymous with the field of minority influence.

ETHICS

It was necessary to deceive participants about the purpose of Moscovici *et al.*'s experiment in order to investigate the hypothesis. Participants were told the true purpose at the end of the experiment, which serves to compensate for the deception. As the deception was relatively harmless and the task did not involve undue stress, we might judge this study to be ethically acceptable.

MOSCOVICI'S RESEARCH INTO CONFORMITY TO MINORITY INFLUENCE

Moscovici *et al.* (1969) aimed to investigate the view that social influence occurs not just through compliance to the views of the majority but through a change to previously held opinions or *internalisation*. In order for this change to occur, Moscovici *et al.* proposed that the minority must be consistent in its views, and that this consistency will create conflict in the rest of the group, leading it to question and possibly change its existing views.

Procedures

Moscovici *et al.* tested 32 groups of six women in each. Of the six participants in each group, two were confederates and four were real participants. The group was shown 36 blue-coloured slides, although the use of filters varied the colour intensity of each slide to give it a slightly different hue. Participants were told that the experiment was about colour perception and that they would be asked to verbally describe the colour they saw. The two confederates, who answered either first and second, or first and fourth, *consistently* reported that the slides were green. In another part of this experiment the confederates answered 'green' 24 times and 'blue' 12 times, i.e. they answered *inconsistently*. In each case there were also control groups with no confederates (i.e. six real participants in each group), so that participants were free to answer without influence.

Findings

Overall, the participants agreed with the minority on 8.42% of the trials (i.e. they agreed that the slides were coloured green). Most impressively 32% gave the same answer as the minority at least once. The physical position of the confederate (i.e. the order in which their responses were given) made no difference. When the confederates were *inconsistent*, however, agreement with the minority was reduced to just 1.25%.

In an interesting variation to this experiment, participants were allowed to write down their responses (private) rather than saying them aloud (public). In this condition there was more agreement with the confederates, suggesting that at least part of the inhibition of minority influence is people's reluctance to be seen as aligning themselves with a deviant minority *in public*.

Conformity (% green responses)

▲ Conformity to a minority as a function of minority consistency

OTHER RESEARCH ON MINORITY INFLUENCE

As we have seen, one way in which minorities can be influential is by being consistent in their arguments. Wood *et al.* (1994) confirmed this with a meta-analysis of 97 studies of minority influence, and found that minorities who were perceived as being especially consistent in their positions were particularly influential. These researchers also established that majority group members tend to avoid aligning themselves with a deviant minority because they do not want to be viewed as deviant themselves. As a result, majority group members were more likely to admit being influenced by the minority privately than they were publicly.

Conversion theory (Moscovici, 1980)

Moscovici's explanation of conformity to minority influence is based on the idea that if an individual is exposed to an argument that is contradictory to a currently held attitude, this creates a conflict. Conversion theory assumes that individuals are motivated to reduce this conflict, and will therefore examine the minority's arguments in order to understand why these people do not hold the same opinions as the majority. With majority influence, individuals are less likely to closely analyse a contradictory argument and will simply adjust their own attitudes in order to conform to the majority position (a process known as *social comparison*). As a result, when a minority attempts to exert its influence, the direction of an individual's attention is on the *content* of a message rather than on the relationship between them and the majority group. As a result, this increases the likelihood that they will *internalise* the message being promoted.

Evaluation of conversion theory

Mackie (1987) challenged Moscovici's explanation. She claimed that it is the *majority* that promotes greater message processing. People generally believe that they share similar views to the rest of the majority group (the *false consensus effect* – believing that most other people think in the same way that we do). When faced with a majority position that appears to be different from their own, an individual engages in careful processing of the majority's message in order to understand *why* there is a difference in opinion. Mackie argues that the opposite is true of minorities – people are not inclined to waste time trying to process why a minority's message is different.

When is internalisation more likely?

The effect of minority influence appears to be different according to whether it comes from an *ingroup* minority (i.e. people who are similar to the majority) or an *outgroup* minority (i.e. people who are different from the majority). Martin (2006) examined the effects of ingroup and outgroup minorities upon public and private levels of influence. His research showed that while ingroup minorities have greater influence in public, outgroup minorities can have as much, if not more, influence when responses are made in private. These results demonstrate that both ingroup and outgroup influence can lead to internalisation, but this effect may be masked when the minority is an outgroup, as people may not want to publicly *align* themselves with a deviant minority.

The lessons of minority influence research

Nemeth (2003) suggests that research into minority influence has provided us with three important insights into how and when social influence works:

1 Minorities can actively promote a differing viewpoint, but need to be consistent in that viewpoint if they are to prevail. Without this consistency their influence is significantly decreased and internalisation is unlikely.

2 Even with consistency and commitment, minorities often do not prevail. The person holding a minority viewpoint is frequently disliked, seen as incompetent and rejected by members of the majority.

3 Exposure to a minority viewpoint stimulates those belonging to the majority to become better and more creative problem solvers as they search for information on all sides of the issue. Minority influence is therefore a valuable part of this process.

Although Kelman (1958) originally intended his distinction between compliance and internalisation to apply to the influence of a majority, for the AQA examination it is appropriate to equate compliance with majority influence and internalisation with minority influence.

▶ The influence of individual members of the suffragette movement is an example of minority influence. In the photo, suffragette Emily Davison lies unconscious after stepping out in front of the king's horse during the Derby of 1913. She never regained consciousness and died four days later.

VALIDITY

It is an assumption of all psychological experiments that the results obtained will have some relevance beyond the experimental situation. However 'real world' research suggests that, in reality, minority influence is relatively rare. In the context of juries, Kalven and Zeisel (1966) claim that it is the *majority* view at the time deliberation begins that determines the final verdict. As we saw on the previous spread, Tanford and Penrod (1986) found that the first vote of the jury determines the outcome of the deliberations in over 95% of cases.

The effect of minority influence in real-life situations is also questioned by Mackie (2006) with her 'unchanging minds hypothesis'. Mackie observes that although discussion is frequently observed in democratic politics, change (what Moscovici would call *conversion*) is rarely observed.

CAN YOU...? No.5.3

...1 Describe **one** study of conformity to minority influence.

...2 Explain how compliance differs from internalisation.

...3 Present evidence to support both types of conformity (i.e. compliance and internalisation).

...4 Explain how internalisation (minority influence) may occur.

KEY TERM

Minority influence A form of social influence where people reject the established norm of the majority of group members and move to the position of the minority.

DO IT YOURSELF No.5.2

One of the important skills in this specification is being able to *apply* your knowledge of psychology. There are many areas of social history where the influence of a minority group has led to an internalisation of the minority position. These include the actions of the suffragettes, the rise of trade unionism, equal rights for gays and lesbians, social change in South Africa and many others (find some of your own).

Choose one area and do some background research into the events surrounding social change, identifying how the features we have discussed (e.g. consistency, innovation etc.) were present as that minority exerted its influence.

Explanations of why people conform

Our social life is characterised by many social influences, some of which we are aware of, and some of which we are not. We give way to this social influence sometimes to 'fit-in' with those around us, and sometimes because we are not sure of the right way to think or act and so use others as a source of information. Our social life is also characterised by social norms, which are generally accepted ways of thinking, feeling and behaving that are shared by the other members of our social group.

People conform for many reasons, ranging from complete acceptance of the majority viewpoint (i.e. internalisation) at one extreme, to simply 'going along' with the crowd at the other (i.e. compliance). Two commonly cited explanations are **normative social influence**, when we 'follow the crowd' and **informational social influence**, when we accept the majority viewpoint because it is most likely to be right. We will look at both of these explanations of why people conform, and at **social impact theory**, which explains how attributes of the group itself determine the likelihood of conformity in group members.

Normative social influence is based on the desire to be liked and accepted.

Informational social influence is based on the desire to be right.

NORMATIVE SOCIAL INFLUENCE

It is possible to behave like the majority without really accepting its point of view. Psychologists have called this type of conformity compliance. A majority may be able to control other group members by making it difficult for them to deviate from the majority point of view, and thus exerting pressure on them to conform. Going against the majority isn't easy, as demonstrated in Asch's study where participants clearly felt uncomfortable deviating from the majority position. Humans are a social species and have a fundamental need for social companionship and a fear of rejection. It is this that forms the basis for normative social influence.

Evaluation of normative social influence

The practical value of this explanation has been highlighted in recent research emphasising the role of normative social influence in bullying. Garandeau and Cillessen (2006) have shown how groups with a low quality of interpersonal friendships may be manipulated by a skilful bully so that victimisation of another child provides the group with a common goal, creating pressure on all group members to comply.

🌐 REAL-WORLD APPLICATIONS

The role of normative social influence was dramatically highlighted in the massacre of the population of Nanking, China, by Japanese troops in 1937. Over a quarter of a million people were murdered and many more raped and mutilated in six weeks of carnage. In 1937 Japanese contempt toward the Chinese had long been an accepted and established norm for members of Japanese society. As the theory of normative influence explains, there is a tendency for members of a group to accept the legitimacy of the group's established norms and make it a priority to act in a way that supports these norms. Shiro Azuma, a former Japanese soldier interviewed by CNN in 1998, explained: *'We (Japanese) were taught that we were a superior race… but the Chinese were not. So we held nothing but contempt for them… the Imperial Army was consumed with a prejudice so intense that killing became easy.'*

INFORMATIONAL SOCIAL INFLUENCE

In some cases individuals go along with others because they genuinely believe them to be right. As a result, we don't just comply in behaviour alone, but we also *change* our own point of view in line with the position of those doing the influencing. Because this involves changing both our public *and* private attitudes and behaviours, this is an example of *internalisation*. In this chapter we have equated internalisation with the influence of a persuasive minority, but it can also occur when exposed to a persuasive *majority*. Informational social influence is most likely when:

- The situation is ambiguous – i.e. the right course of action is not clear.
- The situation is a crisis – i.e. rapid action is required.
- We believe others to be experts – i.e. we believe that others are more likely to know what to do.

Evaluation of informational influence

Although many experiments (including Asch's) have documented the power of normative social influence, the role of informational influence has been less extensively studied. However some studies have demonstrated how exposure to other people's beliefs has an important influence on social stereotypes. Wittenbrink and Henly (1996) found that participants exposed to negative comparison information about African Americans (which they were led to believe was the view of the majority) later reported more negative beliefs about a black target individual.

Fein *et al.* (2007) supported the role of informational social influence in political opinion by showing how judgements of candidate performance in US presidential debates could be influenced by the mere knowledge of others' reactions. Participants saw what was supposedly the reaction of their fellow participants on screen during the debate. This produced large shifts in participants' judgements of the candidates' performance, demonstrating the power of informational influence in shaping opinion.

▶ Japanese soldiers look on impassively as their Chinese victims are buried alive.

◄ Research suggests people conform to informational influence when the situation is both ambiguous and a crisis, as shown in this photo of 9/11.

EXAM TIP
Although we have included three explanations of conformity on this spread, you should concentrate on normative and informational social influence as these are the ones named on the specification. You can use social impact theory if you have to answer the longer 8- and 12-mark questions.

SOCIAL IMPACT THEORY

Latané (1981) developed a theory to explain why people conform in some situations but not others. There are several principles included in this explanation:

- *Number* – the more people present, the more influence they will have on an individual. However, the rate of increase in impact grows less as each new individual is added. For example, Asch found that conformity rates rose dramatically up to three or four, but not much beyond that size.
- *Strength* – the more important the people are to the individual, the more influence they will have. For example in Perrin and Spencer's research (see page 150), when the majority were probation officers and the individual someone on probation, conformity rates were relatively high.
- *Immediacy* – each individual can influence others; but the more people are present, the less influence any one individual will have. Thus, we are more likely to listen attentively to a speaker if we are in a small group than if we are in a large group.

℮ Support for social impact theory

In a test of the principles of social impact theory, Sedikides and Jackson (1990) found that high-strength and high-immediacy sources exerted more impact (i.e. resulted in more conformity) than low-strength and low-immediacy sources.

Latané later revised this theory into the *dynamic social impact theory*:

1 *Consolidation*: Over time, the majority grows in size and the minority decreases in size so that resisting conformity becomes even more difficult.
2 *Clustering*: People are more influenced by their closest neighbours, and so clusters of group members with similar opinions emerge (e.g. cliques).
3 *Correlation*: Over time group members' opinions on other issues, even ones not originally discussed, converge so that their opinions on a variety of matters become similar.
4 *Continuing diversity*: Because of clustering, members of minorities can be shielded from the influence attempts of the majority, and their non-normative beliefs continue on within the group.

THE JACKMANS

Tom's teacher has sent a note home saying that she is worried that he might have got in with a bad crowd as he has started skipping lessons and has been found smoking in the boys' toilets.

Offer **two** explanations to Tom's parents (based on your knowledge of social influence research) explaining why Tom might be acting in this way.

CAN YOU...?   No.**5.4**

...1 Write a sentence summarising each of the **three** explanations on this spread.

...2 Describe *and* evaluate at least **two** explanations of conformity. (You should write about 200 words in total.)

RESEARCH METHODS Qs   No.**5.1**

You will be examined on aspects of research methods in each of the sections of the Unit 2 paper. In other words, in the section on Social Psychology, there will be one question on research in relation to your study of social influence. This means that throughout your study of this chapter (and Chapters 4 and 6), you should think of answers to questions such as the ones below.

1 Outline **two** methods psychologists have used to investigate conformity.

2 Explain **two** methodological problems they have encountered in their research (for example sampling and investigator bias – see pages 92 and 79).

3 Name **two** ethical issues that arise in research on conformity and explain how psychologists might deal with each of these.

4 Describe **two** threats to validity that occur in conformity research.

COMMENTARY CORNER

The art of selectivity
Rather than offering just the bare bones of examination content on these pages, the aim has been to bring the subject alive by embedding it in real-life events. In a typical examination question such as: **Outline two explanations of conformity** *(3 marks + 3 marks)*, your task would be to select two of the explanations on this page and précis each into approximately 50 words. Choose your words carefully though, as accounts of suffragettes throwing themselves under horses are not as useful in an examination context as the underlying explanation for that example.

'Examination stripping' is a useful revision task: once you feel you have mastered each topic, use the revision summaries at the end of the chapter to guide you in retracing your steps through each spread. This helps you to select material for 'Your own little book of revision notes' made up of just the core material.

KEY TERMS

Normative social influence is the result of wanting to be liked and be part of a group (by following social norms).

Informational social influence is the result of wanting to be right – looking to others for the right answer.

Social impact theory states that the likelihood that a person will respond to social influence will increase with *strength* (how important the influencing group is; *immediacy* (how close it is) and *number* (how many members it has).

Obedience to authority

So far in this chapter we have looked at types of *indirect* social influence. A more direct form of social influence where, it might be argued, the individual has less choice in whether they give way or not, is **obedience to authority**. In this form of social influence, the individual is faced with the choice of whether to *comply* with a direct order from a person with higher status, or whether to *defy* the order.

Much of the impetus for research on obedience to authority came from the need to understand the situational conditions under which people would suspend their own moral judgements in order to carry out an order from a malevolent authority figure. The underlying motivation for this, of course, was far more than simple idle curiosity. Stanley Milgram's landmark study of obedience was published in 1963, just six months after the execution of Adolph Eichmann for his part in the murder of European Jews during the Holocaust. At his trial, like many other war criminals when brought to justice, he claimed he was 'only obeying orders'.

WWW All you ever wanted to know about Stanley Milgram and his famous experiment at www.stanleymilgram.com
The Milgram song – take a listen! www.wjh.harvard.edu/~wegner/shock.mp3

► The experimenter (in the lab coat, Milgram's assistant) exerts his authority over the subordinate participant.

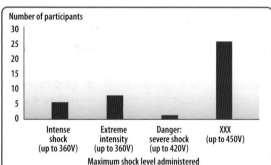

Number of participants

| Maximum shock level administered |
(bar chart showing: Intense shock (up to 360V) ≈ 5; Extreme intensity (up to 360V) ≈ 8; Danger: severe shock (up to 420V) ≈ 1; XXX (up to 450V) ≈ 26)

DO IT YOURSELF

No.**5.3**

Milgram conducted a survey prior to his study, asking people to predict how participants would behave when asked to deliver increasingly severe electric shocks. Write your own questionnaire (see page 94 for advice on questionnaire design) and see what people predict would happen. You might work in small groups and present your results to the class.

▼ The difference between forms of social influence

	Source of influence	Motivation
Obedience	Direct order from someone with perceived authority	Fear of punishment, belief in the legitimacy of authority
Conformity (compliance)	Indirect pressure from majority	Desire to be liked or accepted
Conformity (internalisation)	Indirect pressure from minority (or majority)	Desire to be right

MILGRAM'S STUDY OF OBEDIENCE (MILGRAM, 1963)

Although it makes sense to be obedient in some situations (e.g. obeying a teacher or a policeman), why do people obey when the action required is inhumane or destructive? Stanley Milgram set out to investigate whether ordinary people will obey a legitimate authority even when required to injure an innocent person. He was interested in the circumstances under which people might be induced to act against their consciences by inflicting harm on other people.

Procedures

Milgram recruited 40 male participants by advertising for volunteers to take part in a study of how punishment affects learning, to take place at Yale University. Everyone was paid $4.50 and told that they would receive this even if they quit during the study.

As well as the 'real' participant, there were two confederates: an experimenter (the authority figure), and a 47-year-old accountant who played the part of the 'learner'. The participant drew lots with the second confederate and always ended up as the 'teacher'. He was told that he must administer increasingly strong electric shocks to the 'learner' each time he got a question wrong on the learning task. The machine was tested on the learner to show him that it worked.

The learner, sitting in another room, gave mainly wrong answers and received his (fake) shocks in silence until they reached 300 volts (very strong shock). At this point he pounded on the wall and then gave no response to the next question. He repeated this at 315 volts and from then on said/did nothing. If the 'teacher' asked to stop, the experimenter had a set of 'prods' to repeat such as saying, 'It is absolutely essential that you continue' or, 'You have no other choice, you must go on'.

Findings

Before the experiment, Milgram asked psychiatrists, college students and colleagues to predict how far his participants would go before refusing. Consistently they predicted that nearly all the participants would refuse to obey the experimenter. They expected very few to go beyond 150 volts and only 4% to reach 300 volts. Only a pathological fringe of about 1 in 1000 were expected to administer the full 450 volts.

However, contrary to these expectations, in this (the base-line) part of the study, 65% of the participants continued to 450 volts, the maximum voltage, far beyond what was marked 'Danger: severe shock'. All participants went to 300 volts, and only five (12.5%) stopped at that point, the point when the learner first objected (see graph on left).

Conclusions

These findings demonstrate that ordinary people are astonishingly obedient to authority, even when asked to behave in an inhumane manner. This suggests that it is not evil people who commit atrocities but ordinary people who are just obeying orders. In other words, many crimes against humanity may be the outcome of *situational* rather than *dispositional* factors. It appears that an individual's capacity for making independent decisions is suspended when they find themselves in a subordinate position within a powerful social hierarchy (in this case the relationship with the experimenter).

MILGRAM'S VARIATIONS: SITUATIONAL FACTORS IN OBEDIENCE

In total, Milgram (1974) carried out 18 variations of the obedience experiment, systematically manipulating features of the situation and observing the effects on participants' obedience. Some of these variations are described below.

Proximity of the victim

In the *voice feedback* study, the learner was seated in another room away from the teacher. Although the teacher could hear the learner's protests through the wall, they could not *see* the learner. By contrast, in the *proximity* study both teacher and learner were seated in the same room. Compared to the relatively high obedience rate of 62.5% in the voice feedback study, the obedience rate in the proximity study dropped to 40% as the teacher was now able to experience the learner's anguish more directly. In an even more extreme variation of the proximity study, the teacher was required to force the learner's hand onto a shock plate. In this *touch-proximity* study the obedience rate dropped to 30%, although the *mean* shock level delivered was still nearly 270 volts!

Proximity of the authority figure

In the base-line study, the experimenter sat just a few feet away from the participant, giving them the feeling that they were constantly being monitored. The proximity of the attentive experimenter made participants feel as if they were constantly being monitored. In the *experimenter absent* study, after giving his instructions the experimenter left the room and gave subsequent orders over the telephone. Milgram found that the vast majority of participants now defied the experimenter, with only 21% continuing to the maximum shock level. He also observed behaviours that were not exhibited when the experimenter was physically present, with several participants giving weaker shocks than were required, and some even going as far as repeatedly giving the weakest shock level despite telling the experimenter they were following the correct procedure!

Presence of allies

What do Milgram's studies tell us about the influence of disobedient peers? In the *two peers rebel* study, three participants (two accomplices and the real participant) shared the task of teaching the learner. Teacher 1 read the list of words, teacher 2 told the learner whether his answer was correct, and teacher 3 (the real participant) administered the shocks. When the two bogus teachers refused to carry on, almost all 'real' participants also withdrew their cooperation, with only 4 out of 40 (10%) proceeding to the maximum shock level. Participants had used the defiance of their peers as an opportunity to extricate themselves from causing further harm to the victim.

Increasing the teacher's discretion

Would Milgram's participants have punished the learner with such severe shocks if the choice of the shock level was left to their discretion? In a further variation, the level of shock delivered was left to the participants' discretion. Under these conditions only one participant out of 40 (2.5%) delivered the maximum shock, and 95% of participants refused to deliver any shocks beyond the point where the learner protested for the first time (mean shock level 82.5 volts).

meet the researcher

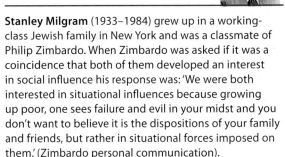

Stanley Milgram (1933–1984) grew up in a working-class Jewish family in New York and was a classmate of Philip Zimbardo. When Zimbardo was asked if it was a coincidence that both of them developed an interest in social influence his response was: 'We were both interested in situational influences because growing up poor, one sees failure and evil in your midst and you don't want to believe it is the dispositions of your family and friends, but rather in situational forces imposed on them.' (Zimbardo personal communication).

▶ The 'touch-proximity condition', where the 'teacher' holds the hand of the 'learner on the shock plate. Obedience rates dropped in this condition, but some participants were very obedient.

CAN YOU...? No.5.5

...1 Outline the main findings and conclusions from Milgram's study in just 120 words.

...2 Draw **three** conclusions about obedience that you have learned from reading Milgram's research.

...3 Briefly outline the difference between obedience and conformity.

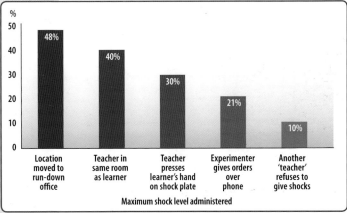

Maximum shock level administered

Chart values: Location moved to run-down office: 48%; Teacher in same room as learner: 40%; Teacher presses learner's hand on shock plate: 30%; Experimenter gives orders over phone: 21%; Another 'teacher' refuses to give shocks: 10%

INDIVIDUAL DIFFERENCES

Who are more obedient – men or women? Milgram found an identical rate of obedience in both groups (65%) although obedient women consistently reported more stress than men. There are about a dozen replications of the obedience experiment worldwide which had male and female subjects. All of them, with one exception, also found no male-female differences (www.stanleymilgram.com).

KEY TERM

Obedience to authority Obedience refers to a type of social influence whereby somebody acts in response to a direct order from a figure with perceived authority. There is also the implication that the person receiving the order is made to respond in a way that they would not otherwise have done without the order.

Evaluating research into obedience to authority

Despite the significance of Milgram's research in social psychology, it has been the subject of a great deal of criticism. Some critics have focused on the questionable ethics of this study, while others have questioned its validity as a representation of real-life obedience. Philip Zimbardo claims that the reason why his former classmate Stanley Milgram's research attracted so much hostile criticism was because of *what* he discovered rather than the way he discovered it.

REAL-WORLD APPLICATIONS
Obedience in the cockpit

An aircraft captain having too much authority may lead to disaster if the captain is in error. The US National Transportation Safety Board (NTSB) reviewed all serious aircraft accidents between 1978 and 1990 where a voice recorder was available on the plane, and where flight crew actions were a contributing factor in the crash (NTSB, 1994). Tarnow (2000) used this data to draw a parallel with findings from psychological research into obedience.

1 **Hesitant challenging** – the teacher's objections to giving shocks were often hesitant and easily overruled by the experimenter. The NTSB study of post-crash voice recorders (the black box) revealed several instances where crew members did not speak up sufficiently when danger threatened.

2 **Lack of monitoring** – the teacher accepts the authority figure's definition of the situation (e.g. that the victim is not really suffering). Again the NTSB study found excessive psychological dependence on the captain's authority and expertise – one second officer claimed that though he noticed the captain taking a particularly risky approach, he said nothing as he assumed, 'the captain must know what he's doing'.

In the aircraft cockpit, suggests Tarnow, the authority figure is the captain, while the first officer takes the equivalent role of the 'teacher' and the harm to the 'learner' is represented by the aircraft crashing. As with obedience experiments, the power of the authority is accentuated further by their close physical proximity. The NTSB report found major 'monitoring/challenging' errors in 19 of the 37 accidents investigated.

INDIVIDUAL DIFFERENCES

Although research has provided evidence for obedience in many different cultures, there are some cultural differences in the *extent* of obedience that has been found. It is worth remembering though, that each of these replications differs slightly both in terms of procedures and types of participants used. Some of these studies are included in the table on the right.

e ETHICAL ISSUES IN OBEDIENCE RESEARCH

Deception and lack of informed consent

Milgram deceived his participants by telling them that they were involved in a study of the effects of punishment on learning, rather than telling them the true purpose of the experiment. Although he argued that the experiment would have been meaningless without some degree of deception, this effectively denied participants the right to informed consent. Despite this, many of the participants subsequently felt they had learned 'something of personal importance' from their participation.

Right to withdraw?

Part of giving informed consent is allowing participants the right to withdraw if at any point during the study they change their mind about participating. In Milgram's study it was not clear to what extent participants felt that they had the right to withdraw. Milgram claimed that participants knew they were free to leave at any time, as demonstrated by the fact that some people did leave. Others argue that the 'prods' from the experimenter (e.g. 'The experiment requires that you continue') made this very difficult for some participants who felt they had no choice about continuing.

Protection from psychological harm

Baumrind (1964) attacked Milgram's study claiming he placed his participants under great emotional strain, causing psychological damage to them that could not be justified. Milgram defended himself in several ways. First, he did not know, prior to the study, that such high levels of distress would be caused. Second, he asked participants afterwards if they had found the experience distressing, and interviewed them again a year later. At this point 84% felt glad to have participated, and 74% felt they had learned something of personal importance.

Darley (1992) proposes a chilling effect of participation in Milgram's study. He suggests that the experience of administering shocks (even though they were not real) may activate a previously dormant aspect of an individual's personality such that they feel more able and more motivated to repeat the actions. Lifton (1986) reported that physicians in the Nazi death camps started out as ordinary people but became killing machines. In other words their personalities altered as a consequence of the activities they were asked to perform.

Why was Milgram's research subjected to so much hostile criticism?

Milgram's findings appeared all the more shocking because they challenged Western assumptions about freedom and personal responsibility. The capacity for moral decision-making, it appeared, is suspended when an individual is embedded within a powerful social hierarchy. This has led some to see such acts as *banal* (i.e. commonplace) rather than being the product of pathological personalities (Arendt, 1963). Milgram's research effectively 'opened our eyes' to the possibility that each of us is capable of performing in the same way as his research participants, and by implication, in the same way as SS guards in the death camps.

Study	Country	Participants	% obedient
Milgram (1963)	USA	**Male general population**	65
		Female general population	65
Mantell (1971)	Germany	**Male general population**	85
Kilham & Mann (1974)	Australia	**Male students**	40
		Female students	16
Burley & McGuiness (1977)	UK	**Male students**	50
Shanab & Yahya (1978)	Jordan	**Students**	62

Realism

According to Orne and Holland (1968) there is doubt about the internal validity of Milgram's research. They claim that participants in psychological studies have learned to distrust experimenters because they know that the true purpose of the experiment may be disguised. For example, despite the fact that the learner cries out in pain, the experimenter remains cool and distant. This leads the participant to suppose that the 'victim' cannot really be suffering any real harm – and this is why so many of the participants were prepared to administer all the shocks.

Milgram challenged this interpretation. Post-experimental interviews showed that, during the study, the vast majority *had* believed they were giving real shocks and that the victim's distress was likewise real.

Generalisability

To test the possibility that obedience may change when in more realistic settings, Hofling *et al.* (1966) conducted a study in a hospital. Nurses were telephoned by a 'Dr Smith' who asked that they give 20mg of a drug called Astroten to a patient. This order contravened hospital regulations in a number of ways: nurses were not to take instructions over the phone from an unknown doctor and the dosage was twice that advised on the bottle. Nevertheless, 21 out of 22 (95%) nurses did as requested.

This study shows that obedience does occur in real-life settings… or does it? Rank and Jacobsen (1975) also asked nurses to carry out an irregular order. This time 16 out of 18 (89%) *refused*. The difference was that on this occasion the drug was familiar (Valium) and the nurses were allowed to consult with peers – a more realistic representation of actual hospital practices.

The obedience alibi

Eichmann's 'alibi' at his trial was that he was just 'doing his duty' when he sent millions of people to their deaths. Did Milgram's research also offer an alibi for the obedience shown by Holocaust perpetrators? That is what David Mandel (1998) has suggested, based on Christopher Browning's detailed analysis of Reserve Police Battalion 101. Mandel has used this information to argue that, in fact, Milgram's conclusions about the situational determinants of obedience are not borne out by real-life events.

- **Proximity of the victim** On July 13, 1942, in Józefów, Poland, Major Wilhelm Trapp, Reserve Police Battalion 101 commander, announced that he had received orders to carry out a mass killing of Jews. His men were to take them in groups to the village outskirts and shoot them. Despite the presence of all of the factors shown by Milgram to increase defiance (e.g. close physical proximity and use of physical force against the victims), only a small minority of men took up Trapp's offer to be 'assigned to other duties' if they felt uneasy about the killing.

- **Proximity of the authority figure** At the Józefów massacre, the killers were *alone* with their victims as they walked them to a killing site and then shot them. Not only were they *not* in the physical presence of their superiors, but also, each killer had a personalised, face-to-face relationship with his victim, a fact that most social psychologists would agree should have produced empathy for the victim.

- **Presence of allies** Although the battalion's men were aware that several of their peers successfully extricated themselves from the killing, the vast majority of those involved in the killing continued to do so until the massacre was completed. In stark contrast, the overwhelming majority of Milgram's participants seized the opportunity to defy authority by extricating themselves from harming the victim.

- **Increasing the 'teacher's' discretion** Browning's analysis revealed that the perpetrators were meticulous in their search to leave no Jew alive and exacted severe brutality on those they 'caught'. The actions of Police Battalion 101 do not indicate that those involved tried to lessen their victims' suffering, even when they had every chance to do so. To the contrary, and unlike the overwhelming majority of Milgram's participants, these killers seemed to enjoy the opportunities they had to exert complete power over their victims (Mandel, 1998).

What would happen if there was absolutely no doubt about the reality of the shocks? Sheridan and King (1972) asked participants to give electric shocks of increasing strength to a puppy. The shocks were genuine, and participants could see and hear the puppy howling in distress. Despite this, 54% of male participants delivered the maximum (non-fatal) shock, but the obedience rate for females was a staggering 100%!

RESEARCH METHODS Qs No.**5.2**

1 Do you think that participants in Milgram's study would have been unduly distressed by taking part?

2 If they were distressed, do you think that this is acceptable?

3 In Milgram's experiment do you think it was acceptable to deceive his participants?

4 Did Milgram obtain informed consent from his participants? Explain your answer.

5 Did Milgram give participants the right to withdraw from his experiment? Explain your answer.

▲ A Reserve Police Battalion receive their orders.

'Even Eichmann was sickened when he toured the concentration camps, but he had only to sit at a desk and shuffle papers. At the same time the man in the camp who actually dropped Cyclon-b into the gas chambers was able to justify his behaviour on the grounds that he was only following orders from above. Thus there is a fragmentation of the total human act; no one is confronted with the consequences of his decision to carry out the evil act. The person who assumes responsibility has evaporated.' (Milgram, 1974)

CAN YOU…? No.**5.6**

…1 Outline **three** studies of obedience.

…2 Describe **three** evaluative points on this spread.

…3 Present evidence that Milgram's research was low in validity.

…4 For each of the arguments in your answer to Question 3 provide a counter-argument, showing that the research was high in validity.

…5 Describe **two** ethical issues raised in Milgram's research.

…6 For each of the issues described in your answer to Question 5, explain how Milgram attempted to deal with the issue.

Explanations of why people obey

Milgram's research into obedience is often described as 'counter-intuitive' in that the results go against what we might reasonably expect, given our knowledge of human behaviour. What Milgram seems to have demonstrated is the power of the situation in shaping behaviour, with moral constraints such as conscience and compassion being sidelined when the individual is confronted by a powerful authority figure. On this spread, we examine *why* people obey, and take a critical look at what Milgram thought to be the prime finding of his work on obedience – that it offered an explanation for the previously inexplicable events of the Holocaust during World War II.

▲ The Abu Ghraib prison abuse showed many similarities with Milgram's obedience research.

REAL-WORLD APPLICATIONS

Milgram's research is not only relevant to the explanation of events in World War II, but has also been used as an explanation of more contemporary atrocities, most notably the abuse of Iraqi prisoners in the Abu Ghraib prison (see right). Milgram's research identified some key conditions for suspending human morality, many relevant to an explanation of events in Abu Ghraib:

- **An acceptable justification for the behaviour.** Many examples of destructive obedience are justified by reference to some underlying ideology (e.g. the importance of science, national security and revenge).
- **An important role for participants.** Milgram's participants had the important role of 'teacher', and as in Zimbardo's Stanford Prison Experiment (see page xii), in Abu Ghraib American guards enjoyed an unusual degree of power over their prisoners.
- **The use of words** such as 'learners' (instead of victims) and 'prisoners', as well as the use of dehumanising acts (e.g. prisoners having to perform simulated homosexual acts) made it easier to aggress against them.
- **A gradual escalation of violence**. This was a key element of abuses at Abu Ghraib, and one of the most important determining factors in Milgram's study. Having given 435 volts he argued, it becomes so much easier to deliver the full 450.

WHY DO PEOPLE OBEY? (MILGRAM, 1974)

Gradual commitment

As participants have already given lower-level shocks, it becomes hard to resist the experimenter's requirement to increase the shocks as the experiment continues. In actuality, no shock level is ever administered that is more than 15 volts from the previous level. Having committed themselves to a particular course of action (i.e. giving shocks), it became difficult for Milgram's participants to subsequently change their minds. This is similar to the *foot-in-the-door* method of persuasion.

Agentic shift

Central to Milgram's explanation of obedience is what he termed the **agentic shift**. The *agentic state* is 'the condition a person is in when he sees himself as an agent for carrying out another person's wishes' (Milgram, 1974). Milgram argued that people shift back and forth between an *agentic* state and an *autonomous* state, the latter referring to the state a person is in when he 'sees himself acting on his own'. Upon entering a hierarchy of authority, Milgram claimed, the individual no longer views himself as acting out his own purposes, but rather comes to see himself as an agent for executing the wishes of another.

The role of buffers

In Milgram's original study, the teacher and learner were in different rooms, with the teacher protected (i.e. *buffered*) from having to see his 'victim', and also from the consequences of his electric shocks. When the learner was in the same room, this buffering effect was reduced, as was the tendency to obey the commands of the experimenter, and therefore the overall levels of obedience. This 'buffering' effect is similarly used to explain the apparent willingness of people to dispatch weapons of mass destruction. A cruise missile does not, after all, have the same immediacy of consequence as a rifle or machete.

Justifying obedience

In Milgram's experiment, the initial justification of the participants' role in delivering electric shocks was given as being that science wants to help people improve their memory through the use of reward and punishment. Dissenters who later tried to extricate themselves from this role were told that they must continue 'because the experiment requires it'. By offering an ideology (good for science, threat to national security etc.), people appear willing to surrender their freedom of action in the belief that they are serving a justifiable cause. During the Holocaust, the Nazis propaganda machine had portrayed the Jews as a danger to all Germans – thus justifying the horrific obedience that was to follow.

DO IT YOURSELF

No.**5.4**

Using the material on this and the previous spreads on obedience to authority, put yourself in the place of the 'authority' figure who sets examination questions in this area. How many different questions can *you* come up with? (Check they are legitimate given the wording of the specification at the start of this chapter.)

'The Nazi extermination of European Jews is the most extreme instance of abhorrent immoral acts carried out by thousands of people in the name of obedience.' (Milgram, 1967)

Although Milgram's research has been influential and revealing, as we have seen Mandel (1998) claims that Milgram's obedience explanation, particularly when applied to the Holocaust, is oversimplified and misleading.

Monocausal emphasis

Mandel (1998) suggests that by focusing solely on obedience as an explanation for atrocities carried out in the Holocaust and other crimes against humanity, Milgram ignored many other more plausible explanations. Goldhagen (1996) identifies anti-Semitism (hostility and prejudice against Jews) as the primary motivation for the actions of those involved in the annihilation of the Jews, rather than obedience. In his book *Hitler's Willing Executioners*, Goldhagen supports this claim with countless examples of voluntary and unnecessary cruelty carried out by ordinary Germans against Jews.

Agentic shift

An important aspect of Milgram's obedience explanation as applied to the Holocaust is the concept of agentic shift. However, unlike the experience of Holocaust perpetrators who carried out their duties over months if not years, Milgram's participants experienced no more than half an hour in the laboratory and were subjected to constant pressure from the experimenter during that time. There is also a crucial distinction in perceptions of harm-doing. The men of Reserve Police Battalion 101 executed 38,000 Jews over a four-year period (Browning, 1992) yet Milgram's participants were reassured that, 'although the shocks may be painful, there is no permanent tissue damage'. Despite these differences, Milgram believed that the same psychological process, agentic shift, was at work in both situations.

The consequences of an obedience alibi

Milgram's original claim that his work offered a situational explanation for Holocaust atrocities is no longer central in social psychology, Mandel (1998) believes the use of an 'obedience alibi' to explain such events has a number of negative consequences.

- The conclusion that obedience had a key role in Holocaust events is unjustified given an analysis of the historical record.
- The suggestion that Holocaust perpetrators were 'just obeying orders' is distressing for those who are or were affected by the Holocaust.
- Such an explanation effectively exonerates war criminals of their crimes.

KEY TERM

Agentic shift
In situations requiring obedience to authority, an individual may shift from an 'autonomous' state (taking responsibility for their own actions) to an 'agentic' level (where they act as an 'agent' for another person rather than acting on their own initiative). In such situations they attribute responsibility for their actions to the authority figure rather than being personally responsible for them.

► Goldhagen believed anti-Semitism, not obedience, was the primary cause of Holocaust events. This 1933 photograph, taken outside a Jewish store in Berlin says 'Germans, defend yourselves, do not buy from Jews'.

internet research

Got a little time on your hands? There are many Internet sites where you can watch online videos of famous studies and world events relevant to this area. Try the following:

www.learner.org/resources/series138.html (The discovering psychology series, with Phil Zimbardo.)

Alternatively, Google video (**video.google.co.uk**) and YouTube (**uk.youtube.com**) are also a good source of video clips for Milgram and associated events; you can also view the film 'Ghosts of Abu Ghraib' where the producer draws parallels between the abuse of Iraqi prisoners and Milgram's obedience experiments.

CAN YOU...? No.5.7

...1 Identify and explain **two** reasons why people obey.

...2 Give **two** criticisms of Milgram's explanation of obedience.

...3 Use your knowledge of why people obey to explain **two** examples of behaviour reported in the media that might be attributable to obedience.

COMMENTARY CORNER

Question: **Give two explanations of why people obey, and offer one criticism of each of these.** *(12 marks)*

This is a straightforward question, although there are pitfalls. First, many students will be desperate to describe a study rather than focusing (as required here) on *explanations* of why people obey. Second, although you may select appropriate explanations (from the left-hand side of this spread), you may not select appropriate criticisms (from the right). Let's look at the possibilities:

Socialisation	Monocausal emphasis – claims that we are socialised into obedience challenged by the claim that Germans were socialised into anti-Semitism.
Gradual commitment	Demonstrated in Abu Ghraib – a gradual escalation of violence was evident in the behaviour of US guards.
Agentic shift	Comparison of Holocaust events and Milgram's research showed significant differences in circumstances.
The role of buffers	Evidence from Milgram's study where obedience levels dropped when buffers (e.g. physical proximity) were removed.
Justifying obedience	Demonstrated in Abu Ghraib – an acceptable justification for behaviour.

Independent behaviour: Resisting social influence

Although the previous spreads have painted a somewhat pessimistic picture of human beings as slaves to situational forces, this need not be the case. Although the *majority* may conform to peer pressure or succumb to the demands of authority, there are always those who refuse to do so. Part of the reason for this refusal may lie in the fact that such people are more aware of the situational pressures around them (as you may be, as you are interested in psychology) and so are better equipped to deal with them. Such people are also more aware of how their own thinking (e.g. the belief that authority figures actually know what they are doing) can distort their perception of a situation, and can engage in critical thinking that goes beyond other people's definition of a situation. On this spread we look at the strategies people may use to resist pressure to conform and pressure to obey authority.

Many of you will have read the preceding spreads and thought 'I would have behaved differently'. This is precisely what Pronin et al. (2007) found in five different studies. People see other people as more susceptible to social influences than themselves. This was found to occur in a variety of situations ranging from consumer purchases to political views.

INDIVIDUAL DIFFERENCES

Griskevicius *et al.* (2006) discovered an interesting gender difference in nonconformity. When men and women are seeking a partner, women are more likely to conform to what they think others want (e.g. what kind of clothes a man finds attractive) whereas men tend to become more nonconformist in their behaviour. This was particularly true when nonconformity made them appear unique (true nonconformity) rather than just difficult or odd. This fits with an evolutionary explanation of male behaviour when seeking romantic partners – nonconformity can be a successful strategy because it offers something different to prospective partners.

DO IT YOURSELF

A day of nonconformity

No.**5.5**

You have read (perhaps with some alarm) of the power of the majority to shape our behaviour, but how easy is it to resist this powerful influence in our day-to-day lives? One way of finding out is to designate one day as a 'day of nonconformity', rather like having a day without smoking or a day without your iPod. Your challenge will be to spend an entire day being as uninfluenced as possible by conformity pressures. This would include pressures shaping what you wear, how you act and what you say or do in order to be liked or accepted by others. In other words, you should spend a full 24 hours living in a way that is true to yourself rather than to those around you. When carrying this out, leave no behaviour unexamined rather than just avoiding obvious acts of phoniness like wearing the same designer clothes as your friends.

The next day, you can ask yourself the following questions?

- How did it feel to not conform?
- Did you prefer it?
- Did other people change their behaviour towards you?
- What are the psychological costs and benefits of resisting day-to-day pressures to conform?
- Do the benefits outweigh the costs?

RESISTING PRESSURES TO CONFORM

Insights from Asch's studies – the role of allies

In one of the variations to his research, Asch showed how the introduction of another dissident gave social support to an individual and caused conformity rates to plummet. This can be explained in terms of informational social influence. The social support provided by a fellow dissenter provides the individual with an independent assessment of reality that makes them feel more confident in their own decision, and more confident in rejecting the majority position.

What happens if the support is not particularly true or valid? In a study by Allen and Levine (1971), there were three conditions in an Asch-type task. In one, the supporter had extremely poor vision (evident from his glasses with thick lenses – i.e. *invalid* social support) and in the second the supporter had normal vision (i.e. *valid* social support). Both conditions were sufficient to reduce the amount of conformity, compared to a condition where there was no support for the lone participant. However, the valid social supporter had much more impact, showing that the presence of an ally is helpful in resisting conformity, but more so when they are perceived as offering valid social support.

Moral considerations

Most of our knowledge about *conformity* comes from research using judgements about *physical* reality (e.g. judging line lengths). Research such as Asch's shows clearly that people are motivated to move toward the majority position, and that at least part of the motivation to conform is about being liked or accepted by the group (i.e. normative social influence). People will conform to the majority even when they know the majority position is wrong, because this is a way of avoiding unwelcome attention. In such situations, the psychological costs associated with abandoning a personal position would be relatively minor compared to the interpersonal benefits achieved as a consequence of fitting in with the rest of the group. However, *if the task involves* judgements with a *moral* dimension, the costs to one's personal integrity may be considerably higher. For example, Hornsey *et al.* (2003) found remarkably little movement towards the majority on attitudes that had moral significance for the individual (e.g. cheating), even when this involved public (rather than just private) behaviours.

The nonconformist personality

The extent to which social influence impacts upon individuals is also affected by their personalities. Individuals who respond to majority influence with *independence* tend to be unconcerned with social norms (Nail *et al.* 2000), or may even not be aware what the social norm is for a particular behaviour. Not conforming to a given norm is usually a result of indifference towards the group norm. Some individuals are predisposed to react to majority influence by actively opposing the norm. They may be fully aware of it, but intentionally choose to oppose it, often on the basis of strong convictions. Such individuals are said to have an *anti-conformity* orientation to their personalities.

As part of his research on obedience, Milgram (1974) noted the background characteristics of those taking part in order to find out which characteristics were consistent with higher or lower obedience. Age, marital status, occupation and military experience had little influence on the person's ability to resist the commands of the experimenter. However, educational history and religious preference did. Less-educated participants were less likely to resist the experimenter's commands than those participants with at least a college degree. Likewise Roman Catholic participants were more likely to obey the experimenter than were Protestant participants.

RESISTING PRESSURES TO OBEY

Insights from Milgram's studies

In Milgram's study of obedience, a high proportion of participants gave the maximum 450 volts, yet others defied the experimenter's instructions and withdrew before this point. Milgram was keen to investigate the situational conditions under which people felt able to defy the orders of an authority figure. The studies described on pages 156–7 tell us as much about resistance to authority as they tell us about obedience itself. This is especially true of those studies where less than 50% obeyed the experimenter. For example, when the study was moved away from the prestigious setting of Yale University to a downtown office, more people felt able to resist authority. This tells us that status is a key factor in obedience/resistance. Resistance was also increased when the victim could be seen, or when other confederates were present. This shows us that being made aware of the effects of your actions and having social support are means of increasing resistance.

Moral considerations

One of Milgram's colleagues, moral philosopher Lawrence Kohlberg (1969), presented a group of Milgram's volunteers with a set of imaginary moral dilemmas. These dilemmas determined not so much what people would do in situations like Milgram's shock experiment, but why they would behave in that way. He found that those who based their decisions on more general moral principles (e.g. the importance of justice over social order), were more defiant in the Milgram study, while most of those at a more restricted level of moral development obeyed the experimenter completely. The American civil rights leader Martin Luther King argued that laws are only valid insofar as they are grounded in justice, and that a commitment to justice carries with it an obligation to disobey unjust laws.

Social heroism

In his book *The Lucifer Effect* (2007) Zimbardo suggests that while the majority of humanity is bowing to unjust authority, the few who resist are really heroes. In this context, heroes are those people who are willing to make sacrifices for the good of others in society. Social heroism involves putting oneself at risk in the pursuit of an important principle. It may be very costly in terms of lowered social status, loss of credibility and in some cases, arrest, torture and even death. The best-known 'hero' is probably Nelson Mandela, imprisoned for 36 years for his resistance to government apartheid policies in South Africa. A less well-known 'hero' is Michael Bernhardt, the US soldier who refused to obey orders to shoot unarmed civilians in the My Lai massacre during the Vietnam war in which nearly 500 Vietnamese died at the hands of US troops. When interviewed by Kohlberg, Bernhardt claimed, 'I can hardly do anything if I know it is wrong. If I think about it long enough, I am just positively compelled'.

Zimbardo believes a key factor that encourages heroic action is stimulation of the 'heroic imagination', a mental orientation that makes people more likely to act 'heroically' when the time comes. This involves imagining facing potentially risky social situations, struggling with the hypothetical problems these situations raise, and considering one's likely actions and their consequences.

REAL-WORLD APPLICATIONS

Perhaps the most important application of obedience research is that it suggests specific actions that people can take to resist pressure to obey.

- **Ask – 'Is this something I would do *without* an order?'** When asked to carry out an order that we find abhorrent, we tend to ignore our personal moral considerations. By reawakening these we can resist this tendency towards blind obedience.
- **Beware the 'foot-in-the-door'** If we agree to even a relatively small initial request (in Milgram's study this was just 15 volts), we may commit to a continuum of increasingly destructive acts and find it harder to extricate ourselves later.
- **Find an ally** It is difficult to be a lone dissenter, but the presence of an ally in the group, as shown in Milgram's study, makes defiance appear more legitimate and easier.

CAN YOU...?   No.5.8

...1 Identify **two** explanations of how people resist conformity and **two** for obedience; expand each of these to about 50 words.

...2 Highlight the main factors involved in each type of resistance and apply these to a novel situation that may involve conformity or obedience.

COMMENTARY CORNER

Applying your knowledge

A common question in AS examinations requires students to *apply* their knowledge, e.g.

Question: **Tom hates the way his friends always drink too much when they go out for the night. He tries to moderate his own drinking on such occasions, but they poke fun and call him names so he just joins in.**

From your knowledge of psychology, suggest two ways that Tom might resist the pressure put on him by his friends to drink heavily. *(6 marks)*

Like many other questions in the AS examination, this one requires you to filter through the material on this spread to convert it into practical advice. This is not that difficult to do, but does require careful consideration. For example, telling Tom to get a nonconformist personality clearly isn't going to work, but suggesting he gets a non-drinking ally, just might do. To make sure you get maximum marks, practice justifying your advice e.g. *'Tom could get an ally to help him resist conformity, such as another friend who he knows also doesn't want to get drunk. This is likely to help because Asch showed that the presence of a fellow dissenter made people more confident in rejecting majority influence.'*

WWW To find out more about the My Lai massacre and the role of obedience in this action, watch the four interviews 'Vietnam My Lai veterans interviewed' on YouTube (www.youtube.co.uk).

Individual differences in independent behaviour

On the previous spread we looked at how people can resist social influence in maintaining independent behaviour. We now turn our attentions to individual differences in independent behaviour, particularly the role of *personality*. The concept of **locus of control** (Rotter, 1966) distinguishes between *internals* – people who attribute the cause of events in their life to their own control, and *externals* – who locate control outside themselves and so tend to feel they have less control over what happens to them. The concept of **attributional style** indicates how people explain to themselves *why* something happens, with people adopting a habitual style that determines the interpretation of future experiences. A positive (or optimistic) style allows the individual to maintain their independence from negative life experiences, whereas a negative (or pessimistic) style condemns the individual to drift helplessly through life at the mercy of their own negative interpretation of events as well as the controlling influence of others.

DO IT YOURSELF

No.**5.6**

You might like to measure locus of control (see below) as a class, and compare (for example) males versus females.

1 How would you go about collecting scores while retaining anonymity?
2 What are the potential ethical issues in a study like this?
3 How could you overcome these ethical issues?
4 Are there any gender differences in locus of control scores?
5 Draw a graph to demonstrate these differences.
6 What does the graph show?
7 If you *did* find gender differences in locus of control, what do you think this means?
8 Is it good to be internal? Why? (Or why not?)
9 What could you do to change someone's locus of control so that they became more internal?

WWW You can take Rotter's locus of control test yourself online at: www.psych.uncc.edu/pagoolka/LocusofControl-intro.html, or print it out and complete it from: wilderdom.com/psychology/loc/Measures.html

INDIVIDUAL DIFFERENCES

Rotter (1966) argues that people high in internality rely more on their own actions and exhibit greater initiative, making them more successful.

Linz and Semykina (2005) used survey data collected from over 2,600 Russian employees between 2000 and 2003. They found significant gender differences, with men being more likely to exhibit an internal locus of control and a need for challenge, with women being more likely to exhibit an external locus of control and a need for affiliation. Although personality appeared to play no part in the *earnings* of men (a measure of success), it did for women, with internals being the higher wage earners.

LOCUS OF CONTROL

What is meant by 'locus of control'?

The term *locus of control* refers to a person's perception of personal control over their own behaviour. It is measured along a dimension of 'high internal' to 'high external'. High internals perceive themselves as having a great deal of personal control over their behaviour, and are therefore more likely to take personal responsibility for it (e.g. 'That happened because I made it happen'). What happens to a person is therefore seen as a product of their own ability and effort. In contrast, high externals perceive their behaviour as being caused more by external influences or luck (e.g. 'That happened because I was in the wrong place at the wrong time').

Internal	LOCUS OF CONTROL	External
A person believes their behaviour is caused primarily by their own personal decisions and efforts.		*A person believes their behaviour is caused primarily by fate, luck or by other external circumstances.*

Internal and external locus of control

Locus of control research has uncovered a number of characteristics of internals and externals that have relevance for the study of independent behaviour. These include the following:

1 High internals are active seekers of information that is useful to them, and so are less likely to rely on the opinions of others.
2 High internals tend to be more achievement-oriented and consequently are more likely to become leaders and entrepreneurs.
3 High internals are better able to resist coercion from others.

Research support: Locus of control and leadership

Research suggests that internals are more likely to become leaders than to follow others. The rationale for this is that individuals who attribute responsibility for their actions to themselves tend to assume they can cause certain changes in their environment, including the behaviour of those around them. Anderson and Schneier (1978) found that group members possessing an internal locus of control were more likely to emerge as leaders in their groups.

(e) Evaluation: Are we becoming more external?

A recent *meta-analysis* by Twenge *et al.* (2004) found that young Americans increasingly believe that their lives are controlled by outside forces rather than their own behaviour. In the studies used in this meta-analysis, researchers found that locus of control scores had become substantially more external in student and child samples between 1960 and 2002. Twenge *et al.* suggest that the implications of this finding are almost uniformly negative, as externality is correlated with poor school achievement, decreased self-control and depression.

Why have we witnessed such a trend? Since the 1960s, most Western countries have seen dramatic social changes, including a significant rise in the divorce rate, increases in the incidence of violent crime and even increases in mental health problems and suicide. Twenge *et al.* suggest that the increase in all of these social factors has seen a corresponding increase in externality, as young people see many aspects of their lives as beyond their control.

INDIVIDUAL DIFFERENCES

As we have flagged up cultural differences in most aspects of behaviour, you might also expect to find them here, given the differences between individualist and collectivist cultures. Anderson (1999) measured attributional style, depression and loneliness in students at a university in China and one in the US. Students in China accepted more responsibility for interpersonal failures than did US students and took less credit for interpersonal success than US students. These relatively maladaptive attributional styles in Chinese students largely accounted for their relatively higher scores on depression and loneliness.

ATTRIBUTIONAL STYLE

What is attributional style?

Attributional style is a personality attribute that indicates how people explain to themselves why they experience a particular event. When people are confronted with situations of success and failure they make causal attributions about these events and learn from the experience, thus developing a particular attributional style. Psychologists have identified three components in attributional style:

- **Personal (i.e. dispositional vs situational).** An individual may see themselves as the cause of an event or may attribute the cause to situational factors e.g. 'I failed my A level because I'm stupid' (dispositional, internal) or 'I failed my A level because I used the wrong textbook' (situational, external).
- **Permanent (i.e. stable vs unstable).** An individual may see the situation as unchangeable or changeable, e.g., 'It's pointless having another go at my A levels, I'm just going to fail again' (stable) or 'Next time it'll be different' (unstable).
- **Pervasive (i.e. global vs local).** An individual may see the situation as affecting all aspects of their life or being restricted to just that event, e.g., 'I can't seem to do anything right' or 'Never mind, I can concentrate on my other subjects'.

Positive and negative attributional styles

Some people generally blame *themselves* for negative events (such as academic failure), believing that such events will continue indefinitely, and tending to let this negativity affect many different aspects of their lives. Such people display what is called a *negative attributional style* (dispositional). Conversely, people who generally blame others for negative events, believe that negative experiences are relatively transient. They do not let the negative events affect too many aspects of their lives, and display what is called a positive *explanatory style* (situational). The positive attributional style is synonymous with independent behaviour, as the person is able to resist the influence of negative life experiences that might otherwise have an adverse influence on their approach to such events in the future.

Research on attributional style

Heaven *et al.* (2005) studied young adolescents in Australia to see if there was an association between attributional style and attitude to school. They found significant differences between self-identified studious students (those who conformed to school, rules and worked hard) and rebel students (those who rebelled against teachers and did not always do homework). Rebels were found to score lowest on positive attributional style and highest on negative attributional style. It is likely that young people who find it difficult to form normal peer relationships, or who have been rejected by their peers, will gravitate to a crowd with similar individuals. It may also be the case that children who have experienced frequent peer rejections or difficulties with schoolwork are more likely to have developed a negative attributional style.

CAN YOU...? No.5.9

...1 Describe **two** ways that locus of control can affect independent behaviour. For each, provide research support.

...2 Describe **two** ways that attributional style can affect independent behaviour, and again provide research support.

WWW You can take the 'optimism test' (an attributional style questionnaire) online at: www.authentichappiness.org/

◀ Sir Alan Sugar receiving an honorary doctorate from Brunel University in 2005. Entrepreneur Sir Alan has displayed fiercely independent behaviour throughout his career, helped no doubt by his positive attributional style.

COMMENTARY CORNER

Question: **Discuss the influence of individual differences on independent behaviour. (12 marks)**

In the 'Can You' box above, you were asked if you could describe two ways that locus of control can affect independent behaviour. As 'locus of control' isn't specified in *this* particular question, you could also use material on attributional style). This could make up the AO1 part of this extended question, e.g.:

1 The nature of locus of control and its relationship with independent behaviour.
2 Characteristics of internal and external locus of control.

For the more critical AO2 component, you have a choice of material from this spread. It is important, however, to make sure that whatever you choose for this component is used as part of a sustained critical commentary, rather than just *described* – remember the advice about using your AO2 vocabulary (see page 43). Therefore, you might start your evaluation thus:

1 The concept of locus of control applied to independent behaviour is *supported by* research by Anderson and Schneier (1978) who found that…
2 A meta-analysis by Twenge *et al.* (2004) found that people are becoming increasingly external over time. *The main implication of this is that…*
3 Research has shown that there are individual differences in locus of control (Linz and Semykina, 2005) *which might explain why…*

KEY TERMS

Locus of control
An aspect of our personality: people differ in their beliefs about whether the outcomes of their actions are contingent on what *they* do (internal control) or on events outside their personal control (external control).

Attributional style A personality attribute that indicates how people explain to themselves why they experience a particular event.

Implications for social change

▲ April, 2006 – Social change through terrorism. Eleven people are killed in Tel Aviv, Israel after a Palestinian suicide bomber attack in April 2006.

Historically, social influence has been one of the most important topics in social psychology. Most research, however, has assumed that social influence is synonymous with social *control* rather than social *change*. But what *is* **social change**? Social change occurs when a society as a whole adopts a new belief or way of behaving which then becomes widely accepted as the 'norm'. Research into social influence does not just tell us how *individuals* change their beliefs and behaviours, but also how whole *societies* might change. If we look around us, we find evidence of social influence in many different types of social change. Sometimes, social influence can be a force for positive social change (e.g. Mahatma Ghandi's dissent against the British salt tax in India acted as the catalyst for widespread social reform). At other times social influence may be a force for negative social change (e.g. the Nazi extermination of Jews during World War II was made easier by the tendency for those involved to obey the orders of their superiors).

CAN YOU...?   No.5.10

...1 Describe **four** implications for social change from research into social influence.

...2 For each implication outline a piece of supporting research evidence.

Implications for social change

How would you begin to answer Question 1 above? Here are some suggestions to get you started. They are not complete answers – each requires some elaboration to turn it into a good exam answer. Where, for example is the *evidence* to support each of these claims?

1 **Terrorist minorities** can bring about social change by being consistent and persistent.
2 **Presence of a dissenter:** a powerful antidote to conformity, enabling others to break free from unjust social pressure.
3 **Widespread motivation to obey** may lead to real-life atrocities (e.g. ethnic cleansing).
4 **Gradual commitment** effect found in Milgram's study can be reversed for positive change.

VALIDITY

We might be tempted to dismiss the relevance of Milgram's experiments (opposite) simply because they were carried out nearly fifty years ago. If this were the case, their value for explaining the process of social change might be challenged. What would happen if the same experiments were carried out today? Blass (1999) went beyond mere speculation on this question, and carried out a statistical analysis of all of Milgram's obedience experiments and the replications conducted by other researchers between 1961 and 1985. By carrying out a correlational analysis relating each study's year of publication and the amount of obedience it found, he discovered no relationship whatsoever, i.e. the later studies found no more or less obedience than the ones conducted earlier. Milgram's findings, and their relevance to social change, still appear to apply as much today as they did back in the early 1960s.

IMPLICATIONS OF CONFORMITY RESEARCH

When minorities become majorities

When a minority succeeds in attracting enough new supporters, it is transformed into the new majority. The former majority is then transformed into a minority. However, a review of studies in this area led Prislin and Christensen (2002) to conclude that losing the majority position can decrease satisfaction and increase hostility and a desire to exit the group. Groups with changed minority and majority positions may suffer an exodus of group members from both minority and majority factions. A real-life example of this effect can be seen in the increase in emigration from South Africa in the aftermath of social change in that country. A newly powerful black South African government led to little reported improvement in people's lives, whereas a newly powerless white South African minority reported a significant deterioration (Finchilescu and Dawes, 1998).

Terrorism as a tactic of social change

Kruglanski (2003) argues that terrorism might be considered a form of social change through the process of minority influence (see page 152). The aim of terrorism is to bring about social change when direct social force is not possible (minorities tend to be relatively weak compared to the dominant majority). The following features of research on minority influence would seem especially relevant to terrorism:

1 *Consistency and persistence* – According to research into minority influence, the influence of a minority is most effective when it shows both consistency and persistence. The persistent suicide bombings by Palestinian terrorists are designed to demonstrate their commitment to overthrowing Israeli occupation.
2 *Internalisation of the minority position* – An effective minority may lead to the internalisation of the minority position. Terrorism attempts to bring about social change by conveying the desperation of minorities, and by drawing attention to the possible legitimacy of their claims.
3 *Conformity to the zeitgeist* – The 'zeitgeist' (meaning 'spirit of the time') is an important concept in minority influence. A group is more likely to internalise a minority position if this position already has widespread popular support. Although we may imagine that the majority of people would object to the killing of innocents in terrorist attacks, this does not always reflect the zeitgeist. For example, a secret poll conducted by the Ministry of Defence in 2005 found that a majority of Iraqis *supported* terrorist attacks against British and American troops stationed in Iraq.

KEY TERM

Social change – when a whole society adopts a new belief or way of behaving which then becomes widely accepted as the 'norm'.

EXAM TIP Remember that social change can be either positive or negative – any widespread change in a society's beliefs or actions would constitute social change.

IMPLICATIONS OF OBEDIENCE RESEARCH

How is obedience related to social change? Milgram's research suggested that although the majority of people might find it difficult to resist authority, this is not always the case, and there are circumstances where people can and do resist obedience. Of particular relevance to social change are the following considerations.

Obedience as a mechanism of social change

On page 156, we saw that the tendency to obey was strong in the majority of Milgram's participants. Unfortunately, human history is littered with examples of this destructive obedience in the name of 'social change'. During the European Holocaust, many Nazi leaders claimed that they were simply following orders to bring about the 'Final Solution', i.e. the total extermination of European Jews. More recently in the 'ethnic cleansing' (eliminating an unwanted group from society) carried out by Serbian soldiers in the former Yugoslavia, soldiers allegedly received orders to rape Muslim women in a direct attempt to undermine the fabric of Muslim family life.

The role of disobedient models in social change

In one variation to his base-line study, Milgram placed the participant with two peers who defied the experimenter and refused to punish the victim against his will. In this setting 36 of the 40 participants also defied the experimenter. Milgram believed that in the base-line study, many participants came near to defiance, but the additional pressure of the defiant peers meant that they were now carried over the threshold of disobedience. The important role of disobedient models has been shown in many movements for social change including the Civil Rights movement in the US and the anti-Apartheid movement in South Africa.

Reversing Milgram's gradual commitment effect: a 'drift to goodness'

Zimbardo (2007) suggests that despite the dangers of a drift into destructive obedience, research also supports the possibility of a reverse 'drift into goodness', making use of the same principles to promote all sorts of *pro*-social behaviour and thus social change.

- *Gradual commitment* – In Milgram's initial studies, the teacher began by delivering just 15 volts, and then continued in small incremental steps up to 450 volts. This is what social psychologists call the 'foot-in-the-door' technique. Researchers have also found that merely signing a petition leads to increased monetary support for charities, and that filling out a short questionnaire increases the willingness of people to sign up as organ donors.
- *Using social models* – Milgram found that the presence of obedient models *increased* obedience in the participant, and the presence of disobedient models *decreased* it. Social role models have been shown to influence positive social change causing an increase, for example, in donations to the Salvation Army and a willingness to share resources with others, and promoting non-violent responses to oppression.

COMMENTARY CORNER

At first glance, you might be forgiven for thinking that the concepts of obedience and conformity have very little to do with social change, and more to do with social *stability*. Obedience is, after all, a compliant response to a direct order from an authority figure, and conformity is likewise characterised by compliance to the majority position, i.e. the status quo. However, people *do* resist authority when obedience would be inappropriate. This is evident from the examples given on this spread. You should, however, ensure that you never lose sight of the underlying psychology when describing the ensuing social change. It is easy to get carried away with the story of Rosa Parks, but you should remember that this is merely an *illustration* of the finding that people with more advanced moral reasoning skills are less likely to obey an unjust order from an authority figure.

It is appropriate, when considering the implications of conformity for social change, to base your answer more on the influence of a persuasive *minority* than on compliance to the *majority* position (which, by definition would make social change less likely).

As a rough guide, when answering questions in this area you should (unless given very specific instructions in the question):

- Outline the relevant psychology, then…
- Illustrate how this has been associated with social change.

◀ Rosa Parks' refusal to obey an unjust law sparked America's Civil Rights movement.

In 1955, she boarded a bus in the city of Montgomery, Alabama, and sat down in the area reserved for white people. At the time, Montgomery's segregation laws meant that black and white people had different seating areas on buses. When Rosa was ordered to give up her seat to a white man, she refused, and was promptly arrested. This simple act of defiance sparked a chain of events throughout the United States. In 1956 the US Supreme Court ruled against segregation laws on the buses, and in 1964, the Civil Rights Act extended desegregation nationwide.

IMPLICATIONS OF RESEARCH INTO INDEPENDENT BEHAVIOUR

Dissent – a catalyst for social change

In Asch's studies on conformity, one of the most important variables for increasing independent behaviour was the presence of a dissenter who expressed a position different from that of the majority. The presence of a dissenter appears to liberate participants from the need to conform to the majority, and leaves them free to express what they truly believe. Dissent has been a catalyst for social change for centuries. In 1930, Mahatma Ghandi and 78 volunteers began a march to protest against the salt tax introduced by the British. Three weeks later, over five million people followed his example of breaking an unjust law, and this eventually led to the overthrow of British colonial rule in India.

The role of moral principles

Kohlberg (see page 163) found that in the Milgram study, those who based their decisions on moral principles tended to be more defiant, while those at a more restricted level of moral development obeyed the experimenter completely. Individuals who resist obedience are freer to be a force for social change. An example of how deep moral convictions might fuel defiance of unjust laws can be seen in the story of Rosa Parks (see right).

We have identified here the key points of the topics on the AQA (A) AS specification, i.e. the bare minimum that you need to know. You may want to fill in further details to elaborate and personalise this material.

SOCIAL INFLUENCE

CONFORMITY

CONFORMITY (COMPLIANCE) MAJORITY INFLUENCE

Types of conformity: compliance, internalisation, identification
- *Compliance* – going along with others to gain approval.
- *Internalisation* – going along with others because you have accepted their point of view.
- *Identification* – going along with others because of a desire to be like them.
- Asch – male US students tested on 12 critical trials (out of 18); 36.8% of these critical trials produced a conforming response, 25% of participants never conformed.
- Why did people conform? Distortion of perception, distortion of judgement and distortion of action.

Variations included:
- Easier task → lower levels of conformity.
- High self-efficacy → less conformity (Lucas *et al.*)
- Majority of 3 led to optimum level of conformity.
- Importance of unanimity – one dissenter → conformity dropped to 5.5%, or dropped to 9% if dissenter gave a different wrong answer.
- Berns *et al.* – conformity produced activity in regions of the brain devoted to perception, whereas independence of judgement produced activity in areas involved in emotion.

 VALIDITY
- Insignificant task (therefore conformity simply to save face), and with strangers, so lacks validity.
- Williams and Sogon – higher conformity with people whom participants already knew.

 ETHICS
- Deception, lack of informed consent, some stress – any harm might have been overcome through debriefing.

 INDIVIDUAL DIFFERENCES
- Females more conformist than males (Eagly and Carli) – may be explained by differences in sex roles; may be experimental artefact as male researchers more likely to find gender differences.
- Collectivist cultures more conformist than individualist cultures (Smith and Bond meta-analysis).

 APPLICATIONS
- Tanford and Penrod – pressure to conform to the majority view is strong in juries – first vote of jury leads to final verdict 95% of the time (conformity to majority position).

⊖ WEAKNESSES
- Asch study a 'child of its time' – Perrin and Spencer (1980) repeated with engineering students and got very little conformity, but with youths on probation got high conformity (costs of nonconformity high).
- Related to era of McCarthyism in 1950s USA, where costs of nonconformity also high.
- Asch's results actually show more independence (two-thirds of trials) than conformity (one-third of trials).

CONFORMITY (INTERNALISATION) MINORITY INFLUENCE

- Moscovici *et al.* – 32 groups, of 6 women in each group, shown series of blue slides. Minority of two confederates identified them as 'green'. In consistent condition, 8.42% of women conformed to minority.
- *Inconsistency* reduced conformity to 1.25%; responding in private led to increased conformity to minority position.
- Importance of consistency shown by Wood *et al.* in meta-analysis of 97 studies of minority influence.

 VALIDITY
- Evidence from 'real world' research suggests conformity to minority influence is relatively rare (e.g. juries – Kalven and Zeisel; democratic politics – Mackie; 'unchanging minds hypothesis').

ⓔ COMMENTARY
- Conversion theory (Moscovici) – minority arguments create conflict, leads to greater message processing.
- Internalisation effect masked when minority is an outgroup, as people may not want to publicly align themselves with a deviant minority.

EXPLAINING CONFORMITY

- Normative social influence – compliance in order to be liked.
- Informational social influence – desire to be right (when situation is ambiguous, crisis and majority seen as experts).
- Social impact theory (Latané) – principles are number, strength and immediacy.

ⓔ EVALUATION
- Garandeau and Cillessen – normative social influence explains bullying.
- Wittenbrink and Henley – informational social influence changed social stereotypes about African Americans.
- Sedikides and Jackson – high-strength and high-immediacy sources exerted more impact than low-strength and low-immediacy sources.
- Latané – dynamic social impact theory – consolidation, clustering, correlation, continuing diversity.

 APPLICATIONS
- Japanese massacre of Chinese at Nanking can be explained using normative social influence because hatred of Chinese was an established norm among Japanese at the time.

OBEDIENCE RESEARCH

Milgram's study
- 40 male volunteers acted as 'teacher'. All went to 300 volts, 65% continued to maximum 450 volts,
- Suggests obedience is due to situational rather than dispositional factors.

Milgram's variations
- Proximity of victim – 62.5% obedience in voice feedback condition, 40% in proximity condition and 30% in touch proximity.
- Proximity of authority figure – 21% obedience with experimenter absent.
- Presence of allies – 10% obedience with two peers rebel study.
- Increasing teacher's discretion – 95% refused to obey.

 INDIVIDUAL DIFFERENCES
- No gender difference in obedience but women report more stress during task.
- Cultural differences in extent of obedience.

 ETHICAL ISSUES
- Deception → lack of informed consent. OK because 74% said they learned something of personal importance, but they were exposed to their 'darker' side (Darley).
- Right to withdraw? Prods may have made this difficult.
- Psychological harm wasn't justified (Baumrind), Milgram said it couldn't be predicted and 84% glad to have participated.
- Study criticised because of findings rather than procedures.

VALIDITY
- Realism – Orne and Holland said participants knew the study was fake; however, Milgram pointed to participants' distress and their comments in post-experimental interviews.
- Generalisability – Hofling *et al.* also found high levels of obedience in nurses but Rank and Jacobsen found opposite in more realistic study.
- Obedience alibi – Mandel looked at WWII police battalion who obeyed despite presence of Milgram's inhibitory factors.

APPLICATIONS
- Tarnow applied findings to airline cockpit – many of Milgram's findings apply to captain/first officer relationship.

EXPLAINING OBEDIENCE

- Socialisation – people trained to obey.
- Gradual commitment – demands in small steps.
- Agentic shift – vs autonomous state.
- Role of buffers – protect from consequences.
- Justifying obedience – because it's an important experiment.

Criticising Milgram's explanation
- Monocausal emphasis – obedience not the only factor in the Holocaust. Alternative explanation e.g. anti-Semitism (Goldhagen).
- Agentic shift – important differences between Milgram's laboratory and Holocaust crimes, therefore comparison not appropriate
- Obedience explanation as 'alibi' – negative consequences because exonerates war criminals.

 APPLICATIONS
- Can explain prisoner abuse at Abu Ghraib – e.g. ideology used as justification, use of labels, gradual escalation.

SOCIAL INFLUENCE IN EVERYDAY LIFE

INDEPENDENT BEHAVIOUR: RESISTING SOCIAL INFLUENCE

Resisting pressure to conform
- Role of allies (Asch); valid social support important (Allen and Levine).
- Morally significant attitude change – Hornsey *et al.* found little conformity.
- Nonconformist personality, or some people just indifferent to norms.

Resisting pressure to obey
- Status and awareness of consequences increases resistance (Milgram).
- Resistance greater in people who base decisions on moral principles (Kohlberg), e.g. Martin Luther King.
- Social heroism can counter obedience (Zimbardo).

INDIVIDUAL DIFFERENCES
- When seeking a partner, women conform more to others, men become more non-conformist (Griskevicius *et al.*).
- Milgram found obedience lower in educated people; Roman Catholics more likely to obey than Protestants.

APPLICATIONS
- Personal application by resisting pressure to obey – e.g. question unjust authority, beware foot-in-the-door approach.

INDIVIDUAL DIFFERENCES IN INDEPENDENT BEHAVIOUR

Locus of control
- Internals rely less on other's opinions, better able to resist coercion.
- Anderson and Schneier – internals emerge as leaders and are effective leaders.

Attributional style
- Positive style linked to independence because can resist influence.
- Heaven *et al.* – rebels scored lowest on positive attributional style and highest on negative attributional style.

INDIVIDUAL DIFFERENCES
- High internals have greater initiative and are more successful (Rotter).
- Men more likely to be internals, (Russian study – Linz and Semykina).
- Anderson – more internal attributions in Chinese (collectivist) students than in US students (individualist).

 EVALUATION
- Externality is increasing (Twenge *et al.*) which has negative implications, e.g. for depression.

IMPLICATIONS FOR SOCIAL CHANGE

From conformity research
- Change from minority to majority may decrease satisfaction and increase desire to leave group, e.g. South Africa (Prislin and Chistiansen).
- Terrorism is a form of minority influence, leading to social change through persistence, and conformity to zeitgeist (Kruglanski).

From obedience research
- Obedience used as explanation for events during Holocaust and ethnic cleansing (examples of social change).
- Disobedient models empower others (civil disobedience, e.g. civil rights).
- Drift to goodness – gradual commitment and using social models (Zimbardo).

From research into independent behaviour
- Importance of dissent, e.g. Gandhi.
- Moral convictions, e.g. Rosa Parks.

VALIDITY
- Blass looked at historical relevance of Milgram's obedience studies, no difference over time.

End-of-chapter review — REVISION QUESTIONS

There are lots of ideas at the end of other chapters that you might adapt and try out here.

CONFORMITY

ACTIVITY 1 pages 148–51

Task 1 Match studies

1 Perrin and Spencer (1980)
2 Lalancette and Standing (1990)
3 Eagly and Carli (1991)
4 Asch (1956)
5 Berns *et al.* (2005)
6 Williams and Sogon (1984)
7 Smith and Bond (1996)

A If stimulus material is more ambiguous than original Asch task then conformity dropped.

B Conducted a meta-analysis of 133 conformity studies in 17 different countries.

C Science and engineering students showed almost no conformity on a conformity task.

D Used a functional MRI scanner to show that exposure to majority views may change the way we think.

E Found that group size only mattered up to a point: three people was a sufficient majority for high conformity rates.

F Conformity was even higher with people who belonged to the same sports club.

G Found that women are more conformist than men probably because they are more interested in social relationships.

Task 2 Validity

It is important to recognise that you can't simply say that a study has no validity – there are always arguments on both sides. It could be argued that a particular study has high validity because of a high level of control, but low validity because of poor realism (see page 68 of research methods).

Present arguments for and against the view that Asch's study has high validity.

- You can set out your arguments in a table.
- You might have a class debate on the topic.
- You can do this for other studies in this chapter.

Task 3 Extended essay

On page 151 we reported a conversation between Tom and Alice on majority influence research. Use their arguments to write an answer to the question: **Discuss research into the influence of majorities on our behaviour.** *(12 marks)*

- You must link all statements to actual research (sometimes Alice and Tom get a bit opinionated).
- Your answer should be about 200–300 words long.
- Decide on an essay plan – will you use the two-paragraph plan, or six paragraphs, or the 'yes but, no but' approach?
- There should be equal amounts of AO1 and AO2 (you can shade in the AO2 bits to show this balance).

CONFORMITY TO MINORITY INFLUENCE

ACTIVITY 2 pages 152–3

Task 1 Understanding minority influence

In the text we presented two studies (Moscovici *et al.* and Wood *et al.*), plus one explanation (conversion theory). Give a brief outline of each of these (two or three sentences – preferably without looking at your book). Compare your answers with someone else in your class to see what points you have omitted.

Task 2 Types of conformity

There are two types of conformity that you are required to study: compliance and internalisation. In this book we have argued that, in general, conformity to a majority results in compliance, while conformity to a minority results in internalisation.

Write an essay on types of conformity, for example:

Discuss two types of conformity. *(12 marks)*

Prepare a 200–300-word answer. Start by drawing an essay planner (grid) to show how you will separate your answer into manageable chunks ensuring an equal balance of AO1 and AO2.

EXPLANATIONS OF WHY PEOPLE CONFORM

ACTIVITY 3 pages 154–5

Task 1 Match explanations

1 Normative influence
2 Informational influence
3 Social impact theory
4 Conversion theory

A Minority views create conflict and people are motivated to resolve the conflict.

B People are more likely to conform as a function of number, strength and immediacy.

C People change their views because they are unsure in a certain situation.

D People change their views because they want to be liked and fit in.

Task 2 Remembering researchers' names

You may find difficulty remembering names such as 'Garandeau and Cillessen' or 'Wittenbrink and Henly'. You don't have to use researchers' names – but if you can, it will impress the examiner. If you have trouble remembering names, you could try breaking the phrase into smaller chunks and thinking of other words that sound similar (such as Grand-oh and Silly-son). Make up your own versions and even illustrate them, linked to the topic studies (in this case it was bullying). The result may be that you don't spell it exactly right in the exam but that is less important than being able to use technical terms.

- Do the same with some of the other names.
- Look back to memory improvement techniques in Chapter 1 (page 22). You could try some of these.

Task 3 Extended writing question

Discuss two or more explanations of conformity. *(12 marks)*

You can argue that both majority influence and minority influence are types of conformity and include them in your answer. But if you do take this route, remember to state at the outset that this is what you are doing.

Now write a 200–300-word answer. It is your choice how many explanations to include but you must cover a minimum of two. Again start by drawing an essay planner (grid) to show how you will separate your answer into manageable chunks.

OBEDIENCE TO AUTHORITY

ACTIVITY 4 pages 156–61

Task 1 *Fill in the blanks*

Stanley Milgram conducted one of the classic studies in psychology. In the study a participant plays the role of _____, while a _____ is the _____ . Before conducting the study, Milgram asked various people such as _____ to predict how participants would behave. They expected only ___% to go as far as 300 volts; In fact ____% continued to 300 volts, and ____% gave the maximum level of shock. These results suggest that _____ factors rather than _____ones cause obedience.

Later Milgram described the process of obedience as an _____ shift where people move from an _____ state to an _____ state.

Task 2 *Psychology in action*

Tom continues to do more babysitting to save up money for a holiday. One of the families he babysits for has three rather unruly children. They never do as he tells them; for example, they run around instead of sitting down to eat their dinner and won't go to bed when told to.

1 What advice could you give him, based on psychological research, that might get them to obey him better? Think of at least **two** suggestions.

Clare is concerned that Alice is being overly influenced by her friends at school. Everything she says, does and wears seems to be an imitation of a certain group of girls.

2 What psychological processes might explain why Alice is behaving like this?

Task 3 *Validity and ethics*

Milgram's studies of obedience are often criticised for (a) being low in validity and (b) failing to deal adequately with ethical issues.

With respect to Milgram's research, provide one or more arguments or examples of each of the following:

1 Low validity (internal or external).
2 High validity.
3 Dealing adequately with ethical issues.
4 Failing to deal with ethical issues.

Task 4 *Criticising Milgram*

There are so many ways to criticise Milgram's research – which means you need to learn to be selective. Identify **four** critical points related to Milgram's research and for each, follow the 'three point rule' (see page 21).

Task 5 *Writing exam questions*

On page 160 we suggested that you work out all the questions that could be set on obedience to authority.

1 Go through this whole chapter and write some possible extended writing questions (6 marks AO1 and 6 marks AO2). You should have some idea what these look like from the ones we have included in commentary corners and in the end-of-chapter reviews.
2 Share your questions with the class and discuss which ones are unlikely to be set.
3 Write model answers to each of your questions. You could work in pairs with each pair doing one question. Your answers should be about 300 words and half description and half evaluation. This model answer bank can then be shared around the whole class.

INDEPENDENT BEHAVIOUR

ACTIVITY 5 pages 162–3

Task 1 *Differences*

You need to study both how people resist pressure to conform *and* how people resist pressure to obey. How are these different? Try to think of at least three differences between resisting pressure to conform and resisting pressure to obey.

Task 2 *How to be independent*

A local school believes it is important for pupils to be independent thinkers. Produce a leaflet for all students, based on psychological advice about how to achieve this.

INDIVIDUAL DIFFERENCES

ACTIVITY 6 pages 164–5

Task 1 *True or false*

If the statement is false, produce a true statement.

Text	T or F
An external locus of control means you feel you have personal control over your behaviour.	
People who have high internal control are more likely to rely on the opinions of others.	
Research by Rotter shows that young Americans are increasingly becoming externals.	
Some research suggests that women are more likely to have an internal locus of control.	
People who have a dispositional (internal) attributional style blame someone else for any failure.	
Attribution retraining can help people be more independent.	

IMPLICATIONS FOR SOCIAL CHANGE

ACTIVITY 7 pages 166–7

Task 1 As this final part of the social psychology section is intended as a way of testing your ability to *apply* your social psychological knowledge, it would be a profitable exercise for you to do just that here. Although much of the material you need is available in what you have just read, there is nothing quite so satisfying as discovering your own material for this topic.

Construct a table like the one below and complete it with at least one example of a psychological principle or research finding and an illustration of social change that might be associated with it.

Research	Principle or finding	Illustration
Obedience		
Conformity		
Independent behaviour		

The Unit 2 exam is divided into three sections. Section B is Social Psychology. The actual number of questions is not fixed but there are likely to be about 4 or 5 and you must answer all of them. The number of marks available for Social Psychology will always be the same – 24 marks; four of these marks will be in a question or questions related to research methods. There may be an extended writing question (see the final question) in this section of the exam but this will not always be the case.

---

1 Two forms of social influence are obedience and conformity. Explain how these **two** forms of social influence are different.
(3 marks)

Alice's answer

Obedience is when someone gives you a direct order and you do what you are told. Conformity on the other hand is when you just go along with what everyone else is doing. So they are different because you do what someone tells you to do in obedience, and not in conformity.

Tom's answer

I think the difference is to do with the source of the influence. Someone in authority has direct power over us, so we obey them because we are subordinate to them. In conformity it tends to be people who are our equals and don't have power over us. We go along with them because we want to be accepted by them.

Examiner's comments

Both Alice and Tom have identified a difference, though Tom does this somewhat better than Alice by starting his answer with a statement of what the difference is. Alice's answer was heading for disaster until the final sentence because she hadn't identified a difference – she just stated what obedience is and what conformity is. However, in the final sentence she improves her answer considerably by trying to explain the difference, as required in the question. However just saying 'one is direct orders and the other isn't', isn't adequate – she really needed to dig a bit deeper for the full 3 marks and say, for example, 'you do what someone tells you in obedience, but in conformity you are copying others not because they tell you to but because you want to'. Tom will get **3 out of 3 marks** whereas Alice gets only **1 out of 3 marks** because she has failed to adequately explain the difference.

---

2 (a) Describe **one** explanation of how people resist pressures to conform. *(3 marks)*

(b) Give **one** criticism of this explanation. *(2 marks)*

Alice's answer

(a) People can restrict pressures to conform by thinking about the moral issues involved. For example, it is one thing to agree that lines are the same length, but not to join in by laughing at racist jokes just because our friends are doing that.
(b) A problem with this is that for many people it just isn't worth going against the group because they don't want to be ridiculed by them. This means they are still likely to join in but disapprove in private.

Tom's answer

(a) Asch found that the presence of an ally helped people to resist conformity. The presence of someone who also disagrees with the majority is sufficient to break the unanimity of the group, and make it easier for the individual to stick to their guns.
(b) The influence of an ally is lessened if they are not seen as particularly valid as an alternative to the majority position e.g. in a perception test if they have very bad eyesight.

Examiner's comments

In part (a) Alice identifies an explanation for resisting pressures to conform, but her example does not make it clear how this helps resistance – instead the example explains what moral issues are, thus **1 out of 3 marks**. In part (b) Alice again misses the point – she is not clearly criticising her explanation; instead she is suggesting why people still conform – **0 out of 3 marks**.

Tom's answer to part (a) is all it should be – appropriate and well-detailed. He identifies one explanation and then provides a clear account of it, **3 out of 3 marks**. In part (b) Tom suggests that the 'ally' explanation only works up to a point, it doesn't work if the ally is not seen as valid. For full marks Tom should have made it clearer how this is a criticism rather than just stating it, so **2 out of 3 marks**.

It is worth noting that a positive criticism would have been creditworthy here – for example, describing a piece of research that supports the explanation presented in part (a).

---

3 A psychologist plans to conduct an experiment to see if males or females are more affected by conformity.

(a) Suggest a suitable procedure for this experiment. *(2 marks)*

(b) Identify **one** potential ethical issue and suggest how the psychologist might deal with this. *(3 marks)*

Alice's answer

(a) You could show people a set of lines and ask them to identify which line is the same length as a comparison line (just like Asch did). You would then arrange for a set of confederates to sometimes identify the wrong answer and see if your participant conformed.
(b) An ethical issue is that people might feel stressed by disagreeing with the confederates. They could be debriefed by the experimenter afterwards, which would make them feel better.

Tom's answer

(a) A suitable task would be to have two groups of students who were all anti animal research, one all males and one all females. They could listen to a tape-recorded presentation of pro-animal-research arguments and then see who changed their attitude.

(b) A problem with this is that the students may feel distressed when they hear arguments from the opposite perspective. This could be dealt with by giving students sufficient information beforehand (i.e. informed consent) so they can make up their minds whether or not to participate.

Examiner's comments

Alice wisely uses Asch's experimental set-up as a suitable procedure for testing conformity, so **2 out of 2 marks**. Tom, on the other hand, tries to develop something original but it isn't clear why this would be testing conformity – what if some of the participants already held anti-animal-research attitudes? Why would they change their minds? Therefore Tom gets **0 out of 2 marks** for part (a). Questions like this are assessing your knowledge of research in this area, not asking you to be inventive.

In part (b) both Alice and Tom identify distress (psychological harm) as an ethical issue and both provide a means of dealing with it (debriefing or informed consent). Tom gets the full marks because he has actually explained *how* he would do this whereas Alice has just said she would debrief participants but not specified what this would involve. Instead Alice explained what the outcome would be ('they would feel better'), which is not relevant to the question of 'how'. For part (b) Alice gets **2 out of 3 marks** and Tom gets **3 out of 3 marks**.

---

4 Some psychologists believe that Milgram's research on obedience is the most important research ever conducted in psychology. Discuss the contribution of Milgram's research to our understanding of obedience. *(12 marks)*

Alice's answer

Milgram asked people to take part in a study of learning and memory, but really it was a study of whether they would obey orders to deliver electric shocks. A problem with this was that he used deception because no electric shocks were really given and people weren't able to give their informed consent to take part. He found that 65% of people did deliver the maximum electric shock, which was a lot more than people predicted would go to this level before the study started. Milgram thought this was why the experiment was so important because it told us something that nobody had expected. This means that the study increased our understanding of human behaviour. We wouldn't have known this if the study hadn't been carried out. He also found that people were more likely to obey the authority figure if they were close to them rather than giving their orders over the telephone and less likely to obey authority when the victim was in the same room. Mandel argues that Milgram's study doesn't really tell us anything about obedience in real life. He studied a group of German policemen during the Holocaust and found that there wasn't much similarity between what happened there and what happened in Milgram's study. For example, being physically close to their victims didn't make them disobey.

Tom's answer

Milgram found that situational factors were important in determining the level of obedience. He found that although two-thirds of participants went all the way to 450 volts, the level of obedience could be changed by altering different aspects of the situation. For example, he found that people were more likely to obey when they couldn't see or hear their victim and when the experimenter was physically close to them. He also found that the presence of peers affected obedience, with disobedient peers making it easier for participants to defy the experimenter and obedient peers making it harder to disobey the experimenter.

Orne and Holland criticised Milgram's research, claiming that the study lacked internal validity because participants did not believe they were giving real electric shocks, and only went along with the experimenter because of this. Mandel claims that Milgram's study also lacked external validity. He claims that Milgram was wrong to suggest that events in the Holocaust could be explained just in terms of obedience, as there were lots of other factors (such as anti-Semitism) involved. Explanations of obedience in Milgram's lab (such as agentic shift) did not apply to the Holocaust because there were important time differences involved. Finally, Baumrind claims that even if Milgram's research had increased our understanding of obedience, the stress caused to participants was just not worth it.

Examiner's comments

This extended writing question starts with a quotation, which is intended to stimulate your thinking. You can, if you wish, ignore it altogether. You must answer the question but can *use* the quotation to help organise your thoughts.

Alice does make reference to the quotation about halfway through her answer, ('Milgram thought this was why the experiment was so important'). She continues to justify why this is a point of criticism and why it is important (the three point rule), providing effective and informed evaluation/commentary (AO2). She makes two other AO2 points – near the beginning she mentions ethical problems raised by the shocks but here fails to remember the three point rule – why is this a criticism? The final AO2 point is made towards the end, using Mandel's arguments. Evidence is provided, but Alice needs to make this point more effectively, perhaps by ending the answer with a sentence saying 'This shows that…'. Overall her evaluation is reasonable – a reasonable range and reasonably effective, thus **4 out of 6 marks for evaluation**.

Alice's answer is nicely balanced with a similar amount of AO1 material and AO2 content. She accurately describes five aspects of Milgram's research (see if you can count them) demonstrating sound knowledge and understanding and appropriate selection, **5 out of 6 marks for description**.

Tom has organised his answer differently from Alice, taking the two-paragraph approach (whereas Alice used the 'yes but, no but' strategy). Both can be equally effective. In Tom's first paragraph he describes the main finding from Milgram's research (that situational factors are important) and gives several examples of particular findings. Some more information on actual obedience rates might have provided sufficient detail for full marks, **5 out of 6 marks for description**.

Tom's evaluation is certainly well informed, identifying and making use of criticisms provided by psychologists. In the case of the first point (on internal validity), there might have been some attempt to say why this is a criticism. Otherwise the points are all effectively made, a broad range of issues in reasonable depth, **6 out of 6 marks for evaluation**.

In total Alice would get **9 out of 12 marks** and Tom would get **11 out of 12 marks**, both good answers.

YOUR OWN LITTLE BOOK OF REVISION NOTES

At the beginning of this book we explained how to produce your own little book of notes and use them for effective revision (see page x).

Remember to keep your notes brief – just record key points which will act as coat pegs for remembering the material.

Column 1: tick when you have produced brief notes.
Column 2: tick when you have a good grasp of this topic.
Column 3: tick during the final revision when you feel you have complete mastery of the topic.

Key terms
3 marks worth of material

Conformity ☐ ☐ ☐
Internalisation ☐ ☐ ☐
Compliance ☐ ☐ ☐
Informational social influence ☐ ☐ ☐
Normative social influence ☐ ☐ ☐
Obedience ☐ ☐ ☐
Independence ☐ ☐ ☐
Locus of control ☐ ☐ ☐

Research studies related to ...
6 marks worth of description
6 marks worth of evaluation (including the issues of validity and ethics)

Conformity ☐ ☐ ☐
Internalisation ☐ ☐ ☐
Compliance ☐ ☐ ☐
Obedience ☐ ☐ ☐
How people resist pressures to conform ☐ ☐ ☐
How people resist pressures to obey authority ☐ ☐ ☐
Influence of locus of control on independent behaviour ☐ ☐ ☐
Influence of attributional style on independent behaviour ☐ ☐ ☐

Factors that affect...
6 marks worth of material

Conformity ☐ ☐ ☐
Internalisation ☐ ☐ ☐
Compliance ☐ ☐ ☐
Obedience ☐ ☐ ☐
Independent behaviour (conformity) ☐ ☐ ☐
Independent behaviour (obedience) ☐ ☐ ☐
Independent behaviour (individual differences) ☐ ☐ ☐
Implications of conformity for social change ☐ ☐ ☐
Implications of obedience for social change ☐ ☐ ☐
Implications of independence for social change ☐ ☐ ☐

Explanations/theories
6 marks worth of description
6 marks worth of evaluation (both strengths and weaknesses)

Conformity ☐ ☐ ☐
Why people obey ☐ ☐ ☐
How people resist pressures to conform ☐ ☐ ☐
How people resist pressures to obey authority ☐ ☐ ☐
Influence of locus of control on independent behaviour ☐ ☐ ☐

Applications of social influence research
6 marks worth of material

Independent behaviour ☐ ☐ ☐
Implications of research into conformity for social change ☐ ☐ ☐
Implications of research into obedience for social change ☐ ☐ ☐
Implications of research into independent behaviour
for social change ☐ ☐ ☐

CROSSWORD

Answers on page 214.

Across
3 In Asch's experiment, the people to answer first were _____ of the experimenter. (12)
4 When people act according to their own principles, they are said to be in an _____ state. (10)
8 The study on blue and green slides was conducted by _____. (9)
10 Mandel argues that Milgram's explanation of Holocaust events is little more than an obedience _____. (5)
14 People who have a positive attributional style are ____ likely to be independent. (4)
16 Milgram claimed people are in this state when they obey authority. (7)
18 Going along with others because you have accepted their point of view because it is consistent with your own. (15)
19 The university where Milgram conducted his experiment. (4)
20 Iraqi prison which provides a real-life example of many of the psychological processes discovered in Milgram's research. (3,6)

Down
1 Kruglanski argued that this was an example of social change through minority influence. (9)
2 People who have a high internal locus of control are ____ likely to conform. (4)
5 US senator who led a communist witch-hunt in the US in the 1950s. (8)
6 Perrin and Spencer claimed that Asch's findings were a _____ of its ____. (5,4)
7 A measure of a person's perception of personal control over their own behaviour. (5,2,7)
8 This type of influence is related to conversion rather than compliance. (8)
9 Conformity levels are higher in this type of culture. (12)
11 One reason why people conform is because they wish to be accepted by the crowd. This is called _____ social influence. (9)
12 Going along with others to gain their approval but with no private attitude change. (10)
13 A form of research study which takes an overview of many different studies, a _____-analysis. (4)
15 Psychologist who investigated the link between obedience and moral principles. (8)
17 Psychologist who conducted a classic study of conformity where participants had to match the length of lines. (4)

Individual differences are the aspects of each of us that distinguish us from others, such as personality and intelligence. Each of us also differs in the extent to which we are 'normal'. Usually, deviation from normality is not a problem, but in extreme circumstances it is – how do we know when abnormality is unacceptable?

CHAPTER

6

Individual differences: Psychotherapy (Abnormality)

Individual differences: Psychopathology (Abnomality)

SPECIFICATION BREAKDOWN

Specification content	Comment
Defining and explaining psychological abnormality	
• **Definitions of abnormality, including deviation from social norms, failure to function adequately and deviation from ideal mental health.** • **Limitations associated with these definitions of psychological abnormality.**	This specification begins with the question 'What is abnormality?' That is, how can we define what we mean when we say a person's behaviour is abnormal? The specification points to three possible ways of defining abnormality. You need to be able to outline these as well as being able to discuss their limitations.
• **Key features of the biological approach to psychopathology.** • **Key features of psychological approaches to psychopathology including the psychodynamic, behavioural and cognitive approaches.**	There are four 'approaches to psychopathology' – one biological and three psychological. 'Psychopathology' refers to *explanations* of abnormality. It is easy to be confused between definitions and explanations but it is an important distinction to understand – a definition sets out the criteria used to decide when a behaviour is abnormal, for example in what way is depression or schizophrenia abnormal? An explanation provides an account of why a person might have developed an abnormal behaviour, for example trying to understand why a particular person became depressed or schizophrenic.
Treating abnormality	
• **Biological therapies, including drugs and ECT.**	Psychologists' greatest concern is in trying to discover effective methods of treating abnormality. These are linked to the approaches to psychopathology – if abnormality is caused by biological factors, then treatments should be biological, such as using drugs or ECT. On the other hand, if the causes of abnormality are psychological then psychological treatments are likely to be effective.
• **Psychological therapies, including psychoanalysis, systematic de-sensitisation and Cognitive Behavioural Therapy.**	The specification lists three psychological treatments which are each linked to the psychological approaches to psychopathology – psychoanalysis is a psychodynamic approach, systematic de-sensitisation is a behavioural approach, and Cognitive Behavioural Therapy is a cognitive approach.

'IF SANITY AND INSANITY EXIST, HOW SHALL WE KNOW THEM?'

This question, posed by Stanford University psychologist David Rosenhan, signalled the beginning of one of the most audacious pieces of psychological research ever carried out. Rosenhan believed that although *we* may be convinced that we can tell the normal from the abnormal, the evidence for this ability is not quite as compelling. There are a great deal of conflicting views about what constitutes 'normal' and 'abnormal' behaviour, made even more confusing by the fact that what may be considered normal in one culture may be seen as quite abnormal in another (Rosenhan, 1973).

Defining behaviour as 'abnormal' (and therefore requiring treatment) presupposes that we have a clear idea of what we mean when we refer to abnormal behaviour. After all, diagnosing a physical illness, such as chickenpox or measles, is fairly straightforward, so why can't we diagnose a *mental* 'illness' with the same level of certainty? The problem appears to be that the very definitions of abnormality itself are considerably less real than we generally believe them to be. Many non-expert definitions of abnormality would focus on the fact that abnormal behaviours are somehow deviant or odd. Yet murder is deviant but not generally regarded as a mental disorder, and musical genius is odd but likewise would not be seen as requiring treatment.

Rosenhan had a plan for testing whether diagnosis of abnormal behaviour could be made as easily as was generally believed. He would send sane people to psychiatric hospitals to see if they would be unmasked as normal by health professionals unaware of their actual mental health status. If they were discovered to be sane, Rosenhan reasoned, this would mean that normality (and presumably abnormality) could be accurately diagnosed regardless of the context in which this diagnosis

STARTER ACTIVITY

Make two copies of the table below and consider the two following issues for each of the cases described on the right:

Table 1: This person suffers from a psychiatric/psychological problem.
Table 2: This person needs treatment for his/her problems.

	Strongly agree	Moderately agree	Do not know	Moderately disagree	Strongly disagree
1					
2					
3					
4					
5					
6					
7					
8					
9					
10					
11					
12					

is made. This would confirm that normality (and therefore also abnormality) was something that resided in the person themselves, something they carried around with them and that was independent of the context in which it was being assessed. If, however, they were not discovered, this would suggest that psychiatric diagnosis of 'abnormality' has less to do with the patient, and more about the (insane) environment in which they are found.

On being sane in insane places

Eight 'pseudopatients' (i.e. normal people *pretending* to be real psychiatric patients) gained secret admission to 12 different hospitals. They were a varied group consisting of: a psychology graduate in his twenties; three psychologists; one psychiatrist; a paediatrician; a painter; and a housewife. They all had one thing in common – they were considered psychologically healthy. They sought admission into a variety of different hospitals presenting just one single symptom. These pseudopatients arrived at the admissions department complaining that they were hearing voices. The voices appeared to be saying 'empty', 'hollow' and 'thud'. Apart from these voices, no other symptoms or evidence of pathological behaviour was presented. Indeed, everything else about the pseudopatient (their background, life history and general behaviour) suggested complete normality. Upon admission, each of the pseudopatients behaved on the ward as they would do normally. When asked by staff how they were feeling, they said they felt fine and no longer experienced any symptoms. When they were admitted, the pseudopatients had no idea when they might be released. They were told by staff that this would be 'when they had convinced staff they were sane'. As a result of this, they were motivated to behave sanely and to cooperate fully toward the goal of release.

Despite this public show of sanity, none of the

"TELL ME ABOUT YOUR FEAR OF POLICEMEN."

pseudopatients were ever detected for what they really were (imposters). With one exception, they were admitted with a diagnosis of schizophrenia, a serious mental disorder. Upon discharge, they were diagnosed as having schizophrenia in remission (the symptoms were no longer evident but it seemed likely that the disease still lurked closely nearby). This research shows the profound impact of an 'abnormal' diagnosis. Once labelled as abnormal (in this case as schizophrenic), a patient is stuck with the label. There is nothing they can do to remove the tag, which in turn profoundly colours others' perceptions of them and their behaviour. In a real-life situation, a patient may eventually accept the diagnosis and behave accordingly.

Schizophrenia

A group of psychotic disorders characterised by behaviours such as: major disturbances in thought, emotion and behaviour; disordered thinking in which ideas are not logically related; faulty perception and attention; bizarre disturbances in motor activity; flat or inappropriate emotions; and reduced tolerance for stress in interpersonal relations. The patient withdraws from people and reality, often into a fantasy life of delusions and hallucinations (Davison and Neale, 2001).

Case histories

1. Mr Smith has always lived in an isolated cottage. He has six dogs which he looks after. He never goes out of the cottage unless absolutely necessary, and has no friends or visitors.

2. Mr Jones is intensely afraid of heights. He has left a job because it was on the fifth floor, and refuses to visit his daughter who lives in Austria because of the mountains.

3. Mrs Jarvis, who was born in Jamaica, is a follower of the Pentacostal Church and believes that on occasions she is possessed by spirits which make her 'speak in tongues'.

4. Mrs Patel was arrested for shoplifting two weeks ago. She blamed the tablets (Valium) that she has been taking for the last five years but had recently discontinued.

5. Mr Khan is a successful executive who has just been told by his GP that he has high blood pressure.

6. Ben is a street musician who recently dropped out of art school. He likes to 'perform' using a variety of vegetables and dead fish!

7. Mrs Lee is a housewife who spends nearly every day at home keeping the house 'spick and span'. He husband returned home from night work early one night last week and found her dusting at 2 a.m.

8. Nadia is 22 years old and a dancer. Although she weighs only six stone she is continually dieting.

9. Bob is a loner who keeps himself to himself because he believes that the Social Security snoopers are out to kill him. Although unemployed, he refuses to seek any welfare benefits.

10. Sue is a six-year-old girl who is extremely shy and seldom speaks. She becomes very upset if her parents alter her playroom furniture.

11. Joe is nine years old and wets the bed about five times a week. His parents' marriage broke up when he was five.

12. Mrs Black is married with two daughters. Last week she confided to her best friend that she had never experienced an orgasm.

Definitions of abnormality

One of the most difficult tasks for those working within the field of abnormal psychology is to *define abnormality*. The definition of what constitutes abnormal behaviour has undergone dramatic transformations throughout history. Before the application of scientific thinking in this field, any behaviour that seemed outside an individual's control was thought to be the product of supernatural forces. The ways in which our ancestors dealt with the problem of abnormal behaviour (e.g. exorcism, the burning of witches, etc.) reflected the very different beliefs they held about the nature and causes of abnormal behaviour. Although we have moved on in our understanding of what constitutes normal and abnormal behaviour (and therefore who requires treatment), the *definition* of abnormality itself inevitably remains a judgement. On this spread and the next we consider some attempts to define this most elusive concept. As will become evident, no single definition is adequate on its own, although each captures some aspect of what we might expect from a true definition of the term. Consequently, abnormality is usually determined by the presence of several of the following characteristics at the same time, rather than one alone.

WWW How do cultures differ in what they regard as 'abnormal'? Read about culture-bound syndromes at: homepage.mac.com/mccajor/cbs_intro.html
For some examples of culture-bound syndromes, try: homepage.mac.com/mccajor/cbs_glos.html

DSM – the Diagnostic and Statistic Manual – is a list of mental disorders which is used to diagnose mental disorders. For each disorder a list of clinical characteristics is given, i.e. the symptoms that should be looked for. In order to diagnose a condition a clinician will look for symptoms. DSM-IV-TR is the current version in use in the US. In Britain clinicians use ICD (Internal Classification of Diseases and Health Related problems).

A clinician or clinical psychologist *is a person who is trained to diagnose and treat mental disorders. A psychiatrist is a person who is trained as a doctor and then studies psychology.*

DEFINITION 1
DEVIATION FROM SOCIAL NORMS

The term 'deviation' in this definition refers to deviant *behaviour* – i.e. behaviour which is considered anti-social or undesirable by the majority of society members. In any society there are social norms – standards of acceptable behaviour that are set by the social group, and adhered to by those socialised into that group. These standards are often in place for good reasons. An example of a social norm is politeness. Politeness oils the wheels of interpersonal relations. People who are rude or surly are behaving in a socially deviant way because others find it difficult to interact with them.

Social standards are not restricted to rules of etiquette but also more serious moral issues, such as what is acceptable in sexual behaviour. Our culture permits sex between consenting adults of any gender but regards some other behaviours as sexually deviant. For example, in the past homosexuality was classified as deviant behaviour in the UK (but not nowadays). Currently the DSM classification scheme contains a category called 'sexual and gender identity disorders' which includes paedophilia and voyeurism. Such behaviours are considered socially deviant.

⊖ LIMITATIONS

Susceptible to abuse

The main difficulty with the concept of deviation from social norms, is that it varies as times change. What is socially acceptable now may not have been socially acceptable 50 years ago. Today homosexuality is acceptable but in the past it was included under sexual and gender identity disorders. Similarly, in Russia 50 years ago, anyone who disagreed with the state ran the risk of being regarded as insane and placed in a mental institution.

If we define abnormality in terms of deviation from social norms we open the door to definitions based on prevailing social morals and attitudes. This then allows mental health professionals to classify as mentally ill those individuals who transgress against social attitudes. In fact, Szasz (1974) claimed that the concept of mental illness was simply a way to exclude nonconformists from society.

Deviance is related to context and degree

Making judgements on deviance is often related to the context of a behaviour. A person on a beach wearing next to nothing is regarded as normal, whereas the same outfit in the classroom or at a formal gathering would be regarded as abnormal and possibly an indication of a mental disorder. In many cases there is not a clear line between what is an abnormal deviation and what is simply more harmless eccentricity. Being rude is deviant behaviour but not evidence of mental disturbance *unless* it is excessive and therefore pathological.

What this means is that social deviance, on its own, cannot offer a complete definition of abnormality, because it is inevitably related to both context and degree.

Cultural relativism

Attempts to define abnormality in terms of social norms are obviously influenced by cultural factors (**cultural relativism**) because social norms themselves are defined by the culture. Disorders are defined or diagnosed in different ways in different places by different groups. This means that a diagnosis may be different for the same person in two different cultures. What may be seen as a diagnosable disorder for a psychologist in the UK may not be viewed that way by a psychologist from another country. Cultural relativism has become such an acknowledged fact that the DSM includes a glossary that describes patterns of behaviour and syndromes that only occur in certain areas (called 'culture-bound syndromes'). What this means in practice is that there are no universal standards or rules for labelling a behaviour as abnormal.

Why do we need to define abnormality?

Whenever we talk about 'abnormality' or 'abnormal behaviour', we inevitably invoke one of the definitions given on this and the next spread. All of you probably have some idea in your heads about what constitutes abnormality, regardless of whether or not you could put this clearly into words (you may have tried to do so in the DIY activity below).

Although this may be acceptable among non-experts, such implicit definitions would not be acceptable among health professionals. If definitions remain implicit, it means that they cannot be challenged, that alternatives are ignored, and that we don't develop our scientific understanding of abnormal behaviour.

DEFINITION 2
FAILURE TO FUNCTION ADEQUATELY

From an individual's point of view, abnormality can be judged in terms of not being able to cope. For example, if you are feeling depressed, this can be coped with as long as you can continue to go to work, eat meals, wash your clothes, and generally go about day-to-day living. As soon as depression, or indeed any other disorder, interferes with such things then the individual might tend to label their own behaviour 'abnormal', and would wish to seek treatment.

▲ As touch, taste, sight, smell and hearing boarded the chartered flight to Havana, Professor Fitzherbert knew in his heart that he had lost more than good friends, In fact, he had finally lost his senses.

LIMITATIONS

Who judges?

In order to determine 'failure to function adequately' someone needs to decide if this is actually the case. It may be that the patient is experiencing personal distress at, for example, being unable to get to work or to manage day-to-day life. The patient him (or her) self then determines that this behaviour is undesirable.

On the other hand, it may be that the individual is quite content with the situation and/or simply unaware that they are not coping. It is others who are uncomfortable and judge the behaviour as abnormal. For example, many schizophrenics do not feel they have a problem, but their erratic behaviour can be distressing to others, and may even be dangerous, as in the case of someone like Peter Sutcliffe, the Yorkshire Ripper.

Adaptive or maladaptive?

Some apparently dysfunctional behaviour can actually be adaptive and functional for the individual. For example some mental disorders, such as eating disorders or depression, may lead to welcome extra attention for the individual. Some individuals who cross-dress make a living out of it, yet transvestitism is in the list of mental disorders and is generally regarded as abnormal.

Cultural relativism

Definitions of adequate functioning are also related to cultural ideas of how one's life should be lived. The 'failure to function' criterion is likely to result in different diagnoses when applied to people from different cultures, because the standard of one culture is being used to measure another. This may explain why lower class and non-white patients are more often diagnosed with mental disorders – because their lifestyles are non-traditional and this may lead to a judgement of failing to function adequately.

◀ Peter Sutcliffe, a serial killer, known as the Yorkshire Ripper, who terrorised the women of Yorkshire and was arrested in 1983. Some mentally ill people like Sutcliffe might behave violently under the delusion that they are defending themselves or others from evil i.e. functioning adequately. Most of Sutcliffe's victims were prostitutes.

DO IT YOURSELF

No.**6.1**

Make a list of behaviours that you consider 'odd' and that break social 'norms'. Your list might include behaviours such as 'talking to oneself in public' or 'persistent rudeness'. When you have finalised your list, ask others to indicate which of the behaviours they consider 'abnormal' and indicative of an underlying mental disorder.

1 How much agreement is there among people asked?
2 What else did you discover?

KEY TERMS

Abnormality A psychological condition or behaviour that departs from the norm or is harmful and distressing to the individual or those around them. Abnormal behaviours are usually those that violate society's ideas of what is an appropriate level of functioning.

Cultural relativism The view that behaviour cannot be judged properly unless it is viewed in the context of the culture in which it originates.

Definitions of abnormality (continued)

The first two attempts to define abnormality that we have looked at were different in several ways, for example '**deviation from social norms**' is based on what others think about us, whereas '**failure to function adequately**' focuses mainly on the individual's own sense of abnormal functioning. The final definition we will look at, **deviation from ideal mental health**, is a mixture of the two – it aims to be objective, yet does take into account subjective feelings.

CAN YOU...? No.6.1

...**1** Write **one** sentence outlining each of the three definitions of abnormality: deviation from social norms, failure to function adequately and deviation from ideal mental health.

...**2** For each definition identify **three** key points.

...**3** For each definition identify and explain **two** limitations.

...**4** Identify **one** similarity and **one** difference between definition 1 (deviation from social norms) and definition 2 (failure to function adequately).

...**5** Identify **one** similarity and **one** difference between definition 1 (deviation from social norms) and definition 3 (deviation from ideal mental health).

KEY TERMS

Deviation from social norms Abnormal behaviour is seen as a deviation from implicit rules about how one 'ought' to behave. Anything that violates these rules is considered abnormal.

Failure to function adequately By using practical criteria of adequate functioning, mentally healthy people are judged as being able to operate within certain acceptable limits. If abnormal behaviour interferes with daily functioning, it may, according to these criteria, be considered abnormal.

Deviation from ideal mental health Abnormality is seen as deviating from an ideal of positive mental health. Ideal mental health would include a positive attitude towards the self, resistance to stress and an accurate perception of reality.

DO IT YOURSELF No.6.2

Try doing an exercise similar to the one using Robert's school phobia (see opposite), using all three definitions of abnormality to determine whether a person's behaviour would count as abnormal.

You can find your own case histories in books on Abnormal Psychology or on the internet, for example: www.belljar.co.uk/cases/1 and www.nlp-hypnotherapy.com/Case%20Histories.htm

meet the researcher

Marie Jahoda (1907–2001) was born in Vienna, Austria, to a Jewish family, and fled to the US at the start of the Second World War. She later settled in the UK and worked at the University of Sussex, where she developed the first department of social psychology in Britain. Throughout her career she focused on issues such as nationalism, anti-Semitism, and the impact of poverty and unemployment.

DEFINITION 3
DEVIATION FROM IDEAL MENTAL HEALTH

Marie Jahoda (1958) pointed out that we define physical illness in part by looking at the *absence* of signs of physical health. Physical health is indicated by having correct body temperature, normal skin colour, normal blood pressure etc., so the absence of these indicates illness. Why not do the same for mental illness? Jahoda conducted a review of what others had written about mental health and identified six categories that were commonly referred to:

- *Self-attitudes*: having high self-esteem and a strong sense of identity.
- *Personal growth and self-actualisation*: the extent to which an individual develops their full capabilities.
- *Integration*, such as being able to cope with stressful situations.
- *Autonomy*: being independent and self-regulating.
- Having an *accurate perception of reality*.
- *Mastery of the environment*: including the ability to love, function at work and in interpersonal relations, adjust to new situations and solve problems.

This model proposes that the *absence* of these criteria indicates abnormality, and potential mental disorder.

⊖ LIMITATIONS

Who can achieve all these criteria?

According to these criteria most of us are abnormal to some degree. Jahoda presented them as ideal criteria and they certainly are, but we also have to ask how many need to be lacking before a person would be judged as abnormal.

Is mental health the same as physical health?

Doctors use signs of health as a means of detecting physical illness, but they also look for signs of illness such as fever or pain. Can mental illness be detected in the same way? In general, physical illnesses have physical causes such as a virus or bacterial infection, and as a result this makes them relatively easy to detect and diagnose. It is possible that some mental illnesses also have physical causes (e.g. brain injury or drug abuse) but many do not. They are the consequence of life experiences. Therefore it is unlikely that we could diagnose mental abnormality in the same way that we can diagnose physical abnormality.

Cultural relativism

Many, if not most, of the criteria of the ideal mental health model are culture-bound. If we apply these criteria to people from non-Western or even non-middle-class social groups we will most probably find a higher incidence of abnormality. For example, the criterion of self-actualisation (reaching one's full potential) is relevant to members of individualist cultures (see page 45) but not collectivist cultures, where individuals strive for the greater good of the community rather than for self-centred goals.

Robert was an underweight eight-year-old who had always been very reluctant to go to school. Every school night he ate little and even that was vomited up later. He twitched and became more and more anxious as the evening wore on. When he couldn't get to sleep he would cry, and his mother would come and sit with him and tell him comforting stories.

In the morning Robert got up early and paced up and down, or sat in a corner occasionally rushing to the toilet to be sick. When it was time to go to school he had to be pushed out of the house, though often his tears and complaints of feeling unwell led his mother to relent and allow him to stay at home – it didn't matter greatly as the boy was unlikely to get much out of school in the state he was in.

If he did go to school, there was some solace in the fact that his mother would visit the school at playtime bringing milk and cookies. She came because that was part of the 'deal' about going to school, but also because she would otherwise worry about Robert.

Robert surprisingly got on quite well with the other children and was well liked, despite crying on the way to school and often acting like a baby. He was good at athletics and quite bright. He did not like being away from home for anything – he did not go to play at friends' houses. However, it wasn't just being away from home that caused the problem, Robert was simply terrified of school. His sorrowful walk to school in the mornings resembled that of a convicted murderer on his way to the gallows.

Is Robert's behaviour abnormal? How does it fit our definitions?

- *Deviation from social norms*: Robert is able to cope with social relations, so he is not deviant in that respect. If, for example, he had constantly got into fights with other children and was considered anti-social by his schoolmates this would be an example of deviation from social norms and undesirable for normal development.
- *Failure to function adequately*: Robert's phobia clearly sometimes prevents him from attending school, which is a part of day-to-day life. However, his behaviour may *appear* to be dysfunctional in one sense but may serve another function – to prevent separation between him and his mother.
- *Deviation from ideal mental health*: Robert's behaviour demonstrates a lack of most of the criteria for ideal mental health, such as poor self-esteem, being unable to cope with stressful situations, lack of autonomy and lack of environmental mastery. It is likely that his behaviour, if it continued, would prevent personal growth.

Robert's mother consulted a therapist who identified the key issue to be Robert's anxious nature. Robert received lots of love from his mother but worried that this would cease if he stopped being good. When he started school he immediately was thrown into a new fear of not succeeding. The anxiety of school coupled with the anxiety of being separated from his mother led to Robert's intense phobia. In the next spread, on models of abnormality, we will look at further explanations of Robert's behaviour.

Source: Oltmanns *et al.* (1999) *Case studies in Abnormal Psychology*. New York: John Wiley and Sons

EXAM TIP
Students often get confused between the three definitions and include characteristics of one definition when explaining a different one. It is worth spending time understanding the similarities and differences between the three definitions to avoid becoming confused.

COMMENTARY CORNER

Question: **Outline and evaluate attempts to define abnormality.** *(12 marks)*

This type of question gives you the chance to utilise many of the techniques covered in our Commentary Corners*, so let's review some of these here:

- The use of the word 'outline' in the question alerts you to the fact that only a summary description is needed (the AO1 content) rather than a detailed account of each.
- The use of the word 'attempts' in the plural tells you that you should write about more than one (but there is no requirement to write about *all* the definitions covered here). In fact, trying to include too broad a canvas in your outline of such definitions may result in either a very superficial coverage, or an unbalanced answer.
- Evaluation (the AO2 content) may be specific (about particular definitions) or general (about the whole idea of trying to define abnormality).
- You are required by the specification to cover *limitations* of each of these definitions of abnormality, but there is no explicit mention of *strengths*. Evaluation, however, could include both limitations *and* strengths, so any strengths of each of these definitions are as relevant to AO2 as the limitations. For example, the 'failure to function adequately' definition of abnormality

recognises the subjective experience of the patient, and allows us to view mental disorder from the point of view of the person experiencing it.
- Whatever the evaluative material, it is a good idea to use appropriate link phrases to introduce your AO2 content. We have met some of these in previous commentary corners (see, for example, page 43). These are fairly simple ('However, an alternative explanation is…', 'In support of this assumption…') but are also extremely effective in focusing the examiner *and* you on the fact that you are doing something different from just describing material.
- The most important thing to bear in mind is that there is no one set route to take when answering this question, no one 'right' answer that an examiner will be looking for.

* Note: if you are starting your studies with Chapter 6 then it may be useful to read through all the Commentary Corners in the book for advice about answering exam questions.

Biological and psychological approaches to psychopathology

Definitions of abnormality are concerned with identifying what behaviours or symptoms are considered abnormal. Now we turn to explaining how these abnormal behaviours might have come about – i.e. using different approaches in psychology to *explain* abnormality. Different approaches within psychology have different views on the nature and causes of abnormal behaviour. In the Middle Ages, abnormal behaviour was most frequently explained in terms of possession by evil spirits or demons. This 'demonological' model of abnormality reflected the medieval preoccupation with religion, superstition and warfare. Each person was viewed as a battleground where the devil challenged God. Abnormal behaviour signalled the devil's victory in this struggle (Comer, 1995).

Whereas just one approach was dominant during the Middle Ages, today there are many different approaches used to explain (and treat) abnormal behaviour. Each of these approaches is based on different assumptions about the nature of human behaviour, and different views on the origins of **psychopathology**. At one extreme, the *biological approach* (also referred to as the *medical* model) stresses the importance of organic (i.e. bodily) processes in behaviour, and therefore sees psychopathology as being caused by either anatomical or biochemical problems in the brain. *Psychological approaches* focus more on the psychological dimensions of human behaviour (e.g. the way a person thinks, feels or acts), and base their interpretation of psychopathology on problems in these areas.

As with the definitions covered earlier, none of the approaches offers a *complete* explanation of psychopathology, and none can explain the entire spectrum of abnormality.

WHAT'S ON A MAN'S MIND

SIGMUND FREUD

OVERVIEW OF THE FOUR MODELS OF ABNORMALITY

The biological approach

In Chapter 4 we explored the **biological approach** to explaining stress. This involved a consideration of how bodily systems can be used to explain the causes and effects of stress.

A biological psychologist explains abnormal behaviour in terms of an abnormal biology, and therefore explains mental disorder as the consequence of malfunctioning of these biological systems. It follows that *treatment* should repair these faulty systems, using somatic (i.e. focused on bodily processes) therapies such as drugs, ECT and psychosurgery.

The biological model of abnormality is also called the medical model because it treats abnormality as a physical condition. The medical model of abnormality is the most widely accepted model of mental illness. In fact, that is why the term mental 'illness' is often used rather than mental 'disorder', because the dominant view in psychiatry is that mental problems are *illnesses*, to be treated much like physical illnesses.

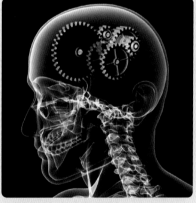

▲ The biological approach sees abnormality as the consequence of malfunctioning of biological mechanisms in the brain, with treatment aimed at 'repairing' this malfunction.

The psychodynamic approach

The essence of a **psychodynamic approach** is to explain behaviour in terms of its *dynamics* – i.e. the forces that drive it. The best-known example of this approach is Freud's psychoanalytic theory of personality, although there are many other psychodynamic theories based on Freud's ideas.

Sigmund Freud was the first to challenge the medical model, claiming that mental disorder was caused by *psychological* rather than physical factors.

Freud believed that much of our behaviour is motivated (i.e. driven) by unconscious desires, i.e. drives that are hidden from our conscious awareness. Abnormal behaviour was seen as being caused by these underlying psychological forces, sometimes originating from childhood experiences or from an unresolved conflict between id and superego. Because the immature ego is unable to deal with them at the time, Freud thought that distressing experiences in childhood could be repressed and eventually re-emerge as psychological problems. Similarly, he believed that if the conflict between id and superego is not managed effectively by the ego, the person might develop a psychological disorder.

The psychodynamic model of abnormality aims to treat mental illness by making the unconscious conscious, through the use of psychoanalytic therapy.

▶ This was the scene in Bedlam, the common name for the mental hospital outside London called Bethlem, as depicted by Hogarth (1735).

DO IT YOURSELF

No.**6.3**

Before reading on, try your own hand at using these four approaches. On page 181 we described Robert's school phobia. Use each of the approaches described on this spread and try to explain *why* Robert might have become phobic about going to school.

KEY TERMS

Psychopathology The scientific study of psychological disorders, their nature and causes.

Biological approach The view that behaviour can all be explained in terms of biological mechanisms such as hormones, neurotransmitters, brain activity and influences inherited via genes.

Psychodynamic approach Literally an approach that explains the *dynamics* of behaviour – what motivates a person. Freud suggested that unconscious forces and early experience are the prime motivators.

Behavioural approach (learning theory) All behaviour is learned through experience as a result of classical or operant conditioning.

Cognitive approach The key influence on behaviour is how an individual *thinks* about the situation.

You are probably familiar with the different 'approaches' that people have to life. For example, some people have a strong belief in their ability to change their own destiny – and so work hard to bring this about. Others believe that they are largely at the mercy of fate – this could result in them doing little to change their lives for the better. These very different beliefs about life cause them to 'approach' it in very different ways.

The behavioural approach

Learning theory (classical and operant conditioning) was described on pages 34–5). This is the bedrock of the **behavioural approach** which is based on the claim that all behaviour is learned. We are born as a blank slate, on which experience writes. 'Behaviourists' believe all behaviour is learned and also believe that behaviour is all that should concern psychology – there is no need to search for the mind or analyse thoughts and feelings. They believe that, in order to develop a truly scientific and objective science of psychology, behaviour alone should be studied.

Behaviourism was first formulated around the start of the twentieth century, at about the same time as Freud's early work. A later development of behaviourism was introduced by Albert Bandura in the 1960s. He pointed out that much of what we learn is not the consequence of direct rewards or punishments but of *vicarious* or second-hand reinforcement. We learn by watching what happens to others and, under certain conditions, *imitating* these behaviours. This is called social learning theory (SLT) – 'social' because the learning process involves other people. SLT is also called 'neo-behaviourism' (a new behaviourism).

A behavioural psychologist explains all behaviour (including abnormal behaviours) in terms of learning and observable phenomena. Neo-behaviourists use the concept of social learning theory. Treatments arising from the behavioural model also involve learning new behaviours through conditioning, and/or unlearning old, maladaptive behaviours.

The cognitive approach

The first module of this book was an example of the **cognitive approach** in psychology – applied to the study of human memory. Cognitive psychology focuses on internal mental processes. It likens the mind to a computer: information is input, processed, stored and retrieved. The different components of the brain function as part of a network, just like a computer.

The emphasis of the cognitive approach is on how thinking shapes our behaviour – quite the opposite of the behavioural approach where the concept of the mind was banished from any explanations. The cognitive approach is more recent than the others outlined here, emerging in the 1950s along with the information-processing revolution. Today it is a dominant approach in the explanation and treatment of mental illness.

A cognitive psychologist explains all behaviour in terms of thoughts, beliefs and attitudes, and studies how these direct our behaviour. Cognitive psychologists explain abnormality in terms of irrational and negative thinking about the world around us. The problem (i.e. abnormality) is the way individuals think about themselves and the world – if that can be changed, the problem will disappear. This is the essence of therapies derived from the cognitive model.

▶ 'Always look on the bright side of life', the song sung at the end of Monty Python's film *The Life of Brian*, is an example of the cognitive approach: dealing with a problem by thinking about it differently.

The biological approach to psychopathology

The biological approach is the view of mainstream *psychiatry*. All behaviour is seen as rooted in underlying physiological processes in the body. Any abnormality must, therefore, have specific causes that lie in some bodily malfunction or in genetic factors. Cure is only possible by removing the root cause and returning the body to its 'normal' level of functioning. Because of its similarity to the diagnosis of *physical* disease, the approach is also referred to as the *medical* model, and mental disorders represented as mental *illnesses*. Because of its emphasis on *scientific* investigation and understanding, the biological approach is the most widely respected approach to psychopathology. However, its representation of mental disorders as 'disease' states equivalent to physical illnesses also makes it one of the most controversial.

Syphilis and general paresis

The medical model of diagnosis can be illustrated by the case of general paresis. From the sixteenth to the nineteenth century, there was a steady increase in the reported incidence of symptoms such as delusions of grandeur, progressive forgetfulness and mental deterioration. People who experienced all these symptoms together also faced an early death. It was not until the nineteenth century that anyone precisely identified these symptoms as a syndrome called general paresis.

The first step in discovering a cure was to find the cause of general paresis. It was thought that it might be caused by the syphilis bacterium. In its early stages, syphilis produces genital sores, but these are short-lived, so it appears that the individual has recovered. However, the suspicion was that the bacterium goes on to cause mental deterioration and eventually death. The problem was that patients with general paresis would not admit to having had syphilis (it was contracted through sexual contact with an infected person) so the link between syphilis and paresis could not be made. However, towards the end of the nineteenth century, Richard Krafft-Ebbing demonstrated the link by selecting nine paretics and injecting them directly with the syphilis bacterium. If they had previously had syphilis they would not be re-infected because they would have developed an immunity. None of them developed the sores associated with syphilis, demonstrating the link. Once the cause was known, a cure could be found, which happened in 1909 with the discovery of arsphenamine as a treatment for the disorder.

The importance of this case study is that it demonstrates: (1) that mental illnesses may have physical causes (2) once a cause has been identified a suitable treatment may be found.

BASIC PRINCIPLES

Abnormality is caused by physical factors

The biological (medical) model assumes that all mental disorders are related to some change in the body. Mental disorders are like physical disorders i.e. they are illnesses. Such changes or illnesses may be caused by one of four possible factors: genes, biochemistry, neuroanatomy and viral infection.

Genetic inheritance

Abnormalities in brain anatomy or chemistry are sometimes the result of **genetic inheritance**, and so are passed from parent to child. One way of investigating this possibility is by studying twins. Pairs of identical twins can be compared to see whether, when one twin has a disorder, the other has it as well. This provides us with a *concordance rate* – the extent to which two individuals are similar to each other in terms of a particular trait. There are low concordance rates for some mental disorders (e.g. phobias) but relatively high concordance rates for others (e.g. schizophrenia). Many of the genes responsible for abnormal behaviours are the product of evolutionary adaptations in our ancestors, despite the fact these traits are no longer useful (see pages 116–17).

Certain genes lead to abnormal biochemistry and/or abnormal neuroanatomy

Genes tell the body how to function. They determine, for example, the levels of hormones and neurotransmitters in the brain (biochemistry). In the chapter on stress we mentioned the neurotransmitter serotonin. High levels of serotonin are associated with anxiety, whereas low levels have been found in depressed individuals. Genes also determine the structure of the brain (neuroanatomy). Research has shown that schizophrenics have enlarged spaces (ventricles) in their brains, indicating shrinkage of brain tissue around these spaces.

Viral infection

Research suggests that some disorders (such as schizophrenia) may be related to exposure to certain viruses *in utero* (i.e. in the womb). For example, Torrey (2001) found that the mothers of many people with schizophrenia had contracted a particular strain of influenza during pregnancy. The virus may enter the unborn child's brain, where it remains dormant until puberty, when other hormones may activate it, producing the symptoms of schizophrenia.

Murderous rampage

In 1966 Charles Whitman strangled his mother, murdered his wife as she lay sleeping, and then installed himself in a tower on the University of Texas campus before shooting 14 people. He was eventually shot down himself. In a letter written beforehand, he expressed a wish that his body be autopsied after his death to see if there was a physical cause for his mental anguish. A small tumour was discovered in his brain, though it is not clear whether this can explain his murderous rampage.

◄ The tower on the Texas campus from where Charles Whitman used a rifle to kill 14 passers by. Was his murderous rampage due to an unhappy childhood with an authoritarian father, or to a brain tumour?

Using the biological approach to explain Robert's school phobia

Robert's separation anxiety may be in part caused by a predisposition to be anxious. He may be anxious by nature and even have inherited a tendency to develop phobias. There is evidence that certain personality traits are inherited. It may be that these innate tendencies, coupled with certain life experiences (e.g. maternal overprotection), could explain his separation anxiety disorder and his school phobia.

 LIMITATIONS

Humane or inhumane?

The emergence of the medical model in the eighteenth century led to more humane treatment for mental patients. Until then mental illness was blamed on demons or on evil in the individual. The medical model offered a different source of blame – the illness, which was potentially treatable. However, more recent critics have claimed that the medical model is inhumane. Thomas Szasz (1972) argued that mental illnesses did not have a physical basis, therefore should not be thought of in the same way. He suggested that the concept of mental illness was 'invented' as a form of social control.

Cause and effect?

The available evidence does not support a simple cause and effect link between mental illnesses such as schizophrenia and altered brain chemistry. For example, schizophrenia is commonly associated with an excess of the brain neurotransmitter dopamine. However, some studies of schizophrenic patients have shown *reduced* levels of dopamine in some brain tissues, meaning that there may be simultaneous excesses *and* deficiencies in different parts of the brain.

Inconclusive evidence

There is no evidence that mental disorders are purely caused by genetic inheritance – concordance rates are never 100%. Gottesman and Shields (1976) reviewed the results of five studies of twins, looking for concordance rates for schizophrenia. They found that in monozygotic (i.e. genetically identical) twins there was a concordance rate of around 50%. If schizophrenia was *entirely* the product of genetic inheritance, we might expect this figure to be 100%. It is likely that, in the case of certain disorders, what individuals inherit is a susceptibility for the disorder, but the disorder itself only develops if the individual is exposed to stressful life conditions (i.e. *stress*). This is called the **diathesis-stress model** ('diathesis' means a constitutional disposition).

METHODS OF INVESTIGATING THE BIOLOGICAL APPROACH

- **Experiments** – If patients fare better when given a drug which alters brain chemistry, this outcome is taken to show the importance of biochemical changes in that disorder. For example, Kirsch *et al.* (2002) reviewed 38 studies of antidepressants and found that patients who received placebos fared almost as well as those getting real drugs.
- **Correlational studies** – Because it is impractical (and immoral) to carry out experiments to test for genetic inheritance, psychologists rely on correlations to investigate the relationship between heredity and the development of mental disorders. Correlational studies provide a comparison of the frequencies of mental disorders in various populations (e.g. children and their parents), but do not demonstrate cause and effect.

CAN YOU...? No.6.2

...1 Identify **six** key pieces of information about the biological approach.

...2 Expand these six points into a 100-word *description* of the biological approach.

...3 Précis this description into a 50-word *outline*.

...4 Identify **three** limitations of the biological approach and then explain each one in detail, using examples.

CULTURAL SIMILARITIES

The evolutionary view argues that mental disorders such as depression are an exaggerated version of a trait that enhanced the reproductive fitness of ancestral humans. This would, therefore, assume that most humans would have the same adaptation. Research supports this, as depression is currently the most common mental disorder, with around 120 million sufferers worldwide.

COMMENTARY CORNER

Can we equate *mental* disorders with *physical diseases*?

The main assumption of the biological model of abnormality is that diseases of the mind are actually diseases of the brain. Contrary to this view, Thomas Szasz (2000) asserts that mental functions are not reducible to brain functions, and that mental diseases are not brain diseases – indeed, that mental diseases are not diseases at all.

Szasz makes the distinction between diseases of the brain (such as epilepsy), and diseases of the mind (such as an irrational belief that one's body is already dead), and states that the two are not equally 'illnesses'. To Szasz, such irrational beliefs cannot be explained by means of physical defects or diseases and therefore cannot be called illnesses in the same way as we would call epilepsy a physical illness.

Of course, disorders such as anxiety and depression *do* exist but they are not diseases in the pathological sense. Diseases are physical phenomena or processes, for example the abnormal metabolism of glucose (diabetes). Mental diseases, on the other hand, are patterns of personal conduct, unwanted by the individual or others. In short, medical diseases are *discovered* and then given a name, such as syphilis. Mental diseases, suggests Szasz, are *invented* and then given a name, such as attention deficit disorder.

RESEARCH METHODS Qs No.6.1

1 Explain **two** ways that psychologists have investigated the biological basis of abnormality.

2 For each of these, describe **one** strength and **one** weakness with the method of investigation.

LINK TO RESEARCH METHODS

See pages 85 and 99 for strengths and weaknesses.

The psychodynamic approach to psychopathology

When used in the context of abnormal behaviour, the term psychodynamic refers to any approach that emphasises the *dynamics* of behaviour, i.e. what drives us to behave in particular ways. As the individual is constantly changing and developing, so do the underlying drives of their behaviour. Those theorists who subscribe to a psychodynamic model believe that an individual's abnormal behaviour is determined by underlying psychological conflicts of which they are largely unaware (i.e. the product of *unconscious* forces). Psychodynamic theorists focus mostly on past experiences, notably early parent-child relationships, because they believe the majority of psychological conflicts are rooted in these relationships. The best-known of the psychodynamic theories of abnormality is Sigmund Freud's theory of *psychoanalysis* (this term applies to both the theory and the therapy). Freud believed that unconscious forces determined all normal *and* abnormal behaviour.

▼ The iceberg metaphor – Freud's view of the human psyche

Conscious
Preconscious   EGO
SUPEREGO
ID
Unconscious

KEY TERMS

Id is the irrational, primitive part of personality. It is present at birth, demands immediate satisfaction and is ruled by the *pleasure principle* – an innate drive to seek immediate satisfaction.

Ego is the conscious rational part of the personality. It develops by the end of the infant's first year, as a child interacts with the constraints of reality and thus is governed by the *reality principle*.

Superego develops between the ages of three and six, and embodies our conscience and sense of right and wrong.

NB These three 'personality structures' are not intended to be real things but to represent aspects of self and motivation

Ego defences
Unconscious methods, such as repression and displacement, which help the ego deal with feelings of anxiety and thus 'defend' the ego.

The basics of Freud's theory of personality

'Personality' refers to the unique character that each of us has. Freud suggested that this developed out of an interaction between innate drives and early life experiences.

Personality structures
In the beginning, at birth, the personality is ruled by the id (Latin for 'it'). The id is driven by the pleasure principle – an innate drive to seek immediate satisfaction. It gets what it wants. By the end of the infant's first year, the ego develops as a consequence of experience with reality (it cannot always get what it wants). The ego or 'I' is driven by the reality principle, which makes the child accommodate to the demands of the environment. Finally, around the age of five, the superego emerges. The superego 'or above-I' embodies our conscience and sense of right and wrong. These three 'personality structures' are not intended to be real things but to represent aspects of self and motivation.

Ego defences
The ego mediates between the id and superego, coping with the conflicting demands. Throughout life the id, ego and superego are inevitably in conflict because each represents different motives – pleasure, reality and ideal behaviour. Conflicts cause the individual to experience anxiety. In order to reduce this anxiety, the ego uses 'defence mechanisms', such as repression (putting unpleasant thoughts in the unconscious) and projection (blaming someone else), denial, displacement (venting angry elsewhere), regression (behaving like a child), and intellectualisation. These ego-defences are unconscious and are a key dynamic of the personality.

Freud in action
Freud recorded the case histories of a number of his patients, using these to support his theory. Two of the best known are Little Hans and Anna O.

BASIC PRINCIPLES

Mental disorder results from psychological rather than physical causes
Freud believed that the origins of mental disorder lie in the *unresolved conflicts of childhood* which are *unconscious*. Medical illnesses are not the outcome of physical disorder but of these psychological conflicts.

Unresolved conflicts cause mental disorder
Conflicts between the **id**, **ego** and **superego** create anxiety. The ego protects itself with various defence mechanism (**ego defences**). These defences can be the cause of disturbed behaviour if they are overused. For example, a boy who cannot deal with what he perceives as maternal rejection when a new baby brother is born may regress to an earlier developmental stage, soiling his clothes and becoming more helpless (regression).

Early experiences cause mental disorder
In childhood the ego is not developed enough to deal with traumas and therefore they are repressed. For example, a child may experience the death of a parent early in life and repress associated feelings. Later in life, other losses may cause the individual to re-experience the earlier loss and can lead to depression. Previously unexpressed anger about the loss is directed inwards towards the self, causing depression.

Unconscious motivations cause mental disorder
Ego defences, such as repression and regression, exert pressure through unconsciously motivated behaviour. Freud proposed that the unconscious consists of memories and other information that are either very hard or almost impossible to bring into conscious awareness. Despite this, the unconscious mind exerts a powerful effect on behaviour. This frequently leads to distress, as the person does not understand why they are acting in that particular way. The underlying problem cannot be controlled until brought into conscious awareness.

Little Hans
Little Hans, aged five years old, had become terrified of horses pulling a laden cart. Freud (1909) suggested that this fear developed because of Hans' unconscious anxieties. For example Hans once heard a man saying to a child 'Don't put your finger to the white horse or it'll bite you'. Hans also once asked his mother if she would like to put her finger on his penis. His mother told him this would not be proper. Hans projected one source of anxiety onto another – he became afraid of being bitten by a white horse whereas he was really scared that his mother would leave him.

Hans saw a horse with a laden cart fall down and thought it was dead.

The horse symbolised his wish that his father (big whiskers and glasses like blinkers) would die and the laden cart symbolised his mother pregnant with his sister, and when it fell over this was like giving birth. Therefore the laden cart symbolised his dying father and his mother giving birth – both events that filled him with anxiety.

Sigmund Freud (1856–1939) was born the son of a Jewish wool merchant in Freiberg, Moravia (now part of the Czech Republic). His theories are based on the principle that unconscious drives have a considerable influence on our lives, and that unless these are understood, then changing the way we feel, think and behave is impossible. Although Freud's ideas were initially greeted with derision in Victorian society, by the 1930s his fame was so great that the Nazis were reluctant to destroy his practice in Vienna and allowed him to emigrate to England. At the time of his death Freud was regarded as one of the major scientific thinkers of his age – equal to Darwin and Einstein.

...1 Identify **six** key pieces of information about the psychodynamic approach.

...2 Expand these six points into a 100-word *description* of the psychodynamic approach.

...3 Précis this description into a 50-word *outline*.

...4 Identify **three** limitations of the psychodynamic approach and then explain each one in detail, using examples.

⊖ LIMITATIONS

Abstract concepts

Abstract concepts such as the id, ego and superego are difficult to define and research. Because actions motivated by them operate primarily at an unconscious level, there is no way to know for certain that they are occurring. As a result, psychodynamic explanations have received limited empirical support, and psychodynamic theorists have had to rely largely on evidence from individual case studies (see right and below).

Sexism

A common criticism of Freud's work is that it (and perhaps Freud himself) was sexist. Freud's theory was undoubtedly sexually unbalanced, and he himself accepted that his theory was less well developed for women (Freud, 1953). Perhaps this is not surprising, given the cultural bias of Victorian society and the simple fact that Freud was male (women were not considered equals in Victorian times). However, the reduced emphasis on the Oedipal complex, and other changes in modern psychoanalysis have made this explanation (and its associated treatment) perfectly applicable to women.

Lack of research evidence

Although a number of researchers have attempted to test Freud's predictions experimentally, the theory is difficult to prove *or* disprove in this way. If an individual behaves in the manner predicted by Freud, this is considered to be supportive of the theory. However, if they do not, the theory is not rejected as it could instead indicate that the person is behaving in this way as a consequence of their defence mechanisms. For example, reaction formation is a defence mechanism that drives a person to hide their real fear by acting in the opposite way (e.g. talking loudly when nervous).

METHODS OF INVESTIGATING THE PSYCHODYNAMIC APPROACH

- **Case studies** – Much of the Freudian theory of psychoanalysis was based on case studies. A case study involves the detailed study of a single individual, such as Little Hans or Anna O. Case studies offer an in-depth data insight into behaviour although it is difficult to generalise from individual cases such as Anna O. because each one has unique characteristics.

- **Experiments** – Although Freud opposed the use of experimental methods to test his theory, many psychologists since Freud have used this technique to test his theory. Fisher and Greenberg (1996) reviewed over 2,500 experimental studies of Freudian hypotheses, with many of Freud's major claims, including the development of depression, receiving experimental support. A major problem for researchers using experimental studies is that positive results may be taken as supporting the hypothesis, but negative results may be taken as indicating the action of a defence mechanism which disguises the *real* underlying conflict.

> **LINK TO RESEARCH METHODS**
> See pages 101 and 85 for strengths and weaknesses.

CASE STUDY

Using the psychodynamic approach to explain Robert's school phobia

Robert may have had a fear of failing and this created anxiety. In order to cope with this anxiety, his feelings about school were repressed and in order to deal with this he had to avoid the object creating the fear. The phobia is the ego's way of not confronting the repressed problem.

In addition to this phobia Robert also suffered from separation anxiety which may have developed out of an insecure attachment to his mother. Such insecurity leads a child to feel anxious when separated. Such anxiety would have been repressed and the method of coping would be to avoid separation.

The implications of this are important. To simply try to get Robert to school (dealing with symptoms) would not overcome the real causes, and his anxieties would remain.

Anna O.

Anna O. (Freud, 1910) suffered severe paralysis on her right side as well as nausea and difficulty in drinking. Freud demonstrated that these physical symptoms actually had a psychological cause. During discussions with her it became apparent that she had developed a fear of drinking when a dog she hated drank from her glass. Her other symptoms originated when caring for her sick father. She could not express her anxiety for his illness but did express it later, during psychoanalysis. As soon as she had the opportunity to make these unconscious thoughts conscious her paralysis disappeared.

RESEARCH METHODS Qs No.**6.2**

1. Explain **two** ways that psychologists have investigated the psychodynamic basis of abnormality.

2. For each of these, describe **one** strength and **one** weakness with the method of investigation.

The behavioural approach to psychopathology

Behaviourists believe that our actions are determined largely by the experiences we have in life, rather than by underlying pathology or unconscious forces. Abnormality is seen as the development of behaviour patterns (established through classical and operant conditioning, or through social learning) that are considered maladaptive for the individual. Most learned behaviours are adaptive, helping people to lead happy and productive lives. However, maladaptive (and therefore undesirable) behaviours can be acquired in the same way. When determining treatment for abnormal behaviour, behaviourists believe that we need only concern ourselves with a person's actions – there is no need to search the mind or analyse thoughts and feelings (a direct contrast to the psychodynamic view of abnormality).

Learning theory is also described on page 34.

Learning theory

Classical conditioning

Learning occurs through association. A neutral stimulus is paired with an unconditioned stimulus, resulting in a new stimulus–response link. The neutral stimulus is now a conditioned stimulus producing a conditioned response.

This process applies to emotional learning as well as to behaviours. For example, behavioural explanations of phobias assume that the feared object (e.g. spiders or rats) was associated with fear or anxiety sometime in the past. The conditioned stimulus subsequently evokes a powerful fear response characterised by avoidance of the feared object and the emotion of fear whenever the object is encountered. The most famous example of the conditioning of a phobic response is 'Little Albert' (see below).

Operant conditioning

Learning occurs through reinforcement. An animal responds to the environment and some of these responses are reinforced, increasing the probability that they will be repeated. If a response is punished, this decreases the probability that it will be repeated.

Psychological disorder is produced when a maladaptive behaviour is rewarded. This means that such behaviours may be functional for the individual, at least at the time they are learned. For example, if a child finds that he or she gets more attention from parents when they have a panic attack, these attacks might well become more frequent until they become difficult to stop. This could lead to the same behaviour with their partner in later life.

Social learning (vicarious conditioning)

Behaviours are learned by seeing others rewarded and punished (social learning). An individual's social context is important when considering the origins of abnormal behaviours, because it provides many opportunities for behaviours to be observed and imitated. When researchers report that some disorders (such as anxiety disorders) run in families, it is difficult to separate the effects of genetics from the effects of social learning (Kendall and Hammen, 1995).

Other concepts: generalisation, discrimination and extinction

If an animal is taught that the sound of a bell is associated with food then the animal will salivate to the sound of any bell (generalisation). If, however, the animal is exposed to trials where food is presented only to the sound of a certain bell but not presented when other bells are rung, then the animal will learn to discriminate between different stimuli. If no food is presented at all the response that was learned will be extinguished.

Many phobic responses are acquired not through direct experience with the feared object, but through generalisation from a conditioned stimulus. For example, people who develop a conditioned fear of rats may also feel anxious when in the company of mice, gerbils, chinchillas, etc.

BASIC PRINCIPLES

Only behaviour is important

The behavioural model concentrates only on behaviours, i.e. the responses a person makes to their environment. Behaviours might be external (e.g. displaying compulsive behaviours such as constant hand washing) or internal (e.g. experiencing a particular feeling). Because the former are more observable, behaviourists tend to focus their attention on the role of external events and behaviours.

Abnormal behaviours are learned through conditioning or social learning

All behaviour is determined by external events. Abnormal behaviour is no different from normal behaviour in terms of how it is learned. We can use the principles of learning theory to explain many disorders for which the major characteristics are behavioural (e.g. the avoidance behaviour that is characteristic of specific phobias). For example, arachnophobia (spider phobia) involves avoidance (external behaviour) and feelings of anxiety when in the presence of a spider (internal behaviour).

Learning environments

Learning environments may reinforce problematic behaviours, for example avoidant behaviour lowers anxiety, depressive behaviours may elicit help from others. Society also provides deviant maladaptive models that children identify with and imitate: for example, a child may engage in drug taking if they judge that by engaging in such behaviour they will be rewarded (e.g. social approval) by their peers. Similarly, people may develop a fear of flying as a result of watching air crashes on TV.

THE JACKMANS

1 Suggest the UCS, CS, UCR, and CR in this scenario:

Many years ago, as a child, Rick used to visit a dentist who thought anaesthetic was just for sissies. The dentist had a large grandfather clock in his waiting room. Years later, Rick still feels uneasy and a little anxious whenever he hears the tick of a grandfather clock.

Little Albert

John B. Watson and Rosalie Rayner (1920) sought to provide experimental evidence that fear could be learned in this way. They worked with an 11-month-old boy called 'Little Albert'. They first tested his responses to white fluffy objects: a white rat, a rabbit, and white cotton wool. He showed no fear response.

Next they set about creating a conditioned response to these previously neutral objects. To do this they used a steel bar that was four feet long. When he reached out for the rat they struck the bar with a hammer behind Albert's head to startle him. They repeated this three times, and did the same a week later. After this, when they showed the rat to Albert, he began to cry. They had conditioned a fear response in him.

...1 Identify **six** key pieces of information about the behavioural approach.

...2 Expand these six points into a 100-word *description* of the behavioural approach.

...3 Précis this description into a 50-word *outline*.

...4 Identify **three** limitations of the behavioural approach and then explain each one in detail, using examples.

RESEARCH METHODS Qs No.6.3

1 Explain **two** ways that psychologists have investigated the behavioural basis of abnormality.

2 For each of these, describe **one** strength and **one** weakness with the method of investigation.

LIMITATIONS

A limited view

Behaviourist explanations of mental disorders have been criticised for offering an extremely limited view of the factors that might cause abnormal behaviours. Behaviourist explanations tend to ignore the role of cognition in the onset and treatment of abnormality, although the emergence of cognitive behavioural theories (see page 197) did take the role of cognition into account.

Counter evidence

Although one of the strengths of this approach is the fact that it lends itself to scientific validation, research has not always supported its claims. For example, conditioning theories of the acquisition of fear would have a problem explaining why many people are unable to identify an incident in their past which led to traumatic conditioning, nor even to recall any contact with the feared object.

By contrast, phobias to many frequently encountered and potentially frightening stimuli, such as fast-moving traffic, are relatively rare (Davey, 1997). Seligman (1970) provided an explanation for this. He suggested that some basic anxieties may be 'hard-wired' into the brain because they provided a survival advantage to our ancestors. As a result, we may be biologically 'prepared' to develop a fear response to small, quick and potentially dangerous animals but not to fast-moving traffic. Despite the fact we no longer live in these conditions, we find it hard to stop responding in this way.

The symptoms and not the cause

Part of the success of this model comes from the effectiveness of behavioural therapies for treating abnormal behaviour. However, such therapies may not provide long-lasting solutions. This may be because the symptoms are just the tip of the iceberg. If you remove the symptoms, the cause still remains, and the symptoms will simply resurface, possibly in another form (called *symptom substitution*). This suggests that although the *symptoms* of many disorders are behavioural, the *cause* of these symptoms may not be.

CASE STUDY

Using the behavioural approach to explain Robert's school phobia

The behavioural account for Robert's phobia might suggest that it developed as a result of classical conditioning, as outlined in the account of Little Albert. School became associated with anxiety, and therefore Robert found that avoidance of the feared object (school) reduced his anxiety. Continued absence served to reduce the fear and was thus reinforcing.

Robert also received a kind of reward for staying away from school – he continued to enjoy his mother's company. In addition when he did go to school she visited him. This meant his phobic behaviour was rewarded.

METHODS OF INVESTIGATING THE BEHAVIOURAL APPROACH

- **Experiments** – Because the behavioural model concentrates only on observable *behaviours*, the most appropriate method of testing behaviourist assumptions is the experiment. For example, the theory predicts that the learning environment of an individual determines the behaviours they acquire (some of which might be maladaptive). Those which are rewarded will be repeated, while those which produce no reward will not. As a result, researchers may use an ABBA design (see page 77), with condition A associated with reward, and condition B with no reward or a punishment). After several trials, the individual should reproduce the behaviour in condition A more readily than the behaviour in condition B.
- **Animal studies** – The same basic laws of learning apply to human *and* non-human animals. This means that it is reasonable to conduct research on non-human animals, such as rats and pigeons, and make generalisations to human behaviour. Much of the behavioural model of abnormality, such as the principles of classical and operant conditioning has been established through the study of non-human animals.

LINK TO RESEARCH METHODS

See page 85 for strengths and weaknesses.

COMMENTARY CORNER

Question: **Outline and evaluate the behavioural approach to psychopathology.** *(12 marks)*

The essence of the behavioural approach to psychopathology is that adaptive *and* maladaptive behaviours are learned by the same procedures. This is also true for the actions that we typically display when faced with an examination situation. During our childhood, we become socialised into associating *more* knowledge with happier outcomes. Having made this link, where does that leave us? Now, at AS level, we need to learn that *more* does not always mean better. In order to answer the above question *effectively*, you need to know what to put in *and* also what to leave out.

To produce a Grade A answer you need to take some important executive decisions about inclusion and exclusion. Look through all the material on this double-page spread. Try to précis the material so that you have a decent 'overview' of the model, and a balanced evaluation. By engaging in this very valuable précis exercise, you are learning *editorial* skills, which are vital in this sort of question. If you have ever marvelled at journalists' ability to capture the gist of a story in a very contained way, you are also being appreciative of their editorial skills, their ability to 'cut to fit'. If you were to repeat your examination many times (let's hope you don't have to…) you would eventually develop the *appropriate* sort of response to maximise your marks. It is hardly surprising, therefore, to learn that operant conditioning is often likened to natural selection. Learn to précis, and you will prosper, fail to do so and you will struggle.

The cognitive approach to psychopathology

Much of contemporary psychology is concerned with human *cognition*, e.g. how people perceive, reason and judge the world around them. The cognitive model of abnormality emphasises that cognitive distortions (dysfunctional thought processes) and cognitive deficiencies (the absence of sufficient thinking and planning) may be at the root of many psychological disorders. Cognitive distortions can be summarised as follows:

- *Cognitive structures* refer to the internal organisation of information. For example, most of us think of dogs (and cats…) as pets that are a source of companionship, sometimes able to do tricks, sometimes well-behaved, totally scatty, and so on. For people who are afraid of dogs, however, they view them on just one dimension, as objects of fear.
- *Cognitive content* is the actual material that the person is processing. We may focus on the negative aspects of a situation ('How can I possibly do this?' or 'I just know I'm going to fail') or the positive ('This is great' or 'I will survive').
- *Cognitive processes* are the ways in which we operate on this information. Anxious people process information differently from those who are less anxious. A girl may overhear a chance remark while at work: 'She really gets on my nerves'. This is a fairly innocuous statement that could apply to anyone, but she is convinced they are talking about her – an example of irrational thinking.
- *Cognitive products* are the conclusions that people reach when they have processed this material. In the example above, the person may conclude that she isn't liked or accepted, a conclusion that may be based on faulty processing.

Cognitive psychologists therefore explain abnormality in terms of *irrational and negative thinking*. Distortions in the way we process information have been implicated in depression, schizophrenia, and other mental disorders.

Common irrational assumptions

All cognitive therapists believe in the idea of faulty thinking. Meichenbaum (1977) called the products of this faulty thinking 'counterproductive self-statements'. Beck (1976) called them dysfunctional 'automatic thoughts', and Ellis (1962) called them 'irrational' assumptions. For example:

- *It is necessary to be loved or approved of by every significant other.*
- *One should be thoroughly competent, adequate and achieving if one is to consider oneself worthwhile.*
- *It is awful when things are not the way I would like them to be.*

An individual who holds such assumptions is bound to be at the very least disappointed, at worst, depressed. An individual who fails an exam might become depressed, not because they failed the exam, but because they hold an irrational belief regarding that failure (e.g. 'If I fail, people will think I'm stupid').

DO IT YOURSELF

No.**6.4**

How much are self-defeating beliefs affecting your life? Try a questionnaire yourself at www.rational.org.nz/public/BeliefsQuestionnaire/indexf2.htm

You could correlate your score on this with some other measure, such as happiness (make up your own scale for this or find one on the web).

BASIC PRINCIPLES

Abnormality is caused by faulty thinking

The cognitive model assumes that thinking, expectations and attitudes (i.e. cognitions) direct behaviour. Mental illness, therefore, is the result of inappropriate, i.e. *disordered* thinking. The focus is not on the problem itself but the way a person *thinks* about it. Faulty and irrational thinking prevents the individual behaving adaptively. Ellis (1962) referred to this as the A-B-C model:

- **A** refers to an **activating event** (e.g. the sight of a large dog).
- **B** is the **belief**, which may be rational or irrational (e.g. 'the dog is harmless' – rational, or 'the dog will attack me' – irrational).
- **C** is the **consequence** – rational beliefs lead to healthy emotions (e.g. amusement or indifference) whereas irrational beliefs lead to unhealthy emotions (e.g. fear or panic).

The individual is in control

In each of the three previous models the view was that an individual's behaviour is caused by forces outside their own control – physiological, genetic, unconscious or environmental factors. Psychologists use the word *determinism* to describe this. By contrast, the cognitive model portrays the individual as being the cause of their own behaviour because the individual controls their own thoughts. Abnormality, therefore, is the product of faulty control.

METHODS OF INVESTIGATING THE COGNITIVE APPROACH

- **Experiments** – As with the behavioural model, assumptions of the cognitive model can be tested experimentally. For example, Thase *et al.* (2007) compared cognitive therapy (CT) with antidepressant medication in the treatment of depression. Results showed that CT was no less effective than antidepressant medications, and was better tolerated by patients. This demonstrates that depression is, at least in part, a disorder of 'faulty thinking'.

- **Meta-analysis** – In a meta-analysis, a researcher looks at the findings from a number of different studies in order to reach a general conclusion about a particular hypothesis. For example, Smith and Glass (1977), in a meta-analysis of research on psychotherapies, cited cognitive therapy as having the second highest average success rate among ten different forms of psychotherapy.

LINK TO RESEARCH METHODS

See pages 85 and 104 for strengths and weaknesses.

Clare is afraid of flying – the family can't go on holiday to foreign places because she simply can't get on a plane.

1 Use each of the four approaches to explain the cause of Clare's fear of flying.

Alice has developed a fear of dogs since she went to stay on a friend's farm over half term.

2 Explain Alice's fear of dogs using the behavioural model.

3 Explain Alice's fear of dogs using the cognitive model.

 LIMITATIONS

Blames the patient rather than situational factors

The cognitive model suggests that it is the patient who is responsible. This may lead one to overlook situational factors, for example not considering how life events or family problems may have contributed to the mental disorder. The disorder is simply in the patient's mind and recovery lies in changing that, rather than the individual's environment.

Consequence rather than cause

It is not clear which comes first. Do thoughts and beliefs really cause disturbance, or does mental disorder lead to faulty thinking? It may be that, for example, a depressed individual develops a negative way of thinking *because* of their depression rather than the other way around. It is also possible that faulty thinking is a *vulnerability* factor for abnormality. People with maladaptive cognitive processes are at greater risk of developing mental disorders.

Irrational beliefs may be realistic

Not all irrational beliefs are 'irrational'. In fact, Alloy and Abrahmson (1979) suggest that depressive realists tend to see things for what they are (with normal people tending to view the world through rose-coloured glasses). They found that depressed people gave more accurate estimates of the likelihood of a disaster than 'normal' controls, and called this the 'sadder but wiser' effect.

RESEARCH METHODS Qs No.**6.4**

1 Explain **two** ways that psychologists have investigated the cognitive basis of abnormality.

2 For each of these, describe **one** strength and **one** weakness with the method of investigation.

◀ The cognitive model emphasises the importance of cognitive processing in psychological adjustment. The sleeping dog, whose real nature is unknown, is seen differently by the two cats.

CAN YOU...? No.**6.5**

...1 Identify **six** key pieces of information about the cognitive approach.

...2 Expand these six points into a 100-word *description* of the cognitive approach.

...3 Précis this description into a 50-word *outline*.

...4 Identify **three** limitations of the cognitive approach and then explain each one in detail, using examples.

CASE STUDY

Using the cognitive approach to explain Robert's school phobia

The cognitive view would be that Robert's phobia was a result of the fact that he placed undue emphasis on negative events in his environment and held irrational assumptions about his abilities to cope. An example of his irrational assumptions was his view that his mother's and teacher's approval were all-important. These 'faulty thoughts' prevented him changing his behaviour.

COMMENTARY CORNER

Question: **Outline and evaluate the biological approach to abnormality.** *(12 marks)*

When students are asked to outline and evaluate an explanation of abnormality, one of the favourite kinds of answer would look like this:

- Paragraph 1: AO1 *The biological explanation of abnormality is ...* *(present a description of the approach)*
- Paragraph 2: AO2 *However the cognitive model is different ...(present a description of the biological approach)*

It is fine to evaluate one explanation by contrasting it with one of the other explanations you know, *BUT* this is only creditworthy if you do present a contrast. There is no credit in simply *describing* the second explanation.

In order to achieve this 'contrast' you should ensure that every AO2 sentence starts with (or contains) AO2 phrases similar to those we have given you (see page 43) and is a genuine point of contrast, for example:

- *In contrast with* the biological model, the cognitive model focuses on the influence of the mind. *This is a strength* because it suggests that a person is capable of changing their behaviour rather than being controlled by their biology.
- The biological approach suggests that abnormality is determined internally, *whereas* the behavioural approach cites external causes.

Biological therapies: Drugs and ECT

The biological approach proposes that the cause of psychological disorder lies in underlying physiological processes in the body, so it makes sense for the treatment to be physical. Thus biological therapies target physiological processes, such as the functioning of neurotransmitters, hormones and parts of the brain. The two main examples of biological therapies are chemotherapy (drugs) and electroconvulsive therapy (ECT).

CHEMOTHERAPY (DRUGS)

A quarter of all the medication prescribed in Britain is 'psychiatric drugs' – drugs which modify the working of the brain and affect mood and behaviour (www.sane.org.uk). In the 1950s, two important discoveries changed the outlook for millions of people suffering with mental illness. Antipsychotics were able to control the symptoms of schizophrenia, making it possible to discharge thousands of people from mental hospitals to lead near-normal lives. Another family of drugs discovered around the same time, the *tricyclics*, would help vast numbers of people suffering from depression until the discovery of the SSRIs (selective serotonin re-uptake inhibitors) in the 1980s. The use of these drugs is not restricted to adults either. In 2003, 40,000 children and teenagers in the UK were taking prescribed SSRIs for the treatment of depression

Antipsychotic drugs

Conventional antipsychotics (such as *chlorpromazine*) are used primarily to combat the positive symptoms of schizophrenia. These drugs block the action of the neurotransmitter **dopamine** in the brain by binding to, but not stimulating dopamine receptors (see diagram).

The *atypical* antipsychotic drugs (such as *clozapine*) act by only temporarily occupying dopamine receptors and then rapidly dissociating to allow normal dopamine transmission. This may explain why such atypical antipsychotics have lower levels of side effects (such as *tardive dyskinesia* – involuntary movements of the mouth and tongue) compared to conventional antipsychotics.

Antidepressant drugs

Depression is thought to be due to insufficient amounts of neurotransmitters such as **serotonin** being produced in the nerve endings. In normal brains, neurotransmitters are constantly being released from the nerve endings, stimulating the neighbouring neurons. To terminate their action, neurotransmitters are re-absorbed into the nerve endings or broken down by enzymes. Antidepressants work either by reducing the rate of re-absorption or by blocking the enzyme which breaks down the neurotransmitters. Both of these mechanisms increase the amount of neurotransmitter available to excite neighbouring cells.

The most commonly prescribed antidepressant drugs are the SSRIs. These work by blocking the transporter mechanism that re-absorbs serotonin into the presynaptic cell after it has fired. As a result, more serotonin is left in the synapse, prolonging its activity, and making transmission of the next impulse easier.

Anti-anxiety drugs

See Chapter 4 (page 136) for details of anti-anxiety drugs which are used to treat stress.

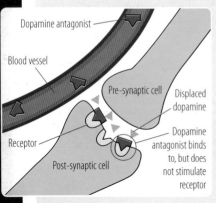

Dopamine antagonist

Blood vessel

Pre-synaptic cell

Displaced dopamine

Receptor

Dopamine antagonist binds to, but does not stimulate receptor

Post-synaptic cell

+ STRENGTHS

Effectiveness

Research evidence indicates that chemotherapies do work. For example, WHO (World Heath Organisation) (2001) reported that relapse rates after one year were highest (55%) when schizophrenics were treated with placebos (a substitute pill with no physiological effects), 25% with chlorpromazine (an antipsychotic) alone and 2%–23% when chlorpromazine was combined with family intervention. This suggests that drugs play an important role, although treatment with drugs alone is less effective than drug treatment *combined with* psychological support.

Ease of use

One of the great appeals of using chemotherapy is that it requires little effort from the user; considerably less than for therapies such as psychoanalysis. In reality, however, many clinicians advocate a mixture of chemotherapy and some form of psychotherapy (Comer, 2002).

− LIMITATIONS

Placebo effects

A significant factor in the effectiveness of drugs may well be their *psychological* effect, as well as their chemical effect. Kirsch *et al.* (2002) reviewed 38 studies of antidepressants and found that patients who received placebos fared almost as well as those getting real drugs. However, other reviews have found rather stronger effects for the real drugs. For example, Mulrow *et al.* (2000) compared the use of tricyclics and placebos in 28 studies and found a success rate of 35% for placebos and 60% for tricyclics.

Tackles symptoms rather than the problem

Drugs only offer temporary alleviation of symptoms. As soon as the patient stops taking the drug, the effectiveness ceases. It may be preferable in the long-term to seek a treatment that addresses the problem itself rather than one that deals only with the symptoms.

Side effects

All chemotherapies have side effects, some more disabling than others. For example SSRIs may cause anxiety, sexual dysfunction, insomnia, nausea and suicidal thoughts – a number of court cases have held drug companies responsible for failing to inform patients about potential aggressive tendencies. For example, in the US in 1998, Donald Schell, 60, killed his wife, daughter and granddaughter and then himself after only two days on Paxil (an SSRI). Surviving family members sued the drug manufacturer and won.

The problem of side effects is one of the main reasons why chemotherapies fail – it leads to patients deciding not to take their medications.

ELECTROCONVULSIVE THERAPY (ECT)

ECT is generally used in severely depressed patients for whom psychotherapy and medication have proved ineffective. It is used when there is a risk of suicide because it often has much quicker results than antidepressant drugs. The National Institute for Clinical Excellence (2003) suggests that ECT should only be used in cases where all other treatments have failed, or when the condition is considered to be potentially life-threatening.

How does it work?

- An electrode is placed above the temple of the non-dominant side of the brain, and a second in the middle of the forehead (unilateral ECT). Alternatively, one electrode is placed above each temple (bilateral ECT).
- The patient is injected with a short-acting barbiturate, so they are unconscious before the electric shock is administered, and given a nerve-blocking agent, paralysing the muscles of the body to prevent them contracting during the treatment and causing fractures. Oxygen is given to the patient to compensate for their inability to breathe.
- A small amount of electric current (approximately 0.6 amps), lasting about half a second, is passed through the brain. This current produces a seizure lasting up to one minute, which affects the entire brain.
- ECT is usually given three times a week, with the patient requiring between 3 and 15 treatments.

Why does it work?

Abrams (1997) has concluded, after studying ECT for 50 years, that we are no closer to understanding why it works. Most researchers agree that ECT causes changes in the way the brain works, but there is disagreement about the exact effects that lead to improvement. In very severe types of depression certain parts of the brain may not work normally, for example different parts of the brain may not be communicating properly with each other. ECT alters the way the chemical messengers (neurotransmitters) are acting in the brain and so helps bring about a recovery.

CAN YOU...? No.**6.6**

All your answers should be about 150 words in length.

...1 Explain how drugs might be used to treat psychological disorders.

...2 Outline **two** strengths and **two** limitations of using drugs to treat a psychological disorder.

...3 Explain how ECT might be used to treat psychological disorders.

...4 Outline **two** strengths and **two** limitations of using ECT to treat a psychological disorder.

 STRENGTHS

ECT can save lives

Supporters of ECT claim it is an effective treatment, particularly for severe depression, which works when other treatments have not. As a result, it can be life-saving, particularly when depression is so severe that it could lead to suicide.

Effectiveness

Comer (2002) states that 60–70% of ECT patients improve after treatment. However, Sackheim *et al.* (2001) found that 84% of the patients they studied relapsed within six months of having ECT.

 LIMITATIONS

Sham ECT

There have been several studies comparing standard ECT with 'sham' ECT, where the patient has exactly the same things done to them, but no electrical current is used and there is no fit. In such studies, patients who had 'real' ECT were much more likely to recover, and did so much quicker than those who had sham treatment. However, a number of the patients receiving sham treatment recovered too, suggesting that the attention received plays an important role in recovery.

Side effects

Possible physical side effects of ECT include impaired memory, cardiovascular changes and headaches (Datto, 2000). Psychological effects may be evident as well. The DOH report (1999) found that among those receiving ECT within the last two years, 30% reported that it had resulted in permanent fear and anxiety.

ETHICS

A meta-analysis of 17 papers covering 134 'testimonies' of ECT patients (Rose *et al.*, 2005) found that approximately half of those who had received ECT felt that they were given insufficient information about the procedure, and approximately a third perceived themselves to have been coerced into having the treatment.

In the UK, patients can be 'sectioned' if a psychiatrist believes that ECT is necessary for the patient's well-being. The term 'sectioned' means 'detained under the relevant section of the Mental Health Act', and refers to the fact that under certain circumstances, patients can be detained and treated without their consent. However, under the amended Mental Health Act (2007), the administration of ECT requires either the patient's consent or a second opinion, *unless* treatment is deemed necessary to save the patient's life or to prevent a serious deterioration in the patient's condition.

KEY TERMS

Dopamine and **serotonin** are both neurotransmitters which have been associated with a number of behaviours. Dopamine is linked to schizophrenia. Low levels of serotonin are related to depression and high levels have been linked to anxiety.

ECT The administration of a controlled electrical current through electrodes placed on the scalp, that induces a convulsive seizure which can be effective in relieving an episode of major depression.

Psychological therapies: Psychoanalysis

Psychological therapies are based on psychological approaches to psychopathology and focus more on the psychological dimensions of behaviour (how people think and feel) than does the biological approach. We have examined three psychological approaches to psychopathology (on pages 186–91) and now will look at one example of a therapy associated with each of these approaches. On this spread we begin with **psychoanalysis** – the therapy developed by Sigmund Freud to make the unconscious conscious and thus deal with the causes of abnormal behaviour.

PSYCHOANALYSIS

Repression and the unconscious mind

As a therapy, psychoanalysis is based on the idea that individuals are unaware of the many factors that cause their behaviour, emotions and general mental health. Some of these factors operate at an unconscious level, and are the result of repressed memories or unresolved conflicts from childhood. During psychoanalysis, the therapist attempts to trace these unconscious factors to their origins and then helps the individual to deal with them. The therapist uses a variety of different techniques to uncover repressed material and help the client deal with it.

Free association

One such technique is known as free association, in which the patient expresses thoughts exactly as they occur, even though they may seem unimportant or irrelevant. Freud believed that the value of free association lies in the fact that these associations are determined by unconscious factors which analysis tries to uncover. This procedure is designed to reveal areas of conflict and to bring into consciousness memories that have been repressed. The therapist helps interpret these for the patient, who corrects, rejects, and adds further thoughts and feelings.

Therapist interpretation

Therapists listen carefully as their patients talk, looking for clues and drawing tentative conclusions about the possible cause(s) of the problem. Patients may initially offer resistance to the therapist's interpretations (e.g. changing the subject to avoid a painful discussion), or may even display *transference*, where they recreate feelings and conflicts and transfer these onto the therapist (e.g. acting towards the therapist as if he were the despised parent).

Working through

Psychoanalysis is not a brief form of therapy. Patients tend to meet up with the therapist four or five times a week. Together the patient and therapist examine the same issues over and over again, sometimes over a period of years, in an attempt to gain greater clarity concerning the causes of their neurotic behaviour.

STRENGTHS

Effectiveness

Bergin (1971) analysed the data from 10,000 patient histories and estimated that 80% benefited from psychoanalysis compared to 65% from eclectic therapies (therapies based on a number of different approaches). Bergin concluded that this is modest support for psychoanalysis.

Length of treatment

Tschuschke *et al.* (2007) carried out one of the largest studies investigating long-term psychodynamic treatment. More than 450 patients were included in the study, which showed that the longer psychotherapeutic treatments took, the better the outcomes were.

LIMITATIONS

Theoretical weaknesses

Psychoanalysis is based on Freud's theory of personality; if that is flawed then the explanations of mental illness arising from this theory must be flawed and the therapy itself must be flawed. Eysenck (1986) argued that '…the obvious failure of Freudian therapy to significantly improve on spontaneous remission or placebo treatment is the clearest proof we have of the inadequacy of Freudian theory'.

Appropriateness

Freud failed to appreciate the differences between individuals in the way that modern psychotherapists do. The development of humanistic or person-centred approaches addressed this problem by putting the client first, rather than imposing specific theories on them.

False memories

Critics of psychoanalysis claim that some therapists are not helping patients to recover *repressed* memories, but are (often unwittingly) planting 'false memories' of sexual abuse or alien abduction. All psychoanalysis assumes that a patient can reliably recall early memories that have been repressed, yet there is little evidence to support this (Loftus, 1995).

ETHICS

Psychoanalysis is potentially fraught with ethical problems. These include the stress of *insight*, as painful memories are brought into the conscious mind; the controversy of *false memories* (see right) and the issue of '*forced termination*', where the therapist must break off from a therapeutic relationship before a client is ready for it. Forced termination may leave clients feeling bereft and provoke a range of negative reactions.

► We looked at the case of Anna O. on page 187, which was Freud's first record of psychoanalysis. Freud introduced the notion that mental illness may have a psychological cause and thus also introduced the idea that treatment should be psychological (Anna O. called it the 'talking cure'). In this sense, psychoanalysis was a trailblazer for all psychotherapies.

...1 Outline how psychoanalysis is used to treat psychological disorders. Your answer should be about 150–200 words and you should identify about **six** key points.

...2 Outline **two** strengths and **two** limitations of using psychoanalysis to treat a psychological disorder.

DO IT YOURSELF   No.**6.5**

Many students are somewhat dismissive of Freudian psychology. Perhaps the following activity – *The Story of Your Life* – may be convincing.

Freud thought that making sense of our past – especially, the events of our childhood – would help us to resolve present conflicts and open up more possibilities for ourselves in the future. Write a short story about yourself. The story should show you in the past, the present, and the future. Include:

- a scene from your early childhood
- a scene about a conflict in your current life, and
- a scene from your imagined future in which the conflict is resolved and elements of the first two scenes are also present.

You may present the scenes in the story in any order you choose. You might then share your story with other students and consider what you learned from the exercise.

Did you make unconscious thoughts and feelings conscious? Do you think this may be helpful? If so, in what way? Has the task changed what you think about psychoanalysis?

COMMENTARY CORNER

Throughout this book we have constantly emphasised the need to fit answers for purpose with regard to exam questions. This very important skill can make all the difference in an examination. All questions set very specific tasks. Rather than throw everything possible in the general direction of a question and hope some of it sticks, it is best to tailor your response to fit the exact requirements of the question.

Consider the following questions – how would you respond to each?

1 Outline how psychoanalysis is used to treat psychological disorders. *(6 marks)*

2 Outline **two** strengths and **two** limitations of using psychoanalysis to treat a psychological disorder. *(6 marks)*

3 Give **one** strength and **one** limitation of using psychoanalysis to treat a psychological disorder. *(3 marks + 3 marks)*

4 Outline and evaluate how psychoanalysis is used to treat psychological disorders. *(12 marks)*

5 Outline and evaluate how psychoanalysis is used to treat psychological disorders. *(8 marks)*

6 Helen is referred to a psychoanalyst to try to cure her fear of commitment in personal relationships. Explain how her analyst might approach this problem. *(6 marks)*

You should have noticed that there is a theme in these questions. At the most you need 150 words of AO1 (Questions 1 and 4) and 150 words of AO2 (Questions 2, 3 and 4). Question 5 requires you to *précis* your Question 4 answer even further, and Question 6 may just leave you bemused – it is actually fairly straightforward. For example:

- What is Helen's 'presenting problem', i.e. why has she been referred for treatment?
- What would the analyst assume was going on, e.g. unconscious forces affecting her behaviour, perhaps a childhood rejection?
- What technique(s) might the analyst employ to 'get at' these unconscious factors, e.g. free association, interpretation?

How do you know if a treatment is effective?

There are many difficulties in evaluating the effectiveness of any treatment for psychological disorders.

First, mental illnesses have psychological symptoms. This means that, in order to evaluate treatments, one needs to measure things like moods, thoughts and unconscious feelings that are not easily quantifiable.

Second is the problem of defining success in this context. It could be measured in terms of various achievements of the patient, including: being able to live at home rather than in an institution; being able to hold down a regular job; being less violent; or feeling happier. Different psychiatrists and different patients have different ideas about what constitutes a successful therapy.

Third, there are difficulties in generalising from research to individual patients. Research is conducted with one group of participants (such as American housewives) and may not apply to other groups or individuals. One drug may have different effects on different individuals. There are also difficulties in generalising from the application of one particular therapy to other instances of the same therapy. Two psychoanalysts may practise the same therapy but in different ways – some may be 'warmer' than others, some talk more, some listen more.

The Dodo bird effect

'But who has won?' This question the Dodo could not answer without a great deal of thought. At last the Dodo said, 'Everybody has won, and all must have prizes.' Alice's Adventures in Wonderland.

Rosenzweig (1936) proposed that there were so many common factors in various different psychotherapies that only small differences would be found when comparing different ones. The commonalities include being able to talk to a sympathetic person which may enhance self-esteem and having an opportunity to express one's thoughts (Sloane et al., 1975). Luborsky et al. (1975, 2002) reviewed over 100 different studies that compared different therapies and did find that there were only small differences.

Such small differences may occur because of difficulties in comparing treatments (Howard et al., 1997). It is also the case that interaction effects between patient qualities and treatment types may reduce effects. For example an introvert personality may do better using one kind of therapy than an extravert, and when treatments were chosen to match patients' personalities, larger effects were reported (Blatt and Ford, 1994).

Psychological therapies: Systematic desensitisation and Cognitive Behavioural Therapy

Altogether this book covers three psychological approaches to psychopathology – psychodynamic, behavioural and cognitive. On the previous spread we looked at psychoanalysis, the method derived from Freud's psychodynamic approach. On this final spread we will look at one therapy for each of the remaining two psychological approaches. Systematic desensitisation is derived from the behavioural approach and is based on classical conditioning. Rational-emotive behaviour therapy (REBT) is a classic example of a cognitive behavioural therapy. In Chapter 4 we covered another cognitive therapy – stress inoculation training (SIT).

Can SD help with your exam anxiety?

If you don't study much, then your anxiety is the result of not knowing the material. If you do know the material but still develop anxiety in exam situations, then SD may be used to desensitise yourself to performance fears.

SYSTEMATIC DESENSITISATION (SD)

An individual might learn that their feared stimulus is not so fearful after all – if only they could re-experience the feared stimulus, but the anxiety it creates blocks such recovery. This is overcome by introducing the feared stimulus *gradually*. This type of behaviour therapy is based on the principle of *counterconditioning* (i.e. teaching a behaviour that is incompatible with the fear response). First developed by Joseph Wolpe in the 1950s, **systematic desensitisation** (SD) enables individuals to overcome their anxieties by learning to relax in the presence of stimuli that had once made them unbearably nervous and afraid. The two responses of relaxation and fear are incompatible and the fear is eventually dispelled.

Use of systematic desensitisation

In the early days of SD, patients would learn to confront their feared situations directly. They would gradually overcome their fears by learning to relax in the presence of objects or images that would normally arouse anxiety. In more recent years, however, rather than actually presenting the feared stimulus, the therapist asks the subject to *imagine* the presence of it.

SD is particularly useful for treating psychological problems in which anxiety is the main difficulty – behaviour therapists will often use this procedure when treating patients with phobias, shyness and related problems. It has also been used in the treatment of fear of flying.

How does it work?

▲ **Problem** – Patient is terrified whenever she sees a spider.

▼ **Result** – After SD, patient has overcome her fear of spiders and feels relaxed in their presence.

Step 1: Patient is taught how to relax their muscles completely. (A relaxed state is incompatible with anxiety.)

Step 2: Therapist and patient together construct a desensitisation hierarchy – a series of imagined scenes, each one causing a little more anxiety than the previous one.

Step 3: Patient gradually works his/her way through desensitisation hierarchy, visualising each anxiety-evoking event while engaging in the competing relaxation response.

Step 4: Once the patient has mastered one step in the hierarchy (i.e. they can remain relaxed while imagining it), they are ready to move onto the next.

Step 5: Patient eventually masters the feared situation that caused them to seek help in the first place.

Other therapies associated with the behavioural model

There are a variety of therapies derived from classical conditioning, operant condition and also social learning theory, including:

Token economy (operant conditioning) aims to reward desirable behaviours with tokens which can then be exchanged for rewards. This can be used to teach patients to look after themselves; rewards are given for things like dressing oneself and making one's own bed.

Modelling (social learning) involves watching a therapist cope in a situation such as handling a feared object, and then imitating the behaviour.

CAN YOU...?   No.6.8

...1 Outline how systematic desensitisation is used to treat psychological disorders. Your answer should be about 150–200 words and you should identify about **six** key points.

...2 Outline **two** strengths and **two** limitations of using SD to treat a psychological disorder.

...3 Answer the same questions for REBT.

⊕ STRENGTHS

Appropriateness

Behavioural therapies in general are quick and require less effort on the patient's part than other psychotherapies where patients must play a more active part in their treatment. Behavioural therapies may be the only treatments possible for certain groups of people, for example for some individuals with severe learning difficulties.

Effectiveness

Research has found that SD is successful for a range of anxiety disorders. For example, about 75% of patients with phobias respond to SD (McGrath *et al.*, 1990). Capafóns *et al.* (1998) reported that when used with aerophobics (who have a fear of flying) those who had undergone SD reported lower levels of fear (compared to a control group) *and* lower physiological signs of fear during a flight simulation.

⊖ LIMITATIONS

The problem of symptom substitution

SD may *appear* to resolve a problem but simply eliminating or suppressing symptoms may result in other symptoms appearing (called *symptom substitution*). Langevin (1983), however, claims that there is no evidence to support this objection.

Reduced effectiveness for some phobias

Öhman *et al.* (1975) suggest that SD may not be as effective in treating anxieties that have an underlying evolutionary survival component (e.g. fear of the dark, fear of heights or fear of dangerous animals) than in treating phobias that have been acquired as a result of personal experience.

COGNITIVE BEHAVIOURAL THERAPY: REBT

Rational-Emotive Therapy (RET) was developed by Albert Ellis (1957), whose ideas were discussed on page 190. It is based on the idea that many problems are actually the result of irrational thinking. Individuals frequently develop self-defeating habits because of faulty beliefs about themselves and the world around them. RET (recently renamed **REBT** – rational-emotive behaviour therapy) helps the client understand this irrationality and the consequences of thinking in this way. It then helps them substitute more effective problem-solving methods. REBT is used in a wide variety of situations where the therapist believes the underlying problem lies in the unrealistic beliefs that individuals have about themselves and their behaviours.

How does it work?

According to the cognitive model of abnormality, our beliefs are the main influence behind our emotional well-being. Irrational beliefs, experienced as self-defeating thoughts, are disruptive and lead to unproductive outcomes. REBT tries to change these self-defeating thoughts and so make people happier and less anxious about life.

Negative Event (A)	Negative Event (A)
↓	↓
Rational Belief (B)	Irrational Belief (B)
↓	↓
Healthy Negative Emotion (C)	Unhealthy Negative Emotion (C)

Challenging irrational beliefs

Because it is not the activating events themselves that cause unproductive consequences, REBT focuses on the self-defeating beliefs that accompany them. During therapy, the patient is encouraged to *dispute* these beliefs:

- *Logical disputing* – self-defeating beliefs do not follow logically from the information available (e.g. 'Does thinking this way make sense?').
- *Empirical disputing* – self-defeating beliefs may not be consistent with reality (e.g. 'Where is the proof that this belief is accurate?').
- *Pragmatic disputing* – emphasises the lack of usefulness of self-defeating beliefs (e.g. 'How is this belief likely to help me?').

Effective disputing changes self-defeating beliefs into more rational beliefs. The individual can move from catastrophising ('I have really let down my family – I am a complete loser') to more rational interpretations of events ('I may have failed but if I work harder, next time I'll nail it'). This in turn helps them to feel better, and eventually become more self-accepting.

Dr. Albert Ellis demonstrated his approach to therapy until recently when he died aged 93. Every Friday night he held lively sessions with audience volunteers at the Albert Ellis Institute in New York – for ONLY $5.00 – including cookies and coffee!

DO IT YOURSELF

No.**6.6**

1. Think of some situations where a person might display irrational thought processes.
2. Identify the *activating event, self-defeating thoughts*, and *consequences* of this irrational thinking.
3. How might REBT be used to change this irrational thinking and bring about more productive consequences for the individual?

KEY TERMS

Systematic desensitisation a form of cognitive behavioural therapy used to treat phobias and other behaviour problems involving anxiety. A client is gradually exposed to (or imagines) the threatening situation under relaxed conditions until the anxiety reaction is extinguished.

REBT a cognitive behavioural treatment that helps people change dysfunctional emotions and behaviours by making them aware of self-defeating beliefs and then modifying these in order to remove the unwanted states.

➕ STRENGTHS

Effectiveness

REBT has generally done well in outcome studies (i.e. studies designed to measure responses to treatment). For example, in a meta-analysis Engels *et al.* (1993) concluded that REBT is an effective treatment for a number of different types of disorder, including obsessive-compulsive disorders and social phobia.

Appropriateness

A particular strength of REBT is that it is not only useful for clinical populations (i.e. people suffering from mental disorders or phobias), but it is also useful for non-clinical populations (e.g., people who might suffer from lack of assertiveness or examination anxiety).

➖ LIMITATIONS

Irrational environments

REBT fails to address the very important issue that the irrational environments in which clients exist continue beyond the therapeutic situation, e.g. marriages with bullying partners, or jobs with overly critical bosses. As a result, these environments continue to produce and reinforce irrational thoughts and maladaptive behaviours.

Not suitable for all

Like all psychotherapies, REBT does not always work, and it is not always what people want. Ellis believed that sometimes people who *claimed* to be following REBT principles were not putting their revised beliefs into action. In other cases, people simply do not want the direct sort of advice that REBT practitioners tend to dispense.

THE JACKMANS

Clare's fear of flying means that the family can't take foreign holidays together. She decides enough is enough and seeks help.

1. How could SD help Clare with her fear of flying?
2. How could REBT help Clare with her fear of flying?

⚖ ETHICS

Disputing irrational beliefs is the most commonly used therapeutic strategy in REBT. However, very little attention has been given to the unique ethical problems that arise when REBT therapists treat devoutly religious clients. Disputing what appears to be an irrational belief *to the therapist* may create moral problems for the client for whom this 'irrational' belief is based on fundamental religious faith.

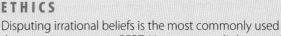

We have identified here the key points of the topics on the AQA (A) AS specification, i.e. the bare minimum that you need to know. You may want to fill in further details to elaborate and personalise this material.

DEFINING AND EXPLAINING PSYCHOLOGICAL ABNORMALITY

DEFINITIONS OF ABNORMALITY

DEVIATION FROM SOCIAL NORMS

- Standards of acceptable behaviour are set by a social group (i.e. social norms).
- Anything that deviates from acceptable behaviour is considered 'abnormal'.
- What is acceptable may change over time.

LIMITATIONS
- Susceptible to abuse e.g. excluding nonconformists or political dissenters.
- Deviance is hard to identify because it is related to context and degree.
- Cultural relativism – DSM includes culture-bound syndromes, acknowledging cultural differences in what is considered 'normal'.

FAILURE TO FUNCTION ADEQUATELY

- Not being able to cope with the demands of everyday life e.g. go to work, eat in public, wash clothes.
- Abnormal behaviour interferes with day-to-day living.
- Individual judges when their behaviour becomes 'abnormal'.

LIMITATIONS
- Who judges? Patient may feel quite content even when their behaviour is clearly dysfunctional.
- Apparently dysfunctional behaviour may sometimes be adaptive e.g. depression elicits help from others.
- Cultural relativism – what is considered 'adequate' differs from culture to culture, so may result in different diagnoses when applied across cultures.

DEVIATION FROM IDEAL MENTAL HEALTH

- Jahoda suggested using the same criteria as for physical illness i.e. absence of signs of health.
- Six categories: self-attitudes, self-actualisation, integration, autonomy, accurate perception of reality, mastery of environment.

LIMITATIONS
- A matter of degree – few people experience all these positive criteria, therefore would be considered 'abnormal'.
- Mental illnesses do not always have physical causes, so are not the same as physical illness.
- Cultural relativism – Jahoda's criteria reflect individualist cultural ideals, e.g. autonomy.

TREATING ABNORMALITY

BIOLOGICAL THERAPIES

DIFFERENCES IN ATTACHMENT

CHEMOTHERAPY

- Conventional antipsychotics used to combat the positive symptoms of schizophrenia. They work by blocking the action of dopamine in the brain.
- Antidepressants increase availability of serotonin e.g. blocking its re-absorption (SSRIs).
- Anti-anxiety drugs e.g. BZs increase effect of GABA.

STRENGTHS
- Effective e.g. better than placebos in treatment of schizophrenia (WHO).
- Relatively easy to use.
- Best used in conjunction with psychotherapy.

LIMITATIONS
- Some studies show placebo just as effective, e.g. Kirsch et al.
- Tackles symptoms not problem, so not a cure.
- Side effects, e.g. SSRIs linked to anxiety or increased aggression.

ECT

- Used for severe depression.
- Unconscious, relaxed patient given 0.6 amps for ½ sec → seizure.
- 3–15 treatments.
- Unilateral or bilateral.
- Not clear why it works, may alter action of neurotransmitters.

STRENGTHS
- Can prevent suicide.
- Effective – 60–70% patients improve (Comer), though Sackheim claims 84% relapse within 6 months.

LIMITATIONS
- Some patients recover even with 'sham' ECT suggesting extra attention important.
- Side effects, e.g. memory loss.

ETHICS
- 50% of patients not well-informed about procedure.

PSYCHOANALYSIS

- Seeks to recover repressed memories or unresolved conflicts.

Techniques:
- Free association.
- Therapist interpretation.
- Working through.

 STRENGTHS
- Bergin analysed 10,000 records, 80% success.
- Longer treatments have better outcome (Tschuschke et al.).

LIMITATIONS
- Based on psychoanalytic theory, but theory is flawed.
- Fails to acknowledge individual differences, imposing same theory on all.
- 'Repressed' memories likely to be false (Loftus).

ETHICS
- Stress from insights, problem of false memories and forced termination.

SD

Systematic desensitisation
- Gradual exposure to feared stimulus.
- Based on counterconditioning.

Steps
- Learn relaxation.
- Construct desensitisation hierarchy.
- Visualise each event while relaxing.
- Work through hierarchy.
- Eventually master fear.

 STRENGTHS
- Quick and requires relatively little effort.
- Useful for e.g. people with learning difficulties.
- 75% recovery for phobics when treated with SD (Capafóns et al.).

LIMITATIONS
- Deals with symptoms not cause – may lead to symptom substitution.
- May be less effective for 'ancient fears' such as fear of the dark.

REBT

Rational-Emotive Behaviour Therapy (Ellis), a form of CBT (Cognitive Behaviour Therapy)
- Irrational beliefs are experienced as self-defeating thoughts.
- Challenge thinking using logical, empirical and/or pragmatic disputing.
- Patient moves from catastrophising to more rational thinking.

STRENGTHS
- More effective than drugs alone.
- Useful for clinical and non-clinical groups.

 LIMITATIONS
- Doesn't address influence of external environment.
- Not suitable for all – e.g. some may reject its direct challenges.

 ETHICS
- May create moral conflicts e.g. people with strong religious convictions.

BIOLOGICAL APPROACH

PSYCHOLOGICAL APPROACHES TO PSYCHOPATHOLOGY

THE MEDICAL MODEL

PSYCHODYNAMIC

BEHAVIOURAL

COGNITIVE

Biological assumptions
- Bodily systems used to explain behaviour.
- Mental disorder explained in terms of malfunctioning of biological systems.
- 'Medical model' because mental disorder regarded and treated like physical illness.

Abnormality caused by physical factors
- Genes – effects demonstrated through high concordance rates for mental disorders in identical twins.
- Traits inherited because at one time may have been adaptive.
- Neurotransmitters associated with mental disorder, e.g. serotonin and depression.
- Viral infection in the womb, e.g. Torrey identified link between influenza and schizophrenia.

⊖ **LIMITATIONS**
- Concept of mental illness invented as a form of social control (Szasz).
- Causal model not supported by individual differences, e.g. many schizophrenics have high levels of dopamine, but some don't.
- No evidence of 100% concordance rates for MZ twins, e.g. Gottesman and Shields estimate 50% for schizophrenia.
- Diathesis-stress model can explain role of biology and experience.

RESEARCH METHODS
- Experiments used to test effect of drugs, and therefore support causal role of neurotransmitters.
- Correlation, e.g. twin or family studies to produce concordance rates.

 CULTURAL SIMILARITIES
- Depression found universally, supporting evolutionary view that it is inherited and linked to once-adaptive behaviour.

Psychodynamic assumptions
- Individual's abnormal behaviour determined by underlying psychological conflicts of which they are largely unaware.
- Freud was first to propose psychological causes for mental illness.

Abnormality caused by unconscious, psychological factors
- Unresolved conflicts between id, ego and superego result in ego defeces (e.g. repression), which may be expressed as mental disorder if used excessively.
- Early experiences, e.g. traumas, can lead to later disorders.
- Behaviour is unconsciously motivated.

⊖ **LIMITATIONS**
- Abstract concepts, e.g. id, ego, difficult to define and research.
- Sexism – theory less well developed for women in part because of historical background. Modern psychoanalysis has addressed this.
- Difficult to prove or disprove the theory, and theory lends itself to turning apparent disproof into support because of the action of defence mechanisms.

RESEARCH METHODS
- Case studies, e.g. Little Hans and Anna O., give rich amount of detail but lack generalisability.
- Experiments – Fisher and Greenberg reviewed over 2,500 experimental studies of Freudian hypotheses, – many received receiving experimental support.

Behavioural assumptions
- All behaviour is learned.
- Maladaptive behaviours are acquired in the same way.

Abnormality caused by learning
- Strict behaviourists believe that only behaviour is important – not thoughts or feelings.
- Classical conditioning – learning as a result of association.
- Operant conditioning – learning as a result of the consequences of behaviour.
- Social learning – observation and vicarious rewards.
- Learning environments reinforce problematic behaviours, e.g. avoidant behaviour lowers anxiety and therefore is rewarding.

⊖ **LIMITATIONS**
- Limited view of factors that cause mental disorder, cognitive behavioural therapies include the role of thought.
- Explanation flawed, e.g. not everyone with a phobia can identify a time when this was experienced and learned.
- Some phobias more likely to develop than others – biological preparedness a key factor rather than just learning.
- 'Symptom substitution' suggests that although symptoms of a disorder may be behavioural, causes may not be.

RESEARCH METHODS
- Experiments easily done because focus is on observable behaviours, can demonstrate the importance of consequences.
- Animal studies used to generalise to human behaviour.

Cognitive assumptions
- The mind is like a computer – processes information.
- Problems arise in the way an individual thinks about the world.

Abnormality caused by faulty thinking
- Cognitive distortions include: structures, content, processes and products.
- Ellis – ABC model (activating event, belief, consequence).
- Rational beliefs → healthy consequences.
- Irrational beliefs → unhealthy emotions.
- The individual is in control of their thoughts, therefore abnormality is the result of faulty control.

⊖ **LIMITATIONS**
- Blames individual rather than situational factors, so real causes may be overlooked.
- Way of thinking may be an effect rather than a cause, e.g. depressed thinking may occur because of depression.
- Faulty thinking may not be a cause but a vulnerability factor.
- Irrational beliefs may be realistic, Alloy and Abrahamson found that depressives were more realistic thinkers.

RESEARCH METHODS
- Experiments, e.g. Thase et al. compared effects of CT to effects of drugs.
- Meta-analysis – e.g. Smith and Glass combined results from many studies to show effectiveness of CT.

End-of-chapter review

REVISION QUESTIONS

There are lots of ideas at the end of other chapters that you might adapt and try out here.

DEFINITIONS OF ABNORMALITY

ACTIVITY 1 pages 178–81

Task 1 Whose limitation?

At the start of this chapter we described three ways to define abnormality: deviation from social norms, failure to function adequately, and deviation from ideal mental health. We also outlined limitations for each of these, some of which are listed below. Identify which definition is linked with each limitation. Sometimes you may identify more than one definition for a limitation.

Limitation	Definition
Who judges what is adequate?	
They are ideal criteria.	
Cultural relativism.	
Attitudes change over time.	
Some abnormal behaviours may actually be adaptive.	
Judgements are related to context.	
Criteria for mental health not the same as those for physical health.	

Task 2 Fill in the blanks

The blanks below have no fixed answers and require one or more words.

One way to define abnormality is in terms of deviation from social norms. Social norms are _____ _____ set by the social group. One example of social deviance is _____. This is socially deviant because _____ _____.

Another way to define abnormality is the failure to function adequately. This refers to how people function everyday, for example _____.

The third deviation of abnormality is deviation from ideal mental health, proposed by _____. Two examples of ideal mental criteria are _____ and _____.

Task 3 Hannibal Lecter

It is clear that Hannibal Lecter's behaviour, as portrayed in the film *Silence of the Lambs*, is abnormal. He ate people. But why is this abnormal? Work in groups and discuss how the three definitions for abnormality fit Hannibal's behaviour. Is it abnormal?

Select some other cases of abnormality and see how the definitions cope with behaviour you would regard as abnormal.

You could also try discussing other examples of behaviours which might count as abnormal using the three definitions, but which you do not regard as abnormal.

Share your ideas with other class members.

Task 4 Concept map

Draw a diagram like the one on the right (except a lot larger). Each circle represents one of the definitions you have studied. Within the circle list the key points of the definition (keep them brief). Draw spokes from the circle and record three limitations of the definition.

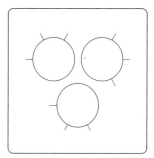

THE BIOLOGICAL AND PSYCHOLOGICAL APPROACHES TO PSYCHOPATHOLOGY

ACTIVITY 2 pages 182–91

Task 1 Similarities and differences

It isn't easy to work out similarities and differences but it helps make you think more carefully about each approach, so give it a go. However make sure you actually identify a difference rather than just stating two aspects of each approach. For example, this is a rather weak attempt: 'The psychodynamic approach uses concepts such as the id and ego whereas the behavioural approach uses conditioning.'

We are looking for something rather more earth-shattering, 'The psychodynamic approach is concerned with the way behaviour is motivated by underlying unconscious feelings whereas the behavioural approach is not concerned with feelings at all but just focuses on how people behave'.

Identify **one** similarity and **one** difference between

- The biological and the psychological approach.
- The psychodynamic and the behavioural approach.
- The psychodynamic and the cognitive approach.
- The behavioural and the cognitive approach.

Task 2 Which research method?

For each of the research methods listed below, state the approach(es) that would be most likely to use it, and give an example.

- Correlational study
- Case study
- Meta-analysis
- Experiment
- Animal studies

Task 3 Psychology in action

A phobia is an illogical, persistent fear reaction to an object or situation, accompanied by a need to flee or avoid whatever is feared.

Ivan has a phobia of driving. As soon as he gets in a car he feels overwhelmed with panic though he can usually manage to cope with short journeys. Sometimes, however, his feelings become so intense that he has been known to try to jump out of the car while it is moving.

(a) Use each of the four approaches you have studied to explain how Ivan's phobia might have developed.
(b) For each explanation you have provided, describe at least one weakness of the explanation.
(c) For each explanation briefly outline how psychologists might conduct research to test whether it is true.

BIOLOGICAL THERAPIES

ACTIVITY 3 pages 192–3

Task 1 Psychology in action

A friend of Tom's has been very depressed and goes to the doctor for help. The doctor prescribes a course of anti-depressants, but Tom is concerned about this. He knows from his psychology course that there are advantages and disadvantages to using drug therapies. What advice do you think he should give to his friend?

1 Discuss the pros and cons with some classmates and then share your ideas with the class.
2 What alternative treatment might you suggest?
3 What are the relative advantage(s) and disadvantage(s) of this method?

Task 2 True or false

Below are some statements about ECT. Which ones are true?

Statements	T or F?
ECT is only done unilaterally.	
Two electrodes are placed on either side of a person's head.	
The electrical current that is applied is moderately strong (about 6 amps).	
The duration of the shock lasts for about half a second.	
Patients are usually given ECT once a week.	
The reason why ECT works is not known.	

PSYCHOLOGICAL THERAPIES

ACTIVITY 4 pages 194–7

Task 1 All mixed up

Below are eight sentences describing systematic densensitisation – except they're all mixed up. Copy the sentences on small slips of paper and try to re-arrange them so they make better sense. Note that there is no 'right' answer and it might be interesting to compare your efforts with someone else's.

- The patient visualises the anxiety-provoking event while trying to relax.
- Patient taught to relax muscles completely.
- Each scene causes slightly more anxiety than the previous one.
- Mastery of each step in the hierarchy is achieved when the patient can remain relaxed when imagining the feared object.
- The patient finally masters the feared situation that caused them to seek help.
- The patient gradually works his/her way through the desensitisation hierarchy.
- Once the patient has mastered one step in the hierarchy, he/she is ready to move on to the next.
- Therapist and patient construct a desensitisation hierarchy.

(You can try the same activity yourself with some of the other descriptions of therapies – you jumble the sentences up and give them to a partner to unjumble.)

Task 2 Approaches and treatments

The _____ approach suggests that all abnormal behaviour is learned. However this approach is based on research with _____, which means that we may not be able to generalise it to human behaviour. The approach has given rise to successful therapies such as _____ , though it can be argued that this method does not treat the _____ , and thus may result in symptom substitution.

By contrast, the _____ approach suggests that some abnormal behaviour may be inherited, or that certain conditions may lead to abnormal levels of _____ and/or _____. One of the difficulties with these explanations is that people who are genetically identical never have a concordance rate of _____ , which means that abnormal behaviour can't just be caused by genes.

The _____ model proposes that abnormal behaviour can be explained in terms of unconscious motives and _____. This approach is based on research with _____, which means it may not be as relevant today. The treatment derived from this approach is _____ , which involves, for example, the use of _____. One criticism of this method of treatment is that it _____.

The _____ approach emphasises the role of thinking in abnormal behaviour, for example a person may _____. An example of a therapy that uses these principles is _____. Both the explanations and treatment have been criticised, because they suggest that _____ is responsible for the illness rather than, for example, a disorder that has been inherited.

Task 3 Compare and contrast

In what ways are biological and psychological therapies different? Draw up a table like the one below and list characteristics of each kind of therapy. In the third column state what the criterion is for comparison. The first one has been done for you. You can include similarities as well as differences. Work in small groups and see which group can come up with the best list.

Biological therapies	Psychological therapies	Difference or similarity criterion
1 Based on biological assumptions i.e. psychopathology is caused by biological factors such as hormones, neurotransmitters, brain structures and genes.	Based on psychological assumptions i.e. psychopathology is caused by psychological factors such as the way people think and feel.	Underlying assumptions are different.
2		
3		

End-of-chapter review

The Unit 2 exam is divided into three sections. Section C is Individual Differences. The actual number of questions is not fixed but there are likely to be about four or five in this section and you must answer all of them. The number of marks available for Individual Differences will always be the same – 24 marks; four of these marks will be in a question or questions related to research methods. There may be an extended writing question (see the final question) in this section of the exam but this will not always be the case.

---

1 There are three statements below. Each one is a central assumption of one of the psychological approaches to psychopathology.

A   All behaviour is learned.

B   It's what you think that counts.

C   Unconscious thoughts affect behaviour.

Match the statements to the approaches listed below. *(2 marks)*

Psychodynamic approach _____

Behavioural approach _____

Cognitive approach _____

Alice's answer

A: *Behavioural*   B: *Cognitive*   C: *Psychodynamic*

Tom's answer

A: *'All behaviour is learned' is the behavioural approach to psychopathology.*

B: *It's what you think that counts is the cognitive approach to psychopathology.*

C: *'Unconscious thoughts affect behaviour' is the psychodynamic approach to psychopathology.*

Examiner's comments

Both students have got the correct three answers and thus gain full marks, but what a lot of time Tom has wasted. You don't gain marks for the amount you write. In fact it is often the case that the less you write, the more marks you will receive! This is because students who are confident in their knowledge focus on what is specifically required and don't worry that they have not given enough information. They know when it is necessary to provide extra detail and when it isn't. In any case Tom hasn't provided extra *detail*, he has just wasted valuable time.

Both Alice and Tom received **2 out of 2 marks**.

---

2 One method that is used to treat abnormality is the use of drugs.

Describe how psychologists have investigated the effectiveness of this method of treating abnormality. *(4 marks)*

Alice's answer

Psychologists have mostly used experiments to investigate the effectiveness of drugs. One type of experiment used in this way is the outcome study, where one group of patients is given a particular type of drug (e.g. an antidepressant) and another control group given a placebo treatment. The groups are then compared to see which shows the greater improvement in their condition.

Tom's answer

The best way of doing this is to use an experiment. In an experiment psychologists can test the effect of an independent variable (e.g. alcohol or coffee) on a dependent variable (i.e. a change in behaviour). This is the only way of testing whether there is a cause and effect relationship between these two variables.

Examiner's comments

Alice and Tom have identified the same method – the use of experiments – but Tom has fallen into the all-too-common trap of simply giving a general description of what is involved in conducting an experiment. Nowhere has he linked this to the investigation of drugs as an effective therapy. He might have said that the IVs were antidepressants and placebos and thus offered some context for his answer. As it stands his answer is almost worthless; he would receive **1 out of 4 marks**. His answer shows lots of knowledge and understanding about experiments – but that wasn't the question.

Alice, on the other hand, gains maximum marks by providing a detailed and well-informed description of exactly how psychologists investigate the effectiveness of drugs, **4 out of 4 marks**.

---

3 Marcus is a man in his twenties. In the last few months he has become withdrawn and depressed. He finds it difficult to get himself to work and when he comes home he just goes to bed.

(a) Identify **one** definition of abnormality and use this to explain in what way Marcus' behaviour is abnormal. *(3 marks)*

(b) Identify **one** other definition of abnormality and give **one** limitation of this definition. *(3 marks)*

Alice's answer

(a) The failure to function properly definition might explain Marcus' behaviour as being a failure to function properly. Most people would not behave in this way, as they would expect to be able to do things like have fun and look after themselves. Marcus doesn't seem able to do this.

(b) Another definition is deviation from social norms. One limitation is that such a definition is culturally relative. It is related to the cultural definition of behaviour and these are different in different cultures.

Tom's answer

(a) Marcus' behaviour can be explained by the deviation from ideal mental health definition. This suggests that a number of things are necessary for ideal mental health and some of these (e.g. being able to function at work and in interpersonal relations) seem to be absent from his behaviour.

(a) The deviation from social norms, one limitation is cultural relativism. A diagnosis may be different for the same person in two different cultures because social norms are influenced by social factors. This means that any definition according to social norms is not universal.

Examiner's comments

In part (a) our students have selected different definitions though each one is perfectly acceptable. And both of them have provided a clear and detailed account of how the definition would explain in what way Marcus' behaviour is abnormal. Therefore they each would both receive **3 out of 3 marks**.

Alice has not done quite as well for part (b). Like Tom she has identified the same alternative definition (deviation from social norms) and the same limitation (cultural relativism), but her explanation of this is rather muddled and repetitive. It is not clear, from what she says, that she really understands what cultural relativism is about. So **2 out of 3 marks** for Alice, whereas Tom gets **3 out of 3 marks** for a very clear response. He has actually written more than is required for a 3-mark answer – he seems to have lots of time to write very full answers but this may well penalise him later in the exam, when it comes to writing answers to the extended writing questions.

---

4 Discuss the key features of the biological approach to psychopathology. *(12 marks)*

Alice's answer

The biological approach to psychopathology explains abnormal behaviour in terms of physical factors. These might be inherited, or might be a consequence of viral infection. Some problems such as schizophrenia have been shown to be passed on from parent to child, and twin studies have shown that if one identical twin has schizophrenia, there is a 50% chance that the other twin also has schizophrenia. This is known as a concordance rate, although if schizophrenia was entirely inherited, this concordance rate should be 100%.

Some researchers (e.g. Torrey, 2001) have found that some mothers of schizophrenics had contracted influenza when they were pregnant, and this virus had entered their brain and re-emerged during adolescence to cause the symptoms of schizophrenia.

Some critics of the biological approach, like Thomas Szasz, claim that physical illness and mental illness are not the same thing, and we do not have the same evidence that something is really wrong when we label someone as 'mentally ill'. Szasz claims that people are labelled as mentally ill as a form of social control.

There is also a problem with cause and effect. It is not known for certain whether the physical symptoms of a mental disorder are what caused the disorder in the first place, or whether the physical symptoms are a consequence of the disorder itself.

Tom's answer

The biological approach explains psychopathology by saying that people with a mental illness have something physically wrong with them, like a virus. When people had general paresis it was thought that they also had syphilis, but they wouldn't admit to it. When these people were injected with syphilis, they didn't get syphilis which meant they must already have it. This proved that general paresis was caused by syphilis. A problem with this is that it isn't ethical to inject someone with something like syphilis, because what would happen if general paresis wasn't caused by syphilis – they would now have syphilis as well!

It is also thought that some mental disorders are caused by genetics. Genes can cause chemical and physical changes in the brain, and it is these changes that are associated with the mental disorder. For example, people may inherit low levels of neurotransmitters like serotonin, and so become depressed. However, biological explanations are not the only explanations, behaviourists claim that people learn mental disorders, either directly through conditioning, or indirectly by observing the actions of others. Cognitive psychologists think mental disorders are caused by faulty thinking. This shows that genetics cannot be the only cause of psychopathology.

Examiner's comments

Both Alice and Tom have recognised that both description and evaluation (AO1 and AO2) are required in this question because it begins with the word 'discuss' and also because it is worth 12 marks (all 12-mark questions have an equal amount of AO1 and AO2). Tom, however, does not seem to have grasped the skill of evaluation.

Alice's answer is exemplary, well almost. She has focused on two key explanations – inherited factors and viruses. For each she has provided some research evidence as a means of expanding her descriptions of each explanation. The question asks for 'key features' so she must provide more than one. She could have given some other features (e.g. discussed the role of neurotransmitters and/or hormones). This would have increased the breadth of her answer and meant that less detail was required – an alternative way of gaining top AO1 marks.

In terms of evaluation, Alice has provided one comment at the end of the first paragraph and then two full paragraphs at the end. Paragraphs 3 and 4 provide some excellent elaboration of critical points. The amount of elaboration again means depth rather than breadth. However the first AO2 point is rather brief and the last paragraph would have benefited by including an example. Therefore AO1 marks are a maximum **6 out of 6 marks**, but AO2 is a less impressive **4 out of 6 marks**.

Tom starts off with a reasonable first sentence, identifying one key feature. But this sets him off on the syphilis 'story'. Such 'stories' are used in textbooks and by teachers to increase student understanding of a topic but are not appropriate in exam answers unless they provide the required material. In this case the details given are almost totally irrelevant.

Paragraph 2 starts again with reasonable and relevant material – in fact several features of the biological approach are given and Tom has demonstrated understanding of these.

In the middle of the second paragraph Tom finally turns to evaluation and hopes to provide this by mentioning some other approaches. But he does what so many candidates do – he says 'however…' (an AO2 'word') and then gives *descriptions* of the other two approaches. This does not count as evaluation. The AO1 material is basic and shows some evidence of selection to address the question, so **3 out of 6 marks**. The AO2 material is rudimentary and so **1 out of 6 marks**.

In total, Alice's mark is **11 out of 12 marks** and Tom's is **4 out of 12 marks**.

YOUR OWN LITTLE BOOK OF REVISION NOTES

At the beginning of this book we explained how to produce your own little book of notes and use them for effective revision (see page x).

Remember to keep your notes brief – just record key points which will act as coat pegs for remembering the material.

Column 1: tick when you have produced brief notes.

Column 2: tick when you have a good grasp of this topic.

Column 3: tick during the final revision when you feel you have complete mastery of the topic.

Key terms
3 marks worth of material
Limitations associated with each definitions

Deviation from social norms ☐ ☐ ☐
Failure to function adequately ☐ ☐ ☐
Deviation from ideal mental health ☐ ☐ ☐

Research studies related to ...
6 marks worth of description
6 marks worth of evaluation (including the issues of validity and ethics)

Drug therapy ☐ ☐ ☐
ECT ☐ ☐ ☐
Psychoanalysis ☐ ☐ ☐
Systematic desensitisation ☐ ☐ ☐
Cognitive Behavioural Therapy ☐ ☐ ☐

Explanations/theories
6 marks worth of description
6 marks worth of evaluation (both strengths and weaknesses)

Deviation from social norms ☐ ☐ ☐
Failure to function adequately ☐ ☐ ☐
Deviation from ideal mental health ☐ ☐ ☐
Biological approach to
  psychopathology ☐ ☐ ☐
Psychological approach:
  Psychoanalysis ☐ ☐ ☐
Psychological approach:
  Behavioural ☐ ☐ ☐
Psychological approach:
  Cognitive ☐ ☐ ☐
Drug therapy ☐ ☐ ☐
ECT ☐ ☐ ☐
Psychoanalysis ☐ ☐ ☐
Systematic desensitisation ☐ ☐ ☐
Cognitive Behavioural Therapy ☐ ☐ ☐

CROSSWORD

Answers on page 214.

Across

2 A criticism of some therapies is that they treat these rather than the cause of the problem. (8)

4 A genetic vulnerability to a particular mental disorder, requiring life stress to trigger it. (9)

5 In Freud's theory, the ego is driven by the _____ principle. (7)

10 The biological model of abnormality is also called the _____ model. (7)

12 Some critics of psychoanalysis claim that what are revealed in therapy are not 'recovered' memories, but _____ memories. (5)

14 Marie _____, responsible for the deviation from ideal mental health definition of abnormality. (6)

16 With some therapies, symptoms may disappear but reappear in a different form. This is known as symptom _____. (12)

19 Another term for drug treatments. (12)

21 Another term for social learning, _____ conditioning. (9)

22 An irrational fear of something. (6)

23 The child conditioned by Watson and Raynor. (6,6)

24 The _____ approach believes that behaviour can be explained in terms of unconscious motives. (14)

Down

1 _____ mechanisms, used by the ego to protect the individual from undue anxiety. (7)

3 An analysis based on the results of many different studies, a _____-analysis. (4)

6 Albert _____, the founder of REBT. (5)

7 Depression is sometimes due to insufficient activity of this neurotransmitter. (9)

8 The _____ approach believes that abnormal behaviour is learned. (12)

9 Thomas _____ believed the concept of mental illness is used to exert social control. (5)

11 Rational _____ behavioural therapy. (REBT) (7)

13 Form of treatment based on classical conditioning _____ desensitisation. (10)

15 One of Freud's most famous case studies. (4,1)

17 In Freud's theory, the part of the personality driven by the pleasure principle. (2)

18 An abbreviation of the treatment which uses electric current to induce convulsions. (3)

20 A substitute treatment which lacks the active component of the treatment, but is otherwise the same. (7)

References

Abrams, R. (1997) *Electroconvulsive Therapy* (3rd edn). New York: Oxford University Press. ▶ page 193

Ainsworth, M.D.S. (1967) *Infancy in Uganda: Child care and the growth of love.* Baltimore: John Hopkins University Press. ▶ pages 40, 44

Ainsworth, M.D.S. and Bell, S.M. (1970) Attachment, exploration and separation: illustrated by the behaviour of two-year-olds in a Strange Situation. *Child Development, 41,* 49–65. ▶ page 34

Ainsworth, M.D.S. and Wittig, B.A. (1969) Attachment and exploratory behaviour of one-year-olds in a strange situation. In B.A. Foss (Ed.), *Determinants of infant behaviour* (Vol. 4). London: Methuen. ▶ page 40

Ainsworth, M.D.S., Bell, S.M. and Stayton, D.J. (1971) Individual differences in Strange Situation behavior of one year olds. In H. R. Schaffer (Ed.) *The origins of human social relations.* New York: Academic Press. ▶ page 40

Ainsworth, M.D.S., Blehar, M.C., Waters, E. and Wall, S. (1978) *Patterns of attachment: A psychological study of the strange situation.* Hillsdale, NJ: Lawrence Erlbaum. ▶ pages 41, 42, 43

Allen, V.L. and Levine, J.M. (1971) Social support and conformity: The role of independent assessment of reality. *Journal of Experimental Social Psychology, 7,* 48–58. ▶ page 162

Alloy, L.B. and Abrahmson, L.Y. (1979) Judgement of contingency in depressed and non-depressed students: Sadder but wiser? *Journal of Experimental Psychology, 108,* 441–85. ▶ page 191

Anastasi, J.S. and Rhodes, M.G. (2006) An own-age bias in face recognition for children and older adults. *Psychonomic Bulletin and Review, 12,* 1043–7. ▶ page 19

Anderson, C.A. (1999) Attributional style, depression, and loneliness: A cross-cultural comparison of American and Chinese students . *Personality and Social Psychology Bulletin, 25,* 482–99. ▶ page 165

Anderson, C.R. and Schneier, C.E. (1978) Locus of control, leader behavior and leader performance among management students. *Academy of Management Journal, 21,* 690–8. ▶ page 164

Andersson, B.E. (1992) Effects of daycare on cognitive and socioemotional competence of thirteen-year-old Swedish schoolchildren. *Child Development, 63,* 20–36. ▶ page 55

Arendt, H. (1963) *Eichmann in Jerusalem,* London: Penguin. ▶ page 158

Arendt, H. (1965) *On Revolution,* London: Penguin. ▶ page 146

Arnetz, B.B., Wasserman, J., Petrini, B., Brenner, S.O., Levi, L., Eneroth, P., Salovaara, H., Hjelm, R. Salovaara, L. and Theorell, T. (1987) Immune function in unemployed women. *Psychosomatic Medicine, 46(3),* 2–12. ▶ page 120

Asch, S.E. (1956) Studies of independence and conformity: A minority of one against a unanimous majority. *Psychological Monographs, 70* (Whole no. 416). ▶ page 148

Ashton, H. (1997) Benzodiazepine dependency. In A. Baum, S. Newman, J. Weinman, R. West, and C. McManus (Eds.), *Cambridge handbook of psychology, health and medicine.* Cambridge: Cambridge University Press. ▶ page 137

Atkinson, R.C. and Raugh, M.R. (1975) An application of the mnemonic keyword method to the acquisition of a Russian vocabulary. *Journal of Experimental Psychology: Human Learning and Memory, 104,* 126–33. ▶ page 22

Atkinson, R.C. and Shiffrin, R.M. (1968) Human memory: A proposed system and its control processes. In K.W. Spence and J.T. Spence (Eds.) *The Psychology of Leraning and Motivation.* Vol. 2. London: Academic Press. ▶ page 8

Baddeley, A.D. (1966a) The influence of acoustic and semantic similarity on long term memory for word sequences. *Quarterly Journal of Experimental Psychology, 18,* 302–9. ▶ pages 7, 76

Baddeley, A.D. (1966b) Short-term memory for word sequences as a function of acoustic, semantic and formal similarity. *Quarterly Journal of Experimental Psychology, 18,* 362–5. ▶ page 7

Baddeley, A.D. (1986) *Working memory.* Oxford: Clarendon Press. ▶ page 12

Baddeley, A.D. (1990) *Human Memory. Theory and Practice.* Boston, MA: Allyn and Bacon. ▶ page 101

Baddeley, A.D. (2000) The episodic buffer: A new component of working memory? *Trends in Cognitive Sciences, 4 (11),* 417–23. ▶ page 12

Baddeley, A.D. (2004). *Your memory: A user's guide* (new illustrated edn). Buffalo, NY: Firefly Books. ▶ page 14

Baddeley, A.D. and Hitch, G.J. (1974) Working memory. In G. H. Bower (Ed.), *The psychology of learning and motivation, Vol. 8.* London: Academic Press. ▶ pages 12, 23

Baddeley, A.D. and Longman, D.J.A. (1978) The influence of length and frequency on training sessions on the rate of learning type. *Ergonomics, 21,* 627–35. ▶ page 69

Baddeley, A.D., Thomson, N., and Buchanan, M. (1975a) Word length and the structure of short-term memory. *Journal of Verbal Learning and Verbal Behavior, 14,* 575–89. ▶ page 13

Baddeley, A.D., Grant, S., Wright, E. and Thomson, N. (1975b) Imagery and visual working memory. In P.M.A. Rabbitt and S. Dornic (Eds.) *Attention and performance, Vol. V.* London: Academic Press. ▶ page 13

Baddeley, A.D., Vallar, G. and Wilson, B. (1987) Sentence comprehension and phonological memory: Some neuropsychological evidence. In M. Coltheart (Ed.) *Attention and performance XII: The psychology of reading.* London: Lawrence Erlbaum Associates. ▶ page 13

Bahrick, H.P., Bahrick, P.O. and Wittinger, R.P. (1975) Fifty years of memory for names and faces: A cross-sectional approach. *Journal of Experimental Psychology: General, 104,* 54–75. ▶ page 4

Bandura, A., Ross, D. and Ross, S.A. (1961) Transmission of aggression through imitation of aggressive models. *Journal of Abnormal and Social Psychology, 63,* 575–82. ▶ pages 83, 86

Barrett, H. (1997) How young children cope with separation: Toward a new conceptualization. *British Journal of Medical Psychology, 70,* 339–58. ▶ page 49

Bartone, P.T. (1999) Hardiness protects against war-related stress in Army reserve forces. *Consulting Psychology Journal, 51,* 72–82. ▶ page 131

Baumrind, D. (1959) Conceptual issues involved in evaluating improvement due to psychotherapy. *Psychiatry, 22,* 341–8. ▶ page 72

Baumrind, D. (1964) Some thoughts on ethics of research: After reading Milgram's behavioural study of obedience. *American Psychologist, 19,* 421–3. ▶ page 158

Baumrind, D. (1985) Research using intentional deception: Ethical issues revisited. *American Psychologist, 40(2),* 165–74. ▶ page 70

Beck, A.T. (1976) *Cognitive therapy and emotional disorders.* New York: International Universities Press. ▶ page 190

Bekerian, D.A. and Bowers, J.M. (1983) Eye-witness testimony: Were we misled? *Journal of Experimental Psychology, Learning, Memory and Cognition, 9,* 139–45. ▶ page 17

Belsky, J. and Rovine, M.J. (1988) Nonmaternal care in the first year of life and the security of parent-infant attachment. *Child Development, 59,* 157–67. ▶ page 52

Belsky, J., and Rovine, M. (1987) Temperament and attachment security in the Strange Situation: A rapprochement. *Child Development, 58,* 787–95. ▶ page 39

Belsky, J., Vandell, D.L., Burchinal, M., Clarke-Stewart, K.A., McCartney, K. and Owen, M.T. (The NICHD Early Child Care Research Network) (2007). Are there long-term effects of early child care? *Child Development*, *78(2)*, 681–701. ▶ pages 52, 54

BEO (2004) Behavioural observation, University of Bern http://www.psy. unibe.ch/beob/home_e.htm (accessed September 2004) ▶ page 90

Bergin, A.E. (1971) The evaluation of therapeutic outcomes. In A.E. Bergin and S.L. Garfield (Eds.), *Handbook of psychotherapy and behaviour change*. New York: Wiley. ▶ page 194

Berns, G.S., Chappelow, J., Zink, C.F., Pagnoni, G., Martin-Skurski, M.E. and Richards, J. (2005) Neurobiological correlates of social conformity and independence during mental rotation. *Biological Psychiatry*, *58*, 245–53. ▶ page 149

Bifulco, A., Harris, T. and Brown, G.W. (1992) Mourning or early inadequate care? Re-examining the relationship of maternal loss in childhood with adult depression and anxiety. *Development and Psychopathology*, *4*, 433–49. ▶ page 49

Blass, T. (1999). The Milgram paradigm after 35 years: Some things we now know about obedience to authority. *Journal of Applied Social Psychology*, *29*, 955–978. ▶ page 166

Blatt, S.J., and Ford, R. (1994) *Therapeutic change: An object relations perspective*. New York: Plenum. ▶ page 195

Blum, D. (2003) *Love at Goon Park: Harry Harlow and the science of affection*. Chichester, West Sussex: John Wiley. ▶ page 38

Bohman, M. and Sigvardsson, S. (1979) Long-term effects of early institutional care: A prospective longitudinal study. *Annual Progress in Child Psychiatry and Child Development*, 148–56. ▶ page 49

Bokhorst, C.L., Bakermans-Kranenburg, M.J., Fearon, P., Van IJzendoorn, M.H., Fonagy, P. and Schuengel, C. (2003) The importance of shared environment in mother-infant attachment security: A behavioral genetic study. *Child Development*, *74*, 1769–82. ▶ page 39

Bouteyre, E., Maurel, M. and Bernaud, J-L. (2007) Daily hassles and depressive symptoms among first year psychology students in France: The role of coping and social support. *Stress and Health*, *23 (2)*, 93. ▶ page 126

Bower, G.H. (1972) Mental imagery and associative learning. In Gregg, L. (Ed.) *Cognition in Learning and Memory*. New York: Wiley. ▶ page 23

Bower, G.H., Clark, M., Lesgold, A. and Winzenz, D. (1969) Hierarchical retrieval schemes, in recall categorised word lists, *Journal of Verbal Learning and Verbal Behaviour*, *8*, 323–43. ▶ pages 23, 81

Bowlby, J. (1951) *Maternal care and mental health*. Geneva: World Health Organisation. ▶ page 36

Bowlby, J. (1958) The nature of the child's tie to his mother. *International Journal of Psycho-Analysis*, XXXIX, 1–23. ▶ page 36

Bowlby, J. (1969) *Attachment and love, volume 1: Attachment*. London: Hogarth. ▶ page 36

Bowlby, J., Ainsworth, M., Boston, M. and Rosenbluth, D. (1956) The effects of mother-child separation: A follow-up study. *British Journal of Medical Psychology, 29*, 211. ▶ page 49

BPS (2006) Code of Ethics and Conduct. www.bps.org.uk. ▶ page 72

Brandimote, M.A., Hitch, G.J. and Bishop, D.V.M. (1992) Influence of short-term memory codes on visual processing: Evidence from image transformation tasks. *Journal of Experimental Psychology: Learning, Memory and Cognition*, *18*, 157–65. ▶ page 7

Brigham, J.C. and Malpass, R.S. (1985) The role of experience and contact in the recognition of faces of own- and other-race persons. *Journal of Social Issues, 41(3)*, 139–55. ▶ page 19

Brody, L.R. and Hall, J.A. (1993) Gender and emotion. In M. Lewis and J.M. Haviland (Eds.), *Handbook of emotions*. New York: Guildford Press. ▶ page 133

Brown, G.W, (1974) Meaning, measurement and stress of life events. In B.S. Dohrenwend and B.P. Dohrenwend (Eds.) *Stressful life events: Their nature and effects*. New York: Wiley. ▶ page 125

Brown, G.W. and Harris, T.O. (1978) *Social origins of depression: A study of psychiatric disorder in women*. London: Tavistock Publications. ▶ pages 53, 123

Browning, C. (1992) *Ordinary men: Reserve Police Battalion 101 and the Final Solution in Poland*. New York: HarperCollins. ▶ page 161

Brugger, P., Landis, T. and Regard, M. (1990) A 'sheep–goat effect' in repetition avoidance: Extra sensory perception as an effect of subjective probability. *British Journal of Psychology*, *81*, 455–68. ▶ page 106

Bryant, B., Harris, M. and Newton, D. (1980) *Children and minders*. London: Grant McIntyre. ▶ page 55

Bunge, S.A., Klingberg, T., Jacobsen, R.B. and Gabrieli, J.D.E. (2000) A resource model of the neural basis of executive working memory. *Proceedings of the National Academy of Sciences of the United States of America*, *97(7)*, 3573–8. ▶ page 13

Burley, P.M. and McGuiness, J. (1977) Effects of social intelligence on the Milgram paradigm. *Psychological Reports*, *40*, 767–70. ▶ page 158

Buzan, T. (1993) *The mind map book*. London: BBC. ▶ page 22

Capafóns, J.I., Sosa, C.D. and Avero, P. (1998) Systematic desensitisation in the treatment of fear of flying. *Psychology in Spain*, *2(1)*, 11–16. ▶ page 196

Carlson, E.A. (1998) A prospective longitudinal study of disorganisation/disorientation. *Child Development*, *69(4)*, 1107–28. ▶ page 38

Charlton, T., Gunter, B. and Hannan, A. (Eds.) (2000) *Broadcast television effects in a remote community*. Hillsdale, NJ: Lawrence Erlbaum. ▶ page 84

Chase, W.G. and Simon, H.A. (1973) The mind's eye in chess. In W.G. Chase (Ed.) *Visual information processing*, 215–81. New York: Academic Press. ▶ page 3

Chase, W.G., Lyon, D. R. and Ericsson, K.A. (1981) Individual differences in memory span. In: M.P. Friedman, J.P. Das and N. O'Connor (Eds.) *Intelligence and Learning*, 29–42. New York: Plenum. ▶ page 22

Christianson, S.A. and Hubinette, B. (1993) Hands up! A study of witnesses' emotional reactions and memories associated with bank robberies. *Applied cognitive psychology*, *7*, 365–79. ▶ page 18

Clarke-Stewart, K.A. (1985) *What daycare forms and features mean for children's development*. Paper presented at the annual meeting of the American Association for the Advancement of Science (AAAS), Los Angeles. ▶ page 54

Clarke-Stewart, K.A., Gruber, C.P. and Fitzgerald, L.M. (1994) *Children at home and in day care*. Hillsdale, NJ: Erlbaum. ▶ pages 53, 55

Clifasefi, S.L., Takarangi, M.K.T. and Bergman, J.S. (2006) Blind drunk: The effects of alcohol on inattentional blindness. *Applied cognitive psychology*, *20*, 697–704. ▶ page 19

Comer, R.J. (1995) *Abnormal psychology*. New York: WH Freeman and Co. ▶ page 182

Comer, R.J. (2002) *Fundamentals of abnormal psychology* (3rd edn). New York: Worth. ▶ pages 192, 193

Coolican, H. (2004) *Research methods and statistics in Psychology* (3rd edn). London: Hodder and Stoughton. ▶ pages 68, 82, 85

Cooper, G., Hoffman, K., Powell, B and Marvin, R. (2005) The circle of security intervention. In L. Berlin, Y. Ziv, L. Amaya-Jackson and M. Greenberg (Eds.) *Enhancing early attachments: Theory, research, intervention, and policy*. New York: Guilford Press. ▶ page 43

Cowan, N. (2001) The magical number 4 in short-term memory: A reconsideration of mental storage capacity. *Behavioral and Brain Sciences*, *24*, 1, 87–114. ▶ page 6

Craik, F.I.M. and Lockhart, R.S. (1972) Levels of processing: A framework for memory research. *Journal of Verbal Learning and Verbal Behavior*, *11*, 671–84. ▶ page 10

Craik, F.I.M. and Tulving, E. (1975) Depth of processing and the retention of words in episodic memory. *Journal of Experimental Psychology*, *104*, 268–94. ▶ page 10

Creps, C.L. and Vernon-Feagans, L. (1999) Preschoolers' social behavior in day care links with entering day care in the first year. *Journal of Applied Developmental Psychology, 20(3)*, 461–79. ▶ page 53

Curtiss, S. (1977) *Genie: A psycholinguistic study of a modern-day 'wild child'.* London: Academic Press. ▶ page 50

Darley, J.M. (1992) Social organisation for the production of evil. *Psychological enquiry, 3(2)*, 199–218. ▶ page 158

Davey, G. (1995) Preparedness and phobias: specific evolved associations or a generalised expectancy bias? *Brain and Behavioural Sciences, 18(2)*, 289–325. ▶ page 189

Davison, G.C. and Neale, J.M. (2001) *Abnormal Psychology* (8th edn) New York: John Wiley. ▶ page 177

de Ridder, D.T.D. (1996) Altijd moe en de psyche. *Psychologie, 2,* 49–50. ▶ page 122

Deffenbacher, K.A., Bornstein, B.H., Penrod. S.D. and McGorty, E.K. (2004) A meta-analytic review of the effects of high stress on eyewitness memory. *Law and Human Behavior, 28,* 687–706. ▶ page 18

DeLongis, A., Coyne, J.C., Dakof, G., Folkman, S. and Lazarus, R.S. (1982) The impact of daily hassles, uplifts and major life events to health status. *Health Psychology, 1,* 119–36. ▶ page 126

DeLongis, A., Folkman, S. and Lazarus, R.S. (1988) The impact of daily stress on health and mood: Psychological and social resources as mediators. *Journal of Personality and Social Psychology, 54,* 486–95. ▶ page 125

Devlin, Hon. Lord P. (1976) *Report to the secretary of state for the home department of the departmental committee on evidence of identification in criminal cases.* London: HMSO. ▶ page 16

Dewe, P.J. (1989) Examining the nature of work stress: individual evaluations of stressful experiences and coping. *Human Relations, 42,* 993–1013. ▶ page 129

Dingfelder, S. (2004) Shortcomings of the 2003 NICHD day care study. *APA Monitor,* 35(9). www.apa.org/monitor/oct04/nichd.html ▶ page 54

Doi, T. (1973) *The anatomy of dependence.* New York: Kodansha International. (Amae no kozo, Japanese text, published in 1966.) ▶ page 46

Dollard, J., and Miller, N.E. (1950) *Personality and psychotherapy.* New York: McGraw-Hill. ▶ page 35

Eagly, A.H. (1978) Sex differences in influenceability. *Psychological Bulletin, 85,* 86–116. ▶ page 78

Eagly, A.H. and Carli, L. (1981) Sex of researchers and sex-typed communications as determinants of sex differences in influenceability: A meta-analysis of social influence studies. *Psychological Bulletin, 90,* 1–20. ▶ page 149

Egeland, B. and Hiester, M. (1995) The long-term consequences of infant day-care and mother-infant attachment. *Child Development, 66,* 474–85. ▶ page 55

Ekman, P. and Friesen, W. V. (1978) *Manual for the facial action coding system.* Palo Alto, CA: Consulting Psychology Press. ▶ page 88

Ellis, A. (1957) *How to Live with a 'Neurotic'.* Hollywood, CA: Wilshire Books. ▶ page 197

Ellis, A. (1962) *Reason and emotion in psychotherapy.* New York: Lyle Stuart. ▶ page 190

Engels, G.I., Garnefski, N. and Diekstra, R.F.W. (1993) Efficacy of rational emotive therapy: A quantitative analysis. *Journal of Consulting and Clinical Psychology, 61(6),* 1083–90. ▶ page 197

Epstein, L.C. and Lasagna, L. (1969) Obtaining informed consent: form or substance. *Archives of Internal Medicine, 123,* 682–8. ▶ page 70

Eslinger, P.J. and Damasio, A.R. (1985) Severe disturbance of higher cognition after bilateral frontal lobe ablations: Patient EVR. *Neurology, 35,*1731–41. ▶ page 15

Evans, P., Bristow, M., Hucklebridge, F., Clow, A. and Pang, F.-Y. (1994) Stress, arousal, cortisol and secretory immunoglobulin A in students undergoing assessment. *British Journal of Clinical Psychology, 33,* 575–6. ▶ page 121

Evans, P., Clow, A. and Hucklebridge, F. (1997) Stress and the immune system. *The Psychologist, 10 (7),* 303–7. ▶ page 121

Evans, P., Hucklebridge, F. and Clow, A. (2000) *Mind, immunity and health: The science of psychoneuroimmunology.* London: Free Association Books. ▶ page 120

Eysenck, H.J. (1986) Can personality study ever be scientific? *Journal of Social Behaviour, 1,* 3–19 ▶ page 194

Farah, M.J., Peronnet, F., Gonon, M.A. and Giard, M.H. (1988) Electrophysiological evidence for a shared representational medium for visual images and visual percepts. *Journal of Experimental Psychology: General, 117,* 248–57. ▶ page 13

Fein, S., Goethals, G.R. and Kugler, M.B. (2007) Social influence on political judgments: The case of presidential debates. *Political Psychology, 28 (2),* 165–92. ▶ page 154

Festinger, L., Riecken, H. W. and Schachter, S. (1956) *When prophecy fails.* Minneapolis: University of Minnesota Press. ▶ page 89

Fick, K. (1993) The influence of an animal on social interactions of nursing home residents in a group setting. *American Journal of Occupational Therapy, 47,* 529–34. ▶ page 89

Field, T. (1991) Quality infant day-care and grade school behaviour and performance. *Child Development, 62(4),* 863–70. ▶ page 53

Finchilescu, G. and Dawes, A. (1998) Catapulted into democracy: South African adolescents' sociopolitical orientations following rapid social change. *Journal of Social Issues, 54 (3),* 563–83. ▶ page 166

Fischer, C.L., Daniels, J.C., Levin, W.C., Kimzey, S.L., Cobb, E.K. and Ritzmann, S.E. (1972) Effects of the space flight environment on man's immune system: II. Lymphocyte counts and reactivity. *Aerospace Medicine, 43,* 122–1125. ▶ page 120

Fisher, R.P., and Geiselman, R.E. (1992) *Memory enhancing techniques for investigative interviewing: The Cognitive Interview.* Springfield IL: Charles C. Thomas. ▶ page 20

Fisher, S. and Greenberg, R. (1996) *Freud scientifically appraised.* New York: John Wiley. ▶ page 187

Fletcher, D. (2005) *British swimming, sport psychology, and Olympic medals: Is it all in the mind?!?* Published on the British Swimming Coaches and Teachers Association website (www.bscta.com), January 31. ▶ page 135

Flett, G.L., Blankstein, K.R., Hichen, J. and Watson, M.S. (1995) Social support and help-seeking in daily hassles versus major life events stress. *Journal of Applied Social Psychology, 25,*.49–58 ▶ page 126

Folkman, S. and Lazarus, R.S. (1980) An analysis of coping in a middle-aged community sample. *Journal of Health and Social Behavior, 21,* 219–39. ▶ page 132

Folkman, S. and Lazarus, R.S. (1985) If it changes it must be a process: Study of emotions and coping during three stages of a college examination. *Journal of Personality and Social Psychology, 48,* 150–70. ▶ page 132

Forer, B.R. (1949) The fallacy of personal validation: A classroom demonstration of gullibility. *Journal of Abnormal and Social Psychology. 44,* 118–123. ▶ page 107

Foster, R.A., Libkuman, T.M., Schooler, J.W. and Loftus, E.F. (1994) Realism and eyewitness person identification. *Applied Cognitive Psychology, 8,* 107–21 ▶ page 17

Fox, N. (1977) Attachment of Kibbutz infants to mother and metapelet. *Child Development, 48,* 1228–39. ▶ page 44

Freud, S. (1909) Analysis of phobia in a five-year-old boy. In J. Strachey (Ed. and trans.) *The complete psychological works: The standard edition* (Vol. 10). New York: Norton, 1976. ▶ page 186

Freud, S. (1910) The origin and development of psychoanalysis. *American Journal of Psychology, 21,* 181–218. ▶ page 187

Freud, S. (1953–66). *The standard edition of the complete psychological works of Sigmund Freud* (J. Strachey, trans). London: Hogarth Press. ▶ page 187

Friedman, M. and Rosenman, R.H. (1959) Association of specific overt behaviour pattern with blood and cardiovascular findings. *Journal of the American Medical Association, 169,* 1286–96. ▶ page 130

Frost, N. (1972) Encoding and retrieval in visual memory tasks. *Journal of Experimental Psychology, 95,* 317–26. ▶ page 7

Gardner, L.I. (1972) Deprivation dwarfism. *Scientific American, 1972 Jul Vol. 227(1)* 76–82. ▶ page 51

Gervais, R. (2005) *Daily hassles beaten back by uplifting experiences*. Poster presented at British Psychological Society Annual Conference, University of Manchester. ▶ page 126

Gilbar, O. (2005) Breast cancer: How do Israeli women cope? A cross-sectional sample. *Family, Systems and Health, 23*, 161–71. ▶ page 132

Gilligan, C. and Attanucci, J. (1988) Two moral orientations: Gender differences and similarities. *Merrill-Palmer Quarterly, 34*, 223–37. ▶ page 95

Ginet, M. and Verkampt, F. (2007) The cognitive interview: Is its benefit affected by the level of witness emotion? *Memory, 15(4)*, 450–64. ▶ page 21

Glanzer, M. and Cunitz, A.R. (1966) Two storage mechanisms in free recall. *Journal of Verbal Learning and Verbal Behavior, 5*, 351–60 ▶ page 9

Glenberg, A.M., Smith, S.M. and Green, C. (1977) Type I rehearsal: Maintenance and more. *Journal of Verbal Learning and Verbal Behaviour, 16*, 339–52 ▶ page 11

Goldhagen, D. J. (1996) *Hitler's Willing Executioners*. New York: Alfred A. Knopf. ▶ page 161

Gottesman, I.I. and Shields, J. (1976) A critical review of recent adoption, twin, and family studies of schizophrenia: behavioral genetics perspectives. *Schizophrenia Bulletin, 2(3)*, 360–401. ▶ page 185

Gregg, P., Washbrook, E., Propper, C. and Burgess, S. (2005) The effects of a mother's return to work decision on child development in the UK. *The Economic Journal, 115*, 48–80. ▶ pages 52, 54, 55

Griskevicius, V., Goldstein, N.J., Mortensen, C.R., Sundie, J.M., Cialdini, R.B. and Kenrick, D.T. (2006) Going along versus going alone: When fundamental motives facilitate strategic (non)conformity. *Journal of Personality and Social Psychology, 91*, 281–94. ▶ page 162

Grossmann, K.E. and Grossmann, K. (1991) Attachment quality as an organizer of emotional and behavioural responses in a longitudinal perspective. In C.M. Parkes, J. Stevenson-Hinde and P. Marris (Eds.) *Attachment across the life cycle*. London: Tavistock/Routledge. ▶ pages 39, 44

Gründl, M. (2007) *Beautycheck – Causes and Consequences of Human Facial Attractiveness*. www.uni-regensburg. de/Fakultaeten/phil_Fak_II/Psychologie/ Psy_II/beautycheck/english/zusammen/ zusammen1.htm ▶ page 33

Guéguen, N. (2007) Courtship compliance: The effect of touch on women's behaviour. *Social Influence, 2(2)*, 81–97. ▶ page 147

Guiton, P. (1966) Early experience and sexual object choice in the brown leghorn. *Animal Behaviour, 14*, 534–8. ▶ page 32

Gulian, E., Glendon, I., Davies, D., Matthews, G. and Debney, L. (1990) The stress of driving: A diary study. *Work and Stress, 4*, 7–16. ▶ page 126

Gunnar, M.R., Brodersen, L., Nachmias, M., Buss, K. and Rigatusso, J. (1996) Stress reactivity and attachment security. *Developmental Psychobiology, 29*, 10–36. ▶ page 118

Hardt, J., Sidor, A., Bracko, M. and Egle, U. (2006) Reliability of retrospective assessments of childhood experiences in Germany. *Journal of Nervous and Mental Disease, 194(9)*, 676–83. ▶ page 125

Harlow, H.F (1959) Love in infant monkeys. *Scientific American, 200(6)*, 68–74. ▶ page 35

Harlow, H.F (1960) Primary affectional patterns in primates. *American Journal of Orthopsychiatry, 30*, 676–84. ▶ page 51

Harms, T., Clifford, R.M. and Cryer, D. (1998) *Early childhood environment rating scale* (revised edn). New York, NY: Teachers College Press. ▶ page 88

Hazan, C. and Shaver, P.R. (1987) Romantic love conceptualised as an attachment process. *Journal of Personality and Social Psychology, 52*, 511–24. ▶ page 42

Heaven, P.C.L., Ciarrochi, J., Vialle, W. and Cechavicuite, I. (2005) Adolescent peer crowd self-identification, attributional style and perceptions of parenting. *Journal of Community & Applied Social Psychology, 15*, 313–18. ▶ page 165

Heikkinen, M.E. and Lönnqvist, J.K. (1995) Recent life events in elderly suicide: A nationwide study in Finland. *International Psychogeriatrics, 7*, 287–300. ▶ page 125

Hilts, P. (1995) *Memory's ghost: The strange tale of Mr. M. and the nature of memory*. New York: Simon and Schuster. ▶ page 100

Hitch, G. and Baddeley, A.D. (1976) Verbal reasoning and working memory. *Quarterly Journal of Experimental Psychology, 28*, 603–21. ▶ page 13

Hodges, J. and Tizard, B. (1989) Social and family relationships of ex-institutional adolescents. *Journal of Child Psychology and Psychiatry, 30*, 77–97. ▶ pages 84, 50

Hofling, K.C., Brontzman, E., Dalrymple, S., Graves, N. and Pierce, C.M. (1966) An experimental study in the nurse-physician relationship. *Journal of Mental and Nervous Disorders, 43*, 171–8. ▶ page 159

Holmes, T.H. and Rahe, R.H. (1967) The social readjustment rating scale. *Journal of Psychosomatic Research, 11*, 213–18. ▶ page 124

Hornsey, M. J., Spears, R., Cremers, I. and Hogg, M. A. (2003) Relations between high and low power groups: The importance of legitimacy. *Personality and Social Psychology Bulletin, 29*, 216–27. ▶ page 162

Howard, K.I., Krause, M. S., Saunders, S. M. and Kopta, S.M. (1997) Trials and tribulations in the meta-analysis of treatment differences: Comment on Wampold *et al.* (1997). *Psychological Bulletin, 122*, 221–5. ▶ page 195

Howes, C. and Hamilton, C.E. (1992) Children's relationships with caregivers: Mothers and child care teachers. *Child Development, 63(4)*, 859–66. ▶ page 55

Hyde, T.S. and Jenkins, J.J. (1973) Recall for words as a function of semantic, graphic and syntactic orientating tasks. *Journal of Verbal Learning and Verbal Behaviour, 12*. ▶ page 11

Jacobs, J. (1887) Experiments in prehension, *Mind, 12*, 75–9. ▶ page 6

Jahoda, M. (1958) *Current concepts of positive mental health*. New York: Basic Books. ▶ page 180

Johansson, G., Aronsson, G. and Lindström, B.O. (1978) Social psychological and neuro-endocrine stress reactions in highly Mechanised work. *Ergonomics, 21*, 583–99. ▶ page 128

Jones, F. and Bright, J. (2001) *Stress, myth, theory and research*. London: Prentice Hall. ▶ page 125

Jones, W.H., Russell, D.W. and Nickel T.W. (1977) Belief in the Paranormal Scale: an instrument to measure beliefs in magical phenomena and causes. *JSAS Catalogue of Selected Documents in Psychology, 7:100* (Ms. no. 1577). ▶ page 107

Joronen, K. and Åstedt-Kurki, P. (2005) Familial contribution to adolescent subjective well-being. *International Journal of Nursing Practice, 11(3)*, 125–33. ▶ page 102

Jost, A. (1897). Die assoziationsfestigkeit in iher abhängigkeit von der verteilung der wiederholungen. *Zeitschrift für Psychologie, 14*, 436–72. ▶ page 69

Kagan, J. (1984) *The nature of the child*. New York: Basic Books. ▶ page 39

Kahn, R.J., McNair, D.M., Lipman, R.S., Covi, L., Rickels, K., Downing, R., Fisher, S. and Frankenthaler, L. M. (1986) Imipramine and chlordiazepoxide in depressive and anxiety disorders. II. Efficacy in anxious outpatients. *Archives of General Psychiatry, 43*, 79. ▶ page 137

Kalven, H. and Zeisel, H. (1966) *The American Jury*. Boston: Little Brown & Co. ▶ page 153

Kanner, A.D., Coyne, J. C., Schaefer, C. and Lazarus, R.S. (1981) Comparison of two modes of stress measurement: Daily hassles and uplifts versus major life events. *Journal of Behavioral Medicine, 4*, 187–212. ▶ page 127

Kebbell, M.R. and Wagstaff, G.F. (1996). *Enhancing the practicality of the cognitive interview in forensic situations. Psycholoquy* [on-line serial], *7(6)*, Available FTP: Hostname: princeton.edu Directory: pub/ harnard/Psycholoquy/1996.volume.7 File: psyc.96.7.16.witness-memory.3.kebbell ▶ page 21

Keenan, A. and Newton, T.J. (1989) Stressful events, stressors and psychological strains in young professional engineers. *Human Relations, 42(11)*, 993–1013. ▶ page 129

Keeports, D. and Morier, D. (1994) Teaching the scientific method. *Review of Educational Research. 76(4)*, 607–51. ▶ page 106

Kelman, H. (1958) Compliance, identification and internalisation: Three processes of attitude change. *Journal of Conflict Resolution, 2*, 51–60. ▶ page 148

Kendall, P.C. and Hammen, C. (1995) *Abnormal psychology*. Boston: Houghton-Mifflin. ▶ page 188

Kerr, G. and Leith, L. (1993). Stress management and athletic performance. *Sport Psychologist, 7*, 221–31. ▶ page 134

Kiecolt-Glaser, J.K., Fisher, L.D., Ogrocki, P. and Stout, J.C. (1987) Marital quality, marital disruption and immune function. *Psychosomatic Medicine, 49*, 13–34. ▶ page 121

Kiecolt-Glaser, J.K., Loving, T.J., Stowell, J.R., Malarkey, W.B., Lemeshow, S., Dickinson, S.L. and Glaser, R. (2005) Hostile marital interactions, proinflammatory cytokine production, and wound healing. *Archives of General Psychiatry, 62*, 1377–84. ▶ page 121

Kiecolt-Glaser, J,K., Garner, W., Speicher, C.E., Penn, G.M., Holliday, J. and Glaser, R. (1984) Psychosocial modifiers of immunocompetence in medical students. *Psychosomatic Medicine, 46*, 7–14. ▶ page 120

Kilham, W. and Mann, L. (1974) Level of destructive obedience as a function of transmitter and expectant roles in the Milgram odeience paradigm. *Journal of Personality and Social psychology, 29*, 696–702. ▶ page 158

Kirsch, I., Moore, T.J., Scoboria, A. and Nicholls, S.S. (2002) The emperor's new drugs: an analysis of antidepressant medication data submitted to the U.S. Food and Drug Administration. Prevention and Treatment 5:Article 23. Available at: journals.apa.org/prevention/volume5/pre0050023a.html. ▶ pages 185, 192

Kivimäki, M., Virtanan, M., Elovainio, M., Kouvonen, A., Väänänen, A. and Vahtera, J. (2006) Work stress in the etiology of coronary heart disease: A meta-analysis. *Scandinavian Journal of work, Environment and Health, 32*, 431–42. ▶ page 129

Kohlberg, L. (1969) Stage and sequence: The cognitive-developmental approach to socialisation. In D.A. Goslin (Ed.) *Handbook of socialisation theory and practice*. Skokie, IL: Rand McNally. ▶ page 163

Kohlberg, L. (1978) Revisions in the theory and practice of moral development. *Directions for Child Development, 2, 83*–8. ▶ page 95

Köhnken, G., Milne, R., Memon, A. and Bull, R. (1999) The cognitive interview: a meta-analysis. *Psychology, Crime and Law, 5*, 1–35. ▶ pages 20, 104

Koluchová (1976) The further development of twins after severe and prolonged deprivation: A second report. *Journal of Child Psychology and Psychiatry, 17*, 181–8. ▶ page 50

Koluchová, J. (1991) Severely deprived twins after twenty-two years' observation. *Studia Psychologica, 33*, 23–28. ▶ page 50

Kruglanski, A.W. (2003) Terrorism as a Tactic of Minority Influence. Paper presented at F. Buttera and J. Levine (Chairs) *Active Minorities: Hoping and Coping*. Grenoble, France. ▶ page 166

Lalancette, M-F. and Standing, L.G (1990) Asch fails again. *Social Behavior and Personality, 18(1)*, 7–12. ▶ page 150

Lamb, M. E. and Roopnarine, J. L. (1979) Peer influences on sex-role development in preschoolers. *Child Development, 50*, 1219–22. ▶ page 86

Lang, H. (2006) The trouble with day care. *Psychology Today*, http://psychologytoday.com/rss/pto-20050504–000004.html ▶ page 54

Langevin, R. (1983). *Sexual strands: Understanding and treating sexual anomalies in men*, Hillsdale, NJ: Erlbaum ▶ page 196

Langlois, J. H. and Roggmann, L.A. (1990) Attractive faces are only average. *Psychological Science, 1*, 115–21. ▶ page 33

Latané, B. (1981) The psychology of social impact. *American Psychologist, 36*, 343–56. ▶ page 155

Lazarus, R. S. (1990) Theory-based stress measurement and reply to commentators. In L.A. Pervin (Ed.), *Psychological Inquiry, 1*, 3–51. ▶ page 125

Lazarus, R. S. (1992) Can we demonstrate important psychosocial influences on health? With commentaries. *Advances, 8*, 5–45. ▶ page 121

Lazarus, R. S. (1995) Vexing research problems inherent in cognitive-mediational theories of emotion, and some solutions. *Psychological Inquiry, 6*, 183–265. ▶ page 129

Lazarus, R.S. (1999) *Stress and emotion: A new synthesis*. London: Free Association Books. ▶ page 127

Leach, P. (1994) *Children first*. Harmondsworth, Middlesex: Penguin. ▶ page 52

Lifton, R.J. (1986) *The Nazi Doctors: Medical killing and the Psychology of genocide*. New York: Basic Books. ▶ page 158

Lindsay, D.S. (1990) Misleading suggestions can impair eyewitnesses' ability to remember event details. *Journal of Experimental Psychology: Learning, Memory, and Cognition, 16*, 1077–83. ▶ page 17

Linz, S.J. and Semykina, A. (2005) Attitudes and performance: An analysis of Russian workers. William Davidson Institute Working Papers Series wp758, William Davidson Institute at the University of Michigan Stephen M. Ross Business School. ▶ page 164

Lockwood, A. H. (1989) Medical problems of musicians. *New England Journal of Medicine, 320*, 221–7. ▶ page 136

Loftus, E. (1995) Remembering dangerously. *The Skeptical Inquirer, 19(2)*, 20–9. ▶ page 194

Loftus, E.F., and Palmer, J.C. (1974) Reconstruction of automobile destruction: An example of the interaction between language and memory. *Journal of Verbal Learning and Verbal Behavior, 13*, 585–9. ▶ pages 16–17, 68

Loftus, E.F., Loftus, G.R. and Messo, J. (1987) Some facts about 'weapon focus'. *Law and Human Behaviour, 11*, 55–62. ▶ pages 18, 82, 83

Loftus, E.F., Miller, D.G. and Burns, H.J. (1978) Semantic integration of verbal information into visual memory. *Journal of Experimental Psychology, 4(1)*, 19–31. ▶ page 17

Logie, R.H. (1995) *Visuo-spatial working memory*. Hove, UK: Lawrence ErlbaumAssociates, Ltd. ▶ page 12

Logie, R.H. (1999) State of the art: Working memory. *The Psychologist, 12*, 174–8. ▶ page 11

Lorenz, K.Z. (1952) *King Solomon's Ring: New light on animal ways*. New York: Thomas Y. Crowell. ▶ pages 32, 38

Luborsky, L., Singer, B. and Luborsky, L. (1975) Comparative studies of psychotherapies. *Archives of General Psychiatry, 32*, 995–1008. ▶ page 195

Lucas, T., Alexander, S.A., Firestone, I.J. and Baltes, B.B. (2006) Self-efficacy and independence to social influence: Discovery of an efficacy-difficulty effect. *Social Influence, 1*, 58–80. ▶ page 149

Mackie, D.M. (1987) Systematic and nonsystematic processing of majority and minority persuasive communications. *Journal of Personality and Social Psychology, 53*, 41–52. ▶ page 153

Mackie, G. (2006). Does democratic deliberation change minds? *Politics, Philosophy & Economics, 5 (3)*, 279–303 ▶ page 153

MacNair, R. M. (2002) *Perpetration-induced traumatic stress: The psychological consequences of killing*. Westport, CT: Praeger Publishers. ▶ page 123

Main, M. (1999) Attachment theory: Eighteen points with suggestions for future research. In J. Cassidy and P. R. Shaver (Eds.) *Handbook of attachment: Theory, research, and clinical applications*. New York: Guilford Press. ▶ page 42

Main, M. and Solomon, J. (1986) Discovery of an insecure-disorganized/disoriented attachment pattern. In T.B. Brazelton and M. Yogman (Eds.) *Affective development in infancy*, 95–124. Norwood, NJ: Albex. ▶ pages 41, 91

Main, M. and Weston, D.R. (1981) The quality of the toddler's relationship to mother and father: Related to conflict behaviour and the readiness to establish new relationships. *Child Development*, *52*, 932–40. ▶ page 42

Malarkey, W.B., Kiecolt-Glaser, J.K., Pearl, D. and Glaser, R. (1994) Hostile behaviour during marital conflict affects pituitary and adrenal hormones. *Psychosomatic Medicine, 56*, 41–51. ▶ page 121

Mandel, D.R. (1998) The obedience alibi: Milgram's account of the Holocaust reconsidered. *Analyse and Krtik: Zeitschrift für Sozialwissenschaften*, *20*, 74–94. ▶ page 159

Manstead, A.R. and McCulloch, C. (1981) Sex-role stereotyping in British television advertisements. *British Journal of Social Psychology, 20*, 171–80. ▶ page 102

Mantell, D.M. (1971) The Potential for Violence in Germany. *Journal of Social Issues, 27*, 101–12. ▶ page 158

Marmot, M., Bosma, H., Hemingway, H., Brunner, E. and Stansfield, S. (1997) Contribution of job control and other risk factors to social variation in health disease incidence. *The Lancet, 350*, 235–39. ▶ page 128

Marucha, P. T., Kiecolt-Glaser, J. K. and Favagehi, M. (1998) Mucosal wound healing is impaired by examination stress. *Psychosomatic Medicine, 60*, 362–365. ▶ page 120

McGrath, T., Tsui, E., Humphries, S. and Yule, W. (1990) Successful treatment of a noise phobia in a nine-year-old girl with systematic desensitization in vivo. *Educational Psychology, 10*, 79–83. ▶ page 196

Meichenbaum, D. (1977) Cognitive-behaviour modification: An integrative approach. New York: Plenum Press. ▶ pages 135, 190

Meichenbaum, D. (1985) *Stress inoculation training*. New York: Pergamon. ▶ page 134

Melchior, M., Caspi, A., Milne, B.J., Danese, A., Poulton, R. and Moffitt. T.E. (2007) Work stress precipitates depression and anxiety in young, working women and men. *Psychological Medicine, 37(8)*,1119–29. ▶ page 123

Melhuish, E., Belsky, J. and Leyland, A. (2005) *Early impacts of Sure Start local programmes on children and families. Report of the cross-sectional study of 9 and 36 months old children and their families.* London: HMSO ▶ page 56

Melhuish, E.C. (2004) Appendix B: A literature review of the impact of early years provision on young children – summary. In *Early Years, Progress in developing high quality childcare and early education accessible to all.* National Audit Office, London. ▶ page 52

Memon, A., Hope, L. and Bull, R.H.C. (2003) Exposure duration: Effects on eyewitness. accuracy and confidence. *British Journal of Psychology*, *94*, 339–54. ▶ page 19

Memon, A., Milne, R., Holley, A., Koehnken, G. and Bull, R. (1994). Towards understanding the effects of interviewer training in evaluating the cognitive interview. *Applied Cognitive Psychology, 8*, 641–59. ▶ page 124

Michael, K. and Ben-Zur, H. (2007) Stressful life events: Coping and adjustment to separation or loss of spouse. *Illness, Crisis and Loss, 15(1)*, 53–67. ▶ page 124

Middlemist, D.R., Knowles, E.S. and Matter, C.F. (1976) Personal space invasions in the lavatory: suggestive evidence for arousal. *Journal of Personality and Social Psychology, 33*, 541–6. ▶ page 71

Milgram, S. (1963) Behavioural study of obedience. *Journal of Abnormal and Social Psychology, 67*, 371–8. ▶ pages 156, 157

Milgram, S. (1967) The small world problem. *Psychology Today, 1*, 61–7. ▶ pages 146, 161

Milgram, S. (1974) *Obedience to authority: An experimental view*. New York: Harper and Row. ▶ pages 146, 157, 159, 160, 163

Miller, D., Staats, S. and Partlo, C. (1992) Discriminating positive and negative aspects of pet interaction: Sex differences in the older population. *Social Indicators Research, 27*, 363–74. ▶ page 127

Miller, G.A. (1956) The magic number seven, plus or minus two: Some limits on our capacity for processing information. *Psychological Review, 63*, 81–93. ▶ page 6

Milne, R. and Bull, R. (2002) Back to basics: A componential analysis of the original cognitive interview mnemonics with three age groups. *Applied Cognitive Psychology, 16*, 1–11. ▶ page 20

Morris, P.E., Gruneberg, M.M., Sykes, R.N. and Merrick, A. (1981) Football knowledge and the acquisition of new results. *British Journal of Psychology, 72*, 479–83. ▶ page 3

Moscovici, S., Lage, E. and Naffrenchoux, M. (1969) Influence of a consistent minority on the responses of a majority in a colour perception task. *Sociometry, 32*, 365–80. ▶ page 152

Moscovici, S. (1980) Toward a theory of conversion behaviour. In L. Berkowitz (Ed.) *Advances in experimental social psychology*, Vol. 13. New York: Academic Press. ▶ page 153

Mulrow, C.D., Williams, J.W., Chiquette, E., Aguilar, C., Hitchcock-Noel, P., Lee, S., Cornell, J. and Stamm, K. (2000) Efficacy of newer medications for treating depression in primary care patients. *American Journal of Medicine, 108(1)*, 54–64. ▶ page 192

Myrtek, M. (2001) Meta-analyses of prospective studies on coronary heart disease, type A personality, and hostility. *International Journal of Cardiology, 79*, 245–51. ▶ page 130

Nachmias, M., Gunnar, M., Mangelsdorf, S., Parritz, R.H. and Buss, K. (1996) Behavioural inhibition and stress reactivity: The moderating role of attachment security. *Child Development, 67*, 508–22. ▶ page 39

Nail, P.R., MacDonald, G. and Levy, D. A. (2000) Proposal of a four-dimensional model of. social response. *Psychological Bulletin, 126*, 454–70. ▶ page 162

Nairne, J.S., Whiteman, H.L. and Kelley, M.R. (1999) Short-term forgetting of order under conditions of reduced interference. *Quarterly Journal of Experimental Psychology, 52A*, 241–51. ▶ page 5

Nelson, T. O. and Rothbart, R. (1972) Acoustic savings for items forgotten from long-term memory. *Journal of Experimental Psychology, 93*, 357–60 ▶ page 7

Nemeth, C.J. (2003) Minority Influence. In M. Cardwell, L. Clark and C. Meldrum (eds.), *Psychology for AS*. London: Harper Collins Publishers Ltd. ▶ page 153

Nesse, R.M. and Young, E. (2000)The evolutionary origins and functions of the stress response. In George Fink (Ed.) *The Encyclopedia of Stress*. New York, NY: Academic Press, NY. ▶ page 116

NICHD Early Child Care Research Network (1997) The effects of infant child care on infant-mother attachment security: Results of the NICHD study of early child care. *Child Development, 68(5)*, 860–79. ▶ page 55

NICHD Early Child Care Research Network (1999) Child care and mother-child interactions in the first three years of life. *Developmental Psychology, 35*, 1399–1413. ▶ page 56

NICHD Early Child Care Research Network (2003) Social functioning in first grade: Associations with earlier home and child care predictors and with current classroom experiences. *Child Development, 74*, 1639–63. ▶ pages 52, 54

Nicholson, N., Cole, S. and Rocklin, T (1985) Conformity in the Asch situation: a comparison between contemporary British and US Students. *British Journal of Social Psychology, 24*, 59–63. ▶ page 150

NTSB (National Transportation Safety Board (1994) A Review of flightcrew-involved, major accidents of U.S. Air Carriers, 1978 Through 1990. *Safety Study: NTSB/SS-94–01. January.* Washington, DC: NTSB. ▶ page 158

Öhman, A., Eriksson, A. and Olofsson, C. (1975) One-trial learning and superior resistance to extinction of autonomic responses conditioned to potentially phobic stimuli. *Journal of Comparative and Physiological Psychology, 88*, 619–27. ▶ page 196

Oltmanns, T.F., Neale, J.M. and Davison, G.C. (1999) *Case studies in Abnormal Psychology*. New York: John Wiley and Sons ▶ page 181

Orne, M.T. (1962) On the social psychology of the psychological experiment: With particular reference to demand characteristics and their implications. *American Psychologist, 17*, 776–83. ▶ pages 71, 79

Orne, M.T. and Holland, C.C. (1968) On the ecological validity of laboratory deceptions. *International Journal of Psychitary, 6(4)*, 282–93. ▶ page 159

Orth-Gomér, K., Wamala, S.P., Horsten, M., Schenck-Gustafsson, K. Schneiderman, N. and Mittleman, M.A. (2000) Marital stress worsens prognosis in women with coronary heart disease: The Stockholm Female Coronary Risk Study. *Journal of American Medical Association, 284*, 3008–14. ▶ page 122

Paivio, A. (1971). *Imagery and verbal processes*. New York: Holt, Rinehart andWinston. ▶ page 23

Parker, J.F. and Carranza, L.E. (1989) Eyewitness testimony of children in target-present and target-absent lineups. *Law and Human Behavior, 13*, 133–49. ▶ page 19

Penley, J.A., Tomaka, J. and Wiebe, J.S. (2002) The association of coping to physical and psychological health outcomes: A meta-analytic review. *Journal of Behavioral Medicine. 6*, 551–603. ▶ page 132

Pennebaker, J.W., Hendler, C.S., Durrett, M.E. and Richards, P. (1981) Social factors influencing absenteeism due to illness in nursery school children. *Child Development, 52*, 692–700. ▶ page 55

Perrin, S., and Spencer, C. (1980). The Asch effect: A child of its time. *Bulletin of the British Psychological Society, 33*, 405–6. ▶ page 150

Peterson , L.R. and Peterson, M.J. (1959) Short-term retention of individual verbal items. *Journal of Experimental Psychology, 58*, 193–8. ▶ pages 4–5, 83, 100, 103

Piliavin, I. M., Rodin, J. and Piliavin, J. A. (1969) Good Samaritanism: an underground phenomenon. *Journal of Personality and Social Psychology, 13*, 1200–1213. ▶ pages 71, 83

Pollock, K. (1988) On the nature of social stress: Production of a modern mythology. *Social Science and Medicine, 26*, 381–92. ▶ page 120

Pomaki, G., Supeli, A. and Verhoeven, C. (2007) Role conflict and health behaviors: Moderating effects on psychological distress and somatic complaints. *Psychology and Health, 22(3)*, 317–35. ▶ page 128

Posada, G. and Jacobs, A. (2001) Child-Mother attachment relationships and culture. *American Psychologist , 56(10)*, 821–2. ▶ page 46

Prior, V. and Glaser, D. (2006) *Understanding attachment and attachment disorders: Theory, evidence and practice*, Child and Adolescent Mental Health Series. London: Jessica Kingsley Publishers. ▶ pages 39, 42, 46

Prislin, R. and Christensen, P.N. (2002) Group conversion versus group expansion as modes of change in majority and minority positions: All losses hurt but only some gains gratify. *Journal of Personality and Social Psychology, 83*, 1095–1102. ▶ page 166

Prodromidis, M., Lamb, M.E., Sternberg, K.J., Hwang, C.P. and Broberg, A.G. (1995) Aggression and noncompliance among Swedish children in center-based care, family day-care, and home care. *International Journal of Behavioral Development, 18*, 43–62. ▶ page 54

Pronin, E., Berger, J. and Molouki, S. (2007) Alone in a crowd of sheep: Asymmetric perceptions of conformity and their roots in an introspection illusion. *Journal of Personality and Social Psychology, 95*, 585–95. ▶ page 162

Quinton, D., Rutter, M. and Liddle, C. (1984) Institutional rearing, parental difficulties and marital support. *Psychological Medicine, 14*,107–24. ▶ page 51

Rabkin, J.G. (1993) Stress and psychiatric disorders. In L.Goldberg and S. Breznitz (Eds.) *Handbook of Stress*, 2nd edn. New York, NY: The Free Press. ▶ page 123

Ragland, D.R. and Brand, R.J. (1988) Type A behaviour and mortality from coronary heart disease. *New England Journal of Medicine, 318(2)*, 65–9. ▶ page 130

Rahe, R.H. (1974) The pathway between subjects' recent life changes and their near-future illness reports representative results and methodological issues. In B.S. Dohrenwend and B.P. Dohrenwend (Eds.) *Stressful life events: Their nature and effects*. New York: Wiley. ▶ page 125

Rahe, R.H., Mahan, J. and Arthur, R. (1970) Prediction of near-future health-change from subjects' preceding life changes. *Journal of Psychosomatic Research, 14*, 401–6. ▶ page 124

Raval, V., Goldberg, S., Atkinson, L., Benoit, D., Myhal, N., Poulton, L. and Zwiers, M. (2001) Maternal attachment, maternal responsiveness and infant attachment. *Infant Behaviour and Development, 24*, 281–304. ▶ page 43

Riniolo, T.C., Koledin, M., Drakulic, G.M. and Payne, R.A. (2003) An archival study of eyewitness memory of the Titanic's final plunge. *Journal of General Psychology, 130(1)*, 89–95. ▶ page 18

Riska, E. (2002) From type A man to the hardy man: Masculinity and health. *Sociology of Health and Illness, 24(3)*, 347–58. ▶ page 130

Ritvanen, T., Louhevaara, V., Helin, P., Halonen, T. and Hänninen, O. (2007) Effect of aerobic fitness on the physiological stress responses at work. *International Journal of Occupational Medicine and Environmental Health, 20(1)*, 1–8. ▶ page 129

Robertson, J. and Robertson, J. (1967–73) *Young children in brief separation*. A film study. Concord Video and Film Council. New York University Film Library. ▶ pages 48, 49

Robertson, J. and Robertson, J. (1989) *Separation and the very young*. London: Free Association Books. ▶ page 48

Roethlisberger, F.J. and Dickson, W.J. (1939) *Management and the worker: an account of a research program conducted by the Western Electric Company, Chicago*. Cambridge, MA: Harvard University Press. ▶ page 83

Rohlf, V. and Bennett, P. (2005) Perpetration-induced traumatic stress in persons who euthanize nonhuman animals in surgeries, animal shelters, and laboratories. *Society and Animals, 13*, 201–19. ▶ page 123

Rosario, M., Shinn, M., Morch, H. and Huckabee, C.B. (1988) Gender differences in coping and social supports: Testing socialization and role constraint theories. *Journal of Community Psychology,16*, 55–69. ▶ page 133

Rose, D.S., Wykes, T.H., Bindman, J.P. and Fleischmann, P.S. (2005) Information, consent and perceived coercion: patients' perspectives on electroconvulsive therapy. *British Journal of Psychiatry, 186*, 54–9. ▶ page 193

Rosenhan, D.L. (1973) On being sane in insane places. *Science, 179*, 250–8. ▶ page 176

Rosenthal, R. (1966) *Experimenter effects in behaviour research*. New York: Appleton. ▶ page 176

Rosenzweig, S. (1936). Some implicit common factors in diverse methods of psychotherapy. *American Journal of Orthopsychiatry, 6*, 412–15. ▶ page 195

Rothbaum, F., Weisz, J., Pott, M., Miyake, K. and Morelli, G. (2000) Attachment and culture: Security in the United States and Japan. *American Psychologist, 55*, 1093–1104. ▶ page 46

Rotter, J.B. (1966) Generalised expectancies for internal versus external control of reinforcement. *Psychological Monographs, 30* (1), 1–26. ▶ page 164

Rozanski, A., Blumental, J.A. and Kaplan, J. (1999) Impact of psychological factors on the pathogenisis of cardiovascular disease and implications for therapy. *Circulatrion, 99*, 2192–2217. ▶ page 122

Ruchkin, D.S., Grafman, J., Cameron, K. and Berndt, R.S. (2003) Working memory retention systems: A state of activated long-term memory. *Behavioral and Brain Sciences, 26(6)*, 709–28. ▶ page 11

Ruffin, C.L. (1993) Stress and health: Little hassles vs. major life events. *Australian Psychologist, 28*, 201–8. ▶ page 126

Rukholm, E.E. and Viverais, G.A. (1993) A multifactorial study of test anxiety and coping responses during a challenge examination. *Nurse Education Today, April 13(2)*, 91–9. ▶ page 132

Russek, H.I. (1962) Emotional stress and coronary heart disease in American physicians, dentists, and lawyers. *American Journal of Medical Science, 243*, 716–25. ▶ page 122

Rutter, M. (1995) Clinical implications of attachment concepts: retrospect and prospect. *Journal of Child Psychology and Psychiatry, 36(4)*, 549–71. ▶ page 39

Rutter, M., Colvert, E., Kreppner, J., Beckett, C., Castle, J., Groothues, C., Hawkins, A., Stevens, S.E. and Sonuga-Barke, E.J.S. (2007) Early adolescent outcomes for institutionally-deprived and non-deprived adoptees. I: Disinhibited attachment. *Journal of Child Psychology and Psychiatry*, 48, (1), 17–30. ▶ page 50

Rymer, R. (1993) *Genie: Escape from a silent childhood*. London: Michael Joseph. ▶ page 50

Sackheim, H.A., Haskett, R.F., Mulsant, B.H., Thase, M.E., Mann, J., Pettinati, H.M., Greenberg, R.M, Crowe, R.R., Cooper, T.B. and Prudic, J. (2001) Continuation pharmacotherapy in the prevention of relapse following electroconvulsive therapy. *Journal of the American Medical Association*, 285, 1299–1307. ▶ page 193

Scarr. S. and Thompson, W. (1994) Effects of maternal employment and nonmaternal infant care on development at two and four years. *Early Development and Parenting, 3(2)*, 113–23. ▶ page 55

Schacter, D.L., Wagner, A.D. and Buckner, R.L. (2000) Memory systems of 1999. In E. Tulving and F.I.M. Craik (Eds.) *Handbook of memory*. New York: Oxford University Press. ▶ page 10

Schacter, D.L., Kaszniak, A.W., Kihlstrom, J.F. and Valdiserri, M. (1991). The relation between source memory and aging. *Psychology and Aging, 6(4)*, 559–68. ▶ page 17

Schafer, W. (1992) *Stress management for wellness* (2nd edn). Fort Worth, TX: Holt, Rinehart and Winston, Inc. ▶ page 127

Schaffer, H.R. (1998) *Making Decisions about Children*. Oxford: Blackwell. ▶ page 56

Schaffer, H.R. and Emerson, P.E. (1964) The development of social attachments in infancy. *Monographs of the Society for Research in Child Development, 29(3)* Serial No. 94. ▶ pages 35, 38, 104

Schaubroeck, J., Jones, J.R. and Xie, J.L. (2001) Individual differences in utilizing control to cope with job demands: Effects on susceptibility to infectious disease. *Journal of Applied Psychology, 86(2)*, 265–78. ▶ page 128

Schellenberg, E.G. (2004). Music lessons enhance IQ. *Psychological Science, 15*, 511–14. ▶ page 84

Schunk, D.H. (1983) Reward contingencies and the development of children's skills and self-efficacy. *Journal of Educational Psychology, 75*, 511–18. ▶ page 83

Schwartz, S. (1992) Universals in the content and structure of values: Theoretical advances and empirical advances in 20 countries. *Advances in Experimental Psychology, 25*, 1–66. ▶ page 151

Scoville, W.B. and Milner, B. (1957). Loss of recent memory after bilateral hippocampal lesions. Journal of Neurology, Neurosurgery, and Psychiatry, 20, 11–21 ▶ page 9

Sedikides, C. and Jackson, J.M. (1990) Social impact theory: a field test of source strength, source immediacy and number of targets. *Basic and Applied Social Psychology, 11(3)*, 273–81. ▶ page 155

Segerstrom, S.C. and Miller, G.E. (2004) Psychological stress and the human immune system: a meta-analytic study of 30 years of inquiry. *Psychological Bulletin,130*, 601–630. ▶ page 121

Seligman, M.E.P. (1970) On the generality of the laws of learning. *Psychological Review, 77*, 406–18. ▶ page 189

Shallice, T. and Warrington, E.K. (1970) Independent functioning of verbal memory stores: a neuropsychological study. *Quarterly Journal of Experimental Psychology, 22*, 261–73. ▶ page 10

Shanab, M.E. and Yahya, K.A. (1978) A cross-cultural study of obedience. *Bulletin of the Psychonomic Society,11*, 267–9. ▶ page 158

Sheehy, R.S. and Horan, J.J. (2004) The effects of stress-inoculation training for first year law students. *International Journal of Stress Management, 11*, 44–55. ▶ page 135

Shepard, R.N. (1967) Recognition memory for words, sentences and pictures. Journal of Verbal Learning and Verbal Behaviour, 6, 156–63. ▶ page 4

Shepher, J. (1971) Mate selection among second generation Kibbutz adolescents and adults. *Archives of Sexual Behaviour, 1*, 293–307. ▶ page 33

Sheps, D.S., McMahon, R.P., Becker, L., Carney, R.M., Freedland, K.E., Cohen, J.D., Sheffield, D., Goldberg, A.D., Ketterer, M.W., Pepine, C.J., Raczynski, J.M., Light, K., Krantz, D.S., Stone, P.H., Knatterud, G.L. and Kaufmann, P.G. (2002) Mental stress-induced ischemia and all-cause mortality in patients with coronary artery disease: results from the Psychophysiological Investigations of Myocardial Ischemia study. *Circulation,105*,1780–4 ▶ page 122

Sheridan, C.L. and King, K.G. (1972) Obedience to authority with an authentic victim. *Proceedings of the 80th Annual Convention of the American Psychological Association, 7*, 165–6. ▶ page 159

Singer, L.M., Brodzinsky, D.M., Ramsay, D., Steir, M. and Waters, E. (1985) Mother-infant attachments in adoptive families. *Child Development, 56*, 1543–51. ▶ page 56

Skeels, H. and Dye, H.B. (1939) A study of the effects of differential stimulation on mentally retarded children. *Proceedings and Addresses of the American Association on Mental Deficiency, 44*, 114–36. ▶ pages 48, 49

Skodak, M. and Skeels, H. (1949) A final follow-up study of 100 adopted children. *Journal of Genetic Psychology, 75*, 85–125. ▶ page 49

Slade, A. , Grienenberger, J., Bernbach, E., Levy, D. and Locker, A. (2005) Maternal reflective functioning and attachment: Considering the transmission gap. *Attachment and Human Development, 7*, 283–292. ▶ page 43

Sloane, R.B., Staples, F.R., Cristol, A.H., Yorkston, N.J. and Whipple, K. (1975) *Short-term analytically oriented psychotherapy vs behaviour therapy*. Cambridge, MA: Harvard University Press. ▶ page 195

Smith, J.C. and Glass, G.V. (1977) Meta-analysis of psychotherapy outcome studies. *American Psychologist, 32(9)*, 752–60. ▶ page 190

Smith, P. and Bond, M.H. (1998) *Social psychology across cultures: Analysis and perspectives* (2nd edition). New York: Harvester Wheatsheaf. ▶ page 151

Sperling. G. (1960) The information available in brief visual presentations, *Psychological Monographs, 74* (Whole no. 498), 1–29. ▶ page 9

Spiers H.J., Burgess N. and Maguire E.A. (2001) Hippocampal Amnesia: A Review. *Neurocase, 7*, 357–382. ▶ page 10

Squire, L.R., Ojemann, J.G., Miezin, F.M., Petersen, S.E., Videen, T.O. and Raichle, M.E. (1992) Activation of the hippocampus in normal humans: A functional anatomical study of memory. ▶ page 9

Sroufe, L.A., Egeland, B., Carlson, E. and Collins, W.A. (2005) *The development of the person: The Minnesota study of risk and adaptation from birth to adulthood*. New York: Guilford. ▶ page 38

Steblay, N.M. (1992) A meta-analytic review of the weapon focus effect. *Law and Human Behaviour, 16*, 413–24. ▶ page 18

Steele, C. M. and Josephs, R. A. (1990) Alcohol myopia, its prized and dangerous effects. *American Psychologist. 45*, 921–33. ▶ page 19

Stein, L. and Memon, A. (2006) Testing the efficacy of the Cognitive Interview in a developing country. *Applied Cognitive Psychology, 20*, 597–605. ▶ page 21

Sternberg, R.J. (2006) *Cognitive psychology* (4th edn). Belmont, CA: Thomson Higher Education. ▶ page 14

Stone, A.A., Greenberg, M.A., Kennedy-Moore, E. and Newman, M.G. (1991) Self-report situation-specific coping questionnaires: What are they measuring? *Journal of Personality and Social Psychology, 61*, 648–58. ▶ page 133

Stueve, A.,Dohrenwend, B.P. and Skodol, A.E. (1998) Relationships between stressful life events and episodes of major depression and nonaffective psychotic disorders: Selected results from a New York risk factor study. In B.P. Dohrenwend (Ed.) *Adversity, stress and psychopathology.* New York: Oxford University Press. pp. 341–57. ▶ page 123

Sylva, K., Melhuish, E., Sammons, P., Siraj-Blatchford, I., Taggart, B. and Elliot, K. (2003) The Effective Provision of Pre-School Education (EPPE) Project : Findings from the pre-school Period. Summary of findings. http://www.ioe.ac.uk/cdl/eppe/pdfs/eppe_brief2503.pdf London: Institute of Education. ▶ page 53, 56

Szasz, T.S. (1972) *The manufacture of madness.* London: Routledge and Kegan Paul. ▶ page 185

Szasz, T.S. (1974) *Ideology and insanity.* Harmondsworth, Middlesex: Penguin. ▶ page 178

Szasz, T.S. (2000) Mental disorders are not diseases. *USA Today Magazine,* January. ▶ page 185

Takahashi, K. (1990) Are the key assumptions of the 'strange situation' procedure universal? A view from Japanese research. *Human Development, 33,* 23–30. ▶ page 44

Tanford, S. and Penrod, S. (1986) Jury deliberations: discussion content and influence processes in jury decision making. *Journal of Applied Social Psychology, 16,* 322-347. ▶ pages 150, 153

Tarnow, E. (2000) Self-destructive obedience in the airplane cockpit and the concept of obedience optimization. In T. Blass (Ed.) *Obedience to authority: Current perspectives on the Milgram paradigm* (pp. 111–23). Mahwah, NJ: Erlbaum. ▶ page 158

Taylor, S.E., Klein, L.C., Lewis, B.P., Gruenewald, T.L., Gurung, R.A.R. and Updegraff, J.A. (2000) Biobehavioral responses to stress in females: Tend-and-befriend, not fight-or-flight. *Psychological Review, 107,* 411–29. ▶ page 118

Thase, M. E., Friedman, E. S., Biggs, M. M., Wisniewski, S. R., Trivedi, M. H., Luther, J. F., Fava, M., Nierenberg, A. A., McGrath, P. J., Warden, D., Niederehe, G., Hollon, S. D. and Rush, A. J. (2007) Cognitive Therapy Versus Medication in Augmentation and Switch Strategies as Second-Step Treatments: A STAR*D Report. *American Journal of Psychiatry, 164,* 739–752. ▶ page 190

Thomas, A. and Chess, S. (1986) The New York Longitudinal study: From infancy to early life. In R. Plomin and J. Dunn (Eds.) *The study of temperament: Changes, continuities and challenges.* Hillsdale, N.J.: Erlbaum. ▶ page 39

Tizard, B. (2005) Personal communication. ▶ page 51

Topal, J., Miklosi, A., Csanyi, V. and Doka, A. (1998) Attachment behaviour in dogs (Canis familiaris): A new application of Ainsworth's (1969) Strange Situation Test. *Journal of Comparative Psychology, 112(3),* 219–29. ▶ pages 42, 88

Torrey, E.F. (2001) *Surviving schizophrenia: A manual for families, consumers and providers.* New York, NY: HarperCollins Publishers, Inc. ▶ page 184

Trojano, L. and Grossi, D. (1995) Phonological and lexical coding in verbal short-term memory and learning. *Brain and Cognition, 21,* 336–54. ▶ page 13

Tronick, E.Z., Morelli, G.A. and Ivey, P.K. (1992) The Efe forager infant and toddler's pattern of social relationships: Multiple and simultaneous. *Developmental Psychology, 28,* 568–77. ▶ page 38

Tschuschke, V., Anbeh, T. and Kiencke. P. (2007) Evaluation of long-term analytic outpatient group therapies. *Group Analysis, 40(1),* 140–59. ▶ page 194

Turner, R.J. and Lloyd, D.A. (1995) Lifetime traumas and mental health: The significance of cumulative adversity. *Journal of Health and Social Behaviour, 36,* 360–76. ▶ page 51

Twenge, J. M., Zhang, L. and Im, C. (2004) It's beyond my control: A cross-temporal meta-analysis of increasing externality in locus of control, 1960–2002. *Personality and Social Psychology Review, 8,* 308–19. ▶ pages 164, 165

Van IJzendoorn, M.H. and Sagi, A. (2001) Cultural blindness or selective inattention. *American Psychologist, 56(10),* 824–5. ▶ page 47

Van IJzendoorn, M.H. and Kroonenberg, P.M. (1988) Cross-cultural patterns of attachment: A meta-analysis of the Strange Situation. *Child Development, 59,* 147–56. ▶ pages 45, 46, 47

Van IJzendoorn, M.H., Schuengel, C. and Bakermans-Kranenburg, M.J. (1999) Disorganized attachment in early childhood: Meta-analysis of precursors, concomitants, and sequelae. *Developmental and Psychopathology, 11,* 225–49. ▶ page 41

Veitch, R. and Griffitt, W. (1976) Good news, bad news: affective and interpersonal effects. *Journal of Applied Social Psychology, 6,* 69–75. ▶ page 83

Violata, C..and Russell, C. (1994) *Effects of non-maternal care on child development: a meta-analysis of published research.* Paper presented at 55th annual convention of the Canadian Psychological Association. Penticon. British Columbia. ▶ pages 52, 57

Vogel, E.K., Woodman, G.F. and Luck, S.J. (2001) Storage of features, conjunctions, and objects in visual working memory. *Journal of Experimental Psychology: Human Perception and Performance, 27(1),* 92–114. ▶ page 6

Warr, P. (1987) *Work, unemployment, and mental health.* Oxford: Clarendon Press. ▶ page 129

Watson, J.B. and Rayner, R. (1920) Conditioned emotional reactions. *Journal of Experimental Psychology, 3,* 1–14. ▶ page 188

Wells, G.L. and Olson, E. (2003) Eyewitness identification. *Annual Review of Psychology, 54,* ▶ page 16

WHO (World Heath Organisation) (2001) *Mental health: New understanding, new hope.* Geneva: World Health Organization. ▶ page 192

Wickens, D.D., Dalezman, R.E. and Eggemeier, F.T. (1976) Multiple encoding of word attributes in. memory. *Memory and Cognition, 4(3),* 307–10. ▶ page 7

Williams, J.E., Paton, C.C., Siegler, I.C., Eigenbrodt, M.L., Nieto, F.J. and Tyroler, H.A. (2000) Anger proneness predicts coronary heart disease risk: Prospective analysis from the atherosclerosis risk in communities (ARIC) study) *Circulation 101(17),* 2034–9. ▶ page 122

Williams, T.M. (Ed.) (1986) *The impact of television: A national experiment in three communities.* New York: Academic Press. ▶ page 84

Williams, T.P., and Sogon, S. (1984) Group composition and conforming behaviour in Japanese students. *Japanese Psychological Research, 26,* 231–4. ▶ page 150

Wittenbrink, B and Henly, J.R. (1996) Creating social reality: Informational social influence and the content of stereotypic beliefs. *Personality and Social Psychology Bulletin, 22,* 598–610. ▶ page 154

Wood, W., Lundgren, S., Ouellette, J., Busceme, S. and Blackstone, T. (1994) Minority influence: A meta-analytic review of social influence processes. *Psychological Bulletin, 115,* 323–45. ▶ page 152

Yuille, J.C. and Cutshall, J.L. (1986) A case study of eyewitness testimony of a crime. *Journal of Applied Psychology, 71,* 291–301. ▶ page 16

Zebrowitz, L.A. (1997) *Reading faces: Window to the soul?* Boulder, CO: Westview Press. ▶ page 33

Zimbardo, P. (2007) *The Lucifer Effect.* London: Rider. ▶ page 163, 167

Zuckerman, M. (1994) *Behavioural experssions and biosocial bases of sensation seeking.* New York: Cambridge University Press. ▶ page 97

Answers

Chapter 1

FOOTBALL KNOWLEDGE TEST ▶ page 3
1 Russia
2 Martin Jol
3 Sunderland
4 Jerzy Dudek
5 Three
6 Blue
7 Real Madrid
8 Norwich
9 West Ham
10 John Motson

CROSSWORD ▶ page 30

Across
2 Devlin
5 Rehearsal
6 Working memory
10 Semantic
11 Adaptive
12 Own-age bias
15 Baddeley
17 Yerkes-Dodson
19 Validity
20 Chunking

Down
1 Phonological
2 Duration
3 Geiselman
4 Everything
7 Weapon-focus
8 Meta-analysis
9 Smashed
10 Sensory
13 Shiffrin
14 Leading
16 Titanic
18 Seven

Chapter 2

CROSSWORD ▶ page 64

Across
1 Disinhibited
3 Primary
7 Privation
10 Ambivalent
13 Secure
16 Tizard
17 Sure Start
18 Lorenz
19 NICHD
20 Ainsworth
21 Strange situation

Down
2 Harlow
4 Individualist
5 Collectivist
6 Five
8 Robertsons
9 Classical
11 Temperament
12 Monotropy
14 Genie
15 Attachment

Chapter 3

MULTIPLE-CHOICE QUESTIONS ▶ page 111

1 a	7 d	13 d	19 d
2 d	8 a	14 d	20 d
3 b	9 c	15 d	21 d
4 d	10 c	16 c	22 c
5 c	11 d	17 b	23 c
6 b	12 d	18 b	24 a

CROSSWORD ▶ page 114

Across
7 Range
8 Double blind
11 Open
12 Scattergram
14 Median
15 Mean
16 DV
18 Qualitative
19 Interview
20 Order effect

Down
1 Bar chart
2 Mode
3 Quantitative
4 Directional
5 Pilot
6 Reliability
9 Opportunity
10 Random
12 Single blind
13 Volunteer
17 IV

Chapter 4

CROSSWORD ▶ page 115

Across
1 Beta blocker
4 Conceptualisation
10 Hypothalamus
11 Pituitary
12 Control
13 Sympathetic
15 GABA
16 Cannon
18 SAM
19 Behavioural
20 Cortisol

Down
2 ACTH
3 Uplifts
5 CRF
6 Type A
7 Leucocytes
8 Daily hassles
9 Hardy
11 Problem
14 Placebo
17 SRRS

HARDINESS TEST SCORING ▶ page 131

For half the questions a high score (e.g. 3) indicates hardiness; for the other half, a low score indicates hardiness (e.g. 0).

To get your score on 'control', add your answers to questions A and G; add your answers to B and H; and then subtract the second number from the first: **[(A+G) – (B+H)]**

To get your score on 'commitment' add your answers to questions C and I; add your answers to D and J; and then subtract the second number from the first: **[(C+I) – (D+J)]**

To get your score on 'challenge' add your answers to questions E and K; add your answers to F and L; and then subtract the second number from the first: **[(E+K) – (F+L)]**

Add your scores on commitment, control, and challenge together to get a score for total hardiness.

The highest score is 18.

(adapted from http://www.suu.edu/ss/wellness/trauma.html)

Chapter 5

CROSSWORD ▶ page 174

Across
3 Confederates
4 Autonomous
8 Moscovici
10 Alibi
14 More
16 Agentic
18 Internalisation
19 Yale
20 Abu Ghraib

Down
1 Terrorism
2 Less
5 McCarthy
6 Child, time
7 Locus of control
8 Minority
9 Collectivist
11 Normative
12 Compliance
13 Meta
15 Kohlberg
17 Asch

Chapter 6

CROSSWORD ▶ page 204

Across
2 Symptoms
4 Diathesis
5 Reality
10 Medical
12 False
14 Jahoda
16 Substitution
19 Chemotherapy
21 Vicarious
22 Phobia
23 Little Albert
24 Psychoanalytic

Down
1 Defense
3 Meta
6 Ellis
7 Serotonin
8 Behaviourist
9 Szasz
11 Emotive
13 Systematic
15 Anna O.
17 Id
18 ECT
20 Placebo

Index